THE MAKING OF THE GEORGIAN NATION

STUDIES OF NATIONALITIES IN THE USSR
Wayne S. Vucinich, Editor
PUBLISHED BY THE HOOVER INSTITUTION PRESS

THE MAKING OF THE GEORGIAN NATION

Ronald Grigor Suny

INDIANA UNIVERSITY PRESS
Bloomington and Indianapolis
in association with
HOOVER INSTITUTION PRESS
Stanford University
Stanford, California

379266

© 1988 by Ronald Grigor Suny
All rights reserved

No part of this book may be reproduced or utilized in any form or by
any means, electronic or mechanical, including photocopying and
recording, or by any information storage and retrieval system, without
permission in writing from the publisher. The Association of American
University Presses' Resolution on Permissions constitutes the only
exception to this prohibition.

Manufactured in the United States of America

Library of Congress Cataloging-in-Publication Data

Suny, Ronald Grigor.
    The making of the Georgian nation.

    (Studies of nationalities in the USSR)
    Bibliography: p.
    Includes index.
    1. Georgian S.S.R—History.   I. Title.
II. Series.
DK511.G4S78   1988   947'.95   87-21367
ISBN 0-253-33623-6
OSBM 0-253-21277-4 (pbk.)

1   2   3   4   5   92   91   90   89   88

For Armena,
in memory of our son,
Grikor Martiros Suni
(1978–1980)

Contents

PART THREE
REVOLUTIONARY AND SOVIET GEORGIA

Foreword

Ronald Grigor Suny's *The Making of the Georgian Nation* is the fifth volume in the Studies of Nationalities in the USSR, a series published by the Hoover Institution Press. The present volume, copublished by Indiana University Press, presents a comprehensive history of Georgia and the Georgians from the earliest times to the present day. Eminently qualified for the task that he has undertaken, Professor Suny is a widely recognized scholar, one of America's leading authorities on the history of Russia, the Soviet Union, and the Caucasus, and the first holder of the Alex Manoogian Chair in Modern Armenian History at the University of Michigan.

With their long history and rich culture, the Georgians hold a unique place among the Soviet nationalities. A good history of Georgia has long been needed. Previous books by W. E. D. Allen (*History of the Georgian People*) and D. M. Lang (*History of Modern Georgia*), though still useful, are antiquated. Although Soviet historiography on Georgia and the Georgians is impressive in quantity and quality, it is marred by vacillating Soviet political and ideological objectives. Professor Suny's main objectives in this book are to trace the Georgians' national formation and to show how history has shaped the Georgians into a self-conscious nationality and a nation. He has sought to produce a balanced work and to unravel and interpret various historiographic controversies.

The first part of the book covers the history of the Georgians from their origin until they came under the rule of imperial Russia. Situated in a strategically valued location between East and West, Georgia was frequently invaded by foreign armies, its lands devastated, and its people subjugated to foreign rule and quarreling native feudatories. Together with local unrest, epidemics, and droughts, the invasions disrupted the social system, depleted the population, and inflicted upon the Georgians foreign rule and culture. Yet, even as Georgians accepted features of other cultures, they maintained their own. Their ethnic community was like a balloon: squeezed at one place, it popped out at another, always outliving its enemies.

In the second, larger part of the book, Suny gives an excellent analysis of the process of integration of the Georgians into the Russian empire and their reaction to Russian rule and culture. The historical significance of Russian rule in Georgia has been a subject of controversy in Soviet historiography. Suny assesses critically this debate and its political implications. In some detail he explores Russia's political, economic, and cultural impact on Georgian society, the conflict between tsarist officialdom and established social conventions, and the relations between social classes in Georgia.

The Georgian Orthodox Church—founded in the fourth century, autocephalous since the sixth century, and a mark of Georgian ethnic identity— was incorporated into the Russian Orthodox Church administration in 1811. The Georgian nobility merged with the Russian nobility. Yet, imperial Russia failed to Russify Georgian society; instead, it stimulated a diverse new Georgian national awareness. The result was that the Georgians emerged as a politically and culturally conscious nationality. Not only did Georgians retain their national identity, but their encounter with Russia actually forged a more cohesive ethnicity with a new national leadership.

By becoming a part of Russia's market system, Georgia's economy developed rapidly, and the nation was more readily exposed to Russian and European cultural and political thought. The literary creations and political movements of Georgia were modeled on those in Russia. And in 1892 Georgia acquired a Marxist organization (*mesame dasi;* "Third Group"). Its leaders, most of whom later became Mensheviks, formed a dynamic political elite that eventually led Georgia into a brief independence. Among those Georgian Marxists who turned to Bolshevism was Josef (Ioseb) Jughashvili—later known as Joseph Stalin.

Among the best pages in Professor Suny's superb study are those, in the third part of the book, on Stalinism and its implementation, including the purges. His discussion of the party structure and analysis of the party cadres also deserve special attention, as does the discussion of the sociopolitical formation and transformation of Stalinism and the results of the policy of *korenizatsiia.* In a masterly fashion Professor Suny shows how Stalin was able to organize a group of dedicated followers in Georgia's governing and party circles, the closest of whom was Lavrenti P. Beria, chief of the secret police.

The fact that Stalin was of Georgian background could not but shape Georgian attitudes toward him and the Soviet Union. Suny notes that despite the Stalinist purges in 1937–1938, the severe repression in Georgia, and Stalin's espousal of "Great Russianism" (which was detrimental to small nations like Georgia), many Georgians consider Stalin a great fellow countryman and attribute Soviet successes in Georgia to him. The museum in Gori, Stalin's birthplace, is still viewed by many Georgians as a shrine. Other Georgians, however, hold Stalin and his brutal rule in disdain, as recently portrayed in a stunning Georgian film, *Repentance*.

The population of Georgia, slightly over five million, is dominantly Georgian (about 60 percent), and there is no danger in the immediate future of the Georgians being overtaken numerically in their own republic by another Soviet nationality. Armenians and Russians each constitute about 10 percent of all inhabitants, and the rest of Georgia's population is principally made up of Abkhazians, Ossetians, Azeris, and Ajars. It is of no small importance that more than 90 percent of ethnic Georgians live in their own republic. The emigration of Georgians to other parts of the Soviet Union has been insignificant.

Georgia entered the Stalinist period largely as a peasant nation. But, as Suny points out, Georgia embarked on industrial development in the second half of the nineteenth century and today boasts an economy based on well-developed industry and agriculture. A new Soviet-born and educated Georgian nation now exists—more industrial, more urban, and still quite nationalistic. But all is not well in Georgia. Suny shows convincingly that the original Soviet goal to achieve a "unitary body" out of diverse Soviet nationalities has failed, as has the drive toward ethnic fusion *(sliianie)* introduced by the Twenty-second Party Congress. Instead, ideologues have recently been speaking of seeking the "full unity" *(polnoe edinstvo)* of the Soviet peoples.

The Georgians themselves seem to want greater autonomy in managing their own affairs. They are critical of aspects of Soviet internal politics, repressive practices, and violation of human rights. They are demanding a higher standard of living and have complained about shortages of food and consumer goods. This dissent and criticism have led to official countermeasures. The Soviet authorities have charged a number of Georgians with economic crimes, illegal business activity, and the use of bribery and extortion; they have periodically accused individual Georgians of promoting national exclusivism.

Suny comments on these and related questions with special insight and objectivity. He has given us an outstanding work in which he covers the wide range of Georgian history, with a focus on how the Georgians developed into a self-conscious nationality and a nation with its own political institutions. The making of the Georgian nation is both a complex and a highly important subject. The depth of the author's research and his analysis make this a book of lasting value.

WAYNE S. VUCINICH

Preface

The writing of national history is most often a labor of love performed by patriots who, in the process of creating a narrative unity for their people's past, serve as both chroniclers and inventors of tradition. Their selection of an ethnic group or a specific territory as the focus of a history spanning many centuries—in the case of the Caucasian peoples, several millennia—is predicated on an assumption that nationality or geographical space is the most appropriate boundary for historical investigation. The consequent synthesis will primarily be meaningful to the inhabitants of that cultural space, either as a contribution to self-knowledge or as advertisement for the outside world. The nineteenth-century flourishing of national histories, in the period of nation-formation and the proliferation of nationalisms, testifies to their importance and influence. Together with grammars, dictionaries, and primers, national histories shaped the self-image and perceptions of ethnic groups as they developed their own cultural and political agenda. "The history which became part of the fund of knowledge or the ideology of nation, state or movement," writes Eric Hobsbawm, "is not what has actually been preserved in popular memory, but what has been selected, written, pictured, popularized and institutionalized by those whose function it is to do so."[1]

The undertaking of a national history by a scholar of another nationality, in a country that has itself been radically "denationalized" and in a time when historians are interested in specific social-historical problems rather than narrative reconstruction of the past, presumes a different motivation. The initiating interest in this work was not a desire to depict past glories or the "rise and fall" of an ancient people, but rather to address the broad sociopolitical question of national formation. The central question posed is, How did the Georgians become the Georgian nation? How did their particular historical experience shape them as a people, later as a self-conscious nationality, and still later as a nation with its own political institutions and the trappings of a kind of sovereignty? More specifically, this study explores the impact on Georgia of its powerful neighbors—Persians, Greeks, Romans, Turks, and Russians—and attempts to understand how the imposition of foreign rule, and change directed by imperial powers, affected the making of the Georgian nation.

The first section of the book, "The Rise and Fall of the Georgian Monarchies," briefly surveys the ethnogenesis of the Georgians and traces their political and social development from a variety of linguistically and culturally affiliated tribes to a single, though still inchoate, ethnic formation divided by loyalty to various princes. The Georgian chronicles *(kartlis tskhovreba)* and their commentaries dictated a primarily political history for the first two millennia of Georgia's evolution. The available sources largely tell us the exploits of royal houses and stories of foreign invasion and domestic revolt. At this level the history of Georgia is a montage of rapidly shifting monarchs, alliances, conquerers, and rebels. But beneath the political veneer much slower, and more permanent, processes of social and cultural formation were shaping Georgian civilization—the adoption of Chalcedonian Christianity, the establishment of a "dynastic-feudal" hierarchy, and the settlement on the land of the great majority of the Georgians. Culturally and politically, Georgia, like its neighbor to the south, Armenia, represented a blend of Western (Greco-Roman and Byzantine) and Eastern (Persian, and to some extent Turkish) influences, which were reflected in language, social structure, and cultural practices. Despite the near-extinction of the Georgians at the end of the eighteenth century, their way of life had retained its time-sanctioned traditions and patterns, which were more similar to those of the Georgians' Islamic overlords than to those of their fellow Orthodox Christians to the north.

Part II of this volume, "Georgia in the Russian Empire," deals with the impact on Georgian society of Russian rule in its bureaucratic-absolutist form. The Georgians' Iranized social conventions, their decentralized political structure, and the customary ties between lords and peasants were radically altered by the arrival of tsarist officials in Tiflis. Within half a century Georgia was integrated into Russian administrative practice, serfdom had been systematized (only to be abolished soon after), and the Georgian nobility had become part of the Russian ruling elite, the *dvorianstvo.* With the integration of Transcaucasia into the Russian empire Western influences, both cultural and material, penetrated Georgia rapidly, creating new social groups to challenge the dominance of the native nobility. Urban life revived, and Armenian merchants secured the dominant position in the local commercial and industrial environment. A Georgian intelligentsia emerged and fashioned both nationalist and socialist ideologies with which to oppose tsarist authority. Ultimately, the Russian impact contributed to a new national awareness among Georgians and their emergence as a culturally and politically conscious nationality. When the Russian monarchy fell, a local Georgian leadership was already in place to assume political authority and to lead the Georgians to nationhood.

Part III, "Revolutionary and Soviet Georgia," parallels Part II. Once again a relatively independent Georgian state was overwhelmed by Russian occupation. Bolshevik troops invaded the Menshevik republic, and a radical transformation of Georgia's social and political life was imposed from above, this time by a Soviet government. Once again the paradoxical impact of the new government was the creation of a deep national awareness and, eventually, a new nationalism. In Georgia, as in other republics of the USSR, the Soviets eliminated full political sovereignty but initiated a process through which Georgians took over the institutions of their own republic, dominated the political and educational system, and expanded their own national cultural production. The Soviet period witnessed both the restraint of separatist and politically nationalist aspirations and the institutionalization of cultural, linguistic, and historical awareness. In a sense the Georgian nation was remade, this time in a Soviet mold. Its current predicament is the product of the tension between Soviet promotion of certain national forms and Soviet restrictions on their full development and expression.

A work of this sort, spanning the history of a people from the "primeval ooze" to the present, can never be the product of one person's research. As a historian of modern Transcaucasia, I am particularly indebted to those scholars who have written on the period before the Russian annexation—Cyril Toumanoff, G. A. Melikishvili, N. A. Berdzenishvili, Sh. A. Meskhia, W. E. D. Allen, David Marshall Lang, and many others both in the West and in the Soviet Union. Part I is the most derivative, based as it is on the expert knowledge of those working in that field and on advice received from friends and teachers. Special thanks are due to Peter Golden and to my teacher of Armenian history, Nina G. Garsoian, for their learned readings of the early chapters. My colleagues at the University of Michigan—Geoff Eley, William G. Rosenberg, and Roman Szporluk—concentrated on the modern period, as did the detailed and perceptive critique of Moshe Lewin. All their comments improved the text in innumerable ways.

Aside from a handful of Soviet works and collections of documents, there are no adequate histories of Georgia in the late nineteenth and twentieth centuries. The bulk of my own research has been concentrated in this period. During the three research trips I made to Georgia under the auspices of IREX, I benefited from consultation with Soviet scholars, most notably Akaki Nestorovich Surguladze. Of the few colleagues in Georgian studies in the West, the most important sources of advice were David Barrett of the Wardrop Collection in the Bodleian Library, L. Hamilton ("Tony")

Rhinelander, and David Marshall Lang. I would like to thank my teachers in Tbilisi, Jondo Metreveli and Nia Abesadze, for their introduction into the beauties and complexities of the extraordinary Georgian language, and our friends, the Mkrtchians, who accepted my wife and me as family and made our lives in Georgia extremely pleasant.

Many institutions have supported my research over the last decade. I would like to express my gratitude to Oberlin College, the National Endowment for the Humanities, the Harriman Institute for Advanced Russian Studies of Columbia University, the Russian Research Center of Harvard University, the University of Michigan and its Center for Russian and East European Studies, and the John Simon Guggenheim Foundation. In addition to these institutions, I have been privileged to work at the New York Public Library, the Library of Congress, the British Library, the Lenin Library, the Karl Marx Library (Tbilisi), the library of Tbilisi State University, the Institutes of Party History in Erevan and Tbilisi, and the Hoover Institution Library and Archives. Special thanks are due to Victor Khomeriki for aid in securing permission to work in the Georgian Archive of the Houghton Library, Harvard University; to Dr. Ramishvili for materials on Georgian social democracy; and to the late Anna Mikhailovna Bourgina for showing me materials in the Nicolaevsky Collection of the Hoover Institution Archives.

Earlier versions of parts of this study have been published in the *Russian Review* and *Nationalities Papers;* in R. G. Suny, ed., *Transcaucasia, Nationalism and Social Change: Essays in the History of Armenia, Azerbaijan, and Georgia* (Ann Arbor: Michigan Slavic Publications, 1983); and in Stephen F. Cohen, Alexander Rabinowitch, and Robert Sharlet, eds., *The Soviet Union Since Stalin* (Bloomington: Indiana University Press, 1980).

Two people made the completion of this project possible. One has no idea of her contribution, but Sevan Siranoush Suni made the sun shine again. Her mother, Armena Marderosian, accompanied me to Tbilisi twice, endured endless conversations in languages she did not understand, and found the courage and joy in life to pull us both through when our lives together almost stopped. It is to her, in the memory of our son, that I dedicate this book.

Note on Transliteration and Dating

Although some exceptions have been made to conform to more familiar usage, in general names and words from Georgian, Armenian, and Russian have been transliterated according to the Library of Congress systems, with a few modifications.

Armenian transliteration is according to the east Armenian dialect, that spoken in the Russian empire and Persia. Georgian words (even titles of books and newspapers) are not capitalized, since Georgian does not use capital letters. Personal names are capitalized, however, and are usually given as they would be transliterated from Georgian. Thus, the more familiar Dzhugashvili (Stalin) is given as Jughashvili, Ordzhonikidze as Orjonikidze. An attempt has been made to transliterate Armenian names according to their Armenian originals (Shahumian instead of the Russian version, Shaumian) and Russian names according to their Russian originals. Certain inconsistencies, however, actually make the text clearer. For instance, the Georgian form is used for the name of the penultimate Georgian king, Erekle II, a monarch who operated in a Georgian context; but the Russian form of the same name has been used for Iraklii Tsereteli, the social democrat who made his reputation in Russia proper.

In Part I the capital of Georgia is referred to by its Georgian name, Tbilisi, and not (except in direct quotations) as Tiflis, the name by which it was generally known to non-Georgians. In Part II Tiflis, the commonly used foreign form, is used. Tiflis is replaced by Tbilisi in chapter 11, that is, from about the year 1936 when the Georgian name was officially revived.

Unless otherwise noted, dates before February 1, 1918, which refer to events in Georgia, Armenia, or Russia are given in the Julian calendar, which was thirteen days behind the Gregorian calendar of the West in the twentieth century, twelve days behind in the nineteenth century, eleven days behind in the eighteenth century, and so on.

THE
MAKING
OF THE
GEORGIAN
NATION

THE RISE AND FALL OF THE GEORGIAN MONARCHIES

PART ONE

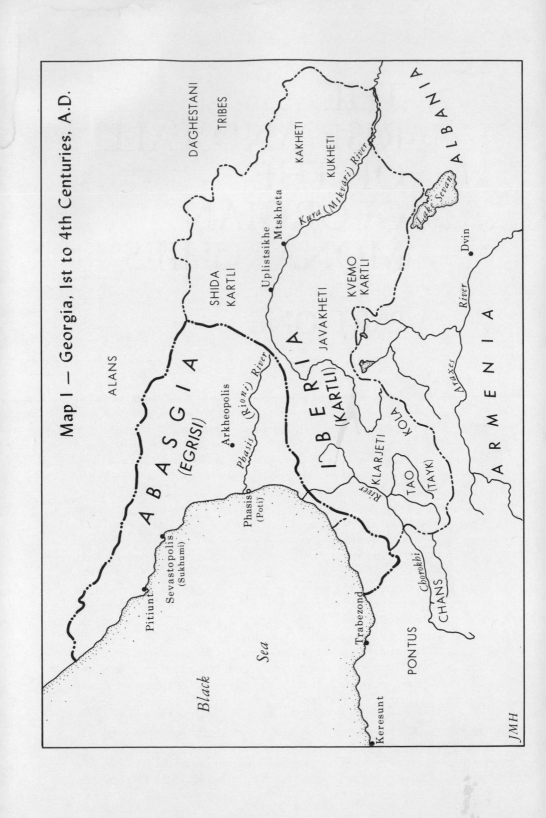

Map I — Georgia, 1st to 4th Centuries, A.D.

1 The Formation of the Georgian Nation

A favorite story of modern Georgians relates how God came upon the Georgians only after he had parceled out all the countries of the world to other nationalities. The Georgians were in a typically festive mood and invited the Creator to join them in wine and song. The Lord so enjoyed himself that He decided to give these merry and carefree people the one spot on the earth that He had reserved for Himself—the valleys and hills that lie to the south of the great Caucasus Mountains.

Unfortunately, the actual ethnogenesis of the Georgian people is far more obscure than this anecdote allows, and to probe its mysteries scholars have used linguistic as well as historical and archaeological evidence. The Georgians call themselves *kartveli* and their country *sakartvelo*, "the place of the Georgians." But the latter term was not used until the eleventh century, when Georgia was first united. Unity was brief, however, and for most of history the lands in which Georgian speakers have lived have been divided into two principal parts, separated by the Surami mountain range. Western Georgia, lying in the basin of the Rioni (Phasis) River, was in ancient times known as Colchis and later as Lazica, Abasgia, or Imeretia. Among the Georgians western Georgia was first referred to as Egrisi, later as Abkhazeti, and most recently as Imereti. Eastern Georgia, larger in territory and running along the Kura (Cyrus) River, was called Iberia (Hiberia) by the classical world and Kartli by the Georgians. Less well known but historically a part of Georgia is an area lying to the southwest of Imereti, in the valleys of the Chorokhi and the upper Kura, a land referred to as Zemo Kartli (Upper Iberia) or Meskhia. The lands to the south of the Kura but east of Upper Iberia are sometimes referred to as Kvemo Kartli (Lower Iberia), while the lands to the north, on the other side of the Kura, are called Shida Kartli (Inner Iberia). Upper Iberia consisted of the lands in the basin of the Chorokhi—Achara, Nigali or Ligani, Shavsheti, Cholarzene or Klarjeti, and Tao—and the lands in the basin of the Kura—Samtskhe or Meskhia, Javakheti, Artani, and Kola. Lower Iberia included the lands of Trialeti, Gachiani, Gardabani, Tashiri, and Abotsi.[1] To the east of Kartli proper lie the regions of Kakheti and Kukheti, the easternmost territories historically inhabited by Georgians. As the eminent scholar of Caucasian history, Cyril Toumanoff, points out: "Most of these lands were, historically no less than geographically, Georgio-Armenian marches, and so a battlefield between two neighboring monarchies. The struggle over them is still going on—on the battlefield of historiography."[2]

The languages of the Georgian peoples are not part of the Indo-European, Altaic, or Finno-Ugric language families. Rather they belong to the southern Caucasian language group known as Kartvelian (kartveluri) and have descended from an original, proto-Georgian language that began to break into several distinct but related languages about four thousand years ago. The first to break away was the Svan language (svanuri), in about the nineteenth century B.C., and by the eighth century B.C. zanuri, the basis of Mingrelian (megruli) and Laz (chanuri), had become a distinct language.[3] On the basis of language it has been established that the Georgians were made up of three principal, related tribes—the Karts, the Megrelo-Chans (Zvans), and the Svans—but in addition there were other Georgian-speaking tribes in Asia Minor, among them the Kashkai (Gashgai, Gashgash, Kashku, Kaska), the Mushki (Moskhi, Moschi, Meskhi), and the Tibal (Tabal, Tibar). The distinguished Soviet investigator of ancient Georgia, G. A. Melikishvili, writes that the peoples speaking these Ibero-Caucasian languages "in all probability have been settled in the territory of Transcaucasia and the North Caucasus from the most ancient times." Ancient place names testify to their presence in the earliest records, and archaeological research does not indicate any great changes in the ethnic composition of the peoples of Caucasia.[4]

The antiquity of the division into myriad language groups is testified to by Herodotus, Strabo, and Pliny. The mountainous terrain tended to separate and isolate related peoples from one another and encouraged the development of dozens of separate languages and dialects. Strabo, for example, writes that in the Greek port of Dioscurias in western Georgia seventy tribes gathered to buy and barter: "All speak different languages because of the fact that by reason of their obstinacy and ferocity, they live in scattered groups and without intercourse with one another."[5]

Evidence indicates that primitive peoples have been living in Georgia since the early Paleolithic period, more than fifty thousand years ago. In southern Oseti and along the Black Sea coast, in Abkhazeti, crude stone tools have been unearthed. Archaeologists have investigated late Paleolithic cave dwellings in Devis Khvreli, Sakazhia, Sagvarjile, and Gvarjilas klde.[6] There have been settlements in the Kura basin since the fifth millennium B.C.

Radiocarbon dating at Shulaveri indicates that the earliest settlements there date from 4659 B.C., plus or minus 210 years. Signs of Neolithic culture, and the transition from foraging and hunting to agriculture and stockraising, are found in Georgia from 5000 B.C., and settlements such as those at Tsopi, Aruchlo, and Sadachlo along the Kura in eastern Georgia are distinguished by a "culture marked by its long duration, its distinctive architecture and its relativity crude but easily recognizable pottery, with its considerable skill in stoneworking."[7] In a very real sense, then, the highlands of eastern Anatolia and Transcaucasia were one of the "cradles of civilization," for in those areas the right combination of domesticable animals and sowable grains and legumes made possible the earliest agriculture. "In short," the *Cambridge Ancient History* states, "the highland zones of the Near (and Middle) East turn out to be the areas in which these earliest developments occurred, and those in the lowland plains date from later periods, thus reversing the old theories that Mesopotamia and Egypt were the birthplaces of civilization."[8]

The entire area of Transcaucasia and eastern Anatolia was, in the period beginning in the last quarter of the fourth millennium B.C., inhabited by people who were probably ethnically related and of Hurrian stock. (The Hurrians, a people spread throughout the Near East in the third millennium B.C., spoke a non-European language closely related to what later became Urartian.) The ethnic and cultural unity of these two thousand years is characterized by some scholars as Chalcolithic or Eneolithic. British scholars Charles Burney and David Marshall Lang refer to these years as the period of "Early Transcaucasian Culture," although some Soviet paleohistorians prefer the term "Kuro-Araxes Culture." Whatever the label applied, it is clear that during this era economic stability based on cattle and sheep raising was achieved, and as a result there was noticeable cultural stability as well. About 2300 B.C. this unified and flourishing culture went into a gradual decline, and after a period of stagnation it broke up into a number of regional cultures. By 2300 B.C. the peoples of the Kura-Araxes area had already made contact with the more advanced civilization of Akkadian Mesopotamia.[9]

At the end of the third millennium, the Indo-European Hittites entered eastern Anatolia and established their rule over Asia Minor and Syria, a dominion that lasted over a thousand years. During the Hittite period Georgia entered the Bronze Age (the Middle Bronze Age in Transcaucasia is dated from 2000 B.C. to 1200 B.C.), and there is evidence of considerable economic development and increased commerce among the tribes. In western Georgia and Abkhazeti, a unique culture known as Colchidic developed between 1800 and 700 B.C., and in eastern Georgia the *kurgan* (tumulus) culture of Trialeti reached its zenith around 1500 B.C. The earliest written records of people living in Armenia come from Hittite tablets, which tell of wars fought by two Hittite kings, Suppiluliumas (1388?–1347 B.C.) and his son Marsilis I (1347?–1320 B.C.), against tribes inhabiting the Armenian plateau.[10] No written records mention the lands of Georgia, but the national epic of Amiriani may have originated in this early period.[11] Late in the Hittite era, by the last centuries of the second millennium, ironworking made its appearance in Transcaucasia but, as Burney and Lang point out, "the true Iron Age only began with the introduction of tools and weapons on a large scale and of superior quality to those hitherto made of copper and bronze, a change which in most of the Near East may not have come before the tenth or ninth centuries B.C."[12]

The Hittite kingdom fell about the year 1190 B.C. under the attack of the mysterious "peoples of the sea" (so called in the sources) and of Indo-Europeans—Thracians, Phrygians, and proto-Armenians—moving from the west into Asia Minor. The political vacuum left by the Hittite collapse was quickly filled by the Phrygians in the west and the Assyrians in the east. The Assyrian king, Tiglath-pileser I (1115–1077 B.C.), led several expeditions into the lands of Nairi, later to be central Armenia. There the Assyrians fought and defeated the Phrygians, whom they called Mushki or Tabal, driving them to the north and west, where they came under the cultural influence of the waning Hittites. In the view of Melikishvili, the Mushki, who settled in the upper Euphrates and along the Murad-su, were Georgian speakers, one of the Kart tribes. After the fall of the Hittites, the Mushki formed their own state in east-central Anatolia, a relatively strong formation, known in the Bible as Mosoch.[13]

Other tribes mentioned in the Assyrian inscriptions may also have been proto-Georgian tribes, notably the Kashkai and the Tibal (the biblical Thubal), who lived in eastern Anatolia. The Kashkai had participated in the destruction of the Hittite empire, then moved westward, where they came up against the Assyrians. The Tibal were, like the Mushki, known for their metallurgy, and the people of Tibal were vassals of the great Assyrian empire from the eleventh century.[14]

The most important tribal formation of possible proto-Georgians in the post-Hittite period was that of the Diauehi (Diauhi, Daiaeni), formed about the twelfth century B.C. southwest of Transcaucasia, in the region to the north of present-day Erzerum. The Diauehi coalition was powerful enough to resist attacks by Assyria, although in 1112 B.C. their king was captured by Tiglath-pileser I. In the ninth and early eighth centuries B.C., Diauehi was the nucleus around which many tribes of southern Transcaucasia gathered, and it was therefore the target not only of Assyria but also of the rulers of the newly emerging state of Urartu. In 845 B.C., Shalmaneser III of Assyria defeated King Arame of Urartu, and King Asia of the Diauehi became his vassal.[15] Sometime in the early eighth century, both Menua and Argishti I of Urartu campaigned against the Diauehi, defeating their king, Utupurshini, and forcing him to pay tribute. The southernmost regions of the Diauehi were annexed by Urartu, and by the middle of the century the blows from Urartu in the east and from the tribes of western Georgia destroyed the Diauehi. This left the tribal formation of Colchis bordering directly on

Urartu, and conflict soon developed between these two political coalitions.[16] The eminent Soviet prehistorian, Igor D'iakonov, believes that Georgian-speaking tribes were already in eastern Pontus (Colchis) in the ninth century B.C. Homer mentions the Halizones in Pontus, and it is supposed that this tribe is the same as the later Chalybes, a proto-Georgian tribe.[17]

The fragility of the various "empires" of the eighth century became evident about 720 B.C. when nomadic peoples from the northern shore of the Black Sea, the Cimmerians, swept down the coast, passing through Colchis and into Urartu. About the same time, the Scythians poured through the Daryal Pass into central Georgia and down the western coast of the Caspian into Urartu. The Cimmerians destroyed the southern Colchian state, known as Kulkha in Urartian inscriptions. Whole regions were emptied of people as the Cimmerians moved south to Syria, Palestine, and the borders of Egypt. Some Mushki and Tibal, pushed aside by the Cimmerians, moved northeast into the Pontic regions, where by the fifth century they had made contact with Greek colonists. For a short time a distinct "kingdom of the Mushki" to the west, a state closely connected with the Phrygians, reigned as the strongest state in Asia Minor. Ruled by Mitas, whom some scholars identify with the legendary Midas of the golden touch, the kingdom of the Mushki had its capital at Gordion, and its people spoke Phrygian, an Indo-European language. The brief ascendancy of the Phrygian-Mushki state came to an end at the hands of the Cimmerians, who were probably allied with Rusa II of Urartu (685–645 B.C.).[18] Some of the Mushki assimilated with local peoples, but others moved northwest out of the area known as Speri, taking with them their Hittite religion and culture.

By the Late Bronze Age, a period that in Caucasia included the end of the second millennium and the first centuries of the first millennium B.C., differentiations in wealth within the tribes are evident in the burial sites. Soviet scholars, including Melikishvili, argue that this "was the period of the disintegration of primitive communal relations among the population of Georgia" and the transition to "class society." Following the linear scheme set out by Friedrich Engels in *The Origin of the Family, Private Property, and the State,* Melikishvili proposes that primitive communal society was replaced by "military democracy" and firm alliances of tribes, which in turn may be seen as the beginning of the formation of a Georgian nationality.[19] Tempting as this theoretical model of Georgian social evolution may be, it must be remembered that there is little available evidence to illuminate the social structure of the tribal societies of this ancient period. It is known that the proto-Georgian tribes (then centered in the Chorokhi basin north of Erzerum) and the proto-Armenian tribes (probably located to the south in the region bordering the Murad-su) were not under a central, unified political authority once the Cimmerians had swept through the area.[20]

The second half of the seventh century B.C. marked the rise of significant political formations that can be identified with proto-Georgian tribes. Some of these tribes, living in the upper reaches of the Chorokhi River, were united under the name *sasperi*.[21] Based in the former territory of the Diauehi, the Sasperi had much of southern Transcaucasia under their sway by the early sixth century and participated in the destruction of the Urartian empire, only to disintegrate under the expansionist thrusts of the Medes in the east. The Sasperi merged with the Urartians in their lands, and, Melikishvili conjectures, borrowed Urartian words that found their way into the Georgian language.[22] At approximately the same time, a new "kingdom" of Colchis was formed in western Georgia, extending from the mouth of the Chorokhi northward but not reaching as far as the Caucasus Mountains. The political center of the kingdom of Egrisi, as it was known to eastern Georgians, was on the Rioni River. Greek migrants from Miletus settled in coastal towns at Trebizond, Kerasunt, Phasis, Dioskuri, and Pitiunt and traded with the native population.[23]

Early in the sixth century, the Urartian empire fell to the Medes, Scythians, and Sasperi, and the Median empire replaced it as the principal political power in Asia Minor.[24] The destruction of Assyria, Urartu, and, not long afterward, of Media created a fluid situation in which tribes of various language groups migrated and settled in new areas that proved to be relatively permanent homes. Armenian tribes moved eastward and occupied Hurrian lands west of Lake Van and to the south of what is today the city of Mush. These lands had been called Arme or Armeni by Urartians, and this may be the source of the name by which Armenians are known to the world.[25] Sometime in the sixth and fifth centuries B.C. some Georgian-speaking tribes, probably the Mushki and Tibal, made their way northeast and settled in the Kura valley, where they formed the nucleus of the Iberian or east Georgian nation.[26] Burney and Lang note the violence that accompanied this migration: "To judge by the abundance of warrior graves of the period the supremacy of the Iberians over the Scythians, Cimmerians and other Indo-European invaders of the Kura Valley was not won without a struggle."[27] Living in troglodytic towns like Uplistsikhe (near Gori), the Iberians moved later to Mtskheta on the Kura. This capital was defended by the fortresses of Armazi on Mount Bagineti and Sevsamora on the Aragvi River.

This transitional phase of Georgian and Armenian national formation is not well illuminated by local historical evidence, and scholars are forced to rely on later classical sources to produce the barest outlines. Herodotus provides us with much of what we know about Caucasia in the sixth and fifth centuries B.C. The first great "world empire," that of the Persians under the Achaemenid dynasty, covered most of Asia Minor and Transcaucasia. The Armenians made up the thirteenth satrapy of the empire; the Sasperi, Matieni, and Alarodi (Urartian and other Hurrian remnants) formed the eighteenth satrapy; and the proto-Georgian Mushki (Moschi), Tibal (Tibareni), Macrones, Mossynoeci, and Mares were included in the nineteenth.[28]

In his descriptions of the military dress of the "Asian" peoples, Herodotus mentions that the various proto-Georgian tribes were similar in uniform and weaponry:

> The Moschi wore wooden helmets on their heads, and carried shields and small spears with long points. The Tibareni and Macrones and Mossynoeci in the army were equipped like the Moschi . . . The Mares wore on their heads the plaited helmets of their country, carrying small shields of hide and javelins. The Colchians had wooden helmets and small shields of raw oxhide and short spears, and swords withal.[29]

The Persian hold over these Georgian tribes was fairly firm until the second half of the fifth century B.C. Georgians marched in the Persian campaigns against the Greeks, and Persian terms in Georgian political vocabulary are eloquent testimony to the depth of Iranian influence in government. Not included in the empire as a satrapy, the kingdom of Colchis was an autonomous vassal state of the Achaemenids. Herodotus tells us:

> Gifts were also required from the Colchians and their neighbors as far as the Caucasian mountains (which is as far as the Persian rule reaches, the country north of the Caucasus paying no regard to the Persians); these were rendered every five years and are still so rendered, namely, one hundred boys and as many maidens.[30]

Colchis in Achaemenid times thus was a tributary state, largely agricultural, with some ironworks, slaves, and commerce in its Greek ports. As a semi-independent kingdom, Colchis-Egrisi existed until the third century B.C. Melikishvili characterizes it as an "early slaveowning society, . . . a relatively underdeveloped class society in which there still were strong remnants of primitive communal society and where the quantity of slaves and the area in which they were used were insignificant."[31]

By the time Xenophon marched through Asia Minor to the Black Sea (401–400 B.C.), the Colchians and other Georgian tribes had freed themselves from Achaemenid rule. As Xenophon and his thousands moved closer to the sea, they came to a mountain pass leading down into the coastal plain. Their path was blocked there by peoples whom Xenophon called the Chalybes, Taochi, and Phasians.[32] The Greeks attacked the defenders of the pass from above, drove them off, and then "descended into the plain on the farther side and reached villages full of many good things." Xenophon's army proceeded deeper into the country of the Taochi, who lived in strong fortifications. The Greeks, in need of provisions, attacked one of the fortresses but were held off for a time by defenders hurling stones and boulders. Once the fortress was taken, "then came a dreadful spectacle: the women threw their little children down from the rocks and then threw themselves down after them, and the men did likewise."[33]

Without many prisoners but with great numbers of oxen, asses, and sheep, Xenophon moved on through 150 miles of the country of the Chalybes.

> These were the most valiant of all the peoples they passed through, and would come to hand-to-hand encounter. They had corselets of linen, reaching down to the groin, with a thick fringe of plaited cords instead of flaps. They had greaves also and helmets, and at the girdle a knife about as long as a Laconian dagger, with which they might be able to vanquish; then they would cut off their [enemies'] heads and carry them along their march, and they would sing and dance whenever they were likely to be seen by the enemy. They carried also a spear about five cubits long, with a point at only one end. These people would stay within their towns, and when the Greeks had pushed by, they would follow them, always ready to fight. Their dwellings were in strongholds, and therein they had stored away all their provisions; hence the Greeks could get nothing in this country, but they subsisted on the cattle they had taken from the Taochians.[34]

After ravaging the country of the Colchians, Xenophon moved on to the west and entered the land of the Mossynoeci, where the Greeks allied themselves with one tribal alliance against another. Xenophon's report about the peculiar activities of the upper class deserves to be mentioned:

> And when the Greeks, as they proceeded, were among the friendly Mossynoecians, they would exhibit to them fattened children of the wealthy inhabitants, whom they had nourished on boiled nuts and were soft and white to an extraordinary degree, and pretty nearly equal in length and breadth, with their backs adorned with many colours and their fore parts all tattooed with flower patterns. These Mossynoecians wanted also to have intercourse openly with the women who accompanied the Greeks, for that was their own fashion. And all of them were white, the men and the women alike. They were set down by the Greeks who served through the expedition, as the most uncivilized people whose country they traversed, the furthest removed from Greek customs. For they habitually did in public the things that other people would do only in private, and when they were alone they would behave just as if they were in the company of others, talking to themselves, laughing at themselves, and dancing in whatever spot they chanced to be, as though they were giving an exhibition to others.[35]

From Xenophon's *Anabasis* it is possible to piece together a picture of the western Georgian tribes at the end of the fifth century B.C. Free from Persian authority (except for the Mossynoeci), they lived in hostile relations with the Greek merchant ports. The various tribal alliances fought with one another, and therefore their lands were covered with fortified settlements. There were no major towns in the area and, in the words of Melikishvili, people "lived in conditions characteristic of the political fragmentation of a primitive communal society, in which separate tribal formations warred constantly with one another."[36]

In the first half of the fourth century B.C., the Persians may have managed to reassert their suzerainty over the western Georgian tribes, for it is known that the Greek cities of Sinope and Amis came under their authority. But the Achaemenid hold over the western satraps was tenuous, and during the reign of Artaxerxes II (405–359 B.C.) several provincial subordinates, including Orontes of Armenia and Datam of Cappadocia, revolted against Persian authority.[37] With the campaigns of Alexander the Great and his decisive victory over the Persians at Arbela (Gaugamela) in 331 B.C., Persian power collapsed in Asia Minor. The Greek expansion not only drove back the Persians but introduced a new cultural and political hegemony over eastern Anatolia. The dominance of Persian and Mesopotamian political culture was both inhibited and complemented by the Greek in a new Hellenistic synthesis, though the influence of Iranian culture remained strong in Georgia and Armenia.

Through the two centuries of Achaemenid dominion over eastern Anatolia and Transcaucasia (546–331 B.C.), several proto-Georgian tribes had migrated north from Anatolia into the Pontic regions along the Black Sea coast, where Xenophon found them, and to the east into the Kura valley. The Tibal and Mushki had moved into eastern Georgia, where they merged with local tribes to form the Georgian people. To the Greeks they were known as Iberoi (Iberians), a name that Melikishvili believes came from the land from which they had migrated, Speri. D. M. Lang mentions the hypothesis that the root *Tibar* in Tibareni (Tibal) gave rise to the form *Iber* from which the Greeks derived their name for the eastern Georgians. From the Mushki (Meskhi, Moskhi) came the name of the chief city of ancient Iberia, Mtskheta. Even more important, the Mushki brought with them from the west the pantheon of Hittite gods, headed by Armazi, the moon god, and Zaden, the god of fruitfulness.[38]

With the elimination of Achaemenid authority the eastern Georgian tribes might have fallen under Macedonian rule, but early in the third century B.C. the ruling dynast of Armazi-Mtskheta in eastern Georgia established his primacy over the other Iberian princes. The Georgian chronicles, *kartlis tskhovreba,* provide the tradition of the first king of Kartli-Iberia, Parnavazi (Farnavazi, Pharnabazus), who, they claim, was a descendant of Kartlosi, the eponymous ancestor of the Georgians. The chronicles state that Parnavazi united Georgians of the east with those of Colchis-Egrisi to drive the "Greeks" from Mtskheta. The overthrow of Azon, founder of the Mtskheta state, and the explusion of the Macedonians left Parnavazi the most powerful ruler in Transcaucasia, and he soon brought western Georgia under his rule. The hegemony of Kartli-Iberia over Colchis-Egrisi meant that the Georgian tribes consolidated around eastern Georgia.[39] Although an older state than Kartli, Egrisi's independence did not prove as durable, and it was successively ruled by Achaemenid Persia, Hellenistic Pontus, Rome, and Byzantium. Parnavazi's new state, on the other hand, soon demonstrated an enviable independence and energy. Kartli not only expanded into western Georgia (with the exception of its northern mountainous regions), but held

Zemo Kartli (Mtskheta), Kvemo Kartli, Shida Kartli, and Kakheti.[40] Parnavazi maintained friendly relations with the heirs of Alexander the Great, and his successors continued this policy and paid tribute to the rulers of the Seleucid empire. Toumanoff suggests that once Seleucid overlordship had been established in Armenia it may have been necessary for the Seleucids to set up a vassal state in Kartli-Iberia to provide pressure on Armenia from the north. In his view, Parnavazi, whose reign he estimates at 299 to 234 B.C., probably operated as such a Seleucid vassal.[41]

Parnavazi is credited by the Georgian chronicles with introducing a military-administrative organization into his kingdom that both Soviet scholars and W. E. D. Allen see as the beginnings of a feudal system.[42] The king appointed a military governor (eristavi) to each of the seven major provinces (Argveti, Kakheti, Gardabani, Tashir-Abotsi, Javakheti-Kolas-Artani, Samtskhe-Ajara, and Kvarjeti) while keeping the central district of Shida Kartli under the administration of his highest official, the spaspeti. Western Georgia was not made into a saeristavo (province) but was a vassal state ruled by Kuji, the man who had aided Parnavazi against the so-called Greeks. The political patterns adopted by the Iberian state were those of its powerful neighbor, Persia, and the term used for a local administrator, pitiaskhshi, was borrowed directly from Persian.[43] Toumanoff sees the new administration as an attempt to impose royal power over the still quite independent tribal leaders. "To ensure its control of the dynastic aristocracy of the sep'ecul-s or mt'avar-s ('royal children,' 'princes'), the youthful Crown instituted the feudal order of the erist'av-s ('dukes') . . . This was not so much a supersedure of the princes, who remained too powerful for that, as the conversion of the more important among them into officers of the State entrusted with the control of others. In this way, the Crown, which was to claim the fulness of sovereignty for itself alone, was able gradually to deprive of it the lesser princes, sharing it, under the guise of delegation, with only a few among them."[44]

Georgia's economy was based on free peasant agriculturalists, though there was apparently some slaveholding. At the top of society stood the royal family, the military nobility, and the pagan priesthood. But the formation of the east Georgian state not only laid the foundation of Georgian social hierarchy but also in its initial stages encouraged the consolidation of separate tribes into a larger ethnic conglomerate. Barriers between tribes were eliminated as a consequence of the political organization established by the Kartveli. "Standing at the head of a powerful state formation, the Kartveli began to assimilate the other tribes who entered into the makeup of the state of Kartli."[45]

With the conquest of Persia by Alexander the Great, a "new epoch of lively commercial and industrial activity" began in Asia Minor. Whereas in the exclusively agricultural economy of Achaemenid times the peoples of Transcaucasia had not been familiar with monetary transactions, at least not until the end of the age, in the Seleucid period money was widely introduced into commercial dealings. Alexandrine drachmas and tetradrachmas were used in western Georgia and Armenia, though not in eastern Georgia, and gold staters of Alexander were used in all three regions. The economic advance of the Hellenistic period was especially keenly felt by the Greek cities of the Black Sea coast. The world trade route from India ran through Media and the Ararat plain to Colchis.[46] This western Georgian state was federated to Kartli-Iberia, and its kings ruled through *skeptukhi* (royal governors) who received a staff from the king. But Iberian power over western Georgia had waned by the late second century B.C., and Colchis-Egrisi proved an easy target for the vigorous ruler of Pontus, Mithradates VI Eupator (111–63 B.C.). Western Georgia thus passed out of the Persian and Iberian spheres of influence into the Greco-Roman culture of the classical cities of the Black Sea littoral.

A new political force entered Asia Minor late in the second century B.C. and changed the balance of forces in eastern Anatolia. In 190 B.C. Roman legions defeated Antiochus III (222–186 B.C.), the Seleucid king of Persia, at the Battle of Magnesia. The weakened Persians were unable to offer opposition when the Armenian kings, Artashes (Artaxias; 189–161 B.C.) of Greater Armenia and Zareh (Zariadres) of Sophene, declared their autonomy from the Seleucid empire. Artashes, founder of an Armenian empire, pushed his border out in a vain attempt to take Sophene. He did succeed in incorporating the southern Georgian regions of Gogarene, Chorzene, and Paryadres. His empire reached the Kura in the north and the Caspian Sea in the east. The Iberian king, Parnajom, fought the Armenians but was killed in battle. His throne was taken by Arshak, son of Artashes, and the Armenian hegemony over eastern Georgia and the trade routes to Colchis lasted well into the first century B.C.[47]

In commercial and cultural contact with Colchis and Pontus, Greater Armenia benefited from the Hellenistic currents from the west. Armenia achieved her greatest expanse in the mid-first century B.C. under the warrior-king Tigran II, "the Great" (95–55 B.C.). In alliance with his father-in-law, Mithradates Eupator of Pontus, Tigran fought the Romans and Persians and conquered Sophene. Disaster befell Armenia when Rome sent Pompey to bring Transcaucasia into submission. In 66 B.C. Tigran was forced to make peace, and Pompey turned north to deal with the Georgians, who had allied themselves with the Armenians. Pompey marched first into Colchis, where he was attacked in the rear by Iberians and Caucasian Albanians. In the spring of 65 B.C., he entered Iberia to fight King Artog (Artoces). Plutarch reports that Pompey subdued the Iberians "in a great battle, in which nine thousand of them were slain and more than ten thousand taken prisoner."[48] As a result of Pompey's expedition, Kartli-Iberia, Armenia, and Caucasian Albania became dependent states of Rome, and Colchis-Egrisi was integrated directly into the empire as part of the province of Pontus.[49] As Toumanoff puts it, "In the years 66–64 B.C., the whole of Caucasia entered the orbit of the nascent *pax romana.*"[50]

Roman power was never very firm in eastern Georgia, and by the second half of the first century B.C. the growing strength of the Parthian successors to the Persian Seleucids was being felt throughout Transcaucasia. For three centuries Romans and Parthians fought over the Armenian and Georgian lands that stood between their rival empires, and the Transcaucasian peoples alternatively sided with one or the other power to maintain their autonomy or to benefit from association with a powerful neighbor. A pattern of Anatolian and Caucasian political maneuvering developed by which the lesser local rulers shifted allegiances, not on the basis of ethnicity or religion, but in desperate attempts to maintain local power in the face of constant threats from larger states. Security could be achieved only temporarily and only in alliance with one of the dominant powers. Rather than an undiluted and consistent struggle for national independence or religious integrity, as is often proposed by modern historians, the struggles of the Armenian, Georgian, and Albanian kings and princes should be seen as a series of constantly changing political orientations. In a treacherous and precarious situation, their lodestar was survival. Often this meant that princes gravitated toward one great power while their monarchs moved toward another.

Gradually, in the second half of the first century B.C., Kartli-Iberia and Albania detached themselves from Roman dominion. When Marc Antony campaigned against Parthia in 36 B.C., neither Iberians nor Albanians joined him. Indeed, in the years 37 and 36 B.C., revolts against Roman authority broke out, first in Albania, then in Kartli-Iberia. The Roman legions under Publius Canidius Crassus entered Georgia to put down the revolt, but Crassus's campaign proved to be the last Roman effort to subdue Georgia. By the last decade of the first century B.C., Kartli-Iberia and Albania were completely free from Rome. The Emperor Augustus recognized Iberia as an ally and lifted Roman taxes from the region. In contrast, Armenia remained a bone of contention between Parthia and Rome into the first century A.D., and as a result Kartli-Iberia emerged as a more powerful state and partook of the spoils to be had in divided and conquered Armenia. In A.D. 35 Parsman I (Farsman, Pharasmanes) of Iberia, an ally of the Romans, defeated the Parthian king of Armenia and placed his brother Mithradates (A.D. 35–51) on the throne. In A.D. 51 Parsman's son, Rhadamistes, defeated his uncle Mithradates at Garni and briefly became king of Armenia, only to be executed by his father. Armenia was taken by the Parthians, who gave the crown to Trdat, the founder of the Parthian Arsacid dynasty in Armenia. Iberia and Rome fought Parthia and Armenia until the Peace of Rhandeia (A.D. 63), when Roman suzerainty over Armenia was recognized by the Parthians in exchange for Roman acceptance of the Arsacid king, Trdat (Tiridates). The terms of the peace destroyed Iberia's chances for aggrandizement at the expense of Armenia, at least in alliance with Rome, and probably influenced Mihrdat (Mithradates) of Iberia, Parsman's son, to ally himself with the fierce Alans, nomads from the north, with' whom he campaigned several times into Armenia.[51]

With the vital issues of security and legitimacy in the balance, the struggle for control of the Iberian and Armenian territories led to almost constant warfare in the first three centuries A.D. between Rome and Parthia, Armenia and Kartli. Toumanoff illuminates the causes of the Roman-Iranian rivalry over Caucasia:

> Juridically, there was the fact that Caucasia had been part of the Achaemenid empire and that, on the other hand, it had subsequently accepted the suzerainty of Rome. Practically, there was the fact that it was necessary to both. Caucasia formed a great natural fortress between the two empires from which each of the rivals could control the delicate frontier-line that lay between them in the south. From it each could strike at the other's sensitive points, Ctesiphon, the "Roman Lake," later, Constantinople.[52]

While Colchis was administered as a Roman province, eastern Georgia generally accepted imperial protection. A stone inscription discovered at Mtskheta speaks of the first-century ruler, Mihrdat I (A.D. 58–106), as "the friend of the Caesars" and the king "of the Roman-loving Iberians."[53] Moreover, Emperor Vespasian fortified Armazi for the Iberian king in the year 75. Rome seemed content for the most part to recognize Kartli-Iberia and Armenia as client states.[54]

Once the Arsacids had firmly established their hold on the Armenian throne in the second century A.D., they extended their rule to Kartli-Iberia. Rev I (*martali*, "the Just"; 189–216), overthrew his wife's brother, Amazaspus II, last of the Pharnabazids. But even as Arsacids triumphed in the Caucasian kingdoms, that dynasty fell from power in its original homeland, Persia, when the dynamic Ardashir overthrew the Parthian dynasty and founded the four-hundred-year empire of the Sassanids (224–651). Led by their warrior-kings, the Sassanids forced Armenia to succumb to their authority, drove back the Romans, captured Emperor Valerian, and invaded pro-Roman Kartli-Iberia and Albania.[55] Shapur I (242–272) placed a vassal, Amazaspus III (260–265), on the throne of Kartli-Iberia, possibly a rival or antiking of Mihrdat II.

The Romans regained Caucasia briefly under Emperor Aurelian (270–275) and again when Carus defeated Iran in 283. The Arsacid line in Kartli-Iberia ended the next year, and the Iranians took advantage of internal strife in the Roman empire to establish their candidate, Mirian III (Meribanes; 284–361), son of the Great King of Iran, on the throne of eastern Georgia.[56] In 298, after a great Roman victory, Iran and Rome signed the Peace of Nisibis, and Mirian was recognized as king, though suzerain rights over Kartli-Iberia and Armenia passed to the Romans. Albania came under

Iranian control. With King Mirian the classical period of Georgian history came to an end, for this monarch was the first of his line to adopt Christianity.

The Greek geographer, Strabo, writing in the first century A.D., permits us to penetrate the military-political veneer of ancient Caucasian history to examine the structure of Colchian and Iberian society. Of the lands around Phasis in Colchis, Strabo writes:

> The country is excellent both in respect to its produce—except its honey, which is generally bitter—and in respect to everything that pertains to ship-building; for it not only produces quantities of timber but also brings it down on rivers. And the people make linen in quantities, and hemp, wax, and pitch. Their linen industry has been famed far and wide; for they used to export linen to outside places.[57]

It is clear that by Strabo's time the period of greatness and prosperity associated with Mithradates Eupator had passed. Some of the tribes near the Hellenistic ports were living in squalor and filth—one received the name *phtheirophagi* ("lice-eaters")—but others reportedly used fleecy skins to pan for gold in the mountain streams (perhaps, as Strabo suggests, the origin of the myth of the golden fleece).[58]

Turning to Iberia, Strabo is full of praise for the country ("fruitful," "exceedingly good pasture"), its towns ("their roofs are tiled, and their houses as well as their market-places and other public buildings are constructed with architectural skill"), and the people. "The plain of the Iberians is inhabited by people who are rather inclined to farming and to peace, and they dress after both the Armenian and the Median fashion; but the major, or warlike, portion occupy the mountainous territory, living like the Scythians and the Sarmatians, of whom they are both neighbors and kinsmen; however, they engage also in farming." Most revealing of all in Strabo's account of eastern Georgian society is his brief description of its four strata:

> There are . . . four castes among the inhabitants of Iberia. One, and the first of all, is that from which they appoint their kings, the appointee being both the nearest of kin to his predecessor and the eldest, whereas the second in line administers justice and commands the army. The second caste is that of the priests, who among other things attend to all matters of controversy with the neighboring peoples. The third is that of the soldiers and the farmers. And the fourth is that of the common people, who are slaves of the king and perform all the services that pertain to human livelihood. Their possessions are held in common by them according to families, although the eldest is ruler and steward of each estate.[59]

Using Strabo and later Georgian and Armenian sources, scholars have developed a picture of Georgian society in classical times. At the top, according to Toumanoff, stood "the dynastic aristocracy of Iberia," which included the royal family *(sepe)* as well as the supreme judge of the land and the commander in chief of the army. Immediately below the aristocracy was the pagan priesthood, which played a diplomatic and probably a judicial role but disappeared with the conversion of Kartli-Iberia to Christianity in the early fourth century. The third class was made up of free agriculturalists and soldiers, the class that in time became the Georgian nobility or *aznaureba.*[60] Akin to the Armenian *azat* class, these small landholders and warriors survived, along with the dynastic aristocracy, well into the twelfth century. The freemen, who lived in territorial communes and held their land as individuals, provided military service and were later known in Georgian as *eri.* For a long time this term meant both "people" and "armed force."[61]

The lowest stratum of society was, in Strabo's terms, *laoi,* semidependent agriculturalists who lived in tribal communes and held their land in common. Both Toumanoff and Melikishvili contend that these people were not slaves in the full juridical sense of that word. They were not the chattel or property of their overlords but were obliged to pay dues in cash and kind and to provide the muscle required by the primitive agrarian economy. They were the *glekhni,* the peasants. Toumanoff asserts that "the rural peasantry, obviously the largest group in Iberian society, had, exactly as in Armenia, come by this time to depend on great landed proprietors, as tenants or *coloni,* and had started on the way towards serfdom." Strabo does not mention artisans, merchants, or real slaves, and it may be that these groups, particularly the latter two, were largely comprised of foreigners.[62]

Although there was some trade between Kartli-Iberia and neighboring countries, the major transit route of Roman times "ran from Southern Russia along the eastern shore of the Black Sea through Colchis and Artaxata-Artašat to Media and thence to the East."[63] The Soviet economic historian, Manandian, does not consider Kartli-Iberia to have been very significant in the transit trade of the first centuries A.D., but Melikishvili takes issue with this view, contending that Manandian underestimates the importance of Kartli in classical trade. Since this was a period of difficulty for Armenia, which was caught between Rome and Parthia, Kartli-Iberia found itself freer to take advantage of transit commerce and developed an interest in trade that probably motivated efforts to control the routes to the south, across Armenia. In Kartli the major trading artery was the Kura, and it is noteworthy that the military-administrative center of eastern Georgia, Mtskheta, was situated at the confluence of the Kura and the Aragvi. Other towns—Kaspi, Uplistsikhe, Urbnisi, Odzrakhe, and Nekresi—were also foci for artisans and merchants *(vachari),* as well as governmental officials and the military.[64]

The first centuries A.D. were the period in which the distinctive features of Caucasian society were molded. Caught between the Roman and Persian worlds, Armenia and Kartli-Iberia were clearly influenced culturally by both, but in the formation of their societies Persian norms played the dominant role.[65] Nicholas Adontz points out the differences from the development of the West, where the state rose from urban settlements to city-states to empires (which in many ways were city-states writ large). In the East, "family relations remained the basic generative principle of political life."[66] Originally a tribal confederation, the Persian empire had evolved by Parthian times into a class society, though one that remained characterized by tribal underpinnings. The Arsacids were kings of kings, rulers of other semiautonomous rulers who paid tribute and gave military service to their overlords.

While Adontz refers to the Arsacid period in Armenia as "feudal," Toumanoff makes an important distinction between "feudalism" and what he calls "dynasticism." Disagreeing with Adontz that the Caucasian social structure was essentially the same as that of Western feudalism, Toumanoff argues that in the Armenian *nakharar* system the princes held their lands absolutely and had much greater local power than did West European nobles, whose tenure was conditional and based on service. Caucasian society was at first dynastic and only later did it approach feudal forms. Toumanoff's dynasticism is marked by princely independence, allodial land tenure, and the primacy of the tribe rather than the state. In Armenia under the Artaxiad dynasty, feudal forms were introduced into a basically dynastic sociopolitical structure. Local princes, whose landholdings existed before their loyalty to the king, became bound to the monarch by ties of political subordination.

"As in Artaxiad Armenia, no doubt under the same imperial influences and probably simultaneously with it, Iberia now evolved that symbiosis of the feudalistic and the dynastic regime which characterizes Caucasian society. The king of Iberia stood at the summit of the two orders, dynasticist and feudal, both as the superdynast and as the theoretical sole source of sovereignty." Toumanoff goes on to explain that "the feudal aspect of the princely class stemmed, in Armenia as in Iberia, from the attempt of the High Kings to involve the dynasts in the service mechanism of the monarchy."[67] A mixture of dynasticism and feudalism emerged in eastern Georgia. Whereas in Armenia the dynastic aspects proved indestructible and prevented the kings from ever fully subordinating the *nakharars* (princes), in Kartli-Iberia monarchical power was exercised more completely and feudal ties were more secure. The Iberian kings were more fortunate than those in Armenia in welding their nobility into a system of service to the monarch, and Iberian monarchs were able at times to unite with their petty nobles against the power of the great princes, something the Armenian kings were unable to do.

The king *(mepe)* of Kartli-Iberia appointed the *spaspeti (erismtavari),* or high constable, to whom all provincial and local officials were subordinated. This office, in contrast to its Armenian counterpart, was not hereditary in one family, though it was usually occupied by a member of the first class, the dynastic aristocracy. The king also recruited some nobles to serve as his royal officers at court *(ezoismodzqvari)* or in the provinces to keep the other nobles in line. In each province an *eristavi* or *pitiaskhshi* governed (the two terms were interchangeable).[68] Most of them came from the highest class. Below the provincial governors were the *spasalarni* (generals) and the *khliarkhni (atasistavni)*, who collected taxes and gathered troops. A few *eristavni* came from the *aznaureba* or nobility, a class that evolved in time from the third class, the free agriculturalists. As warfare increasingly became a matter for mounted warriors *(tskhentartsani)* rather than common foot soldiers *(mkvirtskhlebi)*, military estates were required to support these cavalrymen. The *aznaurni* thus became distinguished from the *tsvrilieri* or "petty people." Already by the fourth and fifth centuries A.D., the *aznaurni* of Kartli-Iberia were becoming a separate social group and were clearly superior to the *tadzdreulni*, the free agriculturists who held allotments on royal lands and served in the king's army.[69]

In its most permanent sociopolitical forms, Georgia was a reflection of Iranian organization rather than Roman. The king of Kartli-Iberia was a hereditary monarch, like the Iranian Great King, not an elected or appointed ruler as in the Roman tradition. Kartli early developed a privileged and hereditary nobility based on the land, just as her neighbor to the east, Iran, had done. In Rome-Byzantium the "ruling class" was an imperial officialdom, nonhereditary and largely the creature of the emperor. As Toumanoff sums up: "Socially the Caucasian polities were similar to the Iranian and utterly unlike the Romano-Byzantine. Armenia and Iberia were even more aristocratic in character than Iran, being, in fact, federations of dynastic princes—each the overlord of a body of lesser nobility—presided over by kings."[70] Yet at the end of the classical period the conversion of Georgia and Armenia to Christianity committed these states to an orientation toward the Romans. Socially akin to the East, Christian Caucasia entered the medieval period with a new cultural and religious allegiance to the West.

2 Christian Georgia: The First Thousand Years

The ancient period of Caucasian history witnessed the transmutation of tribal conglomerations into political societies and can be seen as the gestation period of the Caucasian states; the early Christian period, according to scholars like Nicholas Adontz, Cyril Toumanoff, and Nina Garsoian, can be considered the formative centuries for Caucasian civilization. From the fourth to the eighth centuries, both Kartli-Iberia and Armenia, as well as Colchis-Egrisi and Albania, were divided territorially into "lands" that reflected the ancient tribes and clans that had migrated and merged to form the local nationalities.[1] Attempts by monarchs to centralize their fragmented kingdoms usually were frustrated by local princes, who were always prepared to look beyond the frontier for allies to thwart royal ambitions. "In the polarity of Rome-Iran," Toumanoff tells us, "the Kings of Armenia and Iberia gravitated towards the autocratic and bureaucratic Roman State, and this trend was now enhanced by the meta-political prestige of the Christian Emperors. Their princely vassals, on the other hand, though Christians, were drawn towards the aristocratic realm of the Sassanids."[2] The endless struggle between Rome-Byzantium and Iran, both of which claimed suzerainty over Caucasia, was prolonged precisely because neither great empire was able to overwhelm the other entirely and decisively. This balance between the imperial powers permitted the smaller states of Caucasia to maintain a precious degree of political and cultural autonomy, although the danger of being swept under Iranian or Byzantine hegemony persisted.

The Romans under Diocletian defeated Iran at the end of the third century, ushering in a sixty-five-year period in which the western empire dominated Kartli-Iberia and Armenia. Although relatively brief, this period had long-lasting consequences, for while in the Roman orbit the Caucasian monarchies, first Armenia and then Kartli-Iberia, converted to Christianity. From Cappadocia in the west and Edessa in the south two Christian traditions, one Greek, the other Syriac, penetrated Greater Armenia early in the fourth century. In 314, at Caesarea in Cappadocia, Grigor Lusavorich, "the Illuminator," was consecrated bishop of Armenia. Twenty years later, the king of Kartli-Iberia, Mirian, adopted Christianity. According to Georgian tradition, Christianity was originally brought to Kartli-Iberia by the apostles Saint Andrew and Simon the Zealot; this is testimony, if not to the apostolic origin of the church in Georgia, at least to the antiquity of Christianity in the Caucasus. Trebizond and Pityus were already bishoprics when the illuminatrix of Kartli-Iberia, Saint Nino, began to preach Christ's gospel in 328. The allegiance of the early Iberian church, whether to Constantinople or to Antioch, is unclear, and the possible influence of the Syrian-Iranian or Armenian churches is shrouded in mystery. The western Georgian church, however, was evidently juridically dependent on Constantinople. The first bishop of Kartli-Iberia was consecrated at Antioch at a time when a Roman-Iranian war made the journey to Constantinople impossible.[3]

Whatever the spiritual appeals of the new religion, Christianity in the early fourth century had political and economic attractions for the Iberian state, as Soviet Georgian historians are quick to point out. "The adoption of Christianity," writes V. D. Dondua, "had important consequences for the kings of Kartli. In the first place, it strengthened their alliance with the Roman empire, where Christianity had also been victorious, against the Persians; second, it untied the hands of the kings in the struggle against the pagan priesthood, which possessed immense landholdings and great wealth."[4] Melikishvili claims that the nobility in Georgia quickly adopted Christianity in order to displace the enormously wealthy pagan priesthood, and he believes that a period of intense civil warfare was experienced in eastern Georgia during the conversion. The lowlands quickly converted to the new religion, but it was not until the reign of Mirian's son, Bakur, that the peoples of the mountains became Christian.[5] The former religious elite was replaced by a Christian hierarchy, as each Christian commune or *eklesia* was tied to another under the supervision of priests and bishops. In each town where an *eristavi* sat, a bishopric was established, until by the mid-fifth century there were approximately thirty bishops in Kartli-Iberia.[6] The close ties with Greek Christianity can be seen from the Georgian borrowing of Greek clerical terms: *ekklesia, evangele, diakon, episkop,* and others.

The Roman dominance of Kartli-Iberia was shaken in the year 363 when Emperor Julian was killed in an ill-considered campaign against Iran. His successor, Jovian, was forced to cede the Roman suzerainty over Kartli-Iberia, which had been established three centuries before by Pompey. The Roman vassal in eastern Georgia, Sauromaces II (361–363), was replaced by his younger brother, Bakur I (363–365), called Aspacures II by the Romans, who ruled as an Iranian vassal. Kartli-Iberia became a source of conflict between the two great empires when Emperor Valens briefly restored Sauromaces to rulership in southern Iberia (370–378), leaving only northern Iberia in the hands of the Iranian candidate, Mihrdat III (365–380). But the Roman defeat at Adrianople in 378 restored all of Kartli-Iberia to Iranian control. The chronicles state that the new king, Aspacures III (or Varaz-Bakur II; 380–394), had two wives at once and was irreligious—evidence from a Christian viewpoint of the probable intimacy of this monarch with the Iranians. The situation in Caucasia was somewhat regularized by the Peace of Acilisene in 387, which divided Armenia into two vassal states, with Persia receiving the greater share. By this treaty the Byzantine empire finally admitted the loss of Kartli-Iberia to Iran. From this point on, Iranian influence grew in eastern Georgia, and the ancient teachings of Zoroaster, revived by the Sassanid kings, spread westward, until by the mid-fifth century "Mazdeism appears to have become something like a second established religion of Iberia." Caught between Christianity and Mazdeism (Zoroastrianism), between Rome and Iran, the Georgian monarchy chose Byzantine autocracy as its preferred political model. At the same time the Georgian princes, "albeit Christians, looked in their anxiety to preserve their rights, to the king of kings for protection."[7]

The Georgian noble of the fifth century was already known as *aznauri*, a term that earlier had applied only to the petty nobility. The great dynastic princes—the *mtavarni* or *sepetsulni*—remained a distinct caste within the nobility, close to the king in rank and lineage. The king appointed important members of this dynastic aristocracy to head the seven great principalities of Kartli-Iberia: Shida Kartli, Kakheti, Khunani, Samshvilde, Tsunda, Cholarzene (Klarjeti), and Odzrkhe. These positions were a "feudal" element in an otherwise "dynastic" system. At first the offices were appointed rather than hereditary, but over time each *saeristavo* fell into the hands of a single dynasty. The struggles between this feudal-dynastic aristocracy and the Iberian monarchs are recorded in the Georgian chronicles, the *kartlis tskhovreba*, but a reader must be forewarned that in Georgia, unlike Armenia, the medieval historians were always representatives of the royal house, never of the noble houses. In contrast to Armenia, therefore, there are few references in Georgian historiography to members of the nobility, and even fewer that are favorable to rivals of the royal house.[8]

The growth of Iranian influence in both Kartli-Iberia and Armenia in the fifth century was resisted by the newly established Christian churches and a part of the nobility opposed to the Great King. The most important cultural legacy of this anti-Iranian effort was the invention of the Armenian and Georgian alphabets. Writing in the local languages was needed to combat Mazdaist propaganda. Early in the fifth century, Mesrop Mashtots completed his Armenian alphabet, and then, according to his biographer,

Koriun, set out to devise alphabets for the Georgians and the Caucasian Albanians. This version of the invention of the first Georgian alphabet was later disputed by an eighth-century Georgian historian, Leonti Mroveli, who claimed that a servant of King Parnavazi created the alphabet. A modern Georgian historian, Ivane Javakhishvili, has argued that Georgian writing goes back to the Phoenician-Semitic-Aramaic cultural world and is unrelated to Armenian. Soviet Georgian scholars, including A. G. Shanidze, also dispute the Armenian origin of the first Georgian alphabet, and the controversy continues.[9]

The coincidence of religious and national conflicts was most acutely felt in the mid-fifth century, when the Iranian Great King, Yazdegerd II (438–457), initiated a more active policy of religious and political control over Caucasia, insisting that Armenian, Albanian, and Iberian nobles convert to Mazdaism or risk loss of their rights and properties. At a meeting in Ctesiphon, the nobles feigned agreement, but upon returning home the Armenians and Albanians organized a revolt against Iran. That revolt ended in their defeat at the Battle of Avarair in 451.

The Iberians did not participate in the revolt against Yazdegerd. Indeed, the most powerful prince of eastern Georgia, the *vitaxa* (viceroy) of Gogarene, Arshusha, was kept by the Great King in Ctesiphon, where he became an influential advisor.[10] The Iranians seemingly preferred to deal with the vitaxa rather than the king, the young and vigorous Vakhtang Gorgasali (447?–522). Vakhtang, who had come to his father's throne at age seven, was by age sixteen leading his army against the Osetins (Alans) in the North Caucasus. Loyal to his Iranian suzerain, the young king fought their common enemy, the Roman authorities in western Georgia (455?–458). He married an Iranian princess, Balendukht, and in 472 joined the Iranian Great King in another campaign against Roman west Georgia.

Ten years later, in 482, Vakhtang reversed his political orientation, broke with Iran, and put to death Iran's most faithful vassal, Varsken—Arshusha's son and the new vitaxa of Gogarene. Varsken had taken his pro-Iranian position to the extreme of renouncing Christianity, adopting Mazdaist beliefs, and martyring his Armenian wife, Shushan. In open rebellion against his Iranian overlord, Vakhtang was joined by Prince Vahan Mamikonian, cousin of Shushan and the Iranian-appointed viceroy *(marzpan)* of Armenia. The Armenian chronicler, Ghazar Parpetsi, writes that Vakhtang sent the following message to Armenia: "A powerful Persian detachment has reached the land of Iberia, and I, seeing that I was unable to withstand them, have put my hope in the Armenian mountains, near the border of Iberia, and I await you."[11] The rebels were defeated by the invading Iranian armies, and Vakhtang was forced to flee to eastern Georgia in 484.

In the years of revolt and war with Iran (482–485), Vakhtang formed an alliance with Byzantium, which was sealed by his marriage to Helena, "daughter" (relative) of Emperor Zeno (474–491). The king received permission from Constantinople to elevate the bishop of Mtskheta to the rank of catholicos. As Toumanoff points out, this "can only imply acceptance of Zeno's formulary of faith." Breaking with his Iranophilic past, Vakhtang brought his state and church into line with current Byzantine policy, adopting Zeno's *Henoticon* of 482, which in the East was considered a "veiled condemnation of Chalcedon." After his return to Kartli-Iberia in 485, Vakhtang deposed the prior bishop of Mtskheta, Mikel, presumably for his opposition to the king's new religious position. Mtskheta, the center of the Iberian church, was to be dependent on Antioch, and it was to that Syrian town that the new catholicos and his twelve bishops traveled for consecration.[12] The last decades of Vakhtang's reign marked the zenith of the religious unity of Kartli-Iberia, Armenia, and the Byzantine empire. In 506 at the Synod at Dvin, the moderately Monophysite position of Zeno's *Henoticon* was adopted by the Armenian and Iberian churches. This was precisely at the time when Emperor Anastasius I, a Monophysite, fought the Iranians and made it possible for the Caucasians to declare this religious position.

Vakhtang remained loyal to his Byzantine allies until the end of his life. Early in the sixth century, the Great King of Iran invited Vakhtang to war with him against the Byzantine empire, but Vakhtang refused, thus provoking an Iranian invasion of Kartli-Iberia. Then about sixty, Vakhtang spent the last years of his life in war and exile. The chronology of this period is confused, but it is at least possible to establish that by 518 an Iranian viceroy had been set up at Vakhtang's capital, Tbilisi (Tiflis). In the last year of his life, probably 522, the old king once again had to flee westward to Lazica, where he died.[13]

Much less is known about western Georgia, or Lazica, in the early Middle Ages. A Roman territory since Pompey's conquest, the region experienced a brief flourishing in the mid-fifth century when Laz kings conquered Roman Colchis and founded the Kingdom of Lazica (Egrisi). The new kingdom became an object of desire for the Iberians under Vakhtang, the Iranians, and the Romans under Justinian. Lazica weakened in the 460s and 470s as Vakhtang's Kartli-Iberia became stronger. In 523 the ruler of Lazica, Tsate, broke his alliance with Iran and went to Constantinople, where he adopted Christianity. Soon thereafter a Byzantine garrison was established in Petra (Tsikhisdziri). Iran invaded Lazica several times in the sixth century, but Emperor Justinian (527–565) maintained Roman sovereignty over the western Caucasus. After the Roman-Iranian treaty of 561, in which Iran renounced all claims to western Georgia, Lazica disappeared (at least from the sources) and became a province of the Romans.[14]

In the sixth century Caucasia remained divided between Iran and the Byzantine empire. Western Georgia and part of Armenia were in Roman hands, while the larger part of Armenia (Persarmenia) and much of eastern

Georgia were under Iranian suzerainty after the wars of 526–532. About the year 540, an Iranian viceroy was again reported living in Tbilisi, though the government was being run by local princes, the catholicos, and Grigoli, the *kartlisa mamasakhlisi* (prince-regnant) of Kartli-Iberia. The Iberian monarchs ruled effectively only from their fortress at Ujarma, in the demesne of Kakheti; Tbilisi and Shida Kartli (inner Iberia) were governed more directly by Iran.[15] In 572, anti-Iranian revolts broke out in both Armenia and Kartli-Iberia. Guaram of Klarjeti-Javakheti, the grandson of Vakhtang Gorgasali and his Byzantine consort, Helena, joined Vartan III Mamikonian and his Roman allies in a desperate attempt to break free of Iranian control. Nevertheless, by 575 Iran was again dominant in Caucasia, although the war with the Romans continued for almost two decades.

When the Iberian king, Bakur III, died in 580, the Persians took the opportunity to abolish the monarchy. This was accomplished without resistance from the Iberian aristocrats; the great *eristavni* acquiesced. The Iranian Great King "began negotiations with the Iberian dukes; he promised them great bounties and, by way of blandishment, confirmed their duchies as alods. And the dukes rose and all paid tribute [to the Great King's son]." Just as the Armenian princes had done over a hundred years earlier, the Iberian dynasts collaborated with the Iranian Great King in the elimination of their monarchy. The heirs of Vakhtang Gorgasali remained in their mountain fortresses—one branch in Kakheti, the other in Klarjeti-Javakheti.[16]

The Iberian aristocrats soon had reason to regret their collusion with the Iranians. Direct Sassanid sovereignty led to heavy taxation and a continuation of the Mazdaizing policies of the past. When the Byzantine army under Maurice launched a campaign against Iran in 582, the Iberian princes sent an ambassador to the emperor to request restoration of the Iberian monarchy. Kartli-Iberia's autonomy was restored in 588 by Emperor Maurice, but instead of a king he appointed a curopalates (presiding prince). His ally, Guaram (588–602?), filled the role. Thus a ruling prince appointed from Byzantium replaced the hereditary monarchy. The Iranians accepted this arrangement in the peace of 591, which divided Kartli-Iberia between the two empires at Tbilisi. The treaty placed the old capital of Mtskheta in Roman hands and the new capital of Tbilisi in Iranian hands. The Georgian chronicler, Juansher, makes it clear that the curopalates, although he enjoyed the loyalty of the great nobles, "could not remove the dukes of Iberia from their duchies because they had charters from the Great King and from the Emperor confirming them in their duchies."[17] Thus the period between the death of Vakhtang Gorgasali and the Arab invasions was marked by the ascendancy of the dynastic aristocracy in Kartli-Iberia, the decline and abolition of royal power, and the consequent reduction of the country to the status of a principality—a position shared by Armenia, Albania, and Lazica. By the end of the sixth century the great princes of eastern Georgia, the *eristavni,* "had ceased to be military governors of provinces and had become hereditary proprietors of vast territories, free from royal authority, though required to pay tribute to their distant Iranian sovereign."[18]

Although the chronicler Juansher praises the reign of the Romanophile Guaram, his son and successor, Stepanoz I (590?–627), is condemned as "impious and without fear of God." Whereas Guaram had used the title *mtavari kartlisa* (prince of Kartli-Iberia), his son took the title *eristavt-mtavari* (archduke, or prince of the dukes), possibly in an effort to avoid antagonizing either the Romans or the Iranians.[19] With the Byzantine armies engaged in a difficult struggle against the Avars, a Turko-Mongol horde that was raiding Byzantium, Stepanoz switched his allegiance to Iran and reunited Kartli-Iberia. He made his capital in Tbilisi and from the fortress above the Kura he defied the Roman empire. But Stepanoz had seriously miscalculated. The new emperor, Heraclius I (610–641), called by historian George Ostrogorsky "the creator of Mediaeval Byzantium," launched campaigns, first into Albania (623) and then into Kartli-Iberia (626), and defeated the Iranians. Aided by the Khazars, the Turkic nomads who then dominated the southern Russian steppes, the emperor marched to Tbilisi, captured Stepanoz, and had him flayed alive. Heraclius appointed Adarnase I of Kakheti the ruler of a reduced Kartli-Iberia, and the Khazar overlord, Tong Yabghu Qaghan, was made an *eristavi.*[20] Thus the Byzantine empire quickly re-established hegemony over Caucasia and held that area until the conquest by the Arabs two decades later. By the early seventh century, no kings existed in Caucasia. Albania, Armenia, and Kartli-Iberia were ruled by presiding princes, appointed and sanctioned by the Byzantine emperor.

The political shifts of the late sixth and early seventh centuries were reflected in corresponding changes in religious orientation. The rise of Byzantium's power in Caucasia increased pressure on the local churches to conform to the empire's doctrinal position, even as Byzantium moved from the position of Zeno's *Henoticon* back to the Chalcedonian orthodoxy. It is not clear from the sources if Kartli-Iberia shifted in the sixth century from Monophysitism, which it had accepted late in the fifth century, to the Chalcedonian position. Late in his reign, Vakhtang Gorgasali had allied with Justin I (518–527), and this might have entailed the rejection of the *Henoticon.* There are no indications of Kartli-Iberia's position toward the Armenian church's Second Council of Dvin (555), which officially adopted a moderate Monophysitism. An attempted reunion of the Greek church with the churches of Kartli-Iberia, Albania, Siunia, and part of Armenia did not long endure, and the increase in Iranian power over Caucasia in the 570s discouraged ecclesiastical ties to Byzantium. Only with the successful campaigns of Emperor Maurice in the 580s and the re-establishment of Iberian autonomy under Guaram (588) can we be sure that Kartli-Iberia was restored to the faith of Chalcedon.[21]

In the turmoil of sixth-century politics, this reunion with the church of the Greeks was also short-lived. When Guaram's son, Stepanoz, switched from a pro-Byzantine position to cooperation with Iran, his religious position shifted toward Monophysitism. In 598 or 599 (sources disagree) a Monophysite was chosen to be catholicos of Kartli-Iberia. Hence Juansher refers to Stepanoz as *urtsmuno* (impious). By 608, Iranian authority was predominant in Kartli-Iberia, but soon thereafter the Iberian church swung back to a Chalcedonian position. In 608 or 609, at the Third Council of Dvin, the Armenian church broke with the Iberian church and excommunicated the formerly Monophysite catholicos, Kireon I, for his adoption of the Chalcedonian faith. Apparently Iran at this point was tolerant of Chalcedonians so long as political loyalty to the Great King was assured.

The final victory of the Chalcedonian position in Kartli-Iberia was assured by Heraclius's successful campaigns against Iran and Stepanoz. The emperor was less successful, however, in Armenia. It is true that a union of the Armenian and Greek churches was accepted by Catholicos Ezr (Esdras) in 632 or 633, but this affected primarily Roman Armenians and few of the faithful in Persarmenia. From the early seventh century, then, the Iberian church conformed to the orthodoxy of the Byzantine church, while the Armenian, despite occasional lapses, maintained its own brand of moderately Monophysite Christianity.

In the mid-seventh century, a new element entered Caucasian politics, one destined to remain a potent contender for hegemony over the indigenous peoples to the present day—Islam. Weakened in the wars with Heraclius, Iran was unable to repel incursions by the Arabs, who swept northward in the decades after the death of Muhammad (632). The Byzantine armies also retreated before this new threat. The Arabs penetrated Armenia in 640 and captured the Iberian capital, Tbilisi, in 645. The presiding prince of Kartli-Iberia, Stepanoz II (630?–650?), was forced to recognize the caliph as his overlord. The emergence of this new force in Asia Minor completely changed the centuries-old configuration of Caucasian politics, which had required the Armenians, Georgians, and Albanians to maneuver between the great Christian autocracy to the west and the Mazdaists of Sassanid Iran to the east. As Toumanoff puts it, "The uncouth, vigorous, and egalitarian Islamic empire came to replace the civilized, senile, and aristocratic empire of the Sassanids in the role of the chief foe of Christendom—and to magnify that role."[22]

The Arabs treated Armenia and Georgia as a single frontier province, Arminiya, which was policed by strategically placed garrisons and the viceroy at Dvin and was subject to heavy tributes. But the Arabs made no attempt to colonize Arminiya. The local princes, although recognized as autonomous rulers under the suzerainty of the caliph, were uneasy under Arab rule and frequently rose in revolt. Most notable was the uprising of 681–682 in which Georgians, Armenians, and Albanians participated. For three years Adarnase

II of Kartli-Iberia and Grigor Mamikonian, presiding prince of Armenia, held off the Arabs—until the Khazars joined the fight. Both leaders lost their lives, and the Arabs transferred their favor from the families of the rebels, the Chosroids and the Mamikonians, to rival families, the Bagratids in Armenia and the Guaramids in Kartli-Iberia.[23]

Arab rule in Caucasia was threatened not only by the discontentment of the local dynasts but also by the refusal of Byzantium to relinquish its claims to Armenia and Kartli-Iberia. About the year 689, Justinian II, after a successful campaign against the Muslims, forced the caliphate to cede Caucasia to Byzantium. At the end of the seventh century the Arabs and Byzantines began an intense struggle over Lazica and Abkhazeti, as well as Armenia and Kartli-Iberia. The emperor recognized Guaram II (684–693?) as curopalates of Kartli-Iberia.[24] In Armenia, Justinian pressured the church to accept the Council of Chalcedon. By 693 the Arabs had again taken Kartli-Iberia and Armenia with the help of their Khazar allies, and this time they established direct rule through their viceroy at Dvin. Byzantium did not give up, however, and early in the eighth century the empire aided Armenian rebels under Smbat VI Bagratuni against the Arab viceroy, Marwan ibn Muhammad. The Arabs put down the revolt, and they also dealt a severe blow to the ruling nobility of Armenia in 705, when they arrested and executed hundreds of members of *nakharar* families. This elimination of rival noble families and the subsequent shift of Arab support to the Bagratid (Bagratuni) family greatly aided that dynasty, which emerged as the leading contender for royal power in the next century, not only in Armenia but also in Kartli-Iberia and Albania.

The entire eighth century was marked by Khazar raids, the campaigns and countercampaigns of Byzantine and Arab armies, and periodic Christian resistance to Muslim rule. In 736, Marwan ibn Muhammad, known in Georgia as Murvan Qru, "the Deaf" (because of his cruelty), launched an invasion, probably in an attempt to take western Georgia from the empire. In the 740s Byzantine influence seems to have been restored in Caucasia, although Arab suzerainty continued. Adarnase III (748?–760?) held the title of curopalates, and in 748 the Mamikonians deposed the pro-Arab Ashot III Bagratuni in Armenia. In 771–772 the Armenian Mamikonians made a desperate but ultimately futile attempt to overthrow their Arab overlords, but the disastrous defeat at Bagrevand eliminated many more leading *nakharar*s and further aided the rise of the Bagratunis.[25]

A similar extirpation of the upper nobility took place in eastern Georgia. In 786 the Arab viceroy, Khuzaima ibn Khazim, marched into Kartli-Iberia to take severe measures against the local aristocracy, which had been leading revolts against the Muslims and intriguing with the Khazars. He captured the aristocrats and members of the royal families and " 'cut off their heads, and [in general] treated them in the worst possible manner' . . . Khuzaima's ruthlessness, there can be no doubt, . . . affected, as is clear from the text of

Ya'qubi, a whole social stratum. It is after that date that we hear no more of
the Guaramids and all the other dynasts appear considerably reduced." The
extinction of the Guaramids and the near-extinction of the Chosroids, the
two royal dynasties, allowed a branch of the Armenian Bagratids to gather
their inheritance.[26]

For several decades Kartli-Iberia, like Armenia, had no local dynast as
presiding prince but was ruled directly by an Arab administrator.[27] By the
end of the eighth century, Kartli-Iberia and its neighbor to the south,
Armenia, had clearly reached a political nadir. Toumanoff, however, sees this
time of despair and destruction as a turning point.

> Caucasia was devastated, its aristocracy reduced and decimated by wars and
> repression. Nobles and peasants began removing in large numbers to the
> Empire. And yet these disasters contained the seeds of future recovery. The
> Saracen insistence on collecting taxes and tributes in money, not in kind, led
> to an economic revival. The nobility and peasantry found themselves
> obliged to abandon their autarkic rural economy and to produce a surplus
> of raw and manufactured products for sale. Thus, commerce and urban
> economy, stifled during the upheavals of the Sassanid and Saracen domina-
> tion, recovered; the middle class revived . . . Caucasia once again became
> the nexus of trade-routes connecting Europe and Asia, and the prosperity of
> the medieval period was founded.[28]

Although Kartli-Iberia lived under the direct rule of the Arabs, the
eastern regions of Georgia, Kakheti and Ereti, managed to maintain an
autonomous existence under their local *mtavarni*. "In Kakheti, the native
family of Donauri grew up to independence in the hereditary office of
khorepiskoposi [archbishop]." Elsewhere, in the mountains of Kartli, and in
Abkhazeti, Imereti, and the highlands of the Chorokhi, local lords maintained a degree of freedom from Arab interference. The Arabs, primarily
concerned with maintaining control of the cities and trade routes, cared less
about de facto control of the countryside. Thus an Arab emir sat at Tbilisi,
while the dynasts of Kartli remained at Uplistsikhe.[29] In western Georgia
Leo, prince of Abkhazeti, revolted against Byzantium and conquered Lazica.

After Armenian rebel princes were defeated by the Arabs at Bagrevand,
an Armeno-Georgian prince, Adarnase I Bagratuni, migrated to Klarjeti
(Cholarzene) to the court of his Guaramid cousins, and in the 780s he
acquired the lands of Erusheti (West Javakheti) and Artani. In time, Adarnase
gathered parts of Tao (Tayk) and the duchies of Klarjeti, Ojrkhe, and Tsunda
into his holdings. From these lands the Georgian Bagratunis (Bagratids)
emerged as the most eminent noble family in Kartli. As the surviving
members of the Chosroid house passed away, Adarnase's son, Ashot I, "the
Great" (813–830), became the complete master of the Guaramid state. Ashot
held Shida Kartli, Tao, Artani, Kola, Klarjeti, Javakheti, Samtskhe, and
Trialeti. Only Kakheti to the east eluded him.[30] With his own Arab emirs
growing ever more independent of Baghdad, the caliph decided to rely on the

Bagratids to enforce his authority. When the emir of Tbilisi, Isma'il ibn Shu'aib, revolted against the caliph and was joined by the *mtavari* of Kakheti, the caliph appointed Ashot I Bagratuni the prince of Kartli-Iberia. The rank obliged Ashot to fight the rebel Arabs and their Georgian supporters.[31] The Byzantines recognized the authority of this new prince as well, and Emperor Leo V (813–820) granted Ashot the title of curopalates.

Despite the restoration of the principate in 813, eastern Georgia remained divided among rival authorities. The Bagratids ruled effectively only in western Kartli-Iberia, while the emir of Tbilisi held the capital, and Kakheti had its own *mtavari*. When Ashot I died in 830, his holdings were allotted to his three sons: Adarnase II received Klarjeti and Tao; Bagrat I (842?–876) became prince of Kartli-Iberia; and Guaram ruled Javakheti, Trialeti, Tashiri, Abotsi, and Artani. With the Bagratids divided, the Arab emirs of Tbilisi grew in relative strength. Ishaq ibn Isma'il, emir of Tbilisi (833?–853), was powerful enough to defy the caliph for decades, and he forced the Bagratids to pay him tribute. Finally, in 853, the caliph sent an Arab army under a Turkic officer, Bogha al-Kabir, to put down a rebellion in Armenia and to deal with Tbilisi. Aided in this campaign by the Bagratid curopalates, Bagrat I, the Arab army captured Tbilisi, burned it to the ground, and decapitated the rebellious emir. In the words of W. E. D. Allen, this ended "forever the chance of Tiflis [Tbilisi] becoming the centre of an Islamic state in the Caucasus."[32]

By the middle of the ninth century, the kingdom of Abkhazeti in western Georgia had emerged as a more powerful political authority than Bagratid Kartli-Iberia. At the same time, a renewed danger to Arab hegemony in Caucasia appeared. The armies of the Byzantine emperor, Basil I (867–886), extended the empire's reach to the Euphrates for the first time in a century. The Arabs responded to the threat from the west by consolidating their ties with the Bagratids in both Georgia and Armenia. In 862, the Arabs granted Ashot Bagratuni of Armenia the title of Prince of Princes, clearly favoring him over the other *nakharar*s. Ashot I, "the Great" (862–890), was first among Armenian dynasts and, by aiding Bagrat I of Kartli-Iberia against his brother, Guaram of Javakheti (830–881), he gained great influence in eastern Georgia as well. When Guaram's son, Nasr (881–888), killed Bagrat's son, David I (876–881), Ashot of Armenia again intervened in Kartli-Iberia. Ashot forced Nasr to flee to his allies in the Byzantine empire and supported the legitimate heir to the Iberian rulership, the son of David I, Adarnase IV (II) (888–923).[33] Thus the Armenians under Ashot gained influence in Kartli-Iberia while working, as the Arabs were, to eliminate Byzantine power in the area.

Arab dominion over Caucasia had weakened considerably by the second half of the ninth century, and the developing buffer states in Georgia and Armenia were emerging as a potent bulwark against Byzantine encroachments. In 886, the caliph permitted Ashot the Great to be crowned king of Armenia, thus restoring the monarchy after a lapse of 458 years. Two years later, Adarnase IV was crowned king of Kartli-Iberia by the king of Armenia, and thereby became the first monarch to rule eastern Georgia in over three centuries. These two royal cousins were allies with each other and with the decaying Arab caliphate. Their strategic importance was recognized by the Byzantine emperor, who sent a crown and "a piece of the true cross" to Ashot and in 891 offered Adarnase the dignified title of curopalates. In the absence of Arab or Byzantine power, the Bagratids dominated Kartli-Iberia. From Armenia Ashot's son, Smbat I (890–914), extended his kingdom north to the foot of the Caucasus and west to the frontiers of Colchis-Egrisi, and moved close to Tbilisi and the Kura. When Smbat went to war with the Arab governor of Armenia, his Georgian cousin, Adarnase, came to his aid. Later, when the governor of Azerbaijan attempted to take eastern Georgia, the Georgians supported Smbat's efforts to hold the region. Adarnase even backed Smbat against his own relative, Konstantin of Abkhazeti, who invaded Smbat's territory of Gugark around the year 904. Adarnase captured Konstantin and turned his prisoner over to Smbat, but the Armenian king not only freed his captive, he crowned him king of Abkhazeti. Smbat may have been attempting to balance the power of the Georgian Bagratids by elevating Abkhazeti; this move served to alienate Adarnase, who conspired with the Armenian enemies of the king.[34] In general, however, Adarnase and the Georgians proved to be much more loyal vassals of Smbat than many Armenian princes; the Artsruni family of Vaspurakan, for example, backed by the Arabs, formed their own kingdom in 908. Dynastic ties and considerations of political advantage were far more important in determining strategic connections than ethnic, linguistic, or even religious affinities.

Early in the tenth century, the Armenian and Georgian monarchs were faced by a dangerous alliance between the Arab emir of Azerbaijan, Yusuf, and the Artsrunis of Vaspurakan. After a series of indecisive campaigns, Yusuf managed to defeat and capture Smbat, whom he then executed. The Bagratids of Kartli-Iberia and Giorgi II of Abkhazeti (915?–959?) joined the martyr's son, Ashot II Erkat, "the Iron" (914–928), against the Arabs, and Ashot traveled to Constantinople to form an alliance with Byzantium.[35] Thus the traditional anti-imperial posture of the Caucasian Bagratids was reversed in 921–922, and Ashot was recognized as king of kings (*shahanshah*) in Caucasia as he worked to erase the ravages of Yusuf's invasions. Ashot sought friendship with the rulers of both Abkhazeti and Kartli-Iberia, but when it was discovered that Giorgi II of Abkhazeti had joined in a conspiracy to assassinate Ashot, the Armenian king turned back to his traditional ally, Adarnase of Kartli-Iberia, and together they made war on the Abkhazians. By this time, however, Bagratid unity and power in Armenia had receded. The former Arab province of Arminiya fragmented into small kingdoms and principalities, and from this new political mosaic eastern Georgia was to emerge as the most powerful state in Caucasia.

The Arab danger to Caucasia receded after Yusuf's campaigns, only to

be replaced by the Byzantine empire under the so-called Macedonian dynasty—actually Armenian in origin—which was rapidly expanding eastward. After three hundred years of war with Islam, Byzantine armies were
realizing unprecedented successes in the late tenth century. No single monarch in either Georgia or Armenia was strong enough to resist this imperial
encroachment or to unify the Caucasian principalities, and fragmentation of
political sovereignty increased. In 961 the Armenian Bagratid king moved his
capital from Kars to Ani, and that same year a separate kingdom was created
in Kars. The prince of Siunik in eastern Armenia declared himself king in
970, and two years later the Kingdom of Vaspurakan near Lake Van was
divided among the three sons of the late king. In 982 Lori in northern
Armenia became a separate Bagratid kingdom. In Georgia there were kings
in Abkhazeti (Abasgia) and Kartli-Iberia, a prince *(mtavari)* in Kakheti, and
an autonomous emir in Tbilisi. Against these tiny states the Byzantine
empire moved relentlessly, annexing Taron in 966 and Manazkert in 968,
and threatening a rising new state being formed by David the Great of Tao
(Tayk).

Some historians consider that the Byzantine empire reached its height
under Basil II (975–1025), but before the emperor was able to expand his
realm he had first to establish firmly his power at home. Civil war raged
within the empire from 976 to 979, and in his desperate search for allies Basil
turned to David, the young Bagratid prince of Tao, who sent twelve thousand
cavalry troops. These forces provided the balance needed to overcome the
rebels under Bardas Scleros, and Basil rewarded David with extensive lands
on the frontier of Byzantium.[36] Then the most powerful ruler in Caucasia,
David of Tao used his new prestige and strength to arbitrate dynastic disputes
in both Georgia and Armenia. Himself a Georgianized prince with no
children of his own, David favored the young Bagrat, heir to the Bagratid
throne of Kartli-Iberia, and he made him heir to Tao as well. In 978 David
secured the crown of Abkhazeti for Bagrat by displacing Tevdos III. But
David's plans for his succession went awry when in 981–989 he supported
his friend Bardas Phocus in a revolt against Basil II. Defeated by a combined
Russo-Byzantine force, David agreed to cede his lands to the empire at his
death. Reconciled to his recent foe, Basil II named David the curopalates of
Iberia (990). David was murdered by his nobles in 1000, and Basil II
marched eastward to claim his inheritance. Bagrat III, then king of
Abkhazeti, and his father, Gurgeni of Kartli-Iberia (994–1008), met with
Basil but, unable to prevent the annexation of Tao, were forced to recognize
the new Georgian-Byzantine frontier.[37]

David's legacy to Georgia, however, was far more important than simply
the acquisition of peripheral territories. In 1008 Gurgeni died, and Bagrat III
became the first king of a unified Abkhazeti and Kartli-Iberia (1008–1014).
For the first time since the coming of the Romans the two principal parts of
Georgia were united, and after 1008 a new word, *sakartvelo*, came into use

to refer both to Kartli in the east and Egrisi in the west. "It is only after that moment that one may speak properly of 'Georgia' as a political and ecclesiastical unit."[38]

By the early eleventh century Caucasia had been so fragmented, by what Toumanoff calls a "fissiparous process," that it had "largely lost its raison d'être as a buffer state in the eyes of the [Byzantine] Empire. While Basil II and his successor gathered Armenian and Georgian lands and Armenian nobles left their patrimonies to move deep inside the empire, a profoundly contradictory trend was evident in Georgia proper, where the one surviving Caucasian kingdom was establishing itself. The first king of Abkhazeti and Kartli-Iberia, Bagrat III, made several attempts to incorporate the easternmost Georgian principality, Kakheti, into his realm, but he held that area only briefly. He was more successful in taking over Klarjeti and Artani. From Bagrat's capital at Kutaisi, his son, Giorgi I (1014–1027), launched a campaign to restore the lands of David of Tao to Georgia. In so doing, he broke the peace with Byzantium, first in 1015–1016 when he occupied Tao, and then in 1021 when he faced Basil II and his allies, the Armenian Bagratids of Ani.

The Georgian chronicles, Armenian historian Aristakes Lastivertsi, and the Arab account of Yahya of Antioch all testify to the ferocity of Basil's campaign through Georgia. Prosperous valleys were turned into deserts; old people, women, and children were slaughtered. When a second invasion occurred in 1022, Giorgi submitted to the emperor, relinquished his claims to Tao, and gave the Byzantines his three-year-old son, Bagrat, as hostage. Both Georgia and Armenia lay prostrate before the emperor, whose military and diplomatic efforts had reduced Caucasia to impotence. But just as Byzantine hegemony in the east seemed secure, the harbingers of a major new threat to the heirs of Rome appeared in Caucasia—the Seljuk Turks.[39]

The united Georgian kingdom of Abkhazeti-Kartli was a decidedly decentralized state, in which the great dynasts could successfully challenge the Bagratid king for local power. During the long reign of Bagrat IV (1027–1072), Lipariti Orbeliani, the *eristavt-eristavi*, was the most powerful person in Georgia, and for twenty years he conspired with his Byzantine allies against the monarch in Kutaisi.[40] Bagrat also faced rebellious nobles in Kakheti, where Kvirike III (1010–1029) proclaimed himself king. During his reign Bagrat IV managed to reduce the independent kings of Lori to impotence, and he briefly held the city of Tbilisi. In contradistinction to their predecessors of several centuries earlier, Bagrat III and Bagrat IV were able to reduce mighty princes to lowly status and to elevate their loyal followers into the upper nobility. Clearly, in contrast to Guaram, the late sixth-century curopalates, Bagrat could remove princes holding hereditary possessions. As Georges Charachidzé notes, "This mobile character of a fief conceded by the king seems well established by the tenth century and would no longer be put into question until the end of the fifteenth century."[41]

Despite internal problems, Georgia was by the reign of Bagrat IV the major indigenous power in Caucasia, standing between the Byzantine empire and the emerging Turkish power in Iran. Since much of Armenia was rendered subject to the Seljuks and the Bagratid kingdom of Ani was annexed by Byzantium (1045), Armenian nobles fled to the relatively safer haven of Georgia. There they either joined with Georgian noble families, became merchants and traders, or entered the king's civil service. Toumanoff notes that "Georgian kings entrusted, to the very end of the Georgian polity, their chanceries to houses of Armenian origin and often conducted their correspondence with foreign monarchs in Armenian."[42]

The Seljuks made periodic incursions into Georgia, most notably in 1064–1065 under Alp Arslan. Akhalkalaki in Javakheti was destroyed in 1066, and two years later Kartli and Argveti were ravaged. Tbilisi and Rustavi were retaken from the Georgians and turned over to the Muslim emir of Gandja. No help could be expected from Byzantium, whose influence in Asia Minor suffered a devastating blow in 1071, when Alp Arslan destroyed the imperial army and captured the emperor at Mantzikert. For Georgians this turning point meant that their kingdom was almost alone as a Christian power in the East and was subject to the repeated blows that are known in Georgian history as the *didi turkoba* (the great Turkish troubles). Turkmen tribes began to raid Georgia early in the reign of Giorgi II (III) (1072–1089), enslaving the regions of Asis-Phorni, Klarjeti, Achara, Charcheti, Samtskhe, Kartli, and others.[43] These invasions and settlements had a debilitating effect on Georgia's economic and political order. Cultivated land became pasture for the nomads, and peasant farmers were pushed into the mountains. As a historian of King David wrote: "These were not times of sowing and reaping. The country became empty and turned into forest. And in the place of people, wild animals roamed."[44]

The Georgian king had no choice but to make the trek to Isfahan, just as his contemporaries, Catholicos Vassel of Armenia and King Kvirike of Lori-Tashir, had done. There he submitted to the Seljuk sultan, Malik-Shah, and agreed to pay an annual tribute. The *didi turkoba* greatly weakened Georgian royal power and promoted centrifugal tendencies in the country. Nobles built fortresses and resisted control from the capital. The king of Kakheti, who earlier, under Bagrat IV, had proclaimed himself a vassal of the Georgian king, not only refused to subordinate himself to Giorgi but even converted to Islam.[45] The city of Tbilisi was controlled by its own powerful citizens, who were completely independent of the king. The great nobles of the kingdom finally forced Giorgi to accept his vigorous young son, David, as co-ruler.

David II (III) (1089–1125), known in Georgian history as *aghmas-henebeli* ("the Rebuilder"), was only sixteen years old when he took the reins of power from his impotent father. David began to wage war against the Seljuks at a particularly propitious time. Crusaders from Western Europe had entered the Middle East to liberate the Holy Lands from Islam, and the heirs of Malik-Shah were fighting over his succession. After winning a number of victories over the Turks, King David II refused to pay further tribute to the Seljuks and encouraged his people to return to their homes from their refuges in the mountains.[46]

The renewed force of the monarchy bore down on the most independent *eristavni*, who were either reconciled to the king's new power or were driven from their patrimonies. In 1105, King David defeated the Kakhetian king and annexed Ereti-Kakheti to Georgia. Like Bagrat III before him, David II hoped to eliminate or at least diminish the autonomy of the dynastic princes and to create a more centralized and hierarchical feudal monarchy. Like the unifier of Georgia, so the rebuilder replaced the dynastic aristocrats, who had hereditary claims on provincial holdings, with a service nobility dependent on the king. The king appointed a *mosakargave* (a salaried governor) as his local official in each area he held. The officer's duty was to uproot the *eristavni*, who by the early Middle Ages held their territories in hereditary tenure. In each margravate David appointed a *marzpan* (viceroy) who over time took on the title *monapire* (from the Georgian *napiri* [borderland]).[47]

Unlike his predecessors, David II also re-established royal authority over the church. In 1103 he convened the Ruisi-Urbnisi church council, at which he purged the clerical hierarchy of his opponents. He then combined the highest secular office in his kingdom, the chancellorship or *mtsignobar-tukhutsesi*, with the highest religious office, the bishopric of Chqondideli. To the new post of *mtsignobartukhutses-chqondideli* David appointed his teacher and closest advisor, Giorgi Chqondideli.[48] The new chancellor-procurator also was given judicial powers and influence in both domestic and foreign affairs; he soon came to be called *vaziri* (vizier) in imitation of that powerful office in Islamic countries.

David combined these reforms with a policy of repression and terror against his domestic enemies, directed by his appointed police chief, the *mandaturtukhutsesi*, who ranked just below the *vaziri*. These two officials outranked the commander in chief of the army, the *amirspasalar*, who, under David's supreme command, directed an enlarged army of sixty thousand permanent troops. In the formation of his ruling apparatus, David employed the great *eristavni*, thus making them dependent upon him. The *eristavi* of Svaneti, Iovane Vardanisdze, became the *protostratori* (later called *amirakhori*), the second-in-command of the army, and later was given the post of *mechurchletukhutsesi*, the director of finances. Similarly, members of the Orbeli family occupied the positions of *amirspasalar* and *mandatur-tukhutsesi*.[49]

To build up his army and increase the population of his country, David II invited foreigners to join his forces and to settle depopulated areas in Georgia. Armenians settled in the newly expanded town around the old fortress at Gori.[50] Forty thousand Qipchak Turkish warriors, with their families, moved into Georgia from the north Caucasus and Russian steppe area. The Qipchak nomads soon converted to Christianity and mixed with the Georgian population. Many rose to high state positions, since the king found the Qipchaks useful against both his external enemies, the Seljuk Turks, and the independent nobles who resisted his policies of centralization. David himself married a Qipchak princess. Although many of the former nomads remained in Georgia and played important roles in political and military life, eventually the tribe's leader, Atrak, grew nostalgic for the grass of the steppes and the old nomadic life. He returned to the steppe and presumably was followed by the majority of his people.[51]

The energy David II employed in centralizing his monarchy was matched by his vigor in foreign affairs. His major aims were to clear Georgia of Seljuk intruders, push the frontiers of Christendom eastward, and retake key cities long occupied by Muslims. David worked to maintain peaceful relations with Byzantium, and in 1118 his daughter Kata married Isaac, the younger son of Emperor Alexius Comnenus. As for his neighbors to the north, the Osetins, David pressured them into submission. David's battles were not, like those of the Crusaders, part of a religious war against Islam, but rather were a political-military effort to liberate Caucasia from the nomadic Seljuks.[52] In 1110 David took the city of Samshvilde, and the Seljuks abandoned Kvemo Kartli (Lower Iberia or Somkheti). That same year he defeated the Turks at Trialeti and occupied the town of Gandja. In 1115 Giorgi Chqondideli captured Rustavi, and the following year the king campaigned in Tao and Klarjeti. In 1117 Shirvan, with its fortress at Kalajori, was invaded, and in 1118 the former Armenian kingdom of Lori was liberated from the Turks. But David's successes against the Turks, as well as his demands for tribute from the independent city of Tbilisi, gave rise to an alliance between the Seljuk· sultan and the largely· Muslim merchants of Tbilisi, Gandja, and Dmanisi. The ruling elites in these Caucasian cities requested aid against David, and Sultan Mahmud of Iraq organized a massive levy among Muslims for a campaign against Georgia.[53]

On August 12, 1121, the Georgians and their Armenian, Qipchak, Osetin, and Shirvan allies advanced and attacked the Muslims unexpectedly near Didgori, achieving what in Georgian history is known as *dzleva sakvirveli,* the "wonderful victory." To this day Georgians celebrate the holiday of *didgoroba* in mid-August.

The unification of Georgia and the elimination of Muslim authority was completed in the year following the battle at Didgori. David laid siege to and captured the city of Tbilisi, which for nearly four hundred years had been an Islamic town. Five hundred citizens were tortured to death, and much of the city burned. Tbilisi became a royal town, the capital of Georgia, and in time lost its self-governing status.[54] The population of the city long remained predominantly Muslim, and David gave such religious practices his official protection. But his lenient treatment of Tbilisi Muslims did not end David's struggles with the Seljuks. In 1123–1124, the Georgian king campaigned in Shirvan and annexed that territory to Georgia. In 1123 the Armenian nobles of Ani, the former capital of the Bagratid kingdom, which was then in the hands of the Kurdish Shaddadid dynasty, petitioned David to rule their city.[55]

Thus in the last years of his reign David the Rebuilder ruled over a multinational empire of Abkhazians, Georgians, Armenians, and various Muslim peoples, extending from the Black Sea and the Caucasus south to Greater Armenia and east to the Caspian. But as Speros Vryonis notes, this new state, created by years of fighting, was far from a flourishing economic order: "By the time of his death, David had conquered Tiflis and Ani and extirpated the Turkmen settlements from most of his lands. The half century of warfare between sedentary society and nomadism, however, had left this part of Georgia a semi-inhabited ruin. When Dmitri I (1125–1154) succeeded to the throne, there were inhabitants only in the citadels and towns of Hereth, Somkheth, Tachir, Djawakeheth, and Artahan. Thus both David and Dmitri had not only to rebuild the towns, villages, churches, roads, and bridges, but above all to repeople the desolate ruins."[56]

To his heirs David the Rebuilder bequeathed not only a renewed and expanded Georgia but also a vastly increased royal power and prestige. The lands directly held by the king *(sakhaso)* had grown enormously, since David had appropriated the holdings of the king of Ereti-Kakheti, the emir of Tbilisi, the Seljuks of Kartli, and some of the holdings of his own powerful *aznaurni*. The king had also established new towns, like Gori, in which he settled merchants emigrating from Armenia, and he had promoted learning and culture by founding an academy at Gelati in western Georgia.[57] But, as Allen points out, "the thirty years which followed the death of David II in 1125 were years of stagnation in the political life of the Caucasian lands by contrast with the epic period of the first quarter of the century."[58]

David's successors—Demetre I (1125–1154?), David III (IV) (1156), and Giorgi III (IV) (1156–1184)—were unable to preserve all the territorial gains of their great ancestor. They lost Ani to the Shaddadids and southern Tao to the Seljuks. Even more important, these three kings contended with one another for supreme power in Georgia. David III (IV) dethroned Demetre I briefly, but when his father regained the throne he crowned his youngest son, Giorgi III (IV), bypassing both the rebel son David and another son, Demetre (Demna). In 1174–1177 a group of Georgian and Armenian nobles, the Orbeliani and the Torelis, gathered around Demna and attempted to seize the throne, but Giorgi managed to defeat them and Demna was executed. The next year Giorgi crowned his daughter Tamar co-ruler of Georgia, indicating clearly his chosen successor. He also raised men of low birth to high office in order to break the aristocratic monopoly in the government. On her father's death, Tamar was crowned a second time, this time by the nobles of the council *(darbazi),* who thus reasserted their right to sanction the new monarch.[59]

In the relative security of the eleventh and twelfth centuries, a distinct Georgian Christian culture and civilization emerged, one with affinities to both the Byzantine West and the Iranian East. Georgian society remained, as it had been for centuries, primarily rural, with masses of peasants ruled by a warrior elite that had ultimate authority over the land. Urban life was undeveloped. The "capital," Tbilisi, was held for centuries by Muslims, and Georgian monarchs had no single place of residence. Fortresses were built on nearly inaccessible peaks, and a few fortified settlements, like Ujarma, Urbnisi, Kutaisi, and Tbilisi, were the occasional residence of important officials. One of the most unique settlements in Georgia, the cave complex at Vardzia, with more than five hundred dwellings hewn from the rocks, testifies to the constant insecurity of the sedentary population in the face of invaders and nomads. Georgians lived in the countryside, and from the late Middle Ages until the late nineteenth century the towns of Georgia were largely inhabited by Muslims, Armenians, and other foreigners.

Still, this rural society produced an architecture and a literature that revealed its fundamental values and aspirations. In celebration of their Christian faith, Georgian monarchs and feudal lords ordered and patronized the construction of churches and monasteries. Often built on the sites of pagan temples, the new churches represented the victory of Christ over the idolatry of the past. King Mirian, the first Christian king, had set an example by campaigning against paganism, destroying the old idols, and setting up crosses throughout his kingdom. The earliest Georgian literature, the stories of saints and martyrs, established a pleiade of Christian heroines and heroes—St. Nino, the Cappadocian nun who converted Mirian; St. Shushanik, the martyred wife of an apostate prince; and the ascetic Peter the Iberian—who provided examples of piety and sacrifice for the faithful to follow. In stone, in manuscripts, and in simple illustrations and carvings, artists and writers formulated a Georgian Christianity that was distinct from that of their Armenian neighbors and alien to the Muslim faith of the Arabs and Seljuks. Popular pagan practices were maintained by the peasants, however, even as the church tried to instill a more orthodox worship.

In the early eleventh century a great cathedral was built in Mtskheta, at the confluence of the Kura and Aragvi rivers. Svetitskhoveli, as it was known, became a symbol of the vitality of the Georgian people and the revered burial place for the kings of Kartli. At the height of the Georgian monarchy in the twelfth century, David II built a monastery at Gelati in western Georgia. Attached to it was a noted academy in which philosophers like Ioanne Petritsi and Catholicos Arseni lived and worked.

The Christian literary culture of the upper clergy rivaled the more secular culture of the court. Poets with distinctly Iranian tastes provided the feudal hierarchy with songs and poems that sang of valor, love, adventure, fidelity to friends, and the glory of women. The most enduring monument of Georgian medieval literature, the long epic poem *vepkhistiqaosani* ("The Knight in the Panther's Skin") by Shota Rustaveli, became over time the best-known verses in the Georgian language. Simple people recited long passages from memory; brides were required to know selections for the entertainment of their husbands. High culture mingled with popular culture, just as the religion of the priests coexisted with older, pagan forms. This amalgam of Christian and secular, Byzantine and Iranian influences constituted, by the twelfth century, a recognizable Georgian culture. Rustaveli helped to standardize the spoken language and the church contributed a unifying ideology. The kings and the lords protected the country against the Muslim threat, and Georgians identified with Byzantium rather than with Islam or Iran.[60]

With Queen Tamar (1184–1212) the Georgian medieval monarchy reached its apogee. But this queen (celebrated by Rustaveli, her contemporary and Georgia's greatest poet) initially had to overcome noble resistance to her exercise of power. At the time of her accession, Catholicos Mikel Mirianisdze forced Tamar to make him the *mtsignobartukhutsesi,* thus placing him at the top of both the religious and secular hierarchies. Advisors loyal to Tamar and her father were removed by the *aznaurni,* and Tamar failed in her attempt to use a church council to dismiss Mikel. Her first years on the throne were marked by a circumscription of royal power and an increase in the authority of the noble council. The *darbazi* asserted the right to approve royal decrees.[61] Even the queen's first husband, Prince Iurii, son of Andrei Bogoliubskii of Rostov-Suzdal, was forced on her by the nobles.

The turning point in the queen's fortunes came with the death of Catholicos Mikel and the queen's arrest of her arch-opponent, Qutlu-Arslan, who had planned to build a special palace *(karavi)* in which the noble magnates alone would deliberate and decide policy.[62] Tamar chose to divorce her Russian husband, and in 1189 she wed David Soslan, an Osetin prince raised at the Georgian court. Together the queen and her consort successfully routed a rebellion of west Georgian nobles, who in 1191 had rallied around Iurii, the scorned Russian prince. Tamar elevated her own supporters to high positions at court, most notably the Armenianized Kurdish family of Zakharids, known in Georgia as the Mkhargrdzeli.

In 1191 Georgians celebrated the birth of an heir to the throne by launching military campaigns into Bardav and Erzerum. The Seljuks in Armenia were attacked and pushed back into Anatolia, and the Georgians set up client states on their frontier. Twice Tamar's armies defeated large Muslim forces attempting to reduce the Georgian threat: in 1195 at the Battle of Shamkhor, and in 1203 or 1204 at Basian. The Georgians ruled again in Ani, captured Kars, established their vassals in Shirvan, and helped the Byzantines to establish the Empire of Trebizond. Describing this period,

Toumanoff writes: "Possessed of great commercial and industrial centres—Tiflis, Artanuji, Dmanisi, Samshvilde, Ani, Kars, Dvin, Ganja—Georgia succeeded to Armenia's prosperity. The tribute of her client states and war booty alone brought to the Crown the yearly revenue of 75 million dirhams. The wealth and luxury of the period gave rise to the saying that 'the peasants were like nobles, the nobles like princes, and the princes like kings.' "63

Tamar's son, Giorgi IV Lasha, "the Resplendent" (1212–1223), continued his mother's efforts and was even contemplating a crusade to Palestine when his kingdom was shattered by a new invasion from the east. Early in the fall of 1220, a messenger came to King Giorgi from his highest officials (the *atabeg* [army commander], Ioanne Mkhargrdzeli, and his son, Vahram of Gagi, the *msakhurtukhutsesi* [master of the King's personal estates]), which told of "the arrival of a strange people, speaking a strange tongue, who were devastating Armenia." Thus did the Georgians first hear of the Mongols. The king gathered ninety thousand horsemen and faced the Mongols at Khunani, but his army was decimated. The Mongols moved south to Hamadan, only to return two years later to destroy Somkheti, Shirvan, and the lands of the Qipchaks.64 King Giorgi Lasha, wounded in battle, died in 1223 and was succeeded by his sister, Rusudan (1223–1245). In the third year of her reign, Georgia was invaded by Turkmen tribes under the Khwarazm shah, Jalal al-din. When the commander of the Georgian army, Ioanne Mkhargrdzeli, was defeated at Garni, the roads to Gandja, Kars, Lori, and Tbilisi were open to the conquering shah, who ruled eastern Georgia and much of Armenia until 1230. A third and final invasion of Caucasia by the Mongols in 1236 forced Queen Rusudan to flee from Tbilisi to Kutaisi, leaving eastern Georgia in the hands of the Mkhargrdzelis, who made peace with the Mongols and agreed to pay them tribute.

The Mongols were sovereign over Transcaucasia, which they governed indirectly as the Vilayet of Gurjistan. The most powerful local figures in Georgia and Armenia were Avag Zakharian (Mkhargrdzeli), the atabeg of Queen Rusudan, and the *aznauri* of Kakheti, Egarslani Bakurtsikheli, whom the chronicler described as "an estimable man and very versed in the science of war, [who] had such consideration that he only lacked the name of king. All the Georgians obeyed him as a monarch." Avag Zakharian arranged the submission of Queen Rusudan to the Mongols in 1243, and Georgia officially acknowledged the Great Khan as its overlord. Within the kingdom, the Zakharian-Mkhargrdzelis and the Orbelianis, "both families which were Armenian in religion and not Georgian by origin, represented a definite revival and assertion of Armenian influence throughout the eastern provinces of the kingdom."65 More important, the Mongol and Khwarazmian invasions and the Mongol rulership reduced the power of Georgia's kings, so protractedly struggled for, and increased the independence of her princes.

With the death of Queen Rusudan in 1245, an interregnum began during which the Mongols divided Caucasia into eight provinces or *duman*s.[66] By the mid-thirteenth century, two Georgian kings, both named David, ruled simultaneously. David IV, the bastard son of Giorgi Lasha, and David V, the son of Queen Rusudan, were both cultivated by the Mongols—the former known by the Mongols as Ulu David ("the Elder"), the latter known as Narin David ("the Slender"). In 1250 they were both placed on the Georgian throne by the Mongols, who then abolished the *duman*s. Whether through princes or puppet kings, the Mongols organized their administration with one principal aim in mind: to secure a steady flow of taxes and tributes from the subject peoples. The heavy exactions forced the nobles to sell their lands or attempt to reobtain lands granted by their ancestors to the church. In 1259–1260, Georgian nobles, led by Narin David, revolted against the Mongols, thus separating Imereti from eastern Georgia. Ulu David decided to join his cousin in rebellion but was unable to rally many of his vassals. The eastern Georgians were defeated near Gori and once again submitted to Mongol rule, but the country remained divided, with Imereti free of the Mongols. Eastern Georgia enjoyed a brief period of revival and prosperity during the reign of Demetre II, "the Devoted" (1269–1289), the son of Ulu David and a close ally of the Mongol Il-khans of Persia. Demetre restored the privileges and immunities of the church and successfully maneuvered in the intrigues that divided the Il-khans—until he backed the wrong candidate. To save Georgia from invasion the king agreed to surrender and be executed.[67] Then, as before his reign, Georgia fell into near anarchy.

Under the Mongols Georgia fragmented once again into semi-independent principalities *(samtavro)*, with the consequent rise to power of the great nobles *(mtavarni)*, especially those favored by the Mongols. Most favored was the prince of Samtskhe, Sargis Jaqeli, formerly the *vaziri* of Ulu David, who in 1266 was granted special protection and patronage by the Mongol khan. Thus in the Mongol period a third political entity, besides Kartli and Imereti, evolved and became the most prosperous and cultured of the Georgian lands. While western Georgia maintained a precarious independence from the Mongols, eastern Georgia suffered both the fiscal burdens imposed by the agents of the khan and their direct political interference in the affairs of Kartli. The Mongols raised or brought down the monarchs. At the end of the thirteenth century, a series of joint kings ruled in Georgia. Vakhtang II (1289–1292), placed on the throne by the Mongols, was succeeded by David VII (VIII) (1292–1310), Giorgi V (VI) (1299–1314), Vakhtang III (1301–1307), and Giorgi V, "the Little" (1307–1314?).[67]

As the empire of the Il-khan overlords disintegrated in Persia, the effects of the civil strife were felt in Georgia and Armenia. Raids by the Mongols stimulated peasants to migrate from Armenia to the safer areas of Georgia, and within Georgia peasants moved from Kartli to Samtskhe. A century after the reign of Tamar, her kingdom was divided and destitute. Royal power had but a symbolic hold over the great princes.[68] Medieval Georgia was entering the twilight of her recent glories.

3 The Long Twilight of the Georgian Kingdoms

The term *feudalism* is sufficiently controversial to convince even the least cautious historian to avoid its frequent application. Most scholars writing on medieval Georgia, however, have been willing to borrow this West European concept to describe the system of sociopolitical hierarchy and dependence that characterized Georgia from the eighth through the eighteenth centuries. Georgian feudalism or *patronqmoba,* had three phases. In the first period, from the eighth to the eleventh centuries, Georgian society was organized by a network of personal ties, or, as Georges Charachidzé puts it, by "a series of personal contracts tying the king and the princes, the princes and the nobles."[1] By the year 800 Georgia was already developing a system in which homage was exchanged for benefices.

In the second period, beginning in the eleventh century, this system expanded, and "the relationship between personal ties and the occupation of a territory began to be formalized in official decrees. Some land was given for life [*sakargavi*], other in hereditary tenure [*mamuli*], and the latter, over time, replaced the former."[2] This period in the history of Georgian feudalism can be considered the classical period, and, as the Age of Chivalry, has been immortalized in Rustaveli's epic poem, *vepkhistqaosani* ("The Knight in the Panther's Skin"). "Feudal" ties based on services rendered and mutual affection developed as in medieval France, so that private ties became public ties, and distinctions between private and public disappeared. About the twelfth century, an upper noble was known as a *tavadi,* a term that expressed the dynastic quality of his dignity. The feudal aspect was expressed in the term *didebuli* (grandee). A third usage, *patroni,* had two meanings: seigneur or prince. From the eleventh to the fourteenth centuries, the titles *mtavari* and *tavadi* were synonomous with *eristavi,* and all three terms referred to one of the upper nobles, a prince. Lesser nobles, the *aznaurni*, were divided in the Golden Age into nobles of race (*mamaseulni* or *natesavit aznaurni*) and nobles of patent (*á brevet;* in Georgian, *aghzeebul aznaurni*). The latter were given their noble status in specific charters by the king or a lord.[3]

Throughout the second period, land gradually changed from conditional to hereditary tenure, a process completed only at the end of the fifteenth century. However, the transmission of a holding from father to son was never an absolute right of the vassal but always depended on the vassal's relationship with his lord. During the second period—more precisely, in the twelfth and thirteenth centuries—the power of the feudal nobles over the peasantry increased. The cultivators had formerly possessed personal freedom; this was gradually lost as they were bound to the warrior elite, the church, the dynasts, or the king. The law proclaimed that a lord could search out and return a runaway peasant for up to thirty years after his flight. Thus, in the classical period of feudalism, the Georgian peasantry was reduced to serfdom.

In his careful study of feudalism in Georgia, Charachidzé distinguishes Georgian *patronqmoba* from French *féodalité,* noting that the *aznaurni* were much more subject to the will of their lords than the French vassals. In France the rituals of the oath and of investiture were much more elaborate and precise than in Georgia, where written decrees were preferred. Since the intellectual and juridical influences of Roman law were completely absent in Georgia, Georgian feudalism never developed an abstract theoretical framework. Finally, unlike French society, Georgian society was never neatly divided into three parts—those who prayed, those who fought, and those who worked.[4]

After the feudal revival of the fourteenth century, a long decline set in. "Between the fifteenth and eighteenth centuries, more particularly in the sixteenth and seventeenth, the vassal relations that had formerly united the Georgian princes and their sovereign were found to be in question and their legitimacy ceased to constitute the basis of royal authority." Whereas earlier, in the eleventh to the thirteenth centuries, Georgian monarchs and vassals had fought as adversaries within a feudal hierarchy of dependence, from the fifteenth century on the breakdown of ties of dependence changed the conflict into a struggle between a weak state and increasingly independent princes. In the classical period of feudalism, kings like Bagrat IV (1027–1072) or Giorgi II (1072–1089) had been able to make concessions to rebel princes, even to grant them lands, without weakening the royal authority, for the monarchy was not based on the power of the state opposed to private powers but was itself a private order that rested on personal ties.[5] But between the sixteenth and eighteenth centuries, Georgian feudalism metamorphosed into a new system known as *tavadoba,* the rule of the princes. Princes and nobles broke with their sovereign and became kings of their provinces. The vassal hierarchy no longer had any force. Instead of culminating in royal unity, feudal dependence brought fragmentation and anarchy to Georgia's last independent centuries.

In the fifteenth century the title *didebuli* (with its feudal connotations) began to disappear, and *tavadi* was used in the sense of ruling prince. The old term, *mtavari,* was applied only to one of the five ruling princes of western Georgia or to a chief of an undivided house. The dependent nobility, the *aznaureba,* split into three groups: vassals of the king, vassals of the princes, and vassals of the catholicos; they stood between the peasants and the great nobles. *Aznaurni* were considered to be the slaves (*qmani*) of their lords and were tied more effectively to their princes than the princes were to their king.[6]

The fourteenth century marked the last, desperate attempts of the Georgian monarchs to free their kingdom from Mongol rule and to re-establish the decaying feudal system. The decline of the Il-khans of Persia permitted a brief period of resurgence and reunification. Giorgi V (VI) (1314–1346), called "the Brilliant" (*brtsqinvale*), had for two decades been what W. E. D. Allen refers to as "a shadow king in Tiflis," until he began, at first with the sanction of the Mongols, a program of gathering the Georgian lands. A close friend of Chopan-Noion, the vizier to the Il-khan, Giorgi traveled to the Mongol court in 1316. The already weakened Il-khan granted his loyal vassal all the lands of Georgia. But when Chopan was executed by Abu-Said-Khan in 1327, Giorgi seized this pretext to drive the Mongols out of Georgia, and he stopped payments of tribute to the Il-khan, thus ending the period of Georgian-Mongol cooperation.[7]

In 1329, Giorgi campaigned in western Georgia, reducing the separate royal branch there; five years later he conquered Samtskhe. The great noble families submitted to the king, and Giorgi was able to pass on to his heirs— David VII (VIII) (1346–1360) and Bagrat V (1360–1395)—a relatively stable and prosperous kingdom. As a result of Giorgi's efforts, the kings of the fourteenth century regained their right to cede the possession of fiefs to their princes, a privilege that had been enjoyed by Georgian monarchs since the eleventh century but which had become a mere formality during the Mongol period. Giorgi even extended the feudal structure of his kingdom into the mountainous district.[8] Thus, unlike the Armenian *nakharar* system, which was seriously weakened during the Mongol occupation, Georgian feudalism survived into the fourteenth century and was even briefly revitalized under the renewed monarchy.

As in Europe, the fourteenth century in Caucasia was a time of momentous calamities. In 1366, the Black Death raged through Georgia. Georgian princes, most notably Atabeg Beka, rose against the king, and in 1386 the Mongols appeared again, this time under the ferocious Timur (Tamerlane). In the first of eight invasions, Timur sacked Tbilisi; captured King Bagrat V, Queen Anna, and their son David; and terrorized the countryside.[9] The prince of Imereti, whose predecessors had been reduced to royal vassals, took advantage of Bagrat's predicament and in 1387 declared himself Aleksandre I, king of Imereti.[10] Bagrat's son, Giorgi VII (1395–1405), who became co-ruler in 1369 and reigned during his father's captivity, spent much of his reign fighting the Mongols and died in battle. Thus the century that had opened so auspiciously with the reunification of Georgia and the renovation of its feudal system under Giorgi V (VI) ended under his namesake in gutted towns, ravaged countryside, and a weakened monarchy.

The last king of a united Georgia was the religious Aleksandre I, "the Great" (1412–1442), who married Tamar, princess of Imereti, and so brought western Georgia back under the Georgian crown. But this fragile unity was short-lived, and Aleksandre did not merit the epithet his people bestowed on him.[11] Aleksandre imposed a building tax on his impoverished subjects from 1425 to 1440, but despite the king's efforts many villages were left in ruin and overgrown by forest. Cities declined as commerce and population shrank, and some towns, such as Samshvilde, Tmogvi, Dmanisi, and Zhinvali, simply disappeared.[12] As worldly problems overwhelmed his kingdom, Aleksandre abdicated his crown and withdrew into a monastery.

After the brief reign of Aleksandre's eldest son, Vakhtang IV (1442–1446), a fierce and extended struggle for hegemony in Georgia began, which ended with the fission of the kingdom. Aleksandre's second son, Demetre III (1446–1453), was the rightful king of Georgia, but his younger brother, Giorgi VIII (1446–1465), actually held power. The great nobles of western Georgia, led by a royal nephew, Bagrat, the *eristavi* of Samokalako (Kutaisi and the surrounding area), refused to accept Giorgi's authority and revolted against Kartli. In 1463, Bagrat and the most powerful nobles of the west met and defeated the king at the Battle of Chikhori. Giorgi VIII lost all the western provinces, and Bagrat was crowned king of Imereti. But in return for their aid, the new monarch was obliged to create a principality (*samtavro*) for each of his four major allies. Henceforth the Gelovani clan in Svaneti, the Sharvashidze in Abkhazeti, the Dadiani in Samegrelo, and the Vardanidze in Guria ruled as semi-independent princes.[13]

Giorgi VIII was also threatened by the powerful atabeg of Samtskhe, Qvarqvare III Jqeli. Defeated by the atabeg in 1462, Giorgi attempted three years later to invade Samtskhe, only to be taken prisoner. Then Bagrat of Imereti, taking advantage of the confusion in eastern Georgia, invaded Kartli and ruled as Bagrat VI, king of Georgia (1465–1478). Giorgi found an unexpected ally in his old enemy, Qvarqvare III, who feared Bagrat's new strength, but even together these unlikely partners could not dislodge the usurper. Giorgi retired to Kakheti where he laid the foundations for an independent kingdom and left the field in Kartli to his nephew, Konstantin. Only with Bagrat's death in 1478 was Konstantin II (III) (1478–1505) able to drive out Bagrat's son, Aleksandre II, and become king of a reduced Georgia. As a result of these fratricidal struggles, Georgia by the end of the fifteenth century was divided into three kingdoms and numerous principalities. The son of Giorgi VIII became king of Kakheti and ruled as Aleksandre I (1476–1511). The son of Bagrat VI, Aleksandre II (1491–1510), became king of Imereti. In 1490–1491, Konstantin of Kartli was forced to recognize these rival monarchs as well as the autonomy of Qvarqvare III in the Samtskhe *saatabago* (atabegdom).[14] Georgia was not again united until the annexation by Russia in the nineteenth century.

In the course of the fifteenth century Georgia was the victim of great changes in economic and political life that extended far beyond Transcaucasia. The Ottoman Turks had taken Constantinople in 1453 and Trebizond in 1461, and by subordinating Crimea in 1464 and eliminating the Genoese trading centers in the Black Sea, they established their dominance over the northern, southern, and eastern coasts. Moreover, the Age of Discovery had revealed new routes to the Far East to Europeans, and the most ancient trade routes across Anatolia and Caucasia lost their significance. The Near East, which since earliest recorded history had been a major center of human civilization, declined into a political backwater with less and less importance for the new metropolises in Western Europe. By the end of the century a new dynasty, the Safavids, standard-bearers of Shi'ite Islam, had consolidated power in Iran, and eastern Georgia developed close economic and cultural ties with the Persians.

Divided internally and threatened by the great empires to the east and west, Georgia in the sixteenth century declined economically. The uncertainty of life in the face of raids from the mountaineers in the north discouraged peasants from developing their agriculture. The commercial and agricultural decline affected craft industry and the Georgian towns. By the end of the century, Tbilisi had only two thousand households, that is, not more than about ten thousand inhabitants. Only the towns and countryside of Kakheti appeared relatively prosperous, tied as they were to the economic life of eastern Transcaucasia and Persia. "Kakheti," writes Allen, "had the advantage over other parts of Georgia of flanking the great Ghilan-Shemakha-Astrakhan 'silk route.' The Kakhetian kings, together with their nobles, were able to participate in this trade which had attained an international character. Jewish colonies in Kakheti . . . were seconded by the considerable number of Armenians and Persians who were settled in the market towns . . . This local prosperity encouraged the movement of population from the harassed lands of Kartli." Kakhetian towns, like Gremi, Bazari (Zagemi), Karagaji, and Telavi briefly flourished, while Kutaisi, Batumi, Poti, and others declined, and Akhaltsikhe, Akhalkalaki, and Artanuji fell to the Ottoman Turks.[15]

With the collapse of Georgian unity, princes and nobles gave up the last pretenses of feudal obeisance to their lords and kings, and increasingly their territory was held and ruled as if it were private property (*satavado*).[16] Autonomous seigneuries included the former Ksani and Aragvi *saeristavos*

Samukhranbatono, Saamilalakhvro, Satistsiano, and Sabaratiano in Kartli; and Rachi *saeristavo,* Saabashidzeo, Satseretlo, and others in Imereti. While the Samtskhe *saatabago* was made up of twenty-two large seigneuries, the lord of the area, the atabeg, waged war with the king and became in fact an independent power (*samtavro*).[17] The Dadiani family of Samegrelo (Mingrelia), who also ruled Abkhazeti as part of their principality of Sabediano, refused to pay taxes or supply troops to the king of Imereti and so also became de facto independent. From the mid-sixteenth century, the *mtavari* of Guria also enjoyed a semblance of independence. The princes of western Georgia fought one another for supremacy, particularly the Gurieli and Dadiani. Only at the end of the century, with the decisive defeat of Svimon Gurieli by Manuchar Dadiani (1590–1611) at Opshkviti, was the hegemony of the princes of Samegrelo established among the nobles of the west.[18]

The original tribal-dynastic aspects of the Georgian noble system re-emerged in the fifteenth and sixteenth centuries with the simultaneous collapse of the feudal aspects. Royal authorities, such as David VIII of Kartli (1501–1525), tried to reform the military structure of the realm to revitalize the ties of feudal dependence that pyramided up to the monarch, but with little lasting effect. The secular political, military, and economic functions of the Georgian church remained intact when feudalism was replaced by the rule of the princes. Among the most powerful officials in the kingdom were "princes" of the church. As in Kartli, so in Kakheti, the revival of a royally sponsored feudalism for a time strengthened the monarch's power and increased the number of his supporters among the *aznaurni.*[19] But the feudal revival was of brief duration in Kartli and only of somewhat longer tenure in Kakheti.

Of the three Georgian kingdoms, Imereti suffered most from political disintegration. King Bagrat III (1510–1565) not only faced repeated assaults from the Ottoman Turks but had to contend with ostensible vassals who were joining the enemy. In 1510 the Turks invaded western Georgia and Samtskhe and unexpectedly struck at Bagrat's capital, Kutaisi. Georgians and Turks fought for the next several hundred years over the territory that lay between them. The Turks were determined to incorporate Samtskhe into their empire and considered the atabeg their vassal. At several times, as in 1549, the Safavids too entered the conflict. In no sense can these struggles in western Georgia be seen as national defenses motivated primarily by ethnic or religious commitments. Rather, as so often in Caucasian politics, local dynasts maneuvered among the contenders for political hegemony, sometimes choosing the king, other times the great empires that bordered Georgia. The prince of Samegrelo, Levan II (1533–1572), for example, competed with the Imeretian king for local authority. After escaping from Bagrat's prison in Gelati monastery, Levan hid in Akhaltsikhe and later sided with the Turks, even traveling to Istanbul, where he received gifts and assurances of protection.[20]

For the kings of Kartli the principal military threat came from the Safavids of Persia, who took Tbilisi in 1536 and held the city for two years. From 1541 to 1544, Shah Tahmasp carried on four campaigns against Georgia. He captured fortresses in Kartli, established his garrisons there, and took Tbilisi again in 1548. Both the Safavids and Ottomans penetrated Georgia with the object of establishing their sovereignty over Transcaucasia, and the conflict between the empires had a devastating effect on the states that lay in their path. Finally, after a half-century of war, the Turks and Safavids signed the Peace of Amasa in 1555, which divided Georgia into spheres of influence. Kartli, Kakheti, and the eastern part of Samtskhe *saatabago* were declared to be Iranian, while Imereti, its "vassal" states, and western Samtskhe were to be Turkish.[21]

The king of Kartli, Luarsab I (1530–1556), refused to recognize the terms of the peace and was killed as he resisted the extension of Safavid authority. His son, Kheli Svimon, "Mad Simon" (1556–1569, 1578–1599), carried on the war with the Safavids until he was captured and imprisoned in 1569. Iranian suzerainty was firmly established when the shah placed Svimon's brother, David IX (1569–1578), a convert to Islam, on the throne. Known as Da'ud Khan, the Iranian candidate paid an annual tribute of twenty thousand ducats to his overlord in Tavriz. From this point on and despite temporary reversals, Iranian power and cultural influence dominated eastern Georgia until the coming of the Russians. For two hundred and fifty years, the kings of Kartli and Kakheti ruled at the pleasure of their Safavid overlords, though they made frequent attempts to free themselves of Muslim domination.[22] At the same time the kings and princes of western Georgia lived with the ever-present Turkish menace. Cut off by the Ottoman Turks from Christian Europe and by the mountaineers of the north from Orthodox Russia, Georgia, whose division had been initiated by the Georgians themselves, faced in two directions, both politically and culturally. Imereti looked toward Istanbul, and Kartli-Kakheti toward Safavid Isfahan.

The frontier established in 1555 lasted, in its first incarnation, less than a quarter-century. In 1578, a Turkish army under Mustapha Lala-Pasha defeated the Iranians and moved to establish Ottoman rule over all of Transcaucasia. The Safavids responded by freeing Svimon of Kartli and sending him to Georgia. His brother, Da'ud Khan, gave his fortresses over to the Turks and fled to Istanbul. Svimon began a guerrilla resistance against those Georgian princes who had accepted Turkish sovereignty. Aided by mutiny in the Turkish ranks, Svimon retook most of Kartli, with the notable exception of the citadel at Tbilisi, by 1579 and turned against Aleksandre II of Kakheti (1574–1605). The two kings met at Jotori, and Aleksandre was beaten. Svimon soon ended their quarrel and turned to face a new Turkish invasion of Kartli. In the last decades of the sixteenth century, Kartli's fortunes improved as King Svimon briefly retook the Tbilisi citadel in 1582, reinstated his son-in-law, Manuchar, as atabeg of Samtskhe, and nearly conquered all of Imereti. But this reassertion of Kartlian power was resented by the nobles of Samegrelo, who surprised and defeated Svimon.[23] Captured by the Turks in 1599, Svimon lived out his last years as a prisoner in Istanbul. By the last decade of the sixteenth century, Iran had been forced to recognize Turkish suzerainty over all of Transcaucasia.

The competition for Transcaucasia between the Ottoman and Safavid empires became a triangular struggle when the Russians entered the fray in the late sixteenth century. In 1554, Muscovy had captured Astrakhan at the mouth of the Volga, thus entering the Caspian and Caucasian orbit. About this time a mythical account of the reign of Queen Tamar, *The Tale of Queen Dinara,* spread throughout Russia, and interest in the Christian kingdoms isolated in the Muslim world increased at the court of Ivan IV ("the Terrible"). The first Russian contacts were made with King Levan I of Kakheti (1520–1574) in 1558, but it was during the reign of his son, Aleksandre II of Kakheti, that Moscow sent a series of embassies to Gremi. Aleksandre hoped that Russia would aid Kakheti in its conflicts with Persia and with the powerful ruler of the Kumykhs in Daghestan, *the shevkal (shamkhal)* of Tarku. After exchanging ambassadors in 1586–1587, Tsar Fedor Ivanovich told the envoys from Kakheti that he was prepared to take their king under his protection (1589). That year Aleksandre received Tsar Fedor's ambassadors, Prince Zvenigorodskii and the *diak,* Torkh Antonov. The king declared his fealty to the tsar: "Everything belongs to God and to my great Sovereign, the Tsar and Great Prince Fedor Ivanovich of all Russia. I am their slave, and my wife and my children and all my realm are God's and his, the Great Sovereign's."[24] Russia pledged to fight the shevkal, and Russian troops were sent against the Kumykh chieftain in a brief campaign (1592).

Little else came of the Russian promises. In 1596 Aleksandre complained to ambassadors Sovin and Polukhanov: "We had faith in this royal word and placed our hopes in you; but our land was laid waste in subsequent raids . . . There is nothing more to say." Five years later, Aleksandre repeated his lament to two other Russian envoys, Nashchekin and Leont'ev: "Sixteen years have passed since I grasped the tail of the Muscovite Sovereign's coat, but I have seen no help."[25]

As the seventeenth century opened, the Ottoman Turks remained the dominant power in Transcaucasia, but the vigorous ruler of the Safavid empire, Shah Abbas I (1587–1629), was determined to restore Iranian prestige and power in Asia Minor and Transcaucasia. For nearly three decades this restless and capricious monarch fought in Georgia and Armenia, with devastating results for the Caucasian Christians. In 1602, Shah Abbas renewed his country's war with the Turks, invading Transcaucasia, laying seige to Erevan, and establishing khanates in Lori, Dabeda, and Eniseli. He demanded that Aleksandre II of Kakheti and Giorgi X of Kartli (1599–1605) participate in these campaigns, and the Georgian kings joined the shah against the Turks. But the politics of alliance and allegiance became fatally complex for the Georgians in the next few years. While Aleksandre campaigned with the Iranians, a Russian embassy arrived in Kakheti and was received by his son, Giorgi (Yuri). The Russians beat back a Turkish attack on Zagemi, and Giorgi swore allegiance to the tsar, a particularly dangerous act since his father was serving with the Iranians. The bloody climax of this maneuver occurred in March 1605. Aleksandre arrived in Kakheti, accompanied by his son Konstantin, a Muslim who had been raised in Iran. Within days both Aleksandre and Giorgi lay dead, the victims of Konstantin's loyal execution of the shah's orders.[26] Konstantin was made king of Kakheti, and Safavid influence seemed secure. But the local nobles, inspired by Queen Ketevan, widow of Konstantin's older brother, David, revolted against the patricide, who was killed in the fighting. Ketevan's son, Taimuraz I (1605–1664), was crowned and began a long and difficult reign in conflict with his Safavid overlords.

Shah Abbas reluctantly recognized the Christian kings of Georgia—Taimuraz I in Kakheti and Luarsab II in Kartli (1605–1614). His major concern was the potential interference of Russia in Georgia. Before his death Giorgi X, Luarsab's father, had sworn fealty to the tsar and discussed marriage alliances with Russia.[27] In 1614 the shah renewed his effort to bring Georgia more completely into the Safavid empire with another invasion. This time he was aided by the former *mouravi* (appointed royal official) of Tbilisi, Giorgi Saakadze, an able fighter who had risen from the ranks of the petty nobility to become the most powerful man in Kartli, the *didi mouravi* (Great Lord), until a threat to his life had led him to defect to the shah. The Iranian forces drove both Luarsab and Taimuraz from their realms, and Shah Abbas replaced them with Muslims. Bagrat VII (1614–1619), son of Da'ud Khan, received the throne of Kartli, and Iese Khan, grandson of Aleksandre II, took the throne of Kakheti.

A period of bloodshed and deportation began shortly thereafter. The Kakhetians revolted against Iese in 1615, and as the revolt spread to Kartli, the nobles proposed Taimuraz as king of all of eastern Georgia. The shah took his revenge by torturing to death the king's mother, Ketevan, and by launching a destructive sweep through Kakheti in alliance with the mountain tribes from the north. Sixty to seventy thousand people were killed, and more than one hundred thousand Kakhetian peasants were forcibly deported into Iran. The population of Kakheti dropped by two-thirds. The former prosperity of the kingdom ended abruptly, and its towns shrank into villages; some, like Gremi and Zagemi, never recovered. As the shah's appointed governor, Selim Khan of Ganja, settled Turkish nomads in the area, agriculture declined and commerce came to a standstill. Shah Abbas, like Timur before him, dealt eastern Georgia a body blow from which the tiny kingdom never fully revived. The official Iranian history of his reign, the *Alam-ara,* proclaimed with pride: "Since the beginning of Islam no such events have taken place under any king."[28]

The lengths to which feudal hierarchy (*patronqmoba*) had broken down and been replaced by the rule of independent princes (*tavadoba*) were most visibly evident in western Georgia. Once Manuchar Dadiani had established the primacy of Samegrelo over Guria, the Dadiani princes defied their ostensible king, the *mepe* of Imereti, and tried to avoid paying tribute to the Ottomans. Manuchar's son and heir, Levan II (1611–1657), capitulated, however, when the Turks blockaded the Black Sea ports. Beginning his reign as a minor, Levan was forced to watch as the princes of Abkhazeti grew independent of Samegrelo, but when he came of age, he allied with the Abkhaz and Gurian rulers and fought the Imeretian king, Giorgi III (1604–1639). Taking many prisoners, Levan demanded ransoms, introducing a new practice to Georgia. A Soviet historian notes that this practice "eloquently bears witness to the fact that in the consciousness of the great feudal lords the idea of national and political communality of Georgia had definitely disappeared."[29]

Levan broke with his allies over a personal matter. In order to obtain a divorce so that he might marry his uncle's wife, Levan accused his wife of infidelity, cut off her ears and nose, and drove her from his court. He then invaded her father's land, Abkhazeti, defeated his father-in-law, and turned to put down a rebellion of his uncle, who was unwilling to give up his spouse. All of western Georgia opposed Levan, and warfare tore the country apart. King Aleksandre II of Imereti (1639–1600) asked Moscow for aid against the Dadiani *mtavari*, and in 1651 the king and princes (*didebulni*) swore an oath of allegiance to the tsar.[30]

As a result of Shah Abbas's successes against the Turks and Georgians, Iranian hegemony was re-established in eastern Transcaucasia, and the Iranian-Turkish frontier once again ran along the Likhis-mta (Suram Mountains), as it had in 1555. The deposed king of Kakheti, however, refused to accept the Muslim rulers in Georgia and plotted with the Russians and Turks to regain his throne. While in exile in Imereti in 1615, Taimuraz I joined Giorgi III of Imereti and the Gurieli and Dadiani princes in sending a letter to the Muscovite tsar, Mikhail Romanov, informing him of their opposition to the Iranian shah and requesting aid. The request was repeated in 1624, but Russia, recovering from its Time of Troubles, was not prepared to intervene in the Caucasian maelstrom. Left to their own devices, the Georgian nobles rallied behind Giorgi Saakadze and rose in revolt in 1625. Saakadze, who had learned of Iranian designs to have him murdered, defeated the Iranians in Ganja and Karabagh, annihilated the Turkish migrants in Kakheti, and led a guerrilla force against the Iranian army. The Georgians called on Taimuraz to rule in Kartli-Kakheti, and faced by rebellion, Shah Abbas gave in to the urging of Muscovy and recognized the rebel king.[31] Although his control over Caucasia had been compromised, at his death in 1629 Shah Abbas still maintained paramount influence in eastern Georgia.

The result of this chaos was the decline of the economy, a fall in trade, and a collapse of urban life. By the 1670s the population of Kutaisi had dropped to about one thousand inhabitants, and the once-flourishing Black Sea port cities numbered only a few hundred citizens. A nonmonetary, natural economy operated in most of Samegrelo and Abkhazeti. The remaining trade in western Georgia occurred at fairs (*kalakoba*), and the most lucrative item seems to have been slaves. The only bright spot in this dismal economic picture was the introduction by Laz tribesmen of the cultivation of corn, which in succeeding centuries became a major product of western Georgia. Turkish influence was felt everywhere west of the Suram Mountains, and in 1628 the Ottoman empire abolished the post of atabeg of Samtskhe and incorporated the area into the empire as the pashalik of Akhaltsikhe. The Jaqeli family converted to Islam and remained in power as hereditary pashas. Samtshkhe was thus lost to Georgia, and Georgians migrated from the region, until by the end of the century there were hundreds of abandoned villages. The area became ever more Islamicized.[32]

Warfare and the slave trade combined to reduce severely the population of western Georgia. Traveling through Samegrelo in 1671, French merchant Jean Chardin estimated its population at about twenty thousand inhabitants. He was appalled by the poverty and disorder in the land: "The poor people go almost naked; such is their misery not to be paralleled; as not having anything to cover their nakedness but a pitiful sorry felt like to the *chlamys* of the Ancients . . . Almost all of them go barefoot." The nobility, all armed and spoiling for a fight, were as dangerous to their own peasants as to the Turkish intruders:

> The gentlemen of the country have full power over the lives and estates of their tenants, with whom they do what they please. They seize upon 'em, whether wife or children; they fell 'em, or dispose of 'em, otherwise as they think fit. Every countryman furnishes his lord with so much corn, cattle, wine and other provisions, as he is able. So that their wealth consists in the number of their vassals. Besides, everyone is obliged to entertain his lord two or three days in a year at their own expense. Which is the reason that the nobility, so long as the year lasts, go from one place to another devouring their tenants, and sometimes the tenants of other men.

The prince of Samegrelo had no permanent abode; his realm had no real cities to speak of, only two villages by the sea. The clergy was notoriously ignorant; even the catholicos could hardly read the scriptures. Priests were held in contempt by the nobles. Visiting the local churches, Chardin noted that they were "more nasty than stables; the images mangled and broken, and covered with dust and spiders."[33]

Georgia, as so many times in her long history, was near extinction in the early seventeenth century. The feuding of princes and kings prevented any effective resistance to Turkish encroachments in the west or to Iranian impositions in the east. Western Georgian princes pledged loyalty to the Ottomans, and in Kartli the Bagratid princes ruled at the discretion of the Safavid shah. Yet the first signs of revival, which led tentatively to the so-called Silver Age, began in the second third of the century under an aged administrator in Kartli. Khusrau Mirza, the Muslim son of Da'ud Khan, had been governor of Isfahan when he aided Sam Mirza, grandson of Shah Abbas, to gain the Iranian throne as Shah Safi. In appreciation for his service, the new shah gave his loyal Georgian the title Rustam Khan and installed him as *vali* (viceroy) of Tbilisi, from which city Taimuraz had been expelled. Then sixty-seven years old, Rustam, known in Georgia as King Rostom (1632–1658), ruled Kartli (and from 1648 to 1656 ruled Kakheti as well) and brought relative peace and prosperity to the country.

Loyal to his Safavid overlords, Rostom managed to expand the autonomy of Georgia within the disintegrating empire. He supervised the revival of trade and the growth of cities. Iranian influence grew in eastern Georgia, as Kartli-Kakheti's fate was tied ever closer to that of the empire.[34] Rostom was opposed by the indefatigable Taimuraz until the latter was forced finally to flee Kakheti in 1648.[35] To his people Rostom left a legacy of cooperation with the Iranians and the benefits to be derived from acceptance of the status quo, but it was not an example that his successors were willing to follow.

In the second half of the seventeenth century attempts by Georgians to alter the status quo—to unite the divided kingdoms or to replace Muslim with Russian overlordship—were successfully thwarted by the Ottomans and Safavids. The *vali* of Kartli, Vakhtang V (Shahnavaz I; 1658–1676), tried to find a throne for his energetic son, Archil, first in Imereti (1661) and later in Kakheti (1664–1675), but ultimately the restless prince was driven into exile in Russia. Much more successful were those princes and nobles of Kartli-Kakheti who found positions in the Safavid civil and military service, even as the empire was threatened by invasions from the east. Giorgi XI of Kartli (1676–1688, 1703–1709) enjoyed a splendid career as the Iranian commander in chief of the Afghan front. Known as Gurjin Khan, Giorgi led an Iranian-Georgian army against the rebel Mir Wais. The clever Afghan surrendered without a fight and invited Gurjin Khan to a banquet; there he had his Georgian guests murdered.[36]

Others in Safavid service fared better than Giorgi. A French missionary noted toward the end of the century that the shah "knows how to keep [the Georgians] divided by self-interest. He promotes all the great nobles in such an advantageous manner that they forget their fatherland and their religion to attach themselves to him. The greatest posts of the empire are today in their hands." Chardin reported that "the greatest part of the Georgian lords

are outwardly Mahometan; some professing that religion to obtain prefer-
ment at court and pensions of state. Others, that they may have the honor to
marry their daughters to the king, and sometimes merely to get them in to
wait upon the king's wives."[37]

The choice faced by all rulers of early modern Georgia was between
faithful service to their Muslim sovereigns or pursuit of the elusive prize of
independence. The history of eighteenth-century Georgia is dominated by
two extraordinary monarchs, Vakhtang VI and Erekle II, who between them
managed the affairs of their realms for nearly three-quarters of the century.
Both were, for a time, successful servants of their Iranian sovereigns, yet when
opportunities were presented by civil wars in Iran, both sought the phantom
aid promised by Russia's autocrats. From 1703, Vakhtang ruled as regent for
his uncle, Giorgi XI, and his brother, Kaikhosro (1709–1711). His administration was distinguished by long-needed reforms and the collection of laws
(*dasturlamali*) that he had compiled in 1707–1709. Then, when he should
rightly have received the shah's sanction to ascend the throne of Kartli,
Vakhtang thwarted custom by refusing to convert to Islam, as his predecessors had nominally done. For two years he was a virtual prisoner in Isfahan
while his convert brother, Iese (Ali-Quli-Khan), ruled in Tbilisi. To maintain
his faith, Vakhtang sent his learned uncle and tutor, Sulkhan-Saba Orbeliani, to France to plead with Louis XIV to put pressure on the Iranians.
But nothing came of the mission, and Vakhtang reluctantly converted in
1716. Almost immediately, however, Vakhtang made contact with the Russian ambassador, Artemii Volynskii, and informed him of his true religious
and political convictions. Not long after his return to Georgia, Vakhtang
declared his support for Russian intervention in Transcaucasia.[38] Clearly,
Kartli's leaders, like the Kakhetian kings of the preceding century, calculated
the continued decline of Iran and the expansion of Russia to the south.

After a series of delays, Peter the Great, buoyed by his recent victory over
the Swedes, led a small force of Russians south from Astrakhan in 1722. The
moment was well chosen, for the Iranians were engulfed by chaos, as Isfahan
had fallen to the Afghans. Vakhtang refused to come to the aid of the
Iranians, preferring to await the arrival of the Russians. Unfortunately for the
Georgians—and for the Armenians of Karabagh, also engaged in a complex
struggle against the Muslims—Peter's campaign stopped short of linking
with the Christian rebels, and the tsar withdrew so as not to antagonize the
Turks. Vakhtang was left exposed and alone. Facing a Turkish invasion and
opposed by the king of Kakheti, Konstantin, to whom the shah had given the
throne of Kartli as well, Vakhtang was forced to evacuate Tbilisi. He made his
way across the Caucasus to Russia, where he died in 1737. The first Russian
invasion of Transcaucasia thus proved a disaster for the pro-Russian elements
among the local Christian people. The most immediate result was the establishment of Turkish authority throughout Caucasia, the brief but terrible
period known in Georgian as the *osmanloba* (1723–1735).

Despite their own misfortunes, the Iranians were unwilling to cede eastern Georgia to the Turks, but until the rise to power of the rough and able soldier, Nadir, they were unable to prevent this loss. The revival of Iranian imperialism began in the 1730s and coincided with Georgian resistance to the Turks. In 1732, Konstantin of Kakheti made a fatal attempt to break with the Turks and was murdered. The Turks gave his throne to his brother, Taimuraz II (1732–1744), thus laying the ground for the eventual reunification of Kartli and Kakheti.³⁹ The next year the Abkhaz dealt the Turks a devastating blow in western Georgia, and in 1734–1735, Nadir made two campaigns into Transcaucasia. Taimuraz defected to the Iranians, and together the Iranian-Georgian forces liberated Tbilisi in August 1735. The *osmanloba* was replaced by the *kizilbashoba* (rule by the *kizilbash,* or "redheads," as the Safavids were known).

As long as Nadir Shah (1736–1747) dominated Iran, the Iranians were able to maintain their sway over eastern Georgia, Armenia, and Azerbaijan.⁴⁰ The Russians, who in the post-Petrine period had neither the interest nor the ability to hold their outposts in the Caucasus, signed a treaty by which they abandoned the conquests of Peter the Great south of the Sulak River. Taimuraz ruled in Kakheti as an Iranian governor, while his son, Erekle, campaigned for Nadir in India. The Iranian governor of Kartli, Kilij-Ali-Khan (Khanjal), levied new taxes on the Georgians to finance Nadir's wars. Peasants migrated westward to escape the new burdens, and prominent nobles, like the *eristavi* of Ksani, Shanshe, and the *vakili* (ruler) of Kartli, Givi Amilakhori, rose in rebellion. Taimuraz and Erekle joined forces with the shah and helped to defeat their rebellious countrymen. As a reward, Taimuraz was crowned king of Kartli (1744–1762), and Erekle became king of Kakheti (1744–1762). Thus, all of eastern Georgia was ruled by Kakhetian Bagratids, father and son, but Nadir Shah, their overlord, continued to impose new taxes on his Georgian subjects. In 1746 Kartli-Kakheti was required to pay three hundred thousand *tumanebi* in tribute.⁴¹ When, the next year, Nadir was murdered in his tent while on a campaign in the east, Iran fell into civil disarray, and the wily Bagratid kings of Kartli-Kakheti found themselves arbiters of Transcaucasian politics. In the vacuum left by Iran's troubles and Russia's withdrawal, Taimuraz II and his son set out to rebuild Georgia and create a multinational Caucasian state.

Transcaucasia in the mid-eighteenth century was a mosaic of kingdoms, khanates, and principalities, nominally under either Turkish or Iranian sovereignty but actually maintaining varying degrees of precarious autonomy or independence. Taimuraz and Erekle were faced by three sources of opposition to the expansion of their authority: Georgian rivals, particularly the exiled Mukhranian Bagratids; ambitious Muslim khans of eastern Transcaucasia; and mountaineers from the North Caucasus, who raided the Georgian valleys. In 1748, Erekle recaptured the Tbilisi citadel from the rebel

Georgian prince, Archil, son of Iese, a convert to Islam who had made a desperate attempt to rally the Muslim elements in Georgia. Emerging from this struggle, Erekle was recognized as one of the most powerful princes in Caucasia. He and his father then took on the task of defending Erevan and its Muslim khan against the plundering hordes of Muhammad-Hussan-Khan-Qajar. Within a year the Armenian *meliks* (warrior-nobles) of Karabagh and the khan of Ganja came under Georgian protection.[42]

Despite setbacks, the Georgian Bagratids maintained their hegemony over the smaller Muslim khanates until the last years of the century. When Taimuraz, his aged father, died on a mission to Russia, Erekle succeeded him and thus became king of a united Kartli-Kakheti (1762–1798). At its height eastern Georgia became the nucleus of a large, though fragile, Caucasian empire. Allen describes eloquently Erekle's achievement:

> Irakli [Erekle], with his Georgian nobles, his Armenian diplomats and agents, and his Cherkess, Ossetian and Kalmuk mercenaries, held together for over half a century a strange kingdom of his own creation, which, founded on the nucleus of the derelict appanage of the Mukhranian Bagratids, had become in fact a Caucasian state. Irakli's kingdom stretched from the Daryal to Nakhchevan, from the mountains of Likhi to the foothills of Daghestan and the sandy plains of Shirvan. Not more than half the people living under the authority of the king in Tiflis were Georgian. In the capital and at Gori, Ali and Surami, a large part of the inhabitants were Armenian. The valleys of the Ksani and the Liakhvi were occupied by an Ossetian peasantry owing allegiance to a Georgian feudality. To the south-east of Tiflis in the valleys of the Borchalo and the Akstafa the nomad pastoral tribes were Tatar, and the people of Ganja, Erivan and Nakhichevan were Tatar and Armenian.[43]

Erekle II, known affectionately as *patara kakhi* ("the little Kakhetian"), was an ambitious, energetic, and sometimes arbitrary monarch whose Caucasian empire was, in the words of David Marshall Lang, "essentially a personal creation. The king was in effect his own prime minister, chief justice, and commander in chief." Internally he continued the efforts of his strongest predecessors to reduce the autonomy of the *eristavni* and replace them with royal appointees (*mouravni*). Already in 1743, the *saeristavo* of Aragvi had been abolished, and in 1777 that of Ksani was eliminated. Erekle reformed the system of military service, levied a new state tax (*sursati*) for the army's upkeep, and established a permanent frontier force (*morige*) in which all able-bodied Georgians were to serve.[44] He founded a system of justice built around professional judges (*mdivanbegi*) and encouraged emigration from Armenia to replace the population lost to the incessant raids of the Daghestani mountaineers. The king tried to develop industry and commerce, granting privileges to urban dwellers and importing Greek artisans to work the new mines at Akhtala.[45] But his efforts were thwarted by the mountaineers and the occasional incursions of the Iranians. Kartli remained economically depressed and underpopulated, though Kakheti fared somewhat better. A Russian report notes the difficult straits in which Georgians lived; meat was eaten only once a month, and the daily fare consisted usually of boiled beans and bread dipped in soup.[46] The precondition for significant economic development, physical and political security, had not yet been achieved.

Nevertheless, when compared with the sixteenth and seventeenth centuries, the eighteenth century was a period of material growth and reviving trade. Commercial relations increased as the more traditional, "feudal" forms declined. An early Soviet historian, G. Ia. Natadze, discovered after careful reading of existing documents that increasingly in the eighteenth century there were records of sales of property—fields, gardens, orchards, windmills—whereas earlier, property had been granted by lords to vassals. He also noted that property was more and more sold to adjacent landholders, evidence, Natadze believed, of a developing interest in the rationalization of agriculture, that is, production for sale rather than simple consumption and payment of dues. The relative tranquility of much of the reign of Erekle II permitted the peasants to engage more effectively in agriculture and their landlords to exact more consistently their dues and labor services. Peasant resistance to higher exactions most often took the form of flight, not armed clashes. It is difficult to assess how effective was the peasants' use of their right to petition the king for redress (*deoba*).[47] As for long-distance trade, the road to Russia through Astrakhan became more important, and the ties to Iran weakened. Russian money was increasingly used in commercial transactions in eastern Georgia, and the predominantly natural economy of the sixteenth and seventeenth centuries was challenged by monetary dealings in the major commercial centers—Tbilisi, Gori, Telavi, and Sighnaghi.

Commercial, political, and intellectual ties between Russia and Georgia grew stronger during the reign of Erekle II. When war broke out between Turkey and Russia in 1768, Catherine the Great (1762–1796) resolved to employ the Georgians to tie up Turkish troops in the Caucasus while the major campaigns were fought in the Balkans and Crimea. Erekle, who had earlier been angered by Russian rejections of his late father's pleas for assistance, agreed to cooperate with the Russians only if they promised to protect Kartli-Kakheti against Ottoman reprisals. Although eastern Georgians had grown more ambivalent about the Russian connection, a Russian orientation still found supporters among the Georgian ruling elite, which hoped for Christian aid against Iranian, Turkish, and Daghestani intrusions. On the other hand, the promises of Muscovy had not been fulfilled in the past, leaving the Caucasians vulnerable to their Muslim enemies.

King Solomon I of Imereti (1752–1765, 1768–1784), only recently restored to his throne, was more enthusiastic than most about Russian intervention, since the Turks were a much more immediate danger to him. Solomon had antagonized the Turks early in his reign by prohibiting the lucrative slave trade, and the Turks had responded by invading his kingdom (1757–1758), driving him from Kutaisi (1765), and placing his cousin, Taimuraz, on the throne. In May 1769, Solomon traveled to Tbilisi to meet with Erekle, and the two kings decided to request five Russian regiments and a guarantee that Georgian interests would be protected in the final Russo-Turkish peace agreement. The Georgians' suspicions proved well grounded. The Russians sent a small force of five hundred headed by the impetuous intriguer, General Todtleben, whose rudeness and condescension antagonized the Georgians. At a crucial moment, Todtleben pulled back his troops, and Erekle was left to face a huge Turkish force without Russian help.[48] After receiving reports about her commander, Catherine replaced him, but Russian aid remained too meager to allow the Georgians to win a decisive victory over the Turks.

Erekle decided that Georgia's survival depended on a firm commitment from Russia, and in 1773 his son, Levan, and Catholicos Antoni reached St. Petersburg on a mission to petition the empress to take Kartli-Kakheti under her protection. Erekle asked that four thousand Russian troops be stationed in Georgia, that his heirs be allowed to remain on the throne, that the autocephaly of the Georgian Orthodox Church be maintained, and that the Russians launch an immediate offensive to return Akhaltsikhe to Georgia. The request came at an inopportune moment, for Catherine was faced with the massive rebellion led by Pugachev and was anxiously looking for ways to end the war with Turkey. Instead of more troops and a pledge of support, the empress ordered her soldiers to withdraw from Transcaucasia. On July 10, 1774, the Treaty of Kuchuk-Kainarji was signed, bringing the Russo-Turkish war to an end. Disregarding Georgian interests, the Russians conceded Turkish sovereignty over areas that the Ottomans had held in the past (Imereti). The only gain for the Georgians was the renunciation by the Sublime Porte of tributes of boys and girls.[49] Once again the Georgians had little to show for their appeals to tsarist Russia.

Russian interest in Transcaucasia faded for nearly a decade, and only in the early 1780s did Catherine the Great decide to risk antagonizing the Turks by expanding into Georgia. Despite the losses suffered in the past, Erekle was anxious to ally his small kingdom with the empire to the north. On July 24, 1783, Georgian and Russian plenipotentiaries signed the Treaty of Georgievsk, which placed the kingdom of Kartli-Kakheti under Russian protection. By the treaty's provisions, Erekle's throne was guaranteed, and his heirs were to receive investiture from St. Petersburg. Russian soldiers were to be stationed in Georgia, and the king was to conduct his foreign policy in conformity with Russian preferences.

At first the new Russo-Georgian relationship seemed to promise a revival of Kartli-Kakhetian fortunes. In 1784 the Georgian Military Highway through the Daryal Pass was opened, and a Russian fortress, Vladikavkaz, was built at its northern end. Russia ceased to back Erekle's Mukhranian rivals to the throne, and tsarist troops arrived in Tbilisi. Not only were Iranian and Ottoman influences reduced in the Caucasus, but European states, such as France, were made to realize that the balance of power in the Near East was being fundamentally altered in favor of the newest contender, Russia.

The promise of protection and a more secure future, however, was not fulfilled. When the second Russo-Turkish war broke out in 1787, Catherine ordered her troops to evacuate Georgia in order to concentrate Russian efforts in the Balkans. Georgia was abandoned without a fight, and in 1795 the Iranian shah, Agha Mohammed Khan, invaded Transcaucasia and captured and set fire to Tbilisi. King Erekle was forced to take refuge in Kakheti. Just before her death, Catherine sent an army back into Caucasia, but on ascending the throne her son Paul recalled the expeditionary force and left the aged Erekle to die in Kakheti early in 1798. On Russia's seemingly capricious policy, Lang writes, "By withdrawing her troops in 1787, failing to send them in time against Agha Mohammed in 1795, and again evacuating Georgia in 1797, Russia had undeniably forfeited any juridical right to demand Georgia's continued adherence to the Treaty of Georgievsk." Or, as a Russian statesman evaluated the effect of Russia's role in Georgia, "The simple protectorate which Russia granted Georgia in 1783 had dragged this unfortunate land into an abyss of misfortune which led to its complete exhaustion."[50]

Despite their treatment at the hands of the Russian court, the Georgian leaders had no recourse but to attempt to renew the Russian protectorate. The last king of eastern Georgia, Giorgi XII (1798–1800), opposed by his brothers in a fight for control of the country, made a desperate request that his country be incorporated into the Russian empire. He wrote to General Lazarev, "Our land belongs to his Imperial Majesty, and we have sworn this with our last drop of blood."[51] On December 18, 1800, Tsar Paul (1796–1801) declared Kartli-Kakheti's annexation to the Russian crown. All classes were to retain their privileges, though the question of the continuance of the Bagratid dynasty was left in abeyance. Conveniently, Giorgi XII died just before the first Russian troops arrived in Tbilisi.[52]

After some hesitation, Paul's son, Tsar Alexander I (1801–1825), decided that Russia's interests and Georgia's future could best be guaranteed by outright incorporation into the empire, and in 1801 the young emperor declared that the kingdom of Kartli-Kakheti had been abolished. By unilaterally removing the Bagratids from the throne, Alexander ended any pretense of Georgian acquiescence in Russia's actions. Instead of signing a treaty of mutual consent, the tsar made the final decision without even consulting the Georgian representatives in St. Petersburg. Prince Garsevan Chavchavadze wrote to his relatives in Tbilisi that the Russians had "not fulfilled [even] one of King Giorgi's requirements. They have abolished our kingdom . . . No country has ever been so humiliated as Georgia."[53]

GEORGIA IN THE RUSSIAN EMPIRE

PART TWO

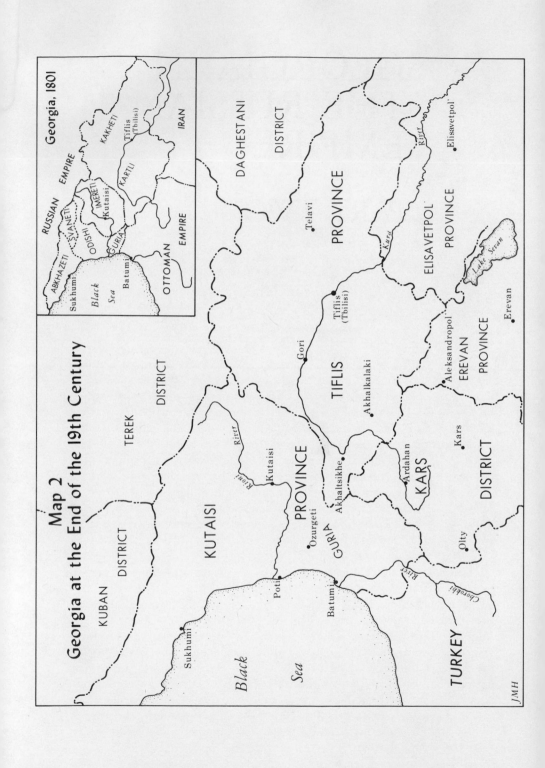

Map 2
Georgia at the End of the 19th Century

KUBAN DISTRICT

TEREK DISTRICT

DAGHESTANI DISTRICT

River

Kutaisi

KUTAISI PROVINCE

Rioni

River

GURIA PROVINCE

Ozurgeti

Akhaltsikhe

Gori

Telavi

TIFLIS PROVINCE

Tiflis
(Tbilisi)

Kura

River

ELISAVETPOL PROVINCE

Elisavetpol

Lake Sevan

Akhalkalaki

Ardahan

Aleksandropol

EREVAN PROVINCE

Erevan

Kars

KARS DISTRICT

Olty

Chorokhi River

Poti

Sukhumi

Batumi

Black Sea

TURKEY

Sukhumi

Black Sea

Batumi

JMH

Georgia, 1801

RUSSIAN EMPIRE

ABKHAZETI

SVANETI

ODISHI

IMERETI
Kutaisi

GURIA

Sukhumi

Black Sea

Batumi

OTTOMAN EMPIRE

KARTLI

KAKHETI

Tiflis
(Tbilisi)

IRAN

4 Russian Rule and Georgian Society

In the half-century from the Russian annexation of eastern Georgia (Kartli-Kakheti) to the outbreak of the Crimean War, Transcaucasian society was irreversibly transformed. The effects of the Georgian metamorphosis were as fundamental and profound as those of the contemporary political and industrial revolutions in Western Europe. Whether the move into the Russian orbit was "progressive," as Soviet historians insist, or a fatal perversion of the nation's natural development, as some nationalists argue, is not a historical judgment capable of empirical demonstration. It can be shown, however, that with the Russian occupation a historical process began that rent the fabric of traditional Georgian society, producing new opportunities and loyalties for some and provoking from others a persistent, if ultimately futile, resistance to centralized bureaucratic rule.[1] Responding to that resistance, the tsarist administration enticed the nobility of Georgia into participation in the new order. By the end of the first fifty years of Russian rule, the once rebellious, semi-independent dynasts of Georgia had been transformed into a service gentry loyal to their new monarch.

At the same time, the Armenian merchants and craftsmen of Caucasia's towns benefited from the new security provided by Russian arms and, while competing with privileged Russian traders, oriented themselves away from the Middle East and toward Russian and European commerce. In the process they laid the foundation for their own fortunes and their future as the leading economic and political element in Russian Georgia. The peasantry of Transcaucasia was forced in the meantime to submit to new exactions as its status became increasingly similar to that of Russian peasants. And the churches of Georgia and Armenia made fundamental and irreversible accommodations to the new political order.

Georgian history before the Russian occupation had been a complex story of division (political and territorial) and periodic attempts at unification. Through its superior military power, the Russian state was able in the first decades of the nineteenth century to "gather" the Georgian lands and establish over them a single political authority. After the incorporation of Kartli-Kakheti in 1801, the Russians moved westward, first taking Samegrelo (Mingrelia) under their formal protection in December 1803, and then forcing King Solomon II of Imereti to accept Russian sovereignty in 1804. During the Russo-Turkish war of 1806–1812 Russian commanders captured Poti, Sukhum-kale, and Akhalkalaki. The princes of western Georgia preferred the Russians to the Ottomans, and in 1809 Safar bey Sharvashidze of Abkhazeti placed his principality under Russian protection. Two years later Mamia Gurieli followed suit, and Guria became part of the Russian empire. Only King Solomon refused to accept Russian authority without resistance. He tried to enlist Turkey, Persia, and France in his cause but, when the Treaty of Bucharest ended the Russian war with Turkey, Solomon received nothing from his erstwhile ally. Poti and Akhalkalaki were returned to the Turks, but when the Turks were defeated in another war (1828–1829) Russia received these two towns and Akhaltsikhe as well. A permanent Russian presence in Transcaucasia was assured by the capture in 1828 of the Iranian fortress at Erevan. Thus eastern Armenia, as well as the greater part of historic Georgia, was brought under Romanov rule, and Russian troops stood between the Christians of the Caucasus and the Muslims to the south.

The long association of eastern Caucasia—Kartli-Kakheti, and the khanates of Erevan, Ganja, and Baku—with the Iranian empire had heavily influenced the social structure and culture of Georgia and neighboring areas. Portraits of the penultimate king of Kartli-Kakheti, Erekle II (1762–1798), and his wife, Darejan, clearly show the Iranicized style of dress common in royal and noble circles. Georgian kings, invested by the shah, were usually permitted to rule within the loose arrangements of the Iranian world, but it was precisely such dependence on his Muslim overlord that Erekle had wanted to exchange for a similar tie with Christian Russia.[2]

The various social classes of Georgia favored the Russian orientation of Erekle II, for the privileges of each were to be maintained. The Georgian monarchy was to remain intact, though investiture would become the prerogative of the Russian monarch. The Georgian Orthodox Church was to remain autocephalic, and the catholicos was to receive a seat on the Holy Synod of the Russian church. The Georgian nobility was to have the same privileges as the Russian *dvorianstvo*. Georgia's merchants were to be given special facilities within Russia, and thus even the flourishing Armenian merchant community in Georgia, by far the most powerful commercial group in Transcaucasia, greeted the Russian protectorate as the necessary guarantor of law and order. Essentially the social structure of Georgia was to remain intact: the church retained its monopoly on education, the nobles their landholdings and dominance over the peasantry, and the merchants their prerogatives in the towns.

At the time of the annexation Georgian society was rigidly hierarchical. A comparatively large proportion, 5 percent of the population, belonged to the nobility. The highest circles of society were occupied by the royal princes and princesses, members of the Bagratid family, which had ruled in Georgia for over a thousand years and still claimed descent from King David of Israel. Immediately below the royal families came the princes, the *tavadni,* organized into great clans. The most prestigious princes were the heads of the five "most noble" clans—the Orbeliani, Amilakhari, Tsitsishvili, and the two Eristavi clans—and the senior Armenian *melik.* Members of these clans outranked other noble clans. Below the princes were the vassal gentry or *aznaurni,* people of status but dependent on the king, the clergy, or the princes. Royal vassals, like the *mouravni* (local governors originally appointed by the king) outranked the vassals of the church, who in turn outranked the vassals of nobles. Many *aznaurni* were quite poor and lived no better than peasants, but their status carried certain privileges and exemptions from obligations.

By the first half of the nineteenth century, Georgian nobles held their estates (*satavadebi*) in one of three ways. Most often the entire noble clan owned the property in common (*sakhaso* or *sasakhlo* tenure), under the rule of the *tavadi* himself.[3] Sometimes a member of a junior branch or several households of a clan together held part of the clan's holdings independently of the head of the clan (*sauplistsilo* tenure). In contrast to the forms of collective ownership, in *satavistavo* tenure individual nobles owned the property outright. Commonly owned land was the general rule among the upper classes, and traditional restrictions to dividing estates were codified in the *dasturlamali,* the law code of Vakhtang VI. Yet even before the Russians arrived, the *satavadebi* were being broken up, and some of the earliest legislation of the Russian government concerning the Caucasus was directed against the entailment of Georgian estates. As a result, the large holdings of such families as the Orbeliani and Bagration-Mukhrani were, through the next half-century, divided among individual households within the noble clan.[4] *Sasakhlo* gradually gave way to *satavistavo* tenure.

Before the Russian annexation, the Georgian princes not only had nearly unlimited power over their estates and the enserfed peasantry but had long been accustomed to exercising police and judicial power. The highest official appointed by the king to govern the towns and countryside, the *mouravi,* was almost always a noble from the upper ranks and often held the position as a hereditary privilege. Almost immediately with his decree to abolish the Georgian monarchy, Tsar Paul ordered that "Georgia" (Kartli-Kakheti) be organized as the *Gruzinskaia guberniia* (Georgian province) and divided into two *provintsiia:* Kartli and Kakheti. A governor-general was to administer Russia's newest acquisition.

But Paul did not live to see fulfilled his plan for the integration of Georgia into the empire. The victim of an aristocratic conspiracy, the capricious tsar was murdered and replaced by his son, Alexander I. Almost immediately, the liberally educated young monarch changed his father's plans and on September 1, 1801, reorganized the Georgian administration. Instead of two provinces, eastern Georgia was divided into five *uezdy* (districts) and at every level of administration Georgian nobles were given a role to play. While real power and final decision-making remained with the Russian *glavnokomanduiushchii* (commander in chief, also referred to as *glavnoupravliaushchii* [head administrator]) and the *pravitel'* (governor), Georgian nobles were to sit as *esaulebi* (*zasedateli,* assessors) on various boards and courts, as *natsvalebi* (police officers), and as magistrates in the towns.[5]

Although these concessions were significant and designed to prevent the incubation of noble resentment against the new government, the consistent aim of the Russian government in the first half of the nineteenth century was to wear away at the peculiarities of the Georgian seigneurial system; that is, to reduce the independent powers of the local nobility and make Georgian practice conform with Russian notions of nobility, serfdom, and bureaucracy. On the very day that he appointed General Karl Knorring the *glavnoupravliaushchii* of the Caucasus, Alexander I wrote to the general, "It goes without saying, all ranks and offices hitherto held by inheritance must be removed."[6] Although some compensation was provided, the abolition of venality was a blow to the prestige of some of the most ancient families in Georgia.

Tsarist officials replaced many of the sixty Georgian nobles who held the powerful and lucrative position of *mouravi* in various parts of the country. But the Russians' lack of familiarity with customary law and practice created friction with the local population. To allay resentment, the early Russian governors assured the local nobles that no more *mouravni* would be removed, although in practice they seized every opportunity to replace one with a government appointee. The persistent sparring over local political influence between the Russian administration and the Georgian nobles usually resulted in incremental victories for the bureaucracy. In 1805, for example, General Tsitsianov recommended that local police officers, formerly elected by the nobility, be appointed by the commander in chief.[7] The princes steadily lost ground, first as hereditary political and police authorities in their districts and later as rulers of their own vassal gentry, the *aznaurni*.

From the Russian point of view Georgian society was peculiar in that the princes held ordinary nobles in subordinate, vassal relations, and held many clergymen as simple serfs. One of the first steps taken to bring Georgian practice in line with Russian norms occurred in 1808, when the clergy was freed from serfdom and all taxes and duties. In 1811, lower nobles who had been vassals of the clergy or of monasteries were freed from dependence on the church and were placed directly under state authority.[8]

Even more important in the formation of a single noble corporation was the emancipation in 1837 of the vassal gentry in eastern Georgia. The *aznaurni* were released from obligations to the princes but were required to prove title to their land; if they could not, they lost the land to their former lords and themselves become state peasants.[9] A decade later the vassal gentry of western Georgia were similarly freed by Viceroy Vorontsov.

An *ukaz* (edict) of February 25, 1827, declared that all Georgian nobles, whether in state service or not, were equal in privilege and status to Russian nobles. But which Georgians' claims to nobility should be recognized by the Russian authorities? The burden of proof was placed on the Georgians. In the absence of reliable written records, the effort to establish social status required years of humiliating petitioning, and many nobles were driven to falsify the necessary documents.[10] As part of the effort to transform Georgian nobles into Russian *dvoriane,* the administration ordered the formation of noble assemblies in Tiflis (formerly Tbilisi) and Kutaisi provinces. The nobles of Tiflis reluctantly formed such an assembly in 1819, and their cousins in Kutaisi followed suit in 1830. The assemblies were charged with defining membership in the nobility, a task that took over thirty years to complete and in the interim created much personal insecurity.

At the same time that Russian legislation was redefining membership in the Georgian nobility, it was also enhancing the nobles' social position in significant ways. In early nineteenth-century Russia the nobility had a legal monopoly on the possession of peasant serfs, but in Georgia the clergy, merchants, and even peasant serfs could own serfs. Not until 1832 was ownership of serfs in Georgia limited to nobles. Those serfs owned by non-nobles had either to be sold or allowed to buy their freedom; otherwise they reverted to state peasants. At the same time nobles were given the right to exile offending peasants to the North Caucasus.[11]

Although the Russian presence thus strengthened the Georgian nobleman's hold over his serfs, it also changed many aspects of the traditional lord-peasant relationship in ways that many nobles found irritating. In the eighteenth century Georgian serfdom had permitted peasants to "volunteer" for bondage, but this practice was ended by the Russians in 1821. At the same time nobles were prohibited from enserfing freemen, a previously common practice. Most disturbing was the 1836 requirement that serf-owners provide documentary proof that their serfs were indeed their property. In the absence of such documentation, the serf could initiate a process of proving that he should be free. Many well-off serfs petitioned the authorities to improve their status, either by becoming freemen or by leaving their lords and becoming state peasants. Serfs were also permitted by law to buy their freedom and land if they had the means.[12] By the early 1830s a Georgian nobleman faced an alien bureaucracy that at one and the same time demanded that he prove he was of noble status and that he owned his serfs. Russian rule had regularized his status and made him a member of the most privileged stratum within Georgian society, but also required that he become the servant of a new master.

The duality of Russian policy, which both encouraged Georgian aristocratic participation and limited the autonomy of local nobles, stemmed from two related but distinct goals. On the one hand, the tsarist government wished to develop an effective Caucasian administration by recruiting loyal men of rank who knew the local conditions and languages. This would have the additional effect of co-opting and rewarding potentially dissident individuals. In the early 1830s, Senator Mechnikov, then on an inspection tour of Transcaucasia, wrote to the minister of justice regarding the desirability of using Georgian nobles: "The landlords in Georgia make up the best and most loyal police, numerous and wide-spread." He recommended that the government "should either not face the Georgian landlords with a free peasantry or should limit that freedom as much as possible."[13] On the other hand, any independent authority of the traditional elite was to be uprooted and replaced by the sovereign authority that directly flowed from the Russian crown. In attempting to realize both these goals the Russians managed simultaneously to alienate a significant number of Georgian nobles and to draw others into the service of the tsar.

These contradictory aims influenced the various Caucasian administrators to different degrees. Knorring's successor as head administrator, Prince Pavel Dmitrievich Tsitsianov (1754–1806), was a Russian-educated Georgian. He won the respect of the Georgians by encouraging their recruitment into state service, opening a noble school in Tiflis (May 1804), abolishing corporal punishment and penal servitude for nobles, and generally displaying interest in Georgian culture. Georgian nobles were even permitted to enroll their children in the Russian cadet corps. When the populace requested that the Russian ban on *krivi*, the native form of boxing, be lifted, Tsitsianov agreed to their petition. But Tsitsianov was killed outside Baku in 1806, and his successor, General Ivan Vasil'evich Gudovich (1741–1820), strove to replace all Georgians in local government with "capable Russian officials." When the Georgian nobility petitioned him to make "Russian justice conform better to local customs" by restoring all the former *mouravni* and removing the Russian officials in local posts, Gudovich refused. His only concession to the nobles was to make them the exclusive arbiters of conflicts arising among their peasants.[14]

Because the Russo-Iranian-Turkish struggle for hegemony over Transcaucasia was not resolved until the end of the 1820s, the military conquerors of the Caucasus, men like Tsitsianov, Aleksei Ermolov, and Ivan Paskevich, also became its first governors.[15] Warfare continued to be a principal concern of the Russian administration for nearly a half-century more, for the mountaineers of the North Caucasus were not subdued until the mid-1860s. Although from our present-day vantage point the frontier established between Russia and the Muslim empires to the south appears remarkably durable, in the first half of the nineteenth century the permanence of these military conquests was by no means certain. The emperor entrusted the governance of the Caucasus to military men in whom he had considerable confidence.

From 1816 to 1827 General Aleksei Petrovich Ermolov, a hero of the Battle of Borodino, ruled the Caucasus as chief administrator while continuing the Russian expansion against the Iranians. Ermolov subdued much of Dagestan, annexed Shirvan and Karabakh, but when he hesitated to capture Erevan, he was replaced by the emperor's favorite, General Ivan Fedorovich Paskevich. Whereas Ermolov had attempted to "establish an effective and lasting balance between customary patterns of life and the requirements of Russian imperial uniformity," Paskevich, an administrative martinet in the mold of his imperial master, was determined to bring the Caucasus more completely into the Russian system of government. The French representative in Tiflis contrasted the two generals in a dispatch to Paris: "[Ermolov] was an administrator, [Paskevich] is nothing more than a soldier; the first understands the power of certain compromises, the other knows nothing but force."[16]

To build a bridge to his Georgian subjects, Ermolov had ordered that the law code of Vakhtang VI be translated into Russian. Yet his successors continued to display an ignorance of and insensitivity to Georgian law and customs. Paskevich, for example, ordered a call-up of six thousand Georgians in March 1829 to fight the Turks, but not a single Georgian answered the call. Paskevich apparently had not been informed that Georgians traditionally responded only to the request of the *sardarebi,* their own local officials, to form militia. When the Russians requested that the *sardarebi* mobilize the Georgians, a militia was promptly formed. Paskevich interpreted this incident not as a warning to respect local traditions, but as a call to root out such disruptive influences.[17]

Russian military government, characterized by arbitrariness and dishonesty, was the reality that lay behind the facade of Russia's civilizing mission in the Caucasus. As Senators Kutaisov and Mechnikov reported after an inspection tour of Transcaucasia in 1830, "Local administrators in Transcaucasia were more the example of breakers of the law than guardians of the law."[18] The rampant corruption and notorious insensitivity of lower-level tsarist officials made significant segments of the Georgian population long for a return to the imperfect independence that they had enjoyed before 1801. In light of the dismal present the past took on the features of a golden age, and it remained only for the noble leaders to articulate the discontents of their estate and lead it to attempt to separate from Russia.

The process of transforming Georgian *tavadni* and *aznaurni* into Russian *dvoriane* was not merely a matter of more clearly defining their tax status and their rights over peasants. It also involved the intellectual evolution of a new type of Georgian noble, one who was better educated, with a smattering of European culture. The ideal Georgian noble of the past had been a brave military servitor, an expansive host, and an absolute ruler in his isolated rural domain; the successful new noble had to earn a rank in state service, and could do so only with a European education and a knowledge of the Russian language. His life was urban rather than rural and much more concerned with events beyond the Caucasus.

The Georgian nobility was from the beginning divided in its attitude toward the Russian occupation.[19] Some nobles were dedicated to careers in state service; others were content to live a life of leisure on their estates; a few simply refused to accept the new political regime. Georgian nobles participated in most of the rebellions against the Russian occupation in the first third of the nineteenth century—the conspiracy of the Kakhetian princes (1802), the insurrection in Mtiuleti (1804), the Kakhetian uprising (1812–1813), and the rebellion in Imereti (1819–1820). Out of such unreconciled aristocrats the first generation of the Georgian oppositional intelligentsia was formed in the 1820s.

From their days as schoolboys these young nobles found it difficult to tolerate the arbitrariness of their Russian overlords, manifested most immediately by the behavior of their teachers. Dmitri Kipiani (Qipiani) (1814–1887) remembered the harsh physical punishment, the learning by rote, and the generally stifling atmosphere of the Tiflis Noble School in the 1820s. Students were often insulted by school authorities, and young Georgians found such humiliations intolerable. Some falsely accused students even considered suicide, itself an act shameful to Georgians.[20] The pettiness and cruelty of most of the teachers and administrators were accentuated by the contrast with the few teachers who managed to awaken intellectual interest in their subjects.

The young nobles, supposedly engaged in the pursuit of Russian culture, imbibed instead the worst aspects of Russian bureaucracy. Throughout the Russian empire serfowning nobles resented the state bureaucrats (the *chinovniki*), who were often of lower birth and less well educated, and formed a potentially rival elite. To this general hostility toward bureaucracy the Georgian nobility added a specific ethnic and cultural dimension. As the third decade of Russian military rule closed, some highly placed Georgian aristocrats planned in secret to overthrow their foreign rulers.

The conspiracy of Georgian nobles was nurtured by the insecurity felt by the most aristocratic families of the Caucasus, the ambitions of royal pretenders, and the irritation with Russian bureaucratic administration. It was further fueled by the political romanticism of the times. The allure of revolutionary societies, felt through much of Metternich's Europe, had in

Russia canonized the exploits of the Decembrists. More than threescore officers associated with the 1825 Decembrist revolt had been exiled to the Caucasus, and they made an indelible impression on certain Georgian aristocrats. In Tiflis Georgian nobles and Russian officers mingled together in the Tiflis Noble Assembly and the restaurant attached to the club, where foreign and Russian newspapers could be read. In July 1828 the Russian authorities authorized publication of the first Russian newspaper in the Caucasus, *Tiflisskie vedomosti* (Tiflis Bulletin), hoping to generate enthusiasm for Russia's military efforts against Turkey. A former Decembrist, Vasilii Dmitrievich Sukhorukov, was appointed editor of the newspaper, and a short-lived Georgian edition, *tbilisis utskebani,* was edited by Solomon Dodiashvili. Decembrists both subscribed to and wrote for the paper. Alexander Pushkin, who visited Tiflis in 1829, wrote to his friend Sukhorukov that the newspaper was "the only one of them in Russia which has an original color and where one can find articles of real and European interest."[21] Although it remained essentially an official gazette, *Tiflisskie vedomosti* provided a focus for Georgian and Russian nobles with political interests.

Shortly after the Decembrist revolt, royalist Georgians in St. Petersburg and Moscow (urged on by the grandsons of Erekle II, Prince Okropir and Prince Dimitrii) tried to convince Georgian students in the two cities that Georgia should be independent. When Okropir visited Tiflis in 1829, a secret society was formed with the aim of restoring the Bagratids to the Georgian throne. Twenty-three-year-old Prince Elizbar Eristavi, an officer in the Russian army, became the acknowledged leader of the conspirators, who included editor Dodiashvili, Iase Palavandishvili, Dmitri Kipiani, Giorgi Eristavi (1811–1864), and the romantic poets Aleksandre Chavchavadze (1786–1846) and Grigol Orbeliani (1800–1883).[22]

Inspired by the French revolution of 1830 and the Polish insurrection of 1830–1831, the conspirators were united in their anti-Russian sentiment but divided in their program. Some favored a restoration of the Georgian "feudal" monarchy, others a constitutional monarchy or republic. In any case, the privileges of the nobility were to be restored. No thought was given to emancipation of the serfs. Their plans were simple and sanguinary: all Russian officers and civil officials were to be invited to a ball where they would be either arrested or murdered. Then Alexander Batonishvili, the royal pretender exiled to Iran, would be invited to rule in Georgia. But before the "Instruction for the First Night" could be implemented, the conspirators were betrayed by one of their own number, Prince Iase Palavandishvili.[23] On December 10, 1832, a mere ten days before the planned murders, the conspirators were arrested. Altogether 145 people were investigated and 18 were brought to trial. Ten were condemned to death, but their sentences were reduced to exile. In fact, the noble status of many of the conspirators saved them from harsh punishment, and most returned from exile before the end of the decade. The non-noble (*raznochinets*) Dodiashvili, however, succumbed to tuberculosis in Viatka in 1836.

Like the Kakhetian revolt of 1812, the noble conspiracy of 1832 starkly illuminated the alienation and hostility that a significant segment of the Georgian nobility felt toward the tsarist regime. After dealing harshly with those involved in the plot, the Caucasian administration groped its way toward piecemeal concessions. The chief administrator of Caucasia at the time, Baron Grigorii Vladimirovich Rozen, understood the need to develop personnel who knew the local languages and could make the alien practices of the bureaucrats accessible to the local peoples. He urged the minister of education, Count Uvarov, to require the children of Russian officials to study Caucasian languages. At the same time, it was hoped that Georgian nobles would learn Russian and thus be able to serve the state more effectively. Rozen also petitioned the government—unsuccessfully—to forbid Georgian peasants from trying to prove they were freemen.[24]

Some of the early Russian administrators of the Caucasus—including Rozen and his predecessors Tsitsianov, Paulucci, Rtishchev, and Ermolov—were relatively sensitive to local customs. Others, notably Gudovich, Paskevich, and Golovin, favored a rapid integration of the Caucasus into a centralized Russian administration. Although Tsar Nicholas I (1825–1855) had no consistent policy toward the region, he was sufficiently troubled by peasant disorders and guerrilla activity in Caucasia to send Baron Pavl Vasil'evich Hahn (Gan) to Tiflis to redesign the territorial administration along central Russian lines. Typically, Hahn, knowing almost nothing about the Caucasus, chose to work alone using Speranskii's law code as a guide rather than to consult with Baron Rozen or other local authorities. Rozen soon offered his resignation, and Hahn had a free hand with his successor, General Evgenii Aleksandrovich Golovin.[25]

The essence of Hahn's program was the immediate and complete incorporation of Transcaucasia into Russia's administrative system, the introduction of Russian law and language into government, and the elimination of local divergences. This bureaucratic vision was put into effect on April 10, 1840, and proved immediately disastrous. Georgian was eliminated as an official language for state business, though the majority of the people of the area did not understand Russian. The law code of Vakhtang VI was rescinded, although it was the only law respected in many districts. Russian officials were to fill all positions in the new bureaucratic structure, and all *mouravni* and Muslim *agha*s (lords) lost their powers. Transcaucasia was divided into two administrative units: the Caspian *oblast'* (region) and the Gruzino-Imeretinskaia *guberniia* (Georgian-Imeretian province). The latter included all of Georgia, Russian Armenia, and the area of the former Ganja khanate. National distinctions were ignored in the administrative divisions, the number of bureaucrats almost doubled, and expenditures rose rapidly.[26]

Hahn further alienated the Georgian aristocracy by announcing that he had discovered a section in the law code of Vakhtang VI stating that serfdom had never existed in Georgia. Prince Aleksandre Chavchavadze, the only Georgian member of the governor's council, protested this threat to the nobles' rights over their peasants. The marshal of the Tiflis nobility, Dmitri Orbeliani, appealed directly to the Ministry of Internal Affairs, and the ministry acted swiftly to rescind Hahn's ruling on Georgian serfdom.[27]

Hahn's entire system, jerry-built on ignorance of local history and practice, soon collapsed under the combined pressure of the local nobility and the resistance of the peasants, who in 1841 rose in rebellion in Guria. Suspecting that the reform was responsible for the disturbances, Nicholas I sent Minister of War Chernyshev and State Secretary Rozen to the Caucasus to review the situation. They reported that Hahn's "institutions were transposed here from Russian provinces and did not correspond to the level of citizenship of the inhabitants, who have totally different conceptions, beliefs, customs, and ways of life."[28] Hahn was rebuked, and concessions were made to Georgian sensibilities. Certain laws of Vakhtang VI were restored, as were the powers of the village elders (*mamasakhlisi*) over small matters. Nicholas placed the area under a viceroy (*namestnik*) with nearly unlimited powers and responsible only to the tsar. The first viceroy Nicholas appointed was Mikhail Semenovich Vorontsov (1782–1856), a man familiar with the Caucasus (he had served under Tsitsianov) and considered a friend of the Caucasian peoples.

In his nine-year reign in the Caucasus (1845–1854) Vorontsov was extraordinarily successful in winning the support of the Georgian nobility. The poet Akaki Tsereteli later wrote, "As long as Georgia is remembered, so will the name Vorontsov live." Ivane Javakhishvili, the dean of modern Georgian historians, also evaluates Vorontsov's achievements positively: "Under the influence of the cultural policy of Prince Vorontsov, a feeling of trust and loyalty toward the highest power in the territory was worked out. The Georgian intelligentsia was inspired, and the hope appeared that the cultural-national progress of the Georgian people would be possible and without obstacles under Russian rule." Even a Soviet historian, I. G. Antelava, comes close to such an assessment: "Vorontsov was actually able to find a common language with the Georgian nobility and make a significant part of it loyal servants of tsarism."[29]

The aim and result of Vorontsov's policies were to reduce opposition to Russian rule in the Caucasus and to forge an alliance between the Russian state and the Georgian nobility at a time when the serfowning system was being questioned throughout the empire. Hahn's reforms were dismantled, and Transcaucasia's administration was simplified, staffed with native officials, and reduced in size. The savings were spent on local schools. Georgia, divided in 1847 into Tiflis and Kutaisi provinces (*gubernii*), disappeared as a political entity, but its traditional elite was enticed into participation in the

Russian system.[30] Vorontsov ordered the liberation of the vassal gentry in western Georgia and, to avoid the hardships that their brethren in eastern Georgia had experienced after their emancipation in 1837, granted the vassals time to prove their gentry pedigree before being demoted to the state peasantry. The former vassals were allowed to keep part of their lands.[31]

The noble monopoly on serfholding was completed in Georgia in 1852 with the transfer of clerical serfs to the state. Landlord peasants found it more difficult to win their freedom after the state in 1849 demanded documentary proof of former freedom before litigation could begin. The landholding and serfowning system was brought under Russian law almost completely. As in Russia, ownership and authority over peasant serfs belonged to the oldest member of the undivided family, that is, to the father or the oldest brother.[32]

Most important, the complex and long-drawn-out process of determining Georgian membership in the nobility was resolved. Immediately before Vorontsov's arrival in Tiflis, the tsar had issued an *ukaz* requiring that forty-eight noble witnesses attest to a candidate's lineage and the authenticity of his documentation. Written records pertaining to grants of nobility were scarce, since traditionally the Georgian kings had known their nobles personally. Further, the documentation was frequently suspect, since nobles had often engaged in forgery to avoid becoming taxable subjects. Dmitri Kipiani pointed out to his superiors in the Caucasian administration that the *ukaz* of 1844 contradicted the treaty of 1783, which had specified that Georgian and Russian nobles were to be equal in privilege. Since Erekle II had provided a list of Georgian noble families at the time of the treaty, Kipiani suggested that Georgians be required merely to prove that they belonged to these families and that a commission of nobles supervise this process.[33] The viceroy agreed to these proposals, and the commissions carried on their investigations for over a decade. Finally, in 1859, 30,000 Georgians received official recognition of their noble status and had their names entered into the Book of Heraldry (*Rodoslovnaia kniga*).

Under the patronage of Count Vorontsov and his wife, the social life of Russian officers stationed in the Caucasus and the Georgian nobility underwent a significant transformation. The brilliance of the viceroy's court, the numerous balls and receptions at the newly built palace, and Princess Vorontsova's insistence on fashionable attire for the women of Tiflis forced the local nobles to spend great sums on their increasingly Europeanized style of life. Renting homes in Tiflis and acquiring the latest Parisian fashions kept the nobles focused on consumption with little effort to increase their income. Not surprisingly, the debt of the nobility of Tiflis province grew from 100,000 to 1,800,000 rubles in the years of Vorontsov's administration.[34] The material dependency of the Georgian nobility on the Russian state strengthened the alliance of the upper classes with the bureaucracy, whose police were the last line of defense of the serfowning system.

The Georgian nobility, which fifteen years earlier had plotted to murder Russian officials and separate Georgia from the empire, made its peace with the tsarist autocracy during the viceroyalty of Vorontsov. Its status and function had been secured. The lower nobles had been freed from dependence on the princes and the church, and all nobles were being integrated into imperial society, adopting a Western cultural veneer and serving with distinction in the military and civil service. The fate of the former conspirators was indicative of the change. Dmitri Kipiani served as a highly placed official in the Caucasian administration and in 1857 became a member of the viceroy's council, the highest governing body in the Caucasus. Prince Grigol Orbeliani was appointed chairman of the viceroy's council in 1857 and three years later became governor-general of Tiflis.

As if to advertise their fidelity to the throne, the nobles of Tiflis province responded to the revolutions of 1848 with a letter to the tsar pledging their willingness to serve outside their country if the "disturbances upsetting Western Europe" should threaten the Russian empire.[35] When danger did approach during the Crimean War, Georgians of all classes rallied to the Russian banner. Joint Russian-Georgian units under a Georgian general, Ivan Andronikov (Andronikashvili), defeated the Turks near Akhaltsikhe in November 1853. In western Georgia popular militia were formed to fight the invading Turks, and when Russian troops were withdrawn from Guria to defend Kutaisi, the Gurian peasants and nobles engaged in partisan warfare. Although some peasants in Samegrelo rallied to the Turkish promises of emancipation, the Turks were forced ultimately to withdraw. Although Russia lost the Crimean War, the resistance in Transcaucasia permitted the empire to keep its Georgian possessions.

The Georgian nobility in the mid-1850s was a self-conscious estate with a new sense of purpose. It had survived the first half-century of Russian occupation by being transformed from a divided political elite in conflict with its own monarch into a united corporation devoted to its new sovereign, the Romanov tsar. Its powers had been both reduced (in terms of local authority) and enhanced (in terms of security of tenure in service and as overlords of the nonstate peasantry). It shared power with Russian officialdom and increasingly defined itself as a service nobility, or *dvorianstvo*, whose identity stemmed as much from its members' performance as state servants as it did from possession of land and serfs.

The noble elite of Georgia lived on the labor of the vast majority of the population—the peasants who worked the fields, herded the livestock, and tended the vineyards. The serfs produced both the product necessary to sustain themselves and their families and the surplus to maintain a large number of nobles. Serfs worked almost all the land; land was seldom set aside specifically as the noble demesne. The land and the peasants belonged to the lords, who had full power over them, although landlords could not maim or kill serfs without penalty of law. Peasants could not leave their lords without permission, though the *dasturlamali* of Vakhtang VI stipulated that runaway peasants could not be forcibly returned to their former masters after thirty years. The law also forbade the selling of peasants without land to infidels; it had nothing to say about such sales to Christians.

Whether these laws were in fact obeyed by nobles is largely a matter of conjecture. In all probability they were effective only when royal power could be brought to bear. In theory at least, a peasant who committed a crime was not judged by his lord (as in Russia), but went before a court. In practice, however, the lord's powers were absolute. As the Georgian historian of serfdom, S. L. Avaliani, writes, "The landlord possessed great rights over the life, personality, and property of the peasant. According to the laws of Vakhtang VI everything, except the soul of the peasant, belonged to the landlord."[36]

Georgia in the days before reform was a country recovering from the ravages of war, plague, and civil disorder. Its agriculture was producing at a subsistence level, and most production was for direct use rather than exchange. The economic insecurity of the Georgian monarchy had not encouraged thoughts of economic development and long-term enterprises. In 1828 a Russian official, General Sipiagin, noted the lack of an entrepreneurial attitude among the Georgians:

> From the time of my arrival in Georgia, I turned much attention to the economic activities of the inhabitants . . . The landlords, having seen no examples on which they might base benefit from the spread of economic improvements, are now satisfied with modest profits, which are attended by very harmful customs; the peasants too, primarily engaged in agriculture, husbandry, and gardening, try to produce to guarantee enough for the year, despite the fact that the fruitful climate of Georgia, the excellent soil, and the rich products of nature here reward richly hard work.[37]

The exiled Decembrist, Baron Andrei Rozen, a German from the much more developed Baltic region, was appalled by the Georgian attitude toward work:

> The children of the soil here looked on any work which they were not obliged to do for their own wants as a disgrace, and gave themselves over to idleness the moment they had procured the necessities of life—which were in general quite easy to obtain; and from this idleness it was impossible to rouse them. The laziness and incapacity of the [Georgian] peasants reaches such a pitch that there are none to be found for ordinary work, even if they are offered splendid wages.[38]

The poverty and indolence of the Georgian peasants were noted repeatedly by travelers and seem to have been even more extreme in western Georgia. English traveler Edmund Spencer noted after a journey through Imereti and Samegrelo in 1836:

It must be confessed that the general appearance of the Mingrelians and Gourials denotes slothfulness and slovenliness. [Given] the consequences of the exuberant fertility of the soil, and of their own low scale in the social state, which, engendering no artificial wants, they are content with merely raising so much grain as may suffice for their own consumption.[39]

Consistently distressed by the Georgians' attitude toward work, economy, and self-improvement, noble officers from the north or travelers from the West found their own explanations in racial, climatic, or educational factors. Often these explanations tell us more about the values of the observer than about the root causes of Georgian work habits. But consideration of the political and cultural past of the Georgians can provide another explanation. Georgians of the early nineteenth century lived in a political economy in which production was geared to local need, not sale in a market or accumulation of limitless wealth. Surpluses would have provoked either thievery or increased dues from local lords. Georgians had neither the security nor the incentive to produce more than was needed. Production only for immediate need was a sign of practical wisdom, not of laziness or lack of imagination. Georgian rural economy was most definitively noncapitalist; only in the towns, among Armenians, might one find the earliest signs of bourgeois development with its accompanying notions of thrift, delayed gratification, and the steady accumulation of wealth.

A contemporary's view of life in the Georgian countryside, perhaps somewhat romanticized, is provided in the memoirs of the poet Akaki Tsereteli, who grew up in the 1840s and 1850s in Imereti (Sachkheri *uezd*, Kutaisi province) as the scion of an old noble family. The Tsereteli household was run by the mother; the father did little but eat, sleep, and give orders to his servants. The estate was a self-contained economic world centering on the "palace," a two-story building surrounded by various outbuildings such as the bakery, kitchen, barns, wine cellars, storehouses, quarters for the women servants, and the *saparesho*, the male servants' quarters. The female servants were divided into three groups: the highly esteemed nursemaids who educated the noble children, the chambermaids who were the personal servants of the noblewomen, and those lowly servants who were at the beck and call of everyone else in the household. Male servants were much more specialized; the bakers, for example, did nothing but bake, and the storehouse keepers were required to do nothing but watch over their stores. Since some peasant families had no obligation to their lord except to provide one servant, there were often too many servants, sometimes as many as sixty, and idleness and laziness characterized the domestics.[40]

Before the house stood a small church that, until Russian influence made itself felt, was divided into a section for men (in the front) and one for women (in the rear). The Tsereteli family had its own priest, who was a serf—though not required, as were others, to kiss the hand of the lord. The dominance of the nobles over these petty clerics compromised their independence in matters spiritual, as reflected in the Georgian saying: "Don't expect paradise from the family priest." Still, for all his limitations, the priest was the only educated person in the village and was often the teacher of the young nobles. Religion was an unquestioned part of village life. Peasants rarely worked on Sunday and faithfully observed religious holidays. The days of rest began with church attendance, and after the service the villagers gathered outside and socialized. After lunch people would congregate once again, play games, and sing. Music was a constant accompaniment to Georgian life, and musicians were highly respected. Occasionally the village was visited by wandering musicians, poets, or clowns, and on holidays the priest or another literate person would read to the peasants from classical Georgian literature, from Rustaveli or other epic poems.[41]

Men and women in the village had separate and distinct roles in work and family life. Men worked in the fields and forests, women worked primarily at home. Sex distinctions were carefully observed; the young Akaki was once prevented from beating wool, a task reserved for females. A popular saying of the time declared: "It is a great sin when a man takes up woman's work."[42]

As a child Tsereteli, like other noble children of the time, was sent to live with the family of his peasant wet nurse for six years. This gave him a firsthand knowledge of peasant life and the conviction that "relations between the upper and lower estates in our country were smoother and more humane than in other countries." This belief was an important element in the self-representation of the Georgian nobility, and the close paternalistic ties between classes, particularly in western Georgia, are repeatedly noted by memoirists. The Russian administrator, Baron A. P. Nikolai, shared this point of view, noting that he could remember only one incident, in 1847, of peasant revenge for landlord cruelty. He later wrote, "One must say, in honor of the Georgian landlords, that their relations with their peasants were for the most part kind and patriarchal."[43]

This apparent social harmony was rooted in the blood ties shared by many nobles and peasants and the often negligible differential in wealth, particularly in western Georgia. But behind the inertia and deference of the serfs was the reality that the ultimate sanction of the serf system was force. As long as obligations were mutual and sanctioned by time and custom, the peasants did not resist. But most peasant males were armed and ready to defend their position should it be threatened by new exactions. Trouble often began when one of the parties, peasant or noble, deviated from the strict observation of their obligations. A peasant might turn to his traditional dagger (*khinjali*) or a noble to the knout.

The somewhat idealized view of the memoirists may have served to contrast the reality of Russian-style serfdom with the dimming memory of the lax norms of the Georgian past. But the real world of the peasantry, even before the Russians arrived, was not as idyllic as Tsereteli, Nikolai, Kipiani, and others would have it. Documentary records show that Georgian nobles were not above selling their peasants without land, having them arrested, or robbing them of their meager possessions.[44]

Yet it is true that Georgian serfdom in the pre-Russian period was an informal institution based on custom rather than written law, and the paternalism and informality of that system continued through the early decades of the nineteenth century. Tsereteli writes:

> Serfdom in our country, unlike other countries, was conditional, not complete. The serfs knew exactly what they had to pay to their owners, the lords what they could demand from their serfs, and both sides without fail fulfilled their mutual obligations. Not all peasants were obligated to the same extent. Some families paid less, others more; still others having paid their *obrok* [dues] in full received their freedom. The *obrok* of one of our peasants, for example, was half an egg. This peasant came to the palace at the beginning of Shrovetide, cooked an egg in the kitchen, peeled it, and with a horsehair cut it into two equal halves, and carried one of the halves to his master as *obrok*.[45]

Georgian peasant society was organized around households, often quite large, and was dominated by the older males. The populist Soprom Mgaloblishvili, writing about life in Imereti in the 1850s, remembered that villagers looked disapprovingly at quarrels in large families or at a brother's attempt to separate from his household. "If blood brothers are unable to find a common language," the saying went, "how can they bear the heavy yoke of life?"[46] In western Georgia the fewer members of a household, the poorer the family was considered. Individual families of twenty to forty members were common and sixty was not unknown. In these households labor was divided quite elaborately, with various members specializing in breadbaking or weaving. Some were shepherds, others kept bees or cleaned house. At the head of this relatively cohesive enterprise was the patriarch, father and grandfather to most of the family members.

Villages were generally governed informally by older men respected for their common sense of wisdom. An elder—the *natsvali* or *mamasakhlisi* or *kevkhi*—was elected by the peasants, sometimes by all the peasants in a village, other times by peasants of one category (a leader might represent only the landlord peasants or only the state peasants). Occasionally pressure was put on the electors to choose a candidate favored by state authorities or the local nobility, and sometimes a noble was elected. The *mamasakhlisi* assessed and collected taxes and called village meetings. Police powers were exercised by the nobles, who also acted as judges in many cases. The separation between the functions and authority of landlords and state officials was blurred, and nobles usually had the final word.

Farming in prereform Georgia was still quite primitive, and productivity was low. In Tiflis province the heavy plow required eight to nine pairs of draft animals and five to seven workers; in one day not more than a third of a desiatina could be plowed. In eastern Georgia there were insufficient hands to farm noble land, so the landlords of the 1840s and 1850s hired peasant laborers from the more densely populated Imereti and even from Iran. In western Georgia agriculture was even less developed. Peasants grew corn and *ghomi* (millet) almost exclusively, and planted just one crop for ten to fifteen years until the land was exhausted and had to be abandoned. This simple system kept the peasants in a half-nomadic state.[47]

In Mgaloblishvili's village, Diabi, the peasants turned over a set share of their grain and wine to the monastery that owned the village and also worked part time on the holdings of the clergy. If the peasants had any surplus after consumption and duties, they were permitted to sell it to merchants who took it to market. They also supplemented their income by sending their young men to towns to become hired workers. As painful as it might be to leave the village, these men were highly respected for their experience and acquired skills.[48] For many peasant households agriculture alone was not sufficient to maintain the family and had to be supplemented by other kinds of work.

Georgian society at the time the Russians arrived was made up mostly of people who were in a variety of ways "bound" or "obligated." Vassal gentry, many clergymen, urban dwellers, and most peasants were to various degrees unfree, required to render service or dues to an overlord. Georgian peasants were categorized by the manner in which they had become enserfed. The majority were hereditary serfs (*samkvidro qmani*), born into serf families that had lived for generations on the lands of their lords. But besides these involuntarily enserfed peasants, there were different kinds of voluntary serfs (*nebieri qmani*) who had become serfs in order to receive protection and land. In the Middle Ages such serfs could leave their lord at will by giving up their land, but by the eighteenth century they had lost this mobility.[49]

Yet another category, the *tskalobis qma,* was a serf given by a lord to his vassal and thus passing into the jurisdiction of a new lord. The *shetsiruli qma* was a serf who had been "sacrificed" by a lord to the church and in that way became a clerical serf. A *naskhidi qma* was simply a peasant bought by one lord from another, either with or without land. Often skilled peasants were bought and sold in their capacity as craftsmen, and their obligations to their lord consisted of performing that craft.[50]

The most unfortunate serf was the *sheudzlebeli movale,* a peasant sold into serfdom in order to pay off a debt, either his own or that of a close relative, and the *tkve,* a captive from another land. In western Georgia some unlucky prisoners were sold to the Ottoman Turks despite the anathema of the Georgian church and the efforts of Solomon I to end the slave trade.[51]

The various categories of "voluntary" serfs were eliminated over time, but among the peasants a rough hierarchy distinguished those with few or limited obligations from those with full obligations. At the top of peasant society was the usually unobligated *msakhuri,* the domestic servant or bodyguard of a powerful lord or of the king himself. Serving as an administrator or warrior, the *msakhuri* was frequently raised to the vassal gentry, freed from peasant stigma though tied as a servitor to his lord's household. The *msakhuri* occupied a position between most peasants and the petty gentry, and his obligations as peasant were considerably lighter than those of other peasants.[52]

Immediately below the *msakhuri* was the *azati,* a peasant freed by his lord either for past service or for payment. He was therefore free from duties to his seigneur but not from royal taxes. Less complete freedom was given to the *tarkhani,* a peasant (or gentryman, for that matter) who was free from certain taxes and obligations but not from others. A peasant who either had escaped and was hiding with another lord or had lost his land to other family members was known as a *bogano.* Usually a poor peasant, the *bogano* had either no land or a plot of no economic significance, but he maintained a house in the village. He paid no taxes to the king and lived as a hired hand, receiving payment in kind.[53]

Near the bottom of peasant society was the *khizani* (sometimes called *stumari* [guest] or *mobarebuli*), a poor peasant forced by material needs to leave the lands of his lord and rent land indefinitely from another landlord. The *khizani* thus had a peculiar dual nature: he remained the serf of his original lord but he acted as a freeman, a tenant farmer renting a plot of land. The *khizani* category was not to be found in the law codes but was a social phenomenon produced by land shortages among some lords. This institution provided some flexibility and labor mobility in the otherwise stagnant serfowning system.[54]

The lowest category of peasant, found primarily in western Georgia, was the *mojalabe,* a near-slave who lived in the home of his lord usually with no land of his own. His obligations included giving one woman from his family to the lord as a *moakhle* (servant girl). The work done by the *mojalabe* was considered the most humiliating in Georgia.

With the economic collapse of Georgia at the end of the eighteenth century, the subtle distinctions among categories of peasants became increasingly blurred. As conditions worsened, the number of *msakhurebi* declined, and the ranks of the poorer peasants—the *boganebi, khizanebi,* and the *mojalabebi*—swelled. The political disintegration permitted some peasants to live more freely from noble supervision and taxation, but in many areas the nobles freed themselves from royal authority and increased their pressure on the peasants. Peasants in the eighteenth century managed to buy and sell land. Their right to purchase land was recognized by Article 160 of the Code of Vakhtang VI, and many peasants used this to acquire new lands, thus breaking the nobles' near-monopoly on land ownership.[55] Once the Russian administration was established, however, the peasants were faced with a new state apparatus—which placed new demands for revenue in addition to the traditional obligations.

Before 1801 there had been no distinction in Georgia between the property and peasants of the king and of the state; obligations were paid to the king. With the abolition of the monarchy in eastern Georgia, the Russian tsar ordered that "all lands of the Georgian royal house forever be included in the properties of the state treasury and the revenues received from them become part of the general Georgian revenues" (September 23, 1804).[56] About 34,000 royal peasants thus became Russian state peasants. Six years later the peasants of Solomon II of Imereti were added to the roster, and the next year (1811) all peasants and lands of clerical nobles were put under the treasury's jurisdiction. In 1813 the holdings of nobles who had participated in the Kakhetian uprising of 1812 were seized by the state, and thirty of Georgia's largest landholding families, among them the Chavchavadze, Amilakhvari, and Eristavi, lost their lands. Twice again noble rebels—in Imereti in 1819 and Guria in 1828—had their lands and peasants confiscated by the state. In this way thousands of royal and noble serfs came under the authority of the tsarist treasury. Peasants themselves preferred being state peasants, for duties were lighter and land more abundant. Indeed, many made every possible effort to free themselves from the hold of their landlords and become state peasants. By the time of emancipation nearly 70 percent of peasants in eastern Georgia were state peasants and over 30 percent in western Georgia.[57]

The collection of taxes and dues was the point at which Georgian peasants and the Russian state made the most palpable contact. Not surprisingly, attempts to collect new payments or to collect old payments in a new way (for example, in cash rather than kind) were often the provocation for peasant violence. Before the arrival of the Russians, Georgian peasants had paid numerous taxes and duties to the royal houses, their landlords, and the church. These obligations varied in amount and nature from district to district but in general could be broken down into two categories: taxes paid by all peasants to the "state"; and payments to overlords—to the ruling families by their own peasants, to the churches and monasteries by clerical peasants, and to noble landlords by serfs. In monarchical Georgia no distinction was made between the state and the person of the king or ruling prince, so "state" taxes were in fact generalized payments to the ruling families for various governmental services. The most widespread "state" obligation was *sursati,* a military tax paid in grain and seed.[58]

When the Russians arrived, additional requirements for tsarist troops *(saruso)* were added to traditional burdens. More important, the intermittency and informality of payments to Georgian rulers were replaced in the early nineteenth century by the permanent tax-collecting presence of the bureaucratic state. The Russian authorities attempted to bring order into the labyrinth of dues and taxes collected. Taxes formerly paid to the Georgian monarchs were to be paid to the Russian government, and exemptions from these taxes that had been granted by the deposed monarchy were abolished in 1807. Three years later a soul tax on each male state, appanage, and landlord peasant was imposed. Because data on the population and productivity of the Georgian countryside were so poor, fair assessment of tax burdens was quite impossible. The Caucasian governor, General Tormasov, warned his superiors that a soul tax would be incomprehensible to the local peasants and would be "considered oppression of the people."[59] His words were not heeded.

The dualistic policy of the Russian authorities toward the Georgian noble elite, which at one and the same time eliminated nobles from traditional political posts and attempted to draw loyal elements into state service, offered no compensating advantages for the peasantry. Tsarist administrators believed that to enhance the state, the Georgian social order had to be integrated into the Russian system as fully as possible. Furthermore, the state's interests coincided with the power of the nobles over the enserfed peasantry. Nobles gained new judicial powers over peasants and state support for dues collection and retrieval of runaway serfs. At the same time Russian state power was used to restrict peasant movement and maintain an agricultural work force for the nobility. When in 1808 a famine forced Imeretian peasants to seek work in Tiflis, General Gudovich ordered such movements halted. Repetitions of the order in 1812, 1830, and 1840 indicate that decrees had little success in stemming the flow of western Georgians into the richer cities of eastern Georgia. By the 1830s almost all hired workers in eastern Georgian cities were Imeretians, and in 1840 the police forcibly removed peasants to their native villages if they had no written proof of permission to migrate—a graphic example of state authorities using the means at hand to maintain the labor force required by the noble proprietors.[60]

Under tsarist authority, the insecurity of the Bagratid kingdom was replaced by militarization of the countryside, a bureaucratic governmental apparatus, and a more effective use of serfs. Russian rule also brought an increase in the use of money. Whenever possible, Russian officials tried to collect taxes and dues in cash rather than kind, but for most peasants in Georgia this innovation was yet another affront to custom. In 1843–1845 the government ordered all payments by state peasants to be made in money; although the peasants protested vigorously, and were joined by seigneurial and clerical peasants, the order stood.[61] In a rural economy that remained nonmonetary long into the second half of the century, these demands created smoldering resentments.

Resistance to the changes brought by the Russians began soon after the first soldier passed through the Daryal. From the first years of the Russian occupation, Georgians in one region or another, members of one class or another, protested the presence of the tsarist forces. In September 1802 royalist disturbances were recorded in various parts of Kartli-Kakheti, and the tsar responded by having Tsitsianov remove members of the Bagratid family from Transcaucasia for fear they would serve as a focus for anti-Russian activity. In May 1804 the Georgian mountaineers of the upper river valleys of the Ksani and Aragvi rose in revolt against Russian demands for money payments, supplies, and labor along the Georgian Military Highway. Cruel fighting ensued, and until Tsitsianov himself entered the fray the people of Khevsureti, Mtiuleti, Pshavi, and Ossetia managed to keep the Russian army at bay. By October the peasants had been defeated, several villages burned, and seventy-three rebel leaders arrested.[62]

By 1812 plague, frosts, and poor harvests combined to create food shortages and high prices in eastern Georgia. The peasants were forced to sell grain to the state for its troops at low fixed prices, while efforts by the government to supply Georgia with surplus grain were thwarted by corrupt local officials. Hunger, sickness, and the forced requisitioning of goods by the army troops quartered in many villages finally resulted in a peasant raid on a requisitioning brigade in the village of Akhmeta (January 31, 1812). The Russian garrison at Sighnaghi was then exterminated, and the town of Telavi was occupied by the rebels, who were joined by noble supporters of the Bagratid pretender, Aleksandre Batonishvili. Inflamed by famine and resentment over arbitrary rule, the revolt spread to Ananuri in Kartli. Russian soldiers suffered more than a thousand casualties. The newly appointed chief administrator of the Caucasus, Marquis Filipp Paulucci, led the campaign against the peasants and somewhat reservedly noted in his report to the minister of police, "It is certain that [the Georgian people] do not care for the Russian government at all." By the end of March the revolt had been crushed; 13 peasants were hanged, 520 were killed in the fighting. Among those exiled to Siberia were 62 *tavadebi*, nobles who had allied with peasants in the hope of ending Russian rule and restoring the decentralized monarchy of the Bagratids.[63]

The Russian administration reacted to the Kakhetian revolt by abolishing the office of *mouravi*, over which the Russians and Georgian nobles had quarreled—thus further restricting noble power. At the same time the Georgian church, a potential center for national opposition, was brought more completely under Russian control. Catholicos Antoni II, a son of Erekle II, who had been called to St. Petersburg in 1811, was not permitted to return to Georgia. After eight hundred years of existence, the autocephaly of the Georgian church was abolished against the will of the Georgian clergy. Briefly a Georgian archbishop, Varlaam, served at the pleasure of the tsar as exarch, but in 1817 Varlaam was called to St. Petersburg and replaced by a Russian archbishop, Feofilakt. The new exarch ordered that services be held in Russian in Tiflis's Sioni Cathedral at least three times a week. Plans were made to reform the Georgian liturgy or to replace it entirely with Slavonic rites.[64]

The affront to the national church was as serious a blow to traditional Georgian society as the removal of the Bagratid house, the replacement of the noble *mouravebi* by Russian officials, and the stiffer requirements placed on the peasantry. Less than a decade after the Kakhetian revolt, the complex of grievances against the Russian bureaucracy congealed into another massive uprising, this time in Imereti. The Georgian church in the west had been independent until 1815, when a new hierarchy was imposed by the Russian administration. Georgian clergymen in western Georgia, like their brethren in the east, became state employees paid by the treasury, and the lands of the monasteries and churches became state property. Then in 1819 the Imeretian clergy, supported by local nobles and peasants, began to resist the tsarist officials taking inventory of church lands and serfs. In June rebellion broke out in Imereti and soon spread to Guria, where fighting went on for another year. In April 1820 Gurians killed the administrator of Imereti, Colonel Puzyrevskii. Once again only the most brutal repression could force the Georgians to submit to the Russian authorities. General Ermolov supervised the systematic ruination of the peasant economy in western Georgia and justified Russian action as appropriate retribution: "Extreme poverty will be their punishment."[65]

The last large-scale peasant uprising before emancipation, the Gurian revolt of 1841, was the product of bureaucratic mishandling of the peasant population. Without regard to local conditions, the government ordered peasants to cultivate potatoes and to pay their taxes with Russian rubles. Gurian peasants still maintained a primarily natural economy based on corn and *ghomi* (millet), and any money found in the local markets was likely to be Turkish. Rumors spread among the peasants that money payments would soon be required and that peasants would be drafted into the army. In May 1841 when the tax collections began, the peasants of Lanchkhuti resisted. The revolt soon spread to the whole of Guria; more than seven thousand peasants refused to pay taxes. All fortified places in the province were seized, and peasant rebels fired on Russian troops, killing seventy-seven in Gogoreti. Twice in August the peasants tried but failed to take the town of Ozurgeti, the last outpost of the Russians. Dissension within the ranks of the rebels led to the defection of many noble allies. In September the Russian forces, aided by a number of Georgian nobles, put down the revolt. Though calm was restored to Guria, the Russians made no further effort to collect taxes in cash or cultivate potatoes.[66]

Despite the evident discontent among the Georgian peasantry, no major changes in state policy toward the serfs were made in the last decade of the reign of Nicholas I. Throughout Russia educated men and women were becoming concerned about the inhumanity and apparent inefficiency of serfdom; even the tsar seemed convinced that emancipation was necessary. But besides extending to Transcaucasia (in 1847) the Law of June 16, 1833, which prohibited the sale of peasants without land, no significant improvement of the peasants' condition occurred. At least this act brought to a halt the grotesque expression of Georgian hospitality by which one noble would give to another a peasant or even an entire family to reciprocate a present of a good horse or rifle. And in this twilight period of serfdom the Georgian nobility managed to convince the government to restrict their peasants' right to petition for freedom. In 1843 Nicholas I ordered that nothing should be permitted "which might encourage peasants to make complaints and suits against their landlords." The act of 1836 that had required serfowners to possess documentary proof of peasant ownership was abolished in 1849, and the burden of proof was put on the peasants themselves.[67] Once more the tsarist government sided with the nobility in an effort to maintain order and the loyalty of the local landed elite.

Serfdom in Georgia had by the mid-nineteenth century been effectively remolded along Russian lines. As a historian of the peasants of Transcaucasia has noted, this transformation had two aspects:

> On the one hand, into the disorderly Georgian institution of bondage Russian legislation had introduced regularity, greater stability and firmness; on the other—thanks to the continual effect of Russian law on the serf population—the Georgian enserfed peasantry more and more entered into those norms which historically had shaped the position of the Russian peasant estates; in other words, toward the end of the first half of the nineteenth century, on the eve of February 19, the Georgian institution of serfdom was governed by the Russian law on serfdom; it is possible to say that Russian and Georgian serf estates were being equalized in their rights and obligations to their landlords and to the state.[68]

These changes brought the state and its officials in much closer contact with the peasants of Georgia than the Georgian monarchy had ever been. The structure of the Russian system—the greater regularity of tax collection, the presence of soldiers, the threat of the draft, and the state's role as policeman enforcing the authority of the landlords—combined with the arbitrariness and willfulness of petty bureaucrats to produce a peasant hostility toward the Russian state that periodically exploded into rebellion. As the alliance between Russian officialdom and the Georgian nobility solidified, the traditionally close ties between the upper and lower classes of rural Georgia were strained.

Before the nineteenth century Georgian society was almost entirely based on an agrarian economy and the age-old relation of lords and peasants in a rural environment. Urban culture and economy were largely foreign to the Georgians, and what trade and craft industry existed was in the hands of

immigrant elements, primarily Armenians. Thus, the division of labor between city and countryside was in Georgia accented by the divisions of
religion, language, and culture of two different peoples. The Armenian
population in Georgian towns dated from the early Middle Ages. After the
collapse of the independent Armenian kingdoms and principalities under the
onslaughts of Byzantium and the Seljuk Turks, thousands of Armenians had
migrated north to the relatively more secure Georgian kingdom. Entering its
Golden Age, Georgia under David *aghmashenebeli*, "the Rebuilder" (1089–
1125), had invited Armenians to settle in its towns, and even built the town
of Gori especially for them. The Georgian empire of Queen Tamar (1184–
1212) included the formerly Armenian towns of Ani and Kars, and for
centuries Armenian merchants and Georgian nobles lived symbiotically as
the fortunes of the Georgian monarchy rose and fell.

The towns in Georgia to which the Armenians were attracted were not
oases of freedom in an otherwise regulated society; they were, in fact, much
more intimately tied to the seigneurial political and social order than towns
in medieval and early modern Europe. In Georgia, as in Russia and Western
Europe, towns could be distinguished from villages by their size, density of
population, and by the fact that in a town, unlike a village, the majority lived
from nonagricultural production. Like towns in Europe, Georgia's towns,
particularly Tiflis, were administrative and religious centers, fortified bas-
tions against enemy invaders, and economic hubs. They served as the sites of
permanent markets and the hosts for a variety of craft industries. But they
differed from European towns in one vivid way: Georgia's urban dwellers
were, for the most part, unfree. The famous phrase from medieval Germany—*Stadtluft macht frei*—simply did not apply in Georgia. As in Russia,
Georgia's towns were not self-governing communes, except in exceptional
cases and for brief times.[69] They were the property of the king or of lords to
whom the king had granted them. In the towns of Georgia runaway serfs
found no haven but rather an urban society made up of serf craftsmen, serf
merchants, and even serf moneylenders. In short, the Georgian town was
part of the seigneurial hierarchical system by which the whole country was
governed.

Most of the craftsmen and merchants of Tiflis, Gori, and other Georgian
towns were serfs bound directly to the king or a member of the royal family,
or to a nobleman, a church, or a monastery. The greatest owner of urban
serfs was the king himself, and second was the Georgian church. Altogether,
in the late eighteenth century, over three-quarters of the population of Tiflis
(77.3 percent) was enserfed. This left about 7 percent free nobles, and 15.6
percent free producers of other classes.[70]

By the seventeenth and eighteenth centuries, Georgian towns were governed by royal officials, the *mouravni,* appointed by the king from among the
aristocrats. Each city also had a "mayor," *mamasakhlisi,* appointed by the
king but usually a member of the merchant class. In Tiflis this office merged

in the eighteenth century with the Armenian community's *melik,* a position that was concerned primarily with economic matters and was usually held in hereditary succession by members of the Bebutov family. The third principal official in Georgia's cities was the *natsvali,* an appointed noble assistant to the *mouravi.* None of the major officials was elected by the urban community.[71]

The most influential urban dwellers in Georgia were the *mokalakebi.* The term *mokalake* (citizen) was originally applied to all inhabitants of Tiflis, regardless of rank or wealth, but in the mid-sixteenth century, it began to refer to a privileged elite of merchants and craftsmen. The *mokalake* was distinguished from the ordinary inhabitant or *temiskatsi* by his wealth, his distinctive dress, and the respect accorded him. By the seventeenth century the term was applied only to those who had been specifically awarded this rank. To qualify as a *mokalake,* a merchant or craftsman had to be a royal serf residing permanently in Tiflis and a person of considerable wealth who paid the large tax corresponding to his position. Eventually a stratum of "first *mokalake*" or "honored *mokalake*" developed within this general category. Of the 556 *mokalake* households in Tiflis in the early nineteenth century, only about a dozen—among them the Amirovs, Takoevs, Mnatsakanovs, Pitoevs, Melikishvilis, and Bebutovs—were included in this elite.[72]

By virtue of their wealth, prestige, and access to people in power, the *mokalakebi* were influential both with their fellow merchants and craftsmen and with the ruling aristocracy. They were sometimes chosen as *ketkhudi* to represent the urban population before the city's administrators. But they remained unfree men—serfs to their monarch. Occasionally, however, the king elevated a *mokalake* to the nobility. In this way, a wealthy merchant might realize his greatest social ambition—not to mention his liberation from bondage and taxation.[73]

When Georgia was annexed by the Russian tsar, the urban political and economic order was strictly controlled by the Georgian royal house. The local merchants and craftsmen were largely serfs of the king, his nobles, and the church; their guilds (*amkarebi*) were under royal control; and no middle-class cohesion or independence from the government had developed.[74] The *mokalake* was not a burgher in the Western sense, with an experience of self-government and a notion of class solidarity. Most urban craftsmen and merchants were distinguished from the rest of Georgia's population not only by their distinct economic position and commensurate political power but also by their ethnic and religious profile. The great majority of the urban dwellers were Armenian; in Tiflis they made up about three-quarters of the population at the time of annexation.[75] In Georgia, from at least the sixteenth century and probably earlier, commercial capital was largely in the hands of the Armenian merchants of Tiflis and Gori. Jews, who lived in Tskhinvali, Ali, Mdzovreti, and other places, played a relatively insignificant role. The particular coincidence of ethnicity and social function in the urban

Armenian community gave rise to a smoldering hostility among many Georgian nobles toward the merchants, even as their monarch supported the Armenian urbanites.

With the coming of the Russians, the Armenians lost their ancient protector, the Georgian monarch, but gained greater physical security behind Russian troops. The troops were the first line of defense against the Iranians and the Lezgin mountaineers; they were also the harbingers of a new civil order. The treaties of Gulistan (1812) and Turkmenchai (1828) inaugurated periods of relative peace with Russia's neighbors; the Russian military presence also put an end to the most abusive treatment of merchants and craftsmen by the Georgian nobility. General Lazarev, who arrived in Tiflis in 1799, reported to St. Petersburg on the violence and exploitation of the urban population:

> Often one sees people who have no means of defending themselves being completely looted. Goods from merchants, edible products from industrialists—all are taken without payment, by *baraty* [orders], given by all the princes, by all the princesses and finally by all who have been given some position. No rank has any salary, and everyone must feed himself from his own place, and from this yet more is tolerated by the merchant and city dweller, by the inhabitant, in a word by everyone.[76]

With the abolition of the Georgian monarchy, the governance of Tiflis and other towns entered a period of uncertainty. The removal of royal power over formerly royal towns and the downgrading of noble officials such as the *mouravni* and *natsvalebi* meant that local guilds, hitherto in virtual subordination to the seigneurial elite, ascended to positions of great power in the city. In the absence of royal control, the guild membership elected its own leaders.

The Russian civil administrator, Kovalenskii, planned a new administration for Tiflis featuring a municipal board chaired by a nobleman but with four seats reserved for "eminent citizens" and four for ordinary urbanites. Not unlike the municipal reform that Catherine the Great had tentatively issued in 1785, the Tiflis plan recognized representation on the basis of estates and property and the principle of election to office. The preponderance of power went to the middle class. The Georgian nobles, not surprisingly, opposed elections to the city board, favored government appointment of all members, and demanded greater noble representation. The *mokalakebi,* for their part, wanted a *mokalake* to chair the board and supported the notion of elections.[77] Unable to resolve this dispute, the government never implemented its plan, and the real running of Tiflis remained in the hands of the guilds.

For nearly forty years, the Russian administration hesitated either to grant formal political institutions to the urban guilds or to take the more drastic step, urged by some, of abolishing them. Not until 1840 was the guilds' influence in urban affairs officially recognized in a municipal statute. Tiflis was given a city board, headed by an elected mayor with six members, two each from the owners of real estate, the merchants, and the craftsmen.[78] For twenty-five years, this board, dominated by the tradition-bound guilds, ran the municipal affairs of Tiflis, even as the guilds steadily lost their economic vitality and *raison d'être*.

As the city grew and trade with the outside world increased, the guilds' monopolies and regulations, their control of production quality and quantity, and their determination to set prices acted to restrain economic innovation and expansion. There were complaints that many goods were too highly priced for the lower classes. Russian craftsmen filtered into the city to compete with local producers, and by the 1840s they numbered more than seven hundred.[79]

By the end of the decade, the city government itself requested that the provincial administration abolish the merchant guilds and issue new rules for the craft guilds. Viceroy Vorontsov received reports damning the activities of the guilds, but he hesitated to thwart centuries of local tradition and antagonize the Armenian middle class. In 1852, however, foreign and Russian craftsmen were ordered not to join local guilds but to organize their own society, thus changing an ancient practice of enrolling immigrant craftsmen into existing *amkarebi*. The debate over the utility of guilds intensified in the mid-1850s, and Viceroy Aleksandr Bariatinskii was nearly convinced to abolish them. But his mind was changed by the eloquent defense of Iu. Akhverdov, a spokesman for the guilds, and the viceroy concluded that the development of industry, trade, communications, and a more enlightened bourgeoisie would eventually bring a natural death to these essentially medieval institutions. At a superficial glance, statistics seem to indicate that the viceroy was probably right in his prediction, for the number of guilds shrank from about one hundred in the 1850s to around sixty-five in the 1860s and 1870s.[80]

The urban economy, while more concerned with production for sale than the self-contained village economies, was nevertheless still largely pre-capitalist in character. Profit was important as an indicator of economic well-being, but other concerns were of equal if not greater importance to the craftsman or petty merchant. Life in town was punctuated by holidays and festivals, public games, and a social life still heavily indebted to Georgian traditions of feasting and drinking. A historian of Tiflis life in the nineteenth century, Sh. Chkhetia, counted more than fifty holidays in the course of a year. Besides Christian holy days, like Easter, Christmas, Assumption, *ninooba* (St. Nino's Day), *surp-sarkisoba* (St. Sarkis's Day), and *mamadavitoba*, there were celebrations dating back to pagan times (*chiakokona, maisoba*), and secular holidays connected with the guilds. The Tiflis *qeenoba* (carnival) was an excuse for the whole town to parade behind their chosen jesters (*qenna* and *beriki*) and to satirize officialdom. The initiation of new masters into the guilds became an occasion for strict and solemn religious ceremonies followed by a feast with a well-laden table and large quantities of wine.[81] The rhythm of the work week was continually interrupted by days of fun and their aftermath. Cool calculation of the monetary losses lay in the future.

From the first years of Russian rule, competition flared up between local and outside merchants. The Russians at first envisioned Transcaucasia as a trade bridge between Europe and Asia, and in the 1820s Russian and foreign businessmen penetrated Transcaucasia. But the area proved somewhat inhospitable to outside merchants and entrepreneurs. As early as 1827, the Russian government lent eighty thousand silver rubles to a Frenchman named Castella to build a silk-spinning mill in Georgia. When Castella died, the state took over the plant and ran it until the 1840s. But this outlay of government capital was exceptional, and by the end of the 1820s Russian authorities began to see the Asian continent as a source of raw materials for the embryonic industry of central Russia.[82]

To enliven commerce in Georgia and entice Middle Eastern merchants to pass through the Caucasus, the tsarist authorities decided in 1821 to permit a low tariff of 5 percent on foreign goods imported into Transcaucasia and a tariff-free transit route to Iran. This policy proved immediately beneficial, particularly to the local Armenian merchants enjoying the first period of security in a generation. Under governmental stimulation, the Armenians traveled to Europe for goods, first appearing at the Leipzig fair in 1824. Their newly awakened preference for European goods led the Tiflis merchants to neglect their former sources at the Nizhegorod fair.[83]

Russian factory owners never liked the tariff-free trade route through Transcaucasia and complained to Minister of Finance Egor Kankrin that they were losing out to the more cheaply produced European goods on the Persian market. The issue of the tariff and the role of Russian merchants in the Caucasus become part of an intense debate within the government on Russian policy toward the southern periphery of the empire. Kankrin, on one side, defended the interests of nascent Russian industry and the need for a tariff. Foreign Minister Karl Nesselrode, on the other side, favored developing Tiflis as a center of trade with the Middle East, arguing that the growth of trade through Georgia was "civilizing." Kankrin emerged the victor in this dispute, and in 1822 a tariff on foreign manufactured goods was imposed on Transcaucasia, thus bringing free transit to an end.[84]

As Russia itself began to initiate some industrial development, Russian officials visualized Transcaucasia as a supplier of raw materials rather than an area to be developed economically. Kankrin stated bluntly in 1827 that "the Transcaucasian provinces not without reason could be termed our colony, which should bring the state rather significant profits from the products of southern climes."[85] Such a colonial relationship would keep Transcaucasia somewhat apart from the empire's political system: "Calling the Transcaucasian territory a colony means that it is not the object of the government to join it to the general state system, that it is not hoped to make of this part of Russia and the Russian people in the moral sense, but to leave this territory as an Asian province, although better governed." While he did not share Kankrin's "regionalist" approach, the newly appointed Caucasian governor, General Paskevich, did agree with the basic economic plans for the exploitation of Transcaucasia: "Should not one look on Georgia as a colony which would deliver raw materials (silk, cotton cloth, etc.) for our factories, in exchange for manufactured goods from Russia?"[86]

Such a colonial policy meant that the local development of industry and the Armenians' near-monopoly of trade would be discouraged by the Russian government. Expressing exactly this view, the journal *Syn otechestva* (Son of the Fatherland) stated in 1835: "As a colony of Russia, Transcaucasia should not have manufacturing, i.e., without destroying that which already exists, no new establishments should be permitted . . . However, we are speaking here only of those manufactures which because of great profits might soon compete with similar enterprises in Russia and thus undermine their well-being." Two years later, Senator Pavl Hahn argued in a similar vein that Transcaucasia should be confined to agriculture and the production of raw materials for Russian industry: "The introduction of factories and manufactures will take away strength so necessary for agriculture and without any benefit, for this territory will harm the industry and commerce of Russia." Besides the short-lived silk mill, no other factory was opened in Georgia in the first four decades after the Russian annexation. Indeed, several large enterprises established under the Georgian monarchy—a glass factory, saltworks, a powder mill, and others—were closed down.[87]

Since its first interest was the development of Russian trade and industry, the Russian government adopted a preferential policy toward Russian merchants and factory owners. Hurt by the new tariffs, many Armenians were forced to cease buying in western markets, and some left Tiflis and crossed the border to Trebizond.

The hold of the Armenians on Caucasian trade was only slightly weakened. Trade and craft industry in Caucasia were still controlled by the *amkarebi,* and as long as the guilds existed, outside penetration of the local economy was inhibited. The Armenian merchants retained the key to the economy, and they found a champion in Baron Rozen, who tried, unsuccessfully, to convince Kankrin to abolish the protective tariff. When Nicholas I visited Erevan in 1837, Rozen presented nine Armenian merchants who petitioned the tsar for permission to open the European trade once again.[88]

Like Ermolov before him, Rozen's interest in the Caucasian economy was an attempt to produce locally the necessary supplies for the army. In these efforts he was opposed by Finance Minister Kankrin, who wanted the Caucasus to supply raw materials to Russian industry and refrain from competing with manufacturers north of the mountains. Kankrin's policies were not notably successful. Little Russian investment took place in the Caucasus, though the basis for a silk industry was laid. Trade with Iran dropped in the early 1830s as English competitors moved into that area, and even with protective tariffs to give them a favored position, Russian goods found few buyers within Transcaucasia.[89]

The viceroyalty of Vorontsov was as much a turning point for the Armenian middle class as it was for the Georgian nobility, not only economically but culturally. As an enlightened imperialist, the viceroy saw Russia's role in Caucasia as not simply an exploiter of local resources but the developer and civilizer of "backward Asiatic" peoples. The clearest physical representation of Vorontsov's vision was the transformation of Tiflis. Before he arrived, the city had changed little under Russian rule. In the 1820s the wreckage left by the last Iranian invasion had finally been cleared away, and streets in the old city had been widened. His predecessor, Ermolov, had torn down the ancient Metekhi fortress on the Kura and had built barracks in its place. (Later these buildings housed prisoners instead of soldiers.)[90] But the serious rebuilding of the city began in the 1840s.

In 1848 Vorontsov removed the remnants of the old city wall, and the town began to expand to the north and west. The former "outer suburb" (Garetubani) became the central part of the city, the site of the viceroy's palace and elegant three-story houses for the nobles and rich merchants. Golovinskii Prospekt (today Rustaveli) was laid out from the reconstructed Erivan Square, site of a new theater, army headquarters, and central police station.[91] Above the square, on the streets leading up the mountain, Sololaki was developed as a European-style residential district for the wealthy, principally Armenian, bourgeoisie. Across the river, on the left bank, Mikhailovskii Prospekt (now Plekhanov) was extended from the square of the same name (now Karl Marx). This boulevard through the area colonized by Germans opened up new housing for the less affluent craftsmen and merchants. Tiflis was growing beyond its old Iranian nucleus into a graceful, lively center of the Russian Middle East.

Vorontsov promoted education and culture in the Caucasus, building the first Russian theater and public library in Tiflis (1846). He remarked in letters that theater would not only allow natives to become acquainted with the art of the stage but aid in the spread of the Russian language. The general cultural level of Tiflis had to be raised so that the Russian officers living there would find it less oppressive. The viceroy was particularly pleased at the reception of an Italian opera company he invited to Georgia, for Rossini, Bellini, and Donizetti could be heard instead of the "semi-barbarous sounds of Persian music" popular a few years earlier. Europeanization of culture was more directly advanced in the state schools, which over three thousand students attended in the late 1840s.[92] Official publications—*Kavkaz* (Caucasus; issued in Russian and Armenian) and *Kavkazskii kalendar'* (Caucasian Calendar)—appeared in 1846. The spread of literary culture in the

Caucasus also required the introduction in 1849 of that guardian of correct expression, the Caucasian Censor's Committee.

In his effort to forge links of mutual interest with the Caucasian peoples, Viceroy Vorontsov became interested in reviving commerce through Transcaucasia. The tariff of 1831 was the principal culprit in the decline of Russian trade with Transcaucasia and Iran and the shift of western trade through Trebizond instead of Tiflis. Vorontsov was an advocate of free trade for the Russian empire in general, and he argued that the free transit of goods through Transcaucasia was "very important for us in political relations" and could lessen Anglo-Russian tensions in the area. He found supporters in the ministry of foreign affairs, but once again the minister of finance, now Vronchenko, was opposed to a lessening of tariffs that might hurt the Moscow industrialists. A compromise was reached; on December 14, 1846, the free transit of West European goods was re-established and tariffs were slightly lowered.[93] The Armenian merchants were pleased, but by this time Trebizond had been well established as a trade rival to Tiflis, and the Iranian trade was securely in the hands of Europeans.

The rivalry between Armenian and Russian merchants did not end with the restoration of lower tariffs, however, and the government remained clearly on the side of the Russians. When two Russian "trading depots" were opened in Tiflis in 1847–1848, Armenian merchants complained to Vorontsov that the Russians were being given an unfair advantage. Although goods bought at the last Nizhegorod fair by Armenians were subject to a 12 percent tariff, goods produced in Moscow and Ivanovo and sold directly through the depots were spared this duty. In a rhetorical reply, Vorontsov asked the Armenians: "Does the Armenian merchant community seriously think that he, the Viceroy, will forbid Russians to do business?" He advised the Armenians to buy goods through the depots.[94]

Despite such official support, the Russian producers and merchants continued to have difficulty in local markets. Vorontsov himself complained that they sold Muscovite goods in Tiflis without buying Tiflis goods for sale in Russia. "Your activities," he told the Russian merchants, "beneficial at first to local consumers because they destroyed the monopoly of Armenian merchants, merely continue the harm you have done them without bringing any benefits to the local producers, industrialists, or craftsmen." Vorontsov's vision, so different from that of Kankrin and Paskevich, included not only the advance of Russian trade but also the economic development of the Caucasus. Therefore his enthusiasm for Russian businessmen flagged, and by the mid-1850s the two associations of Russian merchants in the Caucasus folded. Most government contracts and businesses were handled by the Armenian middle class.[95]

The hopes of the colonialists that Transcaucasia might become a market for Russian manufactures and a source of raw materials for Russian industry were not realized in the first half of the nineteenth century. As Vorontsov reported in 1846, "The market in Transcaucasia for the products of our factories is insignificant." That same year, the Caucasian Committee noted that "the distance of this territory from our manufacturing provinces, the lack of good communication with Russia, the danger of the road across the lands of the mountaineers—all this has hindered so far, and for a long time to come will prevent, the Transcaucasian territory from being supplied only with Russian goods."[96] All these explanations for the failure of Russian trade to develop were at the same time reasons for the indigenous development of Caucasian industry.

Russian rule did not successfully foster Russian trade with Caucasia, but it did permit local merchants to flourish and turned the attention of the Armenian *mokalakebi* toward Europe. From the economic cocoon of the Georgian kingdom, the enserfed *mokalake* was being reborn as a free merchant ready to compete with his commercial rivals in Russia and Europe. Thanks largely to the efforts of the merchants, imports of foreign goods into Transcaucasia rose ninefold from 1821 to 1864 and exports of locally produced goods increased twofold. In recognition of the central role played by the Tiflis merchants, Vorontsov declared in 1854 that the *mokalakebi* were to be "hereditary eminent citizens of the Russian empire." By entering the estate of *pochetnye grazhdane,* which had been established by Nicholas I in 1832, the *mokalakebi* were freed from military recruitment, the soul tax, and corporal punishment.[97] They were already well on the way to becoming full-fledged burghers, at least within the limits set by bureaucratic absolutism.

By the end of the first half-century of Russian rule, Transcaucasia had been administratively integrated into the tsarist empire, and the social elites among the Georgians and Armenians had metamorphosed into estates (*sosloviia*) of the Russian type. The central government, through its most enlightened governors, had by law and by example drawn significant segments of the Georgian nobility and Armenian bourgeoisie into identifying their security, economic well-being, prestige, and political status with the Russian connection. This was no mean achievement. Its permanence can be attested to late in the twentieth century. But at the same time that this pacification and integration was taking place, the stage was being set for a dual confrontation that would mature in the next half-century: between the two leading social and ethnic communities—the Georgian nobility and the Armenian bourgeoisie—and between the Russian autocracy and the intellectual elements emerging from these two classes.

5 Emancipation and the End of Seigneurial Georgia

"I am convinced that sooner or later we must come to this, I think that you agree with me, consequently, it is better that this come from above than from below." With these enigmatic words Alexander II warned his nobles that the time had arrived for serious consideration of emancipation of the serfs.

Russia's defeat in the Crimean War had prompted within the government a movement for reform of basic institutions, most urgently the serfowning system. This monumental undertaking required, in Alexander's view, the participation of the noble estate, for it was noble rights and privileges long protected by the state that were now to be compromised. The hesitant nobility especially feared losing their land, their principal source of income; nevertheless, in the long bureaucratic process of hammering out the terms of emancipation, an irreversible decision was made that obligated the nobles to permit the peasants to redeem the land.[1] On February 19, 1861, emancipation was decreed for Russia proper; it remained to be extended to the peripheries of the empire.

In August 1856 the tsar had appointed Prince Aleksandr Ivanovich Bariatinskii, his friend since boyhood, viceroy of the Caucasus. A courageous veteran of Caucasian wars and former chief of staff to Prince Vorontsov, Bariatinskii had grandiose ambitions for the Caucasus. As he wrote to Alexander, "Russia had become for Asia what Western Europe had represented for so long in Russia—the source and bearer of the world's most advanced civilization. A model administration in the Caucasus would serve as a showcase of Russian colonial policy."[2] Bariatinskii's tasks in the Caucasus were enormous. He came as both conqueror and modernizer. The war with Shamil in the Caucasian mountains was still being fought as discussions of peasant emancipation began.

The Georgian nobility greeted the new viceroy enthusiastically, hosting a ball in Tiflis that was reported in newspapers as far away as Paris. Considering Bariatinskii to have their best interests at heart, the nobles were gratified by invitations to the palace, where the viceroy asked for "their views and opinions in simple, intimate conversations without any official character." In these interviews Bariatinskii made it clear that the time had come to begin reform of peasant-landlord relations in the Caucasus. As in Russia, the government at first moved with extreme caution, appealing to the nobles themselves to make initiatives toward liberating their serfs. Bariatinskii asked Prince Grigol Orbeliani and Dmitri Kipiani to draw up plans for reform. An "opinion" presented to the viceroy early in 1858 was approved but nothing came of it; indeed, the details of the plan remain unknown.[3]

The urgency of resolving the peasant question in Georgia became evident in January 1857 when three thousand peasants in the Jvari district of Samegrelo rose in revolt against the Dadiani family, the *mtavara* or hereditary ruler of the Mingrelian lands. Peasant demands included an end to the sale and purchase of peasants, protection of peasants' rights to own property, creation of courts to decide grievances between landlords and peasants, and the abolition of personal bondage. The Russians responded by abolishing the autonomous powers of the Dadiani *mtavara* and retiring Princess Ekaterina to St. Petersburg, but they would go no further. When peasants continued to attack landlords and refused to work for the nobles, the military moved in and forcibly imposed an armed peace.[4] Thirty-eight peasant leaders were arrested and exiled.

The revolt had been suppressed, but Russian authorities remained concerned about its repercussions. General Koliubakin reported to his superiors: "I do not wish to believe that in the Caucasus in many cases the word of a Russian cannot replace the bayonet and cannon. We cannot forget that each of our shots in Mingrelia against a native—in a coastal country filled with newcomers from Turkey—will have echoes in Constantinople, in Europe and in London at some kind of meeting listening to a drunk orator straining his voice against the inhumanity of Russia." Russian officialdom could hardly afford to forget that just two years earlier, when Omar Pasha had invaded western Georgia, many peasants had responded with enthusiasm to his promises that the allies would emancipate the serfs.[5]

Still, no action was taken toward emancipation in Georgia until after the *Polozhenie* of February 19, 1861.[6] Then, on March 5, the Caucasian Committee in St. Petersburg secretly ordered Bariatinskii to begin the reform in Georgia "with appropriate caution." The viceroy called in representatives of the nobility and informed them of the government's intentions. A Transcaucasian Committee for the Reorganization of the Landlord Peasantry was set up, headed by State Secretary Aleksei Fedorovich Kruzenshtern, and the nobles were told to elect district committees that would supply local plans for reform. The whole apparatus was given six months to complete its work.[7]

In the six decades of Russian administration in Transcaucasia, the Georgian nobility had not only made peace with its Russian conquerors but had consolidated itself as an estate with feet planted firmly in the soil of two alien cultures. With sense of itself as a service nobility loyal to a new sovereign, the Georgian elite had reason to believe that its achievements in the Crimean and Caucasian wars would be rewarded appropriately by the state. The nobles began their deliberations, wary of the consequences of emancipation but also hopeful that their privileged position would not be seriously compromised.

Since the Russian occupation, the relations between the Georgian peasants and the state and nobility had been considerably adapted to Russian norms. The many peasant categories that had existed under the Georgian monarchy had been simplified, as had the labyrinth of local taxation and "feudal" obligations. In general, Georgian peasants at midcentury paid three types of dues to their noble lords—portions of the harvest for the use of the land (*gala* and *kulukhi*) and two kinds of payments for their persons (which, like the land, was owned by the lords): labor services (*begara*), and various customary obligations such as the provision of domestic servants. Russian administration and legislation had strengthened the hold of the lords over the peasantry, reduced peasant mobility and rights, and in many cases turned the traditional paternalistic noble-peasant relationship into a more formal relationship of absentee landlords and peasant serfs.[8]

The primary beneficiaries of Russian rulership were the large landholding aristocrats, the princely Orbeliani, Eristavi, Bagration-Mukhranskii, and Chavchavadze families. Bearers of these prestigious names served in high military and civilian positions, as marshals of the nobility and liaisons between Georgian society and the tsarist bureaucracy. But most Georgian nobles at midcentury were simply not in the economic and social sphere occupied by such aristocrats. Small landowners, those with fewer than twenty-one serfs, made up almost half the nobility in eastern Georgia.[9] In Tiflis province there was also a sizable number of middle gentry, who stood economically between the large magnates and the smallest landholders. They, like the aristocrats, benefited from the potential of state service, but the costs of adopting a European lifestyle drove them, along with many of their wealthier brethren, into debt.[10] Thus, many petty and middle nobles were quite ambivalent about full participation in the Russified culture of the towns, and, as can be seen in the memoirs and literature of this period, many of them lived more traditional lives in the countryside.[11] These small and middle-sized landholders, especially those who remained outside state service and depended on their agricultural income alone, felt the threat of emancipation most acutely. They received little comfort when the tsar visited Georgia in September 1861 and assured them that emancipation would be achieved with "the minimum loss to the landlords."[12]

Emancipation was a direct threat to noble income, as a petition to the government from the Tiflis nobles stated in no uncertain terms: "As soon as the peasants are declared free, our families will immediately be placed in an impoverished condition. We will have to sit sadly in the courtyards and beg for alms. We will have neither servants nor workers for the fields and vineyards, neither shepherds for the livestock nor governesses to bring up our children."[13] Only when the administration threatened to carry out the reform without their participation did the nobles take action, calling an extraordinary meeting of the nobility of Tiflis province for April 20, 1862. After five days of heated discussion the nobles agreed to end personal bondage and free the serfs as persons, but insisted the land remain in their own hands. The peasants would remain on the land temporarily, paying all dues and obligations as before until a voluntary agreement as to future payments was reached with the lords. If no agreement could be reached, the peasants would be free to settle elsewhere, or the nobles could force them to leave.

Dmitri Kipiani was entrusted with the task of formulating the noble position. In his lengthy treatise Kipiani argued that in Georgia the nobles had unlimited authority over the land and the peasants:

> Our property consists of two rights: the right to the people and the right to the land. The juridical right to the people, according to our old law, is outlined rather broadly. "The peasant himself and all that he has belongs to his lord"—so it is written in the law.

Despite this limitless authority, Kipiani went on to say, the peasants had been satisfied with their situation, for relations between estates historically had been devoid of bitterness:

> The relations between ourselves and our peasants, established in ancient times, have been the most intimate relations between members of one house, one family. We have always looked upon them, not as slaves or unfree men, but as producers in a common enterprise. They saw us not as oppressors but as their protectors and as the managers of the domestic economy.[14]

Kipiani proposed that, given these ancient rights and responsibilities, the nobility should be compensated for the loss of its rights over the peasantry and be permitted to keep title over *all* the land. Under his plan the nobles would continue to receive traditional duties without themselves becoming any more involved in agriculture than they had been in the past. On April 30, 1862, Kipiani's treatise was accepted by the noble assembly by a vote of 135 to 4. The negative votes were cast by members of the most exalted families in Georgia, nobles closely allied to the Russian state and least vulnerable, given their immense holdings, to the danger of impoverishment after emancipation.[15]

With the backing of the assembly, Kipiani set to work collecting the nobles' views on emancipation and outlining a model for reform.[16] By late April 1863 he had completed a full report for the nobles of Tiflis province based on his own reading of Georgian history. Central to his conception was the notion that the Russian monarchy was obligated by treaty with the Georgian kings to preserve all rights and privileges of the Georgian nobility, including those specified in the law code of Vakhtang VI, which clearly stated that the nobles had full authority over everything the peasants had. For Kipiani Georgia's feudalism had been the same as that of Western Europe six hundred years earlier, the only difference being that Georgian nobles had never driven their peasants from the land. "Grief and joy," he wrote, "profit and loss, all has been common between us and our peasants as long as the causes for differences had not appeared." The lord was obliged to help the peasant in times of need, and the peasant to supply the lord with produce and labor because the lord owned both the peasant himself and the land he tilled.[17]

Kipiani argued that the Georgian nobles, historically the defenders of the peasants and the nation, more recently the loyal servitors of the Russian tsar, could not, by their very character, engage in agriculture or industry and therefore relied completely on payments and free labor from their peasants. "Our inherited and historically formed character has stubbornly prohibited commercial activity up to now and one must recognize that it is not yet evident that we have any abilities in this area." Kipiani also claimed that farming was not an option for individual Georgian nobles; not only did they lack experience, but their family-owned estates could be broken up into private holdings only with great difficulty. He concluded with an appeal for sympathy: "The peasants have always fed us; we have existed because of them."[18]

Yet, because their sovereign desired emancipation, the nobles were willing to make the sacrifice and give up their powers over the serfs. They would allow the peasants to use all the lands they currently used, but title to the land was to remain with the nobility. Because of land shortage, Kipiani argued, landless emancipation was imperative. If land were distributed to the peasants, the landlords would be left with very small, uneconomical plots. "Where the land will belong to the peasants, there it will be impossible for the landlord to live and everything belonging to him will be ruined."[19] The peasants would continue to pay for the use of the land they cultivated, as well as for the forests and pastures, for three years, during which time they would work out payment terms for a twelve-year agreement.

Essentially all landlord peasants would be reduced to the category of *khizani,* the class of personally free landless peasants who were in fact hereditary tenant farmers.[20] Kipiani conceived that they would continue to pay *gala* (approximately one-sixth of the grain harvest) or *kulukhi* (one-quarter of the grape harvest) and other minor duties. In general, when there was no labor shortage, work obligations (*begara*) would be replaced by payments in cash or kind. Thus, in Kipiani's plan, the serfs were to be bound not to the lord but to the land, in what the historian Avaliani has called "a new economic slavery." Essentially Kipiani's plan replaced the traditional paternalism and protection of the peasants with a more fluid situation, one in which the most basic economic resource of the country—the land—was even more completely in the hands of noble proprietors; peasants were forced to come to terms with the landowners or leave the land.[21]

His program for reform in hand, Dmitri Kipiani traveled from district to district explaining his position to the nobles of Sighnaghi, Telavi, Gori, Dusheti, and Tiflis. Not only were his efforts rewarded with overwhelming support, but in the process a consensus was forged among the eastern Georgian nobility that amounted to their first united political formation since the conspiracy of 1832. At the end of May 1863 a provincial congress of the nobility was held in Tiflis and overwhelmingly approved Kipiani's plan by a vote of 539 to 16. Earlier, the Russian nobility had complained to the tsar about emancipation of the peasants with land, but their protests had occurred before the proclamation of February 19. The Georgian nobles were insisting on keeping all the land, even the peasants' household plots and immovable property, such as houses. Displaying a cohesiveness and self-awareness as they faced the most serious challenge to their sources of income, they were acting in defiance of the reform already promulgated in Russia proper.

Equipped now with a clear ideological position, the nobles of Tiflis province decided to bolster their case with new leadership. At the end of 1863 they invited Kipiani to stand as a candidate for marshal of the nobility of Tiflis province. Members of the most aristocratic families, the Bagration-Mukhranskii and the Orbeliani, objected vehemently to an untitled noble holding a post that had been occupied only by members of their families. Kipiani, angered that the aristocrats refused to accept the wishes of the majority of the nobles, decided to run for the office despite an attempt by a state official to dissuade him. In February 1864 the assembly overwhelmingly elected him, 273 to 4, with 35 of the most prestigious nobles abstaining.[22]

Threatened by a blow to their status, the great majority of the Georgian nobles unhesitatingly threw off their traditional leaders from the *noblesse d'épée* and rallied around Kipiani, the articulate representative of the small and middle nobility.[23] In his acceptance speech Kipiani spoke of the extraordinary and difficult step the nobility had taken, but ended by affirming the complete loyalty of the Georgian nobility to the tsar: "I speak directly that I do not understand any interests outside this rule, that is to say, outside our innate consciousness of our duty and our dignity: noble dignity involves irreproachable service to the throne.[24]

Despite Kipiani's professed loyalty, St. Petersburg, already challenged militarily by the 1863 uprising in Poland, was apprehensive about the shift in noble leadership in Georgia. Baron Aleksandr Nikolai's report to the Caucasian Committee, reassuring the members of Kipiani's devotion to the monarchy, may have helped:

As far as the political convictions of Mister Kipiani are concerned, it is possible to say one thing about them, and that is that he is sufficiently intelligent to comprehend that unconditional submission to the Russian government is the single rule for the survival of his homeland.[25]

In Georgia the Russian government faced a nobility united in its opposition to the state's plans for emancipation, a unanimity that extended even to the few nobles who had voted against Kipiani's program.[26] Their attitudes were gaining attention in the government. When Bariatinskii, for reasons connected with his health, both physical and political, asked to be relieved of his post, he was replaced by Grand Duke Mikhail Nikolaevich. The new viceroy arrived in Tiflis in March 1863 and turned his attention immediately to the peasant question. He wrote to his brother, the tsar, of its increasing seriousness:

I will try to hasten as much as possible the resolution of this important question. Its resolution is essential without delay for the relations of the peasants to the landlords are strained all over Transcaucasia; this is especially evident here and in Gori *uezd,* so that it has been necessary to send expeditions to many villages. Very often the peasants refuse to fulfill those obligations which for ages their fathers and ancestors fulfilled by custom. One can suppose that the peasants, out of impatience to receive freedom, allow themselves such liberties . . . At the same time, it often occurs that landlords, aware of the approaching resolution of the peasant question, try to use the last moments to grab as much as possible for themselves from the peasants and, as they say, squeeze from the last juice.[27]

By the fall of 1863 the debates in the local noble assemblies had ended and the various projects had been submitted to the Transcaucasian Committee for the Reorganization of the Landlord Peasantry. The Kipiani plan represented the clear preferences of a relatively united Georgian nobility, but the committee, now chaired by Baron Nikolai and including both members of the Georgian nobility and the state bureaucracy, developed an alternative plan by early 1864. Believing that the peasantry should not develop into a mobile proletariat but should remain settled on the land and provide tax revenues for the state, the committee decided that the peasants should be given allotments of land for which they would have to pay noble owners.[28]

This proposal was a radical break with the nobles' position, but the government was determined not to create a mass of landless peasants that would "introduce into the state organism a constant element of disorder." The committee was fully aware of the difficulties the loss of land would impose on the nobility—indeed, greater difficulties in Georgia than in Russia, for "the general level of education and economic life of the local landlords lags behind the level of education and economic life of landlords in Russia."[29] In Georgia the peasants generally used all the landlords' lands as their own, whereas in Russia a clearer distinction was usually made between peasant lands and the seigneur's demesne. Thus, division of the land would be much more complicated and threatened to create deep fissures in Georgian rural society.

On October 13, 1864, the tsar authorized the abolition of serfdom in Tiflis province. On November 8 officials sent by the viceroy announced the emancipation at ceremonies in Tiflis, Sighnaghi, Gori, and Telavi. A message in Georgian from the viceroy was read to the peasants, announcing the beginning of a "new life" for them. In Sighnaghi a peasant thanked the tsar and proposed a toast to his health, and one of the local nobles complained publicly that the gentry had just lost the ability to educate its children without aid from the state.[30] A few days later the *ukaz* was read in all the churches of the province.

On the same day that he issued the "Law on the Reorganization of Former Peasant Serfs in Tiflis Province" (November 8), Viceroy Mikhail Nikolaevich ordered the governor-general of Kutaisi, Dmitrii Ivanovich Sviatopolk-Mirskii, to begin a similar reform for western Georgia. Instead of repeating the lengthy process of soliciting opinions from the nobility, the viceroy proposed formation of a noble committee, chaired by the marshal of the provincial nobility, to which each *uezd* would send four representatives, two from the *tavadebi* (princes), two from the *aznaurni* (gentry). A government commission would work out the final proposal on the basis of the nobles' project and the existing reform in Tiflis province. Within four months the nobles had completed their work under the direction of Prince Nestor Tsereteli and sent their *Zapiski* (memorandum) to the governmental commission chaired by Georgii Konstantinovich Bagration-Mukhranskii. Here too the nobles proposed landless emancipation and here too they were rejected. The governor-general, the viceroy's Committee for the Reorganization of the Landlord Peasantry, and the viceroy himself in turn examined, edited, and finally approved the commission's plan.[31] On October 13, 1865, the tsar approved the emancipation of the serfs of Guria and Imereti (Kutaisi, Shorapani, Racha, and Ozurgeti *uezdy*).

Emancipation meant first and foremost that the former landlord peasants received personal liberation from their dependency on the nobles. No longer could the landlords buy, sell, give away, or mortgage peasants. No longer could peasants be involuntarily moved from place to place or sent by will of the landlord into exile. Peasants were free to marry without permission from their lords, engage in business, participate in government and educational institutions, and enter other social orders, such as the townspeople.

Yet at the same time the serf remained dependent materially, and in part legally, on his former master. Central to the terms of emancipation was a two-part principle: while officially recognizing that all the land belonged to the noble landlords, including lands that peasants had worked for centuries, the state nonetheless required that henceforth the land be divided between nobles and peasants. One part was to be fully owned by the lord; the other part, the peasant's *nadel* (allotment), would be used by the peasant, who would pay specific dues for that right. The peasant had the right to redeem his household plot (*usadebnaia osedlost'*, the land immediately around his house), and, if the landlord agreed, to purchase additional arable lands that would then become the peasant's private property.

The Transcaucasian Committee had disagreed with the majority of Georgian nobles, who had argued that even immovable property, such as houses and barns, belonged to them. For the committee, the peasants' right to own immovable property had already been established in the law of February 19, 1861, which recognized both that the nobles owned the land and that peasants' homes were part of the household plots. The boundaries of the household plots were to be determined by voluntary agreement between the peasant and his lord or, if they could not agree, by a *mirovoi posrednik* (peace arbitrator).[32]

The noble was allowed to keep at least half the land he owned before reform; the peasant allotments were to come out of the other half. The committee recognized that the allotments for the peasants would be insufficient "but in its determination to save the nobility, supposedly from ruin, the committee had sacrificed the peasants' interests."[33] Since the nobles had concentrated in their proposals almost exclusively on making a case for a landlord monopoly on landholding, they had not provided the Transcaucasian Committee with specific suggestions on the size of peasant holdings, the amount of dues to be paid the nobles, or the conditions under which peasants could redeem their allotments. On these questions the committee developed its own positions, but sought to protect the nobles from economic hardship.

Maximum peasant allotments, equivalent to what could be plowed in ten or twenty days, were set in various districts. Nobles with small landholdings, however, were permitted to keep at least the equivalent of sixty days' plowing. In the mountainous areas where arable land was scarce and nobles had few holdings, all the land except for pasture was left in the hands of the peasants. They were to continue to pay the *eristavi* the traditional dues and were not permitted to reduce the size of their holdings for ten years. Thus the nobles, who feared that mountain peasants might abandon their harsh way of life and move into the valleys or cities, secured their interests not by receiving half the land but by tying the peasants to the land for a set period and thus maintaining their source of income.[34]

In Tiflis province artificially irrigated land was divided into plots not larger than 5 desiatinas; unirrigated land was divided into plots not larger than 10 desiatinas. In Kutaisi province the maximum size of a plot was 4.5 desiatinas. The basic (*korennoi*) size of most plots in Tiflis was half the maximum, that is, 2.5 desiatinas of irrigated or 5.0 desiatinas of unirrigated land. In Kutaisi, where, the government argued, the land was richer and the peasants could reap two harvests (one in wheat, the other in millet), the basic plot was 1.5 desiatinas.[35]

Peasants could continue to use pasturelands, but the landlords had the right to plow pastures or use them as they saw fit. Forests were left completely in the hands of the lords, and the peasants had to pay to use them. The peasant was obligated to use and pay for his household plot and the basic allotment of arable land for nine years, effectively keeping him, as before, tied to the land. At the end of that time he had two options. He might retain as his private property two *ktseva* (about two acres) of land, foregoing any dues, but also losing any claims on his former allotment. His other alternative was to buy land through a complex system of redemption payments.[36]

There was another pattern: if peasants had received the maximum allotment, the nobles retained all remaining lands. Peasants and nobles could agree to reduce the size of the *nadel* to the basic allotment, with a corresponding reduction in payment. If the peasant wished to redeem his allotment immediately, the *nadel* could be reduced to one-third the maximum. Poor peasants whose *nadel* was smaller than the size of the basic allotment did not have their plots reduced in such transactions, but there was no provision for a minimum allotment size, as there was in Russia. The lord was permitted to grant his peasants land half the size of the basic allotment gratis.[37]

The landlord had the right to retain arable land and meadows of at least 30 desiatinas in Tiflis province and 11.25 desiatinas in Kutaisi province. Petty landlords whose property did not come up to these minimum standards were freed from any obligation to give their peasants arable field allotments. If a noble did not possess even a household garden plot, he was permitted to take over the plot of one of his peasants.[38] The law tried in these ways to secure a livelihood for the nobles, even at the sacrifice of some peasants.

The dues paid by peasants increased significantly after the reform. Dues were levied for the household plots and the rest of the land allotment, the orchards, the arable fields, and the meadows. For the household plot a money payment of three rubles for each half-desiatina in Tiflis province and for each *ktseva* in Kutaisi province was established by law. The dues for the rest of the peasant lands were paid in kind: *kulukhi* (one-fourth of the wine produced); *gala* (one-fourth of the harvest of the fields); and one-third of the mowed hay from the meadows. The obligation of mountain peasants remained the same as before the reform, except now they were fixed by law. Every twenty years the amount of dues in kind could be re-evaluated at the request of either side. Basically payments in kind remained the principal form. *Begara,* the labor obligation, was eliminated with the reform, except in the mountainous region of Georgia. The traditional obligations of *gala* and *kulukhi* had varied from district to district, but they had ranged upward from one-tenth of the harvest, rarely exceeding one-fifth. The peasants, now farming less land, owed more than double their former monetary obligations.[39]

Thus the serf's dependence on his lord did not end with the emancipation. Indeed, the evolution to full free proprietor of his land required several phases, as in Russia. For the first nine years the peasant was obligated to use and pay for his household plot and the basic allotment of arable land. Still tied to the land, the peasant paid the same dues as he had under serfdom, until he reached an agreement (*ustavnaia gramota*) with his lord that set the terms under which he would receive his allotment. These agreements were to be negotiated within two years with the help of the *mirovoi posrednik*. Once such an agreement was reached, the peasant advanced to the status of "temporarily obligated" (*vremennoobiazannyi*). The landlord retained full ownership of his estate, except for the peasant's household plot, but ceded the peasant's allotment in exchange for rent. To acquire full title to the land the peasant had to conclude a redemption agreement (*vykupnaia sdelka*) with his lord and pay off the loan that the government had made to the landlord for loss of land: a process which was to take an estimated forty-nine years. During this period the peasant formally moved into the category of "peasant proprietor," and the state took over the principal responsibility for enforcing peasant payments. If a peasant fell behind, the village leadership could send him or a member of his family to work until he made up the arrears.[40] If the entire process operated as planned, within half a century the former serf would become a free peasant landholder.

The law on the redemption operation for Tiflis and Kutaisi provinces was formally issued on August 14, 1868. As in Russia, the peasant was obligated to come to an agreement with the lord over the terms of purchase of his allotment, but the lord was not obligated to make such an agreement. Thus the lord could keep the peasant in the status of "temporary obligation" indefinitely. Furthermore, in contrast to Russia, in Georgia peasants did not even have an unencumbered right to redeem their household plots except in very limited cases.[41]

The process of redeeming the allotments was quite complicated both in Russia and Georgia. Since peasants lacked the money to buy their land from the landlord, the government paid the nobles what amounted to a redemption loan, which the peasants then had to pay off in installments with interest. The size of the loan was based not on current land values but on the amount of capital that would yield the lord an annual income equal to the former serf's *obrok* (dues). This meant that a year's *obrok* was capitalized at 6 percent, (that is, multiplied by $16\frac{2}{3}$).[42]

In Russia the government loan was 80 percent of the lord's payment; the peasant was required to make up the remaining 20 percent. Redemption payments were fixed at 6 percent of the loan, roughly equivalent to the former *obrok*. With redemption payments set at a level commensurate with the old peasant obligations rather than the market value of the land, the seigneurial aspects of the lord-peasant relationship were preserved, or at least not converted completely into capitalist landlord-tenant relations.

In Georgia, a different system was established. Instead of the government giving the landlords 80 percent of the full redemption payment, a maximum size was set for the loan. Thus, for a peasant household paying *obrok* in money, the loan was 350 rubles for the household plot and other lands. For those peasants paying both in cash and kind, the loan was 250 rubles per household, and it was 180 rubles per household for those peasants in mountainous areas who paid their *obrok* totally in kind.[43] But Georgian land prices at the time were more than twice as high as these maximums, and the landlords were determined their lands would not be redeemed below market value. So if the peasants made redemption agreements with their landlords they were forced to pay more than 50 percent of the total cost, instead of the 20 percent that Russian peasants paid. Furthermore, the rules for redemption did not extend loans to orchards, vineyards, and pastures, which could become peasant property only with the landlord's agreement and full purchase by the peasant. Thus for the great majority of the Georgian peasantry, the possibility of redeeming the land was beyond reach. For the nobles it was more advantageous to maintain the "temporarily obligated" status of their peasants and continue to receive payments from them than unilaterally to abrogate this status and force them to redeem the land. By the latter decision, a landlord would receive the state loan but lose forever the peasants' payments.

Not surprisingly, the process of concluding redemption agreements moved exceedingly slowly in Georgia. In 1879 about 14 percent of former landlord serfs were still "temporarily obligated" in Russia; a decade later 70 percent of their Georgian counterparts were still in that category. Most would remain so until 1912, when the government abolished this relationship in Transcaucasia, thirty years after its elimination in Russia.[44]

The most significant economic consequence of the emancipation in Georgia was the reduction in land under direct peasant control. The land worked directly by the peasants of Tiflis province was reduced by more than 25,000 desiatinas (about one-fifth), and former serfs in Kutaisi province lost about 30,000 desiatinas, one-third of "their" land. A small number of peasants, former household serfs and *khizani*, were liberated completely without land. Although estimates are hard to come by, Soviet historians suggest that about four hundred households in western Georgia received no land, and for Tiflis province estimates run from 9 to 13 percent—at least 1,444 peasant households left without land.[45]

The peasant allotments were very meager in eastern Georgia and even smaller in the west. Historians estimate that the prereform average plot for a peasant in Tiflis province was 5.9 desiatinas. After the reform their actual average allotment was 3.9 desiatinas. This was somewhat less than the average allotment size in European Russia after the reform, where 48.3 percent of the former serfs received from 4 to 6 desiatinas per male serf.

In Kutaisi province, where the land was much richer and the population denser, the average peasant *nadel* after the reform averaged 2.5 desiatinas per household. And in Ozurgeti *uezd* in western Georgia the average allotment was 1.3 desiatinas. Avaliani indicts the government for the effects on the Georgian peasantry: "From the first moment of the dissolution of serfdom the base was laid for the formation of a landless and small landholding peasant proletariat, and this acted as the catalyst for constant ferment and social disorder."[46]

Emancipation led to a new system of self-government. Collectively all peasants in a village were considered a *sel'skoe obshchestvo* or village commune, whether they were former landlord, clerical, or state peasants. This differed from the practice in Russia, where an *obshchestvo* included only peasants of one landlord. Small villages in Georgia were merged into single communes. Each commune was to be administered by a peasant assembly, an elder (*starshina* in Russian, *mamasakhlisi* in Georgian), and a peasant court. Other local appointees included errand boys (*gzirebi*), field guards (*mevelebi*), and irrigation-ditch watchmen (*meruebi*). The powers of all officials and institutions were identical to those provided for the Russian *obshchestvo*, and the landlords were to remain as the guardians of their former serfs with police powers.[47] In Russia several communes made up a *volost*, but no *volosti* were created in Georgia. Thus, immediately above the Georgian village government stood the tsarist administration rather than elected *volost* authorities.

Although in Georgia there had been very little communal landholding by peasants, the Transcaucasian Committee for the Reorganization of the Landlord Peasantry decided to extend *krugovaia poruka*, the collective responsibility of the village commune for paying taxes and debts, to the Georgian villages. The village was responsible for state and land duties, while individual households remained responsible for various social and civil payments.[48] Georgian peasants had never before experienced this kind of collective involvement in tax assessment and collection, and a new element, straight out of Russian peasant practice, was thus introduced into their social life.

The process of emancipating the serfs of Georgia continued through the 1860s into the early 1870s. In 1867 the serfs of Samegrelo were freed. The great majority of the Mingrelian-speaking peasants were landlord serfs (80,000 out of 93,000 male peasants), but the noble landlords were themselves quite poor, and their economic situation differed little from the peasants. In 1870 bound peasants, including slaves, were liberated in Abkhazeti, and finally in 1871 bondage was abolished in Svaneti.

In Abkhazeti peasants had a special relationship to their nobles. Many had the right to leave one owner for another. Besides serfs (*akh-uiu*) who did labor for their lords and paid dues in kind, there were other categories of peasants. In the homes of many lords were *akhashala,* slaves who were the private property of the nobles. Most Abkhazian peasants were landowners, *ankhaiiu,* and had very loose ties to the lords. Peasants considered the land theirs, and when in 1866 they were told that they would be required to redeem it, they rose in revolt. In July a certain Colonel Koniar spoke to a mass meeting of peasants in the village of Lykhny about the coming reform, and the angered peasants set upon him and his staff, killing them. The rebels moved on a few days later to Sukhumi and took the city. Military force was required to retake the town and end the revolt.[49]

With the formal abolition of serfdom in Abkhazeti nearly everyone from noble to slave received some land. The 58,000 peasants received about 192,000 desiatinas, while the 2,245 noble families received 100,000 desiatinas. The former serfs were given four years to pay off their debts to the lords and receive full title to the land, but after a revolt in 1877 the government decided to punish the Abkhaz peasantry and declared that the land was not their private property but was held only in use tenure. All peasants were required to pay off their seigneurial obligations, and like the peasants in Georgia proper they remained "temporarily obligated" until 1912.

Svaneti, the most remote and inaccessible part of Georgia, was distinguished by the ferocity of its people's determination to preserve their traditional way of life. Svaneti was divided into two parts: "princely" Svaneti, ruled by the Dadeshkeliani family, and "free" Svaneti, where serfdom, and indeed nobles, did not exist. Svan peasants (*glekhebi*) paid high dues to their lords. Personal household servants of the Svan nobility, the *mojalabebi,* were little more than slaves, bought and sold without land, and highly valued in a society where servants were hard to come by. The government decided that freeing these servants would cause too much opposition among the nobility, so only their resale and purchase were prohibited; all newborn were automatically free. All peasants with land were set free and given a small plot of land without going through the stage of "temporary obligation." The peasants received about four *ktseva,* half the size of the plots in Samegrelo. The nobles received money payments from the state for the loss of their rights over the peasants, as well as much of the land. Left with very little land, the Svan peasants were forced to rent lands of the nobility.[50]

The Georgian nobles lost much in the reform—part of the lands they had owned for centuries, labor obligations from their serfs, the dues from the serfs—but they also retained much. Former landlord peasants in Tiflis and Kutaisi provinces received 135,000 and 211,000 desiatinas of land respectively, but the nobles received 961,000 in Tiflis province and 815,000 in Kutaisi.[51] Half the land in Georgia was still in the noble domain, and in addition the government decided to recompense the Georgian nobility for their loss of rights over the person of the serfs. For each liberated male serf a lord was to receive twenty-five rubles; lords with less than twenty-one serfs were to receive an additional twenty-five rubles for each male serf. The Georgian and Mingrelian nobility received more than seven million rubles for its lost rights. The tsar in granting this money expressed his hope that "the landlords, comforted by our expression of compassion for their present condition, will use the means given them for the reorganization and improvement of their economy." Kipiani replied in a speech in the viceroy's palace that the tsar's generosity had eliminated the gentry's greatest fear, that of material impoverishment, and he assured the viceroy that the Georgian nobility was prepared to carry out the peasant reform.[52]

The tsar also preserved the nobles' police powers over the peasants. But his trust stopped short of permitting them to nominate candidates for the *mirovye posredniki,* as nobles could in Russia proper. Instead the government appointed these officials usually from the local nobility or state bureaucracy, and did not permit them to gather in congresses as was possible in Russia.[53] Furthermore, the *zemstvo* reform of 1864, which had created elective local administrative bodies, was not extended to Transcaucasia.

The nobles' failure to resist the state's version of emancipation beyond their initial petitions illustrates the degree to which they had been successfully integrated into the tsarist hierarchy. A mere thirty years earlier many of these same men had been prepared to murder Russian officials and to fight to re-establish an independent Georgian kingdom. Yet in the 1860s their opposition to emancipation was contained within legal bounds, and once the tsar's will was announced, they took no further action. Georgian nobles acted precisely like their Russian brethren, though their ties were of more recent vintage and their transformation into service nobles had occurred only a generation earlier. From the age of Paskevich through the reign of Vorontsov to the viceroyalties of Bariatinskii and Grand Duke Mikhail Nikolaevich, the Georgian nobles' fate was increasingly tied to the Russian state, in war and peace. There was no longer any Batonishvili alternative to the Romanovs, no possible hope of restoration of the Bagratid monarchy. Their new sense of self-definition as an estate conformed to that of the Russian nobility. Georgia's finest families were no longer primarily a national elite, as they had been in the first three decades of the century, but a cosmopolitan aristocracy with loyalties extending beyond Georgia, binding them to the Russian autocratic order.

This was not merely psychological or cultural. Thanks to their propensity to consume lavishly, the aristocrats of Georgia increased their material dependence on the Russian state. Their debts grew, and their only source of income came from state service and peasant dues, which ultimately were guaranteed by Russian arms. Like the landed aristocrats in Russia or, indeed, the slaveholders in the antebellum American South, upperclass Georgians regarded an appropriately high standard of living as a necessity for the leaders of society.

In many ways the emancipation settlement had been very generous to the Georgian nobles, and their fellow nobles in Russia might look on them with envy. The corporate solidarity of the Georgian nobles had paid off in important concessions, though they were much further from the government's position on emancipation than many Russian nobles were. As Soviet historian Petr Zaionchkovskii concludes: "As a result of the abolition of serfdom, feudal-serf-owning remnants were preserved in Georgia to a greater degree than in the central regions of Russia."[54] In a sense, then, the emancipation in Georgia stands at the opposite extreme from the reform in the Polish and western provinces where the peasants received a relatively favorable settlement and the nobles, because of their participation in the rebellion of 1863, were treated more harshly than elsewhere in the empire.

Clearly the peasants, the great majority of the people, were the losers in the Georgian emancipation. The final form of the peasant reform was an economic and social disaster, the full consequences of which took nearly forty years to be realized. Acquisition of personal freedom in formal, legal terms was more than offset by the continuing economic dependence on the nobility, a new form of bondage from which they were unable to emancipate themselves. Also, it should be noted that there was no reform of the status of state peasants corresponding to that undertaken in Russia in 1866, and they remained on state land, paying dues to the treasury.

The Georgian peasantry did not at first understand fully the implications of the reform. Even hearing the text of the *Polozhenie,* which had been translated into a rather bookish Georgian, did not clarify the complex provisions of the law.[55] The peasants often interpreted the emancipation as more complete than it actually was. Responding to a few "agitators," peasants would refuse to pay their dues or do *begara* (labor obligations) for their landlords. In the first year of the reform the administration in Tiflis province received almost two thousand complaints from landlords about "temporarily obligated" peasants refusing to pay dues or work for the lords. Peasants also refused to pay their arrears for dues and taxes not paid before the emancipation. Giving up half the land to the nobles proved especially painful to many peasants, and they hesitated to formulate and sign the agreements on land partition (*ustavnye gramoty*). Yet Georgian peasants did not take up arms to protest the terms of emancipation, and indeed they were much more peaceful immediately after the reform than before it. The illusory nature of the freedom granted became more apparent as expected material benefits went unrealized and the impoverishment of the peasantry spread ever further.[56] As the poet Akaki Tsereteli wrote of the reforms in Georgia:

In words everything was as good as possible, but in fact it was good for no one. For example, what kind of abolition of serfdom is it when a state official held in his hands the lord and the serf, tied together by chains, and smothered and fleeced them? What help could be expected from the courts in which one's own language was forbidden and people, thanks to their ignorance of a foreign language, fell into the clutches of every thief and rascal.[57]

The abolition of serfdom in Georgia was initiated, designed, and carried out by the Russian state, by bureaucrats acting in the name of the tsar and his viceroy. It was carried out against the expressed desires of the organized gentry and its newly chosen leadership. Its purpose, like much of the legislation imposed since 1801 by Russian officials on Georgian society, was to bring this anomalous area into conformity with the Russian bureaucratic system, make its institutions as much like those of the Russian empire as possible, while preserving the political and social structure, with the nobility in power. For the first sixty years of Russian rule that process of integration had brought tighter noble authority over the peasant population and tighter ties of the serfs to their lords and the land. But the reform marked a dramatic turning point. Now noble authority, however slightly, was compromised, and peasants, however incompletely, gained a degree of freedom.

No significant group within Georgia was satisfied with the reform. The traditional noble-peasant relationship had been tampered with but not yet fundamentally altered. The reduction of land, the increase of monetary obligations for the peasantry, and the loss of income and labor by the nobility began a process of change that would further erode the customary nexus between estates in Georgia, introducing alien economic and social forces. In time much of the resentment of peasants and nobles alike would be turned against the state, which had attempted in its own interest to transform agrarian relations. Ultimately national and social discontent would converge in a massive revolutionary peasant movement under socialist direction in the early twentieth century.

6   The Emergence of Political Society

An explanation of Georgian political movements in the last third of the nineteenth century does not neatly fit the rather clichéd pattern sometimes proposed for the development of nationalism. For many observers it has been sufficient to explain nationalism as the byproduct of oppression and the instinctive desire of a colonialized people for national independence. Given the "naturalness" of national feelings, there is little need for the historian to explain their appearance and power. But close studies of the historical roots of national movements have exposed a much more complicated picture.

In Georgia, resistance to Russian rule was an extremely differentiated process, one in which pressures for accommodation with the existing regime were as great as (at times greater than) the counterforces that produced resistance. Second, the specifically Georgian nationalist movement, although it shaped a sense of Georgian nationality and alienation from the dominant Russian and Armenian nationalities, was not in the forefront of the liberation movement by the century's end. The relative strength of socialist, rather than nationalist or liberal, answers to Georgia's problems was the historical product of the particular social context and intellectual environment in which all three of these movements arose.

The development of nationality and the conscious expression of its aspirations—nationalism—is analogous to, though in no sense identical to, other social formations, particularly class and class consciousness. A concept borrowed from the Marxist tradition, which posits two distinct though related processes in class formation, might usefully be applied to the history of Georgian national formation. Marx speaks of a class moving from an objective demographic existence as a "class in itself" to a more organized, conscious, and mobilized formation interested and able to act in its interests,

itself." The Georgians, who were incorporated into the Russian
ie first decades of the nineteenth century, were still a divided,
choate people, sharing an ethnicity with recognizable cultural
spite periods of unity and glory in the past, they had faced virtual
extinction by the end of the eighteenth century and, except for a few nobles
and clerics, possessed little sense of their own nationhood.

From this rather desperate and disparate situation, the Georgians under
Russian rule began a gradual resurgence. The consequent economic stability,
the increase in modes of communication among the Georgians, and the
introduction of Western education into the Georgian noble elite—all these
contributed to the formation of a "nationality in itself" by the end of the
second third of the nineteenth century. An ethnic presence existed that would
not be eroded by the efforts of chauvinist administrators or the barely visible
but discernible effects of capitalist development.

From the 1870s to 1890s additional pressures from the government
combined with the new forces of the postemancipation economic environment to encourage a sense of nationality, a national consciousness, and the
first manifestations of political ideologies. By the last decade of the century,
Georgia had developed into a "nationality for itself," complete with a
national leadership and an incipient mass movement for liberation. For many
Georgians the sense of national identity had become their primary loyalty,
replacing older allegiances to regions, religion, or traditional lords. For many
others that national sensibility was intimately tied to an overtly socialist
worldview.

In the first hundred years of Russian rule in Georgia, the efforts of alien
governors to eliminate social and cultural peculiarities in Transcaucasia
resulted, paradoxically, not in the assimiliation of the local peoples, but
instead the remaking of nations. Thanks to centralized Russian administration and the growth of trade and industry, Georgia was reunited, first
politically and then economically. Attempts to impose bureaucratic authority
on a traditionally decentralized and highly flexible civil order brought
resistance by peasants and some nobles, who resented the erosion of their
ancient privileges. Though many in the traditional Georgian elite became
denationalized servants of tsarism, dissident voices could always be heard.

With the emancipation of the serfs and the increasing power of the urban
middle classes (largely Armenian) the Georgian nobility, challenged economically as a social estate, was no longer able as an estate to lead the nation.
There emerged from its midst a series of ideological responses to Georgia's
plight—a westernizing liberalism, a nostalgic nationalism, peasant socialism, and, in the end, Marxism. Educated déclassé noblemen of the last
third of the nineteenth century provided the only leadership to a radicalized
peasantry and the new working class.

The national formation of the Georgian people and their sense of their
own ethnicity were in part shaped by contacts and repeated confrontations

with other nationalities. In the nineteenth century increased contact with the Armenians, who had long dominated Georgia's urban centers, was a prime stimulant to Georgian self-definition. Growing numbers of Georgians moved to towns and came into contact with people of different cultures. One's "Georgianness" now had to be affirmed more consciously. In the multi-ethnic context of Tiflis, the boundaries between ethnicities had to be defined and redefined.

The traditional relationships of Georgians and Armenians shifted rapidly after 1860. The Georgian nobility, once the unquestioned first estate in the land, was threatened by the wealthy Armenian bourgeoisie. And as the agrarian economy turned to increasing involvement with the commercial economy of towns, and peasants and lords migrated to the cities, the new proximity with the Armenians raised the likelihood of bitter confrontation. Georgians of various classes came face to face with a well-entrenched, financially secure, urban middle class whose members spoke a different language, went to a different church, and held very different values. Social distinctions between classes were reinforced by cultural and linguistic differences.

Up to 1864 the principal concern of the Georgian nobility had been the protection of their privileges by the Russian authorities who were steadily eroding their political powers. After the emancipation of the serfs, however, and until the revolution, the principal blows to the status of the nobility no longer came from the state but from the changing economic environment, which increased the wealth and influence of the Armenian middle class. Capitalist concepts of production for market, profitability, and economic efficiency were completely foreign to the vast majority of Georgian nobles, who were accustomed to the free labor and obligatory payments that they had for centuries received from their peasants.

The predictions of the Georgian princes that the loss of serf labor would undermine their economic foundations proved accurate. The last third of the nineteenth century witnessed the rapid economic (and consequently political) decline of the nobility, as most of them failed to meet the challenges of an increasingly competitive economic order. Twelve years after the emancipation, the nobility petitioned the viceroy for relief: "After the abolition of serfdom our situation changed. The serfs were taken away from us; there were no free workers; workers' hands became expensive; we fell into debt, and because we were not able to pay them off in time we lost our estates."[1]

The causes of the precipitate decline of the nobility in the half-century after emancipation were both material and psychological. Nobles were immediately faced with new demands on their capital—hiring workers, buying tools and draft animals—while attempting to pay off old debts incurred during serfdom. The shortage of capital was met by mortgaging or renting their lands, but little effort was made to change from relying on peasant payments to improving productivity. For those who made the adjustment to capitalist agriculture, expanding domestic and foreign markets provided new but precarious opportunities. Competition from more efficient producers abroad and an international grain price depression in the last decades of the century made it all but impossible for Georgian producers to meet their costs.[2]

Taking little interest in their estates, the nobles were in general satisfied to receive their dues or rents and borrow from moneylenders in the towns. Noble indebtedness grew steadily, until by the early twentieth century more than half the privately held land in Tiflis province had been mortgaged.[3] Unlike some of their more enterprising contemporaries in central Russia, Georgian nobles had almost nothing to do with the penetration of capitalism into Transcaucasian agriculture.

While nobles turned away from the countryside to find refuge in state service or a frivolous life in the cities, much of their land fell into the hands of the wealthy merchants and the more well-to-do peasants. When they came into the towns they found that they were forced to do business with an already well-entrenched urban bourgeoisie. The economic and social decline of the traditional Georgian elite was accompanied by the simultaneous rise of the Armenian middle class, particularly the rich *mokalakebi* of Tiflis.

Beginning in the second half of the nineteenth century, Georgians began migrating to Tiflis in significant numbers, and the Armenian demographic dominance over the city began to diminish. Whereas in 1801 nearly three-quarters of the city's 20,000 inhabitants had been Armenian (74.3 percent in 1803) and less than a quarter Georgian (21.5 percent), by 1897 the percentage of Armenians had dropped to 38. By the end of the century Russians made up 24.7 percent of the city's 159,000 inhabitants and Georgians 26.3 percent. In absolute terms all three nationalities were increasing their numbers in the city, but the rate of growth was highest for Russians and lowest for Armenians. Between 1865 and 1897, the number of Russians grew by 190 percent (from 12,462 to 36,113); the number of Georgians rose 158 percent (from 14,878 to 38,357); while the Armenians rose by only 88 percent (28,488 to 55,553).[4] Thus, in the latter half of the nineteenth century, the Armenians no longer had a majority in the city, merely a plurality, and the percentages of each nationality were moving toward equality. The influx of Georgian peasants and Russian officials, army officers, and craftsmen changed the ethnic composition of the town and also created an ever-larger working class made up primarily of Georgians. What distinguished these Georgians most completely from the Armenians and Russians in Tiflis was their almost complete isolation from positions of political and economic power.

This demographic shift increased the weight of non-Armenians in the urban population, but did not displace the Armenians in the economic or political structure of the city. They held the mayoralty, and their guilds guided the life of the city. Attempts by Muscovite merchants in the first half of the century to compete with the Armenians had failed, and the Armenian-dominated guilds maintained control over commerce and production in Tiflis.[5] By midcentury some observers argued that the development of Tiflis's economy was being hindered by the guilds' ancient restrictions on growth, innovation, and foreign craftsmen, but not until 1867 did the state feel confident enough to dissolve the merchant guilds. The craft guilds remained intact, and prior possession, traditions of enterprise, and accumulated wealth helped keep the Armenians in a dominant economic position.

The Soviet historian of Tbilisi, Sh. Chkhetia, paints a detailed picture of the Armenians' complete control of midcentury Tiflis:

> In the second half of the 1860s in Tbilisi there were about 3000 shops and commercial enterprises, among them: 17 caravanserais, 5 hotels, 9 confectioners, 4 saloons, 441 *dukhani* [cafés], 96 *kharchevni* [eateries], 71 wine cellars and warehouses, etc. Most of these commercial enterprises belonged to Armenians, in whose hands was held almost all trade; thus, of the 17 caravanserais, 14 belonged to: Begbutiants, Artsruni, Ananiants, Kherodianants, Korkhmaziants, Shnoiants, Shainiants, Movesiants and Co., Sarkisiants, Vardants, Khalatiants, Tamamshiants, and other Armenian capitalists, who were the spiders [*sic*] of Tbilisi commercial-industrial capital of that time. Armenians also owned most of the hotels, wine cellars, *dukhani*, etc. Approximately two thirds of the commercial-industrial class was made up of Armenians.[6]

As this description makes clear, the economy of Tiflis in the 1860s was still preindustrial. Enterprises were quite small, except for some of the larger caravanserais, which carried on foreign trade. These were almost entirely held by Armenians, although a few Russian and foreign merchants owned "trade houses and stores." Tiflis was the portal through which raw silk and silk goods passed from Iran and eastern Transcaucasia to Russia and Europe. Transit trade rather than local production accounted for most of the goods sold by Tiflis merchants. Much more was imported into Transcaucasia in the 1860s than was exported.[7] In 1821–1831, 1846, and 1864, low tariffs encouraged transit trade from Europe and Iran to cross Russian Transcaucasia rather than go through Turkish Trebizond. The great bulk of this trade went through Armenian hands, and Russians often referred to goods from Iran as *armianskie tovary* (Armenian goods).

An important trading center, Tiflis was also the most important "industrial" city in the Caucasus before the oil boom of the 1880s raised the Caspian port of Baku to predominance. Tiflis industry was dominated by small-scale handwork. Until the end of the nineteenth century, manufacture was carried out either in the more than four thousand artisanal workshops in cities and towns or in individual village households where women used time free from field and housework to make by hand the necessities of life. Figures from 1888 show that 78 percent of workshops in Georgia were either occupied by a single craftsman or run with one assistant.[8]

The economy of Tiflis gradually shifted from transit trade and small craft production to larger-scale industrial production, bringing new opportunities for enterprising people to build their fortunes. Some capital investment came from eager Russian merchants and even from foreigners, but the bulk of the new workshops and factories was built with local Armenian capital. In 1870 the Russian tariff was introduced in the Caucasus, replacing the lower duties imposed six years earlier and creating a protected area in which infant industries could grow without serious competition from cheaper European goods.

Gradually industry became more important than the transit trade. Armenians rapidly entered the world of manufacturing until their position in the economy of Tiflis and western Transcaucasia was unassailable. Of the 9,725 merchants in the city in 1897, 48.6 percent were Armenian (4,727), 26.9 percent were Georgian (2,619) and 6 percent Russian. More impressive, of the 150 largest industrial establishments in Georgia in 1900, 44 percent belonged to Armenians, about the same amount belonged to Russians and foreign capitalists, and only 10 percent were owned by Georgians and 2 percent by Azerbaijanis. When one considers only the city of Tiflis, the Armenian presence is even more striking; about one-half of large enterprises and most of the largest were Armenian. The wealthiest Armenians—the Arzumanovs, Avetisians, and Mantashevs in the oil industry; the Adelkhanovs in leather goods; the Tumaniants, Kevorkovs, Avetisovs and Pitoevs in commerce; the Egiazarovs, Ter-Asaturovs, Bozarjiants, and Enfianjiants in tobacco—made up a fraternity of entrepreneurs who worked together in a variety of joint-stock companies, pooling their capital to maintain the primacy of the local bourgeoisie in the face of Russian and foreign competition.[9]

The urban and bourgeois character of the Tiflis Armenians contrasted sharply with the rural background and agrarian orientation of most Georgians, and familiar attitudes about these two nationalities grew into racial stereotypes in the second half of the century. A Russian observer, S. Maksimov, early in the 1870s echoed many other visitors:

> Trade in the Caucasus is entirely in the hands of clever and calculating Armenians. Armenians are higher than Georgians in intelligence and in love for work, and for that reason there is nothing surprising in the fact that Georgian properties are rapidly falling into Armenian hands. Georgians are dependent on them just as the Poles are on the Jews and similarly feel toward them the same contempt and hatred (if not more than the Poles feel toward the Jews). The commercial Armenians reveal much cleverness, wiliness, are always ready with flattery; their thirst for profit leads them to cheating and swindling.[10]

Russian ethnographer P. I. Kovalevskii spoke of the Georgians as "merry [and] sociable," but also as noted for their "laziness, insufficient energy and enterprise, instability, lack of self-restraint, little ability in work, light-minded and superficial attitude toward business and matters at hand."[11] In the

1880s the British Georgianist and diplomat, Oliver Wardrop, described relations between Armenians and Georgians:

> A local proverb says "a Greek will cheat three Jews, but an Armenian will cheat three Greeks," and the Georgian, straightforward, honest fellow, is but too often cruelly swindled by the artful children of Haik. When the fraud is very apparent, the Armenian often pays for his greed with all the blood that can be extracted from his jugular vein.[12]

However doubtful the accuracy of such stereotypes, it might be noted that they have more to do with the class position of the most visible representatives of either ethnic group than with inherent features of a whole people. There were successful Georgian entrepreneurs equipped with the necessary business acumen; there were also Armenian peasants, both in Transcaucasia and Anatolia, who displayed patterns of life and work much closer to their Georgian counterparts. The dominant elites of each people, to which social inferiors looked for guidance, were quite different, and molded national culture along different lines. The Armenians had long ago lost their nobility, the *nakhararner* of the medieval kingdoms, and were socially and politically dominated by the urban bourgeoisie in cities like Constantinople, Smyrna, and Tiflis; the Georgians, with few native examples of bourgeois leadership, instead had as models a traditional landed nobility then in its final decline.

Armenian dominance in economic life was perhaps the major source of Georgians' resentment that their own increasing presence in the city was not reflected in the distribution of material rewards or political power. But almost as important was the nearly absolute control that Armenians managed to maintain over non-Armenians. Final authority in Transcaucasia always rested with the Russian military-bureaucratic administration, but local government was delegated to the wealthy men of property in Tiflis.

In Russia's history the years after the Crimean War were distinguished by the zealous implementation of liberal reforms, beginning with the peasant emancipation of 1861 and culminating in new institutions of provincial and municipal administration and justice. Only a few of these reforms were extended to Transcaucasia in the 1860s and 1870s, and then usually in incomplete form. In 1866 the Russian judicial reform of 1864 was extended to Caucasia, thus eliminating the local courts and laws and integrating the region into the imperial system. The Transcaucasian administration was revamped the following year, consolidating various departments and abolishing the viceroy's diplomatic chancellory.[13] Yet no *zemstva* were established in Transcaucasia, which meant that the Georgian nobility did not enjoy the local political influence that their Russian brethren exercised.

In Transcaucasia, as in the rest of the empire, municipal administration desperately needed reform, and the tsarist authorities decided in the first half of the 1860s to introduce elected institutions. The imperative for such a reform in Tiflis became suddenly apparent when a popular revolt revealed a threat to Russian authority from the traditional guilds. In June 1865 the mayor of Tiflis and the tsarist treasury decided to impose a new tax on the populace without their prior consent. The guilds responded by shutting down all businesses in the city. The acting governor, Grigol Orbeliani, ordered the strike to end, but the *ustabashebi* (guild leaders) were unable to convince their members and allies to return to work. On June 27, ten thousand artisans, shopkeepers, merchants, and workers marched through the streets to protest the new taxes. They plundered the house of the mayor, Shermazan Vartanov, and stoned and killed the tax collector, Bazhbeuk Melikov. Only on the fourth day, after a new mayor was appointed and the tax revoked, was order restored.

What was most remarkable about the so-called June Days in Tiflis was the cooperation of the Armenian craftsmen and shopkeepers with the poorer Georgian workmen; as the radical publicist Niko Nikoladze put it, the *musha* (worker) shook hands with the *mokalake* "forgetting that yesterday the *mokalake* cheated his ally of today, the *musha*, and that tomorrow the same story will be repeated."[14] Relations between workers and masters in the mid-1860s were still close in this paternalistic preindustrial society; only in the following decades would they be transformed into the less personal labor-management confrontation of emergent capitalism.

On the advice of local officials, the government in St. Petersburg reacted quickly to the events of June 1865 and issued a new plan for the municipal government of Tiflis, one that shifted the balance of local power away from the traditional guilds. Based on similar charters granted to St. Petersburg (1846), Moscow (1862), and Odessa (1863), the law of August 11, 1866, divided the propertied and tax-paying population of Tiflis into four estates for purposes of choosing the city's government. Each estate—the hereditary nobility, the personal nobility and eminent citizens, the "simple citizens" who owned property or were engaged in business, and those who owned no real estate but paid city taxes—elected one hundred electors who then chose twenty-five delegates to the city assembly. A mayor, chosen by electors from all estates, had to be a person of substantial wealth, owning property worth at least ten thousand silver rubles.

This electoral system brought the nobles into urban government for the first time under Russian rule. Combined with eminent citizens, they made up less than 10 percent of the city's population, yet they now became the de facto rulers of Tiflis.[15] The so-called simple citizens made up about 16 percent of the population, and the propertyless about 45 percent, but neither had much influence in the assembly. One-half of the assembly, thus, was elected by 10 percent of the city's inhabitants.

Most affected by these reforms were the guilds, which lost their former prominence. The very next year, the state reduced the powers of the craft guilds, abolished the merchant guilds altogether, and subordinated the remaining *amkarebi* to the city administration. Of approximately one hundred guilds, only seventeen remained after 1867. For the tsarist bureaucracy the lesson of 1865 was well expressed by Baron Nikolai: "The disorders which occurred in Tiflis in 1865 revealed that corporations united thus, without any ties to government, could be harmful to the public tranquility."[16]

The law of 1866 represented the nadir of Armenian power in Tiflis in the nineteenth century and the most concerted attempt to shift municipal power from the Armenian merchants to the Georgian nobility. As destructive as the reform was to the traditional guilds and their influence in government, it was only a temporary encumbrance to Armenian power. The integration of Tiflis into the urban administrative system of the Russian empire was completed in 1874, when the municipal statute granted to Russian cities in 1870 was extended to certain cities in the Caucasus.[17] By this law a municipal duma (council) was to be elected by adult males who owned real estate or paid taxes in the city. This was the widest franchise ever enjoyed by urban dwellers in tsarist Russia and extended even to peasants who met the property or tax qualifications. Three curiae were established, based on the amount of tax paid, and each curia elected one-third of the duma deputies. In practice this meant that a handful of the wealthiest men in the city elected the first third of the duma, the next wealthiest elected a second third, and hundreds of propertied people elected the last third. The duma then would elect an *uprava* (board) and a mayor.

This novel system dispensed with the division of the population into estates (*sosloviia*) and instead distinguished by wealth and property. The *tsenz* or property qualification that gave a man the right to vote established a new principle for political participation, one quite familiar to bourgeois Europe but new to tsarist Russia. The preponderance of power in the new duma lay with the few richest businessmen, who chose one-third of the assembly and from whose number the mayor was likely to emerge. Thanks to this law the Armenian bourgeoisie re-emerged as the leading political force in Tiflis.

Tsarist law had a dual effect on the Armenian bourgeoisie, forcing its modernization by eliminating the merchant guilds and restricting the craft guilds while at the same time preserving, indeed extending, its privileged political position within the municipality. The "bourgeois" principle of representation based on economic status rather than on birth and *soslovie* helped the Armenian *mokalake* maintain his paramount place in the city even as demographic movements were reducing his relative weight in population. Both the Armenian bourgeois and the Georgian noble were reduced to the position of citizen. The influence each held within Tiflis in the next two decades depended not on birth or legal status but on property and wealth. As the Georgian nobility failed to adjust to the spreading market economy and lost its ancient lands to middle-class creditors or land-hungry peasants, it was also pushed aside politically.

By the last third of the century Russian administration and the developing market economy were having profound effects on Georgian national
formation. From the dispersed, insecure pieces of seigneurial Georgia with its
various princely houses and distinct economies, one national political and
economic unit was being formed. The Georgian nation (eri), consolidated
out of the autonomous political units that had been eliminated by the 1860s,
was being further united as the isolated peasant villages, once largely self-
sufficient and only distantly related to towns, were integrated into a national
economy.[18]

As railroads, telegraphs, and improved roads made access to the cities
and the outside world easier, increased contact with the towns, where people
of different nationality lived, forged a growing sense of the distinctions
between Georgians and other peoples. Thus, Russian colonial dominance of
Transcaucasia, which guaranteed a degree of peace, security, and economic
progress in certain sectors, had fostered conditions for both national refor-
mation and ethnic confrontation. Not surprisingly, as this new national
emergence began to be expressed in literature and political journalism, the
deeper question of Georgia's future relationship with Russia appeared at the
center of the national debate.

Like other colonial relationships, Georgia's subordination to Russia was
a mixture of benefits and burdens, and the attitude of many Georgians
toward Russian rule was unavoidably ambivalent. Protection by tsarist arms
was both a necessity and a restrictive imposition for Georgians. The benefits
of European civilization were greatly desired by a thin layer of Georgian
society, and the road to the West lay through Russia. Generations of Georgian students trekked northward to Russian centers of learning to discover
the latest intellectual advances of European thinkers. Enlightenment was the
means by which Georgia could escape the past dominated by the Muslim
East and join the Christian, modern West. At the same time, contact with
Russia and the West worked to awaken consciousness of Georgia's unique
culture and fears that Georgia would be overwhelmed by foreign values, by
Russian political practice and by the alien economic operations of Armenian
middlemen. This ambivalence toward "Europeanization" and Russian rule
was a constant feature of Georgian intellectual life through the nineteenth
century into the twentieth.

The emergence of a modern, secular Georgian national consciousness
should not be understood as the simple product of the confluence of various
social and political currents. The making of a nation in its full demographic,
cultural, and intellectual sense requires more than the coming together of
disembodied social forces or the repressive political intervention of imperial
powers. Historically the creation of a Georgian nation was the result of
imaginative work by intellectuals and political activists who first revived
interest in the national language and historical past and later mobilized

popular sentiment toward a reconceived national whole. Yet the development of national consciousness cannot be reduced to a history of the intelligentsia, for that history is always part of a broader social evolution. Cultural renovation by intellectuals and artists was essential for the development of secular nationalism, with its claims first to cultural autonomy and later to statehood, but the movement was effective because of the new world in which ethnicities found themselves after the French, and the industrial, revolutions.

Moving beyond the earlier work of historians who conceived of nationalism primarily as a problem of intellectual history, more recent studies have emphasized the specific intellectual and political activity of "patriots," which, in an important sense, "invented" modern nationalism in the nineteenth century.[19] From this perspective nationality does not possess an a priori, natural existence, but is the product of a particular cultural intervention by grammarians and philologists, historians and novelists, schoolteachers and journalists. After a series of close empirical studies of small peoples in Eastern and Central Europe, Czech historian Miroslav Hroch proposes that nationalist movements go through three stages of gestation: Stage A, in which a small number of intellectuals begin the cultural work, largely in language studies and the recovery of the national history; Stage B, in which larger groups of "patriots" spread the message of the nation through schools and the press; and Stage C, when broader popular mobilization takes place. Without an unnecessarily rigid application of Hroch's model, it is possible in a discussion of the formation of the Georgian intelligentsia to trace a similar evolution—from the initial revival of the Georgian past and attention to the language in the late eighteenth and early nineteenth centuries through the journalistic activity of the 1860s and 1870s to the active political nationalism of the turn of the century.

In the second half of the eighteenth century, at a time when Russian letters were flourishing under the patronage of Catherine II and the foundation of the Armenian national revival was being laid by Catholic monks in Venice (the Mekhitarist fathers), Georgia was still imperiled by both the Ottoman and Iranian empires. Nevertheless a printing press was set up in Tiflis in 1749, and three decades later the clergyman Gaioz opened a school that taught Russian in the Georgian capital. Unfortunately these tentative shoots of intellectual renewal were cut off by the Iranian destruction of Tiflis in 1795. Learning in Georgia was almost entirely religious, and it is estimated that 85 percent of the output of the Georgian printers was clerical literature.[20] Yet some secular learning also was evident. It may be that twentieth-century historian Ivane Javakhishvili exaggerates somewhat when he speaks of a strong rise in Georgian national self-consciousness in the eighteenth century, but his characterization of the process is very suggestive. "In distinction from the tendencies of the time of Vakhtang VI, when all attention was on the careful gathering of the legacy of centuries, on the preservation of traditions as they had come down to that time, the basic motif of the epoch of Teimuraz and Iraklii was the restoration of ancient Georgian traditions and the establishment and purging from them of foreign influences and distortions."[21]

The history of the Georgian national intelligentsia begins in the romantic age, when educated young Georgians made their desperate attempt to sever the Russian connection. Like the Decembrists, the conspirators of 1832 were much more influential in the afterglow of their failure than they had been before their arrests. Although the example of these last noble plotters was not followed by others, the surviving participants retained enormous prestige, and after they had made peace with the Russian presence many of them became leading figures, not only in Caucasian politics but also in letters.

By virtue both of their aristocratic status and their intellectual abilities, Alexandre Chavchavadze (1786–1846) and Grigol Orbeliani (1800–1883) re-entered state service and rose to high positions. At the same time they became the leading literary lights in the romantic movement in Georgia. The poetry of Chavchavadze lamented the lost past of Georgia. In poems like "vai, droni, droni" (Woe, time, time), "isminet msmenno" (Listen, listener), and "kavkasia" (Caucasia), the Golden Age of Georgia was favorably contrasted with its mundane present. Orbeliani, who eventually became governor-general of Tiflis province, served loyally as a tsarist officer but in his poems called for restoration of Georgia's past glory.

The close social and intellectual ties of the Georgian romantics were exemplified in the life and verse of the finest poet of the period, Nikoloz Baratashvili (1817–1845). The pupil of Soghomon Dodiashvili, one of the conspirators of 1832, and the nephew of Grigol Orbeliani, Baratashvili found his muse in Ekaterina Chavchavadze, the second daughter of Alexandre, and wrote a series of lyric poems to her. The romantic themes of patriotism and nostalgia for a lost past were reflected in Baratashvili's poem "bedi kartlisa" (Fate of Georgia), in which the poet reproduced the debate of Erekle II, penultimate king of Georgia, with an advisor who opposed the union with Russia. The wife of the advisor asks her husband, in a lament that became familiar to all literate Georgians: *"ra khelhqris pativs nazi bulbuli, galiashia datqvevebuli?"* ("What pleasure does the tender nightingale receive from honor if it is in a cage?")

Romanticism in Georgia in the 1830s and 1840s was influenced by Russian poets of the period and by Russian translations of European literature. But the pessimism and patriotism, the lyricism and longing of the romantics was anything but foreign to Georgian literature. Their poets of the seventeenth and eighteenth centuries, writing under Iranian and Turkish influence, had composed lyrical songs, elegant laments, and paeans to nature, quite close to what Baratashvili and his contemporaries produced several generations later.[22] Still, romanticism was the first literary movement in which Georgians engaged along with Russians. In a curious reciprocity,

Russian poetry fertilized the work of Georgian poets, while the Caucasus and Georgia became a rich image for the exotic and romantic in Russian literature. Pushkin, who visited Georgia in 1829, and Lermontov, exiled to the Caucasus in 1840, used Caucasian motifs and characters and helped raise the Caucasus in the popular imagination from a backwater outpost to a land of passion and temper, violence and adventure.

Interest in Georgian history and language expanded along with the new literature. French scholar Marie-Félicité Brosset was invited to St. Petersburg in 1837 and made a member of the Academy of Sciences in order to permit him to continue his Georgian studies. Three years later Brosset published a Georgian-French-Russian dictionary with D. I. Chubinashvili (Chubinov) and a year later completed his translation into Russian of Rustaveli's twelfth-century epic poem, "vepkhistqaosani." Late in the 1840s Viceroy Vorontsov invited Brosset to lead an archæological expedition in Georgia, and thereafter a steady stream of translations and critical editions of the major Georgian chronicles appeared under Brosset's name.

With the attention paid to it by a renowned European scholar and in travel accounts of European visitors as famous as Alexander Dumas, Georgia not only became known in Western Europe but became the subject of heightened literary and scholarly interest among the Georgians themselves. Native Georgian scholarship had already produced a short history of Georgia in Russian, *Kratkaia istoriia Gruzii* (St. Petersburg, 1805) by Prince David Bagrationi, and a geographical survey of the country, *Obozrenie tsarstva gruzinskogo naroda* (St. Petersburg, 1814) by Prince Vakhtang Batonishvili. But the first critical history in Georgian was written by Prince Teimuraz in 1848. Under the impact of Russian rule Georgian intellectuals initiated their own search into their country's past, a search that immediately raised doubts about Georgia's present and future while at the same time it created a congenial view of the past and a source of national pride. Thus historians, like the poets, provided the small Georgian reading public with the images required to regard Georgia as a nation.

The first members of the Georgian intelligentsia, known later as the "fathers," were a small, close-knit group of aristocratic writers who shared with a few others of their noble brothers the benefits of Russian state service. They met occasionally in literary salons to read their works and discuss current issues. With the expansion of education under Viceroy Vorontsov, the number of noble sons and young people of other social classes who gained access to schools rose rapidly. Those who completed their secondary education in the Caucasus and wished to continue had to enroll in one of the half-dozen Russian universities.

From this newly expanding educated group, with its close contact with Russia proper, a rival tendency emerged within the intelligentsia, soon to distinguish themselves as the "sons." Called in Georgian *tergdaleulni* (literally, "those who drank the water of the Terek," the river that separated

Georgia from Russia), the sons were distinguished by their Russian education from their older compatriots, known as the *mtkvardaleulni* ("those who drank the water of the *mtkvari* [Kura]," the river that flows through Tiflis). Together the two groups made up what later would be referred to as the *pirveli dasi,* or "first generation," of the Georgian intelligentsia. The members of this tiny intellectual world were similar in social background but their literary tastes and political outlooks differed greatly, and those differences can be traced to the unique experience of the sons in Russia in the late 1850s and early 1860s.

At the beginning of the reign of Alexander II Russian intellectuals were engaged in an intense public discussion of the backwardness of Russian society, so graphically revealed by the empire's defeat in the Crimean War. The debate over emancipation and the literary-political polemics in the pages of the radical journal *Sovremennik* (Contemporary) stimulated efforts at self-education by the students in Russia's universities. One of those students, the Georgian *raznochinets* Niko Nikoladze (1843–1928), remembered the euphoria of the early 1860s as a kind of "early spring, not only for me, but for all of Russia and even Europe. After the heavy oppression imposed after 1848, here and there flashed the glow of dawn."[23]

Numbering about thirty in the early 1860s, the Georgian students in St. Petersburg lived separately from the Russians. When the various non-Russian minority groups in the university decided to form *zemliachestva* (circles of people from the same town, region, or ethnic group), some Georgians argued in favor of a pan-Caucasian *zemliachestvo.* The majority, however, were convinced by the young writer Ilia Chavchavadze (1837–1907) to form separate Georgian, Armenian, Russian, and "Lezgin" organizations with strong ties among them.[24] At first the Georgians were isolated from the growing tensions in the university, but by the summer of 1861 the radicalization of the Russian and Polish students affected some of the Caucasians. Inspired by the liberation movements in Italy and Hungary, the more zealous among them began wearing their hair like Garibaldi.

Perhaps the most volatile and politically active was the young Nikoladze, an avid reader of *Sovremennik* and *Poliarnaia zvezda* (Polar Star), published abroad by Russian socialist Aleksandr Herzen. Sympathizing with the views of the leaflet *K molodomu pokoleniiu* (To the Young Generation), Nikoladze and his friends joined other students in the demonstrations of September–October 1861. Arrested and expelled from the university, they were ordered to leave the city and return to Georgia. Their formal education in Russia was over, but they were proud of their participation in the first political action against Russian authorities in which Georgians had engaged together with Russians, Poles, and other nationalities. When his father's servant came to fetch him home, Nikoladze went willingly: "Petersburg was oppressive to me; I no longer expected any kind of revolution there."[25]

The acknowledged leader of the *tergdaleulni* was the more moderate Ilia Chavchavadze, the orphaned son of a prominent Kakhetian family. As a child he had learned to love Georgian literature from his mother and to read his native language from a village clergyman. At age eleven he had gone to Tiflis for his studies, first at a private boarding school and later at the noble *gimnaziia*. Fundamentally affected by the time he spent at the juridical faculty at St. Petersburg University (1857–1861), Chavchavadze used these years to write a remarkably rich body of poetry and prose. He and his contemporary, poet Akaki Tsereteli, were the first important Georgian poets to shift from the patriotic romanticism of Orbeliani and Baratashvili to a less rhetorical, more critical realism. In his verse "poeti," written during his student years, Chavchavadze announced his view of his literary and social obligation:

> I do not learn from the birds in flight,
> I listen to another voice.
> Not for sweet songs
> Was I sent by heaven to earth.
> . . . .
> To become a brother to the people,
> A friend in joy and sorrow,
> so that its suffering
> in pain lights fire to my soul.

The Russian radical intelligentsia made social commitment to the people the touchstone of its ideas and behavior and this had a profound effect on the Georgians who studied in the north. Akaki Tsereteli remembered the great influence of the radical "sons" of the Russian intelligentsia—Nikolai Chernyshevskii (1828–1889) and Nikolai Dobroliubov (1836–1861)— though he rejected their almost total denial of esthetic values in literature. The social role of art was a key political issue, and Tsereteli's unwillingness to subordinate his art to political ends cost him his friends.[26] The way that commitment was manifested—whether in practical application of the principles of reform or in alliance with the fledgling revolutionary opposition— deeply divided the Georgian intelligentsia during the years from the emancipation to the revolution.

Returning to Georgia, the *tergdaleulni* arrived just as peasant emancipation was being extended to Transcaucasia. In general, these young noblemen favored a liberal and generous emancipation and were disappointed both by the attitudes of the majority of the nobility and the final settlement granted by the government. But their energies were turned away from specifically political and economic activity to culture and education, journalism and literature. Despite the first stirrings of romantic literature and the promotion of a Georgian drama by Vorontsov, the actual achievements of the literate elite were still quite meager by the 1860s. The Soviet historian Sh. Chkhetia laments:

> In Georgia up to the 1860s, i.e., in the course of almost three-quarters of a century, not more than 160–180 books had been printed in the Georgian language; . . . in Georgia in all that time not one [permanent] Georgian theater had existed; . . . in Georgia in that time not one Georgian cultural and scientific institution had been founded; . . . in all of Georgia up to the 1860s only three Georgian printing presses had existed, and the number of printing presses with Georgian typeface never exceeded two.[27]

Clearly not even the Georgians themselves yet valued their own literature; not enough interested readers could be found to support a modest press for very long. According to the early Marxist historian and activist, Pilipe Makharadze, the Georgian language "gradually lost significance in the eyes of Georgians themselves since knowing only their own language Georgians could not enter state or public service."[28]

Central to the question of ethnic identity in Transcaucasia was the use of language. While Armenians had a distinct brand of Christianity and a separate church with its head at holy Echmiadzin, the Georgians were religiously merged with the Russian Orthodox Church. In terms of social estates Georgian nobles and peasants were roughly equivalent to Russians of the same order, though ethnicity and culture, acceptance and prejudice, always colored social relations and influenced political advancement. But language—the knowledge of Georgian and the degree of fluency in Russian—was a key to social and political mobility and to the degree of identity with one's own people or the dominant nationality.

From 1868 Georgian was clearly inferior to Russian, not only in popular attitudes or the views of officials, but in the law as well. The teaching of Russian was required in all schools in the empire, and Georgian was no longer a required subject. Beginning in the 1870s only private schools taught courses in Georgian, usually on the primary level, with Russian given as a special course. When a student reached middle school the courses were taught in Russian, with Georgian given as a separate course. As the result of state policy and legal discriminations, the percentage of schools that taught a local Caucasian language steadily declined and those that taught all subjects in Russian increased.[29] As early as 1860 Niko Nikoladze discerned this tendency in his first published article, "Do We Need the Georgian Language?"

This painful question was addressed in the first influential and long-lived Georgian journal, *tsiskari* (Dawn), which appeared briefly from 1852 to 1853 under the editorship of playwright Giorgi Eristavi (1811–1864) and enjoyed a longer run (1857–1875) under Ivane Kereselidze (1829–1883). In its pages younger Georgian writers engaged in the debate over serfdom then dividing Russian society, and a novel that passionately attacked serfdom (*suramis tsikhe* [Surami Fortress]) appeared from the pen of Daniel Chonkadze (1830–1860). Yet in 1860 only 180 subscribers could be found to support the journal, and through the decade there was little improvement and occasionally considerable losses.

Tsiskari, propped by the generous subsidies of Alexandre Orbeliani, generally reflected the views of the conservative "fathers" and used an archaic Georgian (*sashualo*) based on the medieval language of the church (*maghali*). The "sons," led by Ilia Chavchavadze, began a campaign for the use of the Georgian vernacular (*dabali*) in published prose and poetry. Up to this time the language of ordinary people was thought appropriate only for the comedies of Giorgi Eristavi and other writers for the theater.

In April 1861 Chavchavadze published his article on Prince Revaz Eristavi's translation of Kozlov's *Bezumna* (Madwoman) in *tsiskari* and thus opened a long feud with the older generation. Chavchavadze's suggestions were rather modest, an orthographic and stylistic reform, but the conservatives were incensed by the attempt to reduce the elevated language of Georgian literature to the level of the spoken word. Similar struggles over the archaic literary language of the upper classes and the church and the "democratic" reform of the written language were then dividing the Armenian intelligentsia and had stirred hostilities a generation earlier among Russian writers.

The debate became heated and took on political overtones when Chavchavadze answered Grigol Orbeliani's "pasukhi shvilta" (Answer to the Sons) with his "pasukhis pasukhi" (Answer to the Answer), which contained the harsh indictment: "Our country, killed by you, did not sell itself for ranks as you did. . . . Liberalism and patriotism, we have not turned into curse words." From St. Petersburg Akaki Tsereteli, Giorgi Tsereteli (1842–1900), and Kiril Lordkipanidze wrote in support of Chavchavadze, signing their letters "*tergdaleuli*." They emphasized that the true Georgian was the peasant; his language was the essence of the national language.

No longer able to work together with the "fathers," the *tergdaleulni* issued their own periodicals. The first, *sakartvelos moambe* (Georgia's Herald), was edited by Chavchavadze; although it lasted only one year, this literary journal was enormously influential. Years later Prince Giorgi Tumanov remembered its impact:

> I speak of 1863 when the journal of I. G. Chavchavadze, *Georgian Herald (sakartvelos moambe)*, began to come out. This was a time of general awakening. This was a time of great hopes. The men in the Sixties—realists and materialists in principle—actually woke up the best feelings of mankind. Even I, a child of eight, was interested in the journal. From Chavchavadze's journal I first learned of the existence of Belinskii, Dobroliubov, Proudhon, and Bastiat. But they were little understood by me, and my sympathies were more attracted by Victor Hugo (his novel *Les*

Miserables was published) and by the editor himself. Here for the first time appeared the novels of Chavchavadze, *Tale of a Poor Man* and *katsia adamiani?*, his best poetry, filled with civic feeling, his "Kako" and his critical-humorous articles, "Conversation of Spiridon and Tadeoz."[30]

With the pages of *tsiskari* closed to him, Chavchavadze published his own and his friends' articles, as well as translations of authors and theorists considered progressive. The ideas of Chernyshevskii, then in prison, were popularized by the *tergdaleulni,* but their hopes for governmental reform or a crystallized revolutionary opposition to tsarism were dashed when tsarist troops crushed the Polish insurrection of 1863. The age of reform quickly came to an end, and years of pessimism stretched into the next decade.

The intellectual awakening in the 1860s had a profound effect on the Georgian intelligentsia. The ideas of the so-called Russian enlighteners (*prosvetiteli*), particularly Nikolai Chernyshevskii and Nikolai Dobroliubov, were as much appeals to emotion and calls to action as they were intellectual stimulants. Dobroliubov's condemnation of Oblomovism, the "disease" of laziness and apathy that infected the Russian gentry, was more than an indictment of Russia's social conditions; it was an attack on passivity, inaction, hypocrisy, and the idle mouthing of humanistic sentiments.[31] For young Russians, Georgians, Armenians, and others in the empire their recently acquired education and privileged social position demanded some kind of moral accounting, a payment of the debt they owed to society and the people. For some this sense of debt could be reconciled in state service, but many others perceived the autocratic state as the enemy of the people and believed that debt could be repaid only in service to the people. Thus, for a significant group in the Russian-educated Georgian intelligentsia, intellectual enlightenment not only changed their perceptions of reality but reforged their life ambitions. And a small number of them turned toward the embryonic revolutionary movement.

The awakening of cultural and intellectual life in Georgia in the 1860s was equivalent to Stage B in Hroch's model of nationalist development. Artistic and scholarly concerns had expanded into broader cultural and even political activities. But the attraction of Western ideas and joint political action with the Russian intelligentsia proved divisive to the Caucasians. In the late 1860s the original *tergdaleulni* ceased to constitute a united group.

Chavchavadze became a *mirovoi posrednik* (peace arbitrator) after the peasant emancipation and worked in Dusheti in Tiflis province until 1874 as a *mirovoi sud'ia* (justice of the peace). His interests turned toward ethnography, and he was one of the first Georgians to study local dialects and to collect folk poetry and music. Politically he became more conservative and dedicated himself to his work in the Georgian Nobles' Bank and the Society for the Spread of Literacy Among Georgians. Liberals like Giorgi Tumanov later regretted this move to the right: Chavchavadze "was wordy, rhetorical, and principally archaic, if one can so express it. His defense of the customs, the fundamentals of old Georgian life, produced an impression of reactionary sympathies. The progressive who had earlier castigated in his best poetic and prose works the old serf-owning system had somehow turned now into an apologist for the old ways."[32] Yet his role as an early patriot and his continuing journalistic activity made Chavchavadze the most influential Georgian nationalist from the emancipation until the 1905 revolution.

Niko Nikoladze, on the other hand, embarked on a different political odyssey. After leaving St. Petersburg he went to study in Western Europe and became the first Georgian to receive a doctorate (in law) from a European university. Through Paul Lafargue he met Karl Marx, who asked the impressive Georgian to become the representative of the Internationale in Transcaucasia. Nikoladze declined the offer. His views at the time were more in tune with the homegrown radicals Chernyshevskii and Dobroliubov, whom he had met in St. Petersburg. While in Europe he also became acquainted with Aleksandr Herzen. Nikoladze briefly collaborated on his influential newspaper, *Kolokol* (The Bell), in 1865, but he soon broke with the "gentry revolutionary" when Herzen attempted a reconciliation with the autocratic government through an open letter to the tsar. Not content with the range of political options, Nikoladze threw himself into his studies.

While Nikoladze was finishing his doctorate in Europe, some of his closest associates founded the newspaper *droeba* (Times) in Tiflis. The group, formed by Giorgi Tsereteli and Petr Umikashvili, declared itself "New Youth" (*akhali akhalgazrdoba*). More radical than most of the *tergdaleulni* from which they had arisen, they were later referred to as the *meore dasi*, or "second generation," of the Georgian intelligentsia. Stimulated by the revival of political activity among Russian intellectuals, the Tiflis literati used the pages of *droeba* to introduce their readers to the ideas of progressive liberal thinkers like John Stuart Mill and "utopian socialists" like Robert Owen, Saint-Simon, Charles Fourier, Pierre Proudhon, and Louis Blanc. Rather than advocate a particular solution to Georgia's backwardness, the *meore dasi* sought widely for a program, ranging from state-regulated capitalism to various forms of "association" and collectivism.[33] Its members were committed to bringing the fruits of European culture and learning to Georgia, but they were also wary of importing an unfettered free-market system. In Russia and in Georgia most intellectuals rejected an unqualified defense of capitalism as it was then developing in the West, preferring some means of ameliorating the struggle between capital and labor through state regulation or "association."[34]

The *meore dasi* was the first group of Georgian intellectuals to become involved primarily in the urban and economic life of Georgia. They responded to the new economic and political forces in Europe, centered in the great cities, and worked to keep the Georgians from being pushed aside by the Russians and Armenians who dominated their cities. In journalism, urban politics, and business, men like Nikoladze, Giorgi Tsereteli, and

Sergei Meskhi operated with a confidence and energy unseen in earlier generations.

In the fall of 1875 Nikoladze returned to Tiflis and began to publish widely in the press associated with the *meore dasi*—*droeba, soplis gazeti* (Rural Newspaper), *krebuli* (Collection), and *Tiflisskii vestnik* (Tiflis Herald). He set forth a full program of municipal reform for Tiflis and revived a forgotten idea for a noble land bank. Despite resistance from influential aristocrats, Nikoladze was able to persuade enough nobles to pool their resources to capitalize the bank at a meager 170,000 rubles.[35] Ilia Chavchavadze agreed to head the bank. The two men, however, soon had a falling out. Nikoladze hoped that the bank would take on a program of agrarian improvement, investment in new productive techniques, and sale of land to peasants so that the farms would remain in the hands of Georgians. But Chavchavadze used the bank's profits to establish schools and cultural institutions. A heated and personal debate over the bank's activities sharply divided the Georgian noble intelligentsia, forcing Chavchavadze to leave the editorial board of *droeba* and found his own newspaper, *iveria* (1877–1906).

As Nikoladze moved toward orthodox liberalism and advocacy of capitalist development for Georgia, Chavchavadze worked to prevent the further decline of the Georgian nobility and to revive interest in Georgian culture. He used his base at the noble bank to promote his own view of Georgia's future. Chavchavadze, known at the time as the "Georgian Gambetta," presided at the public meetings of the bank's shareholders, which were referred to as the *gruzinskii parlament* (the Georgian parliament).

The once-united Georgian intelligentsia was deeply fractured by the late 1870s. Three major political tendencies had appeared; they would dominate Georgian social life until the century's end. On the right was the nostalgic nationalism of the Georgian gentry, led by Ilia Chavchavadze. In the center was the reformist liberalism of Niko Nikoladze and Giorgi Tsereteli. And on the left was the emerging revolutionary movement, first influenced by Russian populism and later by Marxism.

Against the background of developing capitalism, the growing power of the Armenian bourgeoisie, and the steady fall of the Georgian nobility, the newspaper *iveria* and its editor preached an anticapitalist, antisocialist program. Chavchavadze, the former radical and author of a poem celebrating the Paris Commune, turned after 1877 toward loyalty to the Russian throne, orthodox religiosity, and efforts to shore up the falling fortunes of his own estate. Both the liberals and the socialists spoke of the division of society into competing classes, but Chavchavadze and his followers tried to revive the notion of a single, unified, harmonious Georgian society free from class conflict. At all costs capitalism, with its fellow traveler the proletariat, should not be encouraged in Georgia:

> The general sickness of which I want to speak here is a terrible sickness. This sickness has spread all over Europe . . . This horrible and debilitating

sickness chews up, spits out, and corrupts their living corpses; it forces them to lose their human face and turns man into animal. This disease carries the name "proletariat." Proletariat means workers without land, without property, or, as we say here, paupers . . .

Even our *kinto* [peddler] has property: the *tabakhi* on which he lays his fruit, the little money with which he can buy fruit, and his silver belt. All this is his property, and if you add to this his energy he is more or less satisfied. We have no proletariat, but we will have one if our peasants do not buy their land in time. And if before this factories are built here, the peasants incensed that their earnings will go to others, will leave house and land and go to the city to work in the factory . . . We need nothing if our youth is industrious enough to give a hand to the peasant in the form of the organization of banks and consumer societies.[36]

Chavchavadze, Akaki Tsereteli, and others articulated the traditional idea of the Georgian nobility that in their society there had never been serious antagonisms between estates, that the nobility and the peasantry had lived in harmony, and that the ideas of the socialists were destroying the natural bridge that had always existed between lord and serf.

Chavchavadze's social program was founded on preservation of Georgia as an agricultural society with a landed majority. Peasants were to own the land eventually, but at the present time paying one-quarter of the harvest as rent seemed fair to him. He advocated more democratic election of peasant officials and the elimination of police intervention into peasant affairs. His bank would help the nobility keep their land and prevent further penetration of Armenian capital into the countryside.

His cultural program was aimed at reversing the erosion of Georgian traditions and language, and under the leadership of *iveria* a Georgian cultural revival became evident. In 1879 the Society for the Spread of Literacy Among Georgians was founded by Iakob Gogebashvili (1840–1912), a tireless campaigner for education in Georgian and the author of the widely used textbook *deda ena* (Mother Tongue).[37] That same year the first permanent Georgian dramatic troupe was formed, and in 1885 the first chorus for Georgian folksongs was founded by Lado Agniashvili. The Czech conductor Joseph Ratili was invited to Tiflis to assist in this ethnomusicological endeavor, and in 1886 the first concert was held in Tiflis.

Through the 1880s Georgian literature experienced a renaissance with the appearance of works by neoromantic writers like Aleksandre Qazbegi (1848–1893) and Vazha-Pshavela (Luki Pavlis-dze Razikashvili, 1861–1915), men who celebrated the free spirit of the Georgian mountaineers and idealized Georgian life before the Russians arrived. The older generation of Georgian letters—Chavchavadze, Akaki Tsereteli, Dmitri Kipiani—energetically intervened in public affairs to promote Georgian schooling and protest the denigration of the Georgian language.[38]

The dissemination of Georgian national feeling by the patriotic intelligentsia in the last third of the nineteenth century paralleled developments among the Armenians. Inspired by the successes of Russian arms against the

Ottoman Turks in 1877–1878, both the Armenians and the Georgians dared to hope that their brethren living in eastern Anatolia might be liberated from Muslim rule. The historic Georgian region around Batumi was brought into the empire in 1878, as were the districts of Kars and Ardahan, which Armenians claimed as their historic patrimony.

In contrast to gentry nationalism, Caucasian liberalism was based on a respect for the experience of Western Europe and the successes of industrial capitalism. Rejecting revolution and dedicated to reform, the liberals depended on the good will of the state for the implementation of their program. Although they were critical of bureaucratic autocracy, the liberals were anxious not to antagonize Russian authority. At the same time they opposed all forms of national chauvinism and promoted cooperation among the nationalities of Transcaucasia. For liberal reformers like Nikoladze, the Georgian nobility no longer had any historic role to play. The future lay in the new institutions of local government and business, and he encouraged young people to enter the *zemstva*, city government, the railroad, and other businesses where practical intelligence could influence the condition of the mass of people. "In my opinion," he wrote, "the task of liberating the country involves the acquisition by the intelligentsia of sufficient power for that inevitable moment when the government, under the blows of Europe, will again find itself in as helpless a position as it fell into after Sevastopol."[39] Nikoladze took his own advice and went for a time to work in St. Petersburg for a private railroad company. There he tried to convince the Russian revolutionary populists, the *narodniki*, to give up terrorism so that the government would end its repressive policies and take up reform.

The appeal of this liberal, reformist approach was limited to a small number of urban Georgians, the Armenian progressives around Grigor Artsruni's journal *Mshak* (Cultivator), and those men from the "third element" working in city government. It never affected the lower classes or the great bulk of the nobility. By the late 1870s the liberal *Tiflisskii vestnik* had managed to build its circulation to 3,300. Later this antinationalist, antiautocratic, cosmopolitan, procapitalist liberalism was the hallmark of the influential Tiflis daily *Novoe obozrenie* (New Review), which called for a renewal of reforms—increased municipal self-government, the introduction of courts, religious and ethnic tolerance, and an end to racism and chauvinism.

Despite their narrow social base, the liberals achieved notable sucesses in local government. Liberal reformers, led by A. S. Matinov, P. A. Izmailov, and A. A. Tamamshev, introduced a program of municipal improvement in the Tiflis duma. To gain access to the merchants who dominated the assembly, the young intellectuals turned to an Armenian businessman, I. E. Pitoev. Pitoev organized a "party," which met periodically in his apartment, to discuss plans for Tiflis. His influence was paramount; as one contemporary put it, the statement "Isai wants it" had a "magic effect" on the others in the group. Such private meetings of duma deputies were unheard of in the Russia of Alexander II, and according to memoirist Georgii Tumanov, "thanks to the circle of Is. Eg. Pitoev, private conferences of deputies received the right of citizenship here twenty years earlier than in other cities of Russia."[40]

At the end of 1878, the Pitoev-Izmailov party won the elections to the duma. When the deputies met to choose their mayor, bitter differences divided the new members from the old. While the new deputies voted for the Armenian Bebutov, older deputies split their votes between the incumbent mayor, Georgian noble Dmitri Kipiani, and the Armenian M. E. Alikhanov. After much maneuvering an Armenian businessman, A. Korganov, was chosen, but he declined to serve, and A. S. Matinov (1843–1909) was finally elected.[41] The victory of the Pitoev-Izmailov party brought ethnic considerations into duma politics, though they were still muted. Matinov served as mayor of Tiflis until 1890, but the most influential duma member was party leader P. A. Izmailov, the vigorous spokesman for a new water system, bridges, a city hall, and other renovations. This party was responsible for turning Tiflis, or at least part of it, into a modern European city, but its critics condemned the reformers for the "one-sided bourgeois direction of this party." Like the duma that it led, the reform party largely represented the rich Armenian community and the small number of liberal intellectuals.

Liberals like Nikoladze had abandoned their youthful radicalism and turned from revolutionary politics to reform. Meanwhile, in the 1870s a new generation of young noblemen responded to the contradictory messages of the Russian Enlightenment by turning toward populism. In secret circles in their *gimnazii* and seminaries young Georgians read the prohibited works of Belinskii, Pisarev, Dobroliubov, and Chernyshevskii, while disregarding their own native writers. As early as 1865 the editors of *Kolokol* had reported that several *gimnaziia* students in Tiflis had been arrested for membership in a secret society, Molodaia Gruziia i Molodaia Armeniia (Young Georgia and Young Armenia). By 1869 a clandestine library had been established in Tiflis, and seminarians found the home of their teacher, Iakob Gogebashvili, a haven for forbidden discussions of art and politics. One student later claimed that "his house was for the Georgian intelligentsia what Stankevich's home had been for Russian writers."[42] Students at the seminary were close to the editors of *mnatobi* (Luminary; 1869–1872), who expressed socialist views, and themselves put out a handwritten journal, *shroma* (Labor), until March 1871. In general young Georgian intellectuals experienced a new liveliness, and in this stimulating climate they were attracted both by the radical political message of Russian populists and a sense of their responsibility to their own people.

At one extreme, farthest from the Georgian "patriots" (*mamulishvilebi*), were a few Georgian populists who linked their fate directly to that of the Russian revolutionary movement of the 1870s. Men like I. S. Jabadari (Dzhabadari) and Shio Davitashvili saw no contradiction between their commitment to Russian populism and the cause of Georgian liberation. When the patriots complained that Georgia's few educated people should all work for the motherland, Davitashvili answered: "Georgia is closely tied to Russia. The Georgian people can be freed only if the political order in Russia is destroyed. Consequently the Georgian youth are helping the cause of the Russian revolution, and in this way they serve not only the Russian people but the interests of Georgia."[43] Jabadari was even more abrupt in his dismissal of a separate Georgian movement:

> We entered the arena of political activity not as Georgians but as members of the whole Russian revolutionary family. Russian youth was closer to us than the narrowly nationalistic Georgian, Armenian, and other Caucasian . . . We decided to work in Russia hand in hand with Russians, deeply convinced that if sometime it is decreed that we are victorious in Russia then at the same time we will be victorious in the Caucasus; having won freedom for the Russian people we win it for the peoples of the Caucasus at the same time . . . Not separatism but working together was our slogan.[44]

The first generation of Georgian populists came from the same social and educational milieu as the patriots and the *meore dasi,* but their affections were turned toward the larger world outside Georgia. When Jabadari and his friends organized a library for poorer students, they included the works of Louis Blanc, J. S. Mill, Aleksandr Herzen, and Victor Hugo. They read with deep interest the published accounts of the Paris Commune and followed closely the trial of Nechaev. From St. Petersburg they were able to obtain books by Lassalle, the novel *Emma and Lucinda* by Schweitzer, and Marx's *Das Kapital.* This first socialist circle in Georgia (1871–1872) spent much of its energy circulating literature to students, though it had some contact with workers and artisans.[45] But it made no effort to link its socialism with specifically Georgian concerns. It dissolved after a year's existence when its leading members left for St. Petersburg and Zurich.

Their experience in St. Petersburg was different from that of the *tergdaleulni:* it drew them further away from Georgian politics instead of inspiring them to return and work in their homeland. "In Petersburg," Jabadari remembered, "I immediately fell in among young people who spoke, dreamt, and raved only about the people." When he met his old friends from Tiflis, he found them much less interesting than the Russians.[46] Yet the ceaseless arguments among the Russian populists, divided into Lavrovist and Bakuninist camps, fatigued Jabadari, who found them fruitless. When his fellow students decided to "go to the people," he left Russia to continue his studies in Zurich and Paris. There he found colonies of Georgian students attempting to sort out their political alternatives.

In Zurich a largely Georgian circle known as *ugeli* (Yoke) had been formed by Niko Nikoladze. Not revolutionary in its tactics, *ugeli* was a forum for reports on Georgian and general European history, politics, literature, and economics. A similar group was formed by the Armenians in

Zurich, and P. Izmailov and a certain Abelian acted as deputies of that society to its Georgian counterpart. In Paris Nikoladze was publishing a Georgian newspaper, *drosha* (Banner), which advocated a federation of all Caucasian peoples on the basis of economic equality of all citizens.[47] Jabadari was unimpressed by the ideas of federation or the émigrés' emphasis on the political struggle. Like the populists with whom he had been studying, he advocated a joint movement with the Russians and a full social revolution.

In August 1874 Nikoladze organized a congress of Caucasian university students studying in Geneva and invited Jabadari and Mikhail Chikoidze, then living in Paris, to discuss alliance strategy. The main question at the congress was whether to support Nikoladze's notion of a federative republic of Caucasia or to join the all-Russian social revolutionary movement. Jabadari, Domgat from Daghestan, Tsitsianov, Chelokaev, Eliozov, Chikoidze, and a few others found themselves in the minority. The majority proposed Switzerland as a model of what a Russian federal state should be in the future.[48]

This congress marked another decisive bifurcation in the Georgian liberation movement. The more moderate men of the 1860s—Nikoladze, Giorgi Tsereteli, Sergei Meskhi, and others—were dedicated to a Caucasian solution to Georgia's future and to their own political struggle with tsarism, which sought to institutionalize legal restraints on the autocratic power. The populists, on the other hand—Jabadari, Tsitsianov, Zdanovich, and the others—were determined to link the various national liberation movements into one common social revolutionary struggle against tsarism and capitalism.

Given their strategy, it was appropriate that Jabadari and his comrades soon joined forces with a small group of Russian women in Zurich, the so-called Frichi, who had refused to obey their government's command to return home in 1873. United by their opposition to Jacobin centralism, they decided to form a revolutionary party. The All-Russian Social Revolutionary Organization, founded in 1875, included the Georgian-born Georgii Zdanovich (1855–1917), Aleksandre Tsitsianov, and Mikhail Chikoidze, as well as the Russian women from Zurich: Sofia Bardin, Olga Liubatovich, Lydia Figner, and others. It operated as a Bakuninist cell for a few months until April 1875, when Jabadari, Chikoidze, and seven others were arrested. Held in prison for almost two years, they were finally tried in the famous Trial of the Fifty in February 1877, one of a series of mass trials designed by the Russian government to discredit the revolutionary movement. When his lawyer pointed out to him that most of the male defendants at the trial were Georgians, Jabadari seemed genuinely surprised. Ethnicity had never played a very important role in his philosophy.

For all the prominence of Georgians in the Russian populist movement, the movement had very little impact within Georgia itself. A few Tiflis seminarians, led by David Kezeli, met in 1872–1873 to read revolutionary literature. The sons of rural priests and deacons, they were influenced by the radical critic, Dmitri Pisarev (1840–1868), and called themselves nihilists. When the police arrested them, among their books were the incriminating works of Darwin, Mill, and Chernyshevskii. More substantial than the Kezeli circle were the efforts of Ignatii Ioseliani, Mikhail Kipiani, and Isidor Kikodze in 1875–1876. They planned a long campaign of educating and propagandizing the Georgian peasantry for a coordinated insurrection to be timed with the outbreak of war. Overestimating the volatility of the peasantry, the populists believed their organizational tasks would be relatively simple. Visiting from St. Petersburg, Zdanovich met with Kipiani and the others, listened to the local news of revolts in Svaneti and Abkhazeti, and reported back to his comrades that "the Caucasus is on a war footing."[49]

Organizations were formed in Tiflis and Kutaisi, and their members received the simple literature prepared for the peasants—books like *The Clever Mechanic* and *The Tale of Four Brothers*—and translated them into Georgian. They also distributed Russian revolutionary newspapers such as *Vpered* (Forward), *Rabotnik* (Worker), and *Samarskii golod* (Samara Hunger). Their efforts had some success in Tiflis, where they had about two hundred sympathizers, but much less in Kutaisi, where only about thirty people showed any interest before arrests dispersed the populists in 1876.[50]

The government became concerned when peasants in some parts of western Georgia appeared to be influenced by populist rhetoric, particularly by the notion that the land was indisputably theirs and that no one had the right to use their labor. One official wrote to the tsar directly:

> It is impossible not to notice that in the last ten years there has often appeared in Zugdidi district a tendency of the peasants not to fulfill their obligations to the landlords . . . From conversations with peasants I have come to the conclusion that they are motivated by the theory that they have the right to landlord property, [a theory] which has filtered down to them from an alien milieu. Many peasants express themselves on this subject in the identical expressions of the social revolutionary propagandists who were discovered in Kutaisi and Tiflis provinces in April and May of this year (1876) . . . The peasant population is easily affected by these teachings which correspond to their real interests. They now have adopted the notion that he who works the land should have the exclusive right to ownership. The natural consequence of this situation is the refusal to pay the landlord or the treasury for use of the land.[51]

In the 1880s a new generation of Georgian populists appeared, made up of non-nobles. They directed their propaganda to students and the artisanal workers in the towns. The Tiflis seminary was a center of populist activity, and the student Gola Chitadze was instrumental in organizing a student circle (including Is. Ramishvili, Laghiashvili, Uznadze, Menabde, Maglakelikze, and Moseshvili) and a union of journeymen. The circle considered itself close to Narodnaia volia (the People's Will), the terrorist wing of the populist movement. A small committee of these *narodovol'tsy* also existed in the city, made up of three Armenians (Grigor Ter Grigorian, Abraham Dastakian, and Tamara Adamian) and three Georgians (Vasili Sulkhanov, Vasili Rukhiladze, and Anna Sulkhanova); in 1882 the Armenians split off to form their own circle, dedicated, as they put it, to the "undefended claims of the unfortunate Armenian people."[52] Anna Korba and Sergei Degaev, members of the executive committee of Narodnaia volia, formed a military organization in Tiflis, but Degaev was later recruited by the police as a secret agent, returned to Tiflis, and exposed his former comrades. On March 2, 1883, officers of the Sixteenth Grenadier Mingrelian Regiment and other members of the organization were arrested.

For two years (1881–1883) newspapers expressing populist ideas were published legally in Georgian. Both *imedi* (Hope) in Tiflis and its sister paper *shroma* (Labor) in Kutaisi condemned the assassination of Alexander II and moderated their revolutionary sentiments, though many contributors favored a revolution and belonged to secret circles. *Imedi* debated with Chavchavadze's *iveria,* condemning its narrow patriotism and the "nationalization" of the liberation movement. In an article, "Broken Dreams," the populist Chrelashvili charged that Chavchavadze did not understand that the solution to the national question depended on the resolution of the social question.[53] Another prominent populist propagandist, Anton Purtseladze (1839–1913), complained that *iveria* viewed the land problem as underdeveloped agricultural technology, an agronomic problem, whereas it should properly be seen as a social problem, the result of the nobles' ownership of too much of the land. Whereas *iveria* opposed taking the land from the nobility, the populists argued for expropriation and common ownership of the land fund. In opposition to the liberals, the populists opposed private ownership of the land, hoped to introduce communal ownership in the Caucasus, and proposed an equal right to use land and the full right of each producer to the product of his labor.

Although both the liberals and the populists were deeply concerned with Georgia's economic and social problems, they tended to neglect specifically ethnic aspects of the situation. When the hopes of the Great Reforms turned into frustration, an antagonism rooted in social discontent combined with ethnic concerns to produce a volatile political mix. Searching for some explanation of their difficulties, some target on which to fix blame, Georgians often focused on the Armenians of the towns or on Russian officials. With the Georgian nobility rapidly losing its prime position in the social order, Georgians of every level experienced a sense of political powerlessness and fear that all would be lost to rapacious Armenians. Both the socioeconomic structure of Tiflis and the law's bias toward men of great property prevented Georgians from participating in the government of the city that they considered their national capital. The revival of Georgian culture and national consciousness among the gentry and intelligentsia notwithstanding, the political and economic weight of Georgians in their own country was steadily undermined by Russian officialdom and the Armenian bourgeoisie.

Particularly grating was the practice of wealthy Armenians buying up the property of impoverished Georgian nobles. When the Baratovs lost their estate to the merchant Aramiants, the viceroy himself intervened to request that it be returned, but the princes were unable to come up with the necessary 600,000 rubles. The Armenian millionaire Aleksandr Mantashev bought the exquisite home of Prince Mukhranskii in the heart of Tiflis and then rejected an offer by the Georgian Nobles' Bank to buy it back.[54] The Georgian elite was being undermined by the economic and social trends of the last decades of the nineteenth century and appeared powerless to reverse the process. Neither tsarist reforms, liberal politics, nor capitalist economics provided avenues for the advancement of the declining nobility, the emerging intelligentsia, or the peasants forced from their villages into the slums of the town.

At the same time the growth of Russian nationalism in the government bureaucracy and in the population affected the administration of the empire's ethnic periphery. In the 1880s and 1890s a series of laws imposed new restrictions on the Jews, reduced the autonomy of Finland, and reversed the long-standing policy that permitted the Armenian church to run its own schools. One of the first actions of Alexander III affecting Transcaucasia was the abolition of the office of the viceroy and the Caucasian Committee in St. Petersburg. The viceroys had been independent of the various ministries in the capital and could report directly to the tsar, but the administrative system introduced in Janaury 1883 required the governor-general to report routinely through the bureaucracy. The Caucasus lost its special status as a viceroyalty and was reduced to equal footing with other regions of the empire.

The slowly maturing national consciousness of Georgians clashed with the revival of Russian chauvinism, and the governors of the Caucasus attempted to repress, or at least contain, expressions of nationalism while at the same time diverting Georgian hostilities away from the government and toward the Armenians. Nationality was made a consideration in recruitment of state officials. Georgian language studies were further discouraged, even in the Tiflis seminary where a harsh Russianizing regime was installed. The very word Gruziia ("Georgia" in Russian) was prohibited in print. By the mid-1880s, the harsh police rule imposed by the government had effectively contained the revolutionary populists. Only the Chitadze circle continued to function in Tiflis, carrying on propaganda among urban workers.

Suddenly and dramatically, the political tranquility that had deceptively marked the first decade of the new reign was shattered on May 24, 1886, when a student at the Tiflis seminary, Ioseb Laghiashvili, fatally stabbed the Russian rector, Pavl Chudetskii. The seminary had long been a center of student political activity, and, according to a police report, the Russian priests had lost all authority over the Georgian students by the end of the 1870s. Tiflis newspapers continually attacked the seminary administration, thus legitimizing the students' own protests. One young firebrand, Silibistro Jibladze, had earlier slapped the rector and had been sentenced to two years in a disciplinary battalion. Apparently the seminary radicals had decided to avenge Jibladze's treatment with the assassination of the rector. Infuriated by this assault on an official of the Orthodox church, the Russian exarch of Georgia anathematized Georgia and expelled about sixty students from the seminary. Aging patriot Dmitri Kipiani, then marshal of the Kutaisi nobility, wrote an angry letter to the exarch, demanding that he leave Georgia immediately.[55] The government retaliated by exiling Kipiani to Stavropol. There he was mysteriously murdered the following year. It was widely believed that he had been killed by tsarist agents, and his funeral became a massive demonstration against the Russian government. As the 1880s came to a close, social revolutionary and ethnic concerns were gradually merging, and a new stage of political opposition to tsarism was about to open. But in Georgia Hroch's Stage C did not see the unalloyed triumph of the nationalists but the emergence of liberal and Marxist alternatives.

The growing anxiety of Georgians for their future in a Russifying, modernizing autocratic empire found its way into the politics of the Tiflis city duma. Georgians did not participate actively in municipal affairs until the 1890s, and in the duma elections of 1883 and 1887 there had been no intense battles along ethnic or party lines. But in November 1890 the Georgian noble land bank formed a political opposition to the ruling Armenian party and managed to find considerable support in the electors of the "first rank," the richest men in the city, who opposed the reforms of the duma leadership. The "second rank" split between the two parties, and the "third" gave enough support to the opposition to elect a duma divided between the old ruling party and the new opposition. The re-elected mayor, A. S. Matinov, was forced by the opposition to step down, and Prince N. V. Argutinskii-Dolgorukov was chosen in his stead. Still, the duma was dominated by the Armenian bourgeoisie, which held an absolute majority of the seventy-two duma deputies (forty were Armenians and only twenty Georgians).[56]

Ethnic conflicts in the duma heightened in the next few years. In 1892 the municipal counterreform of Alexander III raised the property qualification for duma electors and eliminated the division of the electorate into ranks. This legal maneuver simply strengthened the hold of the wealthiest men in the cities over the dumas, and in Tiflis this meant the even more complete hold of the Armenians. When the city board put forth its list of seventy-seven candidates in 1893, ten were Russian, seven Georgian, and two German; the rest were Armenian. A Georgian opposition re-formed, and the liberal newspaper *Novoe obozrenie* supported its claims to representation, though it was critical of the opposition's use of nationalist rhetoric and its disorganization. This time the opposition was easily beaten; the party of Matinov and Izmailov remained dominant in the duma.[57]

Both in 1893 and again in 1897 almost all the Georgians elected to the Tiflis city council refused to take their seats in protest against the small representation of their community. Liberals like Nikoladze proposed a system of proportional representation by ethnicity, but others like Tumanov opposed the idea, believing that such a system would only increase national tensions. From 1893 to 1897 the council attempted to put aside ethnic considerations in its daily practice and concentrated on sanitation, municipal infirmaries, and better veterinary supervision of the city slaughterhouse, all in response to the cholera epidemic of 1892–1893. The incipient ethnic conflict re-emerged in the elections of 1897 when a Russo-Georgian slate, led by chauvinist writer Vasilii Lvovich Velichko (1860–1904), challenged the dominant board members. By campaigning against all Armenians rather than just the ruling party, the opposition produced a backlash among the electors and assured its own defeat. Young wealthy Armenians were joined by the Avlabar merchants and others who had not previously favored the reform party.[58]

By the turn of the century complaints from Georgian noblemen and the writings of anti-Armenian nationalists fed a growing perception by the authorities that Armenians were a subversive, revolutionary threat to Russian hegemony over Caucasia. The tsarist government began restricting Armenian cultural and political institutions, closing charitable organizations and schools. In May 1899 the government issued a law, applicable only to Caucasian cities, which gave the governor-general the power to remove deputies from the city duma and officials from the municipal administration. With the Armenophobe Prince Golitsyn heading the Caucasian administration, it was not long before the Armenian political and religious hierarchy was attacked. In 1902 the entire Tiflis duma was arraigned for corruption and taken to court.[59] The case was dismissed, however, for lack of evidence.

The next year the government seized the properties of the Armenian church, triggering a revolutionary campaign by the Armenian Revolutionary Federation (Dashnaktsutiun) directed at Russian officials. In 1904 Golitsyn himself was wounded by an Armenian assassin and soon left the Caucasus. Ethnic friction, so long dormant or contained within the confines of the city duma, exploded into the streets, just as the social conflicts between workers and bosses, and intellectuals and the state, coalesced into a broad revolutionary assault on the autocracy.

By the early 1890s Georgian society was being transformed by the new demands of a market economy and early industrialization, but none of the ideological alternatives of the 1880s—liberalism, populism, or gentry nationalism—seemed to provide the mass of Georgians with a way out of their political predicament. Georgian nationalism, in its gentry variant, was too narrowly concerned with the problems and aspirations of the traditional

landed elite to appeal effectively to the Georgian masses. Popu
because of the absence of communal forms of ownership amo
peasants, had limited appeal in the villages and remained attr
radical young intellectuals. Liberalism too had a narrow soci
marily in the Armenian bourgeoisie and intelligentsia. Into the
by the failure of the existing political alternatives came a new social doctrine,
one that appealed broadly to workers and promised a merging of the
national and social struggles.

7 Marxism and the National Struggle

The Georgians of the last decades of the nineteenth century experienced a contradictory process of social formation. Even as villages drew closer to town with the advent of railroads, easier access to markets, and the movement of young people to the city, urban Georgia was becoming a very different place from the traditional settlements of the Georgians. In Tiflis especially, the transformations associated with capitalism and the industrial age created a unique environment, at one and the same time attractive to many Georgians and threatening to their customary way of life. In the towns Georgians came up against Armenians and Russians and were forced to recognize their own ethnicity in a way that would have been irrelevant in the homogeneous village. It was here that the urban intelligentsia had instigated the national revival, the newspapers of the various political tendencies were most accessible, and the celebration of the national folklore found its audience.

Urban life awakened national consciousness, but at the same time divided members of the same nationality into different social classes. The breakup of traditional seigneurial society, with the concomitant decline of the landed nobility, rendered the traditional Georgian elite politically impotent. At the same time, the rise of the Armenian bourgeoisie and the new and brutal isolation of lower-class Caucasians in the poorest sections of the cities rendered the nationalist ideal of a unified social order without class conflict a wistful dream. By the 1890s a Georgian working class, made up of peasants forced off the land into the workshops, factories, and refineries of Tiflis and Batumi, represented a new force to be reckoned with, one almost completely ignored by the nationalists and populists and neglected by the liberals.

Early in the 1890s a small group of Russian-educated intellectuals returned to Georgia from the north, bringing with them an alternative vision of Georgia's future. Noe Zhordania (1868–1953), Pilipe (Filipp) Makharadze (1868–1941), and others had become acquainted with Marxism while studying in Warsaw. From these humble beginnings the Georgian Marxists, soon known as the *mesame dasi* (third generation), developed an intellectual critique of the embryonic capitalist society in Georgia. Their program aimed to overthrow the autocratic monarchy and permit the free evolution of a democratic society, leading eventually to socialism.

By the early twentieth century Marxism provided a political strategy to workers in Tiflis, Batumi, Kutaisi, and elsewhere, and also to the rebellious peasants of western Georgia. By 1905 the Marxists, now adherents of the Menshevik wing of Russian social democracy, were the de facto leaders of a massive national liberation movement, the dimensions of which had not been seen elsewhere in the Russian empire.

The appeal of Marxism, first to Georgian intellectuals and later to workers, was powerful precisely because it gave Georgians both an analysis of their contemporary situation and a solution to it. Despite the demographic decline of the Armenians in Tiflis and the rise of Russians and Georgians, the new relationship among the three ethnic groups had not been reflected in shifts of economic and political power. Georgians remained at the bottom of the economic ladder and nearly totally outside the political arena. The traditional Georgian leaders, the gentry, failed to exercise effective authority in the last quarter of the century, and their form of nationalism had little appeal for the peasants or the new class of urban workers, now strategically located near the heart of economic and political power. Brought together in workshops and factories by the advent of industrialization, even small numbers of workers could make their weight felt much more potently than peasants scattered in isolated villages.

The Marxists provided an ideology that placed workers at the center of the historical moment, a view that accepted the coming of capitalism and rejected nostalgia about the agrarian past. However, unlike liberalism, their doctrine did not stop with a celebration of market society or a rationalization of the power of propertied men, but rather proposed that the contradictory nature of bourgeois society contained the potential for its eventual overthrow. In Marxism Georgians had a non-nationalist idelology that was a weapon against both their ethnic enemies: Russian officials and the Armenian bourgeoisie.

In the view of the Marxists Georgia could be returned to the Georgians only when revolution eliminated the dual domination of Russian bureaucracy and Armenian industrialists. This would require, first, a political revolution and, later, a socialist revolution. To the Georgian working class, separated by language, culture, wealth, and power from the Armenian bourgeoisie, the Marxists made their supranational appeal, exposing a stark world of capitalist exploitation and foreign dominion that they claimed could be overcome only by creating a national liberation movement based on class war. The remarkable success of the Marxists at the turn of the century occurred at a particular conjuncture of social and political forces. Although it is undeniable that the influence of market economies was increasingly being felt in even the most remote parts of Georgia, in no sense had emancipation transformed Georgia into a capitalist economy.

Soviet historians have for decades debated the timing of the introduction and development of capitalism in Georgia.[1] The assumptions on which they have based their calculations were those laid down first by Karl Marx in *Das Kapital* and later applied to Russia by Vladimir Lenin in his *Development of Capitalism in Russia*. Given the Marxist definition of capitalist relations of production, several essential preconditions must exist before any mode of production can be considered capitalist—the separation of the means of production (land, tools of the trade, machinery, etc.) from the direct producers; the concentration of capital and the means of production in the hands of only a part of the population; the transformation of labor itself into a commodity to be bought and sold on the market. Yet the problem of determining as precisely as possible when the creation of a "proletariat" with no ownership of the means of subsistence occurred, and when the concentration of the means of production in the hands of the few began, has not proven to be a simple mechanical task.

To contemporary observers it was clear that rural Georgia was being transformed by market relations in the last decades of the nineteenth century. The older forms of rural authority and deference were breaking down. A significant number of peasants in western Georgia were producing corn, wine, fruit, silk, tobacco, and poultry for commercial sale rather than for their own need. In eastern Georgia their compatriots were marketing wheat, barley, sheep, silk, cheese, wine, tobacco, and fruit. In some areas, like Borchalo, one-third of the wheat crop was marketed, a figure (somewhat exceptional to be sure) which exceeded the amount of gross grain output (26 percent) marketed in Russia.[2] But commodity production and the growth of markets do not in themselves constitute a capitalist transformation. Large-scale landlord agriculture, which accounted for the greater part of commercial production in Russia, did not amount to much in Transcaucasia. The commercial agriculture that remained was in the hands of the peasant smallholders.[3]

Without exaggeration it can be said that commodity production was well established in Georgian agriculture by the end of the nineteenth century, but that rural Transcaucasia was still far from full capitalist relations of production. The great majority of the peasants were not free to move from place to place, sell their labor freely, or buy and sell their land without encumbrance. They had for the most part been transformed neither into free laborers (proletarians with nothing but labor power to sell) nor into propertied freeholders in the image of Marx's rural petty bourgeoisie. The full play of the market was restricted in Georgia by the particular form in which the emancipation had taken place.

Thus, as the twentieth century opened, a tension existed between the forces of the market and "rational" economic activity on the one hand, and the traditional seigneurial patterns of rural exploitation on the other. The peasants were caught in the middle and benefited from neither side—not from the nobility's attempts to enforce their old obligations, not from a free market that, through forces beyond their control and often far from their village, could reduce them to poverty.

Soviet historians customarily refer to the peasant emancipation and accompanying reforms of the 1860s as "bourgeois." As V. D. Mochalov writes: "The bourgeois content of the reform is expressed in the fact that it gave the gestating industrial capitalism the 'free worker,' free before all in the sense of the formal elimination of personal dependence of the peasant on the landowner."[4] Be this as it may, as a means of preparing for "bourgeois" development, the peasant reform was certainly incomplete. The great majority of Georgian peasants found it nearly impossible to free themselves from ties to the landowning class and therefore remained on the land, trying to eke out a living from their ever-diminishing plots. Despite the visible inroads of market relations, the Georgian peasantry remained a precapitalist estate whose methods, mentality, and horizons were much more reminiscent of the centuries spent as serfs than of free farmers producing for a distant market.

The peasant reform, as Petr Struve noted long ago, abolished *krepostnoe pravo* (serfdom, legal bondage) without eliminating *krepostnoe khoziaistvo* (the seigneurial economy). As suggestive as this is for Russia proper, it is even more accurate for the Georgian countryside in the late nineteenth century. As we have seen, the great majority of former serfs in Georgia remained "temporarily obligated" long after their Russian counterparts had been freed from that category. Former landlords and the state bureaucracy retained much of the power they had exercised before 1864, and they continued, all too frequently, to abuse their prerogatives. Georgian peasants had no *volost* (local district) institutions standing between village societies and the provincial administrations. Village elders and assemblies were subject to manipulation by local nobles, the police, and the richer peasants.[5] Conflicts with the landlords could be referred to state officials, but the cases dragged through the bureaucracy for decades.[6] Strains increased, belying the stereotyped image of harmony between rural estates.

Peasants farmed their own plots, and because these plots were too small to support the household they either rented noble lands or worked on them as wage laborers. Noble land was usually rented for only one harvest at a time, and rents and land prices rose constantly as demand remained high.[7] Disputes over the harvest were numerous. Peasants complained about excessive rents; lords complained about lateness of payment, insubordination, and a fall in productivity, which they attributed to peasant laziness. In general the lords wanted the maximum harvest for maximum income, while the peasants worked to produce just enough to feed their family and pay the minimum to the lords. Neither lords nor peasants had much consideration for the land. As one writer pointed out: "The peasant himself was completely uninterested in the fact that hard work would improve his plot; on the contrary, the more valuable his cultivated plot became from his labors, the less he became interested, in a sense, of attaining his allotment as property."[8] Improving one's land only made it more difficult to redeem it, as land values steadily climbed.

The most serious problem facing the peasants after emancipation was land hunger. The population of Georgia was overwhelmingly rural. In 1866, 82 percent of the population in Tiflis province and 95.8 percent in Kutaisi lived in villages rather than towns; by 1897, these percentages had fallen only slightly, to 79 percent in Tiflis and 92.7 percent in Kutaisi. After emancipation the Georgian peasantry was made up of four major groups: the "temporarily obligated" former landlord serfs; state peasants; the *khizani*, who had been freed without land; and a small number of independent landowners. By far the largest group (about 45 percent in the 1880s, leaving out Abkhazeti, Ajaria, and Svaneti) were state peasants; 27 percent were "temporarily obligated" peasants; 21.4 percent were independent land-owners; and 6.9 percent were *khizani*.[9]

In many ways the state peasants were better off than the former landlord serfs; on the average they held more land and had higher incomes. In Tiflis province they held on the average 17.67 desiatinas of land, of which 5.89 were arable. They did not need to buy or rent landlord land, and only about 1 percent of their holdings were private land. In Kutaisi province, however, the average state peasant household had only 4.23 desiatinas, of which only 2.7 were arable; they had to use privately owned land to supplement their holdings. "Temporarily obligated" peasants were still worse off. In Tiflis province an average household that had not yet redeemed its land held 3.7 desiatinas, and in Kutaisi a meager 2.5. For those who had redeemed their land, the figures were a bit higher: 4.3 desiatinas in Tiflis and 3 in Kutaisi province. Compare these figures with the average 13.2 desiatinas held by former serf households in European Russia.[10]

While the state owned vast reserves of land in Georgia (48 percent in Tiflis province and 43 percent in Kutaisi in the 1880s), the best land and by far the greater part of privately owned land (77 percent in 1900) was held by the Georgian nobility.[11] With so much land in their hands, and given their general reluctance to reorganize agriculture on a more productive basis, the nobles constituted the most powerful social barrier to the creation of a capitalist agriculture in Georgia. They were also the principal obstacle to the peasants' acquisition of land.

Because the steady rise of population toward the end of the century was not greatly alleviated by migration to the towns, there were always more mouths to feed in the countryside. Primitive agricultural techniques and the lack of capital prevented a compensating increase in productivity. Even as the Georgian population rose, Russian authorities encouraged the immigration of Russian, German, and other European colonists into Transcaucasia. To survive, the peasants had to rent or buy land from the nobility. A contemporary student of peasant life, I. Bakhtadze, wrote in the mid-1880s: "The peasants are buying land everywhere and primarily, of course, from the princes and the nobles. The latter, who had the best lands of the *uezd* [Shorapani in western Georgia] before the peasant reform, now do not have one-third of it."[12]

Yet because of the rise in population, the per-household decline in allotment size continued. The average holding of a former serf in Tiflis province fell from 3.9 desiatinas in 1864 to about 1.5 in 1901. These figures must be considered against the calculations by Privy Councilor Ia. S. Medvedev, who estimated late in the century that for subsistence peasant families needed a minimum of 18 to 19 desiatinas (8 arable) in Tiflis province, and 11 to 12 desiatinas (10 arable) in Kutaisi. If these estimates are taken seriously, as they are by all Soviet historians, most peasants in Georgia had insufficient holdings. Only 5 percent in Kutaisi province had 10 or more desiatinas. I. G. Antelava has shown that in some districts of Kutaisi province, such as Ozurgeti, Racha, Senaki, and Shorapani, more than 70 percent of state peasant households could not meet these minimal requirements.[13]

Besides population pressure and land hunger, the Georgian peasants were faced by a growing tax burden in the last third of the nineteenth century. From 1843 to 1897 receipts from the household taxes of Kutaisi, Tiflis, and Erevan provinces rose 2.5 times; in Kutaisi they increased fivefold. This increase was not from higher tax rates but increasing population. Peasants tried to merge and abolish households to reduce their tax liability, but the increase in the number of taxpayers allowed the government to expect ever higher revenues. Taxation did not consider ability to pay; there was no calculation of the quantity or quality of the peasants' land in determining the household tax. Thus, the burden hit the poorer peasants much harder than those who were relatively better off. Nobles did not pay household taxes, of course, but they did pay land taxes. The peasants of Transcaucasia, who held more than ten million desiatinas of land, paid twenty times as much in state and land taxes as the nobility, with about five million desiatinas. In addition there were social taxes for the clergy, schools, local police, and village officials. For some former serfs, of course, there were also the redemption payments for their allotments, and for many more there were rents or portions of the crop to pay to the landlords—sometimes one-half the harvest. Most peasants found it impossible to acquire enough capital to make improvements in their land or farming techniques.[14]

The financial burdens that came with the emancipation compelled the peasants to produce for the market. New ports in Poti and Batumi facilitated export abroad; so did the railroads that joined the distant corners of Trans-caucasia together and linked them with Russia proper. Whereas agriculture itself was only partly organized capitalistically—few large estates hired labor or made rational calculations of costs and revenues—farming was in-creasingly geared toward commodity production: growing salable produce for a market. Opportunities were opening up for farmers with surpluses, but the peasants of western Transcaucasia were unable to benefit from them.

As the century came to a close Georgian grain output per desiatina was actually declining because of primitive farming techniques, soil exhaustion, and the decrease in the number of draft animals. In the 1870s a peasant in Kutaisi province could expect 180 to 200 poods of corn from a desiatina of good land; by the early twentieth century he was reaping only 60 to 80 poods. If the payment to his landlord was one-quarter of his harvest, he was left only 45 to 60 poods instead of the former 135 to 150, hardly enough to feed himself, his family, and his livestock.[15] Thus as opportunities opened for the commercialization of agriculture, the Georgian peasant—faced with the far more efficient agriculture of Europe and America—was in a very weak competitive position.

Still, the peasant, particularly in western Georgia, was swept up into the domestic and even the international grain market. The peasants began to move away from localized and subsistence agriculture, producing crops for their own consumption, and toward producing crops that could be sold. For several decades after emancipation the export of grain from Transcaucasia rose steadily. Then, beginning in the 1890s, it began to decline.

The consequences of production for foreign markets were most severely felt by corn producers in western Georgia. When the American Civil War had disrupted corn exports from the western hemisphere and promoted a rise in corn prices around the world, peasant farmers in western Georgia had begun selling corn to middlemen for export. In time they converted land from other crops to the profitable corn. Only by selling to the grain collectors could these peasants hope to make the money necessary to pay off their various obligations to the state and to their landlords. But once agriculture was determined by international exchange rather than local needs, the small producers became vulnerable to the vicissitudes of the market.

The boom and bust of the world market had begun to have disastrous effects in Transcaucasia by the end of the century. From the 1880s Georgian corn met American competition, and a series of events seriously damaged its position in the market. A famine in central Russia in 1891 brought a temporary ban on corn exports. By the time trade was permitted again in 1892, many markets had been lost. World corn prices fell through most of the 1890s, and a pood of Georgian corn sold for an average of thirty-five kopeks instead of the seventy-five kopeks of a decade earlier. The corn crisis was discussed in the press and all over the countryside; as Tiflis's *Novoe obozrenie* reported: "Now in the depths of the villages they are speaking of

American competition, of American corn; the fall of the price of corn is making itself felt more and more."[16]

As corn from America, India, and Australia undersold corn from Kutaisi province, the peasants who had become dependent on foreign markets faced ruin. Guria and Samegrelo were particularly hard hit.[17] Only toward the end of the 1890s and in the 1900s did prices for Transcaucasian grain begin gradually to rise. But by that time some Georgian farmers were converting from grain to cash crops less threatened by competitors—cotton, tobacco, wine, rice, and tea.

Tobacco growing achieved great success around Sukhumi beginning in the 1880s and continuing up to World War I. Cotton production was centered in Erevan, Baku, and Elisavetpol provinces and never spread widely in Georgia. Tea culture was concentrated in Batumi *oblast'*, and since Georgia was the only tea producer in the Russian empire its market was guaranteed. The Georgians' traditional viniculture had been centered in Kakheti, but that easternmost region was not connected by rail to the rest of the world. This isolation, plus an outbreak of phylloxera in the early 1890s, delayed the large-scale commercialization of wine production until after the turn of the century.

Commercial agriculture, with all its vicissitudes, was firmly established in much of Georgia by the early twentieth century. In most areas market relations were the rule. Yet the countryside was only in part transformed by urban and international capitalism. Nobles remained influential in both economic and social life. Although migration to towns increased over time, there was no fully free labor market. In hundreds of legal and customary ways peasants were tied to a more traditional mode of production. Penetrating the market while at the same time preserving seigneurial relations was not unique to Georgia, but there the traditional forms were preserved to a far greater degree and for a longer time than in Russia proper. The unevenness of Georgian development had its most traumatic consequences for those peasants who left their village and moved, even for a time, to Tiflis or Batumi. There they confronted a far more energetic economic environment, but one without the customary protections built into the rural economy.

From the earliest years of Russian rule peasants who could not find work or make a livelihood in their villages migrated, at least for a season, to the towns. After emancipation the areas of western Georgia with the greatest density of population and the most meager land allotments supplied workers for the small workshops of the towns. Niko Nikoladze wrote in *Kolokol* about this first generation of the Georgian working class in the mid-1860s:

> The urban population of Georgia is not numerous. It is concentrated in Tiflis and two or three insignificant cities such as Kutaisi, Gori, etc. In all these places it has up until now been sharply demarcated into two classes: *mokalake (meshchane)* [townsman] and *musha* (worker) . . . The *musha* in

Georgia has no civil rights. He is not even a city dweller and not even temporarily emancipated. He is simply a runaway. Imeretian, Gurian, Mingrelian, and Rachian peasants who cannot bear the landlords' power and "tolerate the lord's whip" run away to Tiflis and, on the other hand, Kartlian and Kakhetian peasants (from Tiflis province) save themselves in Imereti, Guria, etc. . . . The break with family and home saves the peasant from the landlords' power but makes him dependent on the bourgeoisie and bureaucracy, as a slave to a piece of bread. The work of the vast majority consists of carrying stones, sand, and lime for construction, sacks and heavy goods for merchants, water and firewood for householders, and for such work they are rarely paid two or three *abaza* (40, 60 kopeks). The European proletariat has a family—true, aggravating him, but for all that, sweetening often the bitterness of his life; the Georgian *musha* also has a wife and children but "over the mountains, across the plains."[18]

These migrant Georgian peasants, moving between village and town, did not yet constitute a stable social class. Their legal status remained ambiguous; most people considered them peasants. Yet already by the first decades after emancipation, the landless *khizani,* the former house serfs of the nobility, and others of the least fortunate liberated serfs found their precarious place on the fringes of urban society. Usually they maintained a home and a family in the village from which they had come, and this semipeasant aspect of the Georgian worker remained characteristic to the end of the empire.

Viceroy Vorontsov-Dashkov (1905–1915) wrote the tsar:

Almost the entire rural population of working age in Guria, Imereti and Mingrelia is involved in seasonal work, without, however, breaking their ties with their homeland. The Gurians and Mingrelians make up the main contingent of every type of worker in all the Black Sea ports, beginning with Batumi, Poti, and Sukhumi and ending with Odessa and Constantinople. Imeretians also willingly take up any sort of profession when they migrate from their homeland; they make up almost exclusively the contingent of domestic servants in all the cities of the Caucasus and appear in the same kind of work and also as buffet and soup kitchen owners in many cities of the Russian empire all the way to Vladivostok.[19]

The railroads were vitally important in the growth of the new working class, providing employment, transportation, and the single largest industrial enterprise in Georgia, the railroad workshops in Tiflis. The first line, between Tiflis and Poti, was opened in 1872, and by 1883 Batumi on the Black Sea was linked by rail to Baku on the Caspian. It became reasonably profitable to develop manganese extraction in Chiatura and coal mining in Tkibuli, for railroads meant these minerals could be cheaply transported to Black Sea ports for sale in Russia and Europe. And the expansion of oil drilling in the Baku area led to refineries and packing plants in Batumi, whence oil could be shipped to the West.

Thousands of west Georgians migrated by rail to the towns of eastern

Georgia, particularly Tiflis. In 1892 more than 15,000 peasants left the four districts of Zugdidi, Racha, Senaki, and Shorapani, and five years later that number had grown to nearly 26,000, an increase of more than 60 percent.[20] Kutaisi increased its size nearly threefold to 32,000, Batumi to 28,000 by the end of the century, and Tiflis from just under 68,000 in 1865 rose to nearly 160,000 in the census year 1897. For Georgians Tiflis remained the city *(kalaki)*, their capital in all but name; half of all urban dwellers lived there. The city's growth was so rapid after 1880 that only 43.6 percent of its inhabitants could claim local birth in 1897.[21] Nearly a quarter of Tiflis was populated by people from villages.

No rapid program of industrialization transformed the urban economy of Tiflis from the basically small-scale artisanal organization that had characterized it for centuries. But a steady increment of new industrial enterprises appeared in fields where there had been no craftsmen (such as soapmaking, which had been a home endeavor) or where the small workshops simply could not keep up with demand, such as brickmaking. As fashions changed, certain craftsmen suffered, like those who made Oriental slippers *(koshebi)* while others, like those who made European shoes, thrived, even when faced by new competition from mechanized production. Other traditional products, such as the *burka* (felt cloak) were taken over by manufacturers, in this case by G. Adelkhanov, who turned out 100,000 a year, mostly for the Caucasian Cossack troops. A few large factories appeared, producing textiles, tobacco products, and leather goods, but the number of artisans continued to grow: 12,650 in Tiflis alone by 1903. Artisans remained 5 to 7 percent of the city's population well into the twentieth century, though the new factory production reduced their importance somewhat.[22]

The traditional artisanal economy was itself changing rapidly in the last decades of the nineteenth century. A tendency to hire workers, rather than rely solely on the old apprentice system, was already noticeable in the 1840s, and by the late 1880s nearly a quarter of the workshops in Georgia had more than one hired worker. Cheap peasant labor brought in by the railroads and the new machine production challenged the old craft guilds' withering monopolies over employment opportunities and the size of the labor force. In the 1870s the *kharazebi* (cobblers), the *chonebi* (hat makers), and the *dertsikebi* (tailors) had been among the most important guilds of Tiflis; by 1910 they had either disappeared or faced ruin.[23]

Among the crafts that did persevere, the old system of training apprentices and journeymen to become full masters was steadily replaced by harsher and more distant treatment of employees. Apprentices were often kept for years as domestic servants, and journeymen were ruthlessly exploited by the masters or by middlemen who supplied materials and then sold the finished product. A study of Tiflis artisans in 1903 revealed that "the great majority of journeymen receiving payment for piecework . . . work in their own apartments, obtaining orders and materials from the masters. The journeymen receiving fixed money wages spend all day in the shops, usually living in the same buildings in which they work, damp, cold, and completely unsanitary, huddling together at night on the floor, on tables and counters.[24] The gradual transformation of the traditional artisanal economy into a capitalist one affected even the most fiercely individualistic townsmen, the legendary peddlers called *kinto,* who were fast disappearing into the class of wage laborers. The *kinto,* with his colorful songs and fabled rowdiness, gave Tiflis bazaars an almost permanent carnival flavor.

The first stage of the formation of the Georgian working class, the creation of a mass of artisans and wage workers, what Marx called a "class in itself," had essentially been completed by the end of the nineteenth century. The census of 1897 recorded about 26,000 mining and manufacturing workers, about 11,500 of them in factories or mechanized mines. Another 19,000 workers in communication, transportation, repair work, and commercial enterprises can be added to the first category, and yet another 19,000 day laborers and unskilled workers without definite specialty should also be included. Some Soviet historians add to this nuclear "proletariat" the nearly 29,000 *prislugi* (servants in administration, factories, and on estates; domestic servants, cooks, cleaners, and so on); still others expand the figure further by adding the 30,000 agricultural workers. Thus, estimates of the Georgian working class around 1900 range from lows of about 15,500 (Gugushvili) to a high of about 120,000 (Khoshtaria). Most Soviet writers hold to a figure between 25,000 and 40,000.[25]

As a social formation, workers in Georgia were highly differentiated: by occupation, skills, relations to the means of production (master artisan versus *chernorabochii* [unskilled laborer], for example), and, most important, by language and ethnicity. The Georgian-speaking workers, who made up between 40 and 50 percent of the labor force, were the most closely tied to their home village.[26] They had come the shortest distance and could return to their families in the slack season. Armenian, and especially Russian, workers came from greater distances and had less intimate ties with their homeland, but the power of ethnic allegiances was evident in their tendency to work in firms owned by their own countrymen. Muslim workers were a separate category altogether. Azeri workers were still deeply involved in their traditional communities even when physically separated from them. Persian and Turkish workers who emigrated to find work but did not settle in Transcaucasian cities had little commitment to the land of employment and were often the last to become involved in local labor struggles.

Migration and partial industrialization merely brought larger numbers of workers together in close proximity, but this did not lead by itself to a cohesive class, whose members shared a sense of mutual interests and a feeling of distance from other classes. The inchoate quality of Tiflis workers was noted by S. Gulishambarov in his 1888 survey of factories and plants in Tiflis province:

A mass of unskilled workers are coming here from Persia and the Armenian provinces . . . These workers are completely ignorant of factory life, and this means that they must be looked after and directed. Georgians go to factories only in cases of dire need, and not only they, but even Armenians, are very poor workers. Factory life itself shapes the worker type . . . but this occurs only when factory work is the only source of income for a person; when that work takes on an irregular character, then the worker does not adapt to it. Under such conditions the productivity of the Asiatic worker for whom the factory or plant is a temporary refuge is significantly less than the productivity of the Russian worker of the industrial region.[27]

Statistics cannot by themselves reveal the ties that bound or separated these workers. In any period a sense of community or class, a perception of either well-being or exploitation, develop out of a complex process involving both material conditions and cultural perceptions. Probably because of their recent arrival in the city, their maintenance of ties to the villages, and ethnic divisions, the Tiflis workers of the 1880s were not yet a coherent and conscious working class, a class "for itself." As Gulishambarov put it: "Among the workers there is no solidarity . . . They have no interest to cooperate among themselves."[28]

The development of a coherent working-class movement began tentatively in the early 1890s but along two separate tracks—one involving small groups of workers, and the other generated by a somewhat isolated group of socialist intellectuals. These two tracks did not fuse until the early years of the new century.

Workers had periodically and in an uncoordinated manner pushed their grievances to the point of strikes in the last decades of the nineteenth century. In 1872, in the first notable strike by factory workers in Georgia, the 800 textile workers of Mirzoev's mill came into bitter confrontation with the owners, but to no avail. Other protests against low pay, arbitrary treatment by foremen and employers, and fifteen-to-seventeen-hour work days occurred in the Zeitser plant in Tiflis (1878), the Nobel refinery in Batumi (1882), and in the railroad workshops in Tiflis (1880, 1887, 1889).[29]

The first efforts at organization were the creation of *kassy vzaimopomoshchi* (mutual insurance funds) by local artisans. Even domestic servants in Tiflis tried in 1886–1887 to form a Society of Mutual Aid, and they attracted the support of poet Akaki Tsereteli before the government moved in and jailed the leaders. As early as 1889, workers like Arakel Okuashvili produced handwritten newspapers: *musha* (Worker), *gantiadi* (Dawn; 1891), *skhivy* (Ray; 1892), and the journal of the shoemakers, *sinatle* (Light; 1899).[30]

In workshops, particularly among Russians in the railroad yards, populist workers like Fedor Guzenko and Petr Shafranov in 1887 formed study circles and supplied them with illegal literature.[31] In 1891 a Russian worker, Fedor Afanas'ev, formed a circle known to its members as the

"Krasnogorskaia kommuna" (Red Mountain Commune), in which the young writer Aleksei Peshkov (Maxim Gorky) lived for a year.[32] Almost all these circles were Russian-language study groups of radical orientation. As if immune, Georgian, Armenian, and Muslim workers, most of whom could not read Russian, remained untouched by these first stirrings of socialism in the Caucasus. The Georgian workers acted in self-defense, organizing where they could in the traditional guild, independent both of workers of other nationalities and intellectuals of their own nation.

The young intellectuals who gravitated toward Marxism in the 1890s were not the product of the established intelligentsia of urban Georgia, but rather neophytes who emerged from the most backward rural districts of western Georgia, most often from Guria. Officially Guria no longer existed; on Russian maps it was labeled Ozurgeti *uezd*, named after its largest town. Local peasants from the densely populated, land-hungry villages of Guria were drawn by the booming economy in nearby Batumi to work in the refineries or on the docks. Batumi cast an influence over western Georgia that within a few years would transform the peasants of the region from passive loyalists into a major revolutionary force. It was from this peasant milieu, indeed, that several of the early leaders of the labor movement emerged.

One such peasant-intellectual was Egnate Ingoroqva (1859–1894), better known by his nom de plume, Ninoshvili. Like others who aspired to a world wider than their native villages, the young Egnate was sent to the Ozurgeti seminary at fifteen, where he was expelled as a leader in student protests. His educational horizons narrowed by a "wolf's ticket" (being blacklisted), Ingoroqva moved from job to job (first a village teacher, then a railroad worker and a printer in Tiflis) until he went abroad to continue his studies. Poverty forced him home after two years in France, and he found work in the Rothschild refinery in Batumi. There he was thrown into the depths of the agony of the new working class, and he began to describe what he saw in a series of short stories and novels:

> On one side of the city of Batumi, a little above the oil refineries, are strewn in one spot a bunch of wooden structures with large cracks, which more readily deserve to be called hovels than houses. Around them is ubiquitous mud and impassable swamp. The paths leading to them are such that in foul weather, if one is not careful, it is very easy to fall deep into the mud. The swamps in which this area abound are filled with various stinking pieces of filth, and the evil stench rising from them poisons and infects the surrounding atmosphere; such a smell hangs there constantly that a person used to clean air cannot pass through without covering his nostrils.
>
> In these buildings there are no heaters. Each room has only one window, and even on clear, sunny days, darkness and gloom reigns in them. It is true that the rooms have numerous cracks and holes in them, but more often and more strongly wind comes through rather than light. These buildings serve as the place of shelter for several thousand laborers. All the

rooms are damp and too small, though in each of them live ten to twelve workers.[33]

Despite their misery, or indeed because of it, these workers inspired Ingoroqva toward a new political analysis. That summer (1889), as he later wrote to a friend, he "read a great deal" and "seriously studied those questions which interest us. I have come to the conclusion that Marx and Engels and their young Russian disciple, Georgii Plekhanov, are our leaders and teachers lighting for us the way. The working class! Here it seems is the motive force, the wheel of history. The labor movement—here is the turning of the wheel. And if this wheel begins to move here in our country, if the labor movement develops, then a complete change will take place in our life."[34]

Himself too sickly to remain in Batumi, Ingoroqva left for the small town of Kvirili, where he found office work at Gogoberidze's manganese firm. His influence over his fellow workers in Batumi, who continued to look upon him as a friend and protector, hardly diminished after his departure; in the spring of 1890 five hundred Rothschild workers, incensed when their pay was lowered because of falling kerosene prices abroad, formed a union and went on strike.[35]

Attracted as he was by the Marxist reliance on the working class, Ingoroqva-Ninoshvili, like most of the radical activists of the early 1890s, was intellectually still quite close to the dominant populist views of the Russian revolutionary movement. No sharp distinctions were yet made between Russian socialism and its European variants. This same mix of radical ideas could be found in the more politically aware students in the Tiflis seminary, who met in secret circles and read the Russian radical literature available from the bookshop of Zakhari Chinchinadze.

These were years of unrest in the seminary, as a repressive Russifying regime was imposed on the students. It had only been a few years since Jibladze had been expelled for slapping the rector and Laghiashvili had been sentenced to death for killing the hapless priest. The young nobleman Noe Zhordania and his fellow Gurian, Pilipe Makharadze, were in the seminary when these events took place but remained relatively inactive until their last year. When a student disturbance broke out over the poor quality of the food, Zhordania, Makharadze, and T. Kikvadze convinced the seminarians to demand that Georgian language, literature, and history be taught. The student strike was victorious, but its young leaders left the seminary under a cloud.[36]

In 1891 Zhordania and Makharadze embarked together for study at the Veterinary Institute in Warsaw. The city was a revelation to the young Georgians. More highly industrialized than their homeland, with an active working class and an articulate student movement, Poland seemed a completely foreign land, much more European than the rest of the Russian empire. Yet there were striking parallels between Georgia and Poland; both countries were dominated by an alien, Russianizing government, and the anti-Russian feelings of the Poles created a bond of spiritual kinship with the Georgians. In Poland the opposition to Russian rule, much broader than in Georgia, had roots in the working class. Already in the 1880s the "Proletariat" party, an ostensibly Marxist movement with ties to Narodnaia volia, had successfully carried on social revolutionary propaganda among workers and had engaged in acts of terrorism.[37] Bitter debates over conflicting allegiances to patriotism and socialist internationalism divided the Polish students and resonated in the discussions of the Georgians.

Shortly after their arrival in Poland, Zhordania and Makharadze read about the great Lodz strike of more than twenty thousand workers. The combination of palpable worker power with the complex socialist-nationalist dialogue in Poland impelled the Georgians in Warsaw to study Marxism. Zhordania was completely converted, as he remembered later, by the theory of historical materialism: "For the first time I saw that Russian Socialism was really utopian, that it was reactionary. If that socialism were realized we would fall into barbarism. The realization of European socialism was the task of the industrial worker."[38] For Zhordania Marxism was a link with Europe and the most progressive forces of the West. From Plekhanov's polemic against Tikhomirov he understood the need for two revolutions: a political overturn that would permit the organization of a democratic order, and a social revolution based on prior industrial and economic development. He wrote enthusiastically of his new discoveries to Ninoshvili and Jibladze and sent them illegal literature. In the summer of 1892 he left for Georgia because of poor health.

To the dismay of his Marxist comrades in Warsaw, Zhordania began to advocate the formation of a "national democratic" party in Georgia. Makharadze insisted that only a social democratic party, like that in Germany, should be formed. Ninoshvili initiated plans for a preliminary organizational meeting of Georgian socialists, and on December 25, 1892, thirteen men gathered in the home of Ioseb Kakabadze in Kvirili.[39] Both Marxists and populists attended, and most memoirists recall that populist ideas dominated. But when Makharadze's criticism of the Zhordania program was read, it was decided that a new program, more critical of populism and closer to the teachings of Marx, should be drawn up.[40]

A second conference of "Marxists" was held in February 1893 to discuss Zhordania's new program. After objections by Nikolai Chkheidze that the program was not well grounded in economics and lacked a section on the historical development of Georgia, Zhordania's "What Is To Be Done?" was adopted as the platform of the young socialists. A central group of activists was set up to work with workers and poor peasants and to publish Marxist literature legally; for the time being, it was decided not to issue illegal literature. In the spirit of Marxist internationalism a permanent bureau was set up in Tiflis with two Georgians—Ninoshvili and Mikha Tskhakaia—and the Armenian Dandurov.[41]

In the last decade of the nineteenth century a remarkable upsurge of intellectual, political, and economic activity, comparable only to the 1860s, spread through educated society in the Russian empire. Georgia was no exception. In 1893 alone, the Marxist intelligentsia established its organization and the students of the Tiflis seminary renewed their struggle against the school's Russian administration; a tense electoral campaign for the city duma pitted the dominant Armenians against an embittered Georgian opposition; workers in Batumi struck the Rothschild plant again; and a new weekly journal, destined to change the complexion of the educated youth of Georgia, appeared in Tiflis. This illustrated magazine of about twenty pages, *kvali* (Trace), was edited by the liberal writer Giorgi Tsereteli, but for its first five years it had no definite political direction except a dedicated antagonism toward Chavchavadze's *iveria*. Still, the Marxists, particularly Ninoshvili and Zhordania, soon began publishing in *kvali,* which was considered the "most progressive journal of the moment, the organ of young people."[42]

The first public appearance of the young Marxists was in the spring of 1894 at the funeral of Ninoshvili in Chochkhati. In an oration at the grave, Jibladze publicly proclaimed that the members of the new generation, following Ninoshvili's example, would struggle for the "representatives of physical and mental labor" against the "bourgeois capitalist parasites." The speech, reprinted in *kvali,* had a great impact in Georgia. Giorgi Tsereteli was so impressed by the young activists that in his own report on the funeral he named them *mesame dasi,* the "third generation," implying that they were the legitimate successors of the noble nationalists around Chavchavadze and liberals like himself and Nikoladze.[43]

At about the same time Zhordania published the program of the Georgian Marxists as an article, "Economic Development and Nationality," in *moambe* (Bulletin). His strategy was to apply materialism to the history of Georgia's formation as a country. Dismissing racist or individualistic explanations, he argued that material evolution and economic integration were the main forces linking disparate regions into a single nation. "Language is the first sign of nationality," he claimed, but it does not unify people in real life; material changes lead to a consolidation of nationality. Georgian society, he continued, divided as it had been into estates (noble, peasant, and clergy), began to change under the impact of commerce and industry. The noble estate fell apart, and its members lost any mutual interests except the preservation of their rights and privileges. The peasant, at the same time, was freed to sell his own labor. "Looking around he saw that each man works separately for himself, without mutual aid; alone he struggles for a piece of bread; thus in the people's heart new thoughts arose: isolation, loneliness, individualism."[44]

Zhordania wanted to demonstrate that "our country has already imperceptibly stood on the road of industry. The nation has already pushed its head into the capitalist vise." A life and death struggle between rich and poor "is the inevitable requirement of contemporary society. Not one nation can escape this road." Taking aim at both the populist desire to avoid the coming of capitalism and at the nationalists' elevation of the national struggle over the social, Zhordania concluded that the struggle for the nation's freedom and the individual's should be carried on simultaneously. Only with further economic development, the improvement of a "bourgeois" system of law, and unification of the poor could the goals of material, national, and human well-being be achieved.[45]

The *mesame dasi*'s first effort was to attract the intelligentsia to a new view of Georgia's destiny. A dual attack on the gentry nationalism of *iveria* and the residual influences of populism was carried out in the legal press and through propaganda among students. Contacts with workers were minimal, though the first Marxist study circle appeared among Georgian workers in 1894. The *mesame dasi* discovered Afanas'ev and Stanislaw Reniger (Iustin), who were distributing revolutionary literature among Russian workers, and set up "reading circles" in which these translated works were provided for Georgians who did not understand Russian. Like the propaganda circles in Russia proper, these intellectual-led groups provided the workers with a broad new perspective on the world, introducing them to everything from Russian language and history to astronomy and biology. At first there was no discussion of the revolutionary movement, and the intellectuals, fearing police reprisals, kept their distance from the strikes that broke out sporadically.[46] Not surprisingly, officials did not regard the Georgian Marxists as a serious threat at this time; the principal danger was the national separatists, and the most pernicious of these were the Armenians.[47]

In the last half of the 1890s secret workers' circles with ideological ties to the *mesame dasi* began to spring up in Tiflis. Interestingly, only workers actually joined the circles. While some intellectuals like Makharadze, Jibladze, and the young Lado Ketskhoveli worked more closely with workers than most of the social democratic intellectuals, the others stood apart except to act as lecturers or to answer questions about economics. Workers showed little interest in politics, although occasionally someone might ask a question about a constitution.[48]

The experience of the study circles and the contacts, however tenuous, with social democrats had profound effects on the workers. One railroad worker remembered years later that he had been naively nationalist when he first began work at the Tiflis depot: "At the time I considered all Russians to be my enemies"; he and his roommate (Datiko Dvali, later a Menshevik) believed that Ilya Chavchavadze should be king of Georgia. But in his study circle the workers were told that all workers, regardless of nationality, had the same interests and must join together against their common enemy, the rich. The intellectuals introduced the rudiments of class analysis to shape a new, antinationalist perspective. Still, in those early years Armenian, Russian, and Georgian workers maintained separate circles. There was some cooperation between Armenian and Georgian laborers, but greater suspicion of Russians.[49]

By the time Noe Zhordania returned from his four-year odyssey of European universities (1893–1897), the Georgian social democratic movement had outgrown the small *mesame dasi*. Younger comrades were insisting on underground work rather than legal journalistic propaganda. At a long and heated conference in Tiflis the two options were discussed. Zhordania argued for continuation of legal efforts. Eventually, with Jibladze's support, a resolution was adopted to maintain both legal and illegal work. After negotiations with Giorgi Tsereteli, Zhordania was named editor of *kvali*, and Georgia's Marxists were given their own legal organ, a rare advantage in the late 1890s.[50] But the "legal" operatives had to keep clear of direct involvement in the workers' movement, and in time not only age but distinct experiences and outlooks divided the older legalists from the younger underground workers. Among the latter were the volatile Lado Ketskhoveli and a new recruit, Ioseb Jughashvili (Stalin).

Early in 1899 the first Tiflis committee of the Russian Social Democratic Workers' Party (RSDRP) was formed to coordinate the numerous activities of the circles. The self-proclaimed committee was neither elected nor formally representative. Its first leaflet, written by Zhordania, grandly called for unity with the workers of Europe, and organized a celebration of May Day outside Tiflis.[51] Seventy-five workers and intellectuals attended; speeches were made; red flags were unfurled; and a general feeling that a socialist labor movement had made its appearance in Caucasia spread through the dozens of secret circles in the city. As the new century opened, that movement became open knowledge. Workers marched in the funeral demonstration for Giorgi Tsereteli and launched a series of determined strikes. In the three decades from 1870 to 1900 only nineteen strikes were recorded at twelve industrial enterprises in Tiflis; in the year 1900 alone there were seventeen at fifteen enterprises. The number grew steadily, and in the first two months of 1901 fifteen firms were struck in Tiflis.[52]

The epicenter of the labor movement was the railroad workshops in Tiflis, where many of the earliest Russian and Georgian workers' circles had been established and where strikes had occurred periodically since the late 1880s. Then came the strike of August 1900, different in its degree of organization and in the central role played by social democrats. On June 28, the workers presented a list of demands to the administration. Primarily economic in nature (pay raises of 30 to 50 percent, bimonthly wage payments) they also included broader issues affecting the workers' sense of dignity—a demand that officials and foremen use polite forms of address with workers, improvement in hygienic conditions, the end of beatings, and abolition of fines for absence. The demands were rejected on July 1, and on the first day of August more than five hundred workers walked out. Within days three hundred were arrested, and two thousand supporters marched to police headquarters demanding to be arrested. Altogether five thousand workers, many in other industries, went on strike. But after two weeks, with many of the social democrats in prison, the strike ended without a single demand granted.[53]

The effects of this defeat on worker morale are difficult to judge, but the very scale of the strike changed the nature of labor activity and official response. As one worker-socialist remembered: "Until the strike of 1900 we enjoyed full freedom; it is true that meetings were held secretly but no one paid us much attention. During the strike the gendarmes approached the doors of the railroad workshops for the first time." After August workers became more careful; some feared any participation in labor activities, others simply grew cautious—but only for a short time.[54]

The general excitement and activity of workers and students throughout Russia, the turn toward a concerted political attack on autocracy, and the escalation of violent confrontations, which grew into a revolution by 1905, resonated in Transcaucasia with new volume in 1901–1902. The May Day 1901 observance saw larger crowds and bolder displays of antitsarist sentiment. Three thousand people, many of them armed, marched through the streets of Tiflis and fought with police when their flags were torn away. But the police cracked down hard on the known social democrats and, linking the Marxists with kvali, searched the journal's offices. Zhordania was arrested and held for nearly a year before being exiled, first to his village in Guria and then to Ganja.[55]

By the end of 1901 Georgian social democrats had deeply penetrated the workers' milieu, not only in Tiflis, but in Baku, where Georgians had set up the first circles and the famous secret printing press "Nina," and in Batumi, where Jughashvili began in December to organize refinery workers. Almost without exception the Georgian Marxist intellectuals were enthusiasts of the all-Russian newspaper Iskra (Spark), which through its advocacy of an all-nation political struggle against autocracy was winning the scattered social democratic circles of Russia over to its position.[56] Inspired by Iskra, the Baku group headed by Ketskhoveli suggested publishing an illegal newspaper in Georgian. Zhordania and the men around kvali objected, but the Iskra agent Gal'perin supported the notion, and the first issue of brdzola (Struggle) appeared in September 1901. The influence of the old mesame dasi, still strong among intellectuals, was being challenged among the praktiki (activists) of the labor movement. The old traditions of worker self-reliance and suspicion of the intelligentsia were institutionalized by the second Tiflis committee of the RSDRP (the first one to be elected): it was made up almost exclusively of workers.[57]

This phenomenon of the movement outgrowing its intellectual leaders became starkly clear in the labor and peasant activities in western Georgia in

1902. There was no Batumi committee of the RSDRP before 1902; the scattered workers' circles maintained loose contacts with two prominent veterans of *mesame dasi* who lived legally in the city—Nikolai Chkheidze (known to everyone as "Karlo" because of his enthusiasm for Marx's *Das Kapital*) and Isidor Ramishvili. But Chkheidze was extremely pessimistic about the possibility of socialist work among the eight thousand workers in the town.

Then suddenly a massive strike broke out in the Rothschild plant to protest the dismissal of nearly four hundred workers. Arrests followed, and when workers marched on the police station soldiers fired into the crowd, killing fourteen. Only then was a Batumi committee hastily thrown together; two intellectuals, N. Chkheidze and V. Chkhvishvili, served with three workers, G. Kaladze, I. Kopaleishvili, and I. Mgeladze.[58]

The events in Batumi had far-reaching repercussions. Five to six hundred workers were exiled from the city, most of them to their villages in Guria. There they met young social democrats like Grigori Uratadze, and in late spring they organized peasant boycotts against landlords. Beginning in Nigoiti, the boycott movement spread through Guria, and the reluctant Marxists in Batumi and Kutaisi were forced by the movement's success and the intervention of Zhordania and Jibladze to offer help to the peasants.[59]

The first actions had been motivated almost entirely by economic considerations—the harvest of 1901 had been quite poor—but once the police and soldiers intervened on the side of the landlords, the movement broadened into a political struggle against local Russian authority and autocracy itself. In May 1903 the organizers developed an elaborate network of peasant cells of ten members, each of which sent a representative to a higher cell. All of rural Guria was covered by these secret cells, which soon constituted the real governing power in the region. At first the Batumi committee attempted to guide the peasant movement from the city, but by 1903 the Gurian "Committee of Rural Workers" set up by Batumi was replaced with a local Gurian social democratic committee. The resistance of the Marxist intellectuals to organizing peasants under social democratic auspices dissolved in the solvent of the movement's success.

Georgian social democracy was unique in the Russian empire for its close ties with both an ethnic labor movement and a mass peasant organization. In the absence of any rival popular movement, the young Marxists were able to harness economic discontent and ethnic anxieties to their particular organization. Marxism, in its Zhordanian reading, provided both a new interpretation of Georgia's plight and a hope for a future solution. For the first time intellectuals from the traditional Georgian elite worked directly with workers and peasants to change Georgian society.

Despite their national base and involvement with the peasantry, however, the Georgian Marxists conceived of themselves as part of an all-Russian movement to organize workers against the tsarist autocracy. The First Congress of Caucasian Social Democratic Organizations, held at the beginning of 1903, expressed its solidarity with the program of *Iskra*. A nine-member Caucasian Union Committee was formed, and Bogdan Knuniants, Arshak Zurabov (Zurabian), and Dmitri Topuridze were chosen delegates to the upcoming Second Party Congress.[60] The only significant departure from the *Iskra* position was the majority's decision to maintain *elected* city committees rather than appointed ones. Interestingly enough, the future Bolsheviks Tskhakaia and Makharadze defended the principle of co-optation onto committees.[61]

With the phenomenally rapid success of social democracy in the Russian empire, the delegation making its way first to Brussels and then to London for the Second Party Congress probably shared Plekhanov's enthusiastic greeting: "It is a joy to live in such a time." Even as the debates got under way, news of massive strikes and demonstrations in the south of Russia and in Transcaucasia reached the participants. A sense of historic importance, of the need for unity and agreement on a program was so intensely felt that seemingly insignificant points created lengthy disputes.

As is well known, this congress, called to create a united party, produced instead two feuding factions, Bolsheviks and Mensheviks, with conflicting views on the nature of party organization and the terms of party membership. After nearly a month of meeting, the congress had driven the Jewish Bund and the "Economists" out of the party and left the Central Committee and *Iskra* in the control of Lenin and Plekhanov's "majority" faction. The Caucasian delegates—including Zhordania, who attended the congress without a mandate from a local committee—had argued, along with the Iskraites, against the Bund's claim to exclusive sway over the Jewish workers' movement, but once the congress split the Caucasians too divided along factional lines. Knuniants and Zurabov sided with the Bolsheviks, while Toporidze and Zhordania supported the Mensheviks.

In Transcaucasia almost nothing was known of the party schism for more than a year. It was only when Zhordania returned to Tiflis in January 1905 that the local social democrats learned in detail about the factional divisions in their central organizations. The issue of appointment versus election of local committees became the touchstone for factions. The strong elective tradition among Georgian workers and the practice of keeping intellectuals distant from the workers' committees proved to be fertile soil for those who opposed Lenin's more centralized and directed organization of the party. The Caucasian Union Committee remained loyal to the "majority," and for his opposition Toporidze was expelled. But Zhordania toured the local committees and quickly won them over to the Menshevik position. The Bolsheviks were routed from the districts in Tiflis and Batumi but held firm in Baku. From January 1905, Georgian social democracy became an almost exclusively Menshevik movement.

8 The End of Tsarist Georgia

Through 1901 tsarist loyalists gathered at banquets and ceremonies to mark the centennial of imperial Russia's annexation of Georgia. While well-dressed officials, Georgian nobles and clergy, wealthy Armenian businessmen, and ordinary Russian workmen sang "God Save the Tsar," Georgian peasants and workers accelerated their violent protests against the existing social order, and young intellectuals turned toward the embryonic oppositional parties. Social democrats made the most rapid headway among Georgian workers and peasants, and the neopopulists who would soon form the Socialist Federalist Party attracted the moderately nationalist intelligentsia, schoolteachers and students particularly.[1] Clearly a time of social ferment and potential reform, if not revolution, was ahead, and the promise of a future in which Georgians might escape their colonial status encouraged men and women from every social stratum to risk their safety in a bold commitment.

The first decade and a half of the twentieth century witnessed the emergence of mass political movements in Transcaucasia, the brief collapse of imperial authority, its re-establishment by force (though in compromised form), and a long period of sparring between the largely discredited Russian rulers and their political opponents among the ethnic minorities. Between 1905 and 1917, the possibility of a revolutionary overthrow of tsarism remained a vivid hope, even in the dark days of "reaction" and the years of working within the new "constitutional" framework. Through that last decade of Russian imperial rule, resistance to restabilizing tsarism in Transcaucasia was the constant reality to which imperial authority was forced to accommodate itself.

From the centennial year, the tsarist government was faced by a massive agrarian revolt in the western part of Georgia. The dimensions of the Gurian peasants' rebellion had by 1905 expanded beyond the expectations of the social democrats—and beyond the powers of the government to control. Admirers spoke of a "Gurian republic" in which tsarist appointees were replaced by elected officials.

Linguist Nikolai Marr traveled through his native Guria and observed "the intense public life in the villages."

> Meeting follows meeting, and you would be surprised how the peasants, burdened by their work in the fields, hurrying everywhere, take active part in the debates, sitting for long hours, sometimes days, at meetings. Today the court, tomorrow discussion of the principal social questions with a well-known travelling speaker, the day after tomorrow decisions about local affairs: schools, roads, land, etc., etc.

It was clear to Marr that workers from the cities played the most active roles in discussions. The Gurians were indifferent to questions of nationality or the national church and instead concentrated on problems of "material life."[2] The rallying cry was *ertoba* (unity), and the peasants reacted to outside events that they interpreted (with the help of the social democrats) as impinging on their lives. Following the January shootings of "Bloody Sunday," Gurians refused to pray for the imperial family. Portraits of the tsar were destroyed; tsarist supporters were murdered; and a general boycott of all state institutions began.

The dimensions of the peasant revolt were the product of both the peculiarly onerous conditions in Guria and the skill with which the Georgian Menshevik agitators articulated the peasants' pent-up resentments. In Guria, an area of particularly small holdings, the former serfs had suffered from the emancipation even more than in other parts of Georgia. Peasants were still "temporarily obligated" after forty years. The local nobility's advantages in landholding and freedom from tax and labor obligations (like road work) infuriated the peasants. The Russian administration, notoriously insensitive to peasant complaints, only compounded the peasants' alienation from the ruling elites.

Unable to make a living at farming, even after leasing land from nobles, many peasants were forced to seek work in Batumi or other towns. There they made contact with the social democrats, who had already earned a reputation as friends of the simple people. The social democrats, for their part, adjusted their program to fit the aspirations of the Georgian peasants. Self-rule and peasant control over agriculture were emphasized. The official social democratic doctrine on land reform—return of the *otrezki* (lands "cut off" from the peasants) and "municipalization" (control by local authorities) of the land—was conveniently forgotten. In its place the socialists repeated the demands of the peasants themselves—lower rents, abolish certain despised taxes, employ nobles on road work along with peasants. Until such demands were met, the peasants refused to obey or pay dues to the landlords and responded only to their own elected authorities.

The news that demonstrators had been shot by the tsar's soldiers in St. Petersburg on January 9, 1905, also inflamed the already volatile mood among the workers in Transcaucasia. On January 18, railroad employees went out on strike, followed by printers and tobacco workers. A week later the local social democrats proclaimed a general strike in Batumi. Other towns—Sukhumi, Kutaisi, Chiatura, and Poti—soon joined the protest against the deteriorating economic situation and the government's use of military force. The strikes were marked by an extraordinary degree of violence and by overt political expression.

As workers returned to their jobs at the end of the month, their grievances were taken up by the Tiflis city duma and reformist members of the Caucasian administration. The duma voted unanimously in early February to petition the government to grant workers the right of assembly, free expression of their demands, and freedom for unions. Prominent Georgians of various classes visited General Malama, the highest military authority in the Caucasus, to request moderation in dealing with the peasant rebels in Guria. The punitive expedition of General Alikhanov was called off, and a liberal member of the governor-general's council, N. A. Sultan-Krym-Girei, was sent to Guria to investigate the peasants' complaints.[3]

Thus began more than a year of protest, insurrection, and official responses ranging from political concessions to harsh military repression. The waves of activity in Georgia approximated those in the urban centers of Russia. Although its origins, shape, and motivations had distinct characteristics, the movement in Georgia clearly responded to national issues, events far from Transcaucasia, and to the general sense of the fragility of the old order.

To contain the widespread rebellion of west Georgian peasants and pacify the towns of Caucasia, the tsar appointed Count Illarion Ivanovich Vorontsov-Dashkov (1837–1916) viceroy of the Caucasus with extraordinary powers. Promises to restore Armenian church lands seized by the tsarist government in 1903 and to establish *zemstva* and a new judiciary system appeared in the local press. Political prisoners were freed. Shortly after arriving in Tiflis in May, the new viceroy appointed the popular agronomist Vladimir Aleksandrovich Starosel'skii (1860–1916) governor of Kutaisi province and directed him to draw up plans for a land reform.[4] In June police were ordered to stay clear of the huge funeral-demonstration of the social democrat Prince Aleksandre Tsulukidze (1876–1905), in which more than twenty thousand people marched through Kutaisi. On August 1 the acts appropriating Armenian church properties were repealed, thus removing the principal grievance of the Armenian community, and on August 6 the tsar's manifesto establishing a state duma (the so-called Bulygin duma) was published.

Despite these concessions, the fundamental rift between the government and the bulk of Caucasian society could not be bridged. With the social democrats heading the workers' and peasants' movements and calling for a truly representative assembly, and the propertied men of the city dumas agitating for civil rights, *zemstva,* and an end to military intervention, the government found itself almost completely isolated and without support from any significant group. Its ultimate option continued to be the army. When the social democrats called a general strike on June 20, the workers were joined by city employees and many shopowners. To counter such a broad-based movement, martial law was declared and all public meetings prohibited.

A second fissure appeared within society itself in the summer of 1905. Urban groups began to divide as the socialist-led lower classes openly challenged the conciliatory men of the duma. The mayor of Tiflis, the Armenian liberal Khristafor Vermishev, hoped to avoid a confrontation by prohibiting the public from attending the session of the duma planning to discuss the *zemstvo* question. But on August 25, two thousand people crowded into the crescent-shaped duma chamber in the city hall. The deputies left the hall, and the crowd, led by social democrats, held their own meeting. Similar meetings were held the next two days in defiance of the government, but when the crowd broke into city hall on August 29, Cossacks stormed the building, indiscriminately firing. Though reports differ, at least sixty people were killed and possibly two hundred wounded. Tiflis now had its own "Bloody Sunday," and general outrage followed. Sixty-two members of the duma resigned; Mayor Vermishev was dismissed; and a one-day general strike protesting the bloodshed shut down the city.[5]

In October local tensions fused with the all-Russian railroad strike. A strike committee formed in Tiflis by social democrats declared a general strike on October 15 and demanded the end of martial law and the removal of troops from the rebellious villages.[6] Batumi also struck, and the peasants of Guria armed themselves and cut all communication with the rest of the empire. The local "Red Guards" ambushed the district administrator, Lazarenko, and kept him and his men under seige until word was received that the tsar had issued the Manifesto of October 17.

In response to the strikes throughout the empire, Nicholas II had finally agreed to limit his autocratic powers, permit a representative duma to be elected, and guarantee basic rights for his subjects. Many activists on the left were cautious in their appraisal of this "constitution" from above and suspicious of the government's intent. But in Tiflis and other cities crowds surged into the streets overjoyed at society's victory over the government. The city duma adopted the program of the liberal Constitutional Democratic Party (Kadets), but both wings of social democracy called for continuation of the struggle for full democracy. On the right a new and open enthusiasm for the tsar was manifested in several patriotic demonstrations. Twenty thousand people, among them many Russian railroad workers, marched in Tiflis singing "God Save the Tsar." The parade was guarded by soldiers, but as it moved through the center of the city, bombs were thrown and shots rang out. The soldiers fired into buildings from which they thought the first shots had come. Forty-one people were killed, sixty-six wounded.[7]

Sadly for the revolutionary opposition, October marked the high point of the all-nation, united struggle against autocracy. In the coming months the unity of that front was to be steadily shredded as more moderate social groups and parties accommodated themselves to the new "constitutional" order.

The news of the October Manifesto reached Starosel'skii, the governor of Kutaisi province, on the evening of October 21. He set out on his own, without military escort, to meet with the rebels in Guria. A meeting was arranged with the social democratic committee, and the governor urged its members to give up the armed struggle and adopt a parliamentary strategy. Despite the favorable impression made by this modest and sincere man, the committee rejected his proposal.[8] But they did agree to end the strike if Starosel'skii could convince the viceroy not to send in the military. Back in Tiflis, the governor extracted a promise from Vorontsov-Dashkov to remove General Alikhanov and his punitive expedition from Guria. The viceroy hoped that the October Manifesto and the promise of liberal reforms would convince the insurgents to accept a constitutionally limited monarchy. The rebels, for their part, feared that the government would not carry out its promised reforms. Nevertheless, at a congress in mid-November, the social democrats decided to end the boycott of governmental institutions.

The immense influence of social democracy over Georgians in 1905 was not confined to Guria; the government was compelled to deal directly with revolutionary socialists to keep order in the cities of Transcaucasia as well. Late in November the fierce ethnic rivalry between Armenians and "Tartars" (Azerbaijanis) spread from Baku and Elisavetpol to Tiflis. In response to their fighting in the oldest part of the city, the social democrats organized a huge demonstration protesting the divisive actions of nationalists. The viceroy turned to the party to keep peace and issued five hundred government rifles to the socialist *druzhina* (fighting squad).[9] Workers' patrols and the administration's firm stand against any interethnic outbreaks prevented a repetition in Tiflis of the destruction and death that had ravaged Baku twice that year.

But this rare instance of cooperation could not end the strain between the rebellious population and the shaken government. With the disastrous war with Japan concluded and with renewed support from noble circles, the tsarist regime after October was able to reassert its authority, first in the center of the empire and later in the peripheries. In Caucasia the right and the military demanded harsher measures against the revolution. The viceroy's liberalism was rejected by protsarist demonstrators, and the administration was unable to curb attacks by Cossacks in Kutaisi and Batumi. The left

demanded freedom for political activity, local self-government, and the end of
the military threat. Vorontsov-Dashkov was torn between these two poles;
unable to satisfy the insurgents, he opted in the end for military repression.

The final crisis of 1905 began on November 27 with the arrest in St.
Petersburg of the members of the soviet. Within days an armed insurrection
broke out in Moscow, and simultaneously workers and peasants in the Baltic
provinces rose in revolt. In Poland, the Ukraine, and southern Russia, strikes
and street fighting added to the spreading insurgency. Throughout the country railroads came to a halt. On December 10, a strike committee of all the
revolutionary parties was formed in Tiflis, and a general strike was declared.
Armed clashes between workers and the army, bombings, and assassinations
led to all-out attacks on workers' districts by the military. In Guria soldiers
were disarmed and government officials driven out of the area. The pact with
the government had completely broken down. The railroads were in the
hands of the revolutionaries, and Caucasia was cut off from the rest of Russia.

Moderation and promises of reform had failed to end the rebellion.
Nicholas II urged his viceroy to use force:

> I am certain that at that moment when you call out the troops for the
> energetic suppression of disorder, they will rescue [us] from these most
> difficult circumstances . . . Now it is essential to bring the matter to a
> peaceful end by force of arms, not hesitating before the most extreme
> measures.[10]

The tsar advised Vorontsov-Dashkov not to listen to the conciliatory Krym-
Girei and suggested that the best place for Starosel'skii was hanging from a
willow. "The example would be beneficial to many."

With the suppression of the Moscow insurrection in late December, the
revolutionary wave began to recede rapidly. Yet the executive committee of
the Tiflis strike committee, led by Zhordania and Isidor Ramishvili, called
for intensification of the struggle and ordered the bombing of the Cossacks
stationed at Soldatskii Bazar. The Cossacks retaliated by attacking and
burning the party's printing press, killing everyone in the building. The
bombing by the socialists shocked many in the city, and a few days later the
united front of revolutionary parties broke down when the principal Armenian party, the Dashnaktsutiun, unilaterally withdrew from the strike committee.[11] Three days later (December 29), the general strike ended. The
military now had the upper hand. On January 8, 1906, Starosel'skii was
replaced as governor of Kutaisi by none other than General Alikhanov.
Immediately the new governor's troops moved into the province, burning
rebel villages, executing insurgents, and imposing an armed peace. The
social democrats attempted another general strike, this one to mark the first
anniversary of "Bloody Sunday," but the next day party members were
rounded up by the police.

By the end of January 1906, the army had effectively shattered the peasant movement in Georgia, stabilized the government's hold over the towns, and discouraged the more militant socialists from engaging in mass activity. For the next decade the political opposition shifted to a more moderate strategy, in the new state duma and the legal or semilegal press. Mass action was abandoned, but the resort to terrorism—even by the Marxists, who elsewhere in Europe and Russia condemned such tactics—remained a live option. Under orders from the social democrats, a young worker, Arsen Jorjiashvili, threw a bomb that fatally wounded the commander of the Caucasian military region, General F. F. Griaznov. Jorjiashvili was himself wounded and went to his execution without betraying his comrades. But the kind of desperate heroism that preserved Jorjiashvili's memory in songs and poems was an exception to the new tactics adopted by the social democrats. The revolutionary movement became somewhat dormant, though it maintained a dual existence: both underground and openly active in the new legal institutions.

The period 1906–1917 was unique in Russia's history. The Moscovite autocracy, with its unlimited powers in the person of the tsar, was for the first time compromised by laws that provided the people of the empire with elected institutions and certain civil rights. This experiment in limited monarchy was never wholeheartedly endorsed by the tsar or his closest advisors, who steadily pressured him to erode the guarantees of October 1905. The Caucasian administration under Vorontsov-Dashkov (1905–1915) was a somewhat anomalous remnant of governmental liberalism in the era of the much more conservative Prime Minister Petr Stolypin (1906–1911), but the aging viceroy continued to enjoy the confidence of the tsar and worked to ameliorate the strained situation in Caucasia.

Through the last decade of tsarist rule three major areas concerned the Transcaucasian administration: the now somewhat muted tensions with the nationalities; the persistent problem of peasant discontents, particularly with the outmoded "temporarily obligated" status; and the continued activity of the social democrats and the revival of the labor movement after 1912. The liberal policies of Vorontsov-Dashkov had their most palpable effect in the area of ethnic relations, earning the viceroy a reputation for Armenophilia. Reviewing his eight-year rule, the viceroy in 1913 reminded the tsar: "Six years ago I reported to you, Sire, with complete candor that within the borders of the Empire we ourselves created an [Armenian] problem by carelessly ignoring the religious and national views of the Armenians."[12]

By returning the church lands to the Armenians and abolishing the ethnic restrictions on entrance into the state service, Vorontsov-Dashkov went far toward winning over powerful elements in the Armenian community. He rejected the notion, still quite popular among Russian officials, that the Armenians were a dedicatedly separatist and revolutionary people, a nationality in its essence subversive to the Russian imperial idea. "No form of separatism exists among Caucasian Armenians," Vorontsov-Dashkov declared. "Of course, revolutionary parties exist among Armenians, as they do in Russia proper, but to speak of the revolutionary nature of the Armenian people is as strange as to suspect the Russian people of an absence of allegiance to its monarch."[13]

The Georgians also were opposed to separatism, in the viceroy's eyes. "Armenians and Georgians understand quite well and quite realistically that without Russia they will be swallowed up by the Muslims." There were, however, nationalists among the Georgians, and their major concern was the autocephaly of the Georgian church. Nevertheless, the current exarch of Georgia, Innokenti, "has done much to turn this into a theoretical question."[14]

The viceroy showed somewhat more anxiety about the Caucasian Muslims, among whom "ideas of national consciousness are beginning to develop." But he seemed to have faith in education and the power of Russian culture to stem any separatist tides. One of his earliest acts had been to eliminate his predecessors' requirement that instruction in local schools be in Russian from the first year. He returned to the plan adopted in 1881 by Viceroy Mikhail Nikolaevich, which allowed teaching in the local languages in the primary grade. He was particularly pleased that the Armenian church schools, which were not required to teach Russian, had decided to offer Russian language, "though not sufficiently grammatical."[15]

Vorontsov-Dashkov supported the efforts of Caucasian liberals to have provincial and district representative assemblies (*zemstva*) introduced into Transcaucasia. Their absence was regarded as an example of ethnic discrimination by the central Russian government. The liberals also agitated continually for an institute of higher learning; but like the *zemstvo* question, the issue of a Caucasian university remained on the agenda well into 1917–1918. The one notable achievement of the reformers was the government's long-delayed decision to end the status of "temporary obligation" for former serfs. In December 1908, thirty-four members of the Third Duma had introduced a bill to liquidate this status in Transcaucasia. When it was rejected, the issue was taken up by the viceroy's council, and on December 20, 1912, a new bill presented by the viceroy to the duma was adopted. With this law dependent peasants ceased to pay dues to landlords and began redemption payments to the state.[16] Thus the formerly dependent peasants were turned into peasant proprietors, required to buy their land. These compulsory redemption payments were unpopular with the peasants, and in the summer of 1917, in the new revolutionary Transcaucasia, they simply refused to continue.

The viceroyalty had least success with the powerful socialist opposition in the cities. The government was unable to eliminate social democratic influence, though it did enjoy several years of relative political calm as the dominant Menshevik wing of the party turned steadily toward legal pursuits. The last months of 1905 and the early months of 1906 were a period of unusual cooperation and unity within the ranks of social democracy. At the Fourth Party Congress, held in Stockholm in April 1906 and dubbed the "unity congress," both Mensheviks and Bolsheviks made efforts to preserve the united party even though the two factions evaluated the recent past in fundamentally different ways. For the Bolsheviks the new duma was suspect, and for a time Lenin argued that social democrats should boycott the elections. Mensheviks, on the other hand, were inclined to exploit the new legal possibilities, and with their majority at the April Congress they managed to pledge the party to participation. More broadly, the Bolsheviks held out for a strategy based on an armed insurrection and hostility toward Russia's bourgeoisie. The Mensheviks, in contrast, argued that the workers had gone too far late in 1905, had unnecessarily frightened the bourgeoisie, and must now show greater restraint so as to encourage progressive bourgeois forces, like the Kadets. By the time the RSDRP decided to campaign in the elections to the First Duma, almost all returns were in with the exception of the Caucasus. Here the battle was joined, and the social democrats realized an enormous victory.

Most of the duma seats from Georgia were won by the Mensheviks. Noe Zhordania, a member of the RSDRP Central Committee, and his comrade, Semen Tsereteli, were elected from Tiflis, along with the socialist federalist Iosif Baratov and the Kadet Artemii Aivazov. In Kutaisi province the party enjoyed a complete sweep, electing Ivan Gomarteli, Sergei Japaridze, and party veteran Isidor Ramishvili. In Batumi, however, the nonparty conservative, Prince Prokofii Shervashidze, was chosen, though he was to play no significant role in the assembly. The five Caucasian Mensheviks, on the other hand, led the labor bloc of eighteen Mensheviks and workers who made up the left in the duma, and this faction elected Zhordania its chairman.[17]

The duma majority was opposed to the government, and the social democrats supported the Kadet leadership in its demand that the tsar form a government responsible to the duma. Nicholas II rejected the duma's bold "Address to the Throne," and on July 8, 1906, he dissolved the assembly and called for new elections. A stillborn attempt at protest was made by the Kadets, Trudoviks, and social democrats who gathered at Vyborg; Zhordania helped draw up the manifesto and then disappeared into the political underground. The failure of the manifesto to arouse any significant support in the population made it clear to the liberals and socialists that their claims to leadership of the opposition were much less secure than they had been in 1905.

The government's hope that new elections would result in a more pliable or conservative duma were not fulfilled. Indeed the Second Duma was even more radical in composition than the First, and was tolerated for an even shorter time. The social democrats had a faction of sixty-five: thirty-six Mensheviks, eighteen Bolsheviks, eleven nonfactional. The Mensheviks had again swept Georgia.[18] The young Iraklii Tsereteli (1881–1959) became the leader of the social democratic faction in the duma and emerged quickly as a major political figure on the Russian scene. He proved to be an orator of immense power, capable of improvising stirring replies to his opponents. The government acted quickly to stifle the open opposition. On June 3, 1907, Prime Minister Stolypin dissolved the duma, issued a new, considerably less representative electoral law, and arrested the social democratic deputies. This virtual coup d'état ended the first phase of Russian constitutionalism and ushered in a period of repression known to Soviet historians as the "reaction." Tsereteli was to spend the next decade as a political exile in Siberia, while his Georgian comrades continued the antiautocratic struggle both from the underground and in the severely restricted legal institutions.

After the Fifth Party Congress in the spring of 1907, the tentative unity of the RSDRP once again was broken. In Tiflis the Bolsheviks formed a separate organization from a tiny minority of the party's supporters. The Mensheviks remained in control of the old party press and committees, but the Bolsheviks were able to embarrass their rivals by successfully carrying out a bold daytime robbery, the famous "Tiflis ex," organized by Stalin (Jughashvili) and Kamo (Ter Petrossian). Unable to make much headway among workers in Georgia, the leading Bolsheviks, Stepan Shahumian and Stalin among them, left Tiflis in the summer of 1907 for Baku, where Bolsheviks had made inroads among the oil workers. Without any serious rival to their dominance in Georgia, the Mensheviks engaged almost exclusively in legal work, issuing a continuous series of party newspapers and focusing on their elected duma deputies.

In late 1907 "Karlo" Chkheidze was elected to the Third State Duma from Tiflis, and Evgenii Gegechkori from Kutaisi.[19] Though Georgian representation had been severely reduced, these men proved to be important national leaders, especially Chkheidze, who headed the social democratic faction in both the third and fourth dumas. From the duma podium he reported on the situation in Caucasia, where the revolutionary parties faced a revived government ready to use its considerable powers to destroy its adversaries: "The whole Caucasus has been turned into one big prison." Official statistics show that by the first half of 1909 more than eight thousand people in Transcaucasia had been brought to trial for political reasons; thirteen thousand more had been exiled by administrative fiat. Even so Stolypin berated Viceroy Vorontsov-Dashkov for his leniency toward "criminal organizations" on the left.[20]

In a most interesting survey of their activities, the RSDRP reviewed the difficult situation in which party organizations found themselves by August 1908. The section on Georgia is worth reproducing in full:

The party crisis has affected Transcaucasia. Before the London Congress, 15,670 members of the party could be counted, but now, 14,100, i.e., a decrease of 10 percent. In certain organizations this decline is even more noticeable, especially in rural organizations, for example, in Kutaisi province where in all the villages there are punitive expeditions of guards and soldiers; the *starshiny* [village elders] are appointed by the government itself. An exception can be found in Guria, where in all villages there still operate democratic organizations which run all economic, judicial, and school matters, and everyone follows their leadership and decisions. But even here the unchallenged influence of the Social Democrats has been weakened. Georgian Socialist Federalists and Socialist Revolutionaries have appeared who compete with the Social Democrats. The absence of party literature inhibits party work too much. Earlier there were 5000 members of the party in Guria but now only 4500.

In some parts of Transcaucasia the [party] crisis has been influenced by the economic crisis. For example, the export of Chiatura manganese has declined. The number of members of the organization in Chiatura district, as well as in Poti, has fallen. In these areas the number of organized workers has noticeably declined. But in the principal organizations—Tiflis and Baku—on the contrary, the number of members in the organizations not only has [not] declined but has grown. In the Tiflis organization there are 4000 members instead of the earlier 3,032. There are no large factories or plants in Tiflis; small workshops and enterprises operate, but the work here is hard, and there are no propagandists anywhere. Legal Social Democrats, it seems, can work. In May 1907, there were twenty-eight trade unions with 13,000 members who united in a Central Bureau. Most of these unions are now closed and exist semi-legally.[21]

The crisis in the party was reflected in the Georgian and Russian socialist press, in articles dealing with the party's tactics in the post-1905 era. In 1908 Zhordania wrote a series of articles in *azri* (Thought) and *dasatsqisi* (Beginning) on the need to abandon revolutionary actions and operate legally in the duma, trade unions, cooperatives, and elsewhere. He coupled his recommendations with a theoretical innovation: the rejection of the classical Plekhanovian concept of the Russian proletariat as the "hegemon" in the national liberation struggle. Zhordania believed that after October 1905 the bourgeois revolution had to be the product of the Russian bourgeoisie itself, not the proletariat, and that the working class had to restrain itself in order to discourage any move toward counterrevolution or accommodation with autocracy by the industrial-commercial classes.

In two "Letters from the Caucasus" published in *Sotsialdemokrat* in mid-1910, Stalin "exposed" Zhordania's views to the Russian reading public, referring to the Georgian Menshevik program and tactics as "liquidationist," a term of scorn in the party's ranks.[22] None other than the old man of Marxism himself, Georgii Plekhanov, became involved in the controversy and defended his view that "the revolutionary movement in Russia will be victorious as a movement of workers or it will not be victorious at all." Rather than not frightening the bourgeoisie as Zhordania proposed, the proletariat, said Plekhanov, should strengthen the revolutionary movement and thereby "raise to the highest degree the bravery and decisiveness of the 'middle bourgeoisie' represented by the Kadets."[23]

Refusing to become mired in this theoretical debate, the Georgian social democrats, meeting in the fall of 1910 in Guria, rejected the Bolsheviks' charge that *likvidatorstvo* existed in the party and reaffirmed the need for both legal and illegal work.[24] They remained hopeful that a broad unification of the party was possible, and late in 1911 the *Oblastnoi komitet* (regional committee) in Tiflis accepted an invitation to participate in a unification conference. Eight months later, two Georgian delegates, Grigori Uratadze and Vlasa Mgeladze, traveled to Vienna along with various varieties of Mensheviks, Bundists, and other social democrats to discuss an alternative to Lenin's narrow notion of party unity. The so-called August Bloc, initiated by Trotsky, lasted only about half a year before strains in the anti-Leninist camp fractured the group.

A key issue both in social democratic circles and in the general intellectual life of Transcaucasia in the years before World War I was the so-called national question: the problem of ethnic minorities in a multinational empire. Throughout the empire (though less so in Georgia) the revolution of 1905 had vividly demonstrated the implicit violence of nationality discontents, and in the subsequent years the problem was taken up by Marxists and their opponents. Almost from its inception the social democratic party had proclaimed its support for "national self-determination of all nations," but did not prescribe a specific solution to the problem.

The debate centered on questions of territorial versus cultural autonomy, federalism versus centralization, and the right of minority nationalities to separate completely from Russia. Lenin's position was unique: he favored a centralized state rather than federation but at the same time supported the unequivocal right of nations to self-determination, even if they wished independence. Yet the Bolsheviks opposed national-cultural autonomy and held out for territorial autonomy, which would not necessarily take into account ethnic considerations.

In Caucasia, where there had been Azeri-Armenian clashes in 1905, the national question was particularly sensitive, and social democrats made every effort to appear "internationalist" and thus free from any taint of nationalism. In 1903 Caucasians had strongly opposed the claims of the Jewish Bund to special representation and territorial privileges within the party, and in 1906 Caucasian organizations had specifically rejected the proposal of comrades from Kutaisi for national-cultural autonomy. Zhordania in the name of the Mensheviks, and Stalin in the name of the Bolsheviks had argued in favor of "regional self-government for Caucasia."[25] In the next year both the Georgian socialist federalists and the Armenian Revolutionary Federation, the Dashnaktsutiun, adopted the principle of extraterritorial national-cultural autonomy, according to which each person was entitled to ethnic representation no matter where in the empire he or she lived.

Zhordania had long been interested in the national question, but after his early efforts in the 1890s to interest Georgian social democrats in autonomy, he had turned to other issues. In 1908 he returned to this theme and began to raise the issue of protecting national culture. But until 1912 he continued to affirm the basic party position of regional self-government for all of Caucasia. Then, influenced by the work of Austrian Marxists like Otto Bauer, he added the concept of extraterritorial national-cultural autonomy. As he put it:

> The fate of the Georgian language . . . interests a Georgian no matter where he lives. It is very ignorant to say that Georgian culture concerns only Georgians living in Georgia . . . For example, the creation of a Georgian museum interests equally a Tiflis Georgian, a Baku, Kutaisi, Petersburg, or other [Georgian]. This means that management and leadership of all cultural-national affairs ought to be decided by the interested nation itself.[26]

Zhordania's principal Bolshevik opponent was Stalin, who accepted a commission from Lenin to deal with the views of the Austrians, the Bundists, and the Caucasians like Zhordania. In 1913 Stalin's "The National Question and Social Democracy" came out against national autonomy and in favor of regional autonomy. He began by defining a nation as "an historically formed settled community of people which has arisen on the base of a common language, territory, economic life, and psychological makeup, which is manifested in a common culture."[27] Without all these characteristics a people could not be called a nation. Such a definition clearly excluded the Jews, but also was not very congenial to other scattered peoples, like the Armenians. The thrust of Stalin's essay was to promote the seemingly natural historical process of assimilation of smaller nationalities into larger ones. National-cultural autonomy, with its emphasis on preserving cultural differences, would hinder this process; it would artificially maintain distinctions that, left to themselves, would disappear in time.

The essential difference between Stalin and Zhordania was not so much in their specific recommendations for state organization (though Zhordania clearly favored a more decentralized state structure than Stalin) but rather in their sympathies toward national culture. Zhordania placed the weight of his argument on supporting, protecting, and nourishing national culture, whereas Stalin played down the cultural variety of nationalities and encouraged small ethnic groups to gravitate toward what he called "higher culture."[28]

In the last years before World War I, the social democratic party in Georgia was in much less disarray than in most other parts of the empire. The Mensheviks were still dominant, and the Bolsheviks who managed to escape arrest did not formally break with their rivals, though they often met separately and supported Lenin's efforts to form a separate Bolshevik party complete with its own central committee at the Prague Conference in January

1912. In Tiflis the flourishing trade union movement of the years of revolution had all but disappeared by 1911, and the social democrats were limited to their semilegal press and electoral campaigns.

Allying with the liberals, the Mensheviks helped to elect Aleksandr Khatisov (Khatisian), an Armenian Kadet, mayor of Tiflis, and then formed a "new group of voters" to help the liberals win seats in the municipal duma. Their joint efforts also resulted in victories in the Fourth State Duma. Chkheidze was easily returned from Tiflis, but Gegechkori, who was re-elected from Kutaisi, was disqualified on a technicality by a government commission. In the Batumi-Sukhumi-Kars electoral district the social democratic candidate, Akaki Chkhenkeli, defeated the rightist candidate, Shervashidze, despite the government's efforts to have the socialist arrested and exiled. In a spectacularly successful campaign in Baku, organized by Ina Zhordania, Noe's wife, Mikhail Skobelev was elected. Repeatedly the Armenian liberals sided with the Georgian social democrats to defeat the chauvinist candidates.

Even as workers throughout the empire began to revive their strike activities, particularly after the shootings at the Lena gold fields in Siberia in April 1912, the calm and passivity evident since 1907 continued in Transcaucasia. A few activists were arrested with leaflets, and a somewhat greater than usual number of workers were seen walking the streets on May Day, but even the oil workers of Baku exhibited none of their former militance—until the summer of 1913. Early in June the manganese miners of Chiatura went on strike, demanding an eight-hour day, an end to night work, and wage increases. The police permitted their strike committee, made up of social democrats, to function, to keep them from turning a purely economic strike into a political one. After a month and a half, workers returned to the job as individual mine owners came to agree with some of their demands.[29]

Tiflis was relatively quiet (except for a tram workers' strike) in late summer 1913, though the number of sporadic strikes increased in the next year. From the labor press and the speeches of duma deputies, people throughout the empire learned of the growing urban unrest in Russia.[30] Though Transcaucasian workers never reached the level of strike activity or political expression in 1913–1914 that Russian workers in the capitals achieved, on the very eve of the war the oil workers of Baku called a general strike that lasted for over two months and had reverberations in other parts of the country.

With the outbreak of war in early August 1914, Transcaucasia was transformed into a front-line area. Each nationality reacted differently to the threat of a Turkish invasion. The fear of attack mobilized the Armenians of Caucasia under the slogan "the war to final victory and everything for the war." An Armenian National Bureau was organized in Tiflis, to speak for the Caucasian Armenians, and the Russian government gave Mayor Khatisov 245,000 rubles to help form volunteer units. On orders from the government

Khatisov also organized the Union of Caucasian Cities to set up hospitals and aid refugees. Led by the Dashnaks and liberals, the Armenians were enthusiastic about the war, which promised them a long-desired opportunity to liberate their brethren in Turkish Armenia. But, as Khatisov wrote later in his memoirs, "the Georgians and Tatars [Azerbaijanis] were opposed to the war. The Georgians had nothing to expect from the war; on the contrary, they were afraid of the Ajarians who, although Georgians, were Moham-medans and Turcophiles. The Tatars were afraid that the war might weaken Turkey. Only the Armenians wanted war."[31]

Among Georgian social democrats there was little support for Russia's war effort. Following their leaders in the state duma, they refused to work actively for the war and held to the hope that the conflict would lead to political revolution. Among prominent Georgian Marxists, only Zhordania and Uratadze came out for the Allied cause, but they were unable to engage the *Oblastnoi komitet* in debate over the issues of war and peace. Uratadze received permission from the committee to publish a newspaper, *akhali kvali* (New Trace), in Kutaisi to express Zhordania's views on the war. But the success of the paper among workers led the committee to restrict its publica-tion.[32]

The social democrats did not engage in antiwar activity, however, and their neutrality convinced the authorities to allow them to operate freely in Caucasia. A much greater worry for the government was the actions of a small group of Georgian nationalists who lived abroad; they were allied with the Germans, and advocated an independent Georgia. Their leader, Mikhail Tsereteli, made a secret trip to Georgia and met with Zhordania. He urged the social democrats to consider a pro-German orientation, but Zhordania considered any break with the expressed Russian orientation political sui-cide.

In late 1914 when the Turks under Enver Pasha penetrated southern Transcaucasia and rumors spread that the Russians would soon withdraw altogether from the Caucasus, nationalists and some social democrats argued that a Georgian national government be formed. Again Zhordania urged caution, not wishing to provoke reprisals from the government. Only in early 1917 did a secret meeting of social democrats, held near Zhordania's home town of Lanchkhuti, agree that if the Russians pulled out of Caucasia, Georgia should be declared independent.[33]

The pro-German feeling among many Georgians and the cool neutrality of most social democrats toward the Russian government distanced the tsarist officials from Georgian society; at the same time Armenian Rus-sophilia brought the government closer to the middle-class Armenians of Tiflis and Baku who so enthusiastically backed the war effort. Vorontsov-Dashkov's policies favoring Armenians had clearly borne fruit among one nationality but alienated others. The Azerbaijanis, particularly suspect be-cause of their ethnic and linguistic ties to the Turks, were excluded from governmental grace. When Countess Vorontsova-Dashkova set up a committee to aid refugees, and local Azerbaijanis asked that the committee aid "Tatars" [Azerbaijanis] as well, the countess rebuffed them: "I know no Tatar refugees; I only know Tatar traitors." Yet the Armenians too were to be bitterly disappointed in Russian policy. When the Russian army occupied eastern Anatolia in 1916, after the Ottoman government had carried out genocidal massacres against Armenians, Russian officials seriously considered an "Armenia without Armenians." Plans were discussed to settle Russians in the area devastated by the 1915 Turkish deportation and killing of Armenians. By spring 1916, the Armenian volunteer bands were merged with Russian regiments and their Armenian commanders discharged.[34]

In August 1915, Vorontsov-Dashkov was replaced as viceroy by the tsar's uncle, Grand Duke Nikolai Nikolaevich, former supreme commander of the Russian armies. As the veteran administrator prepared to leave Tiflis, the Armenians expressed their grief at his departure, and the city duma made him an honorary citizen of Tiflis. Pointedly, neither the Georgian nobility nor representatives of the Azerbaijani community appeared to bid him farewell.[35]

The war was genuinely unpopular among Georgians and Azerbaijanis, and the steady flow of Armenian refugees from Turkey into Transcaucasia only served to exacerbate the deteriorating economic situation. Social and ethnic tensions fused. Outbursts of resentment against shopkeepers had both a class and national content.[36] Shortages of food and other supplies in the cities of Caucasia, letters from the front complaining of the lack of food, clothing, and even weapons added to the accumulated hostility of many years against the tsarist regime. At all levels of society discontent was turning once again into revolutionary opposition, but no local initiative was taken.

When Khatisov went to Moscow at the end of 1916 for a conference of the Union of Cities, Prince Lvov, the liberal president of the union, outlined a secret plan to have the tsar replaced by Grand Duke Nikolai Nikolaevich. As the new year began, Khatisov visited the grand duke in Tiflis and told him of the conspiracy, but the viceroy rejected the plot. Interestingly enough, the grand duke did not report this "treason" to anyone, indicating how widely the disenchantment with the regime of Nicholas II had spread. Social democrats were discussing Georgian independence, while at the very top of society alternatives to the tsar's rule were being sought. The experiment in constitutional monarchy had failed to bring society and the state together. Within two months women in Petrograd went out onto the streets in demonstrations for bread. The February Revolution of 1917 had begun.

After a century in the Russian empire, Georgia had recovered the possibility of shaping her own political future. Transformed by the Russian "gathering" of Georgian lands, the economic and social integration of diverse Georgian territories under the impact of market relations and easier communication, and the intellectual awakening stirred by the noble intelligentsia, Georgia had acquired many of the attributes of nationhood. The

Mensheviks provided a confident and articulate national leadership with support in almost all classes of society. Both workers and peasants had been mobilized effectively in the quarter-century before the revolution and had created political institutions of their own. Yet the national awakening and the social development in the country had taken place in a particular multinational context, one in which Russians occupied the administrative hierarchy and Armenians controlled the heights of the economy. Georgians were numerically dominant in Tiflis and Kutaisi provinces, but in terms of political and economic power they were the least powerful nationality.

The century of Russian rule had prepared Georgians for statehood, but its full realization presented dangers and difficulties. Aware of the risks of going it alone, the social democratic leadership refrained from declaring Georgia independent in the first year of revolution and sought the best solution to its political dilemmas within the new revolutionary Russia.

REVOLUTIONARY AND SOVIET GEORGIA

PART THREE

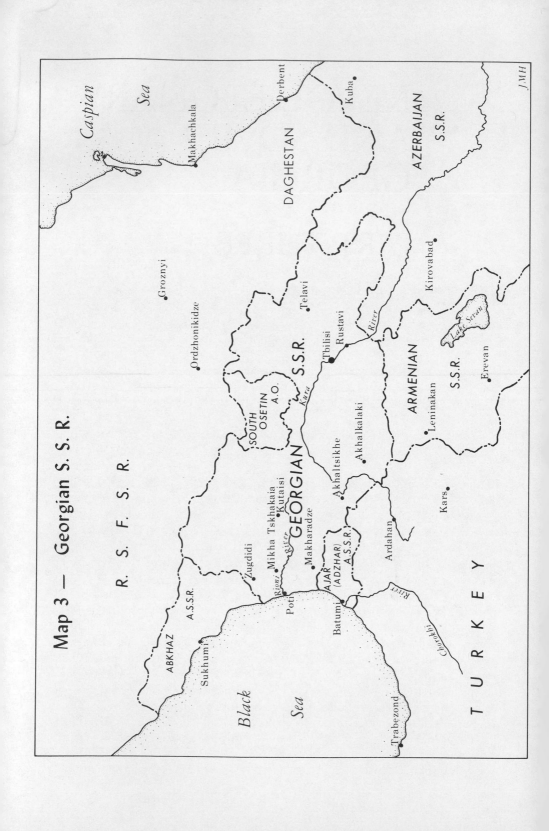

Map 3 — Georgian S. S. R.

9 Revolution and Republic

"Mtavrobadze has died," the telegram read. To the Georgian social democrats in Tiflis, this cryptic communication from their comrades in Petrograd was clear. The government (*mtavroba* in Georgian) had fallen. The long-awaited revolution had come.[1]

The February Revolution of 1917 has been referred to as the "united revolution," or even the "unanimous revolution," for it was a broadly popular event supported by every social class in the country except those closest to the imperial family. Carried out by workers and soldiers in the capital, the revolution was largely spontaneous, the culmination of grievances over the conduct of the war, the lack of food, fuel, and other supplies in the city, and the general disaffection with the government of Nicholas II.[2] The war had placed an insupportable burden on an already weakened political system, which had been unable either to evolve into a truly constitutional monarchy or to revert to the autocracy of the years before 1905.

In the last prewar years a deep social crisis had accompanied the brief spurt of industrial growth, and workers in the capital, particularly those in metallurgy, had accelerated the strike movement and increased their political activity. Already on the eve of the war, as Leopold H. Haimson has shown, the most militant socialists, the Bolsheviks, were making deep inroads among the urban workers in Petrograd and other large cities.[3] Although in the spring of 1917 the alienation of many workers from the rest of society seemed to have abated temporarily and a spirit of cooperation between the government and the lower classes emerged, already by early summer the signs of a rapid radicalization of workers and soldiers were apparent to acute observers.

Both in central Russia and Transcaucasia Marxist intellectuals appeared at the head of the revolutionary workers and soldiers in the course of 1917. In both places they were faced with a fundamental dilemma—the "objective" stage of development of Russian society, which had only partially been transformed by capitalism, was not yet set for the transition to socialism; but the "subjective" aims of many of the key actors in the revolution were directed toward capitalist relations and a more egalitarian and democratic social and political order.

From Lenin's return to Russia in April, the Bolsheviks called for "soviet power," which was equivalent to a demand for moving beyond the "bourgeois-democratic" revolution that most Marxists believed was then appropriate for Russia. But their former comrades, the Mensheviks, refused to disregard the low level of Russian development; they advocated the restraint of radical impulses within the framework of a democratic polity and an essentially capitalist economy. In Russia proper the Bolsheviks would within eight months come to power and attempt to implement their vision of Russia's "socialist" future; only in Georgia would the Mensheviks be able to demonstrate the possibilities of a democratic alternative in the midst of an intensifying social revolution.

In Transcaucasia as in central Russia, the February Revolution gave birth, not to a single political authority, but to what contemporaries referred to as *dvoevlastie* (dual power). Even before the new Provisional Government in Petrograd could designate its local agency in Transcaucasia (the Osobyi Zakavkazskii Komitet or Ozakom), the workers of Tiflis and Baku had elected their own representatives to local soviets (councils). At first the soldiers met separately, and the old city dumas continued to function. But very soon after the tsarist authorities abdicated their power, the workers' soviets emerged as the principal centers of power in Caucasian cities. In Tiflis the Georgian social democrats, under the leadership of Noe Zhordania, took control of the soviet. The soviet moved into the palace evacuated by the last viceroy, and the tricolor flag of the Romanovs was replaced by a red flag.[4]

But in contrast to the conflicts in central Russia, the political struggle of the workers' soviet with the local government and the propertied middle class was quite muted. The Tiflis executive committee, made up of spokesmen of various social and political groups, very rapidly came under the influence of the soviet. With the democratization of political power in the city and the entrance of the lower classes into politics through the soviet, the power of the bourgeois-dominated municipal duma simply eroded. The Ozakom, as Zhordania pointed out to the soviet leadership, was made up of nationalists who did not have the confidence of the "democracy."[5] In the spring of 1917 official authorities sanctioned by the Provisional Government had only as much power as they had support from the soviet and the populace. The soviet alone could bring crowds into the streets, order the soldiers to fire, and compel obedience to its decrees.

The Tiflis soviet adopted the basic view of the revolution outlined by its chairman, Zhordania. Three main forces, he argued, had made the revolution: the working class, the revolutionary army, and the progressive bourgeoisie. Unity among these three groups was imperative for victory. In essence this meant that the proletariat should curb its demands for the immediate future in order not to frighten the bourgeoisie and drive it into alliance with the Right. The errors of 1905, which had led to the isolation of the working class, should not be repeated. Therefore the soviet resolved to support the Provisional Government "insofar as" (*postol'ku, poskol'ku*) it would support the interests of the democratic republic. Both the workers' soviet and the soviet of the Tiflis garrison came out in favor of the Petrograd soviet's March 14 declaration on the war: refusing to support the war effort unconditionally "to a victorious conclusion," but rather advocating the pursuit of a "democratic peace without annexations or indemnities."[6]

The fragile unity of the revolutionary front was breached in the second month of revolution. The soldiers, the great majority of whom were Russian and whose party sympathies were closest to the Socialist Revolutionaries (SRs), became agitated in April over nationalist efforts to establish autonomy for Georgia. The soldiers opposed any movement toward separation from Russia, and the social democratic leaders of the soviet assured the garrison that "extraordinary measures" would be taken against the nationalists. Discussion of autonomy was curtailed in the press, and armed units formed by the various nationalities were disbanded. When the First Congress of the Caucasian army met in late April, the soldiers made clear their opposition to separatism by urging postponement of the "national question" until the constituent assembly.[7]

In the stratified ethnic conglomerate of Tiflis, Zhordania's three major revolutionary forces were three different social classes made up predominantly of three different ethnic groups and influenced primarily by three different political parties. The workers, as noted, were largely Georgian and Menshevik; the soldiers were Russian peasants and supported the SRs; and the "progressive bourgeoisie" was largely Armenian and politically divided between the Dashnaks and the liberal parties (the Kadets and their local Armenian ally, the Armenian People's Party). Every issue that arose in 1917—the eight-hour day, the question of the war, the coalition government, Georgian national autonomy, or soviet power—was debated and decided by balancing the competing interests of these contending political actors.

The loose alliance of the parties in the Tiflis soviet was sorely tested by the successive political crises in Petrograd. The Provisional Government's inability to maintain credibility without the active participation of prominent members of the Petrograd soviet forced the Mensheviks and the SRs to agree reluctantly at the end of April to a coalition government. But the Mensheviks in Tiflis vigorously opposed socialists sitting in the same government with members of the propertied classes. Zhordania argued for a purely bourgeois government, without Kadet leader Pavl Miliukov and those like him who favored an "annexationist" peace. For the Georgian Mensheviks, like their comrades in Russia, the issue of the nature of the government was crucial, for it would establish not only which social class would have its interests promoted by the state but also whether the "bourgeois-democratic" revolution would continue or be transformed into a "socialist" one.

Sharing the Menshevik view that the essential preconditions for a socialist revolution simply did not exist in Russia, Zhordania concluded that the parties of the "democracy" should neither form their own government nor join an essentially bourgeois coalition. For the Mensheviks in Georgia (unlike Tsereteli and Chkheidze in Petrograd), the interests of the lower classes were simply understood to be opposed to those of the propertied classes. Gegechkori told the Tiflis soviet: "If the socialist wing of the Provisional Government acts in the interests of the democracy but without a socialist outlook, then it will deserve the just protests of the proletariat; if it acts in the interests of the proletariat, then this will alienate the bourgeoisie from the other revolutionary strata of society, and this will be the beginning of the end."[8]

Early in April the Petrograd soviet clashed with Miliukov over the government's war policy. Crowds in the street backed the soviet and forced Miliukov's resignation. The "April Crisis" forced changes in the first Provisional Government and intensified the tensions in the democratic alliance of workers and soldiers in Tiflis. The Menshevik-led workers' soviet opposed formation of a coalition government (April 29) and promised it only conditional (*postol'ku, poskol'ku*) support (May 6). The soldiers' soviet, led by the Socialist Revolutionaries, came out for unconditional support of the new government (May 16), defeating a motion by Zhordania. The Mensheviks tried to hold the front together by merging the two soviets (May 26), and Bolsheviks who agitated among the soldiers against the war were arrested.[9] Not surprisingly, Menshevik efforts to keep the Bolsheviks within a common social democratic organization failed. The Bolsheviks formed their own party in early June, sharply separating themselves and their advocacy of "all power to the soviets!" from the moderate socialists who supported, however tentatively, the coalition government.

The Tiflis Bolsheviks were supported largely by militant soldiers and, to some extent, Russian workers. For the first two months of revolution the only social democratic newspaper in the Russian language was *Kavkazskii rabochii* (Caucasian Worker), the organ of the Bolshevik faction; the Mensheviks' *Bor'ba* (Struggle) did not appear until May. Bolsheviks began to make serious inroads among the soldiers once it became clear that the government, instead of bringing the war to a speedy conclusion, was planning a major campaign in the summer.

Embarrassed by the so-called Kerensky offensive, a desperate attempt by the weakened Russian army to reverse recent losses to the Germans, the Tiflis soviet on June 23 adopted a lukewarm resolution calling the offensive "one of the military episodes in the world war which in no way changes our aims in it." The next day four thousand soldiers gathered in the Aleksandr Garden and adopted a Bolshevik resolution calling for the end of the offensive.[10] Following the lead of their comrades in Petrograd, the Tiflis Bolsheviks organized a protest march for June 25. As in the capital, the moderate socialists tried to coopt the demonstration by rescheduling it and providing their own slogans and orators, but the demonstrators, some ten thousand soldiers, shouted down the Menshevik speakers and applauded only the Bolsheviks. This meeting also adopted a Bolshevik resolution opposing the Kerensky offensive, and added a call for a government dominated by the soviet.

The sudden radicalization of the Tiflis garrison was a great victory for the Caucasian Bolsheviks and a most serious threat to the Mensheviks. The army, the most potent force in the revolution, had moved from patriotic support for the war effort to an active opposition to any offensive action. Its enthusiasm for the Provisional Government, on which it had based its hopes for an end to the war, had simply evaporated with the June offensive.

The Mensheviks, fearing civil war in the city, acted resolutely to head off a crisis. When the Left demanded that new elections be called for the Tiflis soviet, to reflect the shift toward greater radicalism, the Mensheviks rejected the demand and decided instead to form a new military force from among their supporters. Mensheviks and Bolsheviks began an intensive campaign for the loyalty of the Tiflis garrison. It was also a struggle for power in the city, and its outcome would determine whether the Georgian working class or the Russian soldiery would decide the political fate of central Transcaucasia.

Events in Petrograd in July—the ill-fated uprising of radical military units with the tentative support of the Bolshevik party, the subsequent suppression of the Bolsheviks, and the formation of a new government under Aleksandr Kerensky—marked a temporary halt in the leftward drift of the revolution both in the capital and in Tiflis. For the first time the Tiflis soviet approved the coalition government and warned of the danger of counter-revolution from the Left. Rallying behind the Central Executive Committee (TsIK) of the Petrograd soviet, the Tiflis soviet prohibited any further meetings of soldiers in the Aleksandr Garden.[11]

By the late summer of 1917 the question of power, of the kind of authoritative government to be formed, was the central political issue in Petrograd and in Tiflis. Despite the compounded difficulties of maintaining a government of "all the vital forces of the nation," the SRs and the majority Mensheviks in Petrograd, led by Iraklii Tsereteli, backed Kerensky as he negotiated with representatives of the propertied classes. But their view that the coalition government must be continued was no longer shared by significant political forces, including members of the major liberal party, the Constitutional Democrats (Kadets), who had already concluded that compromise with the soviet would lead the country into anarchy. Leading political figures and conservative elements in the army conspired to eliminate soviet influence and establish a dictatorship headed by General Kornilov. The attempted coup in late August was thwarted by railroad workers, and all over the country workers and soldiers registered their hostility toward the upper and middle classes (*tsenzovoe obshchestvo*) by passing resolutions of no confidence in the government. When news of Kornilov's mutiny arrived in Tiflis, the soviet came out once again against coalition with the bourgeoisie and this time called for a democratic socialist government (September 2).[12]

Having failed to convince the party leadership in Petrograd that the coalition must be abandoned, the Georgian Mensheviks were isolated, along with Iulii Martov's small group of Menshevik Internationalists. At the Democratic Conference, called in Petrograd to solve the power question, the majority of Russia's Mensheviks stubbornly held on to the notion of coalition, even as popular support for the Kerensky government evaporated.

The major beneficiaries of the radicalization of the lower classes were the Bolsheviks, and on October 25 they seized power in Petrograd. The Mensheviks of Georgia refused to compromise with this "usurpation" of state power, and within weeks the deadly struggle over the Tiflis garrison was revived. The Mensheviks acted swiftly and disarmed the Bolshevik soldiers with the aid of their own Red Guards (November 29).[13] As winter approached, the soldiers drifted northward, leaving the front bare, Georgia in the uncontested hands of the Mensheviks, and the Bolsheviks with no significant base of support in Transcaucasia, except in the city of Baku.

Through much of 1917 the long-established social classes of Transcaucasia had provided the lines along which conflicts broke out. Economic pressures and the question of state power, along with the issue of the war, had relegated ethnic matters to the background. Occasionally they had come to the fore, but usually intertwined with social issues or the political debates then raging. Ethnic conflicts had appeared most volatilely in the newly elected municipal duma, consistently dominated by the Armenian middle class before 1917. With a fully democratic franchise the Georgian Mensheviks were swept to power in the duma, and they effectively excluded the Armenians from city government. The Armenian mayor, Khatisov, was replaced by a Georgian, Nikolai Eliava. Within the ornate duma building the Dashnaks accused the social democrats of being "Georgian chauvinists," and serious debate was drowned by mutual accusations of nationalism. Muslims too complained through their representatives to the Transcaucasian Central Muslim Committee that the Islamic masses were being systematically ignored and demanded representation in the Ozakom.[14]

But as deeply felt as these ethnic tensions were, the hope persisted through 1917 that democratization and national self-determination would resolve them constitutionally. However, after the October Revolution and the dispersal by the Petrograd Bolsheviks of the Constituent Assembly (January 5 [18], 1918), the institution on which constitutional hopes had been pinned, the overt expression and manifestation of nationalist feelings began to dominate the political scene in Transcaucasia.

By early 1918 the political situation in Transcaucasia had changed dramatically, as the Russian army "voted with its feet" against the war. Early in February the Turkish army began moving across the prewar border, a serious threat to the Caucasian peoples; the only resistance came from irregular Armenian units. With the army abandoning Transcaucasia, the Russian national element was severely reduced in the territory. Inhibitions to discussing the national question and moving toward separation from Russia were removed. Soldiers leaving the front met hostility from the local peoples; in one incident, at Shamkhor, they were forcibly disarmed and hundreds were massacred. The central political issue became self-defense, and in the context of Russian retreat and Turkish advance, it inevitably took on an ethnic dimension.

Since both the Georgian Mensheviks and the Tiflis Dashnaks considered the Bolshevik government in central Russia illegitimate and irresponsible and since no local organ of authority existed for Transcaucasia, a debate on the regional government began. None of the major political parties was yet prepared to move toward separation, and the SRs particularly were suspicious of any separatist tendencies. But the need to create a united regional political authority led first to the creation of the Transcaucasian Commissariat (Zavkom; November 14, 1917) and later to the establishment of a legislature, the Seim (January 23, 1918).[15] Bolshevik sympathizers in the Aleksandr Garden protested the opening of the Seim on February 23 (new calendar); they were met by machine-gun fire.

In response to the real separation from Russia and the advancing threat from Turkey, whether one was a worker or an industrialist became less relevant than one's relationship to the Muslim danger and the loss of Russian protection. The central Bolshevik government was forced to sign away Kars, Ardahan, and Batumi to the Turks at Brest Litovsk, and Armenian and Georgian military units at the front were left alone in a life-and-death struggle with a foreign enemy. The Azerbaijanis, who had long felt victims of the Christian overlords and bourgeoisie in Caucasia, welcomed the support and leverage offered by their Turkish brethren. Thus, within months of the October Revolution, the Caucasian political order had totally fragmented along ethnic lines.

On April 22, 1918, the Seim, pressured by the Turkish military to separate Transcaucasia from Russia, voted to declare independence.[16] The pro-Turkish Musavat party enthusiastically supported the decree of separation, but the Mensheviks and Dashnaks took this step reluctantly. The Kadets and Russian SRs opposed the declaration and were joined in their feeble opposition by the Bolsheviks. The fragile Democratic Federative Republic of Transcaucasia lasted only a month before each major nationality decided to take its fate into its own hands. The Turks took the fortress of

Kars and the port of Batumi, invading Erevan province while officially recognizing the new republic. From Batumi they delivered ultimatums to the government of Transcaucasia demanding territory and extraterritorial rights. As they continued their advance toward Baku, the Turks met with a sympathetic response from local Muslims.

The Armenians managed to prevent the capture of Erevan, but with no mutual interests holding the three Caucasian nationalities together they were soon abandoned by the Georgians and Azerbaijanis. The Georgian leaders realized that the embryonic republic was doomed, and on May 26, 1918, they responded to offers of German aid and declared Georgia an independent state.[17] After 117 years Georgia's official connection to Russia was severed, and a brief experiment in independence could be attempted while Bolshevik Russia was embroiled in civil war.

By 1917 Georgians not only had a sense of their own history and national character, but they had also developed their own national leadership in the social democrats, a cohesive and confident group of national Marxist intellectuals who enjoyed support among the peasants as well as among their original constituents, the workers. But population increase and growing cultural awareness had not given the Georgians political or economic power in their own country until the revolution of 1917 provided the Georgians with the first important political institution (the soviet) they had controlled since the 1870s.

Because the social democrats so easily dominated Georgian politics through 1917, there was no particular urgency about implementing political autonomy. The conjuncture of events that led to independence was in no sense the controlled result of social democratic aspirations or planning. Despite the hopes of the small number of Georgian nationalists, independence was not the desired goal. Rather it was the physical and political separation from Bolshevik Russia created by the civil war and the immediate threat of a Turkish invasion that forced the Georgians, Azerbaijanis, and Armenians to break officially with Russia. The Georgians now had the full panoply of political power and the possibility of building a new sovereign state.

On May 26, 1918, a new Georgian national flag (crimson with one black and one white stripe) was raised over the palace of the former viceroy in Tiflis and flew alongside the red flag as the leaders of the new government spoke to the crowds from the balcony and national songs were sung. The first task of the prime minister, Noe Ramishvili, and the foreign minister, Akaki Chkhenkeli, was to open secret negotiations with the Germans in Poti. Without the knowledge of the Turkish diplomats waiting in Batumi, the new Georgian government signed agreements with General von Lossow that established a German protectorate over the fledgling republic. In exchange for diplomatic recognition and protection from the increasing territorial appetite of the Turks, the Georgians gave the German empire use of their railroads, free circulation of German money in Georgia, all ships in Georgian ports, and a monopoly over mining and the export of raw materials. A few days later Ramishvili concluded an agreement with the Turkish command in Batumi, accepting the loss of Akhaltsikhe and Akhalkalaki and permitting Turkish use of Georgian railroads.[18] On June 4, the Ottoman empire formally recognized the Georgian state. German troops arrived in Tiflis on June 10.

Independence and the turn toward Germany were defended by Georgian leaders as the only alternative left after Russian withdrawal and Turkish advance, but in fact, like the "Russian orientation" of the century before, the alliance with Germany was more than an expediency. The shift to the Germans had its roots in a long and growing intellectual affection for Germany as a center of European culture. Georgian social democrats had been admirers of German social democracy since the late nineteenth century and had looked with envy at its firm roots in the trade unions and its successful participation in parliamentary politics. At the other extreme of the political spectrum, Georgian nationalists had nourished dreams of restoring the Georgian monarchy with German help, and early in the war had established ties with the German foreign ministry.[19]

Zhordania later remembered that a "Germanophile mood dominated in Georgia" at the beginning of the war, but no one was prepared to join the pro-German nationalists in their plans for an anti-Russian uprising.[20] Now, nearly four years later, the Georgian Mensheviks tied themselves to imperial Germany for reasons of expedience and affection for the advanced West. German power in Eastern Europe was so great at the time that not only had the Bolsheviks been forced to make concessions at Brest Litovsk, but their opponents, the Kadets, had allied with the once-hated enemies of Russia in their efforts to overthrow the Soviets.

As the summer of 1918 turned to fall, Georgia's leaders were made aware of the consequences of their German orientation. When negotiations with the Germans had begun in May, the outlook for a Central Powers victory in Europe seemed bright. Paris was bombarded by German artillery in June. The Turkish advance eastward climaxed in the fall of Baku on September 15. But by the end of September Bulgaria was unable to carry on its military efforts and left the war. Within a month the Turks were suing for peace, and in early November Germany signed an armistice to prevent further losses at the front and revolution at home. "The catastrophe came unexpectedly for everyone."[21] Georgia's German orientation was now bankrupt, and its most enthusiastic advocate, Chkhenkeli, who had spent nearly his whole tenure as foreign minister in Berlin, resigned his post to Evgenii Gegechkori. Within weeks the British replaced the Germans and the Turks as the dominant foreign power in Transcaucasia. The British were cool toward the Georgians, suspicious of a government so willing to ally with Germany. Given the hostility between the British and Georgians, British influence in the country was limited. In the absence of overwhelming outside direction the Georgian leaders set out to establish their independent course.

From its inception in the mid-1890s, the Georgian social democratic movement had accommodated within its ranks both dedicatedly internationalist socialists and a variety of socialist nationalists. Zhordania's earliest drafts of a party program had been criticized by several of his comrades for their implicit nationalism, and in later years both Georgian and non-Georgian social democrats had repeatedly raised alarms at manifestations of support for national autonomy or cultural nationalism. Indeed the social democratic movement in Georgia did become so closely identified with one ethnic group, the Georgians, that its more "internationalist" leaders, like Iraklii Tsereteli, were never really included among the core leadership. Tsereteli's Russophilia stood in sharpest contrast with Chkhenkeli's ethnocentrism. Zhordania steered a middle course; willing as he was to find a political solution within a Russian federation, at key moments he reaffirmed an enthusiasm for political autonomy.

The issue remained a sensitive if somewhat muted subject in party circles until the splintering of Transcaucasia along ethnic lines forced all the Transcaucasian leaders to confront the question of national independence. The *Oblastnoi komitet* (Obkom, the social democrats' regional committee) and the Tiflis Menshevik committee resolved that Georgia must be declared independent. The next day, one of the founders of Caucasian social democracy, the Armenian S. T. Arkomed (Gevork Gharajian) resigned from the Obkom "because of the impossibility for me to go along with the policy of Chkhenkelism, which had sustained victory over revolutionary Social Democracy," a symbolic but politically impotent gesture. The Menshevik movement had, in the views of its socialist critics, moved closer to those parties whose advocacy of Georgian autonomy or independence had made them the bitterest enemies of the socialists. A small group of internationalist social democrats, most of them Armenian and Russian, began issuing their own newspaper (*Sotsial-Demokrat*) directed against the nationalism of their former Georgian comrades.[22]

The enthusiasm many social democrats may have felt for Georgian independence was tempered by the dilemma posed for socialists as the ruling party in what they conceived to be a "bourgeois" republic. At the first general session of the Tiflis soviet after independence (June 1, 1918), Iraklii Tsereteli defended the party's actions as the only alternative to total destruction, and the soviet accepted the necessity of the act. Following the same instincts that had led him to take a hard line against Bolshevik opposition in Petrograd, Tsereteli advocated strong measures against the opponents of independence. The new government closed *Znamia truda* (Banner of Labor), the local organ of the SRs, for editorializing against independence.[23]

A week later Tsereteli told the joint meeting of the Transcaucasian Center of Soviets and the Tiflis executive committee that the mistakes of the moderates in central Russia should not be repeated in the Caucasus: there should be no duality of power. The soviets had to surrender their power to a legally constituted government.

> The cause of our defeat was the absence of one fully-empowered democratic state authority. The democracy ought to create one. The revolutionary organizations of one class must refuse to take on state functions and return to their true role, to the leadership of their class.[24]

The meeting voted to back a strong government and to limit the activity of the soviets to the defense of working-class interests. This policy was adopted the next day by the Tiflis soviet and the staff of the Red Guards, both of which repudiated any pretensions to governmental power. All power was delegated to a "united democratic government" to be headed by Noe Zhordania.[25]

As prime minister in a socialist government, Zhordania understood the paradox of administering a bourgeois state. A year earlier he had strongly condemned Tsereteli's policy of participation in the coalition government in Petrograd. But rather than abdicate power to the feeble Georgian bourgeoisie, represented ostensibly by the National Democratic Party, Zhordania now implemented his notion of a government of the "democracy," a government representing the lower classes but carrying out the reforms appropriate to the bourgeois stage.

Borrowing from the German socialist theorist Karl Kautsky, Zhordania argued that "the first steps of the victorious proletariat will be, not social reforms, but the introduction of democratic institutions, the realization of the party's minimum program, and only afterwards the gradual transition to the socialist maximum program."[26] The Georgian state, limited as it had to be by the level of social development, "cannot avoid serving in one way or another . . . the interests of the bourgeoisie." Social democracy was compelled to "play the principal role in building a modern state . . . The question arises: how to reconcile our Social Democratic ideology with the work of creating bourgeois institutions; how to do this so that in the process the party does not go off the track of Social Democracy and turn into a petty-bourgeois party." At the same time there was no reason to fear opposition to socialist rule from the upper and middle classes. Given the weakness of the Georgian aristocracy and bourgeoisie, Zhordania concluded that there was "no social base for reaction here, for restoration or constitutional monarchy." The major danger to democracy in a primarily peasant country like Georgia, he asserted, comes from the village, but the government can guarantee "support for the revolution and the rule of democracy" by satisfying the peasants' foremost demand and promulgating a land reform.[27]

The peasantry presented the most serious internal problem for the

Mensheviks. The fall of the monarchy had led to a general questioning of authority, and Caucasian peasants had almost immediately ceased paying their redemption payments and other taxes to the state and either refused altogether to pay dues to the landlords or demanded that they be reduced. Nobles in Georgia protested to the impotent Ozakom, the local agency of the Provisional Government, that the peasants were cutting down forests and using pastureland that belonged to the landlords or the state. The Ozakom issued a decree requiring peasants to pay their prerevolutionary obligations, but peasants simply disregarded the order. When the commissar of Gori tried to enforce the Ozakom decree, the peasants appealed to the chairman of the local Menshevik organization, who in turn sent a delegation to Zhordania in Tiflis. The commissar was replaced, and to the chagrin of the nobles further attempts to collect dues and taxes proved futile.[28]

In the first days of the revolution Zhordania had set forth his analysis that its moving forces were the proletariat, the army, and the liberal bourgeoisie; the peasantry was not mentioned. Despite their long experience in organizing a peasant revolutionary movement in western Georgia, the Menshevik leaders shared with their Russian comrades a deep suspicion of the progressive potential of the peasantry. The Transcaucasian Bolsheviks, more because of their greater opposition to cooperation with the bourgeoisie than any genuine faith in the peasants, included the peasants and urban poor alongside the proletariat in their list of moving forces, while conspicuously leaving out the bourgeoisie.[29]

Yet the Mensheviks, more than any other party in Transcaucasia, had roots in the countryside and palpable support from the villagers. The Caucasian SRs held a dominant position only among the "peasants in uniform," and the First Congress of the Caucasian army (April–May 1917) had voted overwhelmingly for the SR resolution calling for socialization of all land. The Menshevik program, which asked only for confiscation of state and church lands, had been rejected, though all parties agreed that full implementation of the land reform should await the constituent assembly. A few weeks later, the Mensheviks won the crucial vote at the Transcaucasian Congress of Soviets of Workers' and Peasants' Deputies (in which peasants were poorly represented), where it was decided that *otrezki* (the lands cut off from peasant holdings and given to nobles in the emancipation settlement) would be returned to peasants, and lands confiscated from the state and church could be rented by peasants.[30]

By late spring 1917 the Mensheviks had been sufficiently impressed by the activity of the peasants to include them in their formulation of the "moving forces" of the revolution.[31] But they consistently opposed the more radical stand of the Bolsheviks and the SRs in favor of abolishing private property in land. Their prerevolutionary efforts in the countryside made them nearly invulnerable in rural Georgia; the June Congress of Peasant Deputies of Transcaucasia adopted the moderate social democratic agrarian program by a nearly two-to-one margin. Georgian and Azerbaijani deputies voted for the Menshevik proposal; most Armenians followed the Dashnaks and the Russians followed the SRs, both parties having come out for nationalization.[32] All parties, except the Bolsheviks, were committed to delaying a final solution of the land question until the constituent assembly, so no further action was taken by the leaders of the Caucasian soviets or party organizations until the October Revolution.

Faced with the Bolshevik "Decree on Land," which essentially adopted the SR principle of socialization, and the signs of growing impatience among Caucasian peasants, the Mensheviks of Tiflis decided to implement their own local land reform. The Zavkom, the successor to Ozakom, which from November 1917 acted as a fully empowered government, had to contend with opposition to nationalization from the Muslim leaders and decided to avoid confrontation by excluding *wakuf* lands (lands held by religious institutions) from the reforms. The attempt by the Armenian catholicos to exempt their church lands as well was rejected, however.[33] On December 16, 1917, the Zavkom decreed that state, church, and private land above a certain norm was to be transferred to a national land fund to be directed by land committees. Three months later the Seim established the norms—seven desiatinas for plots producing valuable cash crops, fifteen for grain-producing land, and forty for pastureland. Exceptions were later made for larger holdings deemed to have value for the national economy.[34] Basically the laws of December 16 and March 20, 1918, took the bulk of noble land away from the nobles without compensation, leaving them significantly smaller plots in most cases. Poor peasants whose land fell below the norms were able to lease land from the state land fund, but the private market in land was eliminated.[35] The reform had relevance only for Georgia, for the Muslim landlords who controlled much of the land in the Azerbaijani and Armenian areas opposed these laws. Ironically the decrees of 1917–1918 passed by all-Transcaucasian governments marked the high-water mark of a leftist agrarian policy in the region. With the establishment of the independent Georgian republic in May 1918, the social democratic leaders took another look at the land question.

The first months of the new republic were not only occupied with the crucial problems of forming ties with the Germans and fending off the Turks but also with serious internal threats to the establishment of order and authority. In the northern mountainous regions of Georgia, first in Dusheti and later in Racha, Tianeti, and Lechkhumi districts, peasant dissatisfaction with terms of the land reform and the activity of the land committees created conditions for open rebellion. The smallholders of Dusheti were incensed that large estates were being transferred to state control rather than turned over to the nearest village.[36]

Bolsheviks, many of them former soldiers, began agitating in these areas and organized armed detachments of peasants, one of which attacked (but failed to take) the town of Zugdidi on June 27. In Racha Shamshe Lezhava led a guerrilla band, and in Lechkhumi Sasha Gegechkori commanded three hundred men. The Ossetians of Sachkheri also worked with the Bolsheviks, who were in close touch with the territorial center of the Communist party in the North Caucasus and the soviet government in the Terek region.[37] With little hesitation the Mensheviks sent Jugeli's People's Guards (formerly the Red Guards) to the north, where they carried out a brutal campaign against the rebels. Villages were burned; the death penalty was reinstated, as was censorship; and one by one the insurrections were put down.[38] Minister of Agriculture Noe Khomeriki realized early that the land reforms of 1917–1918 did not go far enough for the peasants, who opposed leaving the land in the control of local government and renting it to the peasantry. They looked upon the lands leased to them as their own private property and wanted to buy the remaining land from the noble landlords. Buying and selling went on, despite the legal prohibitions. Khomeriki was convinced that the government had no choice but to deal with this strong tendency toward private property by transferring much of the state land fund into private hands. At conferences of the land committees and at the Menshevik party congress in November the view prevailed that land should pass to the peasantry as private property. The congress resolved that most land should go to landless peasants, that other land could be sold at low prices, and that only land with "broad social significance" would be held by the state or transferred to *zemstva* (local governing bodies).[39] Finally, by the law of January 28, 1919, the peasants were given the land as private property with the right to buy and sell. The SRs, Socialist Federalists, and National Democrats voted against the bill, but Khomeriki answered those critics who opposed turning confiscated land over to private smallholders: "Our agrarian reform destroyed the principle of feudal property. In general we neither establish nor reject bourgeois private property; this is a fact of life with which, of course, the law has to deal."[40]

Inevitably complaints and resentments about the redistribution surfaced. In some districts where there were few large estates to be confiscated, the land shortages could not be alleviated locally; elsewhere the population was so dense that farmers received only tiny supplements to their small plots. In no district of Kutaisi province, for example, did the average peasant farm exceed 1.6 hectares; the situation was considerably better in Tiflis province, where the average plot ran from 4 to 7 hectares. To alleviate shortages, from the second half of 1918 the ministry moved more than eight thousand families to free lands in other districts. Besides the evident economic motivations, there were political considerations in some of these transfers. Georgian peasants were installed in the district of Gagra, for instance, a border region contested with the anti-Bolshevik Volunteer Army of General Denikin, and in Akhalkalaki and Akhaltsikhe, areas with Armenian populations that had been the source of considerable conflict between the Armenian and Georgian republics.[41]

The effects of the Georgian land reforms remain difficult to assess, but their basic contours can be discerned. A year and a half after the final reform law, Khomeriki confidently told the congress of Georgian social democrats that confiscation of noble lands above the set norms had been completed and that nine-tenths of that confiscated land had been turned over to peasants with little or no land. Nearly five thousand estates had been affected by the reform. More than 660,000 hectares of land had been taken from noble landlords, who were left with about 37,000 hectares. On the average, a noble ended up with a holding of about 10 hectares, usually more than his peasant neighbor.[42] The least fortunate peasants received the most land from the reform, and the state held the forests, much of the pastureland, and the waterways. The extent to which the confiscation and redistribution was actually carried out was quite extraordinary, given the fact that the Georgian lands had not been surveyed, that the ministry had few qualified people to carry out the technical aspects of the reform, and that the whole operation was largely completed in two years while the government was fighting off external enemies and internal rebellions.

Essentially the existing smallholding agricultural system that had always existed in Georgia was sanctified by the reform, although at long last the greater part of the nobles' lands (which peasants had always worked) was now in peasant hands. Since Georgia had had little large-scale production, the economy lost little in output as a result of confiscation, but more of the surplus was now consumed by the direct producers. The ultimate rationale by the Mensheviks for abandoning their 1906 program of municipalization of confiscated lands for outright grants to private property holders was simple expedience. There was no desire to thwart peasant desires and risk more unrest and economic dislocation. The socialists were content to oversee the abolition of "feudal vestiges," to live with private farming, and to leave a portion of the land to the nobles in order to maintain social peace.[43]

Both critics and sympathizers of the land reform have pointed out that turning the confiscated land over to private smallholders neither alleviated the problem of land shortage—there were still too many people on the land for the amount of cultivated land available—nor worked to increase output. Russian Menshevik M. Liadov argued that the only solution was formation of larger farms and intensification of agriculture.[44] In his generally supportive account of social democratic Georgia, Kautsky worried about the small surplus produced by small-scale agriculture and hoped that in the future the Georgian form of cooperative agriculture (*nadi*) would evolve into a widespread system of cultivation by the village communes.[45]

But a much more telling critique came from Bolsheviks like Pilipe [Filipp] Makharadze who condemned the reform for preserving noble property. The norms set by law (seven to forty desiatinas) gave nobles allotments large enough to be worked by hired labor. Moreover, in the absence of cadastral surveys, nobles fictitiously divided their families in order to receive additional allotments. The peasants were aware that land that could have been turned over to them had been left in the hands of a privileged class that had never worked the land. Now that buying and selling land was legal, norms for size of holding were meaningless and eventually would work to the benefit of the wealthy.[46] In another early Soviet work, Ia. Shafir, writing about the peasant uprising in Guria in 1919, reproduced a dialogue between a peasant and a Bolshevik agitator found in a report to the Menshevik government:

> "If the Menshevik government is not a noble [government], why does it leave the land to the nobles?" asked the peasants. They were answerd by the agitators: "The Mensheviks promised the land, but they do not want to give it because they themselves are nobles."[47]

The effect of the land reforms of 1917–1920 was to abridge the privileged status of the Georgian nobility but not to eliminate it as a class of landowners. Fifty years after the emancipation, Georgia's peasants finally held full title to their plots, the large estates had either been broken up or taken over by the state, and nobles had been reduced to petty proprietors like their peasant neighbors. The last vestiges of the seigneurial system had been removed, but, unlike Bolshevik Russia, Menshevik Georgia did not take all the land away from the nobility. To the Mensheviks the "bourgeois transformation" that had taken place with the establishment of private property in land conformed to the wishes of the majority of the peasantry and was consistent with the Mensheviks' understanding of the nature of the revolution at hand.

Given their position at the helm of a "bourgeois" state, their broad base among the peasantry, and the fact that they were now a party of the whole nation, the social democrats of Georgia were nevertheless careful to maintain and nurture their special relationship with the small and variegated working class. While the Bolsheviks managed at various times to find sympathizers among soldiers, mountaineers, and national minorities, very seldom were they able to make inroads into the Georgian working class. Workers not only made up the most active elements within the Menshevik party but were the backbone of the People's Guards, the weapon on which the government depended to disarm the Bolshevized soldiers of 1917, to disperse the rebel peasants of 1918–1919, and to defend the shifting frontiers of the republic against Armenians (1918), Denikin's Volunteer Army (1919), and finally the invading Red Army (1921).

Georgia's isolation from Russia, Azerbaijan, and the West in the years of independence had a devastating effect on its industrial economy. Though not nearly as miserable and helpless as the tiny Armenian republic, Georgia suffered from the disruption of trade with the other parts of the former tsarist empire and a general breakdown of internal economic relationships. Soviet scholars estimate that coal production fell nearly 50 percent from 1913 to 1919 and manganese dropped to about 13 percent of prewar production by 1920. The shortages of raw material caused reductions in industrial output; only about 60 percent of Georgia's largest plants managed to operate steadily.[48] The total number of workers fell. Unemployment, inflation and the resultant fall in real wages increased labor unrest and presented the Mensheviks with one of their most vexing dilemmas: how to reconcile their role as the traditional representative of working-class interests and their new position as head of a government representing the interests of the whole nation.

The two decades of social democratic activity among Georgian workers had established a trust in the Menshevik intelligentsia that served the government well. When workers began to question the wisdom of Georgia's separation from Russia and Bolsheviks argued that the shortages of goods were a direct result of that break, the minister of labor, Giorgi Eradze, was able to convince a mass meeting that independence had in fact saved Georgia from the ravages of the Russian civil war and the forced requisitioning of foodstuffs from the peasantry that the Bolsheviks had imposed on Russia. When Tiflis city workers went on strike to protest the municipality's failure to pay them, a united front of Menshevik-led institutions condemned the walkout. Not only the Tiflis soviet but even the council of trade unions opposed the strike and demanded sacrifices in the national interest.[49] In general workers showed restraint in their protests, though strike activity was widespread.

To stop the cycle of inflation and rising wages, the Ministry of Labor established a *tarifnaia palata* (wage board) in May 1919 to set wage rates.[50] Representatives of the trade unions (more than 56,000 workers were organized in Georgia) sat down with representatives of industry, the banks, and government in an official arbitration process expected to bring some order into the highly individualized negotiations between workers and employers. The Mensheviks preferred such policies of state mediation of economic disputes, rather than the outright nationalization favored by the Bolsheviks. Their success testifies to their skills in labor relations and the fact that class antagonisms in Georgia were not nearly as deep as they were in central Russian cities or even in Baku.

Georgian social democratic leaders frequently contrasted their moderate and democratic system of government and economy with the more centralized and dictatorial system in Soviet Russia. Based on their conviction that the preconditions did not exist for socialism, the Mensheviks held back from assaults on the capitalist mode of production. In August 1919, a state monopoly on manganese export to Europe was established, the forerunner of a general state monopoly on foreign trade. But such state intervention was exceptional, and the opposition parties called for more radical measures. The Bolsheviks demanded an end to capitalism; the SRs and Socialist Federalists more modestly argued for a "deepening of the revolution" and more radical economic policies as an alternative to political repression in the struggle against Bolshevism.[51]

The Mensheviks' hegemony over the urban workers of Georgia was so complete that they made few concessions to the left. The major representative body of workers, the Tiflis soviet, had given up its prerogatives to the government and the Georgian constituent assembly and was rarely called into session except to sanction positions taken by the government. In a real sense Georgia exemplified the social democratic ideal—a working class deferring to its socialist intelligentsia, prepared to follow its lead in building a democratic nation-state, and willing to wait for the distant victory of socialism.

Land reform and the economy were the social issues that concerned most people in Georgia, but three other critical problems occupied the bulk of the government's time from the declaration of independence to the invasion of the Red Army two years and nine months later: relations with Georgia's neighbors—Armenia, Azerbaijan, and the portion of southern Russia occupied by Denikin; the search for recognition of Georgian independence from the major Western powers; and the danger posed to the Mensheviks by local Communists and Soviet Russia.

Shortly after the republic was founded, conflict with the Armenians broke out over the border regions of Akhalkalaki, Borchalu, and Lori. These Armeno-Georgian marchlands had been held at various times by Turks, Armenians, and Georgians, but in the nineteenth century (and even more so during World War I), the Muslim population had been reduced and refugees from the Turkish massacres swelled the Armenian population. With the withdrawal of Turkish armies from Transcaucasia, Georgian forces occupied parts of northern Lori and Akhalkalaki, and Armenians moved into southern Lori and Pambak. Efforts at a peaceful solution to the territorial dispute failed, and in December 1918 fighting commenced.[52] Armenians in Georgia were subjected to a series of repressive measures—the suspension of their newspapers, arrests of Dashnak deputies to the city duma, extortion of money—in the name of state security. Only British intervention brought this short, inconclusive war to an end, but relations between the two republics and between Armenians and Georgians within the Georgian republic remained strained.

Georgia had no serious quarrels with Azerbaijan, but both faced a menacing presence on their northern frontiers—the Volunteer Army of General Anton Denikin. On June 16, 1919, delegates from Tiflis and Baku signed a mutual defense pact against the Russian threat. Although Georgia hoped to remain neutral in the Russian civil war, then raging between the pro-Bolshevik forces of central Russia and the anti-Soviet White armies, the antipathy between former tsarist officers and the social democrats who headed the Georgian government soon turned into open conflict. Denikin, attempting to reunite the old Russian empire, opposed Georgian separatism. After the failure of British efforts to mediate the border disputes between the Whites and the Georgians, Volunteer Army forces attacked the Georgians in the Sochi region (February 1919). A year later when peasant rebels near the Black Sea threatened the rear of the Volunteer Army, the White generals imagined Georgian complicity, and Denikin declared war on Georgia. By this time, however, the White armies were being driven back by the Red Army, and no real struggle with Georgia was undertaken. Indeed, a short time later the British, who were attempting to maintain cordial relations with both Denikin and the Georgians, convinced the general to recognize Georgian independence.[53] These good feelings had no consequences, however, for by early 1920 Denikin was about to leave Russia forever, and a new danger faced Georgia from the north—the Red Army.

Georgia, Armenia, and Azerbaijan managed to maintain independence in the brief period when the empires that had ruled Caucasia for centuries were themselves in disarray. As long as Russia was a defeated nation split by civil war and Turkey a vanquished empire with its coastal cities in the victors' hands, the peoples of Transcaucasia were able to contemplate a future free from their former overlords. But to guarantee their precarious and fragile independence, the three republics believed that they required material, military, and political support from the Western powers that had emerged victorious from World War I.

After November 1918, the dominant military authority in Transcaucasia was the British expeditionary force under Major General William M. Thomson, headquartered in Baku. At first British relations with the Germanophilic Georgians were cool, and Thomson had to pressure Foreign Minister Gegechkori into accepting an Allied occupation of Georgia. The British hoped to unify the anti-Bolshevik forces in Caucasia and Russia, but they were frustrated by a series of ethnic, territorial, and political disputes that ultimately reduced their policy in the Russian civil war to ruin. They managed to bring the border war between Armenia and Georgia to an end in late December 1918, but were less successful in reconciling the separatist ambitions of the Georgians with the British-sponsored Volunteer Army's plans for a unitary Russian state.[54]

The British government was divided on the degree of intervention into Transcaucasia. Lord Curzon, a leading member of Prime Minister Lloyd-George's war cabinet, argued for British support of the independent republics and advocated an active British presence in Baku and on the Baku-Batumi railroad, both to protect British interests and "to set the people on their legs there." Montague, secretary of state for India, objected to stationing troops in Caucasia, and Curzon replied, "You cannot take them away and have everybody cutting everybody else's throat." Foreign Secretary Balfour joined Montague in opposition to Curzon: "If they want to cut their own throats why not let them do it . . . I should say we are not going to spend all our money and men in civilising a few people who do not want to be civilised. We will protect Batum, Baku, the railroad between them, and the pipeline." After long discussions in December 1918, the British government decided to keep its troops in the Caucasus without clearly determining their future disposition. On December 31, the foreign office indicated to Georgian representatives in London that it viewed Georgia's independence "with sympathy" and would urge recognition at the forthcoming peace conference in Paris.[55]

The Transcaucasian republics each sent a delegation to the Paris peace conference in January 1919. All their appeals, however, failed ultimately to interest any major power in taking a mandate over the area or even one of the republics. Moreover, de facto recognition of their independence was delayed until all Western troops had been withdrawn from Transcaucasia (except for the British forces in Batumi). Only on January 12, 1920, did Chkheidze, Tsereteli, and the other members of the Georgian delegation in Paris receive from the Supreme Council of the Allied powers the de facto recognition of their government that they had been seeking for a year. Azerbaijan was recognized on the same day and Armenia on January 19. And that same day the Allied heads of government meeting in Paris decided that no troops would be sent to Transcaucasia to prevent a Bolshevik invasion; only arms, munitions, and food would be available. Britain, the principal power in the collapsing anti-Bolshevik intervention, was rapidly re-evaluating its policy toward Lenin's government, seeking an alternative to military confrontation.[56] On July 9, 1920, the last British troops were evacuated from Batumi and the city handed over to the Georgians. By that time the Red Army was already in Azerbaijan, and the Western powers had conceded the likelihood of a Soviet future for Georgia and Armenia.

Neither the Soviet Russian government nor the Caucasian Bolsheviks were consistent or united in their strategy for coming to power in Transcaucasia. In the weeks after the October Revolution, at the very moment when the Russian soldiers of the Caucasian front and the garrisons in Tiflis and Baku were turning to the Bolsheviks, local party leaders like Pilipe Makharadze were calling for restraint and caution.[57] The Transcaucasian regional committee proposed the "peaceful transfer of power" on the local level. Stepan Shahumian, the militant leader of the Baku Bolsheviks, convinced his associates in the spring of 1918 to adopt a more aggressive attitude, and from the end of March to the end of July 1918 Bolsheviks dominated the Baku soviet. But the siege of the city by the Turks and the soviet's decision to invite the British to defend Baku led to the fall of the Bolsheviks and the collapse of the so-called Baku Commune.[58]

In Georgia, on the other hand, Menshevik hegemony over most workers and peasants and their successful seizure of the arsenal in November 1917 influenced the local Bolsheviks to maintain a cautious and peaceful approach. After a Bolshevik-organized protest meeting at the opening of the Transcaucasian Seim was fired upon by forces sent by the Menshevik authorities (February 1918), the Bolsheviks decided to shift to an "underground" strategy. In western Georgia local Bolsheviks called for an armed uprising and began agitating among the peasants. But the Menshevik People's Guard was able to thwart the activity of the insurrectionists everywhere. At the end of May 1918 the Bolshevik Caucasian regional committee (Kavkraikom) was forced to move out of Georgia to Vladikavkaz in the North Caucasus, where they remained until early 1919.

The year 1919 marked the nadir of Bolshevik fortunes in Caucasia. Driven out of the North Caucasus by Denikin's advances, leading communist cadres such as "Sergo" Orjonikidze hid like fugitives in Tiflis. Only in Baku were the Communists able to secure a base of support among workers, though the existing trade unions and the "workers' conference" (which had replaced the disbanded soviet as the principal representative body for workers) were led by Mensheviks and SRs.[59] There was little contact between the Communists in Tiflis and Baku and even less with Moscow.

In the spring of 1919, the Baku Bolsheviks, influenced by the young survivor of the Baku Commune, Anastas Mikoyan, decided to adjust their strategy to take into account the fact that three national republics existed in Transcaucasia and enjoyed considerable support from the lower classes. They called for transforming the "bourgeois" republics into independent Soviet republics. The Bolsheviks of Georgia and Armenia were outraged by this concession to nationalist sentiments, but late in May the Kavkraikom resolved that Communists should support the idea of national Soviet republics. On July 19, the Politburo in Moscow approved the new line, and within the next year separate communist parties were established for Azerbaijan (February 1920), Georgia (May 1920), and Armenia (June 1920).[60] A Caucasian bureau (Kavburo) of the Central Committee of the All-Russian Communist Party (Bolshevik) [RKP(b)] was also set up (April 8, 1920) to coordinate the work of Communists in Caucasia. While nominally autonomous in their work, the individual national communist parties were understood to be branches of the RKP(b).

On April 28, 1920, the Red Army, facing almost no armed resistance, forced the retirement of the Baku government led by the Muslim nationalist Musavat party, and a Soviet republic of Azerbaijan was proclaimed. Despite treaty obligations, the Georgian government prudently decided not to come to the aid of Azerbaijan and take on the Red Army. Lenin was enthusiastic about Soviet control of the Baku oil fields, lost in the summer of 1918, but he cautioned his lieutenants to "act carefully and show the maximum consideration for the Muslims."[61] Always wary of ethnic sensitivities and determined that the Soviet government should not appear to reproduce the "Great Russian chauvinism" and imperialism characteristic of the tsarist regime, Lenin repeatedly warned Caucasian Communists to show patience and restraint in dealing with non-Russian peoples.

Lenin's comrades on the local level, however, were seldom willing to wait for conditions to favor the Bolsheviks; rather they sought to use the Red Army to accelerate the pace of Sovietization. Already in early May 1920 Orjonikidze was wiring Lenin and Stalin that "events are developing such that we hope to be in Tiflis no later than the 15th." Indeed, panic that an invasion was imminent had spread through Georgia, and there were clashes on the border between the People's Guard and the Red Army. But facing an invasion of the Ukraine by Pilsudski's Poland and unsure of the popular Georgian response to the Red Army, the government in Moscow strongly opposed a thrust into Georgia, and the Central Committee ordered Orjonikidze to desist. To the surprise of the local Georgian Communists, the Soviet government signed a peace treaty with Georgia on May 7. Instead of an active policy of forcibly overthrowing the governments of Georgia and Armenia, Moscow in its hour of danger turned toward a peaceful cooperation that would last for the next six months.[62]

By the fall of 1920, the political-military context in which Georgia existed had changed dramatically. Soviet forces stood on the northern and eastern frontiers. Dashnak Armenia was at war with the Turkish nationalists under Mustapha Kemal over their conflicting claims to northeastern Anatolia. The civil war in Russia was coming to an end, and only Poland seemed an active threat to Soviet power. Within Georgia economic difficulties and demoralization had taken their toll on the formerly unchallenged Menshevik hegemony. Foreign observers reported a growing "Bolshevik mood" among soldiers and in the countryside.[63] Still it was clear to the local Communists that they had no hope of coming to power soon without the intervention of the Red Army.

As winter neared, the Turks were advancing into Armenia, and the Soviet forces in Azerbaijan pressured the Dashnaks to come to terms with the "lesser evil" of Bolshevism in order to prevent a Turkish occupation. On December 2, the Dashnak government signed an agreement with the representative of the Russian Socialist Federated Soviet Republic (RSFSR), and a Soviet Republic of Armenia was declared.[64] Georgia now was nearly surrounded by the Soviets, and the Red Army was poised for a final assault on the Menshevik capital.

Repeatedly Orjonikidze requested permission from Moscow to begin operations against Georgia, but the Politburo insisted on its peaceful policy. From Baku arrangements were made for an uprising in the disputed Lori district, and when the insurrection broke out on February 11, 1921, the Red Army in Armenia was prepared to come to its aid. Moscow finally, reluctantly, consented to the invasion of Georgia (February 14). The next day the Eleventh Red Army crossed the border from Azerbaijan into Georgia. The Mensheviks tried in vain to contact Moscow and come to terms, but the Bolsheviks had already set up a revolutionary committee (Revkom) for Georgia, a body that would soon acquire the functions of a government. On February 25, the Mensheviks left Tiflis for a last stand in Batumi. Three weeks later Zhordania and his government sailed into exile.[65]

The political and intellectual dominance of the Mensheviks in Georgia had lasted for nearly three decades. Their odyssey from the graveside of their mentor, Ninoshvili, to a chateau in Leuville, outside of Paris, wound through two revolutions, civil war, and national independence. Their achievement in building a Georgian political nation was extraordinary. Their support among all classes of the Georgian people was genuine. And however ephemeral their accomplishments in the brief episode of national independence, the most impressive testimony to their successes is the fact that they could not be dislodged from Georgia except by a militarily superior force from outside.

Politically the Georgian Mensheviks had jumped from one strategy to another as the pressures of the changing situation and the opportunities shifted. For the first year of the revolution the social democrats tried to hold together the revolutionary alliances of workers and soldiers that had placed de facto power in the local soviets. But conflicts over the national question and ties to Russia fractured the alliance. The Mensheviks then used their political and military muscle to disarm the garrison and send the soldiers packing. In the immediate post-October period they worked together with Armenians and Azerbaijanis to hold Transcaucasia together against the centrifugal ethnic tensions and the invading Turks, but the three major nationalities could not unite against the Muslim threat. At this point the Georgian socialists accepted Germany's offer to establish a protectorate over Georgia. This option, they believed, would save Georgia from the Turks, protect it against Bolshevik Russia, and provide a vital economic and political link with a major European power. But this strategy also proved short-lived. Within months Germany had lost the war and the British, suspicious of Georgia's flirtation with Germany, had become the most potent military force in the region.

The establishment of the independent Georgian republic, though forced on the social democrats, had a profound effect on their political and ideological profile. The more internationalist aspects of their socialism disappeared as the Mensheviks identified most immediately with the national cause of independence and sovereignty. All social groups within the nation soon came around to favor independence, and the social democrats, who had begun their history as the self-proclaimed representatives of the working class, saw themselves as the voice of the Georgian nation as a whole. This profound ideological shift toward nationalism divided them from the Russian and Armenian social democrats, from the independent republics of Armenia and Azerbaijan, and from the Bolsheviks both in Georgia and to the north.

Two fundamental weaknesses in the strategy of independence were that Bolshevik Russia ultimately would not accept separation of the Caucasian republics and that no Western power was willing to give more than financial aid. Within the possibilities offered, the social democrats managed to maximize Georgia's political benefits. But finally the brief experiment with independence—possible only because of the power vacuum left when neither Bolshevik Russia nor Turkey was able to impose its traditional authority over the region—collapsed. Once Russia and Turkey revived and the European intervention ended, it was only a matter of time before the two powers that bordered Transcaucasia would re-establish their hegemony. As it turned out, the bulk of historic Armenia, now scourged of Armenians, fell to the nationalist Turks under Kemal Pasha, while eastern Armenia, Azerbaijan, and Georgia came under Soviet power.

Yet it must be added that, although independence was forfeited, the political experience of the national republics remained important. For the existence and popularity of the republics convinced the Communists to adjust their attitude toward national republics. In an important sense the legacy of the Dashnak, Musavat, and Menshevik national revolutions continued long after the invasion of the Red Army, in the Soviet socialist republics that exist to the present time.

10 Bolshevik Georgia

The flight of the Mensheviks from Tiflis on February 25, 1921, and the Red Army's arrival early the next morning have remained indelibly etched in the minds of those still alive who witnessed this imported revolution. A ten-year-old street-wise boy, Gurgen Mirzoev, heard the desperate Menshevik leaders harangue their followers to defend the capital against the invaders, just before they themselves left the city.[1] When the fleeing Georgian soldiers followed, throwing down their arms, Gurgen and his brother Ruben gathered up rifles, wrapped them carefully in canvas, and buried them in their yard. Their sisters, Seda and Siranoush, fearing that the Bolsheviks would rape young women, fled to the home of left-wing cousins. After long silent hours, whistling could be heard in the distance, and the Bolshevik soldiers marched into the town center. An unknown commissar called upon the citizens to bring their surplus grain, soap, and other foodstuffs to Erivan Square for distribution; harsh penalties were promised for hoarders. The Mirzoevs' landlord was to learn a few days later that the Bolsheviks were serious about their commandments. When a large sack of flour was discovered in his basement, he was led away, never to be seen again.

A new government had been installed. Soon it became clear to all that a far-reaching transformation was about to begin. The Sovietization of Transcaucasia was not the result of the simple application of Marxist principles, nor of their cynical abandonment at an inconvenient juncture. Rather it was the product of conflict between ideological considerations and realistic assessments, between the strategic requirements of Soviet Russia and the aims of local Communists. Baku-based and Tiflis-based Communists advocated strongly divergent strategies on the scene. At the same time, Bolshevik leaders in Moscow had diametrically opposed views of the most appropriate way to deal with local populations and recent enemies. Most important, Lenin's own sense of the peculiar needs of the Caucasian peoples ran up against the hardened attitudes of Stalin, Orjonikidze, and others who time and again opted for a tough line toward the local peoples and seized any advantage that would lead to more centralized control from Moscow. Lenin's position found allies among Georgian Communists in Tiflis, but their struggle against the centralizers became fatally uneven when Lenin's illness removed him from the equation and allowed Stalin and his supporters to make the final calculations.[2]

As we have seen, conflict between Bolsheviks about the fate of Georgia preceded the Red Army's invasion. When Orjonikidze, early in February 1921, urged the immediate Sovietization of Menshevik Georgia by the Red Army, the Moscow party leaders divided on the issue. Stalin supported his Georgian comrade, but Trotsky "stood for a certain preparatory period of work inside Georgia, in order to develop the uprising and later come to its aid."[3] Lenin, on the other hand, wavered, apparently fearful of the international consequences and the possible opposition of Kemalist Turkey, with whom Soviet Russia was soon to begin negotiations in Moscow. Three days after the insurrection in the neutral zone of Lori was initiated, Lenin agreed, somewhat reluctantly, to "allow the XI Army to give active support to the uprising in Georgia and to occupy Tiflis provided that international norms are observed and on condition that all members of the Military Revolutionary Council of the XI Army, after a thorough review of all the data, guarantee success."[4] Repeatedly Lenin complained about the lack of precise and consistent information from the Caucasus, and it seems clear from the available evidence that his final agreement to the invasion took place in the face of a fait accompli by the Baku-based Bolsheviks.

On February 16, the revolutionary committee (Revkom) for Georgia was formed in the town of Shulaveri. Its choice for chairman fell on Pilipe Makharadze. Then still in Moscow, Makharadze conferred with Lenin, who impressed upon him the need for moderation and caution in dealing with the Georgian population.[5]

To underscore his concerns Lenin sent a telegram to Orjonikidze in Baku (March 2) outlining his preferred policy for Georgia:

> Give the Georgian Communists and especially all members of the Georgian Revkom my warm greetings to Soviet Georgia. I ask particularly that they communicate to me if we are in full agreement on three points:
> First: it is necessary to arm immediately the workers and poorest peasants, creating a strong Georgian Red Army.
> Second: essential is a special policy of concessions toward the Georgian intelligentsia and small traders. It is necessary to understand that it is not only improvident to nationalize them but that it is necessary even to make certain sacrifices, if only to better their situation and leave them the possibility to carry on small trade.
> Third: it is gigantically important to search for an acceptable compro-

mise for a bloc with Zhordania and similar Georgian Mensheviks, those who before the uprising had not been absolutely hostile to the idea of a Soviet order in Georgia under certain conditions.

I ask you to remember that the internal and international situation of Georgia demands from the Georgian Communists, not the application of the Russian pattern, but the skillful and flexible creation of a distinctive tactic based on the greatest compliance with all kinds of petty-bourgeois elements.[6]

The "Russian pattern" of which Lenin spoke was in fact the harsh series of emergency measures known as "War Communism," which the party leaders were already planning to abandon in favor of a more accommodating approach, the so-called New Economic Policy (NEP) adopted at the Tenth Party Congress in March 1921. War Communism had involved nationalization of almost all industry, the elimination of private trade in most commodities, regimentation of labor, and the mustering of all social and economic resources in order to win the civil war. Now the defeat of the anti-Bolshevik forces permitted the abolition of forced requisitioning of grain and its replacement by a tax in kind, denationalization of much of industry, and a more relaxed attitude toward private enterprise.

In his famous letter to the Communists of Caucasia (April 14, 1921), Lenin analyzed the differences between Russia and the Caucasus. In the years of civil war the RSFSR had had no political or military support from any quarter, Lenin reminded his readers, and was under constant threat from the Entente. The Caucasus was now free from that danger and could depend on support from Russia. Moreover, "the Caucasian republics are countries even more peasant than Russia." Yet Russia was cut off economically from the leading capitalist nations; Caucasia could coexist and trade with the West much more easily. To nurture such possibilities and smooth an establishment of Soviet power required "more softness, caution, conciliation in relations with the petty bourgeoisie, the intelligentsia, and especially the peasantry . . . A slower, more careful, more systematic transition to socialism is what is possible and necessary for the republics of the Caucasus in contrast to the RSFSR."[7] Lenin, like Stalin and Orjonikidze, was committed to keeping Georgia Soviet, but unlike them, he preferred a moderate approach toward the local intelligentsia and peasantry.

By the time Caucasia was fully in Soviet hands, the Russian republic had "retreated" to a more tolerant form of what Lenin referred to as "state capitalism." But both in Russia and Caucasia many Communists found it difficult to abandon the methods and measures adopted during the civil war and make the adjustment to the more flexible policy. Conflict soon broke out between those who tried to apply Lenin's new directives and those who sought to tighten and centralize party control over the newly Sovietized republics.

From Baku Orjonikidze assured Lenin that "the Georgian Communists are in complete agreement with us," that a delegation had been sent to the former Menshevik government "with a proposal to end further fighting and to recognize Soviet power," and that there was "full solidarity" on the question of small trade. No mention was made, however, of including Mensheviks in a new government, as implied in Lenin's telegram of March 2. Only on March 8, two days after Makharadze had reached Tiflis, did the Revkom inform the Mensheviks that "the question of the entry of representatives of these parties into the revolutionary government will be the subject of special serious negotiations after the cessation of military activities." In his speech that same day, Orjonikidze again took a more uncompromising position than Lenin, while speaking as if their views were consistent. Though he mentioned adapting to local conditions, he also emphasized the need to remove all nonworking elements from power, "the complete destruction of capitalist property, the full transfer of all land to the peasants."[8] Two days later Lenin wrote to Orjonikidze that he must "establish full contact with the Revkom of Georgia, conform strictly to the Revkom's directives, take no steps which could affect the interests of the population without coming to an agreement with the Georgian Revkom, behave with particular respect toward the sovereign institutions of Georgia, and show particular attention and discretion toward the Georgian population."[9] A division was developing, though not yet openly, between Lenin and his sympathizers in the Georgian Revkom on the one hand, and Orjonikidze, whose views were closer to those of Stalin, and the Kavburo majority in Baku on the other.

The growing conflict among the Communists was not merely a psychological or constitutional matter; nor was it simply a question of the future shape of the Soviet republics and their relationship to Moscow. It was also a debate about the way social transformation would occur in Georgia and the other national republics: whether change would come gradually and with due consideration for national peculiarities and sensitivities, or more rapidly with less regard for local priorities. The "revolutions" in Transcaucasia that had brought the Communists to power had not been popular in origin but imposed by a superior military force. Support for Soviet power in these republics was limited to some disaffected elements and remained for a long time dependent on physical force. The possibility of revolt and civil war was great. Indeed, Armenia had risen briefly against the Bolsheviks in February 1921 when the Red Army moved north into Georgia. For moderates like Makharadze their task as laid out by Lenin was to secure for Soviet power a broad base of support, beginning with the intelligentsia. This precluded an assault on Georgian national institutions, the extirpation by force of Menshevik influence, or any hint that Georgian sovereignty was to be compromised by Soviet Russia and its agents.

For Communists like Orjonikidze and Stalin the task of Soviet power was quite different. They were most concerned about the twin dangers of economic collapse and ethnic particularism, both of which could lead to internal conflict and external threats. Orjonikidze repeatedly proposed the economic unification of the three Transcaucasian republics, beginning with the amalgamation of the Transcaucasian railroad system and the merging of the foreign trade commissariats.[10] In these economic plans he enjoyed the full support of Lenin, who was particularly anxious that Caucasia lead the way in stimulating foreign trade and granting foreign entrepreneurs economic concessions. A regional economic authority might assist in these efforts for increased economic ties with the West.

But Stalin and Orjonikidze's concern for unity and their fear of local nationalism was accompanied by an insensitivity to Caucasian hostility to impositions by central Russia. When Stalin spoke to the Tiflis party organization in July 1921, he railed against the rise of local nationalism among the Caucasian peoples and grew nostalgic for the years after 1905 when, as he remembered, workers of all ethnicities worked harmoniously. He called for a cleansing of the party and the elimination of both careerist and nationalist elements, but he failed to mention that high-handed actions by cadres from the RSFSR offended the local peoples. The warning that Communists must be wary of their own Russian nationalism had already been taken up in earnest by Lenin, and the "danger of Great Russian chauvinism" had been specifically condemned at the Tenth Party Congress just four months earlier.[11]

The enthusiasm of the moment of victory and the genuine feeling that Soviet power could create a new era of solidarity among the peoples of Caucasia overcame for a time the misgivings of certain national Communists about the extent of extra-Caucasian influence in the area. Soviet power, it was announced, would resolve the constant quarrels between Armenians, Azerbaijanis, and Georgians that had plagued the period of the "bourgeois" republics. On April 14, the amalgamation of the Transcaucasian railroad system was declared. Less than two weeks later (April 26) a conference of local economic officials decided to form a joint Transcaucasian authority to oversee foreign trade (Obvneshtorg).[12] In May and June customs barriers and border guards between the three republics and between Transcaucasia and the RSFSR were removed. Work began on the touchy matter of delineating the frontiers of the republics and determining the fate of areas like Akhalkalaki, Lori, Karabakh, and Nakhichevan, which were claimed by several republics.

Although these decisions were appreciated by most Communists, the fact that they were handed down from above by the Kavburo, often without consultation with party officials in the republics, created animosity and resistance from below. The emerging spokesman for Georgian national sensitivity, Budu Mdivani, warned the Kavburo in June that issuing such decrees without preparatory work among the masses made it appear as if orders had come from Moscow.[13]

Georgian Communists were well aware of the weakness of their party's social base and the continuing sympathy for the Mensheviks. The Communist Party of Georgia (KPG) was top-heavy with leaders and short on cadres, particularly from the very class they purported to represent. Of the party's fifteen thousand members, only 13 percent were workers. The great majority were peasants.[14] Many were illiterate, few had any higher education.

At the top of the party hierarchy stood an impressive array of Old Bolsheviks, men who had for many years worked closely with Stalin and other powerful Georgian Communists, men like Avel Enukidze and Orjonikidze, who had made party careers largely outside their homeland. But they were not a very cohesive group. Besides those who favored the positions of Orjonikidze (most important were Mamia Orakhelashvili and Shalva Eliava), the party was divided between followers of Makharadze ("Filippists") and Mdivani ("Budists"). There was also a small left wing (Jelava, Kuralov, Oboladze) reluctant to give up the norms of War Communism and determined to push for a hard line against the Mensheviks.

In an early attempt to bring unity to the party, Stalin and Orjonikidze had the Georgian Central Committee remove Makharadze as Revkom chairman and appoint Mdivani in his place (July 7). A "Budist" majority was formed in the new Politburo in August—Mdivani, Okujava, Kavtaradze, Eliava, and Orakhelashvili—and Makharadze was posted to Moscow.[15]

The tensions between the Georgian leadership in Tiflis and the Kavburo in Baku broke into open conflict in August 1921. When the Kavburo decided to form an economic council to direct the railroads, foreign trade, and electrification, the Georgians protested to Moscow. The Politburo sided with Baku, and a few months later the Kavburo put forth plans for the *political* unification of Transcaucasia. In November the Red armies of the three republics were merged into the Detached Caucasian Army (OKA).[16] That same month party organizations in Armenia and Azerbaijan approved the proposal for Transcaucasian federation. In Georgia, however, the Mdivani group argued that such plans were premature and were being pushed through by Orjonikidze undemocratically. In Moscow the Politburo decided to support the idea of federation but using Mdivani's method of implementing it from below. Orjonikidze had been restrained and a compromise reached, though not for long.

Late in January 1922, the Georgian Communist Party held its first congress. The crucial issues of land reform, private trade, and party policy toward the Mensheviks and other non-Bolshevik parties divided the congress between the supporters of Mdivani and those of Orjonikidze. The Central Committee, with its Old Bolshevik membership, backed Mdivani, but Orjonikidze had a majority among the party rank and file. Newer party members favored the harder line of the Kavburo and agreed with Orjonikidze that Mdivani's positions were nationalist. Mdivani defended his opposition to the imposition of a Transcaucasian federation from above by warning: "If [you] find [us] guilty of nationalism, then you must also find Comrade Lenin and the Central Committee of the RKP(b) guilty."[17] But the congress voted in favor of federation of the Transcaucasian republics and with the RSFSR, and declared the work of the former Central Committee "unsatisfactory." The supporters of Orjonikidze now formed the majority in the new Central Committee of the Georgian party. On March 12, 1922, representatives from Georgia joined those from Armenia and Azerbaijan and signed the treaty forming the Federal Union of Soviet Socialist Republics of Transcaucasia (FSSSRZ).

Through 1922 the central party organs, the Central Committee and the Organizational Bureau (Orgburo), tried repeatedly, but in vain, to end the infighting in the Transcaucasian parties. Step by step the centralizers, led by Orjonikidze, reduced the prerogatives of the separate republics and increased those of the Union Council *(Soiuznyi Sovet)* of the FSSSZR. In each instance the Mdivani group, now joined by Makharadze and his followers, protested the infringement on Georgian sovereignty and did everything in its power to prevent implementation of the federal union's directives. A stalemate was reached, and the Union Council found it difficult to operate. Still the efforts to centralize decision-making at the Transcaucasian level and higher, at the all-Russian level, went on.

In early September Stalin introduced a plan to bring the various Soviet republics into the RSFSR as autonomous republics. The leaders of Azerbaijan and Armenia responded enthusiastically, but the Georgians opposed the so-called autonomization plan. In Tiflis the Georgian Central Committee met with Orjonikidze, Kirov, Enukidze, and others who spoke in favor of Stalin's plan, but Mdivani and his followers carried the day. The Central Committee resolved:

> Union in the form of autonomization of the independent republics proposed on the basis of Stalin's theses is premature. The unification of economic affairs and general policy is necessary, but with the preservation of all the attributes of sovereignty.[18]

Stalin's plan was approved by the Orgburo in Moscow and seemed headed for passage in the Politburo, when it met stiff resistance from Lenin. On September 26, Stalin visited the ailing leader at his villa at Gorki outside Moscow for discussions about his plan. Immediately after Stalin left, Lenin wrote to Kamenev, rejecting Stalin's theses and in its place offering a fresh proposal. Instead of the various Soviet republics entering the RSFSR on the basis of broad autonomy, a wholly new political formation—the federation that would eventually become the Union of Soviet Socialist Republics—was to be formed by the six Soviet republics entering on an equal basis.[19] Though Stalin at first resisted Lenin's formulation as "national liberalism," he quickly decided not to confront Lenin on this issue and altered his plan to conform with Lenin's suggestions. On October 6, the Central Committee of the RKP(b) approved the idea of forming a Union of Soviet Socialist Republics.

As he left for Europe on diplomatic business, Mdivani felt vindicated, confident that the "great power tendencies" among members of the Russian Central Committee had "received such a slap in the face that [they] will not soon decide to poke out of the hole into which Lenin drove [them]."[20] But one extremely important matter had yet to be decided: whether the republics of Transcaucasia would enter the new USSR individually or as part of the Transcaucasian federation. As far as Stalin and Orjonikidze were concerned, the Central Committee in Moscow had decided on October 6 to have Transcaucasia enter the union as one unit, but the Georgian leadership in Tiflis insisted on Georgia's separate entry. Tempers flared. Orjonikidze began purging leading Georgian officials. From Tiflis the Georgian leaders wired Moscow in protest and heatedly criticized the authoritarianism of the Transcaucasian Territory Party Committee (Zakkraikom), which had replaced the Kavburo.

When Lenin received word of the Georgians' protests, he was infuriated by their "undignified tone," and expressed anger that the issue of separate entry, which he believed had already been rejected by the Moscow Central Committee, should be raised again by the Georgians. Faced with Lenin's fury and isolated from the central leaders, the Georgian Central Committee took an unprecedented step: on October 22 they resigned en masse. Orjonikidze quickly appointed a new Central Committee of people who agreed with the positions taken in Moscow, but the Mdivani-Makharadze forces stepped up their protests.

A special commission headed by Felix Dzerzhinskii went to Tiflis to sort out the sources of conflict, which had become so intensely personal that one evening late in November Orjonikidze lost control and slapped a Mdivani supporter. Such behavior was unheard of in party circles, and this incident, along with the steady stream of disquieting protests, led Lenin to begin his own personal investigation of Georgian affairs. Again stricken by illness in December, the weakened, semiparalyzed leader embarked on what Moshe Lewin has called his "last struggle," a desperate attempt to support the Georgian Communists, to limit the power of Stalin and the burgeoning bureaucracy in party and state, and to prevent a triumph of "Great Russian chauvinism" in nationality policy.[21]

As Lenin in convalescence became increasingly troubled by Stalin and Orjonikidze's activities, the centralizers managed to reconstitute the FSSSZR into a single Soviet republic, the Transcaucasian Federated Soviet Socialist Republic (ZSFSR) (December 10, 1922). Three weeks later the ZSFSR entered the newly formed Union of Soviet Socialist Republics (December 30). That same day Lenin, now convinced that he had underestimated the depth and power of Great Russian chauvinism within the bureaucracy, began dictating his notes on the national question.[22]

Though few were yet aware of it, Lenin had already bluntly called for Stalin's removal from his post as general secretary. "Stalin is too rude," he had written, "and this defect, though quite tolerable in our midst and in dealings among us Communists, becomes intolerable in a General Secretary." Now he focused on "measures to protect really the national minorities from the truly Russian *Derzhimordy*" [brutal police types] who had peopled party offices. Ironically, the most chauvinistic "Russian" officials were assimilated non-Russians like Stalin, Orjonikidze, and Dzerzhinskii. Lenin wrote:

> In regard to the Georgian nation, a truly proletarian attitude on our part demands extraordinary caution, courtesy, and conciliation. That Georgian who is disdainful to this side of the matter, who disdainfully flings accusations of "social-nationalism" (when he himself is not only a real and true "social-nationalist" but a crude Great Russian *Derzhimorda*), that Georgian, in essence, hurts the interests of proletarian class solidarity . . . That is why in the given case it is better to oversalt on the side of conciliation and softness toward the national minorities than to undersalt.[23]

Lenin ended by declaring that Orjonikidze must be punished as an example, that Stalin and Dzerzhinskii must be held politically responsible for "this whole truly Great Russian nationalist campaign," and that the abuses against the nationalities carried out in the name of unification be ended. Lenin's vision was directed beyond the expedient requirements of forming the new Soviet Union and toward the goal of maintaining the prestige of the Russian Revolution and its liberating mission among the "awakening millions" of Asia.[24]

Physically unable to carry on the fight himself, Lenin instructed his secretaries to inform the Georgians accused of nationalism that he was "on the side of the insulted." He sent a warm note to Trotsky, imploring him to "take on himself the defense of the Georgian matter." In his very last letter, Lenin wrote to Mdivani and Makharadze:

> Respected comrades!
> With all my soul I am following your case. I am indignant at the crudeness of Orjonikidze and the connivances of Stalin and Dzerzhinskii. I am preparing notes and a speech for you.
> Respectfully, Lenin[25]

Never the one to confront Lenin directly, Stalin warned Orjonikidze not to pressure the Georgian Communists and to obtain a compromise. Kamenev arrived in Tiflis for the Second Congress of the KPG, both as a part of a second commission of inquiry and in order to unify the party "internally through agreement and not with some kind of operation from above." A compromise was worked out: the ZSFSR was to "take on such flexible form that it would in no way compromise the independence of the republics in the fields of economy and governance"; but the land reform was to be implemented immediately and the struggle against the Mensheviks was to be carried forward. Though Mdivani and his ally Kote Tsintsadze were not elected to the Georgian Central Committee, three members of the opposition were—Makharadze, Okujava, and Malakia Torosheldize.[26] An outsider, Beso Lominadze, was elected party secretary. An old friend of Stalin's and the choice of the Orgburo in Moscow (but not the local party), Lominadze was nevertheless somewhat above the infighting that was tearing the KPG apart.

Lenin had feared what he called "a rotten compromise" and had planned to use the Georgian case as a "bomb" to dislodge Stalin from his position of power. Instead he lay paralyzed, unable to speak. Trotsky's motion in the Politburo on March 26 to recall Orjonikidze, decentralize the ZSFSR, and recognize that the minority in the KPG had not been "deviationists" failed six to one.[27] Five days later the Central Committee in Moscow decided to return the commissariats of labor, supply, and worker-peasant inspection to the separate Transcaucasian republics and abolish them at the Transcaucasian level. This left only the Commissariat of Finance and the Sovnarkhoz, the supreme economic council, at the federal level. But these mediating shifts were less significant than something that did not happen. When Lenin's theses on Stalin's nationality policy reached the Politburo on the eve of the Twelfth Party Congress, it was decided not to reveal them to the congress delegates. Trotsky would not drop the bomb, and Stalin ultimately had his way in Georgia.

For nine days in mid-April the Russian Communist Party met in Moscow, and a major debate raged over the party's nationality policy, particularly toward Georgia. Orjonikidze accused the "deviationists," Mdivani and Makharadze, of a series of improper activities—refusing to take down customs barriers, selling a Soviet ship to foreigners, negotiating with the Ottoman Bank, and closing the frontiers of Georgia to hungry refugees from the North Caucasus and the Volga region. "For such behavior we squeezed you," Orjonikidze proclaimed, "and will go on squeezing you. More important, he condemned the Georgian government's failure to implement a radical land reform and eliminate once and for all the noble landlords, and castigated them for softness toward the Mensheviks. "We decided to end the amnesty and arrest the Mensheviks," he told the delegates, "while our opponents wavered."[28]

Makharadze defended his faction and told of the authoritarianism of the Zakkraikom, which attempted to direct the Tiflis party committee and the Georgian council of trade unions "over the head of the [Georgian] Central Committee." He maintained that the Orjonikidze majority in the KPG was not representative of the tried and experienced Georgian Communists. "We know on what elements Comrade Orjonikidze leans—these are the least dependable and the most recent elements to have entered our party. These elements hold a course on the most left leftism."[29]

The key speech at the congress on nationality policy was given by Stalin, the commissar of nationalities and long acknowledged as a principal spokesman on this issue. Stalin argued that Great Russian chauvinism was the principal danger to national peace in the Soviet republics, but local nationalisms also presented a danger, "threatening to turn some republics into arenas of national squabbles, tearing there the ties of internationalism." He mentioned Georgia as a country in which "the attitude of some . . . Communists toward minorities in the republic is chauvinistic."[30] Georgia was a relatively privileged republic with its access to the West through Batumi and the railroad center, Tiflis, and opposition to federation was a way to protect that privileged status.

For Stalin the central concern was the strengthening of the proletarian dictatorship. Since the Great Russian proletariat was the backbone of that dictatorship and the peripheral nationalities were primarily peasant, he warned those who feared Great Russian chauvinism not to go too far toward appeasing the peasant peripheries. Turning around Lenin's phrase about the need for concessions toward minorities, Stalin said: "It is just as forbidden to oversalt in politics as it is forbidden to undersalt."[31]

Stalin spoke in favor of industrial development and the strengthening of national cadres in the national republics, but he combined his program of local "nationalization" with a firm commitment to political centralization. Power was to flow downward and outward, and attempts by national Communists to maintain political or cultural autonomy were to be opposed. Local organs of government would be made up of local people using the local language and familiar with national customs, but local decision-making would be strictly subordinated to the "class interests" of the Soviet proletariat as a whole.

Stalin's resolution was adopted by the congress and set the pattern for future political practice. Lenin undoubtedly would have seen that resolution as lacking the necessary guarantees for national autonomy, but mortally ill and with less than a year to live, he was never again able to intervene in the politics of the state he had founded.

The last year of Lenin's life and the year that followed, the so-called interregnum, were among the most crucial in the formation of the Soviet political system. With Lenin eliminated as the effective leader of the party, the helm fell to a newly formed triumvirate of his lieutenants—Grigorii Zinoviev, Lev Kamenev, and Stalin—whose principal motivation seemed to be the isolation and weakening of Lev Trotsky. As the best known of the Bolshevik leaders and the one thought by many to be the appropriate successor to Lenin, the commissar of war was also the most feared by his associates, even as he studiously avoided all displays of power hunger. Crucial issues of economic policy, international communist strategy, and intraparty democracy separated Trotsky from the triumvirs through 1923. More ominously, the decisive strength of the central party's secretariat, headed by Stalin since 1922, was making itself felt in both local and upper party institutions.

Behind the personal and political infighting, Stalin was inexorably emerging as the major leader of the post-Lenin party. His emphasis on unity and discipline reflected deeply felt Bolshevik preferences, but the combination of the secretariat's appointment and assignment powers and the restrictions on factional activity within the party proved fatal to the lively debate and disagreements that had formerly characterized Bolshevik political discourse.

In the fall of 1923 Trotsky openly raised objections to the practice of nominating rather than electing party officials, claiming that the secretarial apparatus was becoming all-powerful and that mass participation in party organizations was "illusory." But by December the Politburo majority had launched an open campaign against Trotsky and the opposition. At the Thirteenth Party Conference in January Trotsky's "errors" were condemned, and the dominant force within the party remained with the secretarial apparatus. Two weeks later Lenin was dead.[32]

For Georgia, the implications of the rise of the secretariat and Stalin had already been demonstrated by the defeat of the Georgian "national Communists" in late 1922 and early 1923. The Stalin-Orjonikidze line had prevailed, and the constitutional integration of the republic into the ZSFSR and the USSR was completed by early 1924. The political triumph of one faction of the communist party over others, particularly more decentralist and "democratic" elements, set the stage for the elimination of non-Bolshevik influences in Georgian society. The first tasks facing the new Georgian leadership were to eradicate the still-powerful Menshevik movement and recruit members of the local intelligentsia and working class into the Communist Party. These efforts were carried out in line with the nationality policies elaborated at the Twelfth Party Congress and a subsequent meeting of non-Russian activists that discussed the threat of "national communism," local variants that favored different degrees of accommodation to cultural particularities.

In June 1923 representatives from the national borderlands met in Moscow with members of the Central Committee. Stalin's predominance was evident, as he put forth the main resolutions and interpreted the decisions on the national question made at the recent congress.[33] He appeared much more conciliatory toward the non-Russian peoples than he had during the Georgian controversy. Staking out a position in the ideological center, he castigated both the right and left wings within the party:

> If the Right threatens by their tendency toward nationalism to hinder the growth of our communist cadres in the border areas, the Left threatens . . . by their infatuation with an oversimplified and hasty "communism" to isolate our party from the peasantry and the broad strata of the local population.

Moreover, he added later, the greater danger at the time came from the Left applying Russian practices mechanistically and disregarding the particularities of various nationalities.[34]

The whole thrust of the conference resolutions and of Stalin's remarks was to attract "more or less loyal elements of local intelligentsia" to work within Soviet institutions. Support for the regime was to be established through "nationalization" of the local governing institutions, or what had been referred to as *korenizatsiia* ("rooting" or "nativization" of the Soviet superstructure in the non-Russian areas), but overt nationalism was not to be tolerated within the party or state apparatus.

> It is essential to remember that our communist organizations in the bor-
> derlands, in the republics and regions, can develop and stand on their feet,
> make of themselves real internationalist Marxist cadres, only if they over-
> come nationalism . . . Various bourgeois, and among them Menshevik,
> influences can penetrate into our borderland organizations only under a
> nationalist cover.[35]

Stalin was critical of party work in Turkestan and the Ukraine, where leaders like Khristian Rakovskii and Mykola Skrypnyk were still contesting the tight federative ties with the all-union center. But he had only praise for Georgia where, he maintained, the high level of literacy had enabled the Georgian Communists to set the best example of linking the apparatus with the masses.

Within a month of the Moscow conference, a campaign was begun in Georgia to liquidate the remaining Menshevik party organizations. A promi-nent former Menshevik, A. S. Martynov, arrived from Russia to participate in a series of local conferences of former Mensheviks, culminating in a congress in August 1923, convened for the purpose of disbanding the party. Martynov explained his own evolution to Bolshevism:

> In the October days history placed before us the question: for a dictatorship
> of the proletariat or for democracy? At that time all the Mensheviks,
> including we internationalists, fell into the swamp of opportunism . . . You
> see, comrades, my break with the Menshevik party is only the logical
> outcome of that struggle which Martov and I carried on within this party
> for many years against its opportunism. The only thing that kept me from
> breaking with it [was] the prejudice that the road to the victory of socialism
> lies through democracy and not through dictatorship. When I found myself
> in Ukraine, on the front line, in the very cauldron of counterrevolution where
> revolutionary and counterrevolutionary elements clashed, it became com-
> pletely clear to me that the revolution can win only by means of iron-willed
> and ruthless dictatorship. Then the last obstacle separating me from the
> Communist Party fell away.[36]

Discussions were heated. From Paris the exiled Central Committee of the Georgian Social Democratic Party issued a statement denouncing the resig-nations of Mensheviks, which they claimed were the result of coercion and persecution by the Cheka (secret police). At one meeting in Tiflis the Men-shevik Targamadze boldly spoke up against the campaign, saying it had been "carried out by threatening workers with loss of work, imprisonment, the 'basements of the Cheka,' and exile." The Menshevik party had numbered more than 50,000 before 1921, he asserted, and their sympathizers ran into hundreds of thousands. "After the Sovietization of Georgia, not only Mensheviks but the whole people were hostile to the Communists, and, I will say openly, they were ready to fight against them." The hostility remained. "Instead of a dictatorship of the proletariat we received a dictatorship of a bunch of people, a group of people over the proletariat."[37] Other speakers denied that they had been coerced to renounce Menshevism, but it seemed clear that two years of Bolshevism in Georgia and the probability that Russian backing would keep the new government in power made recantation a more realistic alternative to holding unfurled the Menshevik flag. The reports from the conferences indicate that sympathy for the old social democratic leaders remained intact. Zhordania's name evoked applause. A play touring the provinces, *Mensheviks in Paris,* was attacked for insulting Zhordania. Resolutions that the Mensheviks were guilty of counterrevolutionary activity had to be rewritten in milder form.

In August a congress of Georgian social democrats was permitted to open in Tiflis, despite the fact that two years earlier the party had been officially declared liquidated by the Soviet authorities. Delegates representing more than 11,000 members heard Pilipe Makharadze, one of the first Marxists in Georgia and formerly a friend and comrade of Zhordania, praise the work of the Mensheviks in the early years of the revolutionary movement, particularly in 1905. In an obvious effort to conciliate the gathered Mensheviks, the Bolshevik leader declared that enough invective had been directed at Mensheviks. The final resolution of the congress acknowledged past services of the Mensheviks, then stated that the party had "taken a definitely false path during the world war and the February Revolution and found itself in the camp of counterrevolution." Then the Georgian Social Democratic Party was officially disbanded within Georgia.[38]

Though the visible shoots of Georgian Menshevism were effectively plowed under by the public campaign of recantation, the roots of the movement that had dominated Georgian public life for the first two decades of the century were too deep to be destroyed easily. The Mensheviks remained particularly influential among the Georgian intelligentsia and the peasantry of western Georgia. In three and a half years the Bolsheviks had managed to make significant inroads into the working class, at least in Tiflis, and to consolidate their support within the growing state bureaucracy and among the Armenians and Russians living in Georgia. But the base of support for the Soviet government was still quite small, and the great majority of the population—which was peasant—had not developed any great affection for the Communists.[39] This potential weakness, of which the Soviet leaders were only too aware, made the government particularly vulnerable to the underground Menshevik opposition.

Sometime in late 1922 the anti-Bolshevik parties still active within

Georgia—the Social Democrats, Socialist Federalists, Socialist Revolutionaries, National Democrats, and Skhivists (independent social democrats)— agreed to form a secret Committee for the Independence of Georgia (*damoukideblobis komiteti,* or *damkom*). By October 1923, the *damkom* decided to organize an armed uprising. Noe Zhordania wrote to his party's Central Committee in Georgia in full expectation that "the current Russian regime will fall in the not too distant future and will bring about a new regrouping of social forces."[40] He considered the conflict with Soviet power "in essence . . . the same as it had been under the *ancien regime*. A democratic and national revolution remains the goal of our current work." Zhordania once again took a position more militant than Russian Menshevism, which "is not carrying on this revolutionary struggle" and wishes to remain a "loyal opposition," and more than some of his Georgian comrades like Seid Devdariani, who called for accommodation with the Soviet regime. Calculating the real risks involved in an uprising, Zhordania warned that "Georgia alone could not win," that it needed allies in the other Caucasian peoples. But the legacy of the years of independence, with their experience of hostility toward the Armenians and the "unreliability" of the Azerbaijanis, left the Mensheviks with the fragile hope that North Caucasians or perhaps Europeans would come to their aid.

Vaguely aware that preparations were being made for an insurrection, the Soviet government did not expect a rebellion on the scale that occurred. On August 6, 1924, Valiko Jugeli, one of the organizers of the rebellion sent from abroad, was arrested by the Cheka, and he soon concluded that the revolt would be a bloody failure. From prison he wrote to his comrades, urging that they give up their plans, but the *damkom* decided to proceed.

At 4:00 A.M. on August 28 an armed band deposed and arrested the Soviet authorities in Chiatura, the manganese-producing center. The following day there were revolts in Shorapani, Novosenaki, and Zugdidi. Most of the activity took place in western Georgia, except for the small force led by Kakutsa Cholokashvili in Gare-Kakheti. Tiflis, Batumi, and most towns remained quiet, as did Abkhazeti and Ajaria. Workers did not rally to the Mensheviks. In Guria, which had been the center of rural revolution at the beginning of the century, the smallholders joined the insurrection. As Aleksandr Miasnikian, secretary of the Zakkraikom, later admitted:

> In Guria our organization was weaker than the Menshevik. Party members in Guria were about 1,200. Besides that, after the fall of the Menshevik government in Georgia, about 7,000 Mensheviks remained in Guria . . . Guria had risen up against the tsar. The great majority of the leaders of the Menshevik party are Gurians who have maintained kinship and other ties up to now. Besides, it is necessary to note that the Gurian nobles are not like the Russian nobles. This petty nobility, which has eight to ten desiatinas of land, are closer to the Russian kulaks. In Gurian villages they were always

well-liked by their own people. The Gurian peasantry, keep in mind, is a cultured element among whom the percentage of literacy is great.[41]

The uprising of 1924 was testimony to the short-term successes and failures of the embryonic Soviet order. In some sense it was the expected aftermath of the Bolsheviks' rough treatment of Georgian sensitivities and aspirations, the desperate alternative to a more accommodating solution to the problem of Georgian autonomy or "national communism." At the same time the failure of the rebels to arouse the general population, except in specific areas like Guria, suggests that the Bolsheviks' perceived strength, their attempts to solve certain basic social and economic problems, and their success in attracting key groups to accept the new order had undermined much of the Mensheviks' traditional appeal. The revolts were remote from one another, cut off from the major towns. No aid came from other peoples, and the great majority of the Georgian people did not join the rebellion.

Collapse came in a matter of days, as the Soviet forces counterattacked fiercely and ruthlessly cut down the rebel leaders. Nearly four thousand people were killed, and the Mensheviks captured by the Cheka were executed, among them Jugeli and the former Menshevik minister of agriculture, Noe Khomeriki. Others were imprisoned or sent to labor camps such as the infamous Solovki in the far north of Russia. Harsh repression of rebels was in the Bolshevik style, and it was with pride and confidence that a rising party activist, Mikhail Kakhiani, told an audience in Tiflis:

> Let everyone remember that Soviet power cruelly and implacably deals with those who it considers to be the organizers of insurrection. Many *meshchane,* especially women and sentimental ladies, cry and weep crocodile tears because nice people and heroes like Jugeli should not be shot . . . Let them cry. We cannot go along with these petty people. At a time of revolt we must act decisively and firmly . . . If we did not shoot these men we would have committed a great crime against the Georgian working people and have given the Mensheviks ground on which to begin their activity in other areas . . . Only with the language of revolutionary, merciless power can one talk to the pitiful, cowardly Mensheviks.[42]

Stalin told a conference of village party secretaries that in general the uprising in Georgia was "artificial, not popular *[narodnoe].* However, in a few places the Mensheviks managed to involve part of the peasant masses in the uprising because of the poor ties of the Communist Party with the masses." Ironically, those districts with the largest number of communist activists were precisely the districts that revolted. Stalin explained this by the failure of party members to link up effectively with the nonparty peasantry. Four days later (October 26, 1924), Stalin elaborated on the nature of peasant discontent before a plenum of the Central Committee, but here he aimed his attack more narrowly on "kulaks [rich peasants], speculators, and other anti-Soviet elements."

This uprising was, of course, all show, but in some districts, especially in Guria, it had, unquestionably, a mass character. What did the peasants in Guria try to achieve? Cheap [industrial] goods, higher prices for corn. Guria lies on the border with the West; it sees the low prices for foreign goods in comparison with our Soviet goods, and it would like our prices to be lowered, at least to the level of the foreign prices, or to have the prices of corn raised to the level where it would be profitable to buy Soviet goods. Here is the economic basis of the Gurian uprising in Georgia.[43]

This kind of economic reductionism was typical of Soviet officials who attempted to argue that the Menshevik uprising was "artificial," or that whatever discontent might have existed, the actual cause of insurrection was the decision by outsiders to launch an open attack on the Soviet order. Yet those same Soviet officials admitted repeatedly that their party had failed to win over the broad masses of the peasantry and that their pricing policies and restrictions on agriculture had created hostility among villagers. The Georgian revolt came up again and again in party debates as an example of incorrect policy toward the peasantry and was used as part of the general argument in favor of concessions to the better-off peasants. The causes of the revolt were complex and included economic and social discontents, frustrated nationalism, and the residual loyalties of Gurians and others to the old social democratic leadership. Its results were more clear-cut.

With the collapse of the uprising, the "Bolshevization" of Georgia was complete. All significant sources of opposition outside the communist party, as well as the "national communist" faction within the party, had been effectively silenced. The process of integrating the country into the Soviet system could now proceed without resistance from the guardians of Georgian sovereignty. Political conflicts remained, but the principal focus of party attention and of popular concern was now on the economy.

In Georgia, as in much of the Soviet Union, the mid-1920s was a period of recovery, stabilization, and gradual economic growth. When the Red Army arrived in Tiflis, food supplies were extremely low, currency in short supply, and workers were leaving the towns for their villages. The Bolsheviks set about reorganizing the economy, collecting the tax in kind from the peasantry to feed the cities, and using the printing press to issue money. On April 6, 1921, the Revkom nationalized all land in Georgia and prohibited all sale, purchase, and renting of land. Estates and large holdings of the former government, nobility, church, and monasteries were confiscated and placed in the state land fund to be administered by local soviets. Poor peasants were to be given land from this fund, and surveyors were mobilized to help carry out land adjustments. All direct taxes on land were abolished and replaced by the single tax in kind on produce. The poorest peasants, collective farmers, and Red Army men were exempted from the tax.[44]

Despite the far-reaching legislation of spring 1921, the new Bolshevik government, responding to Lenin's cautionary missives, did not in fact expropriate the old landed class. As part of a general effort to broaden the base of support for Soviet power, the chairman of the Revkom, who was simultaneously the people's commissar of agriculture, Pilipe Makharadze, was particularly conciliatory to the petty nobility of Georgia. Only after the October 1922 resignation of the Makharadze-Mdivani Central Committee did the Orjonikidze wing of the leadership move to accelerate the redistribution of the land. On November 27, 1922, the new Central Committee ordered "a broad political campaign" to abolish "feudal relations" in the countryside. The Central Executive Committee (TsIK) of the soviets followed by demanding an immediate seizure of the land and houses of former landlords and their transfer to landless or land-hungry peasants by March 15.[45]

In a passionate article (January 25, 1923), Orjonikidze railed against the policy of tolerance that had left the Soviet government protecting the holdings of the Andronikov, Mukhranskii, and Tumanov princes, the counts Kuchenbach, the Tseretelis, Bagration-Batonishvilis, and even the "worthy public figure" Niko Nikoladze. He expressed alarm that the Georgian intelligentsia remained sympathetic to the old ruling class.

> The Georgian intelligentsia—Mensheviks, National Democrats, Federalists—is flesh and blood, skin and bones part of the Russian counter-revolution. Instead of open sabotage it has chosen a different path: to enter Soviet service and to try in every way to defend the interests of the nobles and princes against the workers and peasants.[46]

This more radical approach, which signified a confrontation with the Georgian upper classes and intelligentsia, was approved by the Second Congress of the Georgian Communist Party in March. Instead of the slow surveying and redistribution by rural land committees, the party now decided to send *troiki* of party members "to lead and guide the work of the rural land committees in a revolutionary way." The committees were re-elected, and the inventory of holdings by nobles, merchants, kulaks, and others completed in the spring of 1923. Then almost fifty thousand desiatinas were expropriated, and additional excess holdings were redistributed to help the poorest peasants.[47]

By the summer of 1923, the last holdings of the nobility had been seized, and the class that had dominated Georgian social life for two millennia lost its last foothold in Georgia. The Bolshevik revolution, like other social revolutions, had transformed the class structure and brought new social groups into power; but in contrast to the great revolutions in England and France, the long civil war in the Russian empire had removed the old ruling elite so completely that restoration was impossible.

In the mid-1920s new problems faced the Soviet leaders, even as agriculture continued a steady recovery. The great bulk of the population was peasant, and the Communist Party had only the most tenuous hold over the countryside. A constant fear of peasant counterrevolution and of the tendency within NEP of aiding a revival of capitalism led the party to warn of danger from the richer peasants, the so-called kulaks. The Third Congress of the Georgian Communist Party echoed the perception of many Moscow leaders when it noted that NEP was producing a powerful stratum of rich peasants who were able to manipulate and control the poorer villagers. The congress pointed out that "the Georgian village in the period of the existence of Soviet power, in contrast to the Russian village, did not experience the influence of War Communism and civil war (requisition of produce, confiscation of grain surpluses from the better-off peasants, committees of poor peasants, etc.), which to a significant degree undermined the strength and power of the rural bourgeoisie in Russia." In Georgia the rural bourgeoisie was always quite weak, except in Kakheti and parts of Borchalo, but with the NEP the kulaks began to grow strong.[48]

To fight this trend, the congress recommended granting credit to the poorer peasants, encouraging peasant cooperatives, forming peasant mutual aid committees, setting up schools in the countryside, sponsoring "the patronage *(shefstvo)* of villages by workers," and recruiting poor peasants into the party.[49] This resolution was only one of a series that party congresses, the Central Committee, and the presidium of the Georgian party passed during the next five years in a continuing effort to bring the poor peasant over to Soviet power and create a gap between the upper and lower strata in the countryside. These efforts were almost completely futile.

Given the different notions of how socialism was to be built in peasant Russia, the central party leadership did not have a completely consistent policy toward the villages in the years 1924–1926, though the lack of party influence among the peasants remained a constant theme. Like several other party chiefs, Zinoviev interpreted the Menshevik uprising in Georgia as a sign that concessions had to be made to the peasantry. Six months later Stalin warned the party Orgburo that "under NEP a new Tambov [revolt] or a new Kronstadt [mutiny] is not at all excluded. The Transcaucasian, Georgian insurrection was an important warning."[50]

In stark contrast to the views of the ruling triumvirate, the left wing in the party drew its own lessons from the current impasse, emphasizing the need for more pressure on the peasantry through taxation and price policy in order to increase investment in industry. But following the publication of Trotsky's "Lessons of October" late in 1924, the Left suffered a defeat at the hands of the party majority, and in 1925 a series of concessions to the peasantry (permission to lease land and to hire labor with fewer hindrances, the lowering of the agricultural tax) culminated in Bukharin's famous call to the peasants to "enrich yourselves" (April 17, 1925).[51]

Georgia, indeed all of Transcaucasia, was slow in adapting to the new propeasant policies emanating from the center. Although Georgia had never experienced War Communism, the activity of many civil war–hardened Communists in the countryside was hardly in the spirit of NEP. Churches had been arbitrarily closed; taxes were collected in a confiscatory manner; local soviets were dominated by Communists with little attention to the opinions of peasants. The party made every effort to win over the small urban working class and potentially sympathetic elements in the intelligentsia, but it looked upon the peasantry as either an inert mass to be molded forcibly or a social class inevitably hostile to socialism.

The first palpable criticism of the party's practice in the villages came from outside Georgia, from the chairman of the Central Executive Committee (TsIK) of the USSR, Mikhail Kalinin, widely regarded as a spokesman for peasant interests. When the TsIK met in Tiflis in early March 1925, Kalinin took issue with the overly bright picture painted in the report by Mamia Orakhelashvili, the chairman of the Transcaucasian Council of People's Commissars (Sovnarkom). The report, he said, lacked a "peasant spirit." It had nothing to say to the nonparty peasant, the very person to whom the party was now appealing. Comrades in Georgia had been too hard on the peasantry and tried to turn them too quickly from religion to communism. Kalinin asked that a broader amnesty be considered for participants in the August 1924 insurrection and that persecutions for religious activities be halted. Orakhelashvili responded contritely, announcing that the local organization's policies were softening, that they now had "complete liberalism" in the area of religion. At the end of the TsIK session an amnesty was declared, and the most prominent prisoner, the catholicos of Georgia, Amvrosi, and other clerics who had been detained were released.[52]

The shifts in the approach to the peasantry through 1925 were evident in the speeches and reports of "Sergo" Orjonikidze, unquestionably the most powerful official in Transcaucasia, who sounded considerably more moderate than he had in 1921–1923. As the highest-ranking representative of the Stalin apparatus in the region, a member of the Central Committee of the RKP(b) since 1921, and secretary of the Zakkraikom from December 1924, Orjonikidze had enormous authority. But the failure to attract the nonparty peasantry and the unemployed intelligentsia to the side of Soviet power now had to be faced. He was forced to acknowledge Kalinin's criticism and told the Tiflis soviet a few days later:

We have not been able up to now to attract the nonparty peasantry into the organs of our power. Often terrible things happened in the villages which drove the peasants to despair . . . Yesterday I spoke with the chairman of a district executive committee. To my question, how is the matter of the churches working out, he answered that the Communists were opposed and, therefore, he was unable to permit the churches to open. But the Communists number not more than three to five people in the village. It seems that the church is not for the faithful in the population, but for our comrades. (Laughter.)[53]

Orjonikidze called for a more active role for nonparty peasants in the soviets, reflecting the central party policy of "revitalizing the soviets." The peasants, who complained about the inequitable tax burden, should themselves participate in the distribution of taxes.[54] He cautioned party members not to label peasants arbitrarily as kulaks, illustrating the current practice with an example from a recent report of a commission sent to investigate the peasants' situation:

> Buniat Zade says that he asked to be shown a *bedniak* [poor peasant]. They showed him a man who was covered by a sack, and said: "Here is a *bedniak*." The commission asked to be shown a *sredniak* [middle peasant]. They showed it a man half in a sack, half in rags. The commission asked: "Who is a kulak?" They showed him a man who lived in a cave, had no less than twenty family members and two to three cows. This is whom they consider a kulak, and all these kulaks, it turns out, lose their right to vote.[55]

Like his superiors in Moscow, Orjonikidze was anxious to broaden the base of the Soviet government in the countryside, but at the same time he was careful to tread a fine line between opening the rural economy to market forces, which in the view of most Communists would have benefited the kulaks, and maintaining some restraints on the richer peasants.

The propeasant policy was extremely attractive to the Georgian peasants and also to their supporters within the state apparatus. In July 1925, the People's Commissariat of Agriculture of Georgia drafted a plan that went beyond the limits of party policy and permitted the sale and purchase of land.[56] The plan was suppressed by higher party officials and condemned at the Fourth Congress of the Georgian Communist Party (November–December 1925) and at the Fourteenth Congress of the Russian Communist Party.[57] Clearly, denationalization of the land was far too extreme a move toward capitalism to be tolerated by most Communists. But within Georgia hundreds of cases of land sales were discovered after 1925, and they continued until the end of the decade.

The pendulum began to swing back away from concessions to the better-off peasants by the fall of 1925. In December Orjonikidze chastized those comrades who earlier had deemed it permissible to buy and sell land, as well as those who in promoting the "revival of the soviets" had minimized party participation:

> Some of our comrades have made mistakes in the question of the revival of the soviets, of promoting soviet democracy. Some of our comrades, not having understood the new course of the party, completely stood aside from the re-elections to the soviets, and the election campaign was carried out without the leadership of our party. As a consequence, kulak elements came to head rural soviets in many places. The soviets must be revived; soviet democracy must honestly be promoted, but the party ought to carry this out under its leadership. The leadership of the party must not be weakened one iota.[58]

The party leaders in Transcaucasia were caught between their desire to win over the nonparty peasantry and their ideological commitment to the proletariat and a program of industrialization. The solution to all problems seemed to be an expansion of the economy, yet that required making the difficult choice between unleashing the kulaks or heavier taxation of the agricultural sector. The often-repeated program of bringing the greater part of the peasantry to socialism through the cooperatives never really got off the ground. Orjonikidze periodically regretted the weakness of cooperatives in Transcaucasia and stressed the need for their expansion. At the end of 1925 there were four hundred thousand members in all cooperatives, and the increase in membership since October 1924 had been considerable (48 percent). But the figures for agricultural cooperatives were far less impressive. In Georgia only 34,591 peasants had joined cooperatives by October 1925.[59] The equivocation and hesitancy in the party line on agriculture can be felt in the awkward phrasing of the resolution by the Fourth Congress of the Georgian party in December 1925:

> Considering that the strengthening of work in the village is one of the most important tasks of the party and noting that, as in other Soviet republics, there are two deviations from the current line of the party on work in the village: first—the underestimation of the significance of the development of NEP in the village and the misunderstanding of its necessity; second—the underestimation of the kulak danger, the congress sets forth as immediate tasks the organization of the village poor and those elements of the peasantry allied to them, in agreement with the resolution of the Central Committee of the RKP(b), in order to stop the growing kulak danger and the activities of former nobles, who as a legacy of local peculiarities and the unique social structure of the Georgian nation ought to be included in the category of the kulaks.[60]

Another theme of Orjonikidze's speeches was the continuing tension between the party and the nonparty intelligentsia, especially in Georgia and Armenia. He came down hard on the chauvinism of the intellectuals and the mutual hostility between the two groups, and feared that the inability of the government to employ the intellectuals would lead to their further alienation from the state. Even though he emphasized the successes of Soviet nationality policy in Transcaucasia—the establishment of national peace among the ethnic communities, the "nationalization" of educational, cultural, and governmental institutions—Orjonikidze began to argue that expertise was more important than nationality as a criterion for selecting cadres for the economic apparatus.

> It is necessary to work for the economic renaissance of our country, and for this it is not enough to be a Georgian, one must also know one's business . . .
> Here workers [rabotniki] are needed, and as much as they cry, I am a Georgian, an Armenian, an Azerbaijani, and you cannot put someone else

in but me, we nevertheless declare that we will invite that person who can best do the job, who is best able to revive our economy, no matter what his national origin: Georgian or Armenian, Azerbaijani or Russian. (Applause.)[61]

Georgia had reached a stable economic and cultural plateau by the mid-1920s. The Soviet government had no organized enemies within the country and could dismiss the impotent maneuverings of the Mensheviks abroad. Though much of the population, especially the intelligentsia, was still hostile or at least unfriendly to the regime, an accommodation to political realities had led to a general acquiescence in Soviet rule. This new stability and acceptance of the new order was aided by both the economic recovery and the concessions made to Georgian national culture and language.

The economic revival was palpable both in agriculture and industry by 1925–1926. Agricultural output in Georgia had reached 94.4 percent of the prewar (1913) level. The attention paid to industry had not only brought prior existing plants back into production but had started up some twenty new enterprises between 1921 and 1925, nine had been launched in 1925 alone. Three-quarters of Georgian industry was nationalized, and although industry still produced only about a quarter of the gross output of the Georgian economy, the recovery by 1925 had reached 86.4 percent of the 1913 level, a figure higher than that of Soviet industry as a whole (75.5 percent).[62]

The most important industry in Georgia, the manganese mines of Chiatura, recovered very slowly, however, and were still producing less than 50 percent of the prewar output in 1924–1925. To accelerate development, the central Soviet government negotiated and signed a concessions agreement with American industrialist Averell Harriman, who agreed to put more than $1,000,000 worth of equipment into Chiatura, build rail connections to Poti ($10,000,000), and improve the port facilities at Poti ($1,000,000). Harriman's firm was to produce 300,000 tons of manganese in the first year, 400,000 the second, and 500,000 the third, for which the Soviet government would receive a royalty of $3 a ton for the first three years on every ton exported, and $4 a ton thereafter. The concession was to run for twenty years.[63]

The firmest support for the Soviet order came from the small Georgian working class, which after a decline in numbers during the Menshevik republic began a steady revival. At the end of 1925 Orjonikidze reported that the number of industrial workers was climbing close to the prewar level. Metalworkers reached 82 percent, tobacco workers 112 percent, printing industry workers 90 percent, and all industrial workers 95 percent of the number in 1913. Two-thirds of the 116,000 Georgian workers (1925–1926) were employed by nationalized industries. Ethnic Georgians made up just over 40 percent of young workers in the republic.[64]

Despite the growth in numbers of employed workers, a chronic problem of unemployment developed as more and more peasants moved from the overcrowded countryside into towns. The number of workers actually fell in many industries in 1922–1923 (28 percent in metallurgy, 58 percent in coalmining). The Georgian Central Committee recognized the crisis in industry, and its June 1923 plenum adopted measures to lower the cost of production and aid growth—laying off "redundant" workers, particularly administrative personnel, lowering tariffs on railroads, granting more long-term credits to industry, reducing trade union interference in the industrial activity of the Supreme Economic Council (VSNKh), and gradually concentrating all enterprises under a central authority.[65] The party maintained its interest in industry and workers, but by the middle of the 1920s its focus shifted to the peasantry, and workers seemed to take second place for several years.

The Fourteenth Party Congress was notable not only for the rout of the Zinoviev opposition but for a shift in economic policy toward industry. As E. H. Carr explains it, "The logic of socialism in one country compelled Stalin to call a halt to the policy of concessions to the *kulak* and, almost in spite of himself, carried him over to the camp of the industrialists." Though some of Stalin's allies, most importantly Bukharin, spoke of industrialization "at a snail's pace" within the confines of the existing propeasant policy, a growing consensus in favor of accelerating the expansion of industry, particularly heavy industry, was emerging within the party leadership. As almost all existing industrial capacity was put into use, the major problem ahead "was the need to achieve in an agrarian environment, a substantially higher level of investment in industry, and to direct this investment towards the construction of new factories." The source of capital in the isolated, backward USSR could only be the working peasantry, but the implications of this harsh reality were difficult for many party members to face. Even Dzerzhinskii, head of VSNKh, queried, "At whose expense should our industrialization be carried out?" and fretted that it was too burdensome for the peasantry at present.[66]

Following the April 1926 plenum of the Central Committee of the All-Russian Communist Party [VKP(b)], the party organizations in Transcaucasia began discussing the need for "socialist accumulation," that is, acquisition of capital to build heavy industry. In Tiflis the party *aktiv* (the most active members) considered accumulation through loans. Orjonikidze outspokenly promoted industrialization. "We have now entered a new stage of NEP," he told the Erevan *aktiv*. "Capitalist encirclement dictates that we throw all our forces toward the development of the industry of our country, for if tomorrow the capitalist countries agree not to give us machines then we will not be able to satisfy the growing demand of the peasantry for industrial goods."[67]

By mid-1926 projects for five-year plans had been prepared by each of the Transcaucasian republics. The backwardness of Transcaucasia, even in comparison with peasant Russia, was stressed repeatedly. If one excluded the two major heavy industries in the region, oil and manganese, industry accounted for only 37 percent of the gross income of Transcaucasia. In December 1926 the Georgian Central Committee acknowledged that artisanal production would remain for some time the "fellow traveler" of socialist industry.[68]

At least as important as the economic recovery to the stabilization of Soviet rule in Georgia were the measures undertaken to promote ethnic Georgian culture—building schools, promoting publication in Georgian, encouraging opera, theater, and film. The 1920s was a period of ferment in Georgian literature with a proliferation of rival literary schools. Besides a group of "proletarian writers," who unequivocally supported the Soviet government, the literary men and women were divided between those who were willing to work with Bolsheviks—Niko Nikoladze, former populist Soprom Mgaloblishvili, Niko Lordkipanidze (1880–1944), and others—and those who were either quietly hostile or apolitical—Aleksandre Abasheli (1884–1954), Konstantine Gamsakhurdia (1891–1975), Shalva Dadiani (1874–1959), Galaktion Tabidze (1891–1959), and the symbolist poets Titsian Tabidze (1895–1937) and Paolo Iashvili (1895–1937). Party policy encouraged competition among writers and artists and denied official recognition to any particular group.[69]

The policy of *korenizatsiia* continued the Menshevik republics approach of bringing Georgians into governmental institutions. By the mid-1920s almost all important posts in the republic were held by Georgians. This policy of "affirmative action" was particularly hard on Russians and Armenians, and many displaced professionals emigrated to the north or to Erevan. Nationalization was fostered in the schools as well. Primary education, though not compulsory until 1930, was expanded, and instruction was introduced in Georgian, Armenian, Azeri, Abkhaz, Osetin, and Russian. A massive campaign for literacy was carried out, and in the first ten years of Soviet rule a half-million people were taught to read and write.[70]

Higher education also expanded. The university, founded in 1918 by the historian Ivane Javakhishvili and other academics, had four thousand students by 1923. That year the council of professors elected Javakhishvili rector: he served until June 1926, when tolerance of non-Marxist intellectuals began to contract. Though tensions persisted between the party and nonparty intellectuals, those scholars trained before the revolution were able to publish and teach without persecution until the last years of the decade. Though overt expressions of nationalism were frowned upon, a gesture of considerable magnanimity was made when Georgian national treasures, which had been seized by tsarist authorities, were returned to Tiflis and placed in the national museum.

Discontent with communist policy both in the economy and in the political sphere found its expression in a new opposition within the party. The two principal anti-Stalin factions within the party, the "Left Opposition" of 1923–1924 and the Zinoviev-Kamenev opposition of 1925, joined in a "United Opposition" in mid-1926, castigating the majority leadership for favoring the "upper strata in the countryside." For his factional activity Zinoviev was expelled from the Politburo (July) and replaced by Rudzutak, a follower of Stalin. Five new candidate members of the Politburo were named, all known to be close to Stalin; three—Orjonikidze, Kirov, and Mikoyan—had worked in Transcaucasia. Orjonikidze was assigned to Rostov to become first secretary of the North Caucasian regional committee of the party, and requests from Transcaucasia that he be allowed to remain in the Zakkraikom were rejected by Moscow. His career soon moved into high gear. On November 3, 1926, Orjonikidze was appointed to succeed Kuibyshev as chairman of the Central Control Commission of the VKP(b), and two days later he was named people's commissar of the Workers' and Peasants' Inspectorate (RKI) as well.

The new head of the Zakkraikom, Mamia Orakhelashvili, was a close associate of Orjonikidze and a man loyal to the party majority. Like his predecessor, he lost no time dealing with the opposition within the Transcaucasian party organizations. Strongest and best organized in Georgia, the leftist opposition there included prominent party members who had fought the Stalin-Orjonikidze line since 1921 and others who had railed against the emphasis on the peasantry. In October several of the leaders—Kote Tsintsadze, L. Dumbadze, M. Okujava, B. Kalandadze, K. Iashvili, N. Kiknadze, P. Zalutskii, V. Tsentsadze, M. Solovian, R. Gladkov, and others—were expelled from the party by the Georgian Central Committee.[71] Finding it intolerable to work outside the party, Dumbadze, Okujava, and Kalandadze petitioned the Central Committee for reinstatement.

Defections notwithstanding, the opposition remained organized in Georgia through 1926 and 1927. The shortages in grain and industrial goods in the fall of 1927 gave added weight to the bloc's criticism of the faltering official policy. Reasserting their opposition, Dumbadze, Okujava, Kalandadze, and others issued the "Declaration of the Fifteen," calling for new elections to party cells and conferences. Early in September Trotsky's "Platform of the Eighty-Three" was printed and distributed illegally. At least twenty-six of the signers were Georgians, and more than two hundred Communists in Georgia put their names to it later. The Young Communist (Komsomol) organizations in Georgia were riddled with sympathizers of the opposition, and "Trotskyist" study groups were set up by young Communists.[72]

But as fear of war and threats were perceived from within the country, as pressure on the opposition intensified (Trotsky and Zinoviev were expelled from the Central Committee in late October), a rapid series of defections from the opposition took place. By the time the Fifteenth Party Congress convened on December 2, the Zinovievites were rushing back into the arms of the party, isolating Trotsky once again. In Georgia the party was now led by a new Central Committee from which all oppositionists had been expelled. Led by Mikhail Kakhiani, the Georgian party was prepared to follow closely the twists and turns of the Stalin line. Its more prominent figures— L. I. Kartvelishvili, Sh. Z. Eliava (candidate of the Central Committee of the VKP[b]), Mikha Tskhakaia, Pilipe Makharadze, and Mamia Orakhelashvili (member of the Central Committee of the VKP[b])—were by this time all supporters of the majority.

The party that ruled Georgia by the end of the 1920s was significantly different from the group of Bolsheviks who had entered the country with the Red Army. From a small group of underground revolutionaries it had been transformed into a broad-based ruling elite. In 1921 there had been just over 9,000 Communists in Georgia, the majority of whom (57 percent) were of peasant origin. Workers made up only 13 percent; most of the leaders came from the prerevolutionary intelligentsia or from the white-collar "employees" (*sluzhashchie*) who made up 22.8 percent of the membership. In 1924 the "Lenin levy" brought more workers into the party, until a high point was reached in January 1925 (44.5 percent was worker by social origin). The following year, when the leadership was attempting to establish links with the peasantry, recruitment of villagers was intensified, and two-thirds of the new entrants into the party were peasants.[73] By the end of the decade a little more than one-third of the party were workers still active at the bench, 28 percent were peasants, and a quarter were white-collar employees.

The party had grown to more than 33,000 members, heavily ethnically Georgian. The percentage of Georgians had fallen from 72.4 in 1922 to 62.5 in 1925 before it began a gradual increase. Russians outnumbered Armenians in the party early in the decade, and only in 1925 did Armenians take second place after the Georgians. In 1929 Georgians made up 66 percent of the party membership, Armenians 12.8 percent, and Russians 9 percent.[74] Georgians dominated state as well as party institutions, and with Tiflis the capital of both Georgia and the Transcaucasian federation, men like Orjonikidze, Orakhelashvili, Eliava, and Makharadze played leading roles in the governance of the whole territory.

With the loss of political independence and the curtailment of much of Georgia's political autonomy, the peoples of Georgia adjusted to a new ruling elite, one that had at the best of times a dual loyalty—to the development of a socialist Georgia and to the maintenance of a strong centralized Soviet Union. Those party members who placed the "imperial imperative" before local considerations won out in the first political struggle after Sovietization, and thereafter the parameters of policy were set outside the republic. The process of economic integration of Georgia, first into Transcaucasia, then into the Soviet Union as a whole, and the increasing emphasis on planning for industrialization removed much of the initiation and control of economic projects from the republic level. Essentially the republic became a unit of local administration. The attributes of full sovereignty, which both the Mensheviks and the "national Communists" had fought to preserve, were gone, and the new stable political order was firmly dominated by the Communist Party, the Georgian branch of which was subordinated to the central leadership.

The political victory of the Stalinists in Georgia was accompanied by moderate economic growth, the spread of literacy, and the "nativization" of administrative and cultural institutions. Each new construction project— irrigation systems, canals, the draining of the Poti swamps, the completion of the Zemo-Avchala hydroelectric station in 1927—was celebrated as an achievement not merely of engineering but of the Soviet system.

Though the great social transformation of Georgia would not occur until the following decade, the Soviet government's cultural Georgianization of the republic and its sponsorship of Georgian art, language, and learning were important factors in lessening opposition to the new order, particularly from the intelligentsia. The extension of the land reform and the relative freedom granted peasant producers also worked to reduce hostility to the Communists. Although it is impossible to estimate the degree of active support the government had, it seems clear that in the first half-dozen years of Soviet power the Georgian party had managed to create a relatively stable society in which the mass of people were prepared to acquiesce to its rule.

11 Stalin's Revolution

Besides quite fascinating memoirs and biographies of Stalin himself, the historical literature on the phenomenon of Stalinism was pathetically meager until the 1970s. A virtual explosion of studies occurred just about a decade and a half after Stalin's death, beginning most significantly with Moshe Lewin's study of collectivization, Robert C. Tucker's early biography and edited volume of essays on Stalinism, Sheila Fitzpatrick's work on the "cultural revolution" and social mobility, and Kendall E. Bailes's investigation of the technical intelligentsia.[1] To the earlier political reconstructions of the period have been added, more recently, social histories.

Yet the focus of most investigators remains on the center and the top of Soviet society, on the political leadership and the planners, on the Russians rather than the minorities of the periphery. No study of the Georgian republic in the period 1928–1953 has been undertaken by Western scholars; only the briefest sketch is provided by D. M. Lang in his *A Modern History of Soviet Georgia*.[2]

The full construction of the sociopolitical system of Stalinism took place in the 1930s, a decade both heroic and tragic. It was a time of compressed industrial revolution, the victory of the Communist Party over peasant resistance to collectivization, and the creation of a new, strictly regimented society. The price paid for the social and economic changes was high indeed: millions of lives lost or broken in the "dekulakization" and the purges; severe contraction of the relative freedoms enjoyed by the population under NEP; the radical lowering of material standards, even as rapid social mobility was promoted.

No easy assessment of the "Stalin revolution (or counterrevolution) can be made, and its very scope defies simple categorization by the historian.

Economic historian Alec Nove goes so far as to claim, "The 'revolution from above' which transformed the entire political, social and economic scene in a sense . . . was more revolutionary than the Bolshevik revolution itself."[3] Moshe Lewin contends that "the period 1929–1933 is probably one of the most momentous quinquennia in the history of Russia, indeed in modern history."

> This was a unique process of state-guided social transformation, for the state did much more than just "guiding": it substituted itself for society, to become the sole initiator of action and controller of all important spheres of life. The process was thus transformed into one of "state building," with the whole social structure being, so to speak, sucked into the state mechanism, as if entirely assimilated by it.[4]

For Georgia it was not only a "revolution from above" but a "revolution from outside," for both its inception and its pace were dictated from Moscow, not Tiflis. But the condensed period of the transformation only made the changes more difficult to endure. As in an earlier period of Russian-imposed changes, the Georgians resisted in a variety of ways, none of which prevented the transformation of their lives. At the end of the Stalin revolution Georgia was fundamentally different from what it had been a decade earlier.

If the early 1930s can be spoken of as the Stalin revolution, the years 1927–1929 can be justifiably characterized as the "prerevolutionary crisis." The optimism bred by economic successes in agriculture and in industry that had marked 1926 faded rapidly at the end of the following year as the amount of grain collected from the peasantry steadily declined. Peasants had little incentive to sell their grain in the face of low prices and a shortage of industrial goods. As the situation grew desperate, the party leaders took "extraordinary measures," traveling out to grain-producing areas and forcing the grain from the peasants with a variety of threats. In January 1928 Stalin himself went to Siberia and spoke in favor of prosecuting grain hoarders as criminals. The drastic campaign of confiscating and squeezing the grain from the villagers temporarily relieved shortages in towns, but the harsh policy stimulated resistance among peasants and crystallized a new opposition. Those who favored a tougher line toward the peasantry in the interest of rapid industrialization were grouped around Stalin, while those who hoped to preserve the essence of the New Economic Policy and accommodate the peasantry gathered around his former ally, Bukharin, who now found himself on the right wing of the party.

The majority of the leadership moved leftward in the summer of 1928, becoming convinced that the individual peasant producer had to be collectivized if grain was to be secured at low prices and industrial production permitted to shift away from consumer goods toward capital goods. The campaign against individual peasant agriculture was to be carried out under the aegis of a struggle against the kulaks and "capitalist elements in the countryside." But in fact it hit hard at the middle peasants as the party tried to create cleavages and "class struggle" within the relatively cohesive mass of peasants.

Abandoning the long-respected views of Engels (repeatedly affirmed by Lenin) that precluded the use of coercion against the peasantry, the Stalin leadership launched a program of rapid industrialization financed by a "tribute" levied on the peasantry. The Bukharin moderates were defeated in the fall of 1928 and systematically excluded from key decision-making positions. The poor harvest of 1928 led to "an unprecedented degree of intervention by the party and state authorities in the affairs of the countryside."[5] In April 1929 the Sixteenth Party Conference adopted the most ambitious variant of the first five-year plan.

The all-union crisis in agriculture was also experienced in Georgia. The peasantry in Transcaucasia was on the whole quite poor in comparison with the peasants of Russia. The average holding in Georgia in 1923 was 2.25 desiatinas of cultivated land. Only a minority (44.6 percent) had any working livestock, and a majority (54.1 percent) had no plows.[6] There was certainly improvement in the 1920s: by the end of 1927, the percentage of peasants with draft animals had risen to 65.6.[7] The overall output of agriculture increased. But the amount of farm produce available for market declined over time. Peasants had little surplus to exchange for industrial goods, and therefore Georgian agriculture could not benefit from improvements in technology.

In his report to the Orgburo of the central party in August 1928, the secretary of the Georgian party, Mikhail Kakhiani, admitted that "in recent years one notices that the tempo of growth in the agrarian economy of Georgia is slowing down." The gross output had been valued at 268,000,000 rubles in 1924–1925 and had risen by 56,000,000 rubles in 1925–1926. But it then fell by 16,000,000 rubles in 1926–1927. Grain suffered particularly. The percentage of landless peasants rose to 8.6, smallholders to 21.6 and middle peasants fell from 71.6 to 68.7.[8]

The Georgian People's Commissariat of Agriculture was committed through most of the 1920s to individual peasant agriculture. In 1922 it abolished its section on collective farms and turned that matter over to the Union of Agricultural Cooperatives *(tsarmokavshiri)*. The peasants were left to run their own economy within the broad limits set by state policy. From 1921 to 1927, the Georgian peasant population grew by 8.2 percent, less than the growth of the urban population (10.9 percent). The 1,926,400 peasants in Georgia at the time of the Bolshevik invasion had made up 85.5 percent of the population, whereas the 2,072,300 in 1927 represented only 77.7 percent. Yet this movement toward town did little to relieve land hunger and the density of population on the land. In 1921 there had been 341,400 peasant households in Georgia; by 1927 there were 428,900, an increase of 33.7 percent. Ominously, the number of households had risen four times the rate of population growth, indicating that the size of households and land-holdings was falling.[9]

Large families divided, sometimes only on paper, in order to receive the land allotment granted to individual households or to escape the agricultural tax from which poor peasants were exempt. There were other advantages unique to the poor peasantry. Large estates and the more substantial hold-ings of better-off peasants were broken up and given to the landless peasants (bogano) and the poor, who also received credits and other aid from the state. Already by 1923, 62 percent of all Georgian peasant households had only one able-bodied worker.[10]

The cooperative movement did not prove popular with Georgia's peas-ants. In 1926 tsarmokavshiri was abolished, after sustaining losses of 5,000,000 rubles, and was replaced by soplis kavshiri (Village Union), which did not do much better. By 1927 most cooperatives in industrial and special crops, like cotton, tea, grapes, and silk, had collapsed, and only 21 percent of the peasants were in any kind of cooperative by the end of the year.[11] In August 1928 that figure had risen to 27 percent as the campaign for cooperatives and collectives accelerated, but only the application of coercion would drive the numbers of collectivized and cooperatively organized peas-ants higher.

The gradual but inexorable policy shift from support for individual farming to collectivization of peasant holdings was neither the result of a predetermined plan of action by the party leadership nor the single viable alternative in the midst of the procurement crisis. Rather, like so many steps taken by the Communist Party, it was adopted hesitantly and repeatedly re-evaluated. Once again a momentous and irreversible transformation in Soviet history was an improvised response to a broad range of problems over which the government had little control. The Fifteenth Party Congress, held at the end of 1927, had made it clear that the time had come to move toward socialization of agriculture, but equally clear was the emphasis on a gradual transition and on the need to avoid coercion. One of the means to be adopted to aid collectivization was the contract system (kontraktatsiia), by which the state agreed to buy produce at a predetermined price and supply the peasants with seed, machinery, and other needed materials.

The Transcaucasian party leadership favored the contract system, for it was committed to collectivization, but resisted the kinds of confiscatory measures that were being applied in Siberia and European Russia. On February 1, 1928, the Zakkraikom sent out a directive to party organizations calling for the development of contracts with producers of such industrial crops as cotton, tobacco, and tea. At first the contracts were made by agricultural cooperatives with the few collective farms that existed, but soon private farmers were included. Only those peasants designated as kulaks were to be excluded.[12]

Some local party organizations called for forced requisitions from richer peasants, but these suggestions were rejected by the top leadership in Transcaucasia, which argued that their region was not a grain-exporting area but one dependent in part on imported grain and meat from the North Caucasus and, therefore, requisitions were unnecessary. On March 28, the Georgian Central Committee informed its lower party organizations that "the application of compulsory methods in the matter of exposing and selling grain surpluses [is] incorrect" and that economic means, such as withholding credit from peasants reported by local authorities to have surplus grain, were to be used instead of force.[13]

Grain shortages were felt in Transcaucasia in the winter and spring of 1928. Toward the end of March riots broke out in Tiflis, as embittered citizens, standing for hours in wet snow for bread, smashed bakery windows and beat up the bakers. Party leaders were concerned that the lack of adequate grain would have widespread implications for the Georgian economy. Industrial crops, like wool, were already being exchanged for grain rather than sold to the state, and there was a real possibility that the sown area of industrial crops would be reduced in favor of grain. Moreover, workers in industry and construction could not be supplied with bread. Still the Zakkraikom decided to allow local authorities to supervise the grain collections and to restrain the use of force. Only in "exceptional cases against malicious speculators" were administrative measures to be used.[14] In August the targets for grain collections in Transcaucasia were raised by local authorities, but by this time the moderation of the Georgians had reached the attention of Moscow.

On September 3, 1928, the Central Committee in Moscow issued a stern critique of the work of the Georgian Communist Party, particularly in agriculture. Not enough attention had been paid to intensifying agriculture, to expanding technical crops, to increasing the number of cooperatives and collective farms. Not enough party work, the resolution went on, had been done among poor peasants and women. The level of literacy was uneven: quite high in Ozurgeti (70 percent) and abysmally low (10 percent) in areas of national minorities. In the eyes of the central party leaders, the Georgian intelligentsia was petty-bourgeois and nationalist in its outlook, and an intense struggle had to be waged against "the remnants of Menshevism."[15]

This severe warning came precisely as the Stalin faction was engaged in its struggle with the Bukharin group. No single position was yet clear on agricultural policy, and the Georgian leaders had a brief breathing spell before a more aggressive policy was forced upon them. As Carr and Davies have written about this period:

The last months of 1928 brought a slow but inexorable widening of the rift between the two groups in the party leadership, between those who believed in the conciliation of the individual peasant as the way to guarantee grain supplies, and those who had become convinced that grain at the prices which the state and industry could afford to pay, could in the long run be got only by fighting the *kulak* and collectivizing production.[16]

Only as a more aggressive posture was adopted toward the villagers in late 1928 and early 1929 were the more moderate voices within the party effectively silenced. From the last year of the decade, political survival in the USSR depended on close identification with the "general line" promoted by the Stalin faction, even as it swayed and swerved through the course of a war initiated by the state against the peasants. "By the autumn and winter of 1928," Moshe Lewin writes, "implementation of the Stalinist version of the *smychka* [unity of peasant and worker] had begun. Stalin's formula was as follows: all possible aid was to be given to the bednyaks [poor peasants], and war was to be waged on the kulaks [rich peasants] in order to achieve mastery over the serednyaks [middle peasants]."[17] The year of drift came to an end; the last opposition was routed; and the campaign against the kulaks began.

By early 1929 a tense atmosphere had developed within the Soviet Union. The political conflict within the party was only part of a more generally strained environment. Perceived dangers from abroad and the isolation of the USSR internationally made solution of the grain crisis imperative. The Soviet harvest of 1928 was 5,000,000 tons lower than the record harvest of 1926. With increased demand for agricultural products, particularly from the state engaged in industrial growth, supply simply could not keep up. Extrarural marketings of grain and milk declined in 1928–1929; meat increased only because of unusually high slaughter. Rationing had to be introduced; the government was forced to buy grain abroad; and collections of grain were accelerated. With too few industrial goods available to sell to the peasants in exchange for grain, artificial "contracts" were drawn up, which, in essence, led to uncompensated requisitions of produce. Increasingly the party located the cause of the crisis, not in its own failures, but with the antistate activity of the kulaks.

"Kulak" was never a precisely defined category in the USSR, and the characteristics of such a peasant shifted in the official view according to political requirements. In Transcaucasia, where the peasantry was far poorer than in Russia, the number of "rich" peasants was smaller. In 1926–1927 about 3.5 percent of peasant households in the USSR had an income of more than a thousand rubles a year. In the ZSFSR only 2.3 percent were that fortunate. In European Russia the per capita holding of a peasant averaged 2 desiatinas of land; in Georgia the average peasant held no more than 0.7. In 1928 per capita income in prewar rubles was 91.6 rubles for the USSR as a whole but only 51.2 for the ZSFSR. Officials of the time and later scholars differ on what percentage of the depressed Transcaucasian peasantry should be labeled "kulak"; estimates range from 15 down to 1.5 percent.[18]

Since statistics in this period are questionable and the categories themselves subject to arbitrary cutoffs, the Georgian scholar of collectivization,

P. N. Lomashvili, rejects the figures of the Central Statistical Board of the Georgian Republic (which estimates 2.8 percent of the peasantry were kulaks at the end of the 1920s) and argues that the best data come from tax rolls. In 1928–1929, only 1.74 percent (15,349) of peasant households in Transcaucasia were considered wealthy enough to be "individually assessed." In Georgia only 1.45 percent or 6,659 households fell into this category. These figures rose and fell slightly in the following years, but Lomashvili feels confident that one can conclude from this data that kulak households in Transcaucasia were never more than 1.5 or 2 percent of the total number of peasant households.[19] The clear implication of this material is that there was no "kulak danger" in Transcaucasia and that the harsh measures taken against peasants designated as kulaks were unnecessary and primarily politically motivated.

Within the Transcaucasian party, discussions about the current course were intense. Though we have little information about positions taken by individual leaders, it seems that as early as the drafting of the First Five-Year Plan in the spring of 1928 there was tension between "local nationalists" (apparently those defending the individual constituent republics) and "left centralist, i.e., great-power chauvinist, tendencies" (those who favored expanding the powers of the Transcaucasian government over the republics).[20] As a result of the debates surrounding its foundation in the early 1920s, the ZSFSR government had been limited in its authority. Its planning organs had little sway over the individual republics. The Supreme Economic Council (VSNKh) of the ZSFSR, for example, had no control or operating functions over local VSNKhs or the most important branches of industry, and there was no effective planning from the Transcaucasian planning authority, Zakgosplan.

At every level moderate views prevailed among local Communists well into 1929. Though no organized faction of the Right existed, many party members held that collectivization was inappropriate in Transcaucasia. Others argued that there were no kulaks south of the Caucasus, or, if there were, they were "good Soviet kulaks." In Kakheti the local executive committees opposed the seizure of "excess" land from kulaks, and in Gori *uezd* Komsomol members requested that the right to vote be restored to kulaks. In South Ossetia party members claimed that "since in 1920 we all fought together against the Mensheviks, there is no difference between the various strata; privileges should be enjoyed equally."[21] There was little enthusiasm for collective farms either among peasants or among party members. But as the line from Moscow clarified and "purges" removed the more moderate elements from the Transcaucasian party organizations (7,625 were expelled in the second half of 1929), the moderates began to lose ground.

The radicalization of the state's policies toward the peasantry and national minorities came from the top down, from Moscow rather than from local Transcaucasian Communists. Orders from the center forced the local cadres to carry out policies that many feared would lead to resistance. At the very beginning of 1929, the central government decreed that Muslim women were to be required to remove the *chadra,* the heavy veil covering their faces. In the debate in the Zakkraikom on whether to publish this decree locally, Old Bolshevik Sargis Ter-Gabrielian spoke out strongly against removal of the veil by force: "*Chadra* ought to be removed by one's own culture . . . When we have such a cultural growth among women, you want at that moment to force it in such a way that this will hit us not from one side alone but will cause more than one bloody victim."[22] Ter-Gabrielian was denounced as a reactionary, and the decision was made to carry out the new antireligious policy.

In Georgia a few days later the party resolved to close "all legal and illegally existing Muslim, Jewish, and sectarian religious schools."[23] The costs of such a policy were soon evident. By March anti-Soviet resistance was widespread in Ajaria, the Muslim enclave in southwestern Georgia. The party leaders admitted that there had been "clumsy, and in some places even incorrect," implementation of the directives on veils and schools, but the damage had been done. In almost all Muslim areas of Transcaucasia opposition to communist policy increased, and the campaigns for collectivization were marked in those districts by an exceptional level of violence.

In the second half of 1929 the central authorities steadily chipped away at the decision-making powers of the local Communists in Transcaucasia. On July 12, ZSFSR grain was included in the centralized plan for collections, and Transcaucasia was told to collect 4,000,000 poods of grain. In August Orakhelashvili, as secretary of the Zakkraikom, complained to the Central Committee that with centralization he had no authority to dispose of the collected grain and was unable to satisfy the demand of local cities and poorer districts. His complaint was rejected by Moscow, and he was informed that Transcaucasian grain was needed to alleviate the food crisis in other parts of the Soviet Union.[24] Within Transcaucasia private sales of grain were largely prohibited; grain could not be transported on trains during the period of collection; and the campaign against speculators was accelerated.

On October 4, the Sovnarkom in Moscow ordered the strengthening of the Transcaucasian-level governmental organs at the expense of the subordinate republics. The ZSFSR was given full control over the activity of the republic Sovnarkoms, and a Transcaucasian People's Commissariat of Agriculture was created to direct the antikulak and collectivization campaigns. At the same time local soviets were given broad powers to levy fines and bring charges against peasants who resisted grain collections. Finally, the direction of the Transcaucasian economy was placed under the VSNKh of the ZSFSR with planning functions centered in Zakgosplan. Decision-making was now to be centralized. As the resolution of Zakkraikom in November put it: "A decisive struggle is needed against the manifestations of federalism, against the holding back by party leaders of the rapid tempos of economic construction, against the tardiness and passivity of party organs in the correcting of all sorts of harmful phenomena in party organizations."[25] The moderates' resistance to the radical policies of the center ended dramatically with Orakhelashvili's removal and his replacement as secretary of the Zakkraikom by an outsider, Aleksandr Ivanovich Krinitskii (1894–1938), brought in from Belorussia.[26]

The next four months (November 1929 to March 1930) were the "great turning point" *(velikii perelom)* in the collectivization campaign throughout the Soviet Union. At the November plenum of the Zakkraikom Krinitskii told local party leaders that their region had fallen behind in collectivization: "We must make the maximum effort to prepare and carry out the spring sowing campaign so that this sowing campaign becomes the take-off point for the further development of the process of collectivization."[27] Immediately following the meeting collectivization was speeded up and force applied to the recalcitrant peasants.

With only 3.62 percent of sown area collectivized, the militant Hamaiak Nazaretian now proposed that some districts be completely collectivized and that about 12 percent of all land be collectivized in the spring campaign. Karaev and Buniatzade of Azerbaijan, Gogoberidze of Georgia, and Aghasi Khanjian, soon to be named first secretary of the Armenian party, all pushed for more rapid tempos, though the latter two suggested that *sploshnaia kollektivizatsiia* (full collectivization) be linked to the availability of tractors. Only one major leader, Ivanov-Kavkazskii, warned against the new tempos and argued that the suggested figures had not been thought through. In December the Zakkraikom decided to expel kulaks from areas of full collectivization, even though such a course had not yet been approved in Moscow. Already the richest 1.8 percent of peasant households in the ZSFSR were paying almost half of all agricultural taxes, while more than 60 percent were completely freed from taxation.[28] Thus, both economic measures and physical force were combined to break the independence of the better-off peasants and make the countryside more amenable to the authority of the Communist Party.

Although the harvest declined in the fall of 1929, especially in Abkhazeti, Ajaria, South Ossetia, and almost all of western Georgia, grain collection plans were overfulfilled. And collections continued even after targets had been met. In Georgia the percentage of collectivized households rose rapidly—from 3.5 in October 1929 to 63.7 by March 1930. In certain districts collectivization percentages were even higher: 70 in Kutaisi and Gori *okrugy* and Ozurgeti *uezd*, 83 in Kakheti *okrug*, and 92 percent in South Ossetia, where there had been almost no collectives a month and a half earlier.[29]

No hesitation about applying force now existed. Late in December 1929 Stalin had given the green light to the strongest measures against resistance to collectivization when he declared that the party "in its practical work [was moving] from limiting the exploitative tendencies of the kulaks to the policy of eliminating the kulaks as a class."[30] Within weeks this new line was approved by the Georgian Central Committee and the Zakkraikom. By the end of January a militant "left" position had completely engulfed the Trans-caucasian Communists. Even such consistent moderates as Pilipe Makharadze joined the chorus, either swept up in the general enthusiasm for a radical solution to the crisis or after calculating the consequences of demurring.

> Dekulakization, the destruction of the kulaks as a class, must be carried out, but the essential question is how to carry it out, slowly or rapidly. It is asked, can we go slowly in this matter? When this question is put point-blank, it is clear that one cannot go slowly, because slowness can lead to the most contradictory facts . . . If we go slowly, then the process of liquidation will be dragged out and will be even more painfully implemented. As a result we might have reduced productive forces. The destruction of live and dead inventory is already occurring.[31]

The question arose at the plenum of the Zakkraikom (January 20): what to do with the kulak families once their land and inventory had been seized and given to the collectives. While kulaks were not to be admitted to collectives, it had been thought by many that dekulakized peasants might be admitted. But the more militant antikulak policy articulated by Stalin on December 27 threw the Transcaucasian party leaders into confusion. There was no open opposition to the policy of full collectivization and liquidation of the kulaks as a class by early 1930, but there was disagreement about the tempo of collectivization and the ultimate fate of the kulaks.

Karaev of Azerbaijan wondered aloud what would be done with forty thousand kulaks:

> Together with members of their families this is a whole army. You can imagine what will happen if this army crawls into the city, into the workers' districts . . . I completely share the view—exile the kulaks. Exile them where? To the poorer lands which we have; let them work there.

Erzinkian of Armenia took a harsher position:

> In individual cases we ought to isolate the active kulaks. We ought not only to exile them but perhaps shoot them . . . But a part of the kulaks we will give lands in the worst, most distant regions, having first taken away their inventory . . . We will liquidate them in various districts of Transcaucasia by various methods.

Mamulia of the Muslim region of Ajaria tried to convince his comrades to exempt his region from full collectivization and permit it to continue the policy of limiting the exploitive tendencies of the kulaks, but he was denounced as an opportunist by Krinitskii. Finally, the representative of Kolkhoztsentr (the Collective Farm Center) in Moscow, Bitenko, reminded the Transcaucasian Communists that orders had been given and must be carried out. [32]

In the ferocious campaign of early 1930, the process of dekulakization was pushed more vigorously than collectivization.[33] Class warfare was declared in the countryside. Poorer peasants were to be incited against the better-off, and the lands and inventories of the kulaks seized for the collective farms. But throughout much of Russia and Transcaucasia class lines within the peasantry were impossible to draw, and a remarkable degree of cohesiveness, even solidarity, was exhibited by many peasant villages as they pulled together to resist the onslaught from outside.

Early in 1930 resistance to collectivization and dekulakization spread through Transcaucasia. The first mass demonstration, typical of later episodes, took place in Kakheti. About 120 "kulak" households, expelled from their lands in Kiziki, gathered at the railroad station in Tsnopi. They elected an elder and decided not to leave the district. The Kakhetian party committee ordered their dispersal, but the peasants demanded the release of arrested kulaks, the return of all their property, and settlement within the district. An armed detachment of Communists then surrounded the peasants' camp, and a fight broke out. Two people were killed, two wounded, and forty arrested.[34]

The antikulak campagin was carried out against the villages with little regard for local sensibilities or needs. Repeatedly workers and "communards" (armed Communists) were sent into the countryside to aid the militia and the army against peasant resisters. Not only were the richest peasants expropriated, but many who were middle peasants by any definition were treated as kulaks. The lines of demarcation were meaningless to the peasants, and time and again entire villages opposed the effort by outsiders to take land from so-called kulaks. A report to the Georgian Central Committee stated:

> Demonstrations of peasants against collectivization have taken place in parts of Georgia with the demands that collectivization be stopped, that existing kolkhozes be broken up, that exiled kulaks be returned, that boundaries not be violated, etc. In the demonstrations primarily women participated, influenced by kulaks (Tiflis, Gori, and Kakheti *okrugy*).

If there were not direct confrontations with authorities, peasants found other means to resist, most importantly the slaughter of livestock. In Georgia the sheep population was reduced by half in 1929–1930.[35]

Although party circulars in February and early March called for caution and moderation toward middle peasants, the tempo of dekulakization and collectivization accelerated. In Georgia "socially alien elements," including kulaks, merchants, and their children, were ordered out of secondary and higher educational institutions. A virtual war between the state and the peasantry raged in Muslim areas of Georgia and Armenia and throughout Azerbaijan. "Crude errors" by party cadres toward Muslim peasants led the

Zakkraikom to modify its policy and to restrict repression and exiling of kulaks in those regions. Still, the "left" course prevailed, and Georgian party secretaries Gogoberidze and Kakhiani told the Central Committee that no mistakes had been made in tempo, only in implementing policies by local organizations at times.[36] Charges that the formation of collectives had been artificial were rejected out of hand.

As the resistance in the countryside increased, Stalin suddenly called a halt to the rapid collectivization. On March 2, 1930, his article "Dizzy with Success" appeared in *Pravda*. As Moshe Lewin says: "This manoeuvre enabled him to save his regime and his own power by smearing the Party cadres. In the villages, editions of the newspaper were passed eagerly from hand to hand. Processions of peasants paraded copies of Stalin's article on banners, while the local officials dared not show their faces in the villages."[37] The *velikii perelom* was over.

Though he would later deny that "Dizzy with Success" represented a fundamental shift in agrarian policy, Stalin made several key points in his article that caused confusion in party ranks and an immediate halt to the headlong rush to collectivize. "The success of our collective farm policy," he claimed, "is explained among other things by the fact that this policy is based on the *voluntary nature* of the collective farm movement and *consideration of the different conditions* in different regions of the USSR. It is impossible to cultivate the collective farms by force. This would be stupid and reactionary . . . It is impossible to transfer mechanically the examples of collective farm construction in developed areas to underdeveloped areas. This would be stupid and reactionary." He insisted that the fundamental form of the collective farm was to be the "agricultural *artel*," rather than the more extreme commune or the moderate "cooperative with joint labor." And he ended by chastising those Communists who, in following the directives sent down from the leadership, had linked the campaigns to collectivize and liquidate the kulaks with a brutal attack on religious institutions and the clergy. "And what about those 'revolutionaries,' if one may call them that, who *begin* the business of organizing the *artel* with the removal of bells from the churches. Removing the bells—think about what kind of revolutionary behavior that is!"[38]

During the next two months the official policy of the Communist Party toward the peasantry reiterated Stalin's criticism of compulsory collectivization and attacks on religion. Lower officials were blamed for "extremely crude, shameful and criminal treatment of the population," and any blame for the failures of collectivization was thus diverted away from the leadership and toward local cadres.[39] Early in April Stalin repeated his charges that provincial officials had been too anxious to collectivize rapidly, and this time he mentioned the Transcaucasians (among others) who "in their zeal to 'reach and surpass' the advanced districts, began to orient toward completion of collectivization 'in the shortest possible time,' although they had a full four years at their disposal (until the end of 1933)."[40]

The first responses from Transcaucasia to the new, more moderate policy were characterized by a reluctance to admit errors and an attempt to maintain the leftist line. The Georgian Central Committee passed a resolution on March 7, which proclaimed that

> the party organizations were basically correct in their approach to the tasks at hand, and that despite the fact that in Georgia the collectivization movement could not but develop more slowly than in the advanced grain growing districts of the Union, here a fundamental turn of the basic mass of the peasantry toward socialism has been noticed.[41]

While some local organizations had made some mistakes, it was conceded, the achievements were impressive. Rather than retreat, dekulakization was to be completed within a week, by March 15.

By mid-March the Transcaucasian Communists began moderating their positions. On March 18 the Georgian Central Committee decided not to socialize household plots, vineyards, and orchards in areas where they were primarily used to produce for sale in markets. This was a considerable step backward for the Georgian leaders, who just two months earlier had been pushing for the formation of communes rather than *artely* as the form for the future collective farms. On April 3, the Georgian leaders allowed the breakup of large collectives if demanded by the peasants and if the *kolkhozy* included several villages. A law was to be drawn up on abuses of the electoral rights of citizens. Kakheti and Khobi (Zugdidi) were exempted from full collectivization.[42]

But the hesitant backing away from their militant policies was complicated for the Transcaucasian Communists by divisions and dissatisfactions among local officials. A note was sent to Iagoda and Evdokimov of the GPU (State Political Administration—the reorganized police agency) in Moscow by S. F. Redens and his deputy, Lavrenti Beria, of the Transcaucasian political police. The Caucasians laid blame for the difficulties in collectivization on local party and state leaders who were reluctant to employ sufficiently repressive measures on local kulaks.

> The demonstrations which have taken place have been liquidated up to now by peaceful means . . . The initiators and direct participants in disturbances and violence have with few exceptions not been arrested. In some cases as we tried to carry out arrests we ran into the general resistance of the whole village, as a result of which the designated arrests were rescinded. All this was interpreted by the population as a sign of the government's weakness and permitted the protestors even greater impudence . . .
> The situation is serious. If decisive measures are not taken, then toward spring we might have serious complications which can spill over into armed uprisings.

Party chief Krinitskii protested the tendentious tone of the note and the consequent order of the central party leaders that the GPU be put in charge of the struggle with the kulaks.[43] But he was soon dismissed, along with Kakhiani, Nazaretian, and Kostanian. The men who had come to power in November 1929 and had led Transcaucasia through the *velikii perelom* had lasted only six months before the militant line was repudiated by Moscow.

The new leadership in Transcaucasia was headed by V. V. ("Beso") Lominadze (1897–1935), an outspoken Georgian who had worked for many years in the Comintern.[44] Shortly after his arrival in Tiflis Lominadze made several important speeches critical of the way collectivization had been carried out in the region. To the Seventh Congress of the Georgian Communist party in May 1930 he condemned the attempt to emulate the efforts of the party in the areas designated for complete collectivization.

> Here in the Transcaucasian village the material productive base which would allow us to undertake such a tempo of collectivization as in the North Caucasus, Lower Volga, or Ukraine does not exist. The right land relations or cultural developments do not exist. There is not the depth of class and political differentiation in our villages, and finally there are not enough strong cadres, without whom nothing can be done. There are no definitive political and organizational preconditions, rural soviets able to work, or good organizations of the poor.[45]

Collective farms had not been firmly established in Georgia, Lominadze went on. Comrades cited victories but failed to mention the areas of national minorities where the campaign had not been successful—in largely Turkish Borchalo or Akhaltsikhe, where Armenians and Turks lived, or Akhalkalaki, which was primarily Armenian in population. As an example he mentioned Kakheti where collectivization had been carried out very gradually until orders came down from the Georgian Central Committee. Then a sharp turn to the left was made, and within a few weeks the collectivized share of agriculture rose from 12 to 80 percent. Once free exit from the *kolkhozy* was permitted, however, the number fell to 10 percent.

Lominadze's speech preceded the adoption of a resolution calling for a milder policy toward the kulaks: they were to be limited and restrained largely through economic means, such as taxation, but not eliminated by force. Later at the Transcaucasian party congress in June he criticized the slowness with which local Communists had abandoned the leftist policy of the pre-March period. Not until mid-April had the central committees of the three Transcaucasian republics unequivocally acknowledged their errors.

Lominadze's real views in mid-1930 are difficult to decipher from his public statements. While in Transcaucasia he directed his criticism against the militant practice of forced, rapid collectivization, but he was careful not to question the general line of the party. "The principal danger is in the village," he maintained, "and in general in all our work it is the right deviation." This right deviation, he claimed, would "find its expression more often than not in a nationalist form."[46] Even as he began to develop a critique of Stalin's position, Lominadze refused to make concessions to local nationalists. When Old Bolshevik Eliava complained that Transcaucasia was still too decentralized, that decisions by the federal-level authorities were often disregarded by the republic-level bodies, Lominadze agreed that in the future Transcaucasian economic organs would have to take the leading role. His authority as a member of the all-union Central Committee helped him to win over many local Communists to his analysis, particularly in the Baku organization.

At the Sixteenth Party Congress in Moscow (June–July 1930), Lominadze's remarks had what R. W. Davies calls "a certain 'Leftist' tinge." He lauded the policy of dekulakization as the first step toward the creation of a classless society in the Soviet Union. But the elimination of this class of peasant exploiters was to be carried out, not by repression and force, but by elimination of the means by which kulaks made their livelihood, namely petty commercial production and small peasant agriculture. At the same time social differentials now existing within collective farms would be eliminated as the "sphere of socialization" spread to other parts of the rural economy. Lominadze spoke forcefully, criticizing the positions of other Communists, and when he finished, his speech was one of the few not greeted by applause.[47]

Both his activities in Transcaucasia and his performance at the party congress indicate a certain independence and boldness on the part of Lominadze. His doubts about the direction of Stalin's policies coincided with those of many others in the party apparatus. Though a militant and outspoken leftist in the past, Lominadze had been appalled by the heavy human costs of the collectivization campaign. Careful not to oppose the formation of collectives or the drive for industrialization, he and like-minded comrades nevertheless began circulating memoranda and lobbying for a more moderate policy. Lominadze found an ally in S. I. Syrtsov, chairman of the Council of People's Commissars of the RSFSR, and the two men met sometime in 1930 in Moscow to discuss political matters. In a careful reconstruction of their probable views, Davies has concluded that Syrtsov and Lominadze believed that "the pace of industrialization was not supportable by existing physical resources: the number of capital projects must be reduced and production plans must not be inflated by the operation of the mechanism of counter-planning." In agriculture they wanted less pressure on the peasantry, and in general they called for less centralization, greater flexibility, and the partial restoration of market incentives.[48]

At some point in the late summer or fall of 1930, Lominadze had the Zakkraikom issue a declaration excoriating "the lordly feudal attitude toward the needs and interests of the workers and peasants" characteristic of the soviets in Transcaucasia. The resolution also took on Stalin directly when it challenged his declaration that the USSR had entered the period of socialist reconstruction.

> If the question "who will defeat whom" is not yet completely resolved within our country (and it is not resolved in the countryside), if three-quarters of peasant households are still outside the kolkhozy, if the existing kolkhozy are still not yet enterprises of a consistently socialist type, then it is hardly possible to say that we have entered the period of socialism.[49]

Despite the economic slowdown in the summer and fall of 1930, Stalin was determined to maintain a rapid pace of industrialization and to resume the collectivization drive. He had told the party congress that

> the Soviet country cannot stand on the road of organizing large capitalist enterprises. It can and must move only toward the organization of large enterprises of a socialist type, armed with new technology. Such enterprises here are the sovkhozy [state farms] and kolkhozy.[50]

Early in November Lominadze's "leftist slogans" were condemned, and a daily campaign was launched in the press against an alleged "Right-Leftist Bloc." On December 1, 1930, Syrtsov and Lominadze were expelled from the Central Committee by order of the Politburo and the Central Control Commission. The challenge to Stalin, however ineffectual, was thus eliminated, and four years later at the Seventeenth Party Congress Lominadze abjectly admitted his errors before his associates and repented. The "greatest sin of our opposition," he told his comrades, was coming "out against the leadership of our party, against the leader of the party, comrade Stalin."[51]

Along with Lominadze other Transcaucasian officials lost their positions: Chaplin, Akhundov, and Rakhmanov were removed from the Zak-kraikom; L. D. Gogoberidze, first secretary of the Georgian party, was replaced by Samson Mamulia and L. Sukhishvili. Lominadze's influence had been widespread enough to cause a major shakeup. The new bureau of the Georgian Central Committee contained some familiar old names—Mamia Orakhelashvili, Mikha Tskhakaia, Shalva Eliava, and Pilipe Makharadze—as well as a new name, Lavrenti Beria. Early in 1931 Lavrenti Iosipovich Kartvelishvili (1891–1938), a Georgian who had spent most of his party career in Ukraine, was brought to Tiflis as the new first secretary of the Zakkraikom.[52] More changes soon took place. All indications are that Stalin's party was not yet unquestioning in its obedience to its leaders, and a kind of rough politics continued within its ranks through the period of the First Five-Year Plan.

The political crisis in Transcaucasia, which had seen two major personnel overhauls within a year, was closely connected with the vicissitudes of the collectivization campaign. And that problem, with its political consequences, had not yet been solved. Even before the fall of Lominadze Moscow ordered a renewed push toward socialization of agriculture, especially in cotton-growing and industrial crop areas. Five hundred skilled workers were sent into the Georgian countryside to work with the new agricultural machinery, and thousands of others were employed to organize collectives. On February 19, 1931, the new Zakkraikom adopted a militant resolution connecting the struggle for collectivization of cotton and industrial crops to the battle against bourgeois nationalism.

> The kulaks and their political inspirers—the Musavatists, the Dashnaks, and the Mensheviks—are developing a rabid struggle against the supplanting of grain cultures by technical ones, against the expansion of the sowing of cotton, against the cotton independence of the Union of Soviet Republics. For this reason the fight for cotton is one of the forms of the struggle against the national bourgeoisie, against local nationalism.[53]

Whereas at the beginning of October 1929, just before the drive for rapid collectivization, only 3.6 percent of peasant households in Georgia had been collectivized, at the height of the forced collectivization about two-thirds had "joined" the *kolkhozy*. But once Stalin's "Dizzy with Success" signaled the possibility of leaving the collectives, the figure dropped to 29.4 percent within a month and continued to fall until October 1930, when it reached a low of 16.2 percent. Only in the last quarter of the year, when Lominadze was in serious political trouble, did the direction of the figures shift. From January 1931 to January 1932 Georgian collectivized households rose from 20.8 to 38.5 percent, a pace somewhat slower than that of Transcaucasia as a whole (17.3 to 41.4 percent).[54]

The reapplication of coercion was resisted by the peasants. Attacks were carried out on party officials and organizers. Little had been reported about peasant resistance, but an émigré journal wrote that there was famine in Georgia in the spring of 1931, and the government was forced to bring in extra grain from Odessa. Several districts in Georgia had been declared areas of full collectivization—Lanchkhuti, Ozurgeti, Ambrolauri, Lagodekhi, Karaiazi—and here the number of collectivized households reached over 90 percent. Only in the second half of 1931 did tempos slow down. Turning the land over to cotton was not popular with the peasants, and to achieve the change the party used coercive methods. By August 1, 1931, 50 percent of cotton lands in Azerbaijan had been collectivized, over 38 percent in Armenia, and 26.7 percent in Georgia.[55] Any opposition to the promotion of cotton and industrial crops was considered a variant of "local nationalism" and equivalent to counterrevolution. Yet the Georgian peasantry in particular was able to drag its heels and keep the rate of conversion and collectivization down below rates in other republics.

Though full collectivization was again declared in certain districts, and particularly in areas of industrial crops, the earlier policy of liquidating kulaks as a class was not resurrected. Efforts were made to restrict the activities of the richer peasants, to impose high taxes and other economic burdens on them, but not to dispossess them of their land by force. Georgian peasants had traditionally moved to towns when conditions in the countryside were difficult, and tens of thousands migrated in the late 1920s and early 1930s. But a great many of them were seasonal workers who maintained their ties with the villages, and only a small percentage became permanent members of the expanding working class. All the evidence points to a deep reluctance on the part of Georgia's peasants to change their customary way of life. The violent collectivization, however, drove thousands from the land and forced changes in the traditional patterns of patriarchy and the place of women. For the first time in Georgian history large numbers of women went into industry, many of them into heavy industry.[56]

The rapid and forced collectivization of early 1931 came in for some criticism from the central authorities early in April, when *Pravda* noted certain "exaggerations" in the practice of *kolkhoz* formation in Transcaucasia. "Crude 'leftist' distortions of the party line," formal bureaucratic methods, and the decree of collectivization from above marked Caucasian policy. Later in the year the Georgian republic was targeted. In September Kartvelishvili replaced Mamulia as party secretary while retaining his post as secretary of the Transcaucasian Territory Party Committee (Zakkraikom). Within a week G. A. Mgaloblishvili replaced V. P. Sukhishvili as the chairman of the Georgian government (Sovnarkom).[57]

But the hard blow fell at the end of October. Kartvelishvili was summoned to Moscow, where he delivered a report to the Orgburo. Stalin then made a motion that the secretariat of the Zakkraikom be reorganized with Kartvelishvili as first secretary and Lavrenti Beria as second secretary. A participant in this meeting, Snegov, later reported that "Kartvelishvili answered that he knew Beria well and for that reason refused categorically to work with him. Stalin proposed then that this matter be left open and that it be settled in the process of the work itself. Two days later a decision was arrived at that Beria would receive the Party post and that Kartvelishvili would be deported from the Transcaucasus."[58]

On October 31 the Central Committee in Moscow sent down a highly critical resolution on economic work in Transcaucasia. At the same time the Zakkraikom was attacked for failing to prepare the peasant masses for collectivization and for inadequate pressure on the kulaks, some of whom had been allowed to join collectives to avoid their obligations to the state. Top party leaders were accused of *atamanshchina*, an unprincipled, individualistic, and personal struggle for influence. In a reversal of earlier directives, the resolution found economic work to be too centralized: republic-level organs had been overlooked, their initiative dampened. Great Russian chauvinism remained the major danger in the area of the national question, the Central Committee reminded its subordinates, though local nationalism was also dangerous.[59]

The crisis over party leadership in Transcaucasia was resolved for the moment when Mamia Orakhelashvili was restored as head of the Zak-kraikom and Beria, who up to this time had been a Chekist (secret police officer), was named first secretary of the Georgian party. Clearly not a popular choice but rather the appointee of Stalin, Beria soon set about "Stalinizing" the Georgian political elite. The dismissed Georgian secretaries, Mamulia and Sukhishvili, were accused of having been "too conciliatory" to the "anti-party group" in the Baku organization, namely, the supporters of Lominadze. The party newspaper, *Zaria vostoka* (Dawn of the East), complained in mid-November that the leaders of the Tiflis party organization—Pantsulaia, Okujava, and Lominadze—had not yet come out in support of the Central Committee resolution of October 31. This was precisely the kind of insubordination and independent-mindedness of regional functionaries that the top party leaders had condemned. When Mamulia, Sukhishvili, Okujava, and others defended their policies at the Eighth Congress of the Georgian party (January 1932), they were attacked by Meladze, a spokesman for Beria, for "right opportunism" in their agricultural work. Kulak resistance to collectivization was blamed on inadequate work among poor peasants.[60]

As a direct result of the October 31 resolution the economic apparatus of the ZSFSR was reorganized, both centralizing and decentralizing decision-making at the same time. The Transcaucasian Supreme Economic Council (Sovnarkhoz) was eliminated and replaced by a People's Commissariat of Light Industry, both on the federal level and in each of the three constituent republics. At the same time heavy industry was placed under the authority of plenipotentiaries from the central, all-union People's Commissariat of Heavy Industry. All *kolkhoztsenty* were abolished, and collectivization was placed under the authority of republic-level commissariats of agriculture. In some ways the economic initiative of the individual republics was to be encouraged, especially in light industry and agriculture, but in fact the planning and control of economic activity was shifted to the Transcaucasian party chiefs.[61]

Along with a general policy move toward moderation throughout the USSR, the pace of collectivization in Transcaucasia slowed down in 1932, except in certain subtropical regions where especially valuable crops were given high priority by state authorities. For the rest of the decade the socialization of agriculture was carried out with less of the violence and physical brutality of the First Five-Year Plan. Confiscatory taxation replaced physical force as the means to "liquidate" the kulaks. As the First Five-Year Plan (1928–1932) drew to a close, the number of collectivized households in the ZSFSR actually fell. In the course of 1932 the percentage of Georgian rural households in collectives declined from 38.5 to 34. Whereas 61.5 percent of the peasantry was collectivized in the USSR as a whole, only 37.9 was collectivized in Transcaucasia at the end of 1932.[62]

In the years of the Second Five-Year Plan (1933–1937), as the costs of remaining outside the *kolkhozy* became unbearable, the collective farms appeared to be more attractive, especially since they received the bulk of the tractors and their income had increased. In Georgia *kolkhoz* income rose 117.6 percent from 1931 to 1933. The overwhelming majority of the peasantry entered the collectives by the end of the decade. Yet progress remained slow, and Georgia lagged behind the rest of the Soviet Union. The figures for collectivized households at the end of the Second Five-Year Plan were:

USSR	93%
ZSFSR	83%
Armenia	88.7%
Azerbaijan	86.5%
Georgia	76.5%

Only on the eve of the Nazi invasion of the Soviet Union, in 1941, did Georgian figures approximate Soviet totals: 92.6 percent of the peasantry were in collective farms, 3 percent in *sovkhozy,* with 3.4 percent remaining individual farmers.[63]

Collectivization of Georgia's peasant farms was the most radical transformation of land tenure and village life in Georgia's history. As the relentless drive to end individual production was pushed by the party, the peasants lost control over their own work and output. The relative freedom that they had enjoyed in the 1920s disappeared, and they fell into a new and degrading "state serfdom," losing even the right to leave the land without special permission. At the same time their village institutions of government were eliminated and replaced by soviets. Real decision-making was in the hands of party members who were responsible not to their local constituents but to their comrades in Tbilisi and Moscow. Though the countryside remained somewhat less dominated by the party than the cities, party control in the villages increased enormously during collectivization.

By breaking up the patterns of peasant life and work through collectivization, the Communist Party established its hegemony over the countryside and eliminated a major rival to its monopoly of political and economic decision-making. In 1933 the number of party cells in Georgian collective farms increased from 621 to 2,700, covering 78 percent of all *kolkhozy.*[64] Moreover, the machine-tractor stations (MTSs), which had a near-monopoly of mechanized power, had a decisive effect on the pace of production. The political bureaus *(politotdely)* set up in the MTSs in January 1933 were assigned the task of ensuring that peasants fulfilled their obligations to the state. These bureaus reported directly to the higher party organs, not to local secretaries, and a GPU officer was assigned to each unit. Ironically, many of these officials began to defend peasant complaints about the heavy burdens imposed from above, and by the end of 1934 the *politotdely* were abolished.

The "war on the peasantry" was the most momentous and most long-lasting of the campaigns of the First Five-Year Plan, but the related processes of industrialization, urbanization, and political mobilization also changed Georgian life. The Georgian intelligentsia, which had already been battered by the defeat and eradication of the old social democratic party and the imposition of Bolshevik cultural policies, faced in these years a militant attack on its independence and autonomy. As Moshe Lewin has argued, "The extraordinary display of mass coercion [of the collectivization drive] . . . contributed heavily to the hardening of Stalin's Russia into a bureaucratic police state. Violence applied to millions of peasants year after year was a training ground for institutions and methods which could later be applied to other groups."[65]

A "cultural revolution" (1928–1931), aimed at replacing the older generation of intellectuals with workers, turned the entire educational system around to promote men and women from the bench into new specializations and administrative positions. From the time of the infamous Shakhty trial of engineers (May–June 1928) until Stalin's speech calling for respectful treatment of the specialists (June 23, 1931), the intelligentsia, particularly "bourgeois-specialists," engineers and technicians, was treated as a class enemy by the party and state. The Shakhty trial, in Sheila Fitzpatrick's estimation, "was a turning point in Soviet policy toward the bourgeois specialist. From this time, the technical intelligentsia ceased to be seen as the party's natural ally in industrialization, and became a potentially treacherous group whose real allegiance was to the dispossessed capitalists and their foreign supporters."[66]

Just as "class origins" became an important criterion for matriculation in institutes of learning or promotion into a responsible position, so during the "cultural revolution" national origin also was often more important than acquired skills. The *korenizatsiia* policy of nativizing the schools and the governing apparatus was put into high gear. At the same time, however, it was accompanied by attacks on local nationalism. In the Ukraine, which was a kind of beacon for other national republics to follow, the long-time commissar of education, Mykola Skrypnyk, made it compulsory for courses and examinations in higher educational institutions to be given in Ukrainian. But in June 1931 Skrypnyk lost his post as director of the Ukrainian Institute of Marxism-Leninism when the institute was condemned for its nationalist interpretation of Ukrainian history.[67] This signaled a shift away from the generous backing of *korenizatsiia* which had accompanied the "cultural revolution."

In Armenia the commissar of education, N. Stepanian, fell from grace for similar reasons, and several of the most prominent cultural figures in the republic—the poet Eghishe Charents, the architect A. Tamanian, the painter Martiros Sarian, and the writer Aksel Bakunts—had their work criticized for nationalism. In Georgia some of the most popular and well-known writers— Konstantine Gamsakhurdia, Shalva Sharashidze, Pavel Ingoroqua, and Ioseb Imedashvili—were expelled from the Federation of Georgian Writers.[68]

That same year, on May 28, 1931, the Commissariat of Public Instruction in Georgia dismissed ten professors from institutions of higher learning, among them Ivane Javakhishvili, the dean of Georgian historians and a founder of Tbilisi State University; Grigori Tsereteli, Mikhail Polievktov, Giorgi Gamkrelidze, and Viktor Tevzaia.[69] Education was too important to the central leadership to be left any longer in the hands of the republics. In September 1931, a detailed outline for the proper operation of all educational institutions was sent out to the republics, and a year later higher education throughout the USSR was placed under the direct supervision of the All-Union People's Commissariat of Education.

Korenizatsiia continued to be official state policy through the Stalin years, but official support for its implementation dissipated rapidly in 1933– 1934, a casualty of new concern for political unity and economic efficiency. Skrypnyk was dismissed as commissar of education in Ukraine, and on July 6, 1933, after being attacked in the press, he killed himself. The demise of "national Communists" in Ukraine had a chilling effect on Communists in other republics. Stalin ominously mentioned that "the fall of Skrypnyk and his group in the Ukraine is not an exception. The same kind of dislocations are observable in certain comrades and in other national republics."[70]

Modifying the formula of Lenin, Stalin settled the question of which national deviation was the "principal danger": local nationalism or Great Russian chauvinism. This was a formal, empty argument, he claimed; "the principal danger is that deviation against which one has stopped fighting and which is, thus, allowed to grow to become a danger to the state."[71] Over the next decade, as the Soviet state attempted to reduce the autonomy of regional authorities, the centralizing tendencies also led to the promotion of Russians and Russian language. Expertise rather than ethnicity was pushed as a criterion for choosing cadres, and Russian as a lingua franca for the whole Soviet Union was encouraged. In 1938 instruction in the Russian language was made a compulsory subject in all Soviet schools.

As the Stalin revolution solidified into a rigid and authoritarian social and political formation in the early 1930s, the bureaucratic-administrative integration of the Georgian republic into the Soviet system was completed. Tensions remained between the imperatives of the central leadership and local cadres, but they henceforth were resolved in favor of the center. The consequences for deviation from the norms set by Moscow became increasingly more brutal. National or ethnic dimensions of Georgia's social and political structure were in no way permitted to stand in the way of the "unity of the Soviet Union," which in practice meant complete subordination of the republic to the central authorities. To enforce that subordination and compliance a new leadership was installed in Georgia, and in time the hold of the police over the party was expanded.

12 Stalinism in Georgia

The years 1932–1934 appear in retrospect like a brief interlude between the catastrophes of the collectivization campaigns and the blood purges of 1936–1938. The economic crisis did not end with the modification of the collectivization policy, but in many ways was made worse by the brutal state intervention into agriculture. The harvests of 1931, 1932, and 1933 were uniformly poor, and a large share of grain had to be requisitioned to supply the towns and sell abroad. In the countryside consumption fell until it reached famine levels in the Ukraine and parts of Transcaucasia.[1] At the same time the rate of industrial growth slowed, and capital investment in the economy declined. Inflation was rampant. As planners worked out the details of the Second Five-Year Plan, targets were revised downward. Though the more radical policies of the collectivization drive had been moderated, the goals of full collectivization were maintained. In the spring and summer of 1932 concessions were made to the countryside. In May grain delivery quotas were lowered, and some private marketing by *kolkhozy* and individual peasants was permitted. In July artisan cooperatives were allowed to sell their products on the free market.

Little is known about the internal politics at the top of the party hierarchy. Available evidence suggests that there was neither unanimity among party leaders as to the appropriate strategy for the crisis nor a single direction imposed by Stalin. Despite an emerging personality cult, Stalin was probably not yet the unchallenged leader of the Communist Party. Clearly the most powerful among the Politburo members, he may have been bound by the majority in that body. On a variety of issues—the use of repressive measures, the tempo of industrialization—the Politburo was divided, and

Stalin maneuvered between moderates, like Orjonikidze, and extremists, like Molotov and Kaganovich. A feeling had developed in certain party circles that, despite his evident excesses, Stalin was irreplaceable. But outside the Politburo other party members, like the authors of the 200-page "Riutin platform" circulated in the summer of 1932, argued that Stalin must be removed. The authors of that document were expelled from the party in the fall of the year. One controversial account claims that Stalin called for Riutin's execution, but moderates within the Politburo, this time led by Kirov, recoiled from the suggestion that the party shed the blood of one of its deviant members.[2]

The year 1932 may very well have been a period of relative vulnerability for Stalin. He made no major speeches or policy statements. Just after the celebrations of the October Revolution, his young wife, Nadezhda Allilueva, killed herself in their Kremlin apartment, apparently after an argument with her husband. Another "antiparty group" calling for Stalin's removal was discovered, and in January 1933, a Central Committee member, A. P. Smirnov, and two other Old Bolsheviks, Eismont and Tolmachev, were expelled from the party.[3] This time the victims were Leninists, not members of any organized opposition. The outwardly monolithic impression that the party presented was evidently not an accurate image, and policy shifts on major issues indicated serious differences within the Stalinist leadership.

By the fall of 1932 a harsher policy was once again taken toward the peasants. On the "grain front," "a new offensive was launched—and first of all a terroristic wave against agencies and local authorities still too reluctant to re-engage in excesses . . . Spurred by a flood of orders and pressures, the local agencies now veered sharply from their alleged 'rotten liberalism' into another batch of 'sharp measures of repression.' "[4] New controls were also introduced in the towns, and in November the government ordered that worker absenteeism be punished by dismissal and loss of ration cards. On December 27, 1932, a system of internal passports was introduced, but the documents were issued routinely only to city and town dwellers, not to peasants. The government was determined to control the flow of peasants to cities and workers from plant to plant. Success would be elusive, and the penalties for leaving one's job or being late for work would increase in severity for the next decade.

The crisis continued into 1933, and a widespread opinion existed among party members that the time had come for a "retreat," a slowdown, consolidation of the gains made in the First Five-Year Plan. At the January 1933 plenum of the Central Committee, Stalin agreed to an annual rate of industrial growth of 13 to 14 percent, a significant reduction from the 22 percent of the First Five-Year Plan. Assimilation (*osvoenie*) of new factories and technology was to be the main task at hand, rather than the breakneck construction of still more enterprises.[5] A series of laws was passed in the first three months of 1933 that ended the *kontraktatsiia* system and established quotas for deliveries of grain *(postavki)*, which were to be paid for by the state at fixed prices.

This new practice might have brought some stability into the procurement system and allowed farmers to know in advance what would be expected from them, but in fact other burdens were imposed on the *kolkhozy*. A certain portion of the crop had to be paid in kind *(naturplata)* to the MTS for its "services." Still later the government offered the peasants higher prices for grain bought after they had paid off their state and MTS obligations. In August 1934 these *zakupki* (purchases) were made compulsory. Only after the *postavki* to the state, the *naturplata* to the MTS, and the *zakupki* to the state were the *kolkhozniki* able to sell any surplus on the *kolkhoz* market or in the illegal black market.[6]

The heavy obligations on the peasantry had by 1934 replaced the physical force of the *velikii perelom*. Stalin and Molotov sent a secret "instruction" to party, soviet, and police organizations in May, ordering the end of mass repression in the countryside and a more selective practice of making arrests. The prison population in the USSR was to be cut in half, from 800,000 to 400,000 within two months.[7]

By 1934 the Stalinist economic structure had been set in place, and its general outlines lasted beyond its originator's death. Supplies were to be allocated to nationalized industries by plan; grain was to be delivered to the state by collectivized peasants before surpluses could be sold. Peasants would continue to enjoy personal plots and the rudiments of a farm market but within strict limits. Most retail trade was carried on by the state or consumer cooperatives. Prices were largely set by the authorities; workers were permitted a degree of movement; and rationing was ended.

In essence the Stalinist "command economy" had curtailed markets and private trade and had centralized decision-making far more than any other economy in history. The country's political leaders were also the directors of a huge economic enterprise. Indeed, economic matters occupied an enormous amount of politicians' time as the state obliterated the autonomy of the economy, and the political career of any middle or lower party or state functionary depended on the success or failure of the enterprises under his control. To make the best of an often impossible situation, officials had to resort to coercion and repression, deception and rule-breaking, protecting their own and shifting blame for failure to invented enemies.

From November 12, 1931, until August 31, 1938, Lavrenti Pavlovich Beria (1899–1953) headed the party in Georgia, and from October 17, 1932, to April 1937 he chaired the Transcaucasian party committee as well. Even after the Transcaucasian Federation had been abolished (1937) and he became people's commissar of internal affairs (head of the NKVD) in

Moscow (December 8, 1938), Beria maintained his influence over Transcaucasia, having appointed his satraps to command the three republics.

Beria's power stemmed from his personal relationship with Stalin and the services he was able to provide his patron. He represented a new kind of party leader, one whose entire career up to his appointment as party secretary in Georgia had been spent in the secret police apparatus, the Cheka (later the OGPU, still later the NKVD). He presided over Transcaucasia during the years in which the Stalin revolution was completed and a new and vicious police regime was gradually extended over the party itself. The Great Purges of 1936–1938, which he directed in Transcaucasia, represented the sanguinary victory of this police state over the remnants of the old party and their replacement by a docile administration loyal to "socialism" as defined by the general secretary.

Like the other Stalinist loyalists who rose to the top during and after the purges, Beria had particular ambitions and abilities that made him appropriate for the new political machine being created. These men, writes Roy Medvedev,

> knew how to make their inferiors work, usually by means of intimidation and coercion. In relation to Stalin they learned only to acquiesce and to be prepared to carry out their leader's every order, even if it was criminal. Anyone who was unable to commit a criminal act was not merely removed from power but physically eliminated.[8]

Born in the village of Merkheuli near Sukhumi, the son of a poor peasant family, Beria entered the Bolshevik party in 1917 while at the Baku Polytechnical Institute. He remained in Baku until 1920, working underground, it was reported, but his exact activities were later questioned by his fellow Communists and historians.[9] He moved to Georgia while the Mensheviks were still in power, where he was arrested and released only after a hunger strike. In the early 1920s he worked in the secret operative division of the Azerbaijani Cheka and later held the same position in Georgia. In 1926 he became head of the Georgian GPU (state police). His acquaintance with Stalin may have dated from this time, for the Georgian GPU was responsible for guarding Stalin's *dacha* (summer home) near Gagra.[10]

When Lominadze and his supporters were purged, Beria was placed in the bureau of the Georgian Communist Party, his first significant political appointment. When his superior in the GPU, S. Redens, was called back to Moscow, he became chief of the Transcaucasian GPU (April 1931). Clearly favored by Stalin, Beria was appointed first secretary of the Georgian party and second secretary of the Zakkraikom a few months later. Beria was not well liked by local party leaders and had no popular base of support; his power stemmed from Stalin. A number of Old Bolsheviks in Georgia protested to the Central Committee in Moscow about Beria's appointment, but to no avail, and several high-ranking officials chose to leave the republic rather than work with the former Chekist.[11]

Though it is not possible to know for certain why Beria was appointed to run Transcaucasia when so many senior and orthodox party members were on the scene, it may have been related to Moscow's constant problem with controlling provincial party organizations. Beria had worked all his life in Transcaucasia and knew the local political environment, but he was not part of the interconnected party elite that had dominated Georgian and Trans-caucasian politics since the early 1920s. He was not a friend or protégé of Orjonikidze, as was Orakhelashvili, nor was he an Old Bolshevik, like Makharadze. Relatively young at thirty-two, an outsider, and a man prepared to use tough measures to please his patron, Beria may have been chosen precisely because he would be able to break through the family circles in Transcaucasia and guarantee that the Kremlin's writ would prevail in the republic. His spectacularly rapid rise coincided with the demise of the Old Bolsheviks, most importantly Orakhelashvili, and much of his energy in his first years as party leader was spent discrediting the veterans of the revolution. Beria replaced middle-level party officials with his own appointees. Med-vedev reports that thirty-two directors of district NKVD agencies were made *raikom* (district party committee) secretaries once Beria was in control.[12]

As a loyal client of his patron Stalin, Beria actively and enthusiastically involved himself in the development of Stalin's personality cult. While there had been sporadic bursts of praise for Stalin in the past, most notably during his fiftieth birthday celebration in 1929, the ritualized lauding of the leader began to take shape in the years 1931–1934. At the Sixteenth Party Congress in 1930, the praise of Stalin had been effusive but not required of every speaker. Four years later at the Seventeenth Congress, the lavish and repeated glorification of the *vozhd'* (leader) marked every speech, even those of former oppositionists. Loyalty to the person of Stalin had become the public ex-pression of one's devotion to the party, its Central Committee, and the whole Soviet enterprise. Stalin himself appeared in print as an unimpeachable authority, not only in politics and economics, but also in philosophy, liter-ature, and history.

On October 28, 1931, Stalin wrote his explosive letter on the history of Bolshevism to *Proletarskaia revoliutsiia* (Proletarian Revolution), the leading journal on party history. Ostensibly Stalin was protesting the historian Slutskii's criticism of Lenin's relationship with the centrists of the German social democratic party (SPD) before World War I, but his intervention into a seemingly esoteric episode in the history of the Second International changed the future course of Soviet intellectual life, not to mention the available historical record.

Slutskii had argued that Lenin had not broken with the moderate centrists in the SPD in the prewar period, underestimating the danger they posed. Stalin was outraged by the suggestion that Lenin might not have understood the threat of centrism and had been conciliatory toward "opportunism." Not to have recognized this danger would indicate that Lenin had not been a real Bolshevik![13] Instead of attempting to investigate the documented facts, as Slutskii had done, Stalin "posited a fixed, unchanging (and unhistorical) concept of Bolshevism," proscribing any criticism of Lenin. "By making the party's previous *vozhd'* an iconographic figure, beyond limitation and beyond criticism, Stalin's letter implicitly nominated the successor-*vozhd'* for similar treatment."[14] Most ominously, the letter's abrasive tone, which spoke of "rotten liberals," "Trotskyist contrabandists," and "hopeless bureaucrats" who relied on paper documents, made sober discussion of party history impossible. A critical Marxist history of Marxism was to be replaced by the required confirmations of the party's political positions of the moment. Orthodoxy and conformity, rather than critical analysis or faithfulness to the sources, were to mark historical writing for the next quarter-century.

In Georgia discussion of Stalin's letter filled pages of the local press, and the party took on the special task of rewriting the history of Stalin's early revolutionary career. First, Comrade "Ruben" in *Pravda* and then Orakhelashvili in *Zaria vostoka* condemned a recent Georgian party history by Tengiz Zhgenti, the director of the Institute of Party History in Tiflis. A resolution from the Tiflis party committee accused historians Talakvadze, Zhgenti, and Khundadze of being "carriers of Trotskyist contraband, recidivists of federalism and national deviationism." But it was Beria who quickly and energetically took over the campaign to change the historical record by downgrading the activities of the Old Bolsheviks and expanding the role of Stalin himself.[15]

Rather than attack professional historians, Beria turned on Makharadze, who was both one of the first Marxists in Transcaucasia and a prolific writer on the early years of social democracy. At the Ninth Congress of the Georgian Communist Party, Beria asserted:

> Almost everything written to date on the history of the Communist Party of Georgia and the revolutionary movement of Transcaucasia does not reflect the genuinely active role of Comrade Stalin, who in fact led for many years the struggle of the Bolsheviks in the Caucasus. Let us take, for example, the works of Comrade Makharadze, from which our young generation is being taught.

Makharadze had played down the importance of the intraparty struggle with Menshevism, Beria claimed, and argued that the social democrats had no social base in Georgia. Stalin, on the other hand, had shown that Menshevism developed in Georgia because of the absence of sharp class conflicts and the lack of heavy industrial centers. Beria ended by suggesting that Makharadze "correct these mistakes immediately." Makharadze "admitted" his errors and accepted his guilt, promising to rewrite his histories. In fact, he never did, and no important works on party history appeared by him after 1933.[16]

The appropriation of party history by the Stalinists was a powerful weapon directed against the old party intelligentsia, whose authority rested on their historical contributions. Old Bolsheviks like Makharadze and Orakhelashvili, who had been active in the party long before Beria, were now "exposed" as disloyal because their versions of the past did not exaggerate Stalin's role. At the Georgian party congress in January 1934, Beria's lieutenant, Bedia, damned Orakhelashvili for his lack of faith in the proletariat of one country overthrowing the world bourgeoisie without aid from the proletariat of other strong states. Someone shouted from the floor, "This is Trotskyism and, therefore, demands to be exposed."[17] In this way Old Bolsheviks who were not actually members of any organized opposition were tarred with the brush of Trotskyism, which had come to mean faintheartedness in commitment to the cult of Stalin.

The culmination of Beria's efforts came on July 21–22, 1935, at a time when the ideological struggle within the party was intensifying and many Old Bolsheviks had already lost their positions. For two days he read a detailed history of Bolshevik organizations in Transcaucasia to a meeting of two thousand party members in Tiflis. This speech, soon reprinted throughout the Soviet Union and translated into dozens of languages, became the official "history" of Stalin's role in the revolutionary movement.[18]

Beria's service to his patron had been to invent a past for him. From a rank-and-file activist, Stalin was blown up in Beria's prose to the paramount leader of Caucasian Bolsheviks, eclipsing Makharadze, the martyred Stepan Shahumian, and Orjonikidze. Although the account was closer to fiction than history, it became the standard reading of Stalin's career, until it was joined by the broader and even more authoritative *Kratkii kurs istorii Vsesoiuznoi Kommunisticheskoi Partii (bol'shevikov)* [Short Course of the History of the All-Union Communist Party (bolsheviks)] in 1938. The achievement was impressive. Stalin had established in 1931 the infallibility of Lenin, and in the course of creating a cult of Stalin his underlings had cloaked him with the same mantle. Beria completed the process by reconstructing the history of Transcaucasian Bolshevism, providing the *vozhd'* with impeccable credentials as a revolutionary commander and simultaneously promoting in general the role of the party in the social struggles of ordinary people. In the Stalinist version of Marxist historiography, the people still made their own history but under the initiation and direction of the party leaders.

In these transitional years, as the Communist Party dealt with serious economic problems and prevented popular discontents from erupting into opposition to the regime, Beria developed a variety of methods to carry out the orders he received from the center and to meet its targets. In 1933 it was officially claimed that alien class and hostile elements, moral degenerates and careerists, had infiltrated the ranks of the party and had to be "cleaned out." A *chistka* (cleansing or purge) was carried out from April 1933 to January 1934, and 22 percent of the all-union party's members were forced to leave the organization. This was not the kind of "blood purge" of the later 1930s, in which alleged enemies of the people were executed or imprisoned. Rather, the purges of 1933–1935 were directed at gaining control over a party marred by poor record-keeping, careerism, and passivity of many members, as well as independent attitudes on the part of local leaders. Admissions to the party were halted, and the number of Communists in the Soviet Union declined from a high of 3,555,000 in 1933 to 2,701,000 in 1934, and continued to fall until 1939. The 1933 level would not be regained until 1940.[19]

In Georgia the party had grown to 57,737 before the *chistka* and shrank to 48,431 by January 1934, a decline of 16.2 percent.[20] Apparently Beria had already put many of his supporters in positions of influence and was less aggressive than some other regional leaders in purging the rank and file. Whatever the reasons for the lower percentage of expulsions in Georgia, Beria had other methods to secure a loyal following within his party.

In the same year as the *chistka,* 1933, the Georgian GPU arrested seventeen agricultural specialists and accused them of economic crimes. The failures of the economy were to be personalized and blamed on "wreckers." When the Transcaucasian-level GPU protested that the arrests had been made improperly, without its sanction, the Georgians informed their superiors that Beria himself had ordered the arrests. The unfortunate specialists "confessed" to the alleged crimes, though no corroborating evidence was produced. Again, it was pointed out, procedure had been violated. Eventually the specialists were released, only to be rearrested in 1937 and shot.[21]

When a regional organization proved reluctant to carry out the orders of the Georgian party bureau, quick reprisals were taken. The South Ossetian region failed to push hard enough against its kulaks, and the Georgian Central Committee dispatched an envoy to purge the local judicial organs for "insufficient vigilance." Short of removals, the leadership also resorted to repeated exhortations, production campaigns, wage incentives, rewards and bonuses for highly productive "shock" workers. And police pressure was also employed. In January 1934 Beria announced to the Georgian party congress that a "Georgian national center" had been discovered. Among the intellectuals who had been conspiring for an independent Georgia were former Socialist Federalists, Trotskyists, and even Communists. Such a center had already been exposed in the Ukraine (in time almost every republic would have an equivalent). Beria was careful to distinguish Georgia from the Ukraine, however, pointing out that the principal danger in the Ukraine was local nationalism whereas in Georgia it was still great-power chauvinism. This maneuver exempted the local leadership from charges of nationalism. Beria went on to say that the Georgian party must "increase its fire against local nationalism" and promote the study of Russian, "the language of the greatest revolutionary achievements."[22]

A few days later at the Seventh Congress of Party Organizations of Transcaucasia, the leaders of each republic reported on political deviance. Khanjian, first secretary of the Armenian Communist Party, told of the exposure of a Trotskyist group led by Kamalian and castigated those "liberal-conciliationist Communists" who "look through their fingers" at nationalist manifestations in Armenia. Bagirov, Beria's former colleague in the Azerbaijani Cheka and now his appointee as first secretary of Azerbaijan, attacked Karo Grigorian, the former *obkom* (regional party committee) secretary of the Mountainous Karabakh Autonomous Region, who had developed a theory that the struggle against the kulaks made a special struggle against the counterrevolutionary parties, the Musavatists and the Dashnaks, unnecessary. The congress, like the Georgian meeting that preceded it, stressed the need for vigilance against suspected enemies, and former leaders, like Orakhelashvili, were condemned for their softness toward Trotskyism.[23]

Late in January 1934 nearly two thousand delegates gathered in Moscow for the Seventeenth Party Congress, the so-called congress of the victors. But the victors did not include most of the Transcaucasian leadership that had been in power during the First Five-Year Plan. Orakhelashvili attended as a member of the Central Committee of the VKP(b), but he was not re-elected. Beria, who entered the Central Committee at the end of the congress, made his first major appearance in Moscow. He spent his alloted time praising the achievements of the party in Transcaucasia since Stalin's intervention in 1931.

> In 1930–1931 there was still a situation in the Transcaucasian village in which many *kolkhozy* were falling apart. Kulaks and the remnants of the defeated anti-Soviet parties—the Dashnaks, the Musavatists, the Georgian Mensheviks—tried to use for their counterrevolutionary work the crude political mistakes made by Transcaucasian party organizations. Only after the intervention of the leader of the party, Comrade Stalin, and the decision of the TsK VKP(b) did the Transcaucasian Bolsheviks undertake the correction of these crude political errors. Now, comrades, the situation in the Transcaucasian village has radically changed.

Transcaucasia had become, according to Beria, a supplier of special crops for the whole Soviet Union. Abkhazeti alone provided 52 percent of the tobacco exported from the USSR. Baku's oil made up 59 percent of all Soviet oil production, and Georgia was the major supplier of wine, tea, and citrus fruit. He did not mention any economic difficulties and avoided referring to Enukidze's earlier criticism of Transcaucasia's misuse of forests.[24]

Public speeches, like the writing of history and the Soviet press, were the media through which a positive, upbeat image of Soviet reality was presented to the populace. Even in the worst of times Soviet leaders emphasized the construction of socialism rather than the costs of the domestic revolution. In his opening speech to the congress Stalin had cautioned, however, that a classless society could be built only "by means of the strengthening of the organs of the dictatorship of the proletariat, by means of the abolition of classes, by means of the liquidation of the remnants of capitalist classes, in battles with both domestic and foreign enemies."[25]

Although the congress was followed by a period of reconciliation with former oppositionists, the new party statute limited the independence of local party organizations and freedom of discussion within the party. There was more talk about re-educating cadres rather than expelling people from the party, but at the same time the appointment powers of the Central Committee were increased and those of regional committees reduced. Both Stalin and Kirov spoke about the need for party members to turn away from direct involvement in economic work toward educational and political preparation of party workers. The feverish campaigns of the First Five-Year Plan were replaced by more sober planning, consolidation of the new economic foundations, and an emphasis on assimilating technology. Production in agriculture slowly increased, and by 1935 rationing was ended.

As the economic crisis abated and the agricultural situation improved, the Soviet government seemed to abandon its recent militance both at home and abroad. The Communist International adopted a strategy of "popular front" alliances with socialist and even liberal parties, and in foreign policy the Kremlin's ties with Germany lapsed and the USSR reoriented itself toward the Western powers. Late in 1933 diplomatic relations were established with the United States, and in 1934 Stalin began a rapprochement with France and discussions of a "Little Locarno" pact with the countries of eastern Central Europe. In September the USSR joined the League of Nations. Once an outlaw nation, the Soviet Union had within a few years significantly reduced its international isolation. To many in the West the building of "socialism in one country" seemed a triumph of human will and effort, the concrete validation of Marxism-Leninism; many intellectuals and politicians were prepared, particularly in the face of the fascist danger, to excuse Stalin's dictatorial rule while admiring Soviet economic achievements.

The history of the second half of the 1930s, and indeed the last decade and a half of Stalin's rule, is not as accessible to the historian as the first fifteen years of Soviet power. Sources on the inner workings of the party are almost nonexistent in this period, though educated guesses have been made through careful Kremlinological research and a close reading of the Soviet press.[26] While more and more memoirs have become available in recent years, they often report rumors or hearsay rather than events witnessed. Extraordinarily moving and revealing as these memoirs are, few tell much about the top levels of decision-making. With the evidentiary base diminished, conclusions about the middle and late Stalin years must be speculative and tentative.

In place of the mundane empirical reconstruction of the history of the

Stalinist years in Russia (and Transcaucasia), political scientists, journalists, and historians have resorted to social scientific models to "explain" or rationalize the Soviet system. The most long-lived of such models, that of totalitarianism, was designed to link Stalinism with its contemporaries, nazism and fascism, which in their political aspects—one-man rule, applied state terror, economic development through state intervention and direction, ideological conformity, and elevation of the party—seemed quite similar.

As a tool of analysis, totalitarianism has largely been abandoned by historians, for its very neatness and superficial comparative dimensions encouraged a neglect of specific features of the Stalinist system. Stalinism on close analysis looks much more messy, internally contradictory, and complex than any simple model allows. All of the original orthodoxies—that decisions flowed downward from Stalin and were unquestioningly obeyed, that the party was monolithic, or that the ideology functioned as a cement holding party and mass together—have to be modified. Unfortunately, it is still too early to replace the model with a complete picture of the Stalinist reality, but the details and partial explanations are being accumulated for a richer historical analysis.

Stalin's personality was a key factor in the way the Stalinist system evolved, though it does not alone explain the eventual contours of Soviet society; the historical context and pressures in which the Soviet Union found itself must be considered. Stalin's personal drive for power, his suspicious nature, and his fear of rivals took on historical significance because he was able to translate that suspicion into policy through his alliance with the police and because others in the party shared his perceptions and ambitions and acted on them. As Stalin became an autocrat with unlimited power, he was aided by underlings anxious to "intensify the class struggle," like Ezhov and Molotov. Others, perhaps like Kirov, wanted to increase the protection of Soviet citizens through a new understanding of "revolutionary legality."[27]

Where Stalin stood on these issues at any particular moment is difficult to ascertain. Robert Conquest argues that the general secretary was preparing for the "Great Terror" even in the early 1930s but was thwarted by moderates like Kirov. J. Arch Getty, on the other hand, holds that Stalin vacillated between the "radicals" and the moderates, fully siding with the former only in 1937.[28] For some writers Stalinism and its apogee in the Great Purges reflected the consequences of Stalin's lust for power; for others the system and the purges were rooted in the need of a small, urban-based party to control an overwhelmingly peasant country while forcibly transforming it into an industrial power. Whatever the motives of its architects, its consequences were as violent as the events of 1917 or 1928–1931.

On December 1, 1934, at 4:30 in the afternoon, Sergei Kirov, party boss of Leningrad and considered by many to be Stalin's likely successor, was assassinated at his headquarters in the Smolny Institute. Twenty years later

Nikita Khrushchev, in his famous speech detailing Stalin's crimes, hinted broadly that the dictator had a hand in dispatching his potential rival. At the time the murder stunned the leaders of the party, and Stalin rushed to Leningrad to carry out the investigation. In a series of panicky moves, an order was issued that expedited investigation, conviction, and execution for terrorist acts. A widespread fear that other leaders might be targets for frustrated oppositionists led to the arrest of Zinoviev and Kamenev. Blame for the assassination was finally laid on the Trotskyists and the Left Opposition. At their trial in January 1935, Zinoviev and Kamenev accepted "the political and moral responsibility" for Kirov's death and were sent to prison. The Central Committee called for "enduring revolutionary vigilance," and a number of additional arrests were made.[29]

After the initial arrests and trials following Kirov's assassination, party work and police activity settled into the usual pattern. Two years were to pass before mass arrests occurred. In May 1935 the Central Committee ordered a *proverka* (checking) of party documents to deal with the chaotic state of record-keeping. This exercise had been planned before Kirov's death and was one of the periodic efforts by the central authorities to control the regional and local organizations. Getty argues that at this time "Stalin displayed a liberal and lenient attitude toward the regional secretaries . . . giving them a free hand to clean up their own machines."[30]

The operation was carried out by Ezhov and soon took on aspects of exposing bureaucratism in party work. The party *aktiv* began criticizing the local leaders, and such "populist" activity directed at the established regional authorities was encouraged by the radicals in the center, like Ezhov and Molotov. Whereas only 9 percent of party members throughout the USSR were expelled, the *proverka* was particularly intense in Transcaucasia, where 26,602 people (18.8 percent) were excluded from the party organizations. In Azerbaijan expulsions totaled 22 percent of all party members. It was later announced that "more than thirty counterrevolutionary, Trotskyist, and harmful organizations" had been discovered and liquidated in the course of the *proverka* in Transcaucasia.[31]

Throughout the Soviet Union attacks on Old Bolsheviks and intellectuals continued into 1935. In May the Society of Old Bolsheviks was dissolved. Historian V. I. Nevskii, director of the Lenin Library and a prominent Old Bolshevik, was arrested. The former oppositionist, Beso Lominadze, who had been allowed to redeem himself and had been appointed secretary of the important Magnitogorsk party committee, suddenly fell from grace. When he was abruptly summoned to Cheliabinsk by the authorities, he shot himself. A ferocious campaign was begun against Avel Enukidze (1877–1937), a member of the Central Committee, secretary of the Central Executive Committee of the Soviets, and a founder of Caucasian social democracy. Enukidze had known Stalin since the turn of the century when both worked in the party underground, but when the historical profession was ordered to rewrite the history of Transcaucasian Marxism, Enukidze only half-heartedly repudiated his earlier accounts.[32]

In June the Central Committee denounced Enukidze for "political and personal dissoluteness" and expelled him from the party. The next month he was targeted by Beria, who, in his celebrated speech on the Bolshevik movement in Transcaucasia, claimed that Enukidze "deliberately and with hostile intent falsified the history of the Bolshevik organizations of Transcaucasia in his authorized biography and in his pamphlet *Our Illegal Printing Shops in the Caucasus,* cynically and brazenly distorted well-known historical facts, crediting himself with alleged services in the establishment of the first illegal printing shop in Baku."[33]

After the assaults on historians, writers came under fire. In March and April 1936, *Zaria vostoka* featured several articles critical of formalism in the arts. Poets Titsian Tabidze and Simon Chikovani, novelist Demna Shengelaia, and critic Gerontia Kikodze were taken to task for recent writings. The people's commissar of education, A. S. Tatarishvili, who also served as chairman of the Union of Writers, regretted that the best writers, those who had been Futurists but had sided with Soviet power, had not fully freed themselves from the old traditions.[34] More contact with the people was required, he said. Some writers accepted the criticism in public recantations, but several of the most prominent—Tabidze, Konstantine Gamsakhurdia, Chikovani, and Shengelaia—either ignored or openly rejected it.

Apparently the real danger involved in such defiance was not fully appreciated by many writers. In a private letter Boris Pasternak, a close friend and translator of Tabidze, urged the poet to disregard the attacks on formalism: "Rely only on yourself. Dig more deeply with your drill without fear or favor, but inside yourself, inside yourself. If you do not find the people, the earth and the heaven there, then give up your search, for then there is nowhere else to search." The advice was honorable and sincere, but honesty and integrity were costly values in 1936–1937. Tabidze was only forty-two and a major influence among Georgian writers when he was arrested and executed in 1937. When his fellow poet, Paolo Iashvili, heard of Tabidze's fate, he went to the Union of Writers and shot himself.[35]

In the state-controlled media an optimistic and harmonious picture of Soviet life was drawn. The Soviet Union appeared to be moving toward a brighter future with greater freedom, democracy, and prosperity. "Life is becoming more joyful," said Stalin. The press was filled with the exploits of Soviet explorers and aviators; films in the socialist realist mode featured positive heroes overcoming adversities with Bolshevik will and determination; mass songs celebrated the dawn of the new age—socialism had been built in one country. And the party discussed and approved a new constitution for the USSR, "the most democratic in the world." The Transcaucasian

Federation was to be abolished after fourteen years in operation, and the three republics were to enter the USSR individually as full-fledged union republics. This reversal of the controversial decision of 1922 was proclaimed an achievement of Soviet development.

At the same time there were ominous signs of a new wave of repression. Budu Mdivani, who had opposed the formation of the ZSFSR in 1921–1922, was dismissed as vice chairman of the Georgian Sovnarkom after he boldly defended his old view of the federation.[36] The official explanation was that the federation had been necessary in 1922 to cement economic cooperation between the peoples of Transcaucasia but had become irrelevant in present conditions. Potentially its dissolution meant a reduction of Beria's power, for the post of Transcaucasian party secretary would be eliminated and he would hold only his Georgian position. But with Beria's long-time colleague, M. D. Bagirov, at the head of Azerbaijan's Central Committee since 1933, only the Armenian party, led by the popular Aghasi Khanjian since May 1930, was somewhat independent of his control.

Armenian Communists, most importantly Commissar of Education Nersik Stepanian, had expressed disgust with Beria's falsification of party history. On July 9, 1936, Khanjian went to Tbilisi for a meeting of the Zakkraikom. That evening it was announced that he had killed himself.[37] With Khanjian out of the way, Beria's appointee, Haik Amatuni, began a purge of the Armenian party to rid it of a newly discovered heresy, *Khandzhianshchina* (Khanjianism), which in the official view was a particularly noxious blend of local nationalism and Trotskyism.

On August 19, 1936, an article appeared in *Pravda* under Beria's name—"Scatter the Ashes of the Enemies of Socialism"—in which he revealed the discovery of Trotskyist-Zinovievist groups in Tbilisi, Erevan, and Baku. In Georgia former party members and national deviationists had been planning terrorist acts; in Azerbaijan Trotskyist terrorists had made contact with the counterrevolutionary Ter-Vahanian, then on trial in Moscow. The worst cases were in Armenia, where party chief Khanjian had done nothing about Stepanian's Trotskyist nationalism. The old intelligentsia of Armenia and Georgia was strongly nationalist and a target of opportunity for the counterrevolution. "A Communist who shows conciliation and rotten liberalism toward double-dealing, in whatever form it takes, commits the greatest crime before the party, before Soviet power, before our motherland," Beria concluded.[38]

Beria's article appeared on the same day that the final trial of Zinoviev and Kamenev began. The police had manufactured, out of forced confessions and circumstantial evidence, a vast conspiracy against the state, allegedly organized by a "Trotskyist-Zinovievist Terrorist Center." Its leaders were convicted of having plotted and carried out the murder of Kirov, and the web of the conspiracy entangled others besides those on trial. The center was "revealed," for example, to have had ties with Georgian deviationists, and Okujava's name was mentioned in the testimony.[39] All the defendants were shot.

A few weeks later, apparently not satisfied with the efforts of the police to date, Stalin and Zhdanov, then vacationing in Sochi, sent a telegram to Moscow:

> We deem it absolutely necessary and urgent that Comrade Ezhov be nomi-nated to the post of people's commissar of internal affairs. Iagoda has definitely proved himself incapable of unmasking the Trotskyist-Zinovievist bloc. The OGPU is four years behind in this matter. This is noted by all party workers and by the majority of the representatives of the NKVD.[40]

Party members had already been warned by Stalin that real enemies were still being concealed within party ranks, and a top-secret letter had been sent to key party organizations mobilizing the membership in a campaign of exposure and denunciation to assist the police in ferreting out the opposi-tion. "The inalienable quality of every Bolshevik under present conditions should be the ability to recognize an enemy of the party, no matter how well he may be masked."[41] With the appointment of Ezhov, a zealot dedicated to exposing Stalin's imagined enemies within the party, a major step was taken to complete the police hegemony over the party elite.

The opening salvo came in November 1936 with a trial of mining officials in Novosibirsk, all of whom were convicted of sabotage. In January 1937 a major show trial of old oppositionists—Piatakov, Sokolnikov, Se-rebriakov, and Radek—opened the way to a full-scale assault on the eco-nomic apparatus. For years Piatakov and other planners, engineers, and industrial officials had been protected by the powerful people's commissar of heavy industry, Orjonikidze.[42] But Piatakov's execution revealed the limits of Sergo's influence. After an angry exchange with Stalin, Orjonikidze shot himself (February 18, 1937), and all obstacles to the full terrorization of the party and state hierarchy were removed. Now the Right Opposition was also to be persecuted, as well as party members who had never joined any deviant group.[43]

In June it was announced that Marshal Tukhachevskii and other top military commanders had been found guilty of treason and executed. By July the *Ezhovshchina* (Ezhov-led terror) was tearing through the party, the gov-ernment, and even the NKVD. Hundreds of thousands of people, most of them in no way connected with the opposition, were rounded up, tortured, forced to confess to imaginary crimes, and then either sent to prison camps or shot. The figures are staggering: 57,000 Old Bolsheviks were lost between 1934 and 1939; nearly 300,000 Communists were expelled from the party in 1937–1938; 110 of the 139 members and candidates of the Central Com-mittee elected in 1934 were arrested and many perished, including Politburo members V. Ia. Chubar, S. V. Kosior, P. P. Postyshev, R. I. Eikhe, and Ia. E.

Rudzutak. The Terror spread through the intelligentsia and every layer of the population, sweeping up wives and children along with the accused. At the very least about one million people in the Soviet Union fell victim to the purges of 1936–1938.[44]

When the regional and republic secretaries throughout the Soviet Union were criticized from below and above in the spring of 1937, Beria too was in danger. Following the instructions of the February plenum of the Central Committee of the VKP(b), Georgian party organizations were permitted to engage in open discussions and elections of party officials by secret ballot. Twenty-one thousand party members, about 63 percent of those attending, spoke in the discussions. Two thousand, about a third, spoke at the regional and city party conferences.[45] Violations of "inner-party democracy" were mentioned, as well as "the dulling of vigilance," "weak ties of Communists in leading party, soviet, and economic organizations with the masses," and a "liberal attitude by party members toward enemies of the people." Yet in the resulting elections only 784 new people were elected to the 2,807 positions in the committees of primary organizations and 643 to the 2,522 positions in plenums of *raikomy, gorkomy* (city party committees), and *obkomy*. Of the 4,464 candidates nominated for leading party committees all but 514 were elected. Not one secretary of a *raikom, obkom,* or *gorkom* was defeated in the election, and 70 percent of former secretaries of primary organizations were re-elected. Beria's machine had largely been reinstalled, seemingly thwarting the intentions of the February plenum.

The Tenth Congress of the Georgian Communist Party was held May 15–21, 1937. Beria opened the meeting with a long review of Georgia's economic achievements, then turned to political work. Most Georgian writers, poets, and artists had been anti-Soviet, he said, and had worked actively against Soviet power. But it was now possible to report that all anti-Soviet groups and tendencies had been liquidated. Georgian poets now celebrated the "image of our leader as a symbol of all our victories." The "Trotskyist Spy Harmful Terrorist Center" of Mdivani, Toroshelidze, Okujava, Kavtaradze, and Kiknadze had been exposed.[46] Beria seemed intent on limiting the purge in Georgia to the most vulnerable former oppositionists, but his maneuver was checked by the central authorities.

The day after the congress ended, an article appeared in *Pravda* by its correspondent in Tbilisi. The writer, who must have represented the view of the central leadership, severely criticized the work of the congress. Self-criticism had been inadequate at the congress, and Gobechia and Agrba of Abkhazeti, as well as Kochlamazashvili of Ajaria, had been insufficiently sensitive to shortcomings in their organizations.[47] That same month articles appeared about the inadequacy of the work of the new Armenian party leadership, which probably reflected on Beria not keeping his Transcaucasian house in order. Beria replied in *Pravda* on June 5, claiming that the Georgian congress had been properly self-critical. He presented a picture of a united party, loyal to Stalin, but at the same time he made it clear that the renewal of party officials, which was to have occurred through the elections and self-criticism campaign, had been successfully avoided in Georgia and Armenia.[48]

The reprieve given the Transcaucasian parties, however, was short-lived. Beria must have quickly realized that he had to "cleanse" his own organization if he was to maintain his position. An attack on the governing apparatus began in the summer of 1937. In the course of the operation, blame for economic shortcomings was placed on individuals and groups of officials who, it was alleged, sabotaged the plans of the party. Popular resentment against the governing apparatus, particularly the political police, was harnessed in a violent persecution of key political cadres. In July 1937 members of the NKVD were arrested, among them its chairman, Tite Lordkipanidze, and the head of the economic section, Suren Gazarian. The arrested oppositionists were put on trial, among them Mdivani, Toroshelidze, Okujava, G. Kurulov, S. Chikhladze, G. Eliava, and N. Kartsivadze. All were executed.[49] The chairman of the Georgian Sovnarkom, German Mgaloblishvili, was replaced by Beria's client, Valerian Minais dze Bakradze, and then simply disappeared.

In August the trial of the Sighnaghi "counterrevolutionary terrorist diversionary-harmful organization of Rights" was held. The chairman of the region's executive committee, Shalva Alaverdashvili, and the former secretary of the *raikom,* Artem Tsitlidze, were accused of attempting to overthrow the Soviet government and to restore capitalism. Tsitlidze "confessed" that Mgaloblishvili had suggested that agriculture should be disorganized in order to discredit the government in the eyes of the peasantry. In the first three days of September prominent Communists were arrested in Transcaucasia.[50] Nearly the entire party elite in Georgia was soon replaced. More than four thousand people were removed at the top of the political and economic hierarchy.

Still the pace and ferocity of the purges were not satisfactory to Stalin. Repeatedly the Armenian party under Amatuni and Agopov was chided for leniency. Instead of being removed by the Armenian party members, they were re-elected. The center decided to intervene directly. On September 8, Stalin wrote to the bureau of the Armenian Central Committee, accusing it of covering up enemies of the Armenian people. He announced that he was sending Malenkov to deal with the problem. On September 15 Malenkov arrived in Erevan with Mikoyan and Beria. The year-old leadership of the Armenian party was arrested, and Beria's close associate Grigor Harutiunian (Arutiunov), former head of the Tbilisi party committee, began the systematic decimation of the Armenian party.[51]

Trials and arrests continued through the fall of 1937. In Batumi the Ajarian communist leadership was found guilty of being agents of foreign intelligence services and most were shot. In Sukhumi the Abkhaz leaders, now labeled counterrevolutionaries, were tarred by their association with their late comrade Nestor Lakoba, who had died in December 1936 of a heart attack. Lakoba was posthumously linked to Trotskyism and national deviationism. Many of his colleagues and relatives were implicated in anti-state activities, and ten of the accused were shot. In December a counterrevolutionary group in the Georgian Commissariat of Agriculture was "discovered" to have been sabotaging livestock production.[52]

As the year closed, *Pravda* announced that several of the most highly placed Caucasian Communists—Enukidze, Orakhelashvili, and diplomat Lev Karakhan—had been executed for terrorism, espionage, and bourgeois nationalism. The last Georgian show trial was held in January 1938. Five employees of the Georgian Animal Husbandry Research Institute were shot for their sabotage.[53] In the frenzy of 1937 economic shortcomings had been linked to counterrevolutionary and foreign espionage. Scapegoats were found for every failure.

By the last months of 1937 a moderate sentiment calling for a "partial amnesty" developed within the Politburo, and the mass purges came to a gradual end in 1938. The January plenum of the Central Committee issued a resolution calling for measures to correct errors in expelling Communists. Many imprisoned or disgraced party members were rehabilitated and readmitted to the party, but those murdered could not, of course, be resurrected. The Terror did not end altogether, however. In March Bukharin and Rykov were put on trial and executed.[54] In May L. I. Mirzoyan, who had worked in Azerbaijan before becoming first secretary of the Kazakh party, was shot. In April Politburo members Eikhe and Kosior were arrested, and in May their colleague Chubar was imprisoned. At the end of July Rudzutak, several military commanders, and prominent officials were executed. Nevertheless, the *Ezhovshchina* was drawing to a close. On August 21, Ezhov was named people's commissar of water transport. His successor as head of the NKVD was Lavrenti Beria.

The toll in Georgia and Transcaucasia was extraordinarily high. Apparently Beria, Bagirov, and Arutiunov were "vigilant" enough Bolsheviks to "discover," "expose," and invent enough plots and conspiracies to satisfy Moscow. All three survived the purges and stayed in power until Stalin's death. The names of their victims read like a roll call of the veterans of the revolution, civil war, and "building of socialism." Besides those already mentioned, among the prominent party members killed were Mikha Kakhiani, Levan Gogoberidze, Iason Mamulia, Soso Buachidze, Petr and Levan Agniashvili, and Ivan Bolkvadze. The old elite had been eliminated, and a new group of party functionaries even more loyal to Stalin and Beria took its place.

Beria's replacement in Georgia was Kandida Nestoris dze Charkviani, who served both as head of the party and the Tbilisi committee.[55] It is difficult to determine exactly what his connections with Beria were once the old leader left for Moscow. Later developments suggest that Charkviani acted as a client of Beria's, maintained the personality cult of Beria in Georgia, but in time (particularly after World War II) began to establish his own political machine in the republic. When Beria was favored by Stalin, however, his influence in Transcaucasia was indisputable.

The Great Purges defy easy explanation. Some Western scholars have interpreted them as a permanent, recurring feature of Soviet totalitarianism (Zbigniew Brzezinski), the product of Stalin's personal paranoia (Robert C. Tucker), or a symptom of the state's inability to command compliance and conformity (Gabor Rittersporn). Others see a struggle of the central political authority against the periphery (J. Arch Getty), a terrible, necessary alternative to real popular support (Robert Conquest), or the need to renew cadres (A. L. Unger, T. H. Rigby, Sheila Fitzpatrick). Most suggestively, Moshe Lewin views the purges as the result of Stalin's determination not to allow the bureaucracy to stabilize (as it would after his death) and thereby limit his personal, arbitrary, autocratic power. Certainly they were possible because of the form into which the Soviet system had hardened by the late 1930s. Without Stalin's agreement, participation, even initiative, the *Ezhovshchina* would not have happened. With his support, it was not only begun, but expanded into a general holocaust within the party and intelligentsia. Stalin as autocrat resisted limits on his will and power. He operated his government through campaigns and explosive efforts. The enormous bureaucracy, which was created as he expanded the area of state activity, tried to work in a more routinized and orderly manner, and by 1935 the dictator and his functionaries were engaged in a bloody, uneven contest.

The purges were particularly ferocious in the national republics, and Transcaucasia stands out for the viciousness and thoroughness of their application. Local party leaders were unable to limit the casualties and, once unleashed, Beria and his subordinates, trained in and enamored of police methods, encouraged a special sadism as they tracked down all opponents, brought old foes back to Tbilisi for punishment, and tortured and murdered men and women with whom they had worked just months before. Their reward was more than survival. Their influence reached beyond Transcaucasia, and when Beria moved on to Moscow he took his most loyal agents with him to the NKVD. Vsevolod Merkulov and Boden Kobulov were placed in Moscow, Sergei Goglidze in Leningrad, Gvishiani in the Maritime Province, Tsanava in Belorussia, Vladimir Dekanozov and Sema Mil'shtein elsewhere.[56] Both Beria and Stalin settled scores with old rivals and opponents; Beria's former boss in Transcaucasia's NKVD, S. Redens, was eliminated, as was Mikhail Kedrov.

But vengeance and personal gain are only a small part of the explanation for the purges. Administratively the entire apparatus of government was centralized. Conflicts between the peripheries and the center were settled once and for all in favor of the center. Transcaucasia, which had repeatedly offered resistance to directives from Moscow, was more fully subordinated to the Kremlin. Structurally the last inhibitions to the personal autocracy of Stalin were eliminated with the full imposition of police power. But ultimately the purges cannot be considered rational acts, for behind the political and personal power considerations were a pathology and criminality that prohibit a reduction of this carnage to rational calculations.

A number of analysts have noted the dramatic shift in the nature of the Communist Party after the Great Purges. Instead of recruiting members for their proletarian origin, as in the period of the "cultural revolution," criteria such as education and technical proficiency became more important. About 70 percent of new recruits now came from the category of *sluzhashchie* (white-collar employees).[57] T. H. Rigby writes:

> The social character of the party being created in the years preceding World War II was almost the direct antithesis of that officially aimed at and in part achieved in the decade following Lenin's death. Supplanting the ideal of a thoroughly proletarian organization with rank-and-file workers and poor peasants forming the vast majority, there was implicit in postpurge recruitment policies the concept of an elite organization of men and women invested with authority, whether by virtue of their commanding position, their expertise, or their productive skill and energy.[58]

Not only were the new people taken from the universities and technical schools, but from the "school of production" itself.

> The most numerous element promoted to head party, police, and government posts in the wake of the purges from 1936 to 1938 . . . appear to have been Stakhanovites, and other promoted workers and party rank-and-file, generally young people under the age of forty, who lacked the combination of higher technical educations, production work, and party affiliation that has increasingly characterized the post-Stalin and post-Khrushchev elites.[59]

But better-educated cadres increased their weight in the party as the country moved toward the war. In Georgia 18,555 new candidates were admitted to the party between November 1, 1936, and March 1939. Of them, the largest contingent, 42.8 percent, were *sluzhashchie*, and only 35.6 percent workers and 18.3 percent collective farmers.[60]

These people made spectacularly rapid career moves upward into positions of leadership and management. The purges and the reorganizations that followed opened up positions for 260 secretaries in Georgian *raikomy, obkomy,* and *gorkomy;* 244 directors of departments and party committee instructors; 201 people's commissars, deputy commissars, and directors of large republic-level organizations; not to mention 166 directors of enterprises, 111 editors of newspapers, and 2,599 secretaries and vice secretaries of local party committees. A whole new elite had been put into place, men and women who were intimately tied to the Stalinist system, which had brought them education, employment, the possibility of a better future, and power.[61]

Though the metaphor of revolution has been too frequently employed in describing changes in Soviet society, the 1930s might be considered a period of "dual revolution"—first the economic turnover of collectivization and industrialization, and then the political upheaval of 1936–1938. Those two "revolutions" left a society in considerable disorder. The army had been severely weakened, as the first campaigns of 1939–1941 demonstrated. Agriculture had barely recovered, and then only in some sectors, to the pre-1928 levels; and in general the economy was quite weak in early 1938. The old leadership was largely gone or traumatized, and the new was as yet untested. Instead of fitting the Western-imposed model of totalitarian efficiency and control, the Soviet Union more readily resembled the ruined landscape following a civil war.

The ruling apparatus had no challengers in society, and it possessed a new status and prestige, though it had little independence or autonomy and only moderate security of tenure. Yet the new rulers of the Soviet Union were able within their competence to dominate and punish their subordinates. Despite the rapid promotion of many former workers upward into management and state-party administration, the "workers' state" had become a repressive mechanism over the workers as well as the peasants. Harsh new laws were promulgated to stop the movement of workers and enforce a draconic labor discipline. A new class had come to power, and any real power of workers over their own lives had been eliminated.

As a sociopolitical formation Stalinism was in place in Georgia by 1939 and remained virtually unchanged through the successive trauma of World War II, the harsh period of postwar reconstruction, and the political and cultural repressions of the last Stalin years. In the quarter-century between 1928 and 1953 Georgia was transformed more fundamentally than in any comparable period in its three-thousand-year history. The population of the republic grew from 2,677,000 in December 1926 to 4,044,000 in January 1959, even after suffering a decline of more than 300,000 during the war. A basically peasant country with over 80 percent of its people living in the countryside at the time of the revolution, Georgia had steadily become an urban society during the Stalin period. In 1926 the rural population was still at 78 percent; thirty-three years later it had fallen to 58 percent. Tbilisi swelled from a small city of 294,000 to one of the largest cities in the Soviet Union (703,000) in the same period. The number of workers and "employees" (sluzhashchie) in the economy had tripled in the Stalin years, numbering over 600,000 in the early 1950s. By then women made up 40 percent of that number, a rise of 15 percent since 1933.[62]

Through the pressures placed on the Georgian population, particularly during the first five-year plans, Georgian peasants were forced into the working class, and workers were shifted into larger enterprises. The share of the national product produced by industry rose from 46 percent at the end of the First Five-Year Plan to 75.2 percent by the end of the second, making industry the most productive sector in the Georgian economy.[63] Besides the old centers of Georgian industry, the manganese mines and the railroad yards, new enterprises were built, among them showplace hydroelectric stations on the Kura and Rioni rivers. At great expense and with little concern for economic rationality, a huge steel mill was constructed in Rustavi, despite its distance from the natural inputs needed for making steel. This plant and an automobile factory in Kutaisi were ordered by Stalin. In this way Georgia became more urban, more industrial, and, after thirty years of Bolshevik rule, more proletarian.

The socioeconomic transformation of Georgia under Stalin made the republic, in one sense, less Georgian, for the traditional peasant life and customs were forced into new molds; but in another sense Georgia's ethnic uniqueness was enhanced by the legacy of the *korenizatsiia* policies. By the early 1950s more people spoke, read, and were educated in the Georgian language than ever before. Georgian national culture was institutionalized in state-sponsored folk dance companies, operas, Georgian-language films, and officially sanctioned literature. Illiteracy had largely been eradicated, and a network of primary, secondary, and higher education was in place. The nativization of schooling, the courts, and governmental institutions gave Georgians the dominant role in a republic that still possessed significant non-Georgian minorities.

Women were more involved in activities outside the home, though they did not share in political decision-making in any meaningful way. While Soviet modernization opened the way for women to enter the work force, traditional Georgian attitudes toward female subordination slowed this movement and presented women with the double burden of new obligations outside the home and the customary female work within the home. In this and many other areas a tension developed between the demands of the new urban, industrial life, with its assimilationist pressures, and the ethnic renationalization of Georgian life, which nourished traditional cultural patterns. That tension lay below the surface and could not be openly expressed in Stalin's time. Only after the heavy hand of Stalinist repression was lifted from the population in the mid-1950s would its manifestations emerge.

After the shocks that Georgian society had experienced during the first five-year plans and the Great Purges, a more conciliatory policy by the party-state toward the intelligentsia and traditional Georgian institutions, like the church, achieved a partial reconciliation between society and the state. The Soviet government was ambivalent in its attitude toward the literary and cultural intelligentsia; on the one hand, it feared its potential independence and authority (Solzhenitsyn once said that a great writer is like a second government); on the other, it wished to appropriate the achievements of the intellectuals as products of the socialist system.

Early in the 1930s the dean of Georgian novelists, Konstantine Gamsakhurdia, had been severely criticized. Yet the publication of two major works in the 1930s—*Abduction of the Moon* (1935) and *The Right Hand of the Great Master* (1939)—were greeted as examples of national art produced under the protection of the party-state. The criticism that attended his works did not prevent the novelist from being officially recognized and honored or being required to participate in public, even political, events. In November 1938, for example, Gamsakhurdia and other leading writers and artists, among them playwright Shalva Dadiani (1874–1959), painter Lado Gudiashvili (1896–1980), and sculptor Iakov Nikoladze (1876–1951) attended a public meeting in Tbilisi to protest the Nazi attacks on the Jews in Germany.[64]

By this time the Georgian intelligentsia, having learned the limits of its own autonomy, had reconciled itself to the existing regime; from its side the regime made few frontal attacks on the intelligentsia. The uneasy compromise was based on mutual need. The intelligentsia gained a degree of security and material rewards; the state gained a voice. Although the full aspirations of Georgian nationalism were not promoted by Soviet authorities, the intelligentsia did receive patronage of the arts and language, satisfying in part its national aspirations.

As Georgia became culturally more Georgian in the Stalin period, the non-Georgian minorities paid a price. Armenians, particularly those intellectuals who had formerly enjoyed Tbilisi as an Armenian cultural center, were pressured to move to Erevan. Armenian cultural monuments, most notably the pantheon of Armenian writers in Hojevank, were closed down. Other minorities also found themselves restricted. When the Arabic alphabets of Muslim peoples in the USSR were replaced, first by Latin and then by Cyrillic alphabets, a new Abkhaz alphabet was introduced based on the Georgian. Thirty-three letters were borrowed directly, and six new letters were formed for specifically Abkhaz phonemes.[65] *Korenizatsiia* had "grown over" into a Georgian chauvinism, parallel to the growth of Russian nationalism (often disguised as Soviet patriotism) on the all-union level.

The rise of patriotism and nationalism was related to the dangers that the USSR faced in Europe from the rearmament of Nazi Germany and in Asia with the expansion of the Japanese empire into China. Stalin's policy of rapprochement with the Western powers had brought some short-term benefits but not a firm alliance against Hitler. At the Eighteenth Party Congress in March 1939, Stalin painted a gloomy picture of a world being repartitioned by means of war. While condemning the aggressors, Germany, Japan, and Italy, he also castigated the West for its policy of neutrality and appeasement and charged that some in the capitalist democracies hoped that Germany would turn eastward toward the USSR. "It is possible to think," he told the congress delegates, "that they gave parts of Czechoslovakia to the Germans as the price for the duty of beginning a war with the Soviet Union."[66]

Five months later the Soviet government reversed its international orientation, to the shock of both Western governments and foreign Communists, and signed a pact with Germany. Within days the Germans invaded Poland, and Britain and France declared war on Germany. The Soviet Union occupied eastern Poland, annexed Ukrainian and Belorussian regions, and soon moved into the Baltic republics, Latvia, Lithuania, and Estonia. A short war was fought with Finland, and territory around Leningrad and Karelia was added to the Soviet Union.

The alliance with Nazi Germany was one of mutual convenience and lasted only until Hitler was ready to implement his plans for *Lebensraum* in the east. On June 22, 1941, without provocation or prior warning, Hitler's armies crossed into Soviet territory, forcing the Red Army into a disorganized retreat. The Nazi advance was spectacularly rapid, and there was fear that the Germans would be able to cross the Caucasus into Georgia and Azerbaijan in their quest for the oil of Baku. But Transcaucasia was spared fighting on the ground when the Germans were stopped on the other side of the mountains. As an area close to the front, Georgia supplied the army with textiles, munitions, and other war material. The primitive workshops and newly built factories of Georgia were refitted to build airplanes, repair tanks, and turn out mortars and bombs.

Georgia's greatest contribution to the war effort was in manpower. Like other Soviet republics, Georgia had had national military units until they were reorganized into mixed Red Army units in 1938. But with the outbreak of war it became clear that national units were imperative, given the difficulties of recruiting and training men who knew little Russian. Both regular regiments and partisan bands were organized. Several were sent to guard the Soviet-Turkish border in anticipation that Turkey might exploit Germany's successes and attack Caucasia. Others were sent to fight in the North Caucasus and in Crimea, where the losses were staggering; most of the 224th Georgian infantry division, for example, died in Crimea.[67]

The entire society was mobilized for the war effort. Schooling was curtailed as students and professors were set to war work or recruited into the army. Artists and writers turned to military themes and became active propagandists. It was reported that in the first year of the war the composers of Georgia, in a burst of patriotic energy, produced sixty-two musical compositions! In 1942 the Tbilisi film studio turned out one film on the war itself, *The Bridge,* and another celebrating the great Georgian warrior of the past, *Giorgi Saakadze.* The latter film won a Stalin Prize for its director, M. Chiaureli. Historical dramas based on the lives of King Erekle, Vakhtang Gorgasali, Queen Tamar, and Bagrationi played in Georgia's theaters. Gamsakhurdia published the first part of his tetralogy, *David the Rebuilder.* Both Soviet patriotism and Georgian nationalism were employed in the cause. The church, which had suffered persecution in the early 1930s, was courted as an ally. No longer were the 145,000 members of the Georgian League of the Militant Godless encouraged to demonstrate against Catholicos Kallistrates at his Sioni Cathedral. In 1943 Stalin ordered the restoration of the auto-cephaly of the Georgian Orthodox Church.[68]

As elsewhere in the Soviet Union, a new national unity was promoted by the very regime that for a decade had stimulated class antagonism. The war, ironically, worked both to end the hostilities between traditional and revolu-tionizing elements in Georgian society and to legitimize the communist regime as the leader of the nation. Whereas earlier it had been easier to contrast Georgia as a nation and the Soviet government as its current state authority, the war brought the two together. The Soviet government suc-ceeded where the tsarist government had failed, in bringing victory over the invaders. Clearly this government was not likely to be replaced.

On May 1, 1945, two Red Army soldiers, M. A. Egorov, a Russian, and M. V. Kantaria, a Georgian, raised the red flag over the Reichstag in Berlin. The war in Europe ended a week later. The four years of fighting cost the Georgian people enormously. Of a population of 3,540,000 in 1939, the Georgian republic had supplied 562,756 people to the armed forces of the USSR by December 1, 1944. Of that number 44,914 were already invalids entitled to pension. The population of the republic fell by 307,000 during the war years to 3,232,700, with the heaviest losses among the rural popula-tion. Overall economic production had fallen by 20 percent and prewar industrial output would not be regained until 1947.[69]

The tragic consequences of the German invasion took almost a decade to overcome. War was followed by a bad harvest throughout the USSR in 1946. With famine stalking some areas, wartime rationing continued. Hopes for a more liberal and tolerant political atmosphere evaporated as relations with the USSR's former allies in the West deteriorated. Cold war descended on Europe, and the Soviet Union was isolated within a bloc of states whose governments it had established.

Just after the war in Europe ended, Soviet Foreign Minister Molotov sent a message to the Turkish ambassador announcing that the Soviet-Turkish agreement of December 17, 1925, "no longer accords with the new situation and calls for serious improvements." The Soviet Union was interested in certain adjustments of its border with Turkey in the regions adjacent to Transcaucasia, revisions in the Montreux Convention governing the Straits, and loosening Turkey's ties with Great Britain. At first the claims to Kars, Ardahan, and Artvin were made in the name of the Armenian republic, but later Georgian irredentist claims were also made. The issue was raised at Potsdam in August 1945 and again in Stalin's meeting with the Western foreign ministers in December. An article appeared in major Soviet newspapers, signed by Georgian academicians S. R. Janashia and N. Berdzenishvili, detailing Georgia's irredenta in northeastern Turkey.[70] A campaign to repatriate diaspora Armenians to Soviet Armenia was begun, and the Armenian church became directly involved in the efforts to regain Kars and Ardahan. Soviet demands alarmed the Turks, as well as the British and Americans, and were a factor in drawing Turkey into the Western alliance.

The entire effort, which continued for several years, may have been personally instigated by Stalin at the urging of Beria. Nikita Khrushchev reveals in his memoirs how Beria taunted Stalin into taking action against Turkey.

> Stalin jealously guarded foreign policy as his own special province. The one person able to advise Stalin on foreign policy was Beria, who used his influence for all it was worth. At one of those interminable "suppers" at Stalin's, Beria started harping on how certain territories, now part of Turkey, used to belong to Georgia and how the Soviet Union ought to demand their return . . . Beria kept bringing this subject up, teasing Stalin with it, goading him into doing something. He convinced Stalin that now was the time to get those territories back. He argued that Turkey was weakened by World War II and wouldn't be able to resist.[71]

Shortly after Stalin's death the whole matter was dropped, and Molotov announced in July 1953 that "the governments of Armenia and Georgia deem it possible to waive their territorial claims against Turkey. The Soviet government consequently states that the Soviet Union has no territorial pretensions against Turkey."[72]

The Kars-Ardahan incident indicates how influential Beria sometimes was over Stalin. From a provincial client he had moved to the very center of Soviet government on the eve of the war. During the war he was a member of the de facto government of the USSR, the State Defense Committee, which was headed by Stalin and included Molotov, Malenkov, and Voroshilov and, later, Voznesenskii, Kaganovich, Mikoyan, and Bulganin. Within the top leadership a rivalry had developed between Malenkov, supported by Beria, and Zhdanov, the head of the Leningrad organization until 1945. Because he was preoccupied with the defense of Leningrad for most of the war, Zhdanov was away from Moscow, and during that time Beria increased his influence with Stalin, even providing the leader with Georgian servants and bodyguards. Beria was named Marshal of the Soviet Union and cited as a "Hero of Socialist Labor" for his achievements in producing armaments. He was put in charge of the Soviet program to build atomic weapons. In March 1946 he and Malenkov were raised to full membership in the party's Politburo.

But in the immediate postwar years Zhdanov emerged as the victor in the competition with Malenkov. His ascendancy from 1946 to early 1948— the *Zhdanovshchina*—was marked by a crackdown on artists and intellectuals. He led a brutal campaign against two gifted Soviet writers, Anna

Akhmatova and Mikhail Zoshchenko, and later against "formalism" in Soviet music, taking to task the Georgian composer Vano Muradeli. The unfortunate Muradeli was accused of having written an "anti-people" opera, *The Great Friendship*. He, Shostakovich, Prokofiev, and Khachaturian were all required to undergo a ritual of self-criticism and publicly repent their errors. In foreign policy Zhdanov was militantly anti-Western and was allied with the more revolutionary East European Communists like Tito.[73]

While Zhdanov and his Leningrad cronies were influential, Beria's position was compromised. In January 1946 he was replaced by S. N. Kruglov as minister of internal affairs, and at the end of that year his associate, V. N. Merkulov, lost his post as minister of state security to Abakumov. A Zhdanov associate, A. A. Kuznetsov, was put in charge of state security organs. In Georgia Beria's clients also suffered. Bakradze was demoted to deputy prime minister; Sturua lost his positions in both government and party in 1948; Sharia was removed; and Raprava was shifted to a less important job.[74] At a dinner at Stalin's residence his concern about Beria's power came to a head and, according to Khrushchev, Stalin asked angrily: "Why am I surrounded by Georgians?" Beria was on his guard and tried to soothe Stalin by pleading that the servants he had hired were all devoted to the leader. "Does that mean that Russians are unfaithful?" asked Stalin. "I don't need their loyalty! Clear these people out of here!" "The Georgians—including the shashlik cook and the provisions officer—were immediately whisked away, and Beria shuffled out of the room like a man who had been beaten up."[75]

Even before Zhdanov died in the summer of 1948, Malenkov and Beria re-emerged as dominant personalities within Stalin's inner circle. Zhdanov's associates were swept away in the notorious "Leningrad Affair." Stalin had Khrushchev brought back to Moscow from the Ukraine in 1949, and Khrushchev sensed that he was relocated to counterbalance the weight of Beria and Malenkov. "It seems sometimes that Stalin was afraid of Beria and would have been glad to get rid of him but didn't know how to do it. Naturally, Stalin never told me this, but I could sense it." At one point Malenkov was sent to Central Asia in disgrace, but Beria arranged his return to Moscow. "From then on Beria and Malenkov appeared to be inseparable friends"—"those two rogues," in Stalin's ominous phrase.[76]

By the last decade of Stalin's life government in the Soviet Union had been centralized to the point that the most important matters of domestic and foreign policy were decided at late-night suppers at Stalin's apartment or *dacha*. The information Stalin received was crucial to the direction of party-state policy, and Beria managed to control much of what Stalin heard.

> Stalin was getting old and didn't realize how powerful Beria still was. For instance, the minister of state security, Abakumov, would report to Stalin only after Beria had reported to Stalin himself and received Stalin's instructions . . . [Stalin] thought he had found in Abakumov a bright young man who was dutifully carrying out his orders, but actually Abakumov was

reporting to Stalin what Beria had told him Stalin wanted to hear. Further-more, Beria still did in fact control Stalin's entourage, even after the Georgian service personnel had been thrown out.[77]

Besides his enormous power in Moscow, Beria retained his control over Georgia. He remained a member of the Georgian Central Committee (as did Stalin) and involved himself in personnel matters. A Beria personality cult was maintained in Georgia, and Beria's name adorned the main square of Tbilisi.[78] He managed Georgia as his own "fiefdom." His control of a local power base was unique among the top Soviet leadership. As one analyst has concluded, his authority over Transcaucasia allowed the Georgians "to escape the degree of Russian supervision (such as Russian second secretaries) that was normal in the other union republics and procured for Georgia, at least, special consideration in the allotment of scarce goods."[79]

Again, Beria was able to keep his personal authority over Georgia by effectively sealing Stalin off from news about his homeland. Khrushchev reports that Stalin once was visited by an old Georgian friend who shocked him with tales about the profligate ways of young Georgian men who had completed their education. Unable to find work in Georgia, they took up illegal economic activity. Stalin, who retained a rather puritanical socialism, asked Khrushchev: "Do you know what's going on in Georgia? The young men are either loafing or profiteering! It's disgusting!"[80]

The very last years of Stalin's life were a harsh, tense period in Soviet history. Economic stagnation at home and political repression throughout the Soviet empire marked the declining years of the old dictator's rule. Stalin himself was consumed by suspicion. He told Khrushchev, "I trust no one, not even myself." No one was safe, and the threat of another purge hung in the air. "In those days," Khrushchev remembered, "anything could have happened to any one of us. Everything depended on what Stalin happened to be thinking when he glanced in your direction. Sometimes he would glare at you and say, 'Why are you averting your eyes from mine?' . . . All of us around Stalin were temporary people." After the Nineteenth Party Congress in 1952, Mikoyan and Molotov were banished from Stalin's presence.[81]

In 1951 Stalin decided to curtail Beria's power. The first signal was the replacement of V. S. Abakumov, who had over time come to serve Beria, with S. D. Ignat'ev, a man hostile to Beria and Malenkov. As Beria's influence over state security was being cut back, Stalin and Ignat'ev fabricated a police case against officials in the Georgian republic—the so-called Mingrelian Affair. Beria was himself a Mingrelian *(megreli)*, and in November 1951 key Mingrelian officials in the Georgian party-state—Second Secretary M. I. Baramia, Minister of Justice A. N. Raprava, and Prosecutor V. Ia. Shonia—were removed for protecting officials who had committed crimes. These dismissals were carried out on Stalin's personal orders.[82]

At about the same time Georgia was divided into two new *oblasti*, Tbilisi and Kutaisi, and the secretaries of the new provinces, Lelashvili and

Mgeladze, were raised to full membership in the bureau of the Georgian Central Committee. More personnel changes occurred in December and January; most of the victims were Mingrelians. Finally, in March 1952, the first secretary since 1938, Charkviani, was replaced by Akaki Ivanis dze Mgeladze. Beria was present at the plenum in April that formally confirmed the succession. Charkviani's followers were replaced by men from Abkhazeti, where Mgeladze had been party chief.[83]

In analyzing these purges Robert Conquest argues that three factions were contending in Georgia: Beria's allies, Stalin's new men of 1951, and a Charkviani contingent somewhat independent of Beria. "No interpretation of Stalin's moves in Georgia in 1951 and 1952 appears reasonable except on the view that Stalin was *gradually* lessening Beria's influence." Charles Fairbanks, Jr., adds to this argument by pointing out that Stalin's anti-Jewish campaign, the "Doctors' Plot," and the persecution of Czech Communists Slansky and Geminder were also connected with his attack on Beria.[84] Elaborating on Conquest's three-faction analysis, Fairbanks says:

> First Stalin arrayed Charkviani's clientele and Mgeladze's against Beria's (or Baramiya's and Zodelava's). At this stage both Charkviani and Mgeladze were allowed to fulfill their obligations as patrons by promoting members of their clienteles . . . In the second stage (April–May 1952) Charkviani's clients were displaced in favor of the appointees of Mgeladze.[85]

Finally, Khrushchev writes:

> Because Stalin was old and sick, he wasn't consistent in following through on his scheme. Beria turned the whole thing around in his favor and shrewdly insinuated himself as Stalin's henchman. None of the rest of us would have dared interfere in a matter relating to the Georgian republic. Beria assigned himself to go to Georgia and administer the punishment of the Mingrels, the imaginary enemies.[86]

Beria's power over Georgia was reduced significantly after 1951, if not eliminated completely. He managed to retain his position in the central Politburo, however, and lived to attend Stalin's funeral. Shortly afterward he reinstated his clients in key positions in Georgia.

At the Nineteenth Party Congress in October 1952 speaker after speaker condemned minority nationalism without mentioning Great Russian chauvinism. Only Beria equated three pernicious influences—great-power chauvinism, bourgeois nationalism, and bourgeois cosmopolitanism. He alone conceded the importance of minority languages and cadres, but probably not out of any residual idealism. "A concrete reason for Beria's favoring the non-Russian nationalities more than other leaders did," writes Fairbanks, "is his territorial fiefdom in the Transcaucasus . . . Beria's freedom to use his power as he wished in the Transcaucasus may still have depended somewhat on the general autonomy granted to the union republics."[87]

By this time, the last months of Stalin's life, the nationality policy of the Communist Party had become a grotesque caricature of what Lenin had spent his last energies attempting to establish. All real political autonomy for the union republics had long since been eliminated in favor of centralized decision-making. Although regional elites and family circles cut across the lines of command from center to periphery and preserved some local discretion, the intention of the center was to combat such centrifugal tendencies. As in the Mingrelian Affair, purges of local officials, even those protected by powerful patrons in the Politburo, were carried out occasionally to re-establish the unlimited authority of Moscow over the borderlands.

The Kremlin's power over the destiny of the non-Russian peoples and the latter's ultimate impotence were most brutally illustrated when several small nationalities were physically moved from their homelands. In the midst of the war with Germany, Stalin had ordered the uprooting and exiling of a number of North Caucasian peoples—the Chechens, Ingush, Balkars, Karachai, and Kalmyks—as well as the Volga Germans and Crimean Tatars, ostensibly for collaboration with the enemy.[88] Toponyms were changed, maps redrawn, and "autonomous regions" and "republics" abolished. Two districts in the former Karachai Autonomous Region, including its capital city, were annexed to the Georgian republic as part of the Klukhori district. More than two thousand Georgians were settled in these depleted lands in December 1943. Four years later about eight thousand Muslims in Georgia, the Meskhian Turks, who lived along the border with Turkey, were deported to Central Asia, and plans were made to exile the Abkhazians as well.[89]

Ethnic discrimination and attacks on nationalism went hand in hand with an aggressive promotion of Russian culture and nationalism. Armenians living in Georgia "were subjected to restrictions, deprived of their rights as Soviet citizens, and in many cases deported," writes Roy Medvedev. Stalin's personal anti-Semitism was written into state policy, and a vicious campaign against "cosmopolitanism" led to the arrests of prominent Jews, including Molotov's wife, Polina Zemchuzhina. Jewish theaters were closed, and a famous Yiddish actor, Solomon Mikhoels, was killed. Late in 1952 the infamous "Doctors' Plot" was concocted. Kremlin doctors, many of them Jews, were implicated in a phony conspiracy to murder Soviet leaders. In Georgia, where there was a large and Georgianized Jewish community dating back to the Middle Ages, there was little traditional anti-Semitism. Beria himself was well known as a protector of the Jews, but in the anti-cosmopolitan campaign of the late 1940s and early 1950s even the Georgian Jews were affected. The Historical and Ethnographical Museum of the Georgian Jews, which had been established in 1933, was closed down, and its director, Aharon Krikheli, was arrested.[90]

The attacks on nationalism hit the Georgian intelligentsia, and at the Fifteenth Congress of the Georgian Communist Party in September 1952, Georgian writers, critics, artists, and film-makers were criticized. Once again

Gamsakhurdia was the principal victim. Party chief Mgeladze told the delegates that "the idealization of the past by the writer Gamsakhurdia is an expression of bourgeois nationalism, the essence of which is concealed in an attempt to isolate and close itself off in the confines of national narrow-mindedness without seeing what is bringing closer together and uniting the laborers of all the nationalities of the Soviet Union." Shalva Dadiani's novel *Iurii Bogoliubskii*, which was based on the life of Queen Tamar's unfortunate Russian first husband, was attacked for distorting the "centuries-long friendship of the Russian and Georgian peoples."[91] Dramatists and cinematographers were damned for the poverty of their work, and translators were told to turn out more Georgian-language editions of the classics of Russian literature.

The promotion of Russian language and culture throughout the Soviet Union set the limits for the development of national cultures. In each union republic the titular nationality used its position to develop its own version of great-power chauvinism, limiting where it was able the expression of its minorities. Georgia became a protected area of privilege for Georgians. They received the bulk of the rewards of the society, the leading positions in the state, and the largest subsidies for cultural projects, while Armenians, Abkhazians, Ossetians, Ajarians, Kurds, Jews, and others were at a considerable disadvantage in the competition for the budgetary pie. Georgian nationalism was self-protection against the pressures and the blandishments of the "higher culture" of the Russians and an argument in favor of preferential treatment of one ethnic group over its rivals. Lenin's nationality policy in the hands of the Stalinists had created nationalized republics even as they tried to develop a multinational unity on the basis of the Russian language.

Perhaps Stalin's greatest legacy was the building of an empire, both within and outside the Soviet Union, that proved to have greater capacity to survive his death than many contemporary analysts expected. The relative stability of that empire was in part due to the fact that the non-Russian nationalities, for all the burdens and pains they had undergone, had also benefited considerably from the forced association with the Russians. In a balanced attempt to calculate the costs and benefits of the Soviet model of development for Transcaucasia and Central Asia, Alec Nove and J. Newth write that these areas should not be seen as colonies of Russia.

> It is a characteristic of colonial status . . . that the dominant Power uses the economy of the colony for its own benefit, keeping it industrially relatively under-developed, extracting profit from investments, underpaying colonial labor, neglecting education and so on. None of these features of traditional colonialism can be discerned in an impartial analysis of Soviet policy in the republics. Far from there being any economic exploitation, it is reasonable on the evidence to assert that industrialization, especially in Central Asia, has been financed with money raised in Russia proper. In other words, capital has tended to move to those outlying under-developed areas and there has been virtually no counterbalancing move of remittances of profit or

interest, because in the Soviet Union capital grants are not repayable and do not bear interest.

The evidence also shows that "each of the republics has very little political power and that this is particularly significant in a country in which politicians claim the right to decide far more than is considered 'political' in a Western country."[92] But political subordination, in their view, is not equivalent to colonialism so long as economic exploitation is missing.

The very ambivalence of the Nove-Newth formulation illustrates the difficulty of rendering judgment on the Stalinist system of political subordination and forced economic development. Another conception of Soviet colonialism, proposed by Alvin W. Gouldner, avoids the ethnic dimension and suggests that "what had been brought into being was an urban-centered power elite that had set out to dominate a largely rural society to which they related as an alien colonial power; it was an internal colonialism mobilizing its state power against colonial tributaries in rural territories."[93]

For the Georgians, who entered the Stalinist period as a largely peasant nation, the relationship with the Great Russian center was marked by this kind of "internal colonialism." As part of the Soviet Union Georgians were "modernized" in a particular way and, like most peasant populations in the world, not by choice. Just as in tsarist Russia or Safavid Iran, Georgians were changed by their imperial experience without having been able to determine their own fate. The Stalin years eliminated once and for all Georgia's basically peasant economy and in one desperate push accelerated the creation of a primarily urban and industrial society. Without gaining the full attributes of political sovereignty, Georgians nevertheless remained a cohesive and conscious nationality in possession of its own territory and prepared, should the opportunity arise, to improve its social, material, and cultural life.

13 Georgia and Soviet Nationality Policy since Stalin

Seldom has the death of an individual, even that of a great tyrant, so definitively marked the end of a political era as did the passing of Joseph Stalin. The Soviet system, in so many essentials the creation of his peculiar understanding of Russia's needs and his personal requirements for the maintenance of a monopoly of power, almost immediately began a process of gradual change that, however incomplete, left a society significantly less terrorized, considerably more prosperous, and much more open to the rest of the world.

In the first three decades after Stalin's death, the central political question facing the Soviet leadership was: in reforming the Stalinist political and economic order, how much of what had become the Soviet system had to be dismantled? Within the ruling party and in society as well two conflicting tendencies could be observed: one committed to change leading to a more flexible social order, and the other dedicated to preservation of the status quo. This reform-preservation conflict was reflected in a number of contradictory movements: decentralization of political and economic decision-making versus conservation of the Stalinist command economy; intellectual tolerance versus repression of deviance and dissent; openings to the West versus maintenance of traditional xenophobia; greater liberty for national and ethnic expression versus the containment of such expression within the Stalinist formula "national in form, socialist in content." The occasionally erratic movement in governmental policy and the apparent loss of direction by the political elite at times resulted in frustration on the part of many in society, an erosion among some intellectuals of commitment to the regime and its ideals, and the partial replacement of the official Marxist-Leninist ideology by patriotism and nationalism.

The enormous changes in Soviet society and political practice since Stalin should not obscure the elements of continuity that run from the stormy years of social reconstruction through the years of moderate reform under Khrushchev, Andropov, and Gorbachev and the long period of conservative retrenchment under Brezhnev. Most of the change occurred on the political and cultural level; much of the continuity was located in the fundamental social, economic, and demographic trends initiated under Stalin. Urbanization, industrialization, the spread of education and technology were gigantic processes affected only superficially by changes in political leadership. While the reduction of police terrorism and decentralization of political power undeniably shaped social developments to a degree, the basic contours of the extrapolitical tendencies had already been well established in the Stalin revolution.

All the constituent peoples of the Soviet Union were affected by the social revolution of the Stalin years as well as by the political changes that followed, but the emphasis of most analysts of the recent Soviet past has been, understandably, on the center and on the top, that is, on the Russian heartland and the ruling communist elite. When attention has been turned to the non-Russian periphery, it has usually been to look at the treatment of the minority nationalities as a separate aspect of Soviet policy, as "nationality policy" or the "national question." Such an approach, while illuminating the vacillations in policy arising from the reform-preservation conflict within the central leadership, usually neglects examination of the underlying indigenous social developments that took place in the ethnic areas.

A study of nationality policy emanating from the center tells us little about the implementation or effectiveness of that policy among the various nationalities. Only an unquestioning acceptance of the outdated totalitarian model of the USSR would permit a researcher to make the facile conclusion that the writ of the Kremlin always ran without resistance in outlying areas. Recent work on Soviet nationalities has already indicated clearly that their recent history has been sufficiently diverse to preclude many all-inclusive generalizations about the non-Russian half of the Soviet population.[1]

Indeed, an in-depth look at the last thirty-five years of the history of Georgia demonstrates that the experience in that country was not shaped to any great extent by the twists and turns of official nationality policy but, while evolving under the influence of general Soviet policy, was rather the product of indigenous social and political developments and local resistance to imperatives from the center. The picture that emerges from Georgia is complex and at times indistinct, but available evidence indicates that modernizing forces from beyond the Caucasus and nationalizing forces within

Georgia itself have been engaged in an intense struggle ever since the heavy hand of Stalinist police rule loosened its grip.

Official statements about state policy toward the nationalities were only occasionally, and then always incompletely, articulated in the 1950s. But in the new party program adopted by the Twenty-second Party Congress in 1961, Khrushchev elaborated the official theory of national development. Soviet nationalities were to continue to evolve through the "flourishing" *(rasvet)* of their ethnic culture, but this process would lead dialectically to a "drawing together" *(sblizhenie)* of these nations until their "complete merger" *(sliianie)* was achieved, with the creation of a new Soviet people.[2] These pronouncements flew in the face of the tendencies that had evolved for the last decade and seemed to signal a political attempt to reverse certain "objective" developments.

With the fall of Khrushchev in 1964, some slight changes were introduced into Soviet nationality policy. Among the minor concessions made to national sensibilities was the elimination of the assimilationist term *sliianie* from official statements about the future of Soviet minorities. The term *sblizhenie* was retained, but party leader Leonid Brezhnev emphasized that rapprochement among the nationalities would occur through the play of "objective" social forces and not as the result of artificial prodding by the party.[3] As if to underline the sincerity of this new approach, the government decided in 1965 to publish once again the laws of the Supreme Soviet and its Presidium in the national languages of the republics, something not done since April 1960.[4] And chairmen of republican supreme soviets, councils of ministers, supreme courts, and planning committees became ex officio members of the corresponding all-union organs.

Essentially the new party leadership turned its attention toward the grave economic problems faced by the Soviet state and abandoned a political solution to the nationality problem. But this Soviet version of "benign neglect" soon proved inadequate, for within a few years it became apparent that two developments were occurring that were undesirable from the Kremlin's position: first, local national elites with a base of support in their republics were acquiring independent attitudes and practices with nationalist implications; and second, a new nationalism with oppositional overtones was being articulated more and more openly.

The embodiment of the state's nationality policy at the end of the 1970s could most clearly be seen in the final draft of the new Soviet constitution adopted on October 7, 1977. Affirming the successful construction of socialism in the USSR, the preamble to the document claimed that a "new historical community of people, the Soviet people, has emerged" as part of that process. At least one Western analyst has argued that this formulation "aims at total deprivation of the Soviet nations of their separate national identities," but the Soviet leadership has been quite circumspect in its statements concerning the meaning of this concept.[5] Three days before the constitution was ratified by the Supreme Soviet, Brezhnev declared:

> The Soviet people's social and political unity does not in the least imply the disappearance of national distinctions . . . The friendship of the Soviet peoples is indissoluble, and in the process of building communism they are steadily drawing ever closer together and their spiritual life is being mutually enriched. But we would be taking a dangerous path were we artificially to step up this objective process of national integration. That is something Lenin persistently warned against, and we shall not depart from his precepts.[6]

The new constitution reaffirmed the right of union republics to secede from the Soviet Union, though there had been much discussion in the early 1960s among the drafters of the constitution to do away with this largely fictitious right. Other prerogatives formerly held in law by the union republics were lost in the new constitution. Republics no longer enjoyed the right to possess their own armed forces as they had in the 1936 constitution. Nor were they permitted to enter into relations with foreign states directly.[7] Most important, the administrative functions of the union republics were no longer as clearly demarcated as they had been in the past, and the central government retained the right to decide on the republics' competence in policy matters.

Although these constitutional clauses simply affirmed in law what had been usual practice, some observers in the West feared that they marked a diminution of ethnic autonomy.[8] Yet it can also be argued that the provisions in the Brezhnev constitution, the result of long discussions and many political compromises, actually represented concessions toward the nationalities as well as some aggrandizement of authority by the central government. In his speech to the Supreme Soviet, Brezhnev noted that there had been proposals "to introduce into the constitution the concept of one Soviet *nation*, to abolish the union and autonomous republics or to limit drastically the sovereignty of union republics by depriving them of the right to secession from the USSR and of the right to enter into foreign relations. The proposals to liquidate the Council of Nationalities and establish a one-house Supreme Soviet would have moved in the same direction."[9] These more drastic assaults on the ethnic minorities were rejected by the government, and the official recognition of the multinational composition of the Soviet people was written into the document. Thus, twenty-five years after Stalin's death, the tensions between assimilationist and nationalizing trends were tentatively resolved in a fragile compromise.

In the recent past the fluctuations of official policy seem to have had less effect on the development of Georgian society than the long-term, underlying dynamics that began in the Stalin years and even earlier. In the most general way one can describe the last 150 years as the period of the "re-formation" of the Georgian nation. With the Russian annexations of Georgian lands (1801–1829), most Georgian-speaking peoples were united under a single political authority for the first time since the fifteenth century. The security provided by the Russians permitted the re-establishment of the agrarian economy and the rebirth of urban life.[10]

The Georgian nobility, which at first resisted Russian rule, was pacified and integrated into the Russian *dvorianstvo,* and by the mid-nineteenth century was loyally serving the tsarist state as civil administrators and military officers. Thus, from the beginning the advantages brought by Russian administration to Georgia diluted the recurring nationalist efforts to resist the new foreign authority. This ambivalence toward Russia remained part of Georgian national consciousness for the next century and a half.

Georgia was only beginning capitalist development when the revolution of 1917 made it possible to break free of Russian control and establish an independent Georgian state, but the process of national consolidation promoted by the Georgian social democrats was far from complete when the Red Army overthrew the Menshevik republic in February 1921. The elimination of political independence and the forced integration into the Soviet Union ended the first period of Georgian national reconstruction.[11]

Even as political autonomy and local initiative were reduced for Georgians, two general developments began to transform the life of all nationalities in the Soviet Union: the socioeconomic shift from an agrarian to an industrial society, and the political-cultural process of renationalization. Initiated in the early Soviet period and accelerated during the Stalin revolution, these two trends continued to influence the life of Soviet ethnic minorities long after Stalin's death.

In Georgia, as in the rest of the USSR, the complex processes associated with industrialization and urbanization were accelerated by the state-directed assault on the peasantry, which reduced the weight of agriculture in economic life and propelled agricultural laborers into the new urban working class. In Georgia industrialization had been quite modest before the revolution, but by 1940 industrial output had increased 670 percent over 1928. Even considering Georgia's low base, this marked a tremendous growth and was well above the USSR average. Between 1940 and 1958 Georgia's industrial output grew by 240 percent, and from 1958 to 1965 by 157 percent. In 1913, industrial production in Georgia amounted to only 13 percent of the value of total production; by 1970 industry, construction, and transportation and communications accounted for 53 percent of Georgian national income.[12]

The urban population of Georgia grew steadily during the Soviet period, from 666,000 in 1913 to 2,241,000 in 1970. In the sixty years of Soviet power Georgian urbanites increased from just over a quarter of the Georgian population to just over half by the end of the 1970s. Yet Georgia did not urbanize as rapidly as many other parts of the USSR; in 1979 Georgia (with 52 percent of its population living in towns and cities) was well behind the USSR as a whole (62 percent) and also behind its neighbors, Armenia (66 percent) and Azerbaijan (53 percent). Moreover, Armenians and Russians still made up a high percentage of Georgia's urban population.[13]

More significant for Georgian social life are the figures for the percentage of the total working population engaged in industry, building, and transportation-communications in contrast to the percentage engaged in agriculture. In 1939 the figure for the first segment was 19.4 percent of Georgia's working population, with 61.9 percent in agriculture. Twenty years later the figure for industry had increased to one-quarter (24.9 percent) of the working population and that for agriculture had fallen to one-half (50.7 percent). By 1970 34 percent of the work force was in the industrial sector while 38 percent was in agriculture and lumbering. By 1979 a majority of the work force (53.5 percent) were industrial workers, while only 16 percent were collective farmers.[14]

These figures show a steady shift from agriculture to industry, though when one compares Georgia with her sister republics in Transcaucasia it is noteworthy that Armenia achieved much more rapid development: in 1939 the percentages were 17.8 in industry versus 65.4 in agriculture; in 1959, 30.6 percent versus 45.7 percent; in 1971, industrial, construction, and transportation-communications workers made up just over 50 percent of the work force, and the percentage of agricultural workers had fallen to 11. Azerbaijan with its oil industry around Baku started with a higher percentage of workers in industry than Georgia or Armenia—23.1 versus 57.5 in agriculture in 1939—but did not show as much of a shift toward industry (in 1959 26.5 percent worked in industry, 49.6 percent in agriculture).[15]

Still, it is clear that Georgian economic development has clearly been aided by its link to the USSR and by the official Soviet industrializing ideology and policy.[16] However incomplete Georgian industrialization and urbanization may be, the society in which Georgians live today is vastly more interconnected with cities, factories, and economic growth than was the society into which Ioseb Jughashvili was born in 1879.

The achievements of the communist leadership in expanding the economic power of Soviet society—what Russians like to call *"nashi dostizheniia"* ("our achievements")—are well known to Western readers. Less easily ascertained is the effect these social and economic changes have had on the minority nationalities as cohesive ethnic groups. Most Western writers, while recognizing the assimilationist pressures that accompany "modernization," would agree with Richard Pipes that the expectations of nineteenth-century liberals and socialists that nationalism would "dissolve in the acid bath of modernity" have proven utopian. Soviet analysts as well have noted that the "construction of socialist nations" in the USSR has not led to the elimination of national differences. Indeed, it is clear that in the last thirty years there has been an increase in national consciousness and the open expression of nationalism in the Soviet borderlands. This phenomenon is difficult to explain, for the expectation remains that in developing societies, traditional ethnic allegiances will become less relevant.[17]

To explain the emergence of the new nationalism it is necessary to look at another dynamic process that occurred simultaneously with industrialization and urbanization in the USSR—renationalization. The social transformation of Soviet society entailed much more than economic development. The shift from agriculture to industry and from village to city was accompanied by an expansion of mass education and welfare services and the creation of a modern multinational army and civil service, as well as a technical intelligentsia. New institutions had the dual effect of opening Western and Russian learning to the minorities as well as raising the literary abilities of these peoples in their own languages. For some nationalities renationalization meant the creation of an alphabet and written language. For others it involved the initial establishment of a political framework. For Armenians it meant a fundamental demographic shift, as thousands migrated from other parts of the Soviet Union and the world to reoccupy a small piece of their ancient territory. For Georgians renationalization involved the gradual re-establishment of their political control and ethnic dominance over their historic homeland, a process that had barely started during the brief period of independence.

Before the revolution the Georgians, still primarily a nation of rural nobles and peasants, remained on the fringe of the emerging urban society both politically and culturally, and a desperate reaction to the displacement of their language and traditions led to the assertion of a new nationalism directed against both Russians and Armenians. With the revolution, however, and the brief period of Menshevik rule, the Georgians displaced the Armenian middle class and began to establish their own demographic and cultural hegemony in the towns of Georgia, especially in their own capital, where they had long been second-class citizens. In the early Soviet period Georgian and non-Georgian cadres coexisted in the party and government apparatus, but steadily the policy of developing national cadres *(korenizatsiia)* led to the Georgianization of the local government. At the same time many Armenians who had not already fled from the new communist republic migrated from Georgia to the Armenian Soviet republic, thus further consolidating the Georgian hold on the Georgian republic.

The demographic consolidation of the Georgian nationality faltered in the Stalin years but accelerated after his death. By 1979 Georgia's population had grown to 5,016,000 from 4,044,000 in 1959. In 1959, 64.3 percent or 2,601,000 were ethnic Georgians; by 1979 that figure had grown to 68.8 percent. This increase in the relative weight of Georgians in Georgia's population is particularly noteworthy for two reasons. First, it marked a reversal of the trend evident since 1897: a fall in the percentage of Georgians (see Table

1).[18] And, second, the Georgians, despite their modest birthrate, showed greater increases than other nationalities in their home republics—with the exception of the Muslim republics with their especially high birth rates.

The corresponding weights of Armenians and Russians in Georgia were falling (see Table 1); Georgia has the distinction of being the only union republic in which there has been an absolute fall in the number of Russians. The number of Armenians in Georgia rose insignificantly between 1959 (443,000) and 1979 (448,000), and their proportion in the population of the republic fell to 9 percent. It is clear that this Georgianization of the republic is primarily the result of an outmigration of Russians, Armenians, and Jews.[19]

TABLE 1

POPULATION OF GEORGIA BY NATIONALITIES
(in percent)

Nationality	1897	1926	1939	1959	1970	1979
Georgians	66.3	66.8	61.4	64.3	66.8	68.8
Armenians	9.2	11.5	11.7	11.0	9.7	9.0
Russians	—	3.6	8.7	10.1	8.5	7.4

SOURCES: Dobson, "Georgia and the Georgians," p. 168; *Vestnik Statistiki*, no. 10, 1980, p. 67.

Yet another demographic datum is worth noting. Although their republic is less homogeneous in population than either the Armenian (in which 88 percent of the population was Armenian in 1959, 88.6 percent in 1970, and 89.7 percent in 1979) or the Azerbaijani (67 percent Azerbaijani in 1959, 73.8 percent in 1970, and 78.1 percent in 1979), the Georgians are much more likely than any major Soviet nationality to live within the confines of their national republic. A startling 97 percent of Georgians lived in Georgia in 1970, with another 2 percent in the RSFSR (96.1 percent and 2.5 percent in 1979). Their neighbors, the Armenians, had the lowest percentage (60 percent in 1970, 65.6 percent in 1979) of any titular ethnic group living in its home republic; 86 percent of Azerbaijanis were living in their republic (both in 1970 and 1979).[20] Georgians, thus, are a people content to remain in Georgia with an insignificant outmigration. Important both demographically and psychologically was the achievement of a Georgian majority in the population of Tbilisi by 1975. All these phenomena argue in favor of the cohesiveness of the Georgian population.

This cohesiveness is also supported by evidence on intermarriage and bilingualism. Soviet statistics are strangely silent on the question of intermarriage, but Wesley Fisher has managed to discover some figures for the year 1969. In that year 93.5 percent of Georgian marriages were endogamous;

only 6.5 percent intermarried.[21] These percentages are surpassed only by the Muslim nationalities. As for bilingualism, high percentages of Georgians had no fluency in Russian. According to the 1970 census and the calculations of Brian Silver, 91.4 percent of rural Georgians and 63 percent of urban Georgians were not fluent in Russian. Looking at the figures for the capital city, we find that even in Tbilisi 56.4 percent of Georgians were not fluent in Russian. That is a higher percentage than any of the other titular nationalities in the capital cities of their republics, with the single exception of the Armenians in Erevan (63.1 percent are not fluent in Russian). Again, the figures for Georgians show little tendency toward assimilation through the acquisition of Russian; indeed, a clear resistance to learning Russian is evident. In 1979, 99.5 percent of Georgians living in Georgia considered Georgian their native language, and only 26.7 percent of ethnic Georgians were fluent in Russian.[22]

Besides demographic changes and political nationalization, Georgians also experienced a cultural revival, essentially a continuation of the rebirth of Georgian culture in the late nineteenth and early twentieth centuries. That part of the old intelligentsia that remained in Georgia after 1921 was complemented by a new Soviet-educated intelligentsia, and state-supported arts and publishing nourished an expanding creativity, though strictly within the framework of Soviet socialist norms. Most important, for the first time in Georgian history a Georgian university had been founded (under the Mensheviks in 1919), and subsidized scientific research could be carried on in Georgian.

National theater, opera, and film flourished as a new audience was prepared for culture in the native language. Folk music and dance became part of officially supported art and were promoted in the towns and cities among people who otherwise might have lost contact with the arts of their village past. Ethnicity was actively fostered by the state even to the extent of forcing ethnic motives on modern architects, painters, and sculptors.

As must already be apparent, a fundamental contradiction existed between these two general tendencies. While the state-initiated economic development was creating a new industrial, urban society with greater mobility and material wealth, and greater opportunities for education and integration into Russian and European life, renationalization was creating a new national culture, preserving and revitalizing local traditions, and in a variety of ways preventing the assimilation of the Georgians into an amorphous interethnic conglomerate. These contradictions went unresolved in official nationality policy and were reflected in the formula designed for the arts—"national in form, socialist in content"—and in the confusion over whether the goal of Soviet policy was to solidify the national or to assimilate the minorities. Yet these contradictions were not articulated during Stalin's rule; only in the more tolerant period after 1953 did the tensions developed during the long years of Stalinism surface in a new nationalism.

One of the most striking changes in the post-Stalin period was the decentralization of political and, to a degree, economic decision-making. During the Stalin era, Georgia was directed almost completely from the center. Economically, the industrial machine was almost entirely controlled by all-union ministries, and the threat of police intervention kept local party officials in line and prevented the emergence of any resistance to Kremlin authority.

Beria's brief ascendancy after Stalin's death was brought to an abrupt end when his fellow Politburo members in Moscow arrested him in June 1953 and had him shot. The elimination of Beria's supporters in Tbilisi was completed in September 1953 when Vasili P. Mzhavanadze, a man who had long served in the Ukrainian party apparatus under Khrushchev and as a political commissar in the army, was elected first secretary of the Georgian party. The Beria-sponsored Central Committee was dismissed, with the exception of two members. Purges continued through the next few months, and by the Sixteenth Congress of the Georgian Communist Party in February 1954, the first secretaries of Abkhazeti, Ajaria, and Tbilisi had been replaced, new elections had been held in nearly nine thousand party cells, more than two thousand secretaries had been removed from these cells, and over one thousand candidate members of the party had been expelled.[23] A new premier, G. D. Javakhishvili, was elected. This new party leadership, which took power in September 1953, proved remarkably durable, and Mzhavanadze dominated Georgian politics for nineteen years.

The fall of Beria can be interpreted as the reassertion of the power of the party over the police with the aid of the army. It represented a reversal of the equation under Stalin in which the police had been the dominant political force by which Kremlin leadership imposed its will on the regional parties. From 1953, the new authority of the party, combined with Khrushchev's policy of economic decentralization, increased the power of local parties in the national republics. Under Khrushchev the central party seemed willing to take the risk of somewhat reduced control over the national republics in the hope that the local parties would be able to gain regional sources of support and provide stable government in the peripheries. A policy of indirect rule through dependent local elites replaced the old Stalinist system of direct control from Moscow. In Georgia the long tenure of Mzhavanadze aided the establishment of entrenched local authorities who developed their own ethnic political base from which they could "negotiate" with central authorities.

In the immediate post-Stalin years, central political interference in the economy of Georgia was notably reduced. The aim of the central government appeared to be the gradual reform, rather than the preservation, of Stalinist practice. The number of administrative personnel was sharply reduced as political operatives in many industries were eliminated. This curtailment of political meddling in the economy resulted in an annual saving of 43,000,000 rubles in salaries by 1958. Many industrial firms in Georgia were transferred from all-union ministries to the republic's control; by 1958, 98 percent of industrial output in Georgia was produced by enterprises under the republic's management.[24]

In all probability the motivation for this industrial decentralization was the poor showing of industry in the last years of Stalin's life. Industry in Georgia was not growing as rapidly as it had in the prewar period, and much of the debate at the Sixteenth Congress of the Georgian Party exposed the inadequacies of the country's largest enterprises—the Rustavi metallurgical complex, the Zestaponi ferroalloy plant, and the Kutaisi auto works.[25]

Georgia's problem with industry seemed chronic. In July 1955 a plenum of the Central Committee of the Communist Party of the Soviet Union (CPSU) further criticized the performance of Georgian industry. At the same time Georgian peasants benefited from the policies of Khrushchev, which raised state prices for agricultural produce, reduced the amounts of compulsory deliveries, and left a greater area of decision-making to the collective farms. These reforms, however, reduced the comparative advantage that Georgian fruit and vegetable farmers had had over northern grain farmers during Stalin's time, for grain prices rose quite considerably.[26]

The political de-Stalinization and cultural "thaw" of the early post-Stalinist period raised hopes for more far-reaching reforms and caused much confusion in Georgia. The party congress planned for May 1953 was delayed, and in the interim local party meetings were held to debate past policies and future plans. The official party history reports that about fifty thousand Communists engaged in this critical and self-critical exercise, and it can be imagined that this period created expectations about the extent of political change that were soon frustrated. Within Georgia a few measures were taken to improve the situation of non-Georgians living in the autonomous regions. The school systems of the Abkhaz ASSR (Autonomous Soviet Socialist Republic) and the South Ossetian region were reorganized; new Abkhaz, Ossetian, and Armenian schools were opened, and a sector for Abkhaz language and literature was established in the Sukhumi Pedagogical Institute. Radio programs in Armenian and Azeri were revived, and new newspapers in Russian, Abkhaz, Azeri, and Georgian were issued.[27]

The costs and limits of reform within the system left by Stalin became apparent within the first few years after his death. Khrushchev's experiments with decentralization led to the explosion of long-latent tensions. One of the most violent within the Soviet Union occurred in Tbilisi in connection with the third anniversary of Stalin's death on March 5, 1956. No official ceremony was held in the USSR. Just a few weeks earlier Khrushchev had made his famous "secret speech" denouncing the "cult of personality" and the crimes of the Stalin era. Although this new turn in Soviet policy was hailed by the Russian intelligentsia and by reformers within the ruling elites, it had a peculiar resonance in Georgia.

On March 5, an unofficial demonstration took place at the monument to Stalin that stood on the bank of the Kura in Tbilisi. Each day thereafter crowds of students and onlookers gathered at the statue to listen to poems and speeches commemorating the deeds of Stalin. On March 9, the Georgian officials permitted a celebration of the anniversary, but as students moved through the central streets of the capital they were fired upon by police and the army. Dozens of young people were killed, hundreds wounded.[28]

The response to the peaceful protest was extreme and only deepened local resentments against the central government. Many in Georgia held Khrushchev personally responsible for ordering the army to fire on the unarmed crowd. From Moscow the Central Committee issued a resolution in July that was critical of the Georgian Central Committee, and in August the second secretary in Tbilisi was replaced by a Russian. Yet the Georgian leadership managed to weather the storm. Party leader Mzhavanadze and university rector Viktor Kupradze attempted in interviews to minimize the number of victims of the shootings, and a campaign of lectures was organized to spread party views.[29] For his success in pacifying the Georgians, the first secretary was raised to candidate membership in the Presidium of the Central Committee of the CPSU in June 1957.

The demonstrations in Tbilisi were seen by many as a revival of Stalinism and by others as the first open expression of Georgian nationalism in forty years. So little of the essential evidence needed for meaningful generalizations about this event is available to Western scholars that one must be cautious about attempting an analysis of its causes and significance. Georgia, like the other republics in the Soviet Union, had emerged from the Stalin years as a fundamentally changed society, more urban and more mechanized, with traditional village life affecting an ever-decreasing part of the population. Yet this new society had been imposed on the Georgians by an alien political elite working through local national cadres. At the same time, Georgian national culture had been revitalized through Soviet sponsorship. Georgians had become a cohesive nationality with large numbers of people educated in the national language and history. By 1956 the growing national awareness, coupled with anxiety about the loss of unique ethnicity in the face of modernization, had led to a strong resurgence among young people of a commitment to Georgian ethnic identity.

For young Georgians, not fully acquainted with the darker side of Stalin's reign, his memory was still sacred, and his career represented a great achievement by one of their nation. Stalin's denigration was an appropriate symbol for the treatment of Georgian national consciousness at the hands of the Russian (Soviet) rulers. Patriotic pride was mixed with political protest in March 1956. The swift and brutal response from the Soviet government illustrated starkly its inability to resolve the dilemma of how much of the Soviet system to change and how much of Stalin's authoritarianism to preserve. The government's confusion in Tbilisi was a bloody sign that reform was limited by the party's determination to preserve its essential monopoly of power.

In the years after the Tbilisi demonstrations the government made some concessions to Georgian national pride and loosened cultural controls on Georgian art and literature. In March 1958, a festival of Georgian culture was held in Moscow, and later that year the 1500th anniversary of Tbilisi's founding was celebrated. But much more important than these ephemeral gestures in the realm of culture was the gradual consolidation of a national communist elite ruling in Georgia with a significantly greater degree of autonomy. The loosening of political controls from the center and the growing ethnic consolidation and consciousness locally merged in a combination dangerous both to the leadership in Moscow and to non-Georgians living in the republic. In the late 1950s, the Georgian party elite increased its hold over political, economic, and cultural institutions in the republic and, while ruling in Moscow's name, actually offered a low-level resistance to policies from the center that attempted to drive the Georgians too fast in economic development or cultural assimilation.

Local political control and ethnic favoritism led to the growth of a vast network of illegal economic operations and exchanges, which produced great private wealth for some Georgians while their republic grew insignificantly according to official statistics. Despite Khrushchev's campaigns against speculators and "privatism," a degree of "capitalist restoration" took place in Georgia and was carried out by people in the government or close to it. Between 1960 and 1971, Georgia's national income grew by only 102 percent, the third lowest rate in the USSR.[30] Yet in 1970, the average Georgian savings account was nearly twice as large as the Soviet average. At the same time the educational system was turning out enormous numbers of specialists who avoided work assignments yet managed to live quite well. By the early 1970s Georgia had a larger percentage of its population in institutions of higher education than any major nationality. Yet continually the press reported that thousands of high school and university graduates in Tbilisi had missed classes and were unwilling to accept work.[31]

Higher education in Georgia had become the prerogative of Georgians, and other nationalities found it difficult to enter schools of higher learning. In 1969–1970, Georgians, who made up about 67 percent of the republic's population, accounted for 82.6 percent of the students in higher education; Russians with 8.5 percent of the population made up only 6.8 percent. Armenians fared even worse; with 9.7 percent of the Georgian republic's population Armenians accounted for only 3.6 percent of the students in advanced courses.[32]

Clearly Georgian control of the local party and republican institutions was not resulting in an egalitarian application of Leninist nationality policy, but in officially sanctioned discrimination against minorities within the republic. The efforts of the early Khrushchev years to reverse such practices fell victim to the decentralization of political authority, which permitted a reassertion of national control manifested in the inequitable treatment of local minorities. National autonomy in Georgia had come to mean, on the one hand, resistance to central Russian authorities and, on the other, the exercise of local power against the unrepresented local minorities.

Concern about growing nationalism was reflected in the party program of 1961, which asserted that "Communists consider it their primary obligation to educate the working people in the spirit of internationalism and socialist patriotism, and [to struggle against] any manifestation of nationalism and chauvinism." In the years between the Twenty-second Congress and the fall of Khrushchev, efforts were directed toward the raising of a "spirit of socialist internationalism" among party cadres in Transcaucasia. Links among the three republics were strengthened by the creation of a Transcaucasian bureau of the Central Committee of the CPSU, by the operation of the Transcaucasian economic administration, and by a variety of interrepublican organizations. The central leadership was particularly concerned about the selection of party cadres on the basis of nationality and was determined to avoid national favoritism in the union republics. Already in the party program "any kind of manifestation of national isolation [*obosoblennost'*] in the education and employment of party workers of different nationalities in the Soviet republics" was declared "impermissible."[33]

Despite these efforts to end ethnic favoritism in Transcaucasia, such practices persisted and in some ways worsened. The Transcaucasian bureau complained that areas inhabited by minorities—for example, the Bolnisi and Akhalkalaki districts in Georgia, the Mountainous Karabakh region in Azerbaijan, and the Basargechar area in Armenia—did not receive adequate films or radio broadcasts in their native languages. At the Twenty-second Congress of the Georgian party, it was noted that Georgian scholars were still carrying on heated polemics with scholars in other republics on historical questions with national implications: "Out of absolute trivia they are trying to inflame what could become a national catastrophe."[34]

The fall of Khrushchev in October 1964 made little difference in the national development of the Georgian republic. The Mzhavanadze leadership remained in power for another eight years, and corruption, inefficiency, and discrimination against minorities continued to mark Georgian economic and political life. The beginning of the end for the Mzhavanadze regime was signaled by an article in *Pravda* on March 6, 1972. A resolution adopted by the Central Committee of the CPSU criticized the organizational and political work of the Tbilisi city committee.[35] Corruption, "liberalism" in personnel matters, and failure to meet economic targets were noted. Although the tone of the resolution was markedly restrained, it had an immediate galvanizing effect on the party *aktiv* in Georgia and initiated an intense internal examination and renewal of party leaders.

In the next few months a series of rapid changes occurred in the most important party offices. On July 25, O. I. Lolashvili, the first secretary of the Tbilisi committee, was replaced by Eduard Amvrosis dze Shevardnadze, the forty-four-year-old minister of internal affairs. Three days later he was made a member of the bureau of the Georgian Central Committee. For a brief time it looked as if the purge of the Mzhavanadze machine might end with these lower-level maneuvers, but Moscow soon promoted the fortunes of Shevardnadze, and on September 29, 1972, he replaced Mzhavanadze as first secretary of the Georgian Communist Party.

The major reason for this change in leadership was the widespread corruption in the administration of the republic, which in turn had caused consistently poor economic performances by Georgian industry and agriculture and the tolerance of nationalist tendencies within the party and intelligentsia. In terms of the growth rate of industrial production, Georgia held twelfth place among the union republics, with 0.2 percent for 1972 instead of the projected 6 percent. Total income for the family of an average worker or office employee had declined by twenty rubles from 1971 to 1972.[36]

Agriculture too, particularly in Abkhazeti, was not meeting plan targets, except in certain specialized crops such as tea, sunflower seeds, and fruit. On collective farms "instances of embezzlement, report padding, bribery, extortion, deception and hoodwinking have been uncovered." The procurement operation was particularly subject to fraud, since state collectors paid farmers in cash and frequently cheated them. Although collective farmers' incomes had increased by ninety-nine rubles between 1971 and 1972, most of their income had come from outside the collective sector. In 1970, for example, farmers received three times as much income from their private plots as from the collective farms. Much produce never reached the state or collective farm markets but was sold illegally. Only 68 percent of fruits and vegetables produced in Georgia in 1970 were marketed, compared to 88 percent in Azerbaijan and 97 percent in Armenia.[37]

The corruption, black marketeering, speculation, and bribe-taking in Georgia had their counterparts throughout the Soviet Union in what is referred to as the "second economy." But, as one observer of this all-union phenomenon has noted, when it comes to illegality and venality "Georgia has a reputation second to none . . . In form this activity may not differ greatly from what takes place in other regions, but in Georgia it seems to have been carried out on an unparalleled scale and with unrivaled scope and daring."[38]

In Georgia uninterrupted power for nineteen years had given the post-Stalinist clique an almost completely free hand within the republic. This, combined with the Caucasian reliance on close familial and personal ties in all aspects of life and the reluctance to betray one's relatives and comrades, led to an impenetrable system of mutual aid, protection, and disregard for those who were not part of the spoils system. "Business as usual" in Georgia meant, in the words of an official report, "favoritism, parochialism, cronyism and careerism flourishing on the basis of family ties and corruption, as well as a broad field for malicious talk and tale-bearing; wives and other family members begin to usurp the positions of their high-ranking husbands and state problems begin to be solved in the narrow circle of relatives, the family or close friends."[39]

Such a self-reinforcing system of favors and obligations could not be reformed from within, and it was only with Moscow's backing that Shevardnadze was empowered to purge the worst offenders of the Mzhavanadze regime. In a speech to the Georgian Central Committee in July 1973, he warned those assembled that "there will be no mercy for bribe-takers and extortionists." One of the first officials to be dismissed was the notorious Gelbakhiani, the rector of the Tbilisi Medical Institute, who, along with the party secretary of the institute, was discovered to have tampered with entrance examinations, excluding qualified students and admitting those who paid bribes or had proper connections.[40] Not surprisingly, Soviet statistics showed that Georgia had the highest number of doctors per ten thousand persons of any country in the world.

Not only corruption but officially condoned nationalism—what Teresa Rakowska-Harmstone calls "orthodox nationalism"—became the target of attack in the public statements of Shevardnadze. In one of his earliest speeches the first secretary complained that under Mzhavanadze "a half-baked nationalism raised its head in some places in the republic; things came to such a pass that attempts were made to rehabilitate émigré writers who are hostile to us. In those years the public psyche, man's inner world and his faith in bright ideas suffered more than the economy."[41] In other speeches the party leader condemned "national narrow-mindedness and isolation," and particularly the reluctance of many Georgians to study Russian. Artists, writers, and film-makers were attacked for exploiting themes with nationalist overtones. The strongest attacks were reserved for that most ideological of sciences, the study of history.[42]

Both the chauvinism of Georgians toward ethnic minorities within Georgia and of the minorities themselves came under fire. The Abkhaz, Ajar, and South Ossetian regions had for years resisted both Russian and Georgian intervention into their internal operations. At the meeting of the Georgian party *aktiv* in April 1973, it was reported that "in Abkhazeti a half-baked 'theory' according to which responsible posts should be filled only by representatives of the indigenous nationality has gained a certain currency . . . No one has been given the right to ignore the national composition of the population or to disregard the continual exchange of cadres among nations and the interests of all nationalities." At the same meeting it was noted that Ajarian officials had discouraged the development of tourism for fear that this would lead to migration from other republics. Yet, the *aktiv* was told, such instances of national isolation were understandable as a form of self-defense against the sometimes high-handed and insensitive treatment of minorities by the Georgians.[43]

The Shevardnadze purges continued for several years, and hopes were aroused that fundamental changes were taking place in Georgia. But resistance to reform was great and sometimes violent. As investigators moved closer to exposing a ring of speculators in Tbilisi who operated out of the opera house, a mysterious fire in that historic building destroyed the evidence. Suspicions of arson were directed at the police themselves.[44] Disillusion soon set in, and, as one citizen of Tbilisi expressed it to a foreign visitor: *"U nas bylo vremennaia sovetskaia vlast'!"* ("We had temporary Soviet power!")

Removing the most flagrant offenders would not change a system so deeply imbedded that the great mass of the party was involved, a system that in fact benefited a large part of the population. Shevardnadze's plaintive remarks about the psychological effects of the corruption were very revealing. In the experience of a whole generation of Georgians the Soviet system had in actuality come to mean, not the establishment of a just and egalitarian society, but rather the creation of a new, privileged elite that had been able to amass private wealth through control of the levers of political power.

The dual processes of economic development and renationalization had not been accompanied in Georgia by a significant democratization of the political superstructure. Despite the reforms of the Khrushchev years, the preservation of Stalinist authority patterns limited the development of legitimate criticism of the status quo. New generations of educated young people with broad intellectual interests came up against immovable restrictions on expression and the exercise of power. The resultant frustration led many young Georgians to adapt to the prevailing norms of personal acquisition and easy-going hedonism, while others placed their hopes either in an idealized version of their own national past or in anticipation of a nationalist solution in the future. The failure of political reform under Khrushchev to challenge fundamentally the old elites and the perceived immobility of the present government encouraged an extralegal expression of political and ethnic discontents both in Georgia and throughout the Soviet Union.

In the 1970s Georgia witnessed the appearance of an "unorthodox" or dissident nationalism. Its most articulate and active advocates were a small group of students and professional people stimulated by their aversion to the all-encompassing corruption around them. Zviad Gamsakhurdia, son of the prominent Georgian writer, Konstantine Gamsakhurdia, was a lecturer on American literature and the English language at Tbilisi State University when he began to complain to authorities about the treatment of various Georgian architectural monuments. In 1972 he and his associates became aware of the theft of religious treasures from the Georgian patriarchate in Tbilisi; Gamsakhurdia phoned Shevardnadze, then still minister of internal affairs, and an investigation was begun. The threads of the investigation led to the wife of First Secretary Mzhavanadze, and though he soon lost his post, an official cover-up of the thefts was maintained.

Gamsakhurdia and V. Pailodze soon publicized their claims and made contact with the Russian dissident movement and the Western press. In mid-1974 Gamsakhurdia, Merab Kostava, O. Tsikolia, and others formed a Human Rights Defense Group in the Georgian capital. After the Helsinki accords of August 1975, a so-called watch committee to observe human rights violations was set up in Tbilisi (January 1977). Until his arrest in April 1977, Gamsakhurdia wrote numerous articles complaining of the condition of Georgian national monuments, of the illegal deportation of Georgian Muslims (the Meskhians) to Central Asia, and in defense of his arrested colleagues. After more than a year in prison, Gamsakhurdia and Kostava were tried and sentenced to three years in prison and two in exile.[45]

Although this dissident nationalism did not spread widely in Georgia, and Gamsakhurdia and his associates were easily isolated from the population, their activity illustrated developing tendencies within the Georgian intelligentsia. Besides the desire for rights of free expression, Georgian nationalist dissidents manifested a revival of religious enthusiasm, anxiety about the demoralization of the Georgian people, and a clear dislike for Russians and Armenians. Their attitudes were expressed in less extreme form by many Georgian intellectuals. At the Eighth Congress of Georgian Writers in April 1976, Revaz Japaridze angrily opposed suggestions by the Georgian minister of education that history, geography, and other subjects should be taught in Russian. He was outraged by an order from Moscow that all textbooks for higher educational institutions be published in Russian and that dissertations and their defenses be translated into Russian. Japaridze's speech was greeted by nearly a quarter-hour of applause, and the audience would not permit the minister of higher education, Giorgi Jibladze, to answer him. When Shevardnadze tried to allay fears of Russification, his speech was interrupted by shouts.[46]

In the spring of 1978 the potency of Georgian nationalism was revealed dramatically. The government made an ill-advised attempt to remove from the draft of the new Georgian constitution a clause that affirmed Georgian as the sole official state language of the republic and attempted to replace it with a clause that gave equal status to Russian and other languages. On Friday, April 14, an estimated five thousand people, primarily university students, demonstrated in the streets as the Supreme Soviet met to consider the draft. Shevardnadze, cursed when he first tried to speak to the crowd, returned later to announce to the demonstrators that the disputed clause would be retained.[47] This was a highly unusual concession to an open expression of opposition to state policy, a clear indication of the uneasiness and caution of government policy toward the new nationalism.

The cohesion and development of civil society in Soviet Georgia forced the government to develop a unique strategy toward its own population. Caught between the relative independence of the Georgians and the demands placed on him by the central authorities to improve economic performance and maintain political control, Shevardnadze sought to satisfy some of the aspirations of his constituents while cracking down on the most flagrant abuses—economic crimes, alcoholism, drug abuse, and "parasitism" (the refusal to work by able-bodied people).

An elaborate system of public opinion polling was established in Georgia, and government policy was shaped to a degree by its sense of popular feelings. A survey, for instance, taken among Georgians who had lived in the mountains and been resettled in the valleys revealed that most of them were unhappy with their forced migration. At considerable expense the government reversed its decision, agreed to resettle the mountaineers in their old homes, and undertook to reconstruct some nine hundred villages. When in March 1981 Tbilisi State University students and faculty demonstrated in protest against the dismissal of a popular literature professor, Shevardnadze spoke to the demonstrators and had the professor reinstated.[48]

Yet the Georgian leader was unwilling to cede to all demands or to give in to the ongoing free-wheeling in the economy. Georgian intellectuals were dissatisfied with the requirements set forth in 1975 by the USSR Ministry of Education that candidate and doctoral dissertations be submitted in Russian. A petition from 365 prominent educators and writers was sent to Shevardnadze and Brezhnev.[49] The intellectuals opposed the forced introduction of bilingualism, "which will eventually lead to a gradual diminution of the role and importance of the Georgian language." Such a rule, they contended, would inhibit the development of Georgian scientific thought and the Georgian language and was a violation of the constitutional principle of equality of all peoples of the USSR. Shevardnadze, however, repeatedly stressed the importance of learning Russian and improving the instruction of Russian in Georgia in order to broaden the horizons of the Georgian people. As he told the delegates to the Twenty-sixth Party Congress in Moscow, the sun rises for Georgia, not in the east, but in the north, in Russia—"the sun of Lenin's ideas."[50]

By the late 1970s the administration of Leonid Brezhnev, marked by an enviable stability and unexpected longevity, could look with some pride at its domestic and international accomplishments through the middle years of the decade (détente with the United States, respectable rates of economic growth), but was beginning to experience the effects of deep and long-term social developments. Low birthrates among Russians and western Soviet nationalities contrasted with the high rates among Muslim peoples and presented the leadership with an industrial and military manpower problem in the future. Economic growth rates were slowing down, and the billions poured into agriculture had not solved the basic structural weaknesses in the collective farm system. Growing hostility from the American governments of

Jimmy Carter and Ronald Reagan was compounded by perceived threats in Afghanistan and Poland.

The choice between reform of the system and preservation of its basic features, a choice that underlay much of the politics of the post-Stalin period, was becoming particularly acute in the late Brezhnev years. The conservative political coalition led by Brezhnev refused to challenge the core values and basic practices carried over from the Stalin years (as ameliorated by Khrushchev) and remained committed to centralized planning and direction of the economy, the high priorities given to the military and heavy industry, and differential rewards for those well placed in the hierarchy. Economic experimentation was discouraged, while foreign policy initiatives were taken to expand economic ties with the developed capitalist nations and import technology.[51]

Within the leadership there were those who potentially might embark on a more reformist course had they the power and support. Among those at the top of the power elite was Yuri Vladimirovich Andropov (1914–1984), who succeeded to Brezhnev's mantle briefly (November 1982–February 1984), and Mikhail Sergeevich Gorbachev (b. 1931), who followed Konstantin Ustinovich Chernenko (1911–1985) as head of the party. On the regional party level, there was Eduard Shevardnadze.

Like Geidar Aliev in Azerbaijan, Shevardnadze had been appointed to sweep out the old, entrenched, and self-serving leadership of the republic. Their former superior in the KGB, Andropov, had opposed the corrupt practices that permeated the party-state elite, up to the family of Brezhnev himself. Not mere time-servers or clients of powerful patrons, Aliev and Shevardnadze were men whose careers depended on their effective performance and who displayed a degree of idealism. Shevardnadze in particular often spoke about resurrecting the ideals of the socialist tradition, contrasting them with the realities of daily practice. He told the delegates to the Twenty-fifth Congress of the CPSU in 1976:

> It is necessary to recognize that many of our contemporaries are not liberated from the remnants of the past, from conservative habits and traditions, from private-property tendencies and egoism, careerism and toadyism, protectionism and conceit. All this seriously limits social and political activity of individuals, holds back the process of intellectualism of all spheres where people create material and spiritual treasures.[52]

In his first two years as party chief in Georgia, Shevardnadze was able to take credit for a rise in industrial output of 9.6 percent, an increase in labor productivity of 7.8 percent, and a growth in gross agricultural output of more than 18 percent (as compared to 1970–1972).[53] At the party congress he thanked the central authorities for their help in restarting the Georgian economic machine and then tried to prod them into additional aid not yet earmarked in the Tenth Five-Year Plan. By the end of that plan in 1980

Georgia was one of the four union republics that had fulfilled its targets. Along with Moldavia it was given the highest projected growth rates in the subsequent plan.

Early in his administration Shevardnadze introduced a bold experiment in agricultural reorganization into a particularly poor district, Abasha, in western Georgia. There a regional production association was formed that included *kolkhozy, sovkhozy,* and all the services and organizations involved in agriculture. Instead of having each branch of the rural economy report separately to the corresponding higher republic or all-union authority, all aspects of the region's economy were controlled locally by the production association. This horizontal integration facilitated decision-making and increased local initiative and coordination. Productivity rose, and incomes doubled. In 1981 Shevardnadze announced that the Abasha model would be applied throughout Georgia, and the secretary of that region, Guram Mgeladze, became chairman of the Committee for Agricultural Production for the entire republic.[54] This kind of piecemeal reform was extended to other parts of the Soviet Union during Andropov's brief rule.

Shevardnadze's success in accelerating economic growth, combating corruption, and instilling a degree of optimism and enthusiasm in his cadres was officially recognized when he was awarded an Order of Lenin on his fiftieth birthday in 1978 and became a "Hero of Socialist Labor" in 1981. In November 1978 he was raised to candidate membership in the Politburo. His political methods contrasted with those prevalent in other parts of Brezhnev's Soviet Union. He called for a new attitude and working relation between communist functionaries and their subordinates.

> Many communist leaders sometimes seem unprepared to understand these complex, deep processes [of bureaucratism and formalism in dealing with subordinates] and are governed by them. From this come well-known difficulties. One of these leaders, for example, prophesied about himself: "This democratization of yours will end up with my being removed from work." (Applause.) And that is what happened. There is nothing that can be done about it; democratic power is the power of the people, and the people are just and strict.[55]

In a gesture reminiscent of a forgotten populism, Shevardnadze had a blue-collar worker elected to the bureau of the Georgian Central Committee in 1981. Two years later in an interview published in *Pravda* he revealed that about three hundred republic-level officials had been dismissed in Georgia in the first seven years of his administration. He was willing to support and promote honest and competent cadres but would not tolerate inefficiency or corruption. Criticism and self-criticism were essential, he said, for cadres to learn from their mistakes. The lack of criticism in the bureau had led him to hold meetings twice a year without an agenda, just so that an open, critical discussion could take place. Even the head of the party was not above criticism, he maintained, and he held himself responsible for the delay in prosecuting the finance minister, Ananiashvili, who was expelled from the party and convicted of bribery in 1981.

> Even earlier, following a checkup on the ministry, alarm signals about him had reached the Central Committee's bureau. It had even been suggested that he be removed from the leadership. However, the arguments didn't seem sufficiently weighty to me. Furthermore, I had known this man for many years as a competent, experienced official. In short, I stuck up for him. As it turned out later, I had made a serious mistake. I had to publicly acknowledge my error from the rostrum of the Central Committee's plenary session and at a meeting of the *aktiv*.[56]

Shevardnadze represented a new kind of political leader in the Soviet Union, one prepared to use tough measures to weed out illegal activities while cultivating support among the population. His methods contrasted with those of his predecessor, Mzhavanadze; he would not permit the unlimited "exploitation" of the state economy for private gain nor would he allow the unfettered growth of Georgian nationalism at the expense of the Russian language or of other ethnic groups in the republic. Even the interests of the small Greek minority in Georgia were quietly accommodated by the Shevardnadze government. After decades of neglect modern Greek was reintroduced into schools in Rustavi, Gudauta, Marneuli, Batumi, and villages in Tetri-Tskaro and Tsalka districts. Teachers were given refresher courses, and a professional Greek song ensemble was organized in Rustavi.[57]

The chronic corruption and "second-economy" activity, as well as the underlying tension between the economic development of the republic and the allegiances to national traditions and the Georgian language, continued to plague Shevardnadze's regime. But his thirteen years of firm administration and mild reform were rewarded by the new government of Mikhail Gorbachev at the beginning of July 1985, when Shevardnadze was made a full member of the Politburo in Moscow and appointed to succeed Andrei Gromyko as foreign minister of the USSR.[58]

14 Conclusion

By the end of the first quarter-century of post-Stalinist evolution, the contradictory developments of the Soviet past, the simultaneous drive toward economic development, and the creation of revitalized nationalities within the Soviet federal structure had produced neither Russification nor assimilation in Georgia. Instead two kinds of nationalism coexisted: a pervasive and growing national consciousness that operated within the system to maximize the benefits to the Georgian people themselves; and an illegal, dissident nationalism still characteristic of only a minuscule minority of the Georgian population. Official nationality policy with its avowedly assimilationist goals had had little real effect on the Georgians, who moved steadily toward greater consolidation of their ethnic separateness. The unresolved tension between the assimilationist tendencies of urban industrial society and the reconsolidation of Georgian ethnicity had produced an increasingly potent nationalist mood in all parts of Georgian society—and counternationalisms among the ethnic minorities within the republic.

The new nationalism was the product both of the continuing social trends carried on from Stalinist times and the freer political atmosphere of the period after 1953. More specifically, four major reasons for the appearance of this nationalism can be elaborated:

First, the reduction in political penalties with the relaxation of the Stalinist terror had made it easier for people to express long-latent national feelings. Whereas other forms of political action and expression were more strictly prohibited, in Georgia the state made significant concessions to the population's national feelings. Thus, it may be that nationalist expression was an outlet for a variety of discontents—political, economic, intellectual, and cultural—a kind of political sublimation for activity and expression that was otherwise too dangerous to articulate.

Second, the national elite in Georgia used the opportunity offered by the Khrushchev years to consolidate local power and with the backing of the local ethnic majority legitimized its rule and gained support vis-à-vis Moscow. The autonomy permitted by Moscow, which now chose to rule indirectly through local cadres, gave the national elite the chance to cultivate popular support through the exploitation of national feelings. Ethnicity in turn became an important criterion for success, as the Georgian leadership patronized members of its own nationality to the exclusion of others. Georgians in the party increased from 73 percent in 1952, already higher than the percentage of Georgians in the population of the republic, to over 76 percent in 1970.[1] Thus, ethnic consolidation both in the republic and in the ruling institutions also contributed to the rise in national identification and pride. That nationalism was expressed in culture, in cadre favoritism, and in the economic "exploitation" of the Soviet system.

Third, nationalist expression is a genuine indicator of the historic fear of small nations that they will be swallowed up by larger nations in the process of modernization. Georgian nationalists feared the loss of their language and its replacement by Russian, the destruction of their ancient monuments, and the elimination of their unique customs, traditions, and way of life. Built into their nationalist fears was a deeply rooted conservatism and apprehension about what the future in a multinational state holds for the minorities. There was also a positive side to this anxiety. Not only did it work to preserve ethnicity in the face of modernizing pressures, it also provided an alternative to the model of development imposed by the dominant Soviet nationality. Many Georgians, in their national pride, came to feel that their further evolution was hindered by the restraints placed on them by the Russians. An attitude arose that, left to themselves, the Georgians could more quickly realize their historic potential.

Finally, the erosion of Marxist ideology within the Soviet Union cleared the way for its replacement by patriotism and nationalism. Ironically, the Soviet government itself aided in this process by transforming Marxism from its original purpose—a critical and revolutionary tool of the working class against the status quo—into a rigid, dull rationalization of the existing order. Nationalism, on the other hand, held out a hope for a better future, with reference constantly to great moments in the national past. The romanticism, irrationality, and utopianism of nationalism at least provided an alternative to the everyday reality of a slowly developing society with all its mundane inadequacies.

Although Georgian society was in many ways fundamentally transformed by the modernizing practices and policies of the Soviet government and party, the result of the coincidental renationalization processes has been to preserve, indeed strengthen, the cultural and social cohesion of the Georgians. The protests over restrictions on the use of the Georgian language were the most visible manifestations of the renewed strength of Georgian national awareness, but in daily life Georgians and the other peoples of Georgia maintain many of the traditions that they had when Georgia was largely a society of villages, religious holidays, and seasonal observances. Georgian life remains centered on the social collectivities of family, circles of friends, and the ritual banquet. Heavy drinking, elaborate feasts, expensively decorated cemetery plots, and spontaneous harmonizing by guests in any social situation are vital traditions that the urbanization and industrialization of Georgia have done little to change.

Just as in early European and American industrialization customary revelries were gradually eliminated from daily life by the demands of enterprise, so in Georgia the guardians of economic progress, in this case the party, had an interest in eliminating such practices. In South Ossetia, for example, an ancient tradition prescribes an elaborate series of banquets to follow the death of a family member, a custom that goes back to Scythian times. Muslim Ossetians traditionally hold seven such banquets in the year following a death; Christians hold twelve. On several occasions, and as recently as August 1981, the local party committee passed resolutions to combat such "harmful traditions and customs" as funeral banquets, but with little effect. In a survey only 24 percent of those interviewed believed that the banquets should be completely banned, though many thought they were a burdensome custom.[2] The party limited its persuasion to educational means, no longer resorting to the kind of violence employed in the Stalin revolution, and therefore had to tolerate the continuance of the customs for the foreseeable future.

Despite more than sixty years of Soviet power, Georgian society has its own networks and codes, which have remained largely intact. It remains a society dominated by men; the traditional role for women is one of subordination, sexual modesty, and domesticity. Observations by two anthropologists about Georgian society today might have as easily applied a century ago.

> Honour, and its corollary shame, are constant preoccupations in Georgia. Within family groups spheres of action are well defined; they do not overlap and they are non-competitive—everyone knows their place. Beyond the family, however, these limitations are reversed. Insecurity and instability in the perpetual ranking and re-ranking of personal relationships is the norm. Males have therefore constantly to prove themselves as men. They are, in this respect, perpetually "on show." They need constantly to demonstrate their worthiness to public opinion in general and to their peers in particular. This requires the demonstration of "manliness" and use of goods in display and consumption.
>
> In this kind of "honour and shame" society where peer approval is so important hierarchical official relations are resented and resisted and are the

source of perpetual conflict. The individual Georgian sees honour accruing to families and sees families linked by a common honour. In such a context there is little role for the state or for any centrally-organized hierarchy.[3]

As intrusive as the state attempts to be in the Soviet Union, it ultimately has only limited power within the world of the Georgians. The specific goals of Soviet nationality policy, the rapprochement and eventual merging of nationalities, are further from realization today than they have been at any time in Soviet history—at least for the Transcaucasian and Central Asian peoples. Georgian society remains a network in which family and kinship ties, ideas of honor and trust, nepotism, and patron-client alliances provide informal links within the population and prevent penetration of outsiders, whether members of other nationalities or representatives of state power.

If there is any conclusion to be derived from such a study of the *longue durée* of a small nation, it might be that a nation is never fully "made." It is always in the process of being made. At any particular moment Georgia was in part formed by its prior history and its underlying deep structure and culture, and in part was being transformed by its present experience and the imperatives of an imperial imposition. Although Georgia was being "modernized," to use an overworked and ill-defined paradigm, it never became fully "modern," for it could never completely reproduce the experience of very different nations in another part of the world whose achievements defined modernization.

The history of Georgia might be read as a series of resistances to foreign domination and alien cultural inputs that threatened to compromise its national integrity. But it is hoped that this study of over two millennia has shown that Georgia's being was in part the *product* of successive foreign impositions, and any unique Georgianness can never be surgically separated from the complex exchange that went on with her neighbors. It may be little comfort to nationalists to point out Georgia's interconnections with Armenia, Iran, Byzantium, Turkey, and Russia, but small nations seldom enjoy the luxury of insularity and independence. Like the human species itself, peoples and nations are constantly evolving under the dual influence of their own nature, whatever that is, and their environment, which inevitably includes intruders, enemies, and benefactors. Just as the Georgian language stayed essentially the same tongue while acquiring new vocabulary and syntax from the languages with which it came into contact, so, over time, did the society of the Georgians preserve certain cultural features while modifying the patterns of previous generations.

To encompass a history of a nation in one volume is ultimately an impossibility. There is no single interpretive strand to hold together a historical experience that includes such diverse figures as Vakhtang Gorgasali, Erekle II, Noe Zhordania, Lavrenti Beria, and Eduard Shevardnadze, or such different experiences as Christianization and collectivization. Taken together, however, this experience can be conceived as a process of national formation.

First, tribes speaking related languages coalesced into a loose confederation under a primitive state and were seen by outsiders as a single people. Later, in the classical age, a social hierarchy was created that evolved over a thousand years and outlasted the more ephemeral political forms. Orthodox Christianity provided an identity and ideology that delineated the Georgians from their Muslim and Armenian neighbors. The development of an integrated market economy broke down the isolation of Georgia's villages, bringing peasants and nobles into closer contact with Russian officials and Armenian entrepreneurs. A secular national awareness came rather recently to Georgians, first to the intelligentsia and later, through the mediation of Marxists, to workers and peasants. By the early twentieth century Georgians were a self-conscious nationality with an articulate political leadership, the Mensheviks, who briefly held power in an independent state. But remarkably, and against the original expectations of many observers, the most complete consolidation of the Georgians as a nation came in the first seven decades of Soviet power. Although the thrust of Marxism had seemed opposed to the creation of a coherent and separate Georgian nation, the actual evolution of Soviet Georgia resulted in the emergence of a compact and conscious nation prepared to act in its own interest, either on its own or in concert with its current government.

Glossary

Amkarbashi (Georgian)—elected leader of a guild.

Amkari (pl. *-ebi*) (Georgian)—(also *asnafi*) guild.

Artel (pl. *-i*) (Russian)—association for common work; more specifically, in the Soviet period, a form of agricultural collective in which most equipment and livestock was collectively held while peasants maintained their own household plots.

Atabeg (Georgian)—official; first an administrator, later, with the decline of the Seljuk dynasty, an independent lord; ruler of a *saatabago*.

Azat (Armenian)—"free"; Armenian minor noble, usually a vassal of a *nakharar* or prince; equivalent to the Georgian *aznauri*.

Azati (Georgian)—former serf freed by his lord.

Aznauri (pl. *-ni*) (Georgian)—Georgian petty noble, landlord, or warrior, parallel to the *azat* of Armenia; the term was first applied to all nobles, but in the later Middle Ages a clearer distinction was made between an *aznauri* (dependent noble) and a *tavadi* and *mtavari* (dynastic prince); from the fifteenth century the *aznauri* was considered a *qma* (slave) of his lord.

Aznaureba (Georgian)—nobility

Bagratids—Armeno-Georgian family that ruled both in Armenia as presiding princes (7–8th centuries) and as kings (884–1045), and in Kartli as presiding princes (from 813) and as kings (888 until the coming of the Russians in the nineteenth century); Bagratids also ruled in Imereti (13–14th centuries) and in other Georgian and Armenian lands.

Begara (Georgian)—duty, service; for peasants, labor obligation (*corvée* in French; *barshchina* in Russian).

Bogano (Georgian)—landless peasant.

Catholicos—primate of the Armenian or Georgian church.

Cheka (Russian)—*Chrezvychainnaia komissiia* (Extraordinary Commission), the first political police formed by the Soviet government in late 1917; the predecessor of the OGPU, GPU, NKVD, MVD, and KGB.

Chistka (pl. *-i*) (Russian)—"cleansing," "purge"; refers most precisely to the dismissal of communist party members in periodical checkups; to be distinguished from the Great Purges of 1936–1938 *(Ezhovshchina).*

Curopalates (Greek)—presiding prince; in Armenia such princes ruled in the seventh to ninth centuries; in Georgia in the sixth to ninth centuries.

Dashnaktsutiun (Armenian)—the Armenian Revolutionary Federation *(Hai Heghapokhakan Dashnaktsutiun),* the principal Armenian nationalist party at the turn of the century. Its members were known as "Dashnaks."

Dasturlamali (Georgian)—the law code of Vakhtang VI (eighteenth century).

Deoba (Georgian)—the right of Georgian peasants to petition the king for redress of grievances.

Desiatina (pl. *-y*) (Russian)—land measurement equal to 2.7 acres.

Didi turkoba (Georgian)—"the Great Turkish Troubles," the invasion and occupation of Georgia by Turkmen tribes in the late eleventh century that forced the Georgian kings to submit to Seljuk overlordship until the reign of David II (III) (1089–1125).

Duma (Russian)—municipal council; also, Russia's parliament between 1906 and 1917.

Dvoevlastie (Russian)—"dual power," the political arrangement from February to May 1917 in Russia, in which political power was divided between the Provisional Government and the Petrograd Soviet.

Dvorianin (pl. *-e*) (Russian)—service noble in Russia.

Eri (Georgian)—nation, people; in classical Georgia, the freemen, people, or an armed force.

Eristavi (pl. *-ni*) (Georgian)—provincial governor; duke; commander of the *eri* (army) of his province; the equivalent of the *nakharar* of Armenia.

Eristavt-eristavi (pl. *-ni*) (Georgian)—archduke; duke of dukes; in the eleventh century this position was held by members of the Orbeliani family, who rivaled the kings of Georgia for power.

Eristavt-mtavari (pl. *-ni*) (Georgian)—(also *erismtavari*) archduke; prince of dukes; the leading Georgian political authority during the principate of Iberia (Kartli) (580–888).

Exarch—a bishop ranking below a patriarch and above a metropolitan; after the abolition of the autocephalous Georgian church by tsarist authorities in 1819, the appointed head of the church.

Ezhovshchina (Russian)—the Great Purges of 1936–1938, carried out under the direction of N. I. Ezhov, People's Commissar of Internal Affairs.

FSSSRZ (Russian)—*Federativnyi Soiuz Sovetskikh Sotsialisticheskikh Respublik Zakavkazii* (Federal Union of Soviet Socialist Republics of Transcaucasia), the union of Armenia, Azerbaijan, and Georgia formed in March 1922 and abolished in December.

Gala (Georgian)—an obligation paid by peasants to lords, usually equal to 10 to 25 percent of the grain harvest.

Gimnaziia (Russian)—secondary school with a classical curriculum to prepare students for entry into university.

Glekhi (pl. *-ebi*) (Georgian)—peasant.

GPU (Russian)—abbreviation for *Gosudarstvennoe politicheskoe upravlenie* (State Political Administration), the political police and successor in 1922 to the Cheka.

Henoticon—theological treatise, *The Edict of Union,* issued by the Byzantine Emperor Zeno in 482 to end the schism between the Chalcedonian Orthodox and the Monophysites.

Ibero-Caucasian—language group that includes Georgian, Abkhaz, and many of the languages of the North Caucasus (Avar, Lezghin, Lak, Cherkess, Ingush).

Kartli (Georgian)—Eastern Georgia; the major Georgian kingdom.

Kartli-kakheti—the joint kingdom of the two major east Georgian regions.

Kartveli (Georgian)—a Georgian person.

Kartvelian—of or pertaining to the Georgian language; the southern Caucasian language group to which Georgia belongs.

Kartveluri (Georgian)—the Georgian language.

Kavburo (Russian)—contraction for the *Kavkazskii biuro* (Caucasian Bureau) of the Communist Party.

Kavkraikom (Russian)—contraction for the *Kavkazskii Kraievoi Komitet* (Caucasian Territorial Committee) of the Communist Party.

Khizani (Georgian)—poor peasant forced from the lands of his lord and obligated to rent land indefinitely from another lord (also called *stumari* [guest] or *mobarebuli*).

Khliarkhi (pl. *-ni*) (Georgian)—tax and troop collector (sometimes called *atasistavi*).

Kolkhoz (pl. *-y*) (Russian)—contraction for *kollektivnoe khoziaistvo* (collective farm).

Kolkhoznik (pl. *-i*) (Russian)—collective farm worker.

Korenizatsiia (Russian)—"rooting," the nativization policy of the Soviet government that promoted indigenous ethnic cadres to run national regions and republics and supported education and cultural development in the national languages.

Ktseva (Georgian)—land measurement equivalent to 4,083 square meters, or slightly less than an acre.

Kulak (pl. *-i*) (Russian)—relatively prosperous peasant.

Kulukhi (Georgian)—obligation of Georgian peasant to his lord equal to 25 percent of the grape harvest or wine output.

Mamasakhlisi (Georgian)—(also *kevkhi, natsvali*) elder elected by the peasants to head the village; mayor of a city appointed by the king, usually from the merchant class.

Mamuli (Georgian)—land granted in hereditary tenure; land; fatherland.

Melik—warrior-noble, particularly in eastern Transcaucasia; official; the mayor of Tiflis.

Meore dasi (Georgian)—"second group," a term applied to the liberal and progressive journalists and writers of the 1870s.

Mesame dasi (Georgian)—"third group," the generation of the Georgian intelligentsia of the 1890s which turned to Marxism and eventually led the social democratic movement in Georgia.

Mojalabe (Georgian)—a near-slave who lived in the home of his lord and had no land of his own.

Mokalake (pl. *-bi*) (Georgian)—a city dweller; in nineteenth-century Tiflis, a wealthy citizen, most often Armenian.

Mouravi (pl. *-ni*) (Georgian)—appointed royal official in the Georgian kingdoms.

Msakhuri (Georgian)—domestic servant; a bodyguard; a serf often raised to vassal gentry.

Mtavari (pl. *-ni*) (Georgian)—dynastic prince, equivalent to the *eristavi* or *tavadi* in the twelfth century, but from the fifteenth century applied only to one of the five most powerful ruling princes of western Georgia or to a chief of an undivided house.

MTS (Russian)—abbreviation for *mashinno-traktornaia stantsiia* (machine-tractor station), the organization that controlled farm machinery for the collective farms.

Nakharar (pl. *-ner*) (Armenian)—Armenian dynastic prince or duke bound to the king by service ties; leader of a noble house *(tun)*.

Natsvali (Georgian)—police officer; in villages, the elder *(mamasakhlisi)*; in towns, the appointed noble assistant to the *mouravi*.

NEP (Russian)—abbreviation for *Novaia ekonomicheskaia politika,* the New Economic Policy that Lenin introduced in 1921. Peasants were given greater freedom to trade their grain surpluses, and a degree of market exchange was introduced in the whole economy.

NKVD (Russian)—abbreviation for *Narodnyi komissariat vnutrennykh del* (People's Commissariat of Internal Affairs) of the USSR; in 1934 the secret police, the former OGPU, was placed within NKVD; in 1941 NKGB *(Narodnyi komissariat gosudarstvennoi besopastnosti)* left NKVD as a separate commissariat; in 1946 NKVD became MVD and NKGB became MGB.

Obosoblennost' (Russian)—detachment, isolation; used to refer to ethnic exclusiveness.

Obrok (Russian)—peasant obligations to be paid in kind or cash.

OKA (Russian)—abbreviation for *Otdel'naia kavkazskaia armiia* (Detached Caucasian Army).

Patroni (Georgian)—lord; master; owner.

Patronqmoba (Georgian)—feudalism; the serf-owning system.

Pood (Russian)—weight measurement equal to 16.38 kilograms or 36 pounds.

Postavka (pl. *-i*) (Russian)—delivery; specifically, compulsory delivery of grain to the state.

Qma (pl. *-ni*) (Georgian)—serf; slave.

Raznochinets (pl. *-tsy*) (Russian)—person not belonging to a well-defined social estate; more specifically, an intellectual not belonging to the nobility in the nineteenth century.

Sakartvelo (Georgian)—Georgia; the term used for the united Georgian kingdom first formed in 1008.

Sakhaso (Georgian)—in the Middle Ages, lands held directly by the king; later, lands held in common by an entire noble clan *(sasakhlo)* under the rule of the *tavadi.*

Satavado (pl. *-ebi*) (Georgian)—landed estate; private property.

Satavistavo (Georgian)—lands held outright by individual nobles.

Sblizhenie (Russian)—rapprochement; the growing closeness among ethnic groups in the Soviet Union.

Seim—the parliament in Transcaucasia in 1918.

Sliianie (Russian)—merging, confluence; the term used in the USSR to describe the assimilation of ethnicities into a single Soviet people.

Sovnarkhoz (Russian)—contraction for *Sovet narodnogo khoziaistva* (Council of People's Economy).

Sovnarkom (Russian)—contraction for *Sovet narodnykh komissarov* (Council of People's Commissars), the Soviet government from 1917 to 1936.

Spaspeti (Georgian)—highest official of earliest Georgian kingdoms; governor of the central province, Shida Kartli; also called *erismtavari* (high constable).

Svaneti—the land of the Svans, the mountainous regions of northwestern Georgia.

Tavadi (pl. *-ebi*) (Georgian)—high noble, prince (twelfth century); synonomous from the eleventh to the fourteenth centuries with *mtavari* and *eristavi*; from the fifteenth century, a ruling prince largely independent of the king.

Tavadoba (Georgian)—late Georgian feudalism, the rule of princes marked by weak royal power.

Tsenz (Russian)—qualification, right; here the right to participate in elections to the state dumas directly.

Tsenzovoe obshchestvo (Russian)—those who possessed the *tsenz*; propertied society.

TsIK (Russian)—abbreviation for the *Tsentral'nyi ispolnitel'nyi komitet* (central executive committee) of the soviets.

Vaziri (Georgian)—vizier; chancellor; advisor to the king and tutor of the crown prince.

Vepkhistqaosani (Georgian)—"The Knight in the Panther's Skin," the epic poem by medieval Georgian poet Shota Rustaveli.

VSNKh (Russian)—abbreviation for *Verkhovnii sovet narodnogo khoziaistva* (Supreme Council of the People's Economy), the highest decision-making body in the economic sphere under the Soviets.

Zakgosplan (Russian)—contraction for *Zakavkazskii gosudarstvennyi planovyi komitet* (Transcaucasian State Planning Committee).

Zakkraikom (Russian)—contraction for the *Zakavkazskii kraevoi komitet* (Transcaucasian Territorial Committee) of the Communist Party.

Zemstvo (pl. -*a*) (Russian)—district or provincial assembly set up by the tsarist government for local administration in 1864.

ZSFSR—abbreviation for *Zakavkazskaia Sovetskaia Federativnaia Sotsialisticheskaia Respublika* (Transcaucasian Soviet Federated Socialist Republic), formed in December 1922 and abolished in 1936.

Notes

PREFACE

1. Eric Hobsbawn, "Introduction: Inventing Traditions," in Eric Hobsbawn and Terence Ranger, *The Invention of Tradition* (Cambridge, England: Cambridge University Press, 1983), p. 13.

CHAPTER 1

1. Cyril Toumanoff, "The Bagratids of Iberia from the VIII to the XI century," *Le Museon* 74 (1961): 234–38, and *Studies in Christian Caucasian History* (hereafter, *Studies*) (Washington, D.C.: Georgetown University Press, 1963), pp. 437–40.

2. Toumanoff, *Studies,* p. 440.

3. G. A. Melikishvili, *K istorii drevnei Gruzii* (Tbilisi, 1959), p. 100; and Hans Vogt, *Grammaire de la langue géorgienne* (Oslo: Universitetsforlaget, 1971), p. 2. See also J. C. Catford, "Mountain of Tongues: The Languages of the Caucasus," *Annual Review of Anthropology* 6 (1977): 283–314; and G. A. Klimov, *Kavkazskie iazyki* (Moscow, 1965), and *Etimologicheskii slovar' kartvel'skikh iazykov* (Moscow, 1964).

4. Melikishvili, *K istorii drevnei Gruzii,* pp. 95, 97; and Cyril Toumanoff, "Introduction to Christian Caucasian History: The Formative Centuries (IVth–VIIIth)," *Traditio* 15 (1959): 18–19, 95.

5. Horace Leonard Jones, trans., *The Geography of Strabo,* vol. 5, Loeb Classical Library (New York, 1928), p. 211.

Today standard Georgian serves as a lingua franca for the mountaineers, who in each major valley have their own dialect. In eastern Georgia *kartluri,* the speech of Georgia's political center, is broken down into *meskhuri* and *javakhuri.* To the east of Kakheti, natives speak both *kakhuri* and *kiziquri.* In the mountains the rugged shepherds and farmers communicate in *pshauri, khevsuruli, tushuri, mokheuri, mtiuluri,* and *gudamagruli.* In western Georgia, besides the related languages of Mingrelian and Svan, one can hear the *imeruli* dialect (with *lech-khumuri*), *rachuli, guruli,* and *acharuli.* In Azerbaijan, a Georgian dialect called *ingiluri* is spoken; in Iran, Georgian settlers speak *pereidnuli,* and in Turkey, *imerkheuri* (Vogt, *Grammaire,* pp. 2–3). On Georgians in contemporary Iran, see P. Oberling, "Georgians and the Circassians in Iran," *Studia Caucasica* 1 (1963): 127–43.

6. Melikishvili, *K istorii drevnei Gruzii,* p. 141; and N.A. Berdzenishvili et al., *Istoriia Gruzii: S drevneishikh vremen do 60-kh godov XIX veka,* vol. 1 (Tbilisi, 1962), pp. 7–8.

7. Charles Burney and David Marshall Lang, *The Peoples of the Hills: Ancient Ararat and Caucasus* (New York: Praeger, 1972), pp. 40, 35.

8. J. Mellaart, "The Earliest Settlements in Western Asia from the Ninth to the End of the Fifth Millennium B.C.,: in *The Cambridge Ancient History,* 3d ed., 12 vols. (Cambridge, England: Cambridge University Press, 1970–75), vol. 1, pt. 1, p. 251.

9. Burney and Lang, *Peoples of the Hills,* pp. 43–85; and J. Mellaart, "Anatolia, c. 4000–2300 B.C.," *Cambridge Ancient History,* vol. 1, pt. 2, pp. 401–3.

10. Dates for monarchs indicate reigns. For a discussion in English of this period, see David Marshall Lang, *The Georgians* (London: Thames and Hudson, 1966), pp. 36–53; and J. Mellaart, "Anatolia, c. 2300–1750 B.C.," *Cambridge Ancient History,* vol. 2, pt. 2, pp. 688–90.

11. Melikishvili writes: "The epic of Amiriani has with time undergone many changes. The succeeding centuries left on it a number of additions, but . . . the tales which lay at the basis of this epic undoubtedly were spread among the Georgian tribes already in the era of Bronze culture" (Berdzenishvili et al., *Istoriia Gruzii,* p. 27).

12. Burney and Lang, *Peoples of the Hills,* p. 114.

13. Melikishvili, *K istorii drevnei Gruzii,* p. 111; and Toumanoff, *Studies,* p. 56.

14. Melikishvili, *K istorii drevnei Gruzii,* p. 175; and Toumanoff, *Studies,* pp. 55–56.

15. Melikishvili, *K istorii drevnei Gruzii,* pp. 179, 203. On Urartu, see B. B. Piotrovskii, *Vanskoe tsarstvo (Urartu)* (Moscow, 1959), and *Urartu: The Kingdom of Van and Its Art,* trans. and ed. Peter S. Gelling (New York: Praeger, 1967).

16. Berdzenishvili et al., *Istoriia Gruzii,* pp. 28–31; Melikishvili, *K istorii drevnei Gruzii,* pp. 204–17. In the mid-eighth century B.C. Sarduri II of Urartu reported invading Colchis several times and once taking the city of Ildamusha.

17. I. M. D'iakonov, *Predistoriia armianskogo naroda: Istoriia armianskogo nagor'ia s 1500 po 500 g. do N. E. Khurrity, Luviitsy, Protoarmiane* (Erevan, 1968), pp. 119–20. Recently an English translation has appeared: I. M. Diakonoff, *The Prehistory of the Armenian People,* trans. Loni Jennings (Delmar, N.Y.: Caravan Books, 1984).

18. Melikishvili, *K istorii drevnei Gruzii,* pp. 112, 225–29. Melikishvili says that this kingdom was known as Phrygia to the Greeks but as the "kingdom of the Mushki" to the Urartians (p. 255).

19. Ibid., pp. 102, 197.

20. G. A. Melikishvili, *Nairi-Urartu* (Tbilisi, 1954), pp. 418–19. The Armenian area was known as Sokhmi or Sukhmi and is the source of the Georgian words for Armenian *(somekhi)* and Armenia *(somkheti).*

21. Berdzenishvili et al., *Istoriia Gruzii,* pp. 33–34.

22. Melikishvili, *K istorii drevnei Gruzii,* p. 233.

23. Burney and Lang, *Peoples of the Hills,* pp. 193–94.

24. Melikishvili, *K istorii drevnei Gruzii,* p. 231; B. B. Piotrovskii has established that Teishebaini (Karmir Blur) was destroyed by the Scythians.

25. Melikishvili, *K istorii drevnei Gruzii,* p. 234; see also Toumanoff, *Studies,* pp. 61–62 n. 58.

26. On the complex question of whether the Mushki were proto-Georgians or proto-Armenians (Melikishvili and D'iakonov disagree) see the discussion in D'iakonov, *Predistoriia,* pp. 214–24.

27. Burney and Lang, *Peoples of the Hills,* p. 194.

28. Toumanoff, "Introduction to Christian Caucasian History: The Formative Centuries," p. 23n; A. D. Godley, trans., *Herodotus,* vol. 2, Loeb Classical Library (Cambridge, Mass., 1938), pp. 121, 123.

29. Godley, *Herodotus* 2:387, 389.

30. Godley, *Herodotus* 2:125.

31. Berdzenishvili et al., *Istoriia Gruzii,* p. 41.

32. O. J. Todd, trans., *Xenophon, Anabasis, Books IV–VII,* Loeb Classical Library (New York, 1922), pp. 59–67. These were probably all Georgian-speaking peoples. The Chalybes may not have been a distinct ethnic group but simply people identified by the Greek used word to describe the ironworking tribes of the area (*khalyps* means "steel" in Greek). Melikishvili argues that the Chalybes mentioned by Xenophon as living in two different places and later by Strabo were not a separate ethnic group but were probably the Khaldi, known to the Armenians as Khaghtik, who in fact were the Chans (Sans) (Melikishvili, *K istorii drevnei Gruzii,* pp. 70–72, 258). The Taochi (Taokhoi) were the people known formerly to the Urartians as Diauehi (Diauhi, Daiaeni) and are mentioned in Sarduri II's records as ironworkers (Lang, *The Georgians,* pp. 59–60).

33. Todd, *Xenophon,* pp. 67, 73.

34. Todd, *Xenophon,* pp. 73, 75.

35. Todd, *Xenophon,* p. 131.

36. Melikishvili, *K istorii drevnei Gruzii,* p. 264.

37. Ibid., p. 263.

38. Lang, *The Georgians,* pp. 57, 75–76; and Melikishvili, *K istorii drevnei Gruzii,* p. 45.

39. Melikishvili, *K istorii drevnei Gruzii,* pp. 125–26. Kartlosi is described in the chronicles as *mamamtavari* ("father of his people") and *targamosis dze* ("born of Targamosi," the great-grandson of the biblical Noah) (*kartlis tskhovreba,* ed. S. Qaukhchishvili [Tbilisi, 1955], vol. 1, pp. 4, 5, 7, 9, 10, 11, 26, 60). The name Parnavaz is Iranian (F. Justi, *Iranisches Namenbuch* [Marburg, 1895; Hildesheim, 1962], p. 92). I am grateful to Professor Peter Golden for these references.

40. Melikishvili, *K istorii drevnei Gruzii,* p. 126.

41. Cyril Toumanoff, "Chronology of the Kings of Iberia," *Traditio* 25 (1969): 9.

42. W. E. D. Allen, *A History of the Georgian People from the Beginning down to the Russian Conquest in the Nineteenth Century* (London, 1932; New York: Barnes and Noble, 1971), p. 41.

43. Melikishvili, *K istorii drevnei Gruzii,* pp. 131, 279, 290.

44. Cyril Toumanoff, "Iberia on the Eve of Bagratid Rule: An Enquiry into the Political History of Eastern Georgia Between the IV and the IX Century," *Le Museon* 65 (1952): 28–30.

45. Melikishvili, *K istorii drevnei Gruzii,* p. 125.

46. Ia. A. Manandian, *O torgovle i gorodakh Armenii v sviazi s mirovoi torgovlei drevnikh vremen* (Erevan, 1945). References are to the English translation by Nina Garsoian: H. A. Manandian, *The Trade and Cities of Armenia in Relation to Ancient World Trade* (Lisbon, 1965), pp. 29, 38–39.

47. Ibid., pp. 50–52; on Artaxias's origins in Media, and Iranian influences on Armenia, see Anahit Perikhanian, "Une inscription araméenne du roi Artašes trouvée à Zangezour (Siwnik)," *Revue des études arméniennes,* n.s., 3 (1966): 17–29, and "Les Inscriptions araméennes du roi Artachès (A propos d'une récente trouvaille épigraphique en Arménie)," ibid., n.s., 8 (1971): 169–74.

48. Bernadotte Perrin, trans., *Plutarch's Lives,* vol. 5, Loeb Classical Library (New York, 1917), p. 207.

49. Some Western scholars, like D. Magie, argue that the Romans aimed at controlling the northern Transcaucasian transit trade route (Kura-Phasis), but Manandian and other Soviet scholars believe that the northern route was much less important than the southern, which ran through Artaxata in Armenia (Manandian, *Trade and Cities,* pp. 48–49).

50. Toumanoff, *Studies,* p. 83.

51. Melikishvili, *K istorii drevnei Gruzii,* pp. 337, 344–45; and Berdzenishvili et al., *Istoriia Gruzii,* p. 61.

52. Cyril Toumanoff, "Caucasia and Byzantium," *Traditio* 27 (1971): 114. Control over the Caucasus meant control over the northern passes through which raiders from the steppe could move down into Iran or the eastern Roman holdings.

53. Allen, *History of the Georgian People,* p. 75.

54. The ambivalence of Roman-Iberian relations is well illustrated in what we know of the reign of the most celebrated of the east Georgian monarchs of the second century A.D., Parsman II (called *kveli,* the "good" or "valiant"), who ruled from 116 to 132. Parsman was a friend of the Emperor Hadrian, who honored him with the gift of an elephant. The Georgian monarch sent gold-embroidered cloaks in return. In 129, however, Parsman refused to pay homage to Hadrian on the occasion of the emperor's visit to the East. Tensions with Rome prompted Kartli-Iberia to ally with the Alans and campaign against the great empires to the south (Toumanoff, "Chronology of the Kings of Iberia," p. 16; Melikishvili, *K istorii drevnei Gruzii,* pp. 353–62). Half a century later, Parsman III (135–185) was the guest of Emperor Antonius Pius and was honored by being permitted to make offerings in the Capitol. His equestrian statue was erected in the Temple of Bellona, and the territory of Iberia was increased (Toumanoff, "Chronology of the Kings of Iberia," p. 17).

55. Ibid., p. 18. On the Sassanids, see A. Christensen, *Iran sous les Sassanides* (Copenhagen, 1944).

56. Toumanoff, "Chronology of the Kings of Iberia," pp. 21–22.

57. Jones, *Geography of Strabo,* p. 211.

58. Ibid., p. 215.

59. Ibid., pp. 217–21.

60. Toumanoff, "Introduction to Christian Caucasian History: The Formative Centuries," pp. 43, 45, and *Studies,* pp. 91, 93–94.

61. Melikishvili, *K istorii drevnei Gruzii,* p. 315; and Berdzenishvili et al., *Istoriia Gruzii,* p. 68. The coincidence of identical terms for "people" and "armed force" was widespread in the early societies; cf. the Indo-European languages: the German *Volk* and the Slavic *polk.*

62. Toumanoff, *Studies,* pp. 94–95; and Melikishvili, *K istorii drevnei Gruzii,* pp. 312–13.

63. Manandian, *Trade and Cities,* p. 73.

64. Melikishvili, *K istorii drevnei Gruzii,* 439–40, 443–44. *Vajari* is an Iranian loanword from the Persian *vazar* (bazaar).

65. For a penetrating study of the Iranian influence in ancient Armenia, see Nina Garsoian, "Prolegomena to a Study of the Iranian Aspects in Arsacid Armenia," *Handes Amsorya* 90 (1976): 177–234.

66. N. Adontz, *Armenia in the Period of Justinian: The Political Conditions Based on the Naxarar System* (Louvain-Lisbon, 1970), p. 291. This is a translation by Nina Garsoian of Adontz's classic *Armeniia v epokhu Iustiniana: Politicheskoe sostoianie na osnove nakhararskogo stroia* (St. Petersburg, 1908).

67. Toumanoff, "Introduction to Christian Caucasian History: The Formative Centuries," pp. 50, 62.

68. Georges Charachidzé, *Introduction à l'étude de la féodalité géorgienne (Le Code de Georges le Brillant)* (Paris, 1971), p. 97.

69. Toumanoff, *Studies,* pp. 96–98; and Melikishvili, *K istorii drevnei Gruzii,* pp. 67–68, 474–75.

70. Toumanoff, "Christian Caucasia Between Byzantium and Iran: New Light from Old Sources," *Traditio* 10 (1954): 123–24.

CHAPTER 2

1. Cyril Toumanoff, "Introduction to Christian Caucasian History, II: States and Dynasties of the Formative Period," *Traditio* 17 (1961): 2.

2. Ibid., pp. 4–5. The noble attraction toward Iran should not be exaggerated, however; certain aristocratic houses, such as Armenian Mamikonians, were oriented toward Rome-Byzantium.

3. Toumanoff, *Studies,* p. 377, and "Christian Caucasia Between Byzantium and Iran," p. 167.

4. Berdzenishvili et al., *Istoriia Gruzii,* p. 85.

5. Melikishvili, *K istorii drevnei Gruzii,* pp. 129–30, 477–78. For an analysis of the persistence of paganism among Georgian mountaineers, see Georges Charachidzé, *Le Système de la Géorgie païénne, analyse structurale d'une civilisation* (Paris, 1968).

6. Berdzenishvili et al., *Istoriia Gruzii,* p. 86.

7. Cyril Toumanoff, "Iberia on the Eve of Bagratid Rule," p. 27n, and "Christian Caucasia Between Byzantium and Iran," p. 124. For the kings in this period, see Toumanoff, "Chronology of the Kings of Iberia," pp. 21–29.

8. Toumanoff, *Studies,* p. 141.

9. Berdzenishvili et al., *Istoriia Gruzii,* pp. 88–89. The chronicles give this version: "And this Parnavazi was the first king in Kartli of the Georgian race. He spread the Georgian language and never spoke another language except Georgian. And he created the Georgian writing" (*kartlis tskhovreba,* vol. 1, p. 26; trans. Peter Golden). See also Toumanoff, *Studies,* p. 105 n. 160).

10. Berdzenishvili et al., *Istoriia Gruzii,* p. 92.

11. Cited in N. Adontz, *Armenia in the Period of Justinian,* p. 173. On Varsken's apostasy, see Toumanoff, *Studies,* p. 364.

12. Toumanoff, "Christian Caucasia Between Byzantium and Iran," pp. 167–169. At the Fourth Church Council at Chalcedon (451), a Christological formulation was adopted that was ultimately rejected by the Armenian church and accepted by the Georgian church. It became the touchstone of the faith of the Eastern Orthodox churches.

13. Toumanoff, *Studies,* pp. 368–72. Tbilisi is the Georgian name of the city known to Armenians, Russians, and others as Tiflis. The latter usage became dominant in the nineteenth century, only to be officially changed to Tbilisi by the Soviet authorities in the 1930s.

14. Ibid., p. 225; "Chronology of the Kings of Abasgia and Other Problems," *Le Museon* 69 (1956): 74 n. 3. See also Z. V. Anchabadze, *Istoriia i kul'tura drevnei Abkhazii* (Moscow, 1964); and Melikishvili, *K istorii drevnei Gruzii,* p. 386.

15. Toumanoff, "Chronology of the Kings of Iberia," pp. 29–31.

16. Juansher, translated in Toumanoff, *Studies,* p. 381. On the sixth century in Georgia, see Charachidzé, *Introduction à l'étude de la féodalité géorgienne,* pp. 97–100; and P. Goubert, *Byzance avant l'Islam,* vol. 1 (Paris, 1951), esp. chaps. 5–8.

17. Toumanoff, *Studies,* p. 386 n. 11. "The dignity of Curopalates, connected at first, apparently, with certain aulic functions, was, from the time of Justinian I to that of the Comneni, one of the highest in the Eastern Empire, ranking next to Caesar and Nobilissimus and, like them, reserved usually for members of the Imperial family. Its conferment upon various Caucasian dynasts is an impressive witness to their political importance on the international scene of the times" (Toumanoff, *Studies,* p. 389). See also N. V. Pigulevskaia, *Vizantiia i Iran na rubezhe VI i VII vekov* (Moscow, 1946).

18. Charachidzé, *Introduction à l'étude de la féodalité géorgienne,* p. 100.

19. Toumanoff, *Studies,* p. 390; Allen, *History of the Georgian People,* p. 78.

20. Speri and southern Klarjeti were annexed by the Byzantine empire (Toumanoff, "Iberia on the Eve of Bagratid Rule," p. 201; *The History of the Caucasian Albanians by Movses Dasxuranci,* trans. C. J. F. Dowsett (London, 1961), pp. 85–90, 94–95).

21. Toumanoff, "Christian Caucasia Between Byzantium and Iran," pp. 172–74, 179–81.

22. Ibid., p. 158. Toumanoff overstates his case here. The Sassanids were hardly "senile." Arab success was aided by the exhaustion both Iran and Byzantium experienced after their long war.

23. Réné Grousset, *Histoire de l'Armenie des origines à 1071* (Paris: Payot, 1947), pp. 306–7. Soviet scholar Aram Ter-Ghevondian has produced two major works on the Arab period in Armenia: *Arabakan amirayutyunnere Bagratunyats Hayastanum* (Erevan, 1965) (English translation by N. G. Garsoian, *The Arab Emirates in Bagratid Armenia* [Lisbon: Calouste Gulbenkian Foundation, 1976], and *Armenia i arabskii khalifat* (Erevan, 1977). See also G. G. Mkrtumian, *Gruzinskoe feodal'noe kniazhestvo Kakheti v VIII–XI vv. i ego vzaimootnosheniia s Armeniei* (Erevan, 1983).

24. Toumanoff, *Studies,* pp. 406–7.

25. Ibid., p. 406; Grousset, *Histoire de l'Armenie,* pp. 323–34.

26. Quoted from the Arabic source, al-Ya'qubi's *Ta'rikh.* See Toumanoff, *Studies,* pp. 409, 410, 412–66.

27. Grousset, *Histoire de l'Armenie,* pp. 337–40.

28. Cyril Toumanoff, "Armenia and Georgia," *The Cambridge Medieval History* (Cambridge England: Cambridge University Press, 1966), vol. 4, pt. 1, p. 609.

29. Allen, *History of the Georgian People*, p. 81; and Berdzenishvili et al., *Istoriia Gruzii*, pp. 126–27.

30. Toumanoff, "Iberia on the Eve of Bagratid Rule," pp. 275, 300–302, and *Studies*, pp. 466, 486–87.

"According to the erroneous tradition of Sumbat . . . this house was deduced in direct male line from an earlier dynasty of Iberian rulers, the Guaramids, and the latter, in turn, was traced back to the official ancestor of the Bagratid race, King and Prophet David. Until recently, this tradition was given a general acceptance. Yet older and more authoritative sources than Sumbat, affirm, in accord with the Armenian historical data, that the Georgian Bagratids branched out of the Armenian Bagratid dynasty; that this branch removed to Iberia only after the defeat of the Armenian princes by the Arabs in 772, in the person of Prince Atrnerseh or Adarnase (grandson of Ashot III the Blind, Prince of the Bagratids and Prince of Armenia in 732–748); that Adarnase's son Ashot the Great attained, the first of the Bagratids, to the Principate of Iberia in 813 and thus founded the last royal house of Georgia; and that finally, the Davidic claim of that house was a further development of the earlier tradition of Hebrew origin entertained by its Armenian ancestors. All this has now come to be accepted in modern Georgian historiography" (Toumanoff, "Iberia on the Eve of Bagratid Rule," p. 22).

The Soviet history of Georgia produced collectively by N. A. Berdzenishvili et al. concludes the following on the Armenian origins of the Georgian Bagratids: "The illustrious dynasty of the Bagrationi originated from the most ancient Georgian district—Speri (today Ispir). Through their farsighted, flexible policies, the Bagrationi achieved great influence from the sixth through eighth centuries. One of their branches moved out to Armenia, the other to Kartli, and both won for themselves the dominant position among the other rulers of Transcaucasia" (Berdzenishvili et al., *Istoriia Gruzii*, p. 129).

31. Grousset, *Histoire de l'Armenie*, pp. 352–53.

32. Allen, *History of the Georgian People*, p. 82; ibid., pp. 352–53, 364; and Berdzenishvili et al., *Istoriia Gruzii*, p. 130.

33. Grousset, *Histoire de l'Armenie*, pp. 391–93. Here and elsewhere certain monarchs will have two numerals after their name, reflecting the disputes among scholars on the number of kings of that name on the Georgian throne.

34. Ibid., pp. 401, 410, 413, 414, 428–29, 432.

35. Adarnase II of Kartli-Iberia returned the favor of Ashot's father, Smbat, and in 915 Adarnase personally crowned Ashot II of Armenia (ibid., p. 442).

36. Thus David's lands increased, though it remains unclear whether his lands were granted conditionally or outright.

37. Grousset, *Histoire de l'Armenie*, pp. 501–2; and Z. Avalichvili, "La Succession du curopalate David d'Iberie, dynaste de Tao," *Byzantion* 8 (1933): 177. For a detailed discussion of Basil II's eastern policy, see John Harper Forsyth, "The Byzantine-Arab Chronicle (938–1034) of Yahya B. Sacid Al-Antaki" (Ph.D. diss., University of Michigan, 1977), 2 vols.

38. Toumanoff, "Introduction to Christian Caucasian History, II," p. 52.

39. Toumanoff, "The Background to Mantzikert," *Proceedings of the XIIIth International Congress of Byzantine Studies* (Oxford, 1966), p. 424; Avalichvili, "La Succession," pp. 179, 199; Grousset, *Histoire de l'Armenie*, pp. 537–38, 547–50, 561; and Allen, *History of the Georgian People*, pp. 87–88.

40. For details, see Allen, *History of the Georgian People*, pp. 88–90; and Toumanoff, "Armenia and Georgia," pp. 621–22.

41. Charachidzé, *Introduction à l'étude de la féodalité géorgienne,* pp. 103–4.

42. Toumanoff, "Iberia on the Eve of Bagratid Rule," p. 258n.

43. Berdzenishvili et al., *Istoriia Gruzii,* p. 152; and Speros Vryonis, *The Decline of Medieval Hellenism in Asia Minor and the Process of Islamization from the Eleventh through the Fifteenth Century* (Berkeley and Los Angeles: University of California Press, 1971), pp. 283–84.

44. S. A. Meskhia, *Didgorskaia bitva* (Tbilisi, 1974), p. 24.

45. Ibid., p. 25.

46. Ibid., pp. 20–27. David "the Rebuilder" is usually designated David II; Toumanoff and some of his followers regard him as David III.

47. Ibid., pp. 28–29.

48. Ibid., p. 30.

49. Ibid., pp. 31, 32, 38, 41.

50. Mariam Davidovna Lordkipanidze, *Istoriia Gruzii XI–nachalo XIII veka* (Tbilisi, 1974), p. 37.

51. For an excellent discussion of the Qipchaks in Georgia, see Peter B. Golden, "Nomads and Sedentary Societies: The Case of the Cuman/Qipcaqs in Georgia" (Paper presented to the American Oriental Society annual meeting, Ann Arbor, Michigan, April 16, 1985), and his earlier "Cumanica I: The Qipčaqs in Georgia," *Archivum Eurasiae Medii Aevi* 4 (1984): 45–87. On the Seljuks in Georgia, see N. N. Sengalia, *seljukebi da sakartvelo XI saukuneshi* (Tbilisi, 1968).

Several Soviet scholars, among them S. Eremian and K. Chkhataraishvili, argue that David settled the Qipchaks in Armenia and that they adopted the Armenian form of Christianity. Meskhia, however, believes that the Qipchaks were settled in the borderlands to protect Georgia from the Seljuk Turks and were converted to Chalcedonian, i.e., Georgian Orthodox, Christianity, not the Armenian faith (the same process that happened to many Armenians in this period of Georgian expansion). Meskhia also argues that Georgia and Kievan Rus' were both interested in having the Qipchak Turks (known to the Russians as the Polovtsi) move south into Transcaucasia, though for very different reasons (Meskhia, *Didgorskaia bitva,* pp. 35–37, 51–52; Vryonis, *Decline of Medieval Hellenism,* pp. 284–85). In his *Rannie Tiurki na Severnom Kavkaze* (Moscow, 1978), Ia. A. Fedorov argues that Rus' did not drive the Qipchaks into Georgia and that the North Caucasus was the *udel* (appanage) of David's father-in-law, the Qipchak chieftain Atrak. See also Golden, "Nomads and Sedentary Societies," p. 16.

52. Meskhia, *Didgorskaia bitva,* pp. 47–49, 59. Minorsky says that David used forty thousand Qipchaks (Polovtsi) and five thousand slaves who had converted to Christianity to throw off Seljuk domination (V. Minorsky, "Tiflis," *The Encyclopedia of Islam,* vol. 4, p. 755).

53. Allen, *History of the Georgian People,* pp. 98–99; and Meskhia, *Didgorskaia bitva,* pp. 64–65, 70, 73. Contemporary accounts (e.g., Mateos Urkhaetsi) estimated the Muslim forces at more than 500,000, but a modern historian, Ivane Javakhishvili, considers 300,000 to be a more accurate number (Meskhia, *Didgorskaia bitva,* pp. 79–82; Ivane Javakhishvili, *kartveli eris istoria* [Tiflis, 1914], 2:202–3). Meskhia estimates that King David had about 56,000 troops.

54. Dmanisi, the other independent town in Georgia, was captured by David "the Rebuilder" in March 1123. Meskhia rejects the view of S. Eremian that David appointed Vahram Artsruni the governor of Tbilisi and that this post became hereditary in the Artsruni family (*Didgorskaia bitva,* pp. 98–99, 100–101).

55. Ibid., p. 101; while a Georgian paid five dinars in annual taxes and a Jew four dinars, a Muslim was required to pay only three dinars. See also V. Minorsky, *Studies in Caucasian History* (London, 1953), p. 84.

56. Vryonis, *Decline of Medieval Hellenism,* pp. 284–85.

57. Berdzenishvili et al., *Istoriia Gruzii,* pp. 166–67. Kirakos Gandzaketsi writes: "And even the merciless Georgians were kind and compassionate to the newcomers, who were searching among them for shelter. In this way, merciful God comforted those who had fallen into misery" (Kirakos Gandzaketsi, *Istoriia Armenii,* trans. from the Armenian by L. A. Khanlarian [Moscow, 1976], p. 167).

58. Allen, *History of the Georgian People,* p. 100. On David's political legacy, see V. V. Abashmadze, *narkvevebi sakartvelos politikur modzghvrebata istoriidan* (Tbilisi, 1969), chap. 3.

59. Lordkipanidze, *Istoriia Gruzii,* pp. 137, 142.

60. Because the central problem of this study is the social and political development of Georgia, questions of art and literature will not be discussed in any detail. For those who would like a broader introduction to Georgian art, see Shalva Amiranashvili, *kartuli khelovnebis istoria* (Tbilisi, 1961) (or the Russian translation, *Istorii gruzinskogo iskusstva [Moscow, 1963];* and Rusudan Mepisashvili and Vakhtang Tsintsadze, *The Arts of Ancient Georgia* (London: Thames and Hudson, 1979). On Georgian literature, I recommend a look at David Marshall Lang, *Lives and Legends of the Georgian Saints,* 2d ed., rev. (Oxford: A. R. Mowbray, 1976); Shota Rustaveli, *The Knight in the Panther's Skin,* trans. Venera Urushadze (Tbilisi, 1968); Aleksandr Baramidze, Shalva Radiani, and Beso Zhgenti, *Istoriia gruzinskoi literatury: Kratkii ocherk* (Tbilisi, 1958); and A. G. Baramidze and D. M. Gamezardashvili, *Georgian Literature* (Tbilisi, 1968).

61. Lordkipanidze, *Istoriia Gruzii,* pp. 142–46.

62. Berdzenishvili et al., *Istoriia Gruzii,* pp. 197–98; and Abshmadze, *narkvevebi,* chap. 4.

63. Toumanoff, "Armenia and Georgia," pp. 624–25.

64. Cited in Allen, *History of the Georgian People,* p. 110.

65. Ibid., pp. 115–16.

66. Berdzenishvili et al., *Istoriia Gruzii,* pp. 229, 232, 236–37; and Toumanoff, "Armenia and Georgia," p. 626.

67. Berdzenishvili et al., *Istoriia Gruzii,* p. 242; and Toumanoff, "Armenia and Georgia," p. 626.

68. Berdzenishvili et al., *Istoriia Gruzii,* p. 248. Charachidzé notes that even in the thirteenth century, when Georgian kings were quite weak, the formality of royal grants of lands to princely heirs was maintained (*Introduction à l'étude de la féodalité géorgienne,* p. 104).

CHAPTER 3

1. Charachidzé, *Introduction à l'étude de la féodalité géorgienne,* p. 16.

2. Ibid., p. 20.

3. Ibid., p. 105; and Cyril Toumanoff, "La Noblesse géorgienne: Sa genese et sa structure," *Rivista Araldica* 59, no. 9 (September 1956): 267. Berdzenishvili writes

that by the fourteenth century the mass of the nobility was already divided into ordinary *aznaurni* and *didebulaznaurni*, the latter a group that eventually evolved into *tavadi* (Berdzenishvili et al., *Istoriia Gruzii*, p. 252).

4. See Charachidzé, *Introduction à l'étude de la féodalité géorgienne*.

5. Ibid., pp. 12, 14.

6. Ibid., p. 113; and Toumanoff, "La Noblesse géorgienne," p. 269. The term "slave" was used more loosely in the East than in Europe and did not refer only to persons as property.

7. Berdzenishvili et al., *Istoriia Gruzii*, pp. 253–56.

8. Charachidzé, *Introduction à l'étude de la féodalité géorgienne*, pp. 106, 133.

9. The king was held prisoner until 1393, when he converted. By the time of his death in 1395, Bagrat had become a Christian again. Cyril Toumanoff, "The Fifteenth-Century Bagratids and the Institution of Collegial Sovereignty in Georgia," *Traditio* 7 (1949–1951): 170–71.

10. Giorgi VII was aided in his struggle against the Imeretian king, Aleksandre I, by the nobles of Imereti. Giorgi gave the Tskhumi *saeristavo* to the Dadiani princes of Samegrelo, thus forming a new and powerful formation known as Sabediano. Z. V. Anchabadze, *Iz istorii srednevekovoi Abkhazii (VI–XVII vv.)* (Sukhumi, 1959), p. 237.

11. W. E. D. Allen writes that Aleksandre "proved that he had some military capacity, and in the first year of his reign he defeated the Atabegi Ioanne at Kokhta. But he was a young man greatly under the influence of his grandmother, and he spent his time and resources in the repair of Sweti-Tzkhoveli and other shrines which had been destroyed during the Timurid wars . . . [His] character found expression in a religiosity which could impose a special tax upon an exhausted peasantry to provide for the restoration and embellishment of churches and convents" (Allen, *History of the Georgian People*, pp. 126–27). For more information on Aleksandre the Great, see Toumanoff, "The Fifteenth-Century Bagratids," pp. 176–82.

12. Berdzenishvili et al., *Istoriia Gruzii*, pp. 260, 264–65. New terms entered the Georgian lexicon to express this decline in population and the phenomenon of abandoned lands and villages: *napuzari* (land that had once been a "living" *pudze*); *nakalakari* (a small town); *partakhti* (an escheated estate); and *nasoplari* (an abandoned village).

13. Toumanoff, "The Fifteenth-Century Bagratids," pp. 185–86; and Allen, *History of the Georgian People*, p. 137.

14. Berdzenishvili et al., *Istoriia Gruzii*, p. 268; Allen, *History of the Georgian People*, pp. 137–39; and Toumanoff, "The Fifteenth-Century Bagratids," pp. 188–89. Allen claims that the nobles of Kakheti who opposed Bagrat elected David, a nephew of their King Giorgi, but Toumanoff shows this story to be fiction.

15. Berdzenishvili et al., *Istoriia Gruzii*, p. 272; S. A. Meskhia, *Goroda i gorodskoi stroi feodal'noi Gruzii XVII–XVIII vv.* (Tbilisi, 1956), pp. 93, 99–102; and W. E. D. Allen, ed., *Russian Embassies to the Georgian Kings (1589–1605)*, texts translated by Anthony Mango (Cambridge, England: Cambridge University Press, 1970), vol. 1, p. 57.

16. The major Georgian source on the sixteenth and seventeenth centuries is the *aghtsera sameposa sakartvelosa* by Prince Vakhushti Bagrationi (1696–1757), the son of Vakhtang VI. It was most recently published by Professor S. Qaukhchishvili in vol. 4 of the *kartlis tskhovreba* (Tbilisi, 1973). A Russian translation by N. T. Nakashidze is now available: Vakhushti Bagrationi, *Istoriia tsarstva gruzinskogo* (Tbilisi, 1976).

17. *Samtavro*, a principality ruled by a *mtavari*, was an independent entity with nothing more than formal ties binding it to a monarch. *Satavado*, a seigneury ruled by a *tavadi*, was an autonomous territorial and economic unit with one tenant, a fortress and monastery, and a number of vassals and serfs (Charachidzé, *Introduction à l'étude de la féodalité géorgienne*, p. 105).

18. Berdzenishvili et al., *Istoriia Gruzii*, pp. 275–76; Anchabadze, *Iz istorii*, pp. 260–61.

19. David divided Kartli into four *sadrosho* (military districts, literally "banner"; *sanjak* in Ottoman usage), each under the command of a royal official, the *sardara*. But this feudal office soon became hereditary in certain families, thus undermining the king's attempt (Berdzenishvili et al., *Istoriia Gruzii*, pp. 277, 279). About the same time the kings of Kakheti eliminated the old *saeristavo* units and replaced them with smaller administrative districts ruled by an appointed royal official, the *mouravi*, who had no military force and was given strictly defined functions and duties. In Kakheti four newly created *sadrosho* were put under the command of bishops, not of *tavadi* as in Kartli.

20. Ibid., pp. 280, 288; and Anchabadze, *Iz istorii*, p. 272.

21. Berdzenishvili et al., *Istoriia Gruzii*, p. 287.

22. N. Nakashidze, "sakartvelo-Ruset-iranis urtiertoba da bakhtrionis ajankheba," *kartuli samepo-samtavroebis sagareo politikis istoriidan*, vol. 1 (Tbilisi, 1970), pp. 78–97.

23. Berdzenishvili et al., *Istoriia Gruzii*, p. 290. Just as Svimon of Kartli reached the pinnacle of his success, his royal cousin in Kakheti was informing the Russian ambassadors that Svimon "has lost nearly the whole of his kingdom for he eats opium and always quarrels with Turkish men" (Allen, *Russian Embassies*, vol. 1, p. 158).

24. Ibid., pp. 146, 37–38, 63.

25. Ibid., pp. 373, 375.

26. Berdzenishvili et al., *Istoriia Gruzii*, p. 295; Allen, *History of the Georgian People*, p. 165, and *Russian Embassies*, vol. 2, pp. 434, 447, 462.

27. Allen, *Russian Embassies*, vol. 2, pp. 489, 499, 510–11.

28. Cited in Minorsky, "Tiflis," p. 759; Allen, *Russian Embassies*, vol. 1, p. 261; Berdzenishvili et al., *Istoriia Gruzii*, p. 297.

29. Anchabadze, *Iz istorii*, p. 263.

30. Ibid., pp. 263–65; Berdzenishvili et al., *Istoriia Gruzii*, p. 313. On the embassy to Imereti in 1650–1652, see M. Polievktov, *Posol'stvo stol'nika Tolochanova i d'iaka Ievleva v Imeretiiu* (Tiflis, 1926); and I. Z. Tsintsadze, ed., *Stateinyi spisok posol'stva v Imeretiiu 1650–1652 gg., sostavlennyi Alekseem Ievlevym (Russkii tekst s gruzinskim perevodom)* (Tbilisi, 1969).

31. Giorgi Saakadze opposed this alliance and had to be driven from Georgia by Taimuraz's forces. He was killed in Turkey in 1629 (Berdzenishvili et al., *Istoriia Gruzii*, pp. 303–4).

32. Ibid., pp. 315, 292–93. Corn was called *lazuti*, a term still used by Turkish speakers in eastern Anatolia.

33. John Chardin, *Travels of Sir John Chardin into Persia and the East Indies, Through the Black Sea and the Country of Colchis* (London, 1691), pp. 87, 86, 97, 89.

34. Political terms in Kartli-Kakheti were Iranicized in the seventeenth century: *msakhurtukhutsesi* became *korchibashi* (head administrator); *msajultukhutsesi* was

replaced by *mdivanbegi* (chief justice); and *khurotmodzgvari* became *saraidar* (commander in chief) (Berdzenishvili et al., *Istoriia Gruzii*, pp. 305–6; David Marshall Lang, *The Last Years of the Georgian Monarchy, 1658–1832* [New York: Columbia University Press, 1957], p. 23). From the early seventeenth century, silver coins minted in Kartli bore the inscriptions of the Iranian shahs, and only copper coins had distinctive Georgian features (Lang, *Last Years*, pp. 29–30). Essentially eastern Georgia had become a province of Iran, with Kakheti completely under Iranian rule and Kartli enjoying somewhat more autonomy under its Bagratid *vali*, usually a nominal convert to Islam.

35. In 1658 Taimuraz was received by Tsar Aleksei Mikhailovich in Moscow. The old king never gave up hope of returning to Kakheti, and during his long exile he participated in a rebellion of Tushin, Pshavi, and Khevsuri tribesmen against Iranian rule. Taimuraz died in 1663(?), a prisoner of his implacable enemy, Iran.

36. Lang, *Last Years*, pp. 96–101.

37. Father P. Sanson, *Voyage de Perse* (Paris, 1695), pp. 176–77; cited in Lang, *Last Years*, p. 95; see also Chardin, *Travels*, p. 205.

38. J. Karst, *Corpus Juris Ibero-Caucasici*, vol. 1, *Code georgien du roi Vakhtang VI*, vol. 2, *Commentaire ou Precis du Droit ibero-caucasien* (Strasbourg, 1935–1937); I. I. Surguladze, ed., *kartuli samartlis dzeglebi* (Tbilisi, 1970), pp. 211–764. For a full treatment of the Russian orientation in Georgia in the first half of the eighteenth century, see G. G. Paichadze, *Russko-gruzinskie politicheskie otnosheniia v pervoi polovine XVIII veka* (Tbilisi, 1970). Earlier Paichadze produced a more specialized monograph: *Russko-gruzinskie otnosheniia v 1725–1735 gg.* (Tbilisi, 1965). For Georgian-French relations, see I. M. Tabagua, ed., *sabutebi sakartvelo-saprangetis urtiertobis istoriidan (1707 tlis marti–1714 tslis dekemberi)*, vol. 1 (Tbilisi, 1975).

39. Taimuraz II of Kakheti had married Tamar, the daughter of Vakhtang VI of Kartli, thus joining the Mukhranian Bagratids of Kartli with the Kakhetian Bagratids. Their son, Erekle II, became king of united Kartli-Kakheti upon his father's death in 1762.

40. The best Western work on Nadir Shah is L. Lockhart, *Nadir Shah* (London, 1938).

41. Allen, *History of the Georgian People*, p. 194; Lang, *Last Years*, p. 145.

42. Allen, *History of the Georgian People*, p. 197; Lang, *Last Years*, p. 149.

43. Allen, *History of the Georgian People*, p. 204.

44. Lang, *Last Years*, pp. 158–59. Berdzenishvili et al., *Istoriia Gruzii*, p. 374.

45. The mountain tribes, called somewhat indiscriminately "Lezgins" by the Russians, were led by the Avar tribesmen but were made up of various ethnic and linguistic groups. For an in-depth treatment of Erekle's economic policies, see A. A. Rogava, *Zachatki kapitalizma v Gruzii i politika Irakliia II* (Tbilisi, 1974).

46. Report by Captain Iazykov to Count Panin, 1770; cited in Lang, *Last Years*, p. 188. For the full text of the report, see A. A. Tsagareli, *Gramoty i drugie istoricheskie dokumenty XVIII stoletiia, otnosiashchiesia k Gruzii*, vol. 1, *S 1768 do 1774 gody* (St. Petersburg, 1891), pp. 183–96.

47. G. Ia. Natadze, "K voprosu ob ekonomicheskom polozhenii Gruzii v kontse XVIII stoletiia," in M. Zhakov, S. Sef, and G. Khachapuridze, eds., *Istoriia klassovoi bor'by v Zakavkaz'i: Sbornik statei, Kniga pervaia* (Tiflis, 1930), pp. 123–52. Natadze found no evidence of resistance leading to armed clashes (p. 139), while his colleague, S. Kakabadze, notes a few manifestations. ("Krest'ianskii vopros i

krest'ianskie dvizheniia v vostochnoi Gruzii v XVIII veke," in Zhakov, Sef, and Khachapuridze, *Istoriia klassovoi bor'by,* pp. 153–94.)

48. Lang, *Last Years,* p. 164, 169–70. There is some discussion of slave trading in Georgia in Ehud R. Toledano, *The Ottoman Slave Trade and Its Suppression: 1840–1890* (Princeton, N.J.: Princeton University Press, 1982).

49. Lang, *Last Years,* pp. 173, 176.

50. Ibid., pp. 227, 232.

51. Ibid., p. 243.

52. N. Dubrovin, *Georgii XII: Poslednii tsar Gruzii i prisoedinenie eia k Rossii* (St. Petersburg, 1897), pp. 171–72.

53. Laurens Hamilton Rhinelander, Jr., "The Incorporation of the Caucasus into the Russian Empire: The Case of Georgia" (Ph.D. diss., Columbia University, 1972), p. 44; Muriel Atkin, *Russia and Iran, 1780–1828* (Minneapolis: University of Minnesota Press, 1980), pp. 60–65.

CHAPTER 4

1. For English-language accounts of the end of the Georgian kingdoms and the early years of Russian administration, see Lang, *Last Years;* and two unpublished dissertations: Rhinelander, "The Incorporation of the Caucasus," and Henry John Armani, "The Russian Annexation of the Kingdom of Imeretia, 1800–1815: In the Light of Russo-Ottoman Relations" (Georgetown University, 1970).

2. See Lang, *Last Years,* photograph facing p. 208. A Russian official visiting Georgia early in Erekle's reign noted the king's Eastern ways and his desire to affect Western manners:

> King Erekle made tables and chairs and ordered from Russia all the tableware and porcelain. When the king had a meal made for me, it was served in European style. Many princes already eat here with spoons, whereas before they ate in the Asian manner, sitting on the floor and without spoons . . . Many fashionable ladies wear hats made of taffeta and net, or covered with galloon and carry umbrellas in their hands. Hats and umbrellas have recently been ordered and imported from Russia (Tsagareli, *Gramoty i drugie,* p. 190).

3. The estates of the noble landlords, whether collectively or individually owned, consisted of two parts: lands supervised directly by the landlords, and those divided among the enserfed peasants. The best lands, including the large vineyards, were as a rule kept by the lords and worked by the serfs to fulfill their labor obligations (A. Ia. Pantskhava, *Ocherki agrarnoi istorii feodal'noi Kartli-Kakheti kontsa XVIII veka* [Tibilisi, 1965], p. 91).

4. On August 7, 1810, the article in the Code of Vakhtang that required nobles to forfeit one-twentieth of a divided estate to the state was rescinded, thus removing the penalty for individualizing collectively owned lands (A. Ia. Pantskhava, *Ocherki agrarnoi istorii Gruzii pervoi poloviny XIX veka* [Tbilisi, 1969], pp. 57, 60).

5. Sh. Chkhetiia, *Tbilisi v XIX stoletii (1865–1869)* (Tbilisi, 1942), pp. 298–301.

6. Rhinelander, "Incorporation of the Caucasus," p. 59; A. P. Berzhe, ed., *Akty sobrannye kavkazskoiu arkheograficheskoiu kommissieiu* (hereafter, *Akty*) (Tiflis,

1866), vol. 1, doc. 548, 12 September 1801. For an extremely suggestive analysis of Russian imperial policy toward non-Russian peoples, see Marc Raeff, "The Style of Russia's Imperial Policy and Prince G. A. Potemkin," in Gerald N. Grob, ed., *Statesmen and Statescraft of the Modern West: Essays in Honor of Dwight E. Lee and H. Donaldson Jordan* (Barre, Mass.: Barre Publishers, 1967), pp. 1–51; and his "Patterns of Russian Imperial Policy Toward the Nationalities," in E. Allworth, ed., *Soviet Nationality Problems* (New York: Columbia University Press, 1971), pp. 22–42.

7. G. V. Khachapuridze, *K istorii Gruzii pervoi polovine XIX veka* (Tbilisi, 1950), p. 69; Rhinelander, "Incorporation of the Caucasus," p. 105. General Tsitsianov's *ukaz* was applied to Imereti and Samegrelo (Mingrelia) in 1841 (S. L. Avaliani, *Krest'ianskii vopros v Zakavkaz'e*, 2 vols. [Odessa, 1912–1914], vol. 1, pp. 113–14).

8. Pantskhava, *Ocherki* (1969), p. 51; clerical peasants became state peasants in 1852. Rhinelander, "Incorporation of the Caucasus," pp. 243–44.

9. *Polnoe sobranie zakonov*, first series, 1649–1825 (St. Petersburg, 1830–1839), no. 921 (February 25, 1827).

10. Dmitri Ivanovich Kipiani, "Zapiski Dmitriia Ivanovicha Kipiani s 1820 goda," *Russkaia starina* 50 (May 1886):277.

11. Berdzenishvili et al., *Istoriia Gruzii*, pp. 447, 449–50.

12. K. Oragvelidze, "K voprosu o razvitii kapitalizma v sel'skom khoziastve Zakavkaz'ia," in Zhakov, Sef, and Khachapuridze, *Istoriia Klassovoi bor'by*, p. 3.

13. Chkhetiia, *Tbilisi*, p. 420.

14. Rhinelander, "Incorporation of the Caucasus," pp. 116–17; on Tsitsianov in Caucasia, see Atkin, *Russia and Iran*, pp. 70–87; and Pantskhava, *Ocherki* (1969), p. 17. See also L. Hamilton Rhinelander, "Russia's Imperial Policy: The Administration of the Caucasus in the First Half of the Nineteenth Century," *Canadian Slavonic Papers* 17, nos. 2 and 3 (1975):224; and A. P. Ermolov, "Dnevnik Alekseia Petrovicha Ermolova v prodolzhenie komandirovaniia v Gruzii do konchiny Imperatora Aleksandra," in M. P. Pogodin, *Aleksei Petrovich Ermolov: Materialy dlia ego biografii* (Moscow, 1864), pp. 235–54.

15. The early Russian governors of the Caucasus were:

Karl F. Knorring (1801–1803)
Pavel Dmitrievich Tsitsianov (1803–1806)
Ivan Vasil'evich Gudovich (1806–1809)
Aleksandr Petrovich Tormasov (1809–1811)
Marquis Filipp Paulucci (1811–1812)
Nikolai Fedorovich Rtishchev (1812–1816)
Aleksei Petrovich Ermolov (1816–1827)
Ivan Fedorovich Paskevich (1827–1831)
Grigorii Vladimirovich Rozen (1831–1837)
Evgenii Aleksandrovich Golovin (1837–1842)
Aleksandr Ivanovich Neidgardt (1842–1845)
Mikhail Semenovich Vorontsov (1845–1854)

16. Dispatch dated 28 June/10 July, 1832, "Memoires et documents: Russie," vol. 36, doc. 25, Paris, Ministère des Affaires Etrangères; Rhinelander, "Incorporation of the Caucasus," p. 178.

17. Khachapuridze, *K istorii Gruzii*, pp. 177–87; Rhinelander, "Incorporation of the Caucasus," pp. 176–77.

18. *Akty,* vol. 8, p. 11; Chkhetiia, *Tbilisi,* p. 310.

19. Georgian historian Ivane Javakhishvili (Dzhavakhov) listed three parties within the Georgian nobility at the time of annexation. The first party favored the re-establishment of the monarchy under David, eldest son of Giorgi XII, who had ruled briefly between the time of his father's death (December 28, 1800) and the arrival of General Knorring (May 24, 1801). The second party offered Prince Iulon, son of Erekle II and Queen Darejan, as the candidate for the throne, and the third party was made up of those pro-Russian nobles prepared to accept the end of Georgia's independence (I. Dzhavakhov, *Politicheskoe i sotsial'noe dvizhenie v Gruzii v XIX v* [St. Petersburg, 1906], p. 10).

20. Kipiani, "Zapiski," 49:519, 522–24. In 1829 the noble *uchilishche* was re-organized as a noble *gimnaziia.*

21. D. L. Vateishvili, *Russkaia obshchestvennaia mysl' i pechat' na Kavkaze v pervoi treti XIX veka* (Moscow, 1973), p. 310. The first Georgian newspaper, *sakartvelos gazeti* appeared in Tiflis in 1819. Under the name *kartuli gazeti,* it continued for three more years. At that time only two other provincial Russian cities, Kharkov and Astrakhan, had local newspapers. The Georgian newspaper had little public support and operated under strict censorship (ibid., pp. 93, 100).

The first *raznochinets* intellectual in Georgia, the philosopher-publicist Solomon Ivanis dze Dodiashvili (1805–1836) was the son of an enserfed clergyman and attended the only school in Tiflis open to non-nobles, the Tiflis seminary, and then went on to university in St. Petersburg, where he published the first textbook on logic in Russian. Returning to Tiflis in July 1827, Dodiashvili began teaching Georgian language and literature at the noble school, and a few years later compiled one of the first grammars of the Georgian language. Dodiashvili's non-noble birth seemed to hinder him little socially, and he was soon involved with the scions of the most noble families in Georgia in a plot against the Russian administration.

22. For an account of Grigol Orbeliani's role, see Igor Bogomolov, *Grigol Orbeliani i russkaia kultura* (Tbilisi, 1964), Bogomolov argues that Orbeliani, Dodiashvili, Chavchavadze and others were not anti-Russian but antiaristocratic. In his words, they were "healthy patriots" and not "anti-Russian nationalists." Soviet writers frequently make a distinction between patriotism, which is officially accept-able national feeling, and nationalism or chauvinism, which expresses unacceptable feelings, particularly the denigration of another nationality.

23. Khachapuridze, *K istorii Gruzii,* pp. 353–54. "Delo o gruzinskom zagovore," *Akty,* vol. 8, pp. 391–423.

24. Chkhetiia, *Tbilisi,* p. 368. Khachapuridze, *K istorii Gruzii,* p. 422.

25. Rhinelander, "Incorporation of the Caucasus," pp. 196–98. One of the best accounts of Baron Hahn's activities in the Caucasus is given in Semen Esadze, *Istoricheskaia zapiska ob upravlenii Kavkazom,* 2 vols. (Tiflis, 1907), vol. 1, pp. 68–82. The Decembrist Baron Andrei Rozen, exiled to Tiflis in 1837, remembered with bitterness Baron Hahn's attempt to centralize the Caucasian administration without consideration of local peculiarities (A. Rozen, *Zapiski dekabrista* [St. Petersburg, 1907], p. 235).

26. For the law itself—"Vysochaishee utverzhdennoe uchrezhdenie dlia up-ravleniia Zakavkazskim kraem"—see *Polnoe sobranie zakonov,* no. 13,368 (April 10, 1840). While all too typical of the Caucasian administration, the high-handed manner of bureaucrats like Baron Hahn found its nemesis in officials like Count Kiselev, the minister of state properties, who believed that the disorders in the Caucasus "derived from the premature introduction of our laws there," and that this opinion was based "on that well-known truth that the civil laws of each country ought

to flow out of the elements of that people's life and correspond to all their civil needs and relationships" (*Akty,* vol. 9, pp. 21–23; Avaliani, *Krest'ianskii vopros,* vol. 1, pp. 95–96). By the late 1830s Kiselev's enthusiasm for the Georgian laws was no longer shared by many members of the Georgian nobility who periodically petitioned the tsarist government to bring legislative order into the territorial administration. In 1846 a commission headed by Prince Bagration-Mukhranskii recommended the exclusive use of Russian laws. This erosion of support for the old Georgian laws seems to have started at the top of Georgian society, with the aristocracy that served the Russian administration. Georgian laws were completely eliminated in 1859.

27. Kipiani, "Zapiski," 53:616–17.

28. Cited in Rhinelander, "Incorporation of the Caucasus," p. 221.

29. Akaki Tsereteli, *Perezhitoe* (Moscow, 1940), p. 120. For the background to Nicholas I's decision to establish the Caucasian viceregency, see L. Hamilton Rhinelander, "The Creation of the Caucasian Viceregency," *Slavic and East European Review* 59, no. 1 (January 1981):15–40. On Vorontsov, see I. Dzhavakhov [Javakhishvili], "Gruziia," in *Entsiklopedicheskii slovar' russkogo bibliograficheskogo instituta Granat,* vol. 17, p. 213; and I. G. Antelava, "Iz istorii sotsial'no-politicheskogo polozheniia i osvoboditel'nogo dvizheniia Gruzii v 30–50 godakh XIX veka," *Matsne* 16, no. 1 (1964):46.

30. Three autonomous principalities remained in Georgia until the late 1850s and early 1860s. While Guria had lost its autonomy in 1828, Samegrelo remained under the rule of its hereditary princes, the Dadiani, until 1856. Svaneti kept its autonomy until 1857–1859, and Abkhazeti until 1864.

31. Rhinelander, "Incorporation of the Caucasus," p. 244. Those who failed to prove their nobility became state peasants.

32. Avaliani, *Krest'ianskii vopros,* vol. 1, p. 125.

33. Kipiani, "Zapiski," 50:277–79.

34. This estimate is by noble publicist Konstantin Mamatsashvili; see the article by I. Antelava, "konstantine mamatsashvilis sazogadoebriv-politikuri shekhedulebani," in *sakartvelos akhali istoriis sakitkhebi* (Tbilisi, 1975), vol. 2, pp. 12–13n.

35. *Akty,* vol. 10, doc. 29, p. 26; Rhinelander, "Incorporation of the Caucasus," p. 344.

36. Avaliani, *Krest'ianskii vopros,* vol. 1, p. 28. On Georgian peasants in the century before the Russian annexation, see Darejan Megreladze, *glekhobis klasobrivi brdzola peodalur sakartveloshi* (Tbilisi, 1979).

37. I. G. Antelava, *Gosudarstvennye krest'iane Gruzii v XIX veke, I: Do krest'ianskoi reformy 1864 g.* (Tbilisi, 1969), p. 121.

38. Glynn Barratt, *The Rebel on the Bridge: A Life of the Decembrist Baron Andrey Rozen (1800–84)* (London: Paul Elek, 1975), p. 181.

39. Edmund Spencer, *Travels in the Western Caucasus* (London, 1838), vol. 2, pp. 51–52.

40. Tsereteli, *Perezhitoe,* pp. 57–59.

41. Sofrom Mgaloblishvili, *Vospominaniia o moei zhizni. Nezabyvaemye vstrechi* (Tbilisi, 1974), p. 23.

42. Tsereteli, *Perezhitoe,* p. 21.

43. Ibid., pp. 19–20. Baron A. P. Nikolai, "Vospominaniia iz moei zhizni. Krest'ianskaia reforma v Zakavkazskom krae," *Russkii arkhiv* 2, no. 5 (1892):98.

44. Avaliani tells of the landlord K. Abashidze who in 1802 gave his loyal peasant S. Dvali a written promise that he would not be sold, arrested, or plundered

(*Krest'ianskii vopros,* vol. 1, pp. 32–33). The fact that such a document was required testifies to the frequent practice.

45. Tsereteli, *Perezhitoe,* p. 60.

46. Mgaloblishvili, *Vospominaniia,* p. 6.

47. Avaliani, *Krest'ianskii vopros,* vol. 1, pp. 177–79. A desiatina equals 2.7 acres.

48. Mgaloblishvili, *Vospominaniia,* pp. 15, 18, 24–25.

49. According to article 198 of the *dasturlamali* of Vakhtang VI; Pantskhava, *Ocherki* (1965), p. 109.

50. Ibid., pp. 110–11.

51. Ibid., pp. 112–14. Only with great difficulty was the Russian government able to eliminate slavery in western Georgia by the middle of the nineteenth century.

52. Ibid., p. 116; Avaliani, *Krest'ianskii vopros,* vol. 1, pp. 50–61; Berdzenishvili et al., *Istoriia Gruzii,* p. 317.

53. Pantskhava, *Ocherki* (1965), pp. 114–15, 117–19.

54. Avaliani, *Krest'ianskii vopros,* vol. 1, pp. 62–63; Pantskhava, *Ocherki* (1965), pp. 115–16.

55. E. V. Khoshtaria, *Ocherki sotsial'no-ekonomicheskoi istorii Gruzii: Promyshlennost', goroda, rabochii klass (XIX v.–nachalo XX v.)* (Tbilisi, 1974), pp. 38–39; I. Antelava, *XVIII saukunis sakartvelos sotsialur-ekonomiuri ganvitarebis khasiatis sakitkhisatvis* (Tbilisi, 1977), passim.

56. *Akty,* vol. 2, p. 91; Antelava, *Gosudarstvennye krest'iane,* vol. 1, p. 7.

57. By the early 1860s the figures for categories of peasants in Georgia were as follows:

	STATE PEASANTS	LANDLORD PEASANTS	CLERICAL
Peasants			
Tiflis province	68.6%	20.8%	10.6%
Kutaisi province	31.0%	56.4%	12.6%
Georgia (total)	56.4%	32.4%	11.2%

(Antelava, *Gosudarstvennye krest'iane,* vol. 1, p. 23).

58. Avaliani, *Krest'ianskii vopros,* vol. 1, p. 149; Antelava, *Gosudarstvennye krest'iane,* vol. 1, pp. 268–69.

59. Avaliani, *Krest'ianskii vopros,* vol. 1, pp. 148–49. Pantskhava, *Ocherki* (1969), p. 18; this law was extended to Imereti in 1821 (Berdzenishvili et al., *Istoriia Gruzii,* p. 450.

60. Khoshtaria, *Ocherki,* pp. 86–87; Avaliani, *Krest'ianskii vopros,* vol. 1, pp. 14–144.

61. Antelava, *Gosudarstvennye krest'iane,* vol. 1, p. 433.

62. Berdzenishvili et al., *Istoriia Gruzii,* pp. 424–25.

63. Rhinelander, "Incorporation of the Caucasus," p. 136. The most complete account of the revolt is O. P. Markova, *Vosstanie v Kakhetii 1812 g.* (Moscow, 1951).

64. Rhinelander, "Incorporation of the Caucasus," pp. 158–59. That same year an Orthodox seminary was opened in Tiflis.

65. Berdzenishvili et al., *Istoriia Gruzii,* pp. 438–39. For the most complete account of the insurrection, see N. B. Makharadze, "Vosstanie v Imeretii 1819–20 gg.," *Materialy po istorii Gruzii i Kavkaza* (Tbilisi, 1942), vol. 3, pp. 3–184.

66. Kipiani, "Zapiski," 50:270–71; Antelava, "Iz istorii," p. 53. On the revolt, see Avaliani, *Krest'ianskii vopros,* vol. 1, pp. 162–64; and G. V. Khachapuridze, *Guriiskoe vosstanie v 1841 godu* (Tiflis, 1931).

67. Pantskhava, *Ocherki* (1969), pp. 24–25, 27; Avaliani, *Krest'ianskii vopros,* vol. 1, pp. 136–38; *Akty,* vol. 10, p. 21.

68. Avaliani, *Krest'ianskii vopros,* vol. 1, p. ix.

69. See Sh. A. Meskhia, *Goroda i gorodskoi stroi feodal'noi Gruzii XVII–XVIII vv.* (Tbilisi, 1956) for an overview of Georgian urban history. On medieval Russian towns, see Lawrence N. Langer, "The Medieval Russian Town," in Michael F. Hamm, ed., *The City in Russian History* (Lexington: University of Kentucky Press, 1976), pp. 11–33.

70. Erekle II held 1,589 serf households in Tiflis, and among his serfs were *aznaurni* and the most powerful merchants and craftsmen of the capital, the *mokalakebi.* The Imeretian king, a considerably poorer monarch, held 110 serf households in Kutaisi in the early nineteenth century. Through the catholicos at Mtskheta, the Georgian church directly owned 198 serf households in Tiflis, and the Armenian catholicos at Echmiadzin owned 49. Noble families owned 724 serf households in Tiflis in 1783; the Mukhranbatoni and Tsitsishvili were among the large proprietors in Tiflis, and the Amilakhvari dominated in Gori. The family of the Armenian *melik-mamasakhlisi* of Tiflis, Agha Bebutov, held more than 65 households in the capital (Meskhia, *Goroda,* pp. 147–48, 150–52, 159).

71. For detailed analysis of the governance of Georgian towns, see Meskhia, *Goroda,* pp. 244–321.

72. Ibid., pp. 170–72, 177–78. A royal decree was required to raise an ordinary merchant or craftsman to the exalted rank of *mokalake.*

73. Ibid., p. 187. The principal tax paid by royal serfs, among them the *mokalakebi,* was *makhta,* usually paid in cash. All merchants and craftsmen paid *mali* and a host of special taxes: *samaspinszlo* to finance royal visits; *sursati* and *saleko* to maintain troops; *saruso* to support Russian troops; *satarguo* and *samouravo* to maintain the *mouravi;* and *maspad* to maintain public buildings, repair bridges, and so on.

74. The economy of Tiflis and other Georgian towns was based on the limited production of craftsmen and the trade of petty merchants. In the late eighteenth century there were 574 shops in the capital, of which 310 were occupied by craftsmen and 264 by merchants (Meskhia, *Goroda,* p. 126). Much of what was produced was sold directly by the producers themselves. What large-scale industry existed—powder mills, mines, some metallurgy, the mint—was owned by the king and usually rented out to middle-class entrepreneurs who then hired workers. The laborers in these "factories" were most often freemen rather than serf laborers, commonly used in Russia (ibid., p. 127). The enserfed craftsmen and merchants who made up the vast majority of the working population of the city were organized into guilds *(amkarebi).* Meskhia believes that such guild organizations existed in Georgia from the tenth century and were of local origin, not simply imitations of Muslim models (pp. 322–23). Other writers, like A. Haxthausen, E. Veindenbaum, N. Dunkel-Welling, Iu. Akhverdov, and N. Berdzenov, believe that these guilds were of later origin, probably first formed in the sixteenth or seventeenth centuries under foreign influence. Meskhia argues that the use of Georgian terms, such as *galatoztukhutsesi* (elder of the stone masons) and *mkervaltukhutsesi* (elder of the tailors), testifies to the existence of indigenous trade organizations in the medieval period. Only later did Turkish and Iranian domination lead to the use of foreign terms like *tabuni* and *asnafi* for the guilds. All ethnic groups were represented in the guilds, which monopolized and

regulated production in each profession, but most of the membership was Armenian. The *amkari* was headed by an *amkarbashi (ostati, ustabashi)*, who was usually elected by the membership. *Amkarbashi* of the largest guilds, however, were appointed by the king, and all guild leaders had to be either nominated or ratified by the king's officials (ibid., pp. 333–38).

75. Chkhetiia, *Tbilisi*, p. 145. Georgians made up a little over one-fifth of the population.

76. N. I. Badriashvili, *Tiflis*, vol. 1, *Ot osnovaniia goroda do XIX v.* (Tiflis, 1934), p. 124.

77. Meskhia, *Goroda*, pp. 239–40. The nobles wished to limit the rights of merchants to serf ownership. Instead of allowing them to buy entire households or even villages, merchants were to be restricted to buying one or two domestic servants.

78. *Polnoe sobranie zakonov*, vol. 15, no. 13,369; Chkhetiia, *Tbilisi*, pp. 259, 313–17.

79. Khachapuridze, *K istorii Gruzii*, p. 464.

80. Chkhetiia, *Tbilisi*, pp. 261, 263–64, 270. Akhverdov's brief was later published as *Tiflisskie amkary* (Tiflis, 1883). The decline in the number of *amkarebi* was due in part to the abolition of merchant guilds and in part to the merging of many craft guilds.

81. Chkhetiia, *Tbilisi*, pp. 293–438.

82. M. K. Rozhkova, *Ekonomicheskaia politika tsarskogo pravitel'stva na srednem vostoke vo vtoroi chetverti XIX veka i russkaia burzhuaziia* (Moscow-Leningrad, 1949), pp. 80–81; I. G. Antelava, E. A. Ordzhonikidze, and E. V. Khoshtaria, *K voprosu o genezise i razvitii kapitalizma v sel'skom khoziaistve i promyshlennosti Gruzii* (Tbilisi, 1967), p. 85; Walter Pintner, *Russian Economic Policy Under Nicholas I* (Ithaca, N.Y.: Cornell University Press, 1967), p. 43n. Several skilled workers came from France to work for Castella, but most of the workers—usually fifteen to twenty but sometimes as many as fifty—were local. Most of the machinery, of course, was imported.

83. Rozhkova, *Ekonomicheskaia politika*, pp. 51–52.

84. Ibid., pp. 86, 93.

85. Firuz Kazemzadeh, "Russian Penetration of the Caucasus," in Taras Hunczak, ed., *Russian Imperialism from Ivan the Great to the Revolution* (New Brunswick, N.J.: Rutgers University Press, 1974), p. 254. Kazemzadeh argues in this essay that trade considerations influenced Russian expansion into the Caucasus but that "trade with Asia was not an end but rather a means to political domination. The economic motive may have been important for a number of individual merchants, but they exercised almost no influence on government policy" (p. 254). While other than purely mercantile motives certainly played a role in Russian expansion into the Caucasus, Kazemzadeh's quotation to prove his point shows the importance of economic considerations and does not demonstrate a strict separation between economic and political ends and means.

86. Rozhkova, *Ekonomicheskaia politika*, pp. 94–95. Kazemzadeh, "Russian Penetration," pp. 254–55.

87. Chkhetiia, *Tbilisi*, pp. 224 (citing *Syn otechestva* 44, no. 38, pp. 44–45), 224n, 225. As part of his colonial policy, Kankrin planned to send Russian peasants to settle in Georgia, and Ermolov was forced to inform him that the treasury owned no free land in Georgia for such settlers (Khachapuridze, *K istorii Gruzii*, p. 140).

88. Rozhkova, *Ekonomicheskaia politika*, pp. 96–101.

89. Ibid., pp. 151, 274.

90. Chkhetiia, *Tbilisi*, p. 102n.

91. Ibid., p. 103.

92. *Akty*, vol. 10, no. 10, p. 9; Rhinelander, "Incorporation of the Caucasus," pp. 341, 321; *Akty*, vol. 10, p. 355. The numbers of students doubled by 1852: 3,000 boys, almost 300 girls (*Akty*, vol. 10, p. 897). Princess Vorontsova organized the St. Nino Philanthropic Society to open schools for poor girls; five were operating by 1852. Nine schools were established for the Muslims. The Armenian patriarch, Nerses, who in 1825 had opened a private Armenian school, the Nersesian Jemaran, again found financial support among the Armenian merchants and organized a commercial *gimnaziia* in 1851. The schools, though not of high quality, managed to teach their pupils Russian as well as two local languages. In Tiflis Georgian and Azeri were studied, and in Kutaisi Georgian and Turkish. Armenian may also have been available; it had been added to the curriculum of the Tiflis nobles' *gimnaziia* in 1831 (Rhinelander, "Incorporation of the Caucasus," pp. 312–32). For a treatment of education in Tiflis in midcentury, see Chkhetiia, *Tbilisi*, pp. 363–93.

93. Rozhkova, *Ekonomicheskaia politika*, pp. 285–88, 294.

94. Konstantin Bukh, "Moskovskoe torgovoe predpriatie v Tiflise, 1846–1854," *Russkaia starina* 53 (November 1886): 383–84.

95. Ibid., pp. 388, 389; Khachapuridze, *K istorii Gruzii*, p. 464.

96. A. V. Fadeev, "Razvitie kapitalizma vshir' v poreformennoi Rossii," *Doklady i soobshcheniia Instituta Istorii*, no. 10, 1956, p. 11.

97. Chkhetiia, *Tbilisi*, p. 206; Khachapuridze, *K istorii Gruzii*, p. 464.

CHAPTER 5

1. For a discussion of gentry opinion on the reform, especially the liberal abolitionist program, see Terence Emmons, *The Russian Landed Gentry and the Peasant Emancipation of 1861* (Cambridge, England: Cambridge University Press, 1968). The Russian literature on the peasant emancipation is extensive. The most respected Soviet account is that of P. A. Zaionchkovskii, *Otmena krepostnogo prava v Rossii*, 3d ed. (Moscow, 1968). For a Western study of the bureaucratic evolution of the peasant reform, see Daniel Field, *The End of Serfdom: Nobility and Bureaucracy in Russia, 1855–1861* (Cambridge, Mass.: Harvard University Press, 1976).

2. Alfred J. Rieber, *The Politics of Autocracy: Letters of Alexander II to Prince A. I. Bariatinskii, 1857–1864* (Paris, 1966), p. 71.

3. Kipiani, "Zapiski," 51:68; Sh. K. Chkhetiia, ed., *Dokumenty po istorii Gruzii. Seriia II. Tom I: Gruziia v period burzhuaznykh reform (1862–1872), Chast' pervaia (1862–1866)* (Tbilisi, 1960), p. xviii.

4. O. K. Zhordaniia, *K voprosu o revoliutsionnoi situatsii v Gruzii v kontse 50-kh–nachale 60-kh godov XIX veka* (Tbilisi, 1971), p. 72; Berdzenishvili et al., *Istoriia Gruzii*, vol. 1, pp. 482–85.

5. Avaliani, *Krest'ianskii vopros*, vol. 1, p. 175; for an account of the revolt in Samegrelo, see pp. 166–75. P. V. Gugushvili, *Sel'skoe khoziaistvo i agrarnye otnoshenii*, vol. 2, *Otmena krepostnogo prava* (Tbilisi, 1950), p. xxv.

6. For evidence of peasant unrest in the years before the emancipation in Georgia, see Zhordaniia, *K voprosu*, pp. 70–113. Following the lead of historians like M. V. Nechkina, Zhordaniia attempts to show that a "revolutionary situation" existed in Georgia, which contributed to the government's resolve to emancipate the serfs. He

produces much evidence of peasant discontents—flight from landlords, complaints to officials, and refusals to pay dues—but it is clear that these incidents were isolated and uncoordinated. Peasant discontents, fostered by the landlords' attempts to get more income from peasants before emancipation, did not lead to a massive peasant movement, except in Samegrelo in 1857.

It does not appear that the emancipation in Georgia was primarily motivated by a developing "revolutionary situation," as Zhordaniia proposes. But it is clear that for at least a decade before the reform, the question of liberation of the landlord peasants, in Niko Nikoladze's words, "stirred all elements of Georgian society" ("Os-vobozhdenie krest'ian v Gruzii," *Kolokol,* no. 198, June 15, 1865). And peasant protests were connected in many minds with the hoped-for reform. Nikoladze believed, for example, that rumors of liberation at the beginning of 1858 led to an increase of peasant revolts. Motivations are difficult to isolate, but it seems likely that the peasants' sporadic resistance and the officials' anticipation of further trouble played a part in the administration's determination to carry out the reform against the expressed wishes of the local nobility. Another important consideration was the administration's plan to integrate as fully as possible the Transcaucasian provinces into the all-Russian governmental system; to eliminate, as much as Transcaucasian conditions would permit, local peculiarities and deviations from the Russian patterns of landholding and peasant-noble relations.

7. Avaliani, *Krest'ianskii vopros,* vol. 1, p. 189; Chkhetiia, *Dokumenty,* p. xix. Despite the government's request, the nobles of Tiflis province did not bother electing the district committees, preferring to work through their traditional assemblies (Gugushvili, *Sel'skoe khoziaistvo,* pp. 13–17). Bariatinskii conceded on this point, though it contradicted his instructions from St. Petersburg and the model adopted in Russia.

8. For descriptions of these changes see the works of Archil Iakobis dze Pants-khava: *K voprosu o razvitii agrarnykh otnoshenii v doreformennoi vostochnoi Gruzii* (Moscow, 1957), *Ocherki* (1965), *Ocherki* (1969), and *Voprosy agrarnoi istorii Gruzii pervoi poloviny XIX veka* (Tbilisi, 1973).

9. Statistics on noble serfowning in Tiflis province (Avaliani, *Krest'ianskii vopros,* vol. 1, pp. 416–17):

No male serfs	2 nobles
Fewer than 21 male serfs	869 nobles
21–100 male serfs	729 nobles
101–500 male serfs	137 nobles
501–1000 male serfs	12 nobles
More than 100 male serfs	2 nobles
Total	1,751 nobles

In the early 1860s the landlord peasants numbered 122,120 in Tiflis province (17,261 households). They lived on 3,242 noble estates and made up 20.5 percent of the peasant population of the province in 1866; church peasants made up 12.9 percent; state peasants, 65.5 percent. Of the total population of Tiflis province, peasants made up 86 percent, nobles 3.5 percent (ibid., pp. 417, 419).

In Tiflis province 14 percent of the serfowners (214 nobles) owned serfs without land; these serfs lived on state lands or lands of other landlords.

In Kutaisi province (Kutaisi, Shorapani, Ozurgeti, and Racha *uezdy*), there were 4,785 landlord families at the time of emancipation with 48,785 peasant households and 96,732 male serfs. More than three-quarters of Kutaisi nobles held fewer than 21 male serfs:

Fewer than 21 male serfs	3,776 nobles
21–100 male serfs	831 nobles
101–500 male serfs	167 nobles
501–1000 male serfs	7 nobles
More than 1000 male serfs	4 nobles
Total	4,785 nobles

The majority of peasants in Kutaisi province were landlord peasants, whereas the majority in Tiflis province were state peasants. Emancipation in Kutaisi province liberated 181,270 serfs of both sexes, compared to 106,634 in Tiflis province (ibid., p. 512).

10. The number of peasant serfs mortgaged from 1848 to 1863—4,316 households in eastern Georgia alone, 26 percent of the landlord peasant households—rose on the eve of the reform to 4,848 households (29.5 percent). This is considerably lower than comparable figures for European Russia, where two-thirds of landlord serfs were mortgaged on the eve of the emancipation. More than 30,000 peasants, however, had been mortgaged in eastern Georgia by the time of the reform. The money raised by these mortgages was not, in general, invested in agriculture but was spent on personal consumption (ibid., p. 418; Geroid Tanqueray Robinson, *Rural Russia under the Old Regime* (New York: Macmillan, 1932), pp. 56–57). In a recent Soviet study, a group of Georgian scholars estimate that by January 1, 1863, the Tiflis provincial nobility had mortgaged 30,714 serfs (one-fourth of the total) and 32 percent of their property (Antelava, Ordzhonikidze, and Khoshtaria, *K voprosu o genezise*, p. 32).

11. See, for example, Tsereteli, *Perezhitoe;* and the short novel by Il'ia Chavchavadze, *katsia adamiani?* (Is This Fellow a Man?), published in 1863.

12. Later the tsar ordered the treasury to set aside 2,000,000 silver rubles as compensation for the nobles' loss, not only of the land but of the peasants' dues as well (Zhordaniia, *K voprosu*, p. 125; Gugushvili, *Sel'skoe khoziaistvo*, pp. 16–17).

13. Chkhetiia, *Dokumenty*, p. xx.

14. G. Megrelishvili, *Gruzinskaia obshchestvenno-ekonomicheskaia mysl' vtoroi poloviny 19-ogo veka i nachala 20-ogo veka* (Tbilisi, 1960), vol. 1, pp. 195–96. The full text of Kipiani's report can be found in Georgian and Russian in Gugushvili, *Sel'skoe khoziaistvo*, pp. 28–117.

Dmitri Ivanovich Kipiani (Qipiani) (1814–1887), a member of the small-landholding nobility of Tiflis province, had participated in the conspiracy against the tsarist authorities in 1832. Having made peace with the bureaucracy, he entered state service and rose rapidly until by 1859 he was a member of Viceroy Bariatinskii's council. From 1864 to 1870 he served as marshal of the Tiflis nobility, and from 1885 to 1886 as marshal of the Kutaisi nobility. When the rector of the Tiflis seminary was killed by a former student, the exarch of Georgia, Pav'l, anathematized Georgia. Kipiani wrote a strong letter of reproach to the exarch. Arrested and exiled to Stavropol, he was mysteriously murdered, possibly by tsarist agents. His memoirs exist in Georgian (Tbilisi, 1930) and in Russian ("Zapiski," *Russkaia starina*, 49–53 [March–September, 1886]). A biography appeared in Georgian during the Soviet period: S. Khundadze, *dmitri qipiani* (Tbilisi, 1936).

15. Chkhetiia, *Dokumenty*, p. xx; Kipiani, "Zapiski," 53:619–20. It should be remembered that the noble assembly included only the wealthy nobles, those who could meet the property qualification for membership. In the Caucasus a nobleman was required to have an annual income or equivalent holdings to produce two

thousand rubles. His holdings had to be in land. These requirements, which applied also to Bessarabia and the Crimea, greatly limited the number of nobles eligible for participation in the noble assemblies (Baron S. A. Korf, *Dvorianstvo i ego soslovnoe upravlenie za stoletie 1762–1855 godov* [St. Petersburg, 1906], pp. 542–43.

16. The "Svod dvadtsati odnogo mneniia dvukhsot soroka gruzinskikh pomeshchikov po krest'ianskomu voprosu" can be found in Sh. Chkhetiia, *K istorii krest'ianskoi reformy v Gruzii* (Tbilisi, 1950), pp. 137–82; his plan for reform is in the same volume, pp. 182–290).

17. Gugushvili, *Sel'skoe khoziaistvo,* pp. 54, 52, 56; Megrelishvili, *Gruzinskaia obshchestvenno-ekonomicheskaia mysl',* vol. 1, pp. 202–3.

18. Gugushvili, *Sel'skoe khoziaistvo,* pp. 60, 62, 64.

19. Ibid., p. 66; Avaliani, *Krest'ianskii vopros,* vol. 1, p. 258.

20. The *khizani* was a legal person with rights and obligations noted in a contract, but had no hereditary claim to the land he worked (Avaliani, *Krest'ianskii vopros,* vol. 1, p. 336).

21. Ibid., p. 267. In Kipiani's plan those peasants who had no land, such as domestic servants, would be freed personally and would have to make their own way in the world. The nobles hoped to delay the final liberation of household serfs as long as possible so as not to be deprived of their servants. The full text of Kipiani's "Project for a Law on the Emancipation from Serfdom of Peasants in Georgia, i.e., Tiflis Province" has been published in Gugushvili, *Sel'skoe khoziaistvo,* pp. 118–28.

22. Kipiani, "Zapiski," 53:624–28.

23. Megrelishvili, *Gruzinskaia obshchestvenno-ekonomicheskaia mysl',* vol. 1, p. 186. This is noted in Baron Nikolai's report to the Caucasian Committee of February 28, 1864.

24. Kipiani, "Zapiski," 53:628.

25. Megrelishvili, *Gruzinskaia obshchestvenno-ekonomicheskaia mysl',* vol. 1, p. 186. Baron Aleksandr P. Nikolai, who replaced A. F. Kruzenshtern as head of the viceroy's administration and as chairman of the Transcaucasian Committee for the Reorganization of Landlord Peasantry in October 1863, served as the viceroy's second in command until 1875. His memoirs are a valuable source on the emancipation of the serfs in Transcaucasia from the point of view of a high official in the state bureaucracy ("Vospominaniia iz moei zhizni: Krest'ianskaia reforma v Zakavkazskom krae," *Russkii arkhiv* 2, no. 5 [1892]: 91–125, no. 6, 222–46, no. 8, 445–78).

26. Separate proposals were submitted by a "minority" of fourteen noblemen, headed by Grigol and Alexander Orbeliani, and privately by Prince Ivan Bagration-Mukhranskii, but they did not differ in substance from the "majority" report (Chkhetiia, *Dokumenty,* pp. xxi–xxiii). A few nobles, considered by Soviet historians to have been relatively progressive, were willing to concede the peasants their household plots. One of them, K. Mamatsev, saw the necessary connection between real freedom and land and supported his view with a patriotic argument: "A person without land cannot be interested in the happiness of his country; for him there is no permanent fatherland, he is a cosmopolitan" (ibid., p. xxv). N. Chavchavadze sent in his "Zapiski" noting that "without land the peasant cannot exist" and arguing for personal and economic independence for the peasant (ibid., pp. xxiv–xxv; Megrelishvili, *Gruzinskaia obshchestvenno-ekonomicheskaia mysl',* vol. 1, p. 254). Chavchavadze's "Zapiski" was published in *saistorio moambe* 3 (1947), but this issue was not available to me.

27. This letter can be found in Antelava, Ordzhonikidze, and Khoshtaria, *K voprosu,* p. 34. Bariatinskii left the Caucasus in the spring of 1862 but retained the title of viceroy until December 1862. Prince G. Z. Orbeliani served as acting viceroy until the grand duke's arrival.

28. Nikolai, "Vospominaniia," 2, no. 5, p. 99.

29. Avaliani, *Krest'ianskii vopros,* vol. 1, pp. 308, 309.

30. Ibid., p. 412.

31. Chkhetiia, *Dokumenty,* pp. xxx–xxxi, ccviii.

32. Avaliani, *Krest'ianskii vopros,* vol. 1, p. 315.

33. Ibid.

34. Ibid., pp. 318, 319–20, 321–22.

35. Nikolai, "Vospominaniia," 2, no. 6, p. 229.

36. Esadze, *Istoricheskaia zapiska,* vol. 1, p. 424. A *ktseva* was slightly less than an acre or 4,083 square meters.

37. For the details on the minimal allotments permitted in Russia, see Robinson, *Rural Russia,* pp. 81–82. Vasilii Dmitrievich Mochalov, *Krest'ianskoe khoziaistvo v Zakavkaz'e k kontsu XIX v.* (Moscow, 1958), pp. 50–51.

38. Mochalov, *Krest'ianskoe khoziaistvo,* p. 51.

39. Ibid., pp. 54, 56; Avaliani, *Krest'ianskii vopros,* vol. 1, p. 424.

40. Mochalov, *Krest'ianskoe khoziaistvo,* p. 61.

41. Ibid., p. 59.

42. For a clear explanation in English, see the translation of N. M. Druzhinin's article in *Istoriia SSSR,* vol. 2, *1861–1917: Period kapitalizma,* 2d ed. (Moscow, 1965), pp. 23–33, published as "The Emancipation Legislation" in Terence Emmons, ed., *Emancipation of the Russian Serfs* (New York: D. C. Heath, 1970), pp. 19–25.

43. Mochalov, *Krest'ianskoe khoziaistvo,* p. 60.

44. Zaionchkovskii, *Otmena,* p. 335; Avaliani, *Krest'ianskii vopros,* vol. 1, p. 427. In the first ten years after the reform only 1,220 peasants in Georgia—all of them in Tiflis province—used their right to redeem their allotments with the help of the government. Many more peasants in both Tiflis and Kutaisi provinces tried to redeem their land without governmental help. This anomaly stems from a provision in the redemption for Transcaucasia that placed ruble limits on payments by the government. Thus, while in Russia the government paid 80 percent of the redemption sum and the peasant paid 20 percent, in Shurapani and Racha *uezdy* (in Kutaisi province), for example, the government paid only fifteen rubles a *ktseva* or about 30 percent of the redemption sum. With peasants obligated to pay 70 percent, landlords were unlikely to take the risk (Esadze, *Istoricheskaia zapiska,* vol. 1, pp. 434–35).

45. Zaionchkovskii, *Otmena,* p. 332; Antelava, Ordzhonikidze, and Khoshtaria, *K voprosu,* p. 36. Peasants in Russia lost about 13 percent of their lands on average; in the black earth and steppe provinces the percentage rose to 23.3. See Mochalov, *Krest'ianskoe khoziaistvo,* p. 52; Avaliani, *Krest'ianskii vopros,* vol. 1, p. 421.

46. Avaliani, *Krest'ianskii vopros,* vol. 1, p. 421; Mochalov, *Krest'ianskoe khoziaistvo,* pp. 52–53; Zaionchkovskii, *Otmena,* p. 242; Iu. Kacharava et al., *Istoriia Gruzii,* 2 vols. (Tbilisi, 1973), vol. 2, p. 23. In European Russia the average male serf had held 5.1 desiatinas of land prior to the reform, a figure that declined to 2.7 desiatinas by 1900 (Francis M. Watters, "The Peasant and the Village Commune," in Wayne S. Vucinich, ed., *The Peasant in Nineteenth Century Russia* [Stanford, Calif.: Stanford University Press, 1968], p. 149).

47. Avaliani, *Krest'ianskii vopros,* vol. 1, 339–40, 421.

48. Ibid., pp. 340–41.

49. Zaionchkovskii, *Otmena*, pp. 330–31.

50. Avaliani, *Krest'ianskii vopros,* vol. 2, pp. 46, 49–50.

51. Orest Semin, *Velikaia godovshchina: Agrarnyi vopros i krest'ianskaia reforma na Kavkaze* (Kiev, 1911), p. 35; Zaionchkovskii, *Otmena*, p. 338.

52. Chkhetiia, *Dokumenty*, p. 232; Gugushvili, *Sel'skoe khoziaistvo*, pp. 279–80; Esadze, *Istoricheskaia zapiska,* vol. 1, p. 344. The state payment to the nobles satisfied one of the demands of the Georgian nobility. In his report to the assembly of nobles of Tiflis province in April 1863, Dmitri Kipiani had argued that "the spirit of the time demands that since the personal freedom of the peasants is restored in view of the benefits to the state, the state ought to incur the unavoidable costs" (P. B. Gugushvili, *Razvitie sel'skogo khoziaistva v Gruzii i Zakavkaz'e v XIX–XX vv.* [Tbilisi, 1968], vol. 1, p. 27).

53. Mochalov, *Krest'ianskoe khoziaistvo*, p. 63.

54. Zaionchkovskii, *Otmena*, p. 333.

55. Avaliani, *Krest'ianskii vopros,* vol. 1, pp. 410–12.

56. Zhordaniia, *K voprosu*, pp. 66, 67, 73, 422. The number of complaints about peasants not working was especially high in the years 1864–1866 in Gori *uezd*, Tiflis province; by law the "temporarily obligated" peasants were supposed to pay all customary dues to their lords until January 1, 1866. The consequences of reform, what he termed the "cutting off" of land, were discussed by A. Kipshidze in an article written during the peasant rebellion of the early twentieth century:

> It would be wrong to forget that up to the reform all landlord land, including forests and pastures, was in the hands of the peasants. The landlords, since they did not engage in their own economic activity, did not need these lands and willingly granted all their lands to their peasants. With the issuance of the reform this situation fundamentally changed. The peasants were given, by household, a definite quantity of land, with access to the rest of the landlord's land forbidden. The small landholding of the noble proprietors in Tiflis and Kutaisi Provinces, on the one hand, and the establishment of precise norms for the household allotments of the Georgian peasants served later as the principal cause of the land impoverishment among peasants in the two Transcaucasian provinces in which serfdom had existed ("Ocherk krepostnogo prava i krest'ianskaia reforma v Gruzii," *Kavkazskii vestnik* 6 (1902):16–17; cited in Mochalov, *Krest'ianskoe khoziaistvo*, p. 54n).

57. Tsereteli, *Perezhitoe*, p. 153.

CHAPTER 6

1. *Droeba,* 1876, no. 48; Antelava, Ordzhonikidze, and Khoshtaria, *K voprosu,* p. 66n.

2. For differing views on the agrarian crisis in the Russian empire in the late nineteenth century, see James Y. Simms, Jr., "The Crisis in Russian Agriculture at the End of the Nineteenth Century: A Different View," *Slavic Review* 36, no. 3 (September 1977): 377–98; G. M. Hamburg, "The Crisis in Russian Agriculture: A Comment," *Slavic Review* 37, no. 3 (September 1978): 481–86; James Y. Simms, Jr., "On

Missing the Point: A Rejoinder," ibid., pp. 487–90; and G. M. Hamburg, "The Russian Nobility on the Eve of the 1905 Revolution," *The Russian Review* 38, no. 3 (July 1979): 323–38.

3. Antelava, Ordzhonikidze, and Khoshtaria, *K voprosu,* p. 66.

4. F. Makharadze, *Gruziia v deviatnadtsatom stoletii. Kratkii istoricheskii ocherk* (Tiflis, 1933), p. 69. A one-day census of Tiflis was held on March 25, 1876. Of the 104,024 inhabitants:

37,610 (36.1%) were Armenian
30,813 (29.6%) were Russian
22,156 (21.3%) were Georgian
13,445 (12.9%) were Germans, Iranians, Tatars, Greeks, Jews, and others.

(*Putevoditel' po Tiflisu* [Tiflis, 1896], p. 39).

5. For more on the Armenians of Russia in the nineteenth century, see Ronald Grigor Suny, "Images of the Armenians in the Russian Empire," in Richard G. Hovannisian, ed., *The Armenian Image in History and Literature* (Malibu, Calif.: Undena, 1981), pp. 105–37.

6. Chkhetiia, *Tbilisi,* pp. 208–9.

7. Ibid., pp. 209, 214.

8. Khoshtaria, *Ocherki,* p. 100. Those with two to four workers made up 21 percent, and those with five to eight workers 0.3 percent.

9. Ibid., pp. 165–66, 166n. The nationality of the remaining 1,784 Tiflis merchants from the 1897 tally (24.5 percent) is not given, many of them may have been foreigners. The foreign capital was primarily attracted to the extractive industries—copper, manganese, and oil in Baku, refineries in Batumi. The single area where native Georgian nobles were able to penetrate the world of capitalist production was in the manganese industry, where they outnumbered all other ethnic groups.

10. S. Maksimov, *Russkiia gory i kavkazskie gortsy* (n.p., 1873), p. 56.

11. P. I. Kovalevskii, *Kavkaz* (St. Petersburg, 1914), vol. 1, p. 234.

12. Oliver Wardrop, *The Kingdom of Georgia; Notes of travel in a land of women, wine, and song; To which are appended historical, literary and political sketches, specimens of the national music, and a compendious bibliography* (London, 1888), pp. 13–14.

13. Esadze, *Istoricheskaia zapiska,* vol. 2, pp. 42–43.

14. *Kolokol,* no. 204, September 15, 1986.

15. Chkhetiia, *Tbilisi,* p. 327.

16. Chkhetiia, *Tbilisi,* pp. 277–79; Kacharava et al., *Istoriia Gruzii,* vol. 2, p. 28. After 1867, craft *amkarebi* were united under an *uprava* (board) made up of the *ustabashebi* and a chief *starshina* (elder). But the board could not call a general meeting of the *amkarebi* without police permission, and individual *amkarebi* lost their judicial powers, their authority over initiation of apprentices, and the ability to rid themselves of an undesired leader. All these prerogatives were given to the *uprava.* Whereas earlier an *amkari* had been able to install its own *ustabashi,* now the elected leader had to be approved by the governor.

17. Walter Hanchett, "Tsarist Statutory Regulation of Municipal Government in the Nineteenth Century," in Hamm, *City in Russian History,* pp. 102–7; Esadze, *Istoricheskaia zapiska,* vol. 2, pp. 72–73. Baku received municipal self-government in 1878 (A. Sh. Mil'man, *Politicheskii stroi Azerbaidzhana v XIX-nachale XX vekov* [Baku, 1966], p. 208). Kutaisi and Batumi received it in 1888, Sukhumi and Poti in

1892, and Gori, Dusheti, Akhaltsikhe, Akhalkalaki, Sighnaghi, and Telavi in 1894 (Kacharava et al. *Istoriia Gruzii,* vol. 2, p. 29).

18. For a theoretical discussion of the role of social communication in the formation of nationality and nationalism, see Karl Deutsch, *Nationalism and Social Communication: An Inquiry into the Foundations of Nationality* (Cambridge, Mass.: MIT Press, 1953).

19. Miroslav Hroch, *Die Vorkämpfer der nationalen Bewegung bei den kleinen Völkern Europas* (Prague, 1968); *Social Preconditions of National Revival in Europe: A Comparative Analysis of the Social Composition of Patriotic Groups Among the Smaller European Nations* (New York: Cambridge University Press, 1985); Elie Kedourie, *Nationalism* (London, 1960); Hobsbawm and Ranger, *The Invention of Tradition;* Geoff Eley, "Nationalism and Social History," *Social History* 6, no. 1 (January 1981): 83–107.

20. D. L. Vateishvili, *Russkaia obshchestvennaia mysl',* p. 46.

21. I. Dzhavakhov (Javakhishvili), "Gruziia," in *Entsiklopedicheskii slovar' russkogo bibliograficheskogo instituta Granat,* vol. 17, p. 204.

22. As literary critic Georgii Dzhibladze put it: "The lyrical poetry of Besiki, Guramishvili, David the Rector, Tsaritsa Ketevan and others, the *Wisdom of Falsehoods* of Sulkhan-Saba Orbeliani—all these represented something very closely related to the creations of the Romantics" (*Romantiki i realisty v gruzinskoi literature XIX veka* [Tbilisi, 1963], p. 29).

23. Niko Nikoladze, "Vospominaniia o shestidesiatikh godakh," *Katorga i ssylka* 33 (1927): 29.

24. Ibid., p. 34.

25. Ibid., p. 45.

26. Tsereteli, *Perezhitoe,* pp. 140–44.

27. Chkhetiia, *Tbilisi,* p. 335.

28. *Gruziia v deviatnadtsatom stoletii, Kratkii istoricheskii ocherk* (Tiflis, 1933), p. 90.

29. *Russkaia shkola* 1 (1901): 76. The percentage of schools teaching a local Caucasian language dropped from 33.3 in 1879 to 28 in 1888 and then precipitously to 9 in 1898. The percentage of schools teaching all subjects in Russian rose from 49.8 in 1879 to 71 in 1888 and 91 in 1898.

30. Georgii Mikhailovich Tumanov, *Kharakteristiki i vospominaniia, Zametki kavkazskogo khronikera* (Tiflis, 1900), vol. 1, pp. 178–79.

31. Dobroliubov's influential essay, "What Is Oblomovism?" used the apathetic hero of Goncharov's novel, *Oblomov,* as an example of a "superfluous man" incapable of taking action as required by Russia's situation.

32. Tumanov, *Kharakteristiki,* vol. 1, p. 170.

33. The newspaper *droeba* sold between 400 and 500 copies in the 1860s, primarily in Tiflis; indeed, early in the 1870s the only subscriber in Gori was the nobles' club (Mgaloblishvili, *Vospominaniia,* p. 57; Chkhetiia, *Tbilisi,* p. 348).

34. See, for example, G. A. Tarkhan-Mouravi's article, "The Causes of Our Poverty," *droeba* 6, 8 (1870); Megrelishvili, *Gruzinskaia obshchestvenno-ekonomicheskaia mysl',* vol. 1, pt. 2, pp. 126–40.

35. V. S. Bakhtadze, *Ocherki po istorii gruzinskoi obshchestvenno-ekonomicheskoi mysli (60–90 gody XIX stoletiia)* (Tbilisi, 1960), p. 81. On Nikoladze's Russian journalism, see G. D. Dzhavakhishvili (Javakhishvili), *Niko Nikoladze i russkaia zhurnalistika* (Tbilisi, 1978).

36. "Movement of the Working People in Western Europe and Thoughts about Our People," *iveria* 41 (1877); Bakhtadze, *Ocherki,* p. 54.

37. Tumanov, *Kharakteristki,* vol. 3 (1907), p. 174; Akaki Surguladze, *kartuli sazogadoebrivi azri XIX saukunis meore nakhevarshi* (Tbilisi, 1973), pp. 283–95.

38. Bakhtadze, *Ocherki,* p. 161.

39. Niko Nikoladze, "Osvobozhdenie N. G. Chernyshevskogo," *Byloe* 1, no. 9 (September 1906): 244.

40. Tumanov, *Kharakteristiki,* vol. 2 (1905), p. 110.

41. Ibid., pp. 91–92; Kacharava et al., *Istoriia Gruzii,* vol. 2, p. 29.

42. Mgaloblishvili, *Vospominaniia,* p. 57. Nikolai Stankevich (1813–1840) was a leading noble intellectual in the 1830s, the organizer of an influential circle in Moscow, and a proponent of Hegelianism.

43. Megrelishvili, *Gruzinskaia obshchestvenno-ekonomicheskaia mysl',* vol. 1, pp. 460–461.

44. I. S. Dzhabadari, "Protsess 50-ti. (Vserossiiskaia Sotsial'no-Revoliutsionnaia Organizatsiia) 1874–1877 gg.," *Byloe,* 2, no. 9 (21) (September 1907): 185–86.

45. P. V. Gugushvili, *Karl Marks v gruzinskoi publitsistike i obshchestvennosti do 1898 goda* (Tbilisi, 1963), pp. 149–51. The members of this early populist circle included Varlam Cherkezishvili, I. Jabadari, G. Zdanovich, Mikhail Chikoidze, and Prince Aleksandr Tsitsianov.

46. Dzhabadari, "Protsess 50-ti," *Byloe* 2, no. 8 (20) (August 1907): 9, 11.

47. Gugushvili, *Karl Marks,* p. 103.

48. Dzhabadari, "Protsess 50-ti," *Byloe* 2, no. 9 (21) (September 1907): 177–78.

49. E. Korol'chuk, "Pis'ma G. F. Zdanovicha," *Krasnyi arkhiv,* no. 1 (20) (1927): 189; Megrelishvili, *Gruzinskaia obshchestvenno-ekonomicheskaia mysl',* vol. 1, pp. 428–35; Zhakov, Sef, and Khachapuridze, *Istoriia klassovoi bor'by,* pp. 80, 82.

50. Zhakov, Sef, and Khachapuridze, *Istoriia klassovoi bor'by,* pp. 37–39.

51. Antelava, *Gosudarstvennye krest'iane,* p. 146n.

52. Louise Nalbandian, *The Armenian Revolutionary Movement: The Development of Armenian Political Parties Through the Nineteenth Century* (Berkeley and Los Angeles: University of California Press, 1963), p. 137; Kristapor Mikaielian, "Bekorner im husherits," *Hairenik Amsakir* 2, no. 10 (August 1924): 56–57; Ronald Grigor Suny, "Populism, Nationalism and Marxism: The Origins of Revolutionary Parties Among the Armenians of the Caucasus," *Armenian Review* 32, no. 2-126 (June 1979): 134–51; Norman M. Naimark, *Terrorists and Social Democrats: The Russian Revolutionary Movement Under Alexander III* (Cambridge, Mass.: Harvard University Press, 1983), p. 116.

53. *Imedi,* no. 3 (1882).

54. Alexander Khatissian, "The Memoirs of a Mayor," *Armenian Review* 2, no. 3 (7) (September 1949): 43.

55. Zhakov, Sef, and Khachapuridze, *Istoriia klassovoi bor'by,* pp. 87–92; P. Makharadze, "rogor gavkhdi marksisti. (chemi magonebata erti gverdi)," *revoliutsiis matiane* 1 (March 1923): 73–74. Laghiashvili was condemned to death, but the sentence was commuted to twenty years' imprisonment. He was sent to Siberia but later escaped to the United States, where he became a citizen.

56. For accounts of these elections, see *Novoe obozrenie,* no. 2366, November 5, 1890, no. 2378, November 17, 1890, no. 3132, February 2, 1893, no. 3155, February 28, 1893, and no. 3167, March 12, 1893.

57. *Novoe obozrenie,* no. 3218, May 6, 1893. When Argutinskii-Dolgorukov

retired in September, Izmailov himself was chosen (62–8) to become mayor of Tiflis, the first mayor from the "third element." Izmailov was politically liberal but able to work with the bureaucracy. He was interested in developing the *samodeiatel'nost* of urban society, its "self-activity." A man of power and influence in Tiflis, he was responsible for building the theater, trolley lines, schools, and hospitals, and introducing insurance programs (Tumanov, *Kharakteristiki*, vol. 1, pp. 94–95).

58. D. M. Tumanov, *Zametki o gorodskom samoupravlenii na Kavkaze* (Tiflis, 1902), pp. 4, 22–23, 45–47.

59. Khatissian, "Memoirs of a Mayor," p. 43.

CHAPTER 7

1. In the first years after Stalin's death, when the possibility for such debate reappeared among historians, M. K. Dumbadze and Z. V. Anchabadze argued that there had been no significant capitalist production in Georgia before the 1860s. This view was supported by G. K. Bakradze in a detailed study of the coming of capitalism in industry in the post-Emancipation decades (G. K. Bakradze, *Vozniknovenie i razvitie kapitalisticheskoi promyshlennosti v Gruzii XIX veka* [Tbilisi, 1958]). In contrast to this postponement of the arrival of capitalism, a historian of the reign of Erekle II, A. A. Rogava, put forth the extreme proposition that capitalism actually came to Georgia in the late eighteenth century (A. A. Rogava, *Zachatki kapitalizma v Gruzii i politika Irakliia II* [Tbilisi, 1974]). Earlier, historical sociologist P. V. Gugushvili had defended the notion that the manufacturing enterprises of the late eighteenth century should be considered the foundation of capitalist production in Georgia, but most historians working on the question—I. G. Antelava, A. Ia. Pantskhava, E. A. Orjonikidze, E. V. Khoshtaria, D. A. Gogoladze, and M. M. Samsonadze—settled on dating the breakdown of "feudal" relations and the origins of capitalism to the first half of the nineteenth century.

2. Mochalov, *Krest'ianskoe khoziaistvo*, p. 441.

3. Mochalov, a Soviet authority on Transcaucasian agriculture, sums up the argument in favor of capitalist development in an appropriately cautious fashion:

> An investigation of the development of commercial agriculture in Transcaucasia leads one to the conclusion that commodity production in the rural economy of the area had been established almost everywhere toward the end of the nineteenth century. The natural economy in most places had moved into the background and in Georgia and Armenia wide areas of capitalist [i.e., commercial] agriculture had even managed to be developed (ibid., p. 450).

4. Ibid., p. 73.

5. I. I. Uturashvili, *Realizatsiia krest'ianskoi reformy v Gruzii* (Tbilisi, 1976), pp. 48–49.

6. Ibid., pp. 62–63.

7. Oragvelidze, "K voprosu o razvitii," pp. 38–39. One desiatina of land in Guria (Ozurgeti *uezd*) cost on the average 21 rubles, 16 kopeks in 1869–1879, and four times more—86 rubles, 48 kopeks—in the next decade (1877–1888). Prices of land rose 192.3 percent from 1891 to 1911 in Tiflis province and 110.5 percent in Kutaisi province (ibid., p. 40).

8. Uturashvili, *Realizatsiia*, pp. 150–51; Esadze, *Istoricheskaia zapiska*, vol. 1, pp. 422–23.

9. Antelava, *Gosudarstvennye krest'iane Gruzii*, vol. 2, pp. 44, 51–52.

10. Mochalov, *Krest'ianskoe khoziaistvo*, pp. 103–4; Orest Emin, *Velikaia godovshchina: Agrarnyi vopros i krest'ianskaia reforma na Kavkaze* (Kiev, 1911), p. 34; Robinson, *Rural Russia*, p. 34.

11. Antelava, *Gosudarstvennye krest'iane*, vol. 2, pp. 70–71.

12. Antelava, Ordzhonikidze, and Khoshtaria, *K voprosu*, p. 64.

13. Antelava, *Gosudarstvennye krest'iane*, vol. 2, pp. 74–75, 86; Uturashvili, *Realizatsiia*, p. 106.

14. Oragvelidze, "K voprosu," pp. 10, 24.

15. Ibid., p. 33; I. I. Vorontsov-Dashkov, *Vsepoddanneishaia zapiska po upravleniiu kavkazskim kraem generala adiutanta grafa Vorontsova-Dashkova* (St. Petersburg, 1907), p. 35.

16. *Novoe obozrenie*, no. 4141, January 20, 1896; Mochalov, *Krest'ianskoe khoziaistvo*, p. 139.

17. Antelava, *Gosudarstvennye krest'iane*, vol. 2, pp. 30–31.

18. *Kolokol*, no. 204, September 15, 1865.

19. Vorontsov-Dashkov, *Vsepoddanneishaia zapiska*, p. 26.

20. Antelava, Ordzhonikidze, and Khoshtaria, *K voprosu*, pp. 60–61.

21. Khoshtaria, *Ocherki*, pp. 175–76.

22. Ibid., pp. 46–47, 80; Gugushvili, *Karl Marks*, p. 38. For a treatment of artisans in central Russia at the turn of the century, see Victoria E. Bonnell, "The Roots of Rebellion in Urban Working-Class Life: A Study of Artisanal Trades in St. Petersburg and Moscow on the Eve of 1905," paper read at American Association for the Advancement of Slavic Studies annual meeting, New Haven, Conn., October 1979.

23. S. T. Arkomed (Gevork Gharajian), *Rabochee dvizhenie i sotsial-demokratiia na Kavkaze (s 80-kh godov po 1903 g.)*, 2nd ed., (Moscow-Petrograd, 1923), pp. 35–36.

24. Gugushvili, *Karl Marks*, p. 39.

25. Khoshtaria, *Ocherki*, pp. 181–85.

26. Ibid., p. 195. In the 1890s Georgians were almost 85 percent of the work force in the Chiatura mining district, 44 percent of the workers in the Tiflis railroad workshops (Slavs were over 50 percent, Armenians 6 percent), and 46 percent of the work force in five Batumi plants on which figures are available. Armenians made up the largest ethnic contingent among artisans in Tiflis (44 percent), followed by Georgians (33 percent) and Russians (11 percent).

27. S. Gulishambarov, *Obzor fabrik i zavodov Tiflisskoi gubernii* (Tiflis, 1888), p. 232; cited in Khoshtaria, *Ocherki*, p. 191.

28. Cited in Khoshtaria, *Ocherki*, pp. 34, 89.

29. *Droeba*, 1872, no. 15; F. Makharadze, *Ocherki revoliutsionnogo dvizheniia v Zakavkaz'i* (Tiflis, 1927), pp. 45, 47–48; Mikh. Chodrishvili, "chemi avtobiograpia," *revoliutsiis matiane* 4–5 (9–10) (1924), passim.

30. L. Asatiani, *Zhizn' Akakiia Tsereteli* (Tbilisi, 1971), p. 317; F. Makharadze, *K tridtsatiletiiu sushchestvovaniia tiflisskoi organizatsii: Podgotovitel'nyi period, 1870–1890 (Materialy)* (Tiflis, 1925), p. 18.

31. Khoshtaria, *Ocherki*, p. 207. All members of the Guzenko-Safranov circle were

Russian. For more on this circle, see Naimark, *Terrorists and Social Democrats*, pp. 188–89.

32. *Delo o Maksime Gor'kom: Materialy tiflisskogo gubernskogo zhandarmskogo upravleniia* (Tiflis, 1928), pp. iv–v.

33. G. Tsereteli, *Ignatii Ingorokva* (Tiflis, 1905), pp. 11–12.

34. Megrelishvili, *Gruzinskaia obshchestvenno-ekonomicheskaia mysl'*, vol. 2, p. 256.

35. Tsereteli, *Ignatii Ingorokva*, pp. 12–14.

36. Noe Zhordania, *Moia zhizn'* (Stanford, Calif.: Hoover Institution Press, 1968), pp. 11–13; N. B. Makharadze, *Filipp Makharadze* (Tbilisi, 1960), pp. 8–9.

37. Pilipe Makharadze, "'revoliutsionuri mogonebata' saghamo. (stenograpiuli angarishebi)," *revoliutsiis matiane* 1 (March 1923): 85. For a recent study in English of Polish socialism in the 1880s, see Norman M. Naimark, *The History of the "Proletariat": The Emergence of Marxism in the Kingdom of Poland, 1870–1887* (New York: Columbia University Press, 1979). One of the leaders of "Proletariat" was a half-Georgian, Stanislaw Kunicki.

38. Zhordania, *Moia zhizn'*, p. 14.

39. The thirteen who gathered in Kvirili were Egnate Ninoshvili, Noe Zhordania, Ioseb Kakabadze, Mikhail Tskhakaia, Silibistro Jibladze, Nikolai Chkheidze, Isidor Ramishvili, Evgenii Vatsadze, Arsen Tsitlidze, Razhden Kaladze, Dmitrii Kalandarishvili, Isidor Kvitsaridze, and S. Kiladze.

40. Zhordania, *Moia zhizn'*, pp. 16–17; F. Makharadze, *K tridtsatiletiiu*, pp. 4, 36–37; S. Talakvadze, *K istoriiu kommunisticheskoi partii Gruzii* (Tiflis, 1925), pp. 14a, 16; A. V. Maskuliia, *Mikhail Grigor'evich Tskhakaia* (Moscow, 1968), pp. 26–29.

41. Maskuliia, *Tskhakaia*, p. 32.

42. Ninoshvili's letter to G. Tsereteli, February 1894, published in Egnate Ninoshvili, *Izbrannaia proza: Pis'ma* (Tbilisi, 1959), p. 384.

43. *Kvali,* no. 21, May 15, 1894, pp. 1–4; for Jibladze's speech, see *kvali,* no. 22, May 22, 1894, pp. 14–16.

44. *Moambe,* 1894, nos. 5 and 6; a Russian translation of Zhordania's article is available in the Georgian Collection, no. 16, of the Inter-University Project on the History of the Menshevik Movement, Columbia University.

45. Ibid.

46. F. Makharadze, *K tridtsatiletiiu,* pp. 48–49; Grigorii Uratadze, *Vospominaniia gruzinskogo sotsial-demokrata* (Stanford, Calif.: Hoover Institution Press, 1968), p. 18; S. Todriia, "Na zare rabochego dvizheniia (1893–1903 g.g.)," in Orakhelashvili et al., eds., *Chetvert' veka bor'by za sotsializma* (Tiflis, 1923), pp. 195–96.

47. Anahide Ter Minassian, "Le Mouvement révolutionnaire arménien, 1890–1903," *Cahiers du monde russe et soviétique* 14, no. 4 (October–December 1973): 578–79. The newspaper *iveria* was closed down by the government for eight months in 1896 because of "harmful propaganda, aimed principally at students, against Russian authority in the Caucasus, against the Russian language, and in general against Russian influence in any form" (from a government order, cited in Bakhtadze, *Ocherki,* p. 166).

48. Talakvadze, *K istoriiu,* p. 43; G. Chkheidze, "dzvirpasi da mudam dauvitsqari zakro chodrishvili," *revoliutsiis matiane* 1 (March 1923): 95.

49. G. Chkheidze, "chemi mogonebani," *revoliutsiis matiane* 4 (1923): 172–73;

5: 87–88.

50. There were a few other legal Marxist periodicals in the Russian empire, namely *Samarskii vestnik* (1895) and *Novoe slovo* (1897).

51. The Tiflis committee members were Silibistro Jibladze, Severian Jugeli, Al. Shatilov, Vasilii Tsabadze, Dmitrii Kalandarishvili, Razhden Kaladze, Zakro Chodrishvili, Arakel Okuashvili, and Mikho Bocharidze (Georgian Collection, no. 11, p. 9, Inter-University Project on the History of the Menshevik Movement, Columbia University). This was the second May Day celebrated in Transcaucasia; the first was in 1898.

52. Khoshtaria, *Ocherki,* pp. 213, 216–17.

53. Talakvadze, *K istoriiu,* pp. 33–35; F. Makharadze, *Ocherki revoliutsionnogo dvizheniia,* pp. 78–81; Khoshtaria, *Ocherki,* pp. 213–15.

54. Talakvadze, *K istoriiu,* p. 35; Chkheidze, "dzvirpasi," p. 97.

55. G. Khachapuridze, ed., *Noi Zhordaniia i tsarskaia okhranka: Arkhivnye dokumenty* (Tiflis, 1931), pp. 22–23; Zhordania, *Moia zhizn',* pp. 32–35.

56. Tengiz Zhghenti, "batumi 1901–1905 tslebshi," *revoliutsiis matiane* 3 (20) (1928): 93–94. Social democrat Giorgi Eradze told Professor Leopold H. Haimson in a taped interview that among workers in Tiflis only Russians read *Iskra* (interview no. 4, p. 8; transcript is available at the Inter-University Project on the History of the Menshevik Movement, Columbia University).

57. A. Enukidze, "Istoriia organizatsii i raboty nelegal'nykh tipografii RSDRP na Kavkaze za vremia ot 1900 po 1906 god," *Proletarskaia revoliutsiia,* no. 2 (14) (1923): 117. The second Tiflis Committee included Zakro Chodrishvili, Arakel Okuashvili, G. Chkheidze, Vaso Tsabadze, Kalistrate Gogoua, G. Gharajian, Severiane Jugeli, Keshishiants, and Starosenko (Chkheidze, "chemi mogonebani," p. 91).

58. Georgian Collection, no. 1, p. 22, Inter-University Project on the History of the Menshevik Movement, Columbia University.

59. Uratadze, *Vospominaniia,* pp. 32–48.

60. The other six members of the Caucasian Union Committee were M. Tskhakaia, P. Makharadze, A. Tsulukidze, M. Bochoridze (the only worker among them), S. Jibladze, and N. Zhordania.

61. Razhden Arsenidze, interviews with Leopold H. Haimson, no. 1, pp. 3, 102; transcript at the Inter-University Project on the History of the Menshevik Movement, Columbia University.

CHAPTER 8

1. The Georgian Socialist Federalist Party was founded in April 1904 at a conference in Geneva. Its leader was Archil Konstantinis dze Jorjadze, the editor of the Paris-based journal, *sakartvelo* (Georgia). Opposed to the antinationalist stance of the social democrats, the Socialist Federalists called for autonomy for every nationality in Russia and a federal link among them. The party adopted the Socialist Revolutionary (SR) program on the agrarian question (full socialization of the land) and committed itself to a revolutionary struggle against absolutism.

2. N. Marr, *Iz guriiskikh nabliudenii i vpechatlenii* (St. Petersburg, 1905), pp. 15, 19.

3. *Revoliutsiia 1905 goda v Zakavkaz'i (Khronika sobytii, dokumenty i mate-*

rialy). Po materialam Muzeia Revoliutsii Gruzii (Tiflis, 1926), p. 16; Uratadze, *Vospominaniia,* p. 104.

4. Opposed by the landed nobility and the military, Starosel'skii drew close to the revolutionary movement and soon was completely discredited in the eyes of his governmental sponsors.

5. *Revoliutsiia 1905 goda v Zakavkaz'i,* pp. 65, 158. For an account of these events by the French consul, Alexandre Chayet, see Jacques Baynac, "Aspects caucasiens," in his *Sur 1905* (Paris, 1974), p. 135.

6. *Revoliutsiia 1905 goda v Zakavkaz'i,* p. 78.

7. Ibid., pp. 83–84, 161–63.

8. Uratadze, *Vospominaniia,* p. 117.

9. *Revoliutsiia 1905 goda v Zakavkaz'i,* pp. 109–11; Khatissian, "Memoirs of a Mayor," pp. 45–46.

10. S. V. Maglakelidze, *Vladimir Aleksandrovich Starosel'skii (Dokumenty i materialy)* (Tbilisi, 1969), pp. 114–15; *Revoliutsionnoe dvizhenie v Armenii 1905–1906 gg. Sbornik dokumentov i materialov* (Erevan, 1955), p. 166.

11. Razhden Arsenidze, Interviews with Leopold H. Haimson (1961), Inter-University Project on the History of the Menshevik Movement, Columbia University, no. 2, p. 23; *Revoliutsiia 1905 goda v Zakavkaz'i,* p. 137; Baynac, "Aspects caucasiennes," pp. 142–43. An interesting observation on the Tiflis general strike was made by P. D. Sakvarvelidze, a Bolshevik delegate to the Fourth Congress of the RSDRP:

> In Tiflis in December our ranks were disorganized and demoralized; there was no kind of fighting spirit, no real possibility to carry out an armed struggle, not one real possibility to carry out an armed struggle, not one real chance for victory. But . . . comrade K. [Zhordania] ignored all these conditions and insisted on immediate action. (*Chetvertyi [Ob"edinitel'nyi] S"ezd RSDRP, Aprel' [Aprel'–Mai] 1906 goda: Protokoly* [Moscow, 1959], pp. 386–87).

12. I. I. Vorontsov-Dashkov, *Vsepoddanneishii otchet za vosem' let upravleniia Kavkazom* (St. Petersburg, 1913), p. 6.

13. Ibid., p. 7.

14. Ibid., pp. 9, 8.

15. Ibid., pp. 10, 14, 32–33.

16. Uturashvili, *Realizatsiia,* pp. 194–96, 203.

17. Zhordania, *Moia zhizn',* p. 49.

18. Elected from Tiflis were Arshak Zurabov (Zurabian), Archil Japaridze, Severian Jugeli, N. A. Katsiashvili; elected from Kutaisi were I. G. Tsereteli, V. B. Lomtatidze, and G. F. Makharadze.

19. Chkheidze was elected by the deciding votes of the Armenian liberals, led by Tiflis mayor Aleksandr Khatisov, who preferred to vote for a social democrat rather than for Lurasab Andronikashvili, who, although a Kadet, was perceived by the Armenians as a Georgian nationalist (Zhordania, *Moia zhizn',* p. 55).

20. *Rechi N. S. Chkheidze* (Petrograd, 1917), p. 15; Uratadze, *Vospominaniia,* p. 214; P. A. Stolypin, "Bor'ba s revoliutsionnym dvizheniem na Kavkaze v epokhu stolypinshchiny (iz perepiski P. A. Stolypina s grafom I. I. Vorontsovym-Dashkovym)," *Krasnyi arkhiv,* no. 3 (34) (1929): 201.

21. "Obzor deiatel'nosti sotsial-demokraticheskikh organizatsii sostavlenii soot-

vetstvenno pis'mami svedeniiam poluchennykh s mest," published in *revoliutsiis matiane* (no date) and reproduced in a letter from G. Uratadze to B. I. Nicolaevsky, January 27, 1958 (Nicolaevsky Collection, Hoover Institution, uncatalogued).

22. I. V. Stalin, *Sochineniia*, vol. 2, *1907–1913* (Moscow, 1946), pp. 174–96; originally published in *Sotsial-Demokrat*, no. 11, February 13, [26], 1910; and *"Diskussionnyi listok (Prilozhenie k gazete 'Sotsial-Demokrat')*, no. 2, May 25 [June 7], 1910. The first article is on Baku, the second on Tiflis.

23. G. V. Plekhanov, "Predislovie," in Arkomed, *Rabochee dvizhenie*, pp. 30–31.

24. *Golos Sotsialdemokrata* (Paris), no. 25, May 1911.

25. I. V. Stalin, "Na puti k natsionalizmu (Pis'mo s Kavkaza)," *Sochineniia*, vol. 2, p. 288.

26. *Chveni tskhovreba* (Our Life), no. 12, July 1912; cited in Stalin, *Sochineniia*, vol. 2, p. 349.

27. Stalin, *Sochineniia*, vol. 2, p. 296.

28. Ibid., pp. 351-52.

29. On this strike, see G. A. Arutiunov, *Rabochee dvizhenie v Zakavkaz'e v period novogo revoliutsionnogo pod"ema (1910–1914 gg.)* (Moscow-Baku, 1963), pp. 276–91.

30. For a view of the growing social crisis in urban Russia on the eve of World War I, see Leopold H. Haimson, "The Problem of Social Stability in Urban Russia, 1905–1917," *Slavic Review* 23, no. 4 (December 1964): 619–42; 24, no. 1 (March 1965): 1–22.

31. Khatissian, "Memoirs," vol. 3, no. 1 (9) (March 1950), p. 106.

32. Uratadze, *Vospominaniia*, pp. 268–75; Zhordania, *Moia zhizn'*, p. 66.

33. Zhordania, *Moia zhizn'*, pp. 69–70.

34. Khatissian, "Memoirs," vol. 3, no. 2 (10) (June 1950), pp. 90, 84.

35. Ibid., vol. 3, no. 3 (11) (October 1950), pp. 102, 105.

CHAPTER 9

1. *Izvestiia* (of the Tiflis soviets), no. 50, March 4, 1918.

2. For a detailed discussion of the February Revolution, see Tsuyoshi Hasegawa, *The February Revolution: Petrograd 1917* (Seattle: University of Washington, 1981).

3. Haimson, "Problem of Social Stability," pp. 1–22.

4. *Izvestiia*, no. 50, March 4, 1918.

5. Ia. Shafir, *Ocherki gruzinskoi zhirondy* (Moscow, 1925), p. 8.

6. *Protokoly zakavkazskikh revoliutsionnykh sovetskikh organizatsii, I* (Tiflis, 1920), pp. 125–26, N. N. Zhordaniia (Zhordania), *Za dva goda (S marta 1917 po 1 marta 1919 g.): Doklady i rechi* (Tiflis, 1919), pp. 5–6; *Izvestiia*, no. 2, March 28, 1917.

7. *Izvestiia*, no. 8, April 7, 1917, May 14, 1917.

8. *Bor'ba*, no. 6, May 11, 1917.

9. *Protokoly*, pp. 41–44, 145–58; *Izvestiia*, no. 34, May 9, 1917, no. 41, May 19, 1917, no. 42, May 20, 1917, and no. 50, May 31, 1917.

10. *Izvestiia*, no. 72, June 25, 1917; *Kavkazskii rabochii*, no. 86, June 28, 1917.

11. *Izvestiia*, no. 96, July 25, 1917, no. 97, July 26, 1917; S. E. Sef, *Revoliutsiia 1917 goda v Zakavkaz'i* (Tiflis, 1927), pp. 192–93.

12. Sef, *Revoliutsiia*, pp. 211–15. For a fuller discussion of the political alternatives available in 1917, see my review essay, "Toward a Social History of the October Revolution," *American Historical Review* 88, no. 1 (February 1983): 31–52.

13. Zhordania, *Moia zhizn'*, pp. 80–81.

14. *Bor'ba*, no. 82, August 12, 1917; no. 85, August 17, 1917. *Kaspii* (Baku), no. 207.

15. For detailed treatment of these developments, see Firuz Kazemzadeh, *The Struggle for Transcaucasia (1917–1921)* (New York: Philosophical Library, 1951).

16. Ibid., pp. 103–7.

17. For discussion of the complex diplomatic, military, and political events in early 1918, see Richard G. Hovannisian, *Armenia on the Road to Independence, 1918* (Berkeley and Los Angeles: University of California Press, 1967); and Ronald Grigor Suny, *The Baku Commune, 1917–1918: Class and Nationality in the Russian Revolution* (Princeton, N.J.: Princeton University Press, 1972).

18. Kazemzadeh, *Struggle*, pp. 57–60, 122–23; Zurab Avalov (Avalishvili), *The Independence of Georgia in International Politics, 1918–1921* (London: Headley Brothers, 1940), pp. 57–60.

19. Fritz Fischer, *Germany's Aims in the First World War* (New York: Norton, 1967), pp. 134–36.

20. Zhordania, *Moia zhizn'*, p. 68.

21. Avalov, *Independence*, p. 102.

22. Arkomed, *Rabochee dvizhenie*, pp. 12–13n. *Sotsial-Demokrat* appeared in Tiflis from June 10, 1918, as the organ of a group of Mensheviks who opposed the creation of independent republics in Transcaucasia and the separation from "Russian democracy." Of the eighteen members of the editorial collective only one was clearly a Georgian; the others were Armenian, Russian, and Jewish.

23. *Bor'ba*, no. 84, June 4, 1918.

24. *Sotsial-Demokrat*, no. 1, June 10, 1918; *Bor'ba*, no. 90, June 11, 1918, no. 91, June 12, 1918.

25. *Bor'ba*, no. 90, June 11, 1918, and no. 91, June 12, 1918.

26. *Bor'ba*, no. 153, August 28, 1918, no. 154, August 29, 1918, no. 155, August 30, 1918, and no. 156, August 31, 1918.

27. The speech was reprinted in Zhordania, *Za dva goda*, pp. 109–35. "Social relationships in Georgia," Zhordania argued, "have given rise to three democratic classes—the workers, the peasants, and the petty bourgeoisie—which constitute the social basis for the building of the Georgian state. In such circumstances the state can only be democratic or it cannot exist at all" (p. 113).

28. Giorgi Eradze, Eighteen interviews with Leopold Haimson, Menshevik Project, Columbia University, interview no. 10, p. 38.

29. *Kavkazskii rabochii*, no. 4, March 15, 1917.

30. *Bor'ba*, no. 7, May 13, 1917; *Izvestiia*, no. 38, May 16, 1917, and no. 52, June 2, 1917.

31. *Izveshchenie o shestoi oblastnoi s"ezde zakavkazskikh rabochikh organizatsii RSDRP* (Tiflis, 1917), p. 3.

32. *Delo naroda* (Petrograd), no. 127, August 15, 1917.

33. Georgian Archive, Harvard University, boxes 1, 2, no. 3 (film 76-4545, reel 2), pp. 1309–16.

34. The text of this law can be found in *Sbornik izdannykh s nachala revoliutsii po l noiabria 1918 goda zakonov, instrutsii i raz'iasnenii po ministerstvu zemledeliia*

(Polozhenie o zemel'nykh komitetakh, o konfiskatsii zemel' i pr.), compiled by L. G. Asatiani (Tiflis, 1918), pp. 42–48. The supplementary law of May 2, 1918, can be found on pages 53–54. This law left larger holdings in the hands of nobles and other proprietors.

35. Ibid., pp. 27–28. The category of *khizani* was abolished, and those peasants were given the land they had cultivated. Later it was decided that peasants who used land that had been left to nobles were required to pay dues on that land and were retroactively responsible for a proportionate amount of dues for 1917.

36. *Bor'ba,* no. 106, July 2, 1918.

37. The Terek People's Soviet Socialist Republic, centered at Vladikavkaz, was established in March 1918 and headed by the Georgian Bolshevik, Noe Buachidze. A month later it recognized the sovereignty of the RSFSR. In August local Cossacks drove the Bolsheviks from Vladikavkaz briefly, but in alliance with Ingush tribesmen the Bolsheviks retook the city a few weeks later. In 1919 Denikin's Volunteer Army moved into the area. It was not until late March 1920 that the Whites were driven out of Vladikavkaz.

38. Kazemzadeh, *Struggle,* pp. 189–93.

39. Interview with N. G. Khomeriki in *Bor'ba,* no. 109, July 5, 1918, and no. 221, November 17, 1918.

40. *Zakavkazskoe slovo,* no. 5, January 24, 1919. In a contemporary study of the Georgian land reform, S. Avaliani presents the following figures to illustrate the decline in the nobles' economic position by 1918:

NOBLES' LANDHOLDINGS

	TIFLIS PROVINCE	KUTAISI PROVINCE
1860s	961,502 desiatinas	815,321 desiatinas
c. 1900	992,216	495,125
January 1, 1918	511,538	110,157

(S. Avaliani, *mitsismplobeloba sakartveloshi* [Kutaisi, 1920], p. 12).

41. M. Khomeriki, *La Réforme agraire et l'économie rurale en Géorgie: Rapport au Congrès du Parti Social-Democrate de Géorgie, en juillet 1920* (Paris, 1921), pp. 28–31.

42. Ibid., pp. 23, 19.

43. Ibid., pp. 36–37.

44. *Bor'ba,* no. 11 (267), January 16, 1919.

45. Karl Kautsky, *Georgia, a Social-Democratic Peasant Republic: Impressions and Observations* (London, 1921), pp. 54–55.

46. Filipp Makharadze, *Diktatura men'shevistskoi partii v Gruzii* (Moscow, 1921), pp. 39, 44, 45.

47. Shafir, *Ocherki,* p. 46.

48. M. V. Natmeladze and N. I. Sturua, *Iz istorii rabochego klassa Gruzii (1921–1958 gg.)* (Tbilisi, 1961), p. 10.

49. Eradze, Interview no. 17, pp. 95–102. *Bor'ba,* no. 70 (326), March 28, 1919, and no. 71 (327), March 29, 1919.

50. *Bor'ba,* no. 104 (360), May 14, 1919.

51. Grigorii Uratadze, *Obrazovanie i konsolidatsiia Gruzinskoi Demokraticheskoi Respubliki* (Munich, 1956), p. 106. *Bor'ba*, no. 250 (508), November 2, 1919, no. 251 (509), November 4, 1919, and no. 253 (511), November 6, 1919.

52. See Richard G. Hovannisian, *The Republic of Armenia*, vol. 1, *The First Year, 1918–1919* (Berkeley and Los Angeles: University of California Press, 1971), pp. 66–78, 93–125; Kazemzadeh, *Struggle*, pp. 174–83.

53. For a detailed description of these events, see Peter Kenez, "The Relations Between the Volunteer Army and Georgia, 1918–1920: A Case Study in Disunity," *The Slavonic and East European Review* 48, no. 112 (July 1970): 403–23.

54. On British involvement in Transcaucasia, see Artin H. Arslanian, "The British Decision to Intervene in Transcaucasia during World War I," *Armenian Review* 27 (Summer 1974): 146–59; Artin H. Arslanian and Robert L. Nichols, "Nationalism and the Russian Civil War: The Case of Volunteer Army—Armenian Relations, 1918–1920," *Soviet Studies* 31, no. 4 (October 1979): 559–73; and Richard H. Ullman, *Britain and the Russian Civil War, November 1918–February 1920* (Princeton: Princeton University Press, 1968), particularly pp. 66–86.

55. Ullman, *Britain and the Russian Civil War*, pp. 73, 77–78, 81. Avalov, *Independence*, p. 146.

56. Ullman, *Britain and the Russian Civil War*, pp. 329–46.

57. *Kavkazskii rabochii*, no. 185, October 28, 1917; on the entire question of Bolshevik tactics in Transcaucasia after the October Revolution, see S. Kh. Karapetian, "K voprosu o prichinakh zaderzhki pobedy Oktiabr'skoi revoliutsii v Armenii," *Izvestiia Akademii nauk Armianskoi SSR (seriia obshchestvennykh nauk)* 12 (1962): 15–30.

58. Suny, *Baku Commune*, pp. 306–24.

59. A. I. Mikoian, *Dorogoi bor'by* (Moscow, 1971), pp. 305–7.

60. S. V. Kharmandarian, *Lenin i stanovlenie Zakavkazskoi Federatsii, 1921–1923* (Erevan, 1969), p. 30. The early history of the Transcaucasian communist parties is quite complex. For a short account of some of the problems involved, see Stephen Blank, "Bolshevik Organizational Development in Early Soviet Transcaucasia: Autonomy vs. Centralization, 1918–1924," in Ronald Grigor Suny, ed., *Transcaucasia, Nationalism and Social Change: Essays in the History of Armenia, Azerbaijan, and Georgia* (Ann Arbor: Michigan Slavic Publications, 1983), pp. 305–38.

61. V. I. Lenin, *Polnoe sobranie sochineniia*, 5th ed. (Moscow, 1958–1966), vol. 51, p. 175.

62. Kharmandarian, *Lenin*, pp. 41, 43; Lenin, *Polnoe sobranie sochineniia*, vol. 51, p. 191.

63. *Times* (London), January 8, 1921.

64. Kazemzadeh, *Struggle*, pp. 286–93.

65. Ibid., p. 328.

CHAPTER 10

1. Gurgen Mirzoev later emigrated to the United States with his family. He is my father, George Suny.

2. For discussions of these events, see Richard Pipes, *The Formation of the Soviet Union: Communism and Nationalism, 1917–1923* (Cambridge, Mass.: Harvard

University Press, 1957), pp. 263–82; and Moshe Lewin, *Lenin's Last Struggle* (New York: Pantheon, 1968).

3. Leon Trotsky, *Stalin: An Appraisal of the Man and His Influence* (New York: Harper, 1941), p. 268.

4. Central Committee resolution of February 14, 1921, published in Lenin, *Polnoe sobranie sochinenii,* vol. 51, p. 71.

5. Kharmandarian, *Lenin,* p. 59.

6. Lenin, *Polnoe sobranie sochineniia,* vol. 42, p. 367.

7. Ibid., vol. 43, p. 199.

8. *Revoliutsionnye komitety Gruzii v bor'be za ustanovlenie i uprochenie sovetskoi vlasti (Fevral' 1921 g.–mart 1922 g.): Sbornik dokumentov i materialov* (Sukhumi, 1963), p. 38. G. K. Ordzhonikidze (Orjonikidze), *Stat'i i rechi, vol. 1, 1910–1926 gg.* (Moscow, 1956), pp. 172–81.

9. Lenin, *Polnoe sobranie sochineniia,* vol. 43, p. 128.

10. Kharmandarian, *Lenin,* pp. 127–28.

11. Stalin, *Sochineniia,* vol. 5, pp. 88–100.

12. Kharmandarian, *Lenin,* p. 135.

13. Ibid., p. 140.

14. *Ocherki istorii kommunisticheskoi partii Gruzii,* vol. 2 (Tbilisi, 1963), p. 25.

15. Kharmandarian, *Lenin,* p. 84.

16. Ibid., pp. 201, 165.

17. Kharmandarian, *Lenin,* p. 223; V. S. Kirillov and A. Ia. Sverdlov, *Grigorii Konstantinovich Ordzhonikidze (Sergo): Biografiia* (Moscow, 1962), p. 166.

18. Lenin, *Polnoe sobranie sochineniia,* vol. 45, p. 556. Among those attending the meeting, Orjonikidze, Kirov, Enukidze, Eliava, and Kakhiani favored Stalin's plan, but Mdivani and the majority of the Georgian Central Committee opposed it (Kharmandarian, *Lenin,* p. 341).

19. Lenin, *Polnoe sobranie sochineniia,* vol. 45, pp. 211–13.

20. Kharmandarian, *Lenin,* pp. 347–48.

21. Lenin, *Polnoe sobranie sochineniia,* vol. 54, pp. 299–300; Lewin, *Lenin's Last Struggle.*

22. Lenin, *Polnoe sobranie sochineniia,* vol. 45, pp. 356–62.

23. Ibid., pp. 346, 359–60, 357.

24. Ibid., pp. 361–62.

25. Ibid., pp. 607, 54, 329–30.

26. Kharmandarian, *Lenin,* pp. 398–401, 405.

27. Ibid., pp. 411–12.

28. *Dvenadtsatyi s"ezd RKP (b), 17–25 aprelia 1923 goda: Stenograficheskii otchet* (Moscow, 1968), pp. 175, 178–79.

29. Ibid., pp. 172, 173.

30. Ibid., pp. 481, 487.

31. Ibid., pp. 649–50.

32. For discussions of this period, see E. H. Carr, *The Interregnum, 1923–1924* (New York: Macmillan, 1954); and Robert Vincent Daniels, *The Conscience of the Revolution: Communist Opposition in Soviet Russia* (Cambridge, Mass.: Harvard University Press, 1960), pp. 172–235.

33. Stalin had to defend himself against charges that he had been too lenient in

dealing with Muslim "national communism" in the Sultan Galiev affair. On Sultan Galiev, see Alexandre Bennigsen and Chantal Quelquejay, *Les Mouvements nationaux chex les musulmans de Russie*, vol. 1, *Le "Sultangalievisme" au Tatarstan* (Paris: Mouton, 1960); and Alexandre A. Bennigsen and S. Enders Wimbush, *Muslim National Communism in the Soviet Union: A Revolutionary Strategy for the Colonial World* (Chicago, Ill.: University of Chicago Press, 1979), esp. pp. 81–94.

34. Stalin, *Sochineniia*, vol. 5, pp. 311–12; Bennigsen and Wimbush, *Muslim National Communism*, p. 164.

35. Stalin, *Sochineniia*, vol. 5, p. 310.

36. *Konferentsiia byvshikh men'shevikov 1-ogo raiona zheleznodorozhnykh rabochikh Tiflisa: Stenograficheskii otchet* (Tiflis, 1923), pp. 27–28.

37. *Konferentsiia byvshikh men'shevikov 4-ogo raiona: Stenograficheskii otchet* (Tiflis, 1923), pp. 31–39; *Konferentsiia byvshikh men'shevikov 2-ogo raiona: Stenograficheskii otchet* (Tiflis, 1923), p. 5.

38. *Vsegruzinskii s"ezd sotsial-demokraticheskoi rabochei partii (men'shevikov) Gruzii. 25–30 avgusta 1923 goda: Stenograficheskii otchet* (Tiflis, 1924), pp. 156, 322, 325.

39. Calculations about relative Menshevik and Bolshevik support after the invasion of 1921 are by necessity impressionistic. The Bolsheviks at times were surprisingly frank about the limits of their social base, but the estimation of gradually growing acceptance of the Soviet order by some social groups is based here on the uprising itself, where it took place and where it made no headway at all, as in Tiflis.

40. Letter from N. Zhordania, June 2, 1924, printed in part in *Rabochaia gazeta* (Tiflis), no. 207 (453), September 9, 1924.

41. Report by A. Miasnikov (Miasnikian) in *Zaria vostoka*, no. 677, December 1, 1924.

42. *Rabochaia pravda*, no. 207 (453), September 11, 1924.

43. Stalin, *Sochineniia*, vol. 5, pp. 316–17, 308. For a recent Soviet study of the Menshevik uprising, see I. Ia. Trifonov, "Razgrom men'shevistsko-kulatskogo miatezha v Gruzii v 1924 godu," *Voprosy istorii*, no. 7 (July 1976): 41–55; an English translation is available: "The Smashing of the Menshevik-Kulak Revolt in Georgia in 1924," *Soviet Studies in History* 16, no. 2 (Fall 1977): 3–31.

44. *Bor'ba za uprochenie sovetskoi vlasti v Gruzii (Sbornik dokumentov i materialov) (1921–1925 gg.)*, compiled by Iu. M. Kacharava et al. (Tbilisi, 1959), pp. 34–35; 160–67, 170–71.

45. Ibid., pp. 171–72, 177.

46. Ibid., p. 176.

47. Ibid., pp. 192, 177–78. As a result of the land reforms, 141,801 desiatinas were taken from large landowners by early 1925, most of which went to peasants. A significant equalization of peasant holdings occurred. The number of poor peasant households (with holdings of 0.25 desiatinas or less) fell from 13.8 to 4.4 percent; the number of middle households (with holdings from 1.25 to 4 desiatinas) rose from 42.3 to 61.1 percent, and the number of richer households (over 4 desiatinas) fell from 43.9 to 34.5 percent (P. N. Lomashvili, *Velikii perevorot* [Tbilisi, 1972], pp. 99–103).

48. *Bor'ba za uprochenie*, p. 182.

49. Ibid., pp. 181–90.

50. Stalin, *Sochineniia*, vol. 7, p. 22. E. H. Carr, *Socialism in One Country, 1924–1926*, (New York: Macmillan, 1958), vol. 1, p. 199.

51. Carr, *Socialism in One Country*, vol. 1, pp. 240–82. As the propeasant policy unfolded and Stalin's program of building "socialism in one country" was more clearly articulated, a new opposition began to crystalize, this time around Zinoviev and Kamenev. The triumvirate fell apart over both personal jealousies and substantive issues of policy, but Stalin's firm hold on the party apparatus doomed his opponents. At the Fourteenth Party Congress (December 18–21, 1925), Stalin and his new ally, Nikolai Bukharin, emerged victorious in the intraparty struggle. A few months later Zinoviev lost his post as head of the Leningrad party organization and was replaced by a loyal Stalin supporter then based in Azerbaijan, Sergei Kirov.

52. *Pravda*, no. 56, May 8, 1925, and no. 57, May 10, 1925. Catholicos Amvrosi had been arrested in 1923 after sending a memorandum to the Genoa conference (1922) protesting confiscation of church treasures. He was tried in March 1924 (G. Uratadze, "Gruziia pod sovetskoi okkupatsiei," Nicolaevsky Collection, Hoover Institution, uncatalogued).

53. Ordzhonikidze, *Stat'i i rechi*, vol. 1, pp. 388–89.

54. Ibid., p. 405.

55. Carr, *Socialism in One Country*, vol. 1, p. 287; *Leningradskaia pravda*, December 23, 1925; *Chetyrnadtsatyi s"ezd VKP (b): Stenograficheskii otchet* (Moscow, 1926), pp. 118, 223.

56. Trotsky writes the following about this incident:

> Shortly after Lenin's death [Stalin] made a clandestine attempt to transfer the nationalized land as private property to the peasants of his native Georgia under the guise of "possession" of "personal parcels" for "many years." Here again he showed how strong were his old agrarian roots and his dominant and deep-seated Georgian nationalism. Upon Stalin's secret instruction, the Georgian people's commissar of agriculture prepared a project to transfer the land to the possession of the peasants. Only the protest of Zinoviev, who got wind of the conspiracy, and the alarm raised by the project in Party circles, compelled Stalin, who did not yet feel sure enough of himself, to repudiate his own project. Naturally, the scapegoat in this case proved to be the unfortunate Georgian people's commissar (*Stalin*, p. 397).

57. P. V. Gugushvili et al., eds., *Istoriia kollektivizatsii sel'skogo khoziaistva Gruzinskoi SSR (1927–1937 gg.)* (Tbilisi, 1970), p. 123.

58. Ordzhonikidze, *Stat'i i rechi*, vol. 1, p. 442.

59. Ibid., p. 431; T. I. Zhgenti, *Istoriia kolkhoznogo stroitel'stva v Gruzii (1921–1950)* (Tbilisi, 1977), p. 34.

60. *Bor'ba za uprochenie*, p. 411.

61. Ordzhonikidze, *Stat'i i rechi*, vol. 1, pp. 386–87.

62. *Ocherki istorii kommunisticheskoi partii Gruzii, 1883–1970* (Tbilisi, 1971), pp. 460–62.

63. Carr, *Socialism in One Country*, pp. 484–85; *New York Times*, June 15, 1925, p. 14. On Harriman and other American capitalists doing business in the Soviet Union, see Joseph Finder, *Red Carpet* (New York: New Republic/Holt, Rinehart & Winston, 1983).

64. Ordzhonikidze, *Stat'i i rechi*, vol. 1, p. 432; Natmeladze and Sturua, *Iz istorii*, pp. 19–21.

65. *Bor'ba za uprochenie*, pp. 288–90. On the composition of the Georgian work

force in the 1920s, see M. V. Natmeladze, *Istoriia rabochego klassa Gruzii (1921–1941 gg.)* (Tbilisi, 1981), vol. 2, pp. 5–113.

66. Carr, *Socialism in One Country*, vol. 1, p. 352; E. H. Carr and R. W. Davies, *Foundations of a Planned Economy, 1926–1929* (New York: Macmillan, 1969), vol. 1, pt. 1, pp. 275–76.

67. Ordzhonikidze, *Stat'i i rechi*, vol. 1, p. 448.

68. *Ocherki istorii kommunisticheskikh organizatsii Zakavkaz'ia, II, 1921–1937 gg.* (Baku, 1971), pp. 94–96; *kommunisti*, no. 281, December 8, 1926; Natmeladze and Sturua, *Iz istorii*, p. 32.

69. Soviet policy toward the intelligentsia proscribed only overtly anti-Soviet activity and expression. As Orjonikidze warned the Georgian intellectuals in 1925:

> To those who honestly stand on the soil of the Soviet system, we offer full opportunity to display their talent and to create. We open a broad road to Georgian literature, the theater, music, science, painting, but if art, culture wish to serve our enemy, counterrevolutionary ends, then our struggle with them will become merciless (*drosha*, 1925, no. 28, pp. 19–20; trans. in *Istoriia gruzinskoi sovetskoi literatury* [Moscow, 1977], p. 11).

At the end of February 1926 the First Congress of Writers of Georgia was held, and a loose federation of literary groupings was formed into the Union of Writers of Georgia. The intense debates, with separate literary journals and declarations, continued until 1932.

70. *Gruzinskaia SSR: Kultura* (Tbilisi, 1971), p. 15.

71. *Ocherki istorii kommunisticheskoi partii Gruzii* (1971), p. 478.

72. Ibid., pp. 490–91; *Pravda*, no. 220, September 27, 1927, and no. 232, October 11, 1927.

73. *Kommunisticheskaia partiia Gruzii v tsifrakh (1921–1970 gg.) (Sbornik statisticheskikh materialov)* (Tbilisi, 1971), pp. 7, 26, 33.

74. Ibid., p. 45.

CHAPTER 11

1. Moshe Lewin, *Russian Peasants and Soviet Power: A Study of Collectivization* (Evanston, Ill.: Northwestern University Press, 1968); Robert C. Tucker, *Stalin as Revolutionary, 1879–1929: A Study in History and Personality* (New York: Norton, 1973), and *Stalinism: Essays in Historical Interpretation* (New York: Norton, 1977); Sheila Fitzpatrick, ed., *Cultural Revolution in Russia, 1928–1931* (Bloomington: Indiana University Press, 1978), and *Education and Social Mobility in the Soviet Union, 1921–1934* (Cambridge, England: Cambridge University Press, 1979); and Kendall E. Bailes, *Technology and Society Under Lenin and Stalin: Origins of the Soviet Technical Intelligentsia, 1917–1941* (Princeton, N.J.: Princeton University Press, 1978).

2. David Marshall Lang, *A Modern History of Soviet Georgia* (New York: Grove Press, 1962), pp. 245–62.

3. Lewin, *Russian Peasants*, p. 7.

4. Lewin, "Society, State, and Ideology During the First Five-Year Plan," in Fitzpatrick, *Cultural Revolution*, p. 41.

5. R. W. Davies, *The Industrialization of Soviet Russia*, vol. 1, *The Socialist Offensive: The Collectivisation of Soviet Agriculture, 1929–1930* (Cambridge, Mass.: Harvard University Press, 1980), p. 51.

6. Zhgenti, *Istoriia kolkhoznogo stroitel'stva*, p. 45.

7. Gugushvili et al., *Istoriia kollektivizatsii*, p. 121.

8. Ibid.

9. Zhgenti, *Istoriia kolkhoznogo stroitel'stva*, p. 44.

10. Ibid., p. 45.

11. Gugushvili et al., *Istoriia kollektivizatsii*, pp. 121, 52.

12. Lomashvili, *Velikii perevorot*, pp. 111–12.

13. Ibid., p. 150.

14. Ibid., pp. 149–51.

15. *Pravda*, no. 212, September 12, 1928; Gugushvili et al., *Istoriia kollektivizatsii*, pp. 126–28; *Ocherki istorii kommunisticheskoi partii Gruzii, 1883–1970* (Tbilisi, 1971), pp. 497–98.

16. Carr and Davies, *Foundations*, p. 95.

17. Lewin, *Russian Peasants*, p. 286.

18. Lomashvili, *Velikii perevorot*, pp. 133, 226, 132; for a full discussion of the statistics on "kulaks," see pp. 390–401.

19. Ibid., pp. 399, 401.

20. Ibid., p. 174.

21. Ibid., pp. 159–61.

22. Ibid., p. 145.

23. Ibid., pp. 145–46.

24. Ibid., pp. 152–53.

25. Lomashvili, *Velikii perevorot*, pp. 177–78, 156, 174–75; Kharmandarian, *Lenin*, p. 433.

26. There was much shifting of top-level personnel in 1929–1930 in Transcaucasia. In October 1929, Levon Isaevich Mirzoian (1878–1938), a secretary of the Central Committee (CC) of the Azerbaijani party since Kirov's departure in 1925, was posted to the Urals. The first secretary of the Azerbaijani CC since 1925, Aligeidir Agakerim-ogly Karaev (1896–1938), was made a secretary of Zakkraikom. In August 1930, Vladimir Ivanovich Polonskii (1893–1939) became first secretary of the Azerbaijani CC, as well as a secretary of the Zakkraikom in November 1930.

In Georgia Lavrenti Iosebis dze Kartvelishvili (1890–1938), secretary of the Georgian CC from 1925 and briefly chairman of the Sovnarkom, was sent to the Ukraine. Levan Davidis dze Gogoberidze (1896–1937), second secretary of the Georgian CC (1926–1929), was raised to first secretary briefly in May 1930 before being transferred to Moscow. He had replaced M. Kakhiani, who was shifted to Central Asia.

In Armenia a military man, Haik Hovsepian, briefly headed the party in 1927, followed by Haikaz Kostanian (1897–?) as first secretary in 1928–1930. He was replaced in May 1930 by Aghasi Khanjian (1901–1936), a young, energetic activist who had worked in Leningrad until his transfer to Armenia in April 1928.

27. Lomashvili, *Velikii perevorot*, p. 180.

28. Ibid., pp. 182, 185, 187, 417.

29. Ibid., pp. 156–57, 218–19, 419. The figure for Georgian households collectivized is given elsewhere as 67.7 percent.

30. Davies, *Industrialization of Soviet Russia*, vol. 1, p. 202.

31. Lomashvili, *Velikii perevorot,* pp. 195–96.

32. Ibid., pp. 196, 198.

33. Lewin, *Russian Peasants,* p. 488.

34. Lomashvili, *Velikii perevorot,* pp. 275–76.

35. Ibid., pp. 275, 274.

36. Ibid., pp. 238–39, 252, 262–64, 270.

37. Lewin, *Russian Peasants,* p. 515.

38. Stalin, *Sochineniia,* vol. 12, pp. 193, 198. The Toz (*Tovarishchestvo po obshchestvennoi obrabotki zemli;* cooperative with joint labor) was the simplest form of collective farm. Only the land and heavy equipment were held in common, while livestock, implements, housing, and some land were privately owned and worked. The *artel* was a more socialized form in which land, most equipment and livestock were collectively held and worked but in which peasants maintained household plots. In the *kommuna* all property was collectively owned and families lived in communal housing and usually ate together. Each of these forms was considered a *kolkhoz (kollektivnoe khoziaistvo)* until 1930, when Stalin declared the *artel* to be the preferable form of collective farm.

39. Davies, *Industrialization of Soviet Russia,* vol. 1, pp. 273–74.

40. *Pravda,* no. 92, April 3, 1930; I. V. Stalin, *Sochineniia,* vol. 12, p. 209.

41. Lomashvili, *Velikii perevorot,* p. 306.

42. Ibid., pp. 316, 319–20.

43. Ibid., pp. 312–14.

44. Bessarion ("Beso") Lominadze was the son of a teacher and had been active in Transcaucasian party affairs since the revolution. He was elected a candidate member of the Central Committee RKP(b) in 1925. Usually on the left in party circles, in July 1927 the Comintern sent him to China to urge a more militant policy on the Chinese Communist Party. He was a severe critic of Bukharin and was even chided by Molotov for "ultraleftism." At the Sixteenth Party Conference in April 1929 he called for excluding kulaks from collective farms except under unusual circumstances. Along with his associates, Komsomol leaders Shatskin and Sten, Lominadze was openly critical of party policy in 1929 and was demoted to the provincial post of secretary of *agitprop* (agitation and propaganda) in Nizhnyi Novgorod. His assignment as first secretary of the Transcaucasian party committee represented a kind of rehabilitation, but his identification with the "Right-Leftist" opposition later in 1930 cost him his high posts. His last assignment was as party chief in Magnitogorsk, where American worker John Scott met him (*Behind the Urals: An American Worker in Russia's City of Steel* [Cambridge, Mass., 1942; Bloomington: Indiana University Press, 1973], pp. 82–83). Roy Medvedev reports that in 1935 Stalin circulated copies of testimony by Kamenev about a conversation with Lominadze: "At a reception for metalworkers in the Kremlin, Stalin acted as if he did not recognize Lominadze. Soon after his return to Magnitogorsk, Lominadze was summoned to Cheliabinsk. He shot himself in an automobile on the way" (*Let History Judge: The Origins and Consequences of Stalinism* [New York: Knopf, 1972], p. 167).

45. *Zaria vostoka,* no. 144, June 21, 1930.

46. Ibid., no. 164, June 22, 1930.

47. R. W. Davies, "The Syrtsov-Lominadze Affair," *Soviet Studies* 33, no. 1 (January 1981): 35; *XVI s"ezd Vsesoiuznoi Kommunisticheskoi Partii (b): Stenograficheskii otchet* (Moscow-Leningrad, 1930), pp. 194–99.

48. Davies, "The Syrtsov-Lominadze Affair," p. 45.

49. Ibid., pp. 42, 41.

50. Stalin, *Sochineniia*, vol. 12, p. 279.

51. *XVII s"ezd Vsesoiuznoi Kommunisticheskoi Partii (b), 26 ianvaria-10 fevralia 1934g.: Stenograficheskii otchet* (Moscow, 1934), p. 119.

52. *Pravda*, no. 325 (4770), November 26, 1930. Kartvelishvili was born in a peasant family in Ianeti, Georgia, and joined the revolutionary movement in 1905. From 1911 when he entered the Kiev Commercial Institute until 1923 when he was elected secretary of the Georgian Central Committee, he worked in the Ukraine. After a brief stint as chairman of the Sovnarkom of Georgia in 1929, he returned to the Ukraine. He was elected a candidate member of the Central Committee of the VKP(b) in 1930. From 1931 until 1933 he worked in Transcaucasia, then in western Siberia and Crimea, before his death in the Great Purges (*Bolshaia sovetskaia entsiklopedia*, vol. 11, p. 464; Boris Levytsky, *The Stalinist Terror in the Thirties: Documentation from the Soviet Press* [Stanford: Hoover Institution Press, 1974], pp. 242–43).

53. Lomashvili, *Velikii perevorot*, pp. 349–50, 348.

54. Ibid., pp. 218–29, 351, 358. The highest gains were in Azerbaijan (16.6 to 46.1 percent) and Armenia (12.1 to 40.2 percent). On p. 353, Lomashvili gives the figure of 49 percent for collectivized peasant households in Transcaucasia on October 1, 1931.

55. *Promethée* (Paris), no. 55 (June 1931), pp. 22–23; Lomashvili, *Velikii perevorot*, pp. 351, 356–58.

56. Lomashvili, *Velikii perevorot*, pp. 361–62; M. V. Natmeladze, "Nekotorye voprosy razvitiia rabochego klassa Gruzii v period sotsialisticheskoi industrializatsii," in *Rabochii klass i industrial'noe razvitie SSSR* (Moscow, 1975), pp. 169–73.

57. *Ocherki istorii kommunisticheskikh organizatsii Zakavkaz'ia* (1971), p. 206; *Zaria vostoka*, no. 252, September 13, 1931, no. 261, September 22, 1931.

58. Roy Medvedev cites information from Snegov, who in 1931 was head of the organizational section of the Zakkraikom. Beria, says Snegov, met Stalin when he went to Tskhaltuba in Georgia for a rest cure. For a month and a half Georgian GPU men guarded Stalin, and Beria frequently spoke with him. When Stalin returned to Moscow, he requested a report for the Politburo on Transcaucasian affairs. All the top leaders were summoned to Moscow, and at a meeting chaired by Kaganovich, L. Kartvelishvili, G. Davdariani, V. Polonskii, and A. Khanjian were invited to speak. Stalin then spoke at length and proposed Beria as second secretary of the Zakkraikom. Kartvelishvili protested: "I will not work with that charlatan." The majority of the Zakkraikom rejected the suggestion. Stalin was furious: "Well, so what, we'll settle this question the routine way."

When the meeting ended, the Zakkraikom members went to see Orjonikidze, who had refused to attend "the coronation of Beria." He was depressed about the decision and told his old associates: "For a long time I've been telling Stalin that Beria is a crook, but Stalin won't listen to me, and no one can make him change his mind." The next day the personnel changes were made: Orakhelashvili became first secretary of Zakkraikom, Beria second secretary. Kartvelishvili, Davdariani, Snegov, and A. I. Iakovlev all left Transcaucasia for work elsewhere. (Medvedev, *Let History Judge*, pp. 242–43.) From all indications the appointment of Beria seems to have been a challenge to Orjonikidze, but at the same time his old comrade Orakhelashvili was put in charge, probably as a compromise or interim measure.

Snegov, who spent seventeen years in prison camp, was rehabilitated after Stalin's death, and his report was quoted by Nikita Khrushchev in his famous "secret speech" of 1956 denouncing the crimes of Stalin. Khrushchev went on to say: "The long unfriendly relations between Kartvelishvili and Beria were widely known. They date back to the time when Comrade Sergo [Orjonikidze] was active in the Transcaucasus; Kartvelishvili was Sergo's closest assistant. The unfriendly relationship impelled Beria to fabricate a 'case' against Kartvelishvili. It is characteristic that in this 'case' Kartvelishvili was charged with a terroristic act against Beria" (*Khrushchev Speaks: Selected Speeches, Articles, and Press Conferences, 1949–1961,* edited by Thomas P. Whitney [Ann Arbor: University of Michigan Press, 1963], p. 250).

59. *Zaria vostoka,* no. 302, November 6, 1931, and no. 306, November 10, 1931; Kharmandarian, *Lenin,* pp. 433–34; Gugushvili et al., *Istoriia kollektivizatsii,* pp. 369–70.

60. *Zaria vostoka,* no. 311, November 15, 1931, no. 309, November 13, 1931, and no. 313, November 19, 1931. Gugushvili et al., *Istoriia kollektivizatsii,* pp. 391–92. Beria's speech was published in *Zaria vostoka,* no. 22, January 27, 1932, no. 23, January 28, and no. 24, January 29.

61. *Ocherki istorii kommunisticheskikh organizatsii Zakavkaz'ia* (1971), p. 212; *Ocherki istorii kommunisticheskoi partii Gruzii* (1971), pp. 341–42; Kharmandarian, *Lenin,* pp. 433–34.

62. Lomashvili, *Velikii perevorot,* p. 435. P. N. Lomashvili, "K voprosu ob osobennostiakh stroitel'stva sotsializma v Zakavkaz'e (1921–1936 gg.)," *Voprosy istorii KPSS* 5 (May 1964): 100.

63. Lomashvili, *Velikii perevorot,* pp. 447, 455–56; Zhgenti, *Istoriia kolkhoznogo stroitel'stva,* p. 135.

64. Lomashvili, *Velikii perevorot,* pp. 442, 444.

65. Moshe Lewin, "'Taking Grain': Soviet Policies of Agricultural Procurements Before the War," in Chimen Abramsky, ed., *Essays in Honour of E. H. Carr* (Hamden, Conn.: Archon Books, 1974), p. 314.

66. Fitzpatrick, *Cultural Revolution,* p. 10.

67. For a full discussion of national communism in the Ukraine, see James E. Mace, *Communism and the Dilemmas of National Liberation: National Communism in Soviet Ukraine, 1918–1933* (Cambridge, Mass.: Harvard Ukrainian Research Institute, 1983).

68. *Promethée* (Paris), no. 56 (July 1931), pp. 23–24.

69. *Kommunisti,* June 6, 1931; *Promethée* (Paris), no. 56 (July 1931), p. 22.

70. *XVII s"ezd,* p. 31.

71. Ibid., p. 32.

CHAPTER 12

1. R. W. Davies, "The Soviet Economic Crisis of 1931–1933," CREES Discussion Papers, Soviet Industrialization Series no. 4, University of Birmingham, 1976; Dana G. Dalrymple, "The Soviet Famine of 1932–1934," *Soviet Studies* 15, no. 3 (January 1964): 250–84.

2. Boris I. Nicolaevsky, "The Letter of an Old Bolshevik," in Janet D. Zagoria, ed., *Power and the Soviet Elite* (New York: Praeger, 1965), pp. 28–30.

3. *Pravda,* January 13, 1933; Medvedev, *Let History Judge,* p. 155.

4. Lewin, "Taking Grain," p. 297.

5. Davies, "The Soviet Economic Crisis," p. 21; Stalin, *Sochineniia,* vol. 13, p. 186.

6. Lewin, "Taking Grain," p. 313.

7. Merle Fainsod, *Smolensk Under Soviet Rule* (Cambridge, Mass.: Harvard University Press, 1958; Vintage paperback, 1963), pp. 185–88.

8. Roy Medvedev, *All Stalin's Men* (Oxford: Basil Blackwell, 1983), p. viii.

9. The Chekist Mikhail Sergeevich Kedrov (1878–1941) was sent to Baku in the early 1920s to investigate the operations of the local Cheka. He apparently discovered something compromising about the young Beria and recommended that he be dismissed from the service. After Beria became head of the NKVD, Kedrov and his youngest son, Igor, sent Stalin letters accusing Beria of treacherous activities. Igor Kedrov was arrested and shot; Mikhail Kedrov was arrested in 1939, tried by the military collegium of the Supreme Court, acquitted, but then ordered shot by Beria (*Leningradskaia pravda*, February 25, 1964; Werner G. Hahn, *Postwar Soviet Politics: The Fall of Zhdanov and the Defeat of Moderation, 1946–53* [Ithaca, N.Y.: Cornell University Press, 1982], pp. 163–64; Levytsky, *Stalinist Terror*, pp. 485–89).

10. Suren Gazarian, "O Berii i sude nad Berievtsami v Gruzii," *SSSR. Vnutrennie protivorechiia* 6 (1982): 113. This is a published excerpt from the *samizdat* manuscript by a former Chekist who worked in Tiflis until his arrest in 1937 (*Eto ne dolzhno povtorit'sia* [1958–1961]).

11. Suren Gazarian, *Eto ne dolzhno povtorit'sia*. Among those whom Gazarian mentions as having left Transcaucasia because of Beria was Ervand Asribekov, secretary of the Tiflis city committee.

12. In his memoirs Konstantin Konstantinovich Orjonikidze, Sergo's brother, relates that Stalin did not like Orakhelashvili and had to be persuaded by Sergo to visit him when in Tiflis. The arrests of Orakhelashvili and his wife followed Orjonikidze's suicide in February 1937. When Beria visited Orjonikidze's widow after Sergo's death, Zinaida Gavrilovna slapped him and called him *"negodiai"* (scoundrel) in the presence of Stalin, Molotov, Zhdanov, and others (*Politicheskii dnevnik* 55 [April 1963]; Medvedev, *Let History Judge*, pp. 196, 243).

13. Stalin, *Sochineniia*, vol. 13, pp. 84–102.

14. John Barber, "Stalin's Letter to the Editors of *Proletarskaya Revolyutsya*," *Soviet Studies* 28, no. 1 (January 1976): 32; Robert C. Tucker, "The Rise of Stalin's Personality Cult," *American Historical Review* 84, no. 2 (April 1979): 356.

15. *Zaria vostoka*, no. 90, April 17, 1932, no. 69, March 23, 1932, no. 83, April 9, 1932, and no. 85, April 11, 1932. For a discussion of the rewriting of Caucasian party history in the Stalinist mode, see the still-interesting Bertram D. Wolfe, *Three Who Made a Revolution: A Biographical History* (New York: Dial Press, 1948; Stein and Day, 1984), pp. 399–474.

16. *Zaria vostoka*, no. 11, January 12, 1934, and no. 13, January 14, 1934. Suren Gazarian, who was then working in the Tiflis NKVD, writes that Beria's men were preparing a case against Makharadze. Bogdan Kobulov was assigned to gather incriminating material on the Old Bolshevik and to establish that he headed all counterrevolutionary work in Georgia. Depositions to this effect were given by German Mgaloblishvili, Karp Modebadze, David Bagrationi, Budu Mdivani, Shalva Eliava, and many others. But the case was never used against Makharadze ("O Berii," p. 199). Instead of imprisonment or execution, Makharadze was elected chairman of the presidium of the Supreme Soviet of the Georgian republic in 1938, a largely ceremonial position. He died on December 10, 1941 (Makharadze, *Filipp Makharadze*, pp. 147, 149).

17. *Zaria vostoka*, no. 13, January 14, 1934.

18. L. Beria, "K voprosu ob istorii bol'shevistskikh organizatsii v Zakavkaz'i,"

Zaria vostoka, no. 170, July 24, 1935; no. 171, July 25, 1935. Medvedev reports that the real author of the history was the Georgian commissar of education, Bedia, who later was falsely accused of political crimes and killed (*Let History Judge,* p. 327).

19. T. H. Rigby, *Communist Party Membership in the U.S.S.R., 1917–1967* (Princeton, N.J.: Princeton University Press, 1968), pp. 52, 204; *Zaria vostoka,* no. 15, January 16, 1934. The distinction between various purges has been clearly drawn in J. Arch Getty, "Party and Purge in Smolensk: 1933–1937," *Slavic Review* 42, no. 1 (Spring 1983): 66–67; and in his book, *Origins of the Great Purges: The Soviet Communist Party Reconsidered, 1933–1938* (Cambridge, England: Cambridge University Press, 1985).

20. *Kommunisticheskaia Partiia Gruzii v tsifrakh (1921–1970 gg.): Sbornik statisticheskikh materialov* (Tbilisi, 1971), pp. 62, 65.

21. Gazarian, *Eto ne dolzhno povtorit'sia,* pp. 44–48.

22. Gugushvili et al., *Istoriia kollektivizatsii,* pp. 466–68. *Zaria vostoka,* no. 11, January 12, 1934.

23. *Zaria vostoka,* no. 15, January 16, 1934; no. 19, January 20, 1934.

24. *XVII s"ezd,* pp. 129–30, 117.

25. Ibid., p. 28.

26. See, for example, Getty, *Origins of the Great Purges;* Gabor T. Rittersporn, "L'État en lutte contre lui-meme: Tensions sociales et conflicts politiques en U.S.S.R. 1936–1938," *Libre* (Paris) 4 (1978): 3–38 [English translation: "The State Against Itself: Socialist Tensions and Political Conflict in the U.S.S.R. 1936–1938," *Telos* 41 (Fall 1979): 87–104]; "Société et appareil d'état soviétiques (1936–1938): Contradictions et interferences," *Annales E.S.C.* 4 (1979): 843–67; "Staline en 1938: Apogée du verbe et défaite politique, Eléments pour une étude du 'stalinisme réel,' " *Libre* 6 (1979): 99–164 [English translation: "Stalin in 1938: Political Defeat Behind the Rhetorical Apotheosis," *Telos* 46 (Winter 1980–81): 6–42]; "Du Goulag de la littérature à l'histoire de la politique pénale en Union soviétique, 1933–1953," *Critique politique* 7/8 (1981): 3–68; "The 1930s in the Longue Durée of Soviet History," *Telos* 53 (Fall 1982): 107–16.

27. See the interesting essay by Francesco Benvenuti, "Kirov in Soviet Politics, 1933–1934," CREES Discussion Papers, Soviet Industrialisation Series no. 8, University of Birmingham, 1977, pp. 20–23.

28. Robert Conquest, *The Great Terror: Stalin's Purge of the Thirties* (London and New York: Macmillan, 1968), chap. 1, "Stalin Prepares"; and Getty, *Origins of the Great Purges.*

29. Conquest, *Great Terror,* pp. 58–60. Twenty-two years after Kirov's assassination, Nikita Khrushchev hinted in his famous "secret speech" to the Twentieth Party Congress that Stalin had been involved in the killing, and Western historians and Soviet dissidents developed a theory that Kirov had become a rival to Stalin. But other historians, among them Francesco Benvenuti, J. Arch Getty, and Adam Ulam, doubt Stalin's complicity or the suggestion that Kirov opposed Stalin in any threatening way. Circumstantial evidence suggests, however, that the Leningrad NKVD functionaries were involved in some way.

30. Getty, *Origins of the Great Purges,* p. 64.

31. Ibid., and Lomashvili, *Velikii perevorot,* p. 443.

32. *Pravda,* May 26, 1935, and January 16, 1935; Medvedev, *Let History Judge,* p. 167.

33. L. Beria, *On the History of the Bolshevik Organizations in Transcaucasia,*

Speech Delivered at a Meeting of Party Functionaries, July 21–22, 1935 (New York: International Publishers, n.d.), p. 35; *Pravda*, June 8, 1935; Conquest, *Great Terror*, p. 88.

34. *Zaria vostoka*, no. 73, April 4, 1936.

35. Boris Pasternak, *Letters to Georgian Friends*, trans. David Magarshack (London: Secker and Warburg, 1967), p. 65. In despair Pasternak wrote to Iashvili's widow: "When again and again I come to the realisation that never again shall I see that wonderful face with its high, inspired forehead and laughing eyes and never hear the voice whose very sound was fascinating from its overflow of ideas, I burst into tears, I toss about in anguish and can find no place for myself" (pp. 70–71).

36. Gazarian, *Eto ne dolzhno povtorit'sia*, p. 163.

37. A quarter-century later it was claimed that Beria had killed Khanjian in his office. See Shelepin's speech at the Twenty-second Party Congress, *Kommunist* (Erevan), November 15, 1961; November 28, 1963; Conquest, *Great Terror*, pp. 248–49; Medvedev, *Let History Judge*, pp. 367–68.

38. *Pravda*, August 19, 1936; *Zaria vostoka*, no. 193, August 20, 1936.

39. *Report of the Court Proceedings: The Case of the Trotskyite-Zinovievite Terrorist Centre* (Moscow, 1936), pp. 109–10.

40. Bertram D. Wolfe, *Khrushchev and Stalin's Ghost: Text, Background and Meaning of Khrushchev's Secret Report to the Twentieth Congress on the Night of February 24–25, 1956* (London: Atlantic Press, 1957), p. 173; Conquest, *Great Terror*, p. 155.

41. Fainsod, *Smolensk Under Soviet Rule*, p. 233.

42. Bailes, *Technology and Society*, pp. 76, 275–84; Victor Kravchenko, *I Chose Freedom: The Personal and Political Life of a Soviet Official* (Garden City, N.Y.: Garden City Publishing Co., 1946), pp. 215, 232; *Pravda*, November 17, 1964, reports Orjonikidze's protection of the Caucasian Old Bolshevik Hamaiak Nazaretian.

43. Rittersporn, "Staline en 1938," pp. 104–5.

44. For a brief and sober discussion of the dimensions of the Great Purges, see Jerry F. Hough and Merle Fainsod, *How the Soviet Union Is Governed* (Cambridge, Mass.: Harvard University Press, 1979), pp. 176–77. The conclusion here is that "the number of deaths in the purge would certainly be placed in the hundreds of thousands rather than in excess of a million. A figure in the low hundreds of thousands seems much more probable than one in the high hundreds of thousands" (p. 177).

45. *Pravda*, no. 153, June 5, 1937. I am grateful to Gabor Rittersporn for alerting me to the criticism of the Georgian party in mid-1937.

46. Ibid.

47. Of the men specifically criticized by the *Pravda* correspondent, several perished in the purges. A. S. Agrba was later shot; Gobechia's fate is unknown to me; and I. D. Kochlamazashvili escaped harm and in June 1938 was named second secretary of the Georgian Central Committee, just behind Beria (*Zaria vostoka*, no. 142, June 21, 1938). (I am presuming that this is the same Kochlamazashvili; no initials are given in the *Pravda* report.) When Beria moved on to Moscow, Kochlamazashvili did not succeed him, however, but was appointed chairman of the Tbilisi soviet (ibid., no. 200, September 1, 1938).

48. *Pravda*, no. 143, May 26, 1937, no. 145, May 28, 1937, no. 153, June 5, 1937, and no. 154, June 6, 1937.

49. Conquest, *Great Terror*, pp. 248–49. The arbitrariness of the Great Purges is illustrated by the survival of one of the most vulnerable Old Bolsheviks, Sergei

Ivanovich Kavtaradze, who had been a member of the Trotskyist opposition in the 1920s. Medvedev reports that Kavtaradze was exiled after Kirov's assassination until he wrote to Stalin saying that he was not working against the party. Stalin brought him back from exile, and soon after an article by Kavtaradze appeared in central newspapers on his underground work with Stalin. Suddenly at the end of 1936 he and his wife were arrested, tortured, and sentenced to be shot. He was implicated in Mdivani's alleged plot to kill Stalin. Yet both he and his wife were eventually released, given work and an apartment, and were visited by Stalin and Beria. "When he had Kavtaradze to dinner, Stalin himself would pour the soup, tell jokes, and reminisce. But during one of these dinners, Stalin suddenly went up to his guest and said, 'And still you wanted to kill me.' " This story was told to Medvedev by Kavtaradze himself (*Let History Judge*, pp. 310–11).

50. *Zaria vostoka*, no. 195, August 26, 1937; typed copy is available in the archives of the Hoover Institution, (ms) DK 511 G47T88; Conquest, *Great Terror*, pp. 249–50.

51. *Ocherki istorii Kommunisticheskoi partii Armenii* (Erevan, 1967), p. 387. While the Russian edition of 1967 does not mention Malenkov's name, the Armenian version of 1963 does. See *Hayastani Komunistakan partiayi batmutyan urvagtser* (Erevan, 1963), p. 488.

Malenkov and Mikoyan were sent with Beria to purge the Armenian party and other high officials, like Kaganovich, were sent to other regions and republics, but no prominent outsider was sent to Georgia. Beria was permitted to "cleanse" his own machine in the fall of 1937. Yet he still may have been in trouble by the end of that year or early in 1938, if a rumor reported by Gazarian has any validity. According to this memoirist, Goglidze, the commissar of internal affairs in Georgia and a Beria loyalist, received a telegram from Ezhov ordering Beria's arrest and transport to Moscow. Goglidze showed the message to Beria but did not arrest him. Beria flew to Moscow, met with Stalin, and instead of going to jail was soon positioned to replace Ezhov (Gazarian, "O Berii," pp. 119–20; Conquest, *Great Terror*, p. 452).

52. *Zaria vostoka*, no. 220, September 26, 1937, no. 249, October 29, 1937, and no. 275, December 2, 1937. A study of the purges in Abkhazeti concluded: "The weight of circumstantial evidence points to the fact that the terror was directed against a coalescing governing stratum that refused to subject its inner circle to a thorough purge, and probably manifested autonomist strivings in other realms . . . the most plausible explanation seems to lie in the resistance of the regional leadership to premature collectivization and its destructive effects on agricultural productivity and the social fabric of the province." (Patrick Flaherty, "Stalinism in Transition, 1932–1937," *Radical History Review* [1987], p. 60.)

53. *Pravda*, December 30, 1937; *Zaria vostoka*, no. 19, January 25, 1938.

54. Rittersporn argues that this trial signaled to the new people in the state and party apparatus that they would be relatively safe, for the accused were guilty of crimes linked to their oppositional past or, in the case of Iagoda, to police excesses ("Staline en 1938," p. 147).

55. An émigré reported later that Beria had proposed V. M. Bakradze, the chairman of the Sovnarkom, as party chief, but Stalin appointed Charkviani. The two men became rivals and formed separate clientele within the Georgian party (Sandro Anageli, "K politicheskim sobytiiam v Gruzii," *Ob"edinennyi Kavkaz* 5 [22] [May 1953], p. 20).

56. Conquest, *Great Terror*, pp. 464–65; Gazarian, "O Berii," p. 120.

57. See A. L. Unger, "Stalin's Renewal of the Leading Stratum: A Note on the Great Purge," *Soviet Studies* 20, no. 3 (January 1969): 321–30.

58. Rigby, *Communist Party Membership*, pp. 230–31.

59. Kendall E. Bailes, "Stalin and the Making of a New Elite: A Comment," *Slavic Review* 39, no. 2 (June 1980): 268.

60. Jashi's speech in *XVIII s"ezd Vsesoiuznoi Kommunisticheskoi Partii (b), 10–21 marta 1939 g.: Stenograficheskii otchet* (Moscow, 1939), p. 577.

61. Ibid., p. 578. For a discussion of the creation of the new ruling elite in the USSR, see Sheila Fitzpatrick, "Stalin and the Making of a New Elite, 1928–1939," *Slavic Review* 38, no. 3 (September 1979): 377–402.

62. *Narodnoe khoziaistvo Gruzinskoi SSR: K 60-letiiu Velikogo Oktiabria. Iubileinyi statisticheskii ezhegodnik* (Tbilisi, 1977), pp. 10, 134, 137; *Sovetskaia Gruziia k 50-letiiu Velikoi Oktiabr'skoi Sotsialisticheskoi Revoliutsii* (Tbilisi, 1967), p. 197. Not until 1975 did 50 percent of Georgia's population live in towns and cities; that same year Tbilisi passed one million in population. During World War II, female employment had reached a high of 42 percent of the work force in Georgia.

63. Natmeladze and Sturua, *Iz istorii*, p. 92.

64. *Zaria vostoka*, no. 273, November 29, 1938.

65. Ibid., no. 31, February 8, 1938.

66. *XVIII s"ezd Vsesoiuznoi kommunisticheskoi partii (b), 10–21 marta 1939 g.: Stenograficheskii otchet* (Moscow, 1939), p. 14.

67. I. P. Babalashvili, *Gruzinskaia SSR v gody Velikoi Otechestvennoi voiny, 1941–1945* (Tbilisi, 1977), pp. 87, 157.

68. Ibid., p. 152; David M. Lang, "Religion and Nationalism: A Case Study: The Caucasus," in Max Hayward and William C. Fletcher, eds., *Religion and the Soviet State: A Dilemma of Power* (New York: Praeger, 1969), pp. 178–79.

69. Babalashvili, *Gruzinskaia SSR*, pp. 200, 318–19. Between 1939 and 1946 urban population in Georgia rose by 20,000; rural population fell by 327,000.

70. Bruce R. Kuniholm, *The Origins of the Cold War in the Near East: Great Power Conflict and Diplomacy in Iran, Turkey, and Greece* (Princeton, N.J.: Princeton University Press, 1980), pp. 255–70, 287.

71. *Khrushchev Remembers: The Last Testament*, trans. and ed. Strobe Talbott (Boston: Little, Brown, 1974), pp. 295–96.

72. *Pravda*, July 19, 1953.

73. For a discussion of the Muradeli affair, see Alexander Werth, *Musical Uproar in Moscow* (London: Turnstile Press, 1949). There are two recent studies of the Zhdanov period: Gavriel D. Ra'anan, *International Policy Formation in the USSR: Factional "Debates" During the Zhdanovshchina* (Hamden, Conn.: Archon Books, 1983); and Hahn, *Postwar Soviet Politics*. Hahn argues that Zhdanov was a moderate; Ra'anan sees him as a militant. See also William O. McCagg, Jr., *Stalin Embattled, 1943–1948* (Detroit, Mich.: Wayne State University Press, 1978).

74. "The replacement of Merkulov by Abakumov in the M.G.B. was at best the removal of one of Beria's oldest and closest associates in favour of one whose connection with him was at any rate rather slighter" (Robert Conquest, *Power and Policy in the U.S.S.R.: The Struggle of Stalin's Succession, 1945–1960* [London: Macmillan, 1961; Harper Torchbook, 1967], pp. 87–88).

75. *Khrushchev Remembers*, trans. and ed. Strobe Talbott, intro. and notes by Edward Crankshaw (Boston: Little, Brown, 1970), pp. 311–12. (Hereafter, *Khrushchev Remembers*, vol. 1.)

76. Hahn, *Postwar Soviet Politics*, pp. 122–35, 137; *Khrushchev Remembers*, vol. 1, pp. 250, 313.

77. *Khrushchev Remembers,* vol. 1, pp. 296–301, 312.

78. Conquest, *Power and Policy,* p. 136. The most important square in Tbilisi had historically been known as Erivan Square. Later its name was changed to Transcaucasian Federation Square, then to Beria Square. One does not anticipate another name change as long as the Soviet government rules in Georgia; it is now called Lenin Square.

79. Charles H. Fairbanks, Jr., "National Cadres as a Force in the Soviet System: The Evidence of Beria's Career, 1949–53," in Jeremy R. Azrael, ed., *Soviet Nationality Policies and Practices* (New York: Praeger, 1978), p. 156.

80. *Khrushchev Remembers,* vol. 1, p. 305.

81. Ibid., pp. 307, 257–58, 310.

82. Hahn, *Postwar Soviet Politics,* pp. 141–42; Conquest, *Power and Policy,* p. 139; Fairbanks, "National Cadres," p. 150.

83. Charles H. Fairbanks, Jr., "Clientelism and Higher Politics in Georgia, 1949–1953," in Suny, *Transcaucasia, Nationalism and Social Change,* p. 343. V. K. Balavadze headed the party organs department, later became first secretary of the Tbilisi *gorkom;* Ia. Zarandia became first secretary of the Poti *gorkom,* and R. S. Kandelaki headed the Komsomol.

84. Bakradze, Mirtskhulava, G. F. Sturua, and the deposed Mingrelians were Beria's men; Chkhubianishvili and Gogua were Charkviani's; V. D. Bujiashvili, Ketskhoveli, Mgeladze, the Balavadzes, and Getia were Stalin's (Conquest, *Power and Policy,* pp. 150–52; Fairbanks, "National Cadres," pp. 160–61.)

85. Fairbanks, "Clientelism and Higher Politics," p. 358.

86. *Khrushchev Remembers,* vol. 1, p. 312.

87. Fairbanks, "National Cadres," pp. 155, 146–49; *Pravda,* no. 283, October 9, 1952.

88. For the most complete account of these events and their consequences, see Aleksandr M. Nekrich, *The Punished Peoples: The Deportation and Fate of Soviet Minorities at the End of the Second World War* (New York: Norton, 1978).

89. Ibid., pp. 42, 104–5.

90. Medvedev, *Let History Judge,* p. 452; Mordechai Altshuler, "Georgian Jewish Culture Under the Soviet Regime," *Soviet Jewish Affairs 5,* no. 2 (1975): 37.

91. "XV s'ezd KP(b) Gruzii," *Pravda,* no. 264, September 20, 1952. For the treatment by historians of Iurii Bogoliubskii, see Lowell Tillett, *The Great Friendship: Soviet Historians on the Non-Russian Nationalities* (Chapel Hill: University of North Carolina Press, 1969), pp. 327–29.

92. Alec Nove and J. A. Newth, *The Soviet Middle East: A Communist Model for Development?* (London: Allen and Unwin, 1967), pp. 113–14, 120.

93. Alvin W. Gouldner, "Stalinism: A Study of Internal Colonialism," *Telos 34* (Winter 1977–78: 13.

CHAPTER 13

1. A lengthy, though uneven, attempt to examine the indigenous development of Soviet nationalities is the collection of essays edited by George W. Simmonds: *Nationalism in the USSR and Eastern Europe in the Era of Brezhnev and Kosygin: Papers and Proceedings of the Symposium Held at University of Detroit on October 3–4, 1975* (Detroit, Mich.: University of Detroit Press, 1977).

2. *XXII s"ezd Kommunisticheskoi Partii Sovetskogo Soiuza, 17–31 oktiabria 1961 goda: Stenograficheskii otchet,* III (Moscow, 1962), p. 314.

3. Teresa Rakowska-Harmstone, "The Dialectics of Nationalism in the USSR," *Problems of Communism* 22, no. 3 (May–June 1974): 18–19.

4. *Vedomosti verkhovnogo soveta,* 1965, no. 36, p. 839.

5. A. Shtromas, "The Legal Position of Soviet Nationalities and Their Territorial Units According to the 1977 Constitution of the USSR," *Russian Review* 37, no. 3 (July 1978): 267.

6. *Izvestiia,* October 5, 1977; trans. in E. Bagramov, "A Factual Survey of the Soviet Nationalities Policy," *Reprints from the Soviet Press* 27, no. 5 (September 15, 1978): 49.

7. Shtromas, "Legal Position," p. 271.

8. Ibid.

9. *Izvestiia,* October 5, 1977; trans. from Shtromas, "Legal Position," pp. 271–72.

10. The historian of this period, David Marshall Lang, writes: "By the year 1800, the process of disintegration of the Georgian state had reached a critical stage . . . Left to itself, it is doubtful whether the Georgian nation would even have been assured of physical survival" (*Last Years,* pp. 282–83).

11. The revolution in Georgia and the controversy over Georgian autonomy after 1921 are discussed in Pipes, *The Formation of the Soviet Union.* See also Kazemzadeh, *Struggle.*

12. Richard B. Dobson, "Georgia and the Georgians," in Zev Katz, ed., *Handbook of Major Soviet Nationalities* (New York: Free Press, 1975), p. 162; Nove and Newth, *Soviet Middle East,* p. 40. Of the least developed republics in the USSR, those of Central Asia and Transcaucasia, Georgia has in the post-Stalin period been growing slower than most. From 1940 to 1958 only Azerbaijan and Turkmenistan grew less rapidly than Georgia, and in the period 1958–1965 Georgia finished next to last, with only Turkmenistan behind.

13. *Vestnik Statistiki,* no. 5, 1979, pp. 68, 72–73.

14. Dobson, "Georgia and the Georgians," p. 162; *Vestnik Statistiki,* 1981, no. 1, pp. 66–67. However, among ethnic Georgians only 49 percent were "workers" in 1979 (this figure included agricultural workers), 32 percent were "employees," and 19 percent were collective farmers (Iu. Arutiunian, "Korennye izmeneniia v sotsial'nom sostave sovetskikh natsii," *Sotsiologicheskie issledovaniia,* no. 4 [October–December, 1982], p. 23).

15. Katz, *Handbook,* pp. 147, 194.

16. This argument is made by Nove and Newth, *Soviet Middle East.*

17. Richard Pipes, "Introduction: The Nationality Problem," in Katz, *Handbook,* p. 3. The contradiction between modernization and ethnic revival was explored by V. Stanley Vardys in an excellent short study of Baltic nationalism and modernization, but his conclusion that modernization has been ineffective in eroding nationality begs the question of why this paradox exists ("Modernization and Baltic Nationalism," *Problems of Communism* 24, no. 5 [September–October 1975: 32–48]. A partial answer is provided by Teresa Rakowska-Harmstone, who argues that the "powerful integrative forces" of modernization, which one would expect to work against the preservation of ethnicity, have been modified somewhat in the national republics where "the retention of a federal administrative framework safeguarded the territorial loci and formal ethnocultural institutions of most minorities, thereby preserving the bases for potential manifestations of national attitudes" ("Dialectics of Nationalism,"

p. 2). Trond Gilberg demonstrates the limits of Karl Deutsch's modernization model, which predicts cultural assimilation of minorities, in an interesting article on modernization in Romania ("Romania: Problems of the Multilaterally Developed Society," in Charles Gati, ed., *The Politics of Modernization in Eastern Europe: Testing the Soviet Model* [New York: Praeger, 1974], pp. 117–59).

18. J. A. Newth, "The 1970 Soviet Census," *Soviet Studies* 24, no. 2 (October 1972): 215; *Vestnik Statistiki*, no. 10, 1980, p. 67; Dobson, "Georgia and the Georgians," p. 168.

19. The number of Russians in Georgia fell from 408,000 in 1959 to 397,000 in 1970. In 1979 the number of ethnic Georgians in the USSR was 3,571,000; the population of the republic was 4,993,000. The number of Armenians in Georgia rose by only 2 percent while the number of Armenians in Azerbaijan rose by 9.5 percent and those in Armenia rose by 42.3 percent between 1959 and 1970. The number of Azerbaijanis in Georgia, a group that is largely rural, has a high birthrate and apparently does not migrate, rose in the same period by 41.6 percent. (Newth, "The 1970 Soviet Census," pp. 216, 218.)

20. Ibid., p. 215; Teresa Rakowska-Harmstone, "The Study of Ethnic Politics in the USSR," in Simmonds, *Nationalism in the USSR*, p. 24.

21. Wesley A. Fisher, "Ethnic Consciousness and Intermarriage: Correlates of Endogamy Among the Major Soviet Nationalities," *Soviet Studies* 29, no. 3 (July 1977): 398. These figures are for marriages within the Georgian republic.

22. Brian D. Silver, "Methods of Deriving Data on Bilingualism from the 1970 Soviet Census," *Soviet Studies* 27, no. 4 (October 1975): 592–97; J. W. R. Parsons, "National Integration in Soviet Georgia," *Soviet Studies* 34, no. 4 (October 1982): 556; *Current Digest of the Soviet Press* (hereafter, *CDSP*) 34, no. 49 (January 5, 1983): 4. Erevan is a special case because of the large number of immigrants from outside the Soviet Union, who usually do not speak Russian.

23. John Ducoli, "The Georgian Purges (1951–53)," *Caucasian Review* 6 (1958): 58–59; *Zaria vostoka*, October 4, 1953.

24. *Ocherki istorii Kommunisticheskoi Partii Gruzii*, II (Tbilisi, 1963), p. 252.

25. *Ocherki istorii Kommunisticheskoi Partii Gruzii, 1883–1970* (Tbilisi, 1971), p. 686.

26. *Ocherki*, II (1963), p. 262; Nove and Newth, *Soviet Middle East*, pp. 59–60, 62–63.

27. *Ocherki* (1971), p. 684; II (1963), pp. 250–51.

28. G. Charachidze, "The Riots at Tiflis: An Analysis," *Caucasian Review* 3 (1956): 99–104.

29. *Zaria vostoka*, August 9, 1956; *Ocherki*, II (1963), p. 270. Yaroslav Bilinsky suggested to me that Khrushchev's patience with Mzhavanadze might in part have been due to their close acquaintance dating back to the 1940s, when both worked in the Ukrainian party.

30. *Narodnoe khoziaistvo SSSR 1922–1972: Iubileinyi statisticheskii ezhegodnik* (Moscow, 1972), p. 515 ff; Dobson, "Georgia and the Georgians," p. 163.

31. Dobson, "Georgia and the Georgians," pp. 163, 177; *Zaria vostoka*, March 24, 1956; *Ocherki*, II (1963), p. 269.

32. Dobson, "Georgia and the Georgians," p. 177.

33. *XXII s"ezd KPSS*, III, pp. 245, 315; K. B. Udumian, "Iz opyta partiinykh organizatsii Zakavkaz'ia po internatsional'nomu vospitaniiu trudiashchikhsia," *Voprosy istorii KPSS*, 1964, no. 12 (December), p. 17.

34. *Zaria vostoka*, February 2, 1964; Udumian, "Iz opyta," pp. 25–26.

35. *Pravda,* March 6, 1972: "V tsentral'nom komitete KPSS: Ob organizatorskoi i politicheskoi rabote Tbilisskogo gorkoma Kompartii Gruzii po vypolneniiu reshenii XXIV s"ezda KPSS." An English translation of this resolution is available in *CDSP* 24, no. 10 (April 5, 1972): 7–9.

36. *Zaria vostoka,* February 28 and July 31, 1973; *CDSP* 25, no. 13 (April 15, 1973): 1; no. 31 (August 29, 1973): 5.

37. *Zaria vostoka,* February 28, 1973, November 25, 1972, July 31, 1973; *CDSP* 24, no. 50 (January 10, 1973): 5, 25, no. 13 (April 25, 1973): 2, 25, no. 31 (August 29, 1973): 5, 25, no. 12 (April 18, 1973): 9–10; *Izvestiia,* March 23, 1973.

38. Gregory Grossman, "The 'Second Economy' of the USSR," *Problems of Communism* 26, no. 5 (September–October 1977): 25–40.

39. *Zaria vostoka,* February 28, 1973; CDSP 25, no. 13 (April 25, 1973): 5. See also Konstantin Simis, *USSR: The Corrupt Society, the Secret World of Soviet Capitalism* (New York: Simon and Schuster, 1982), pp. 53–60. For a most interesting analysis based on interviews with Georgian Jewish emigrants, see Gerald Mars and Yochanan Altman, "The Cultural Bases of Soviet Georgia's Second Economy," *Soviet Studies* 35, no. 4 (October 1983): 546–60.

40. *Zaria vostoka,* July 31, 1973, November 3, 1973; *CDSP* 25, no. 31 (August 29, 1973): 6, 25, no. 44 (November 28, 1973): 4; Simis, *USSR: The Corrupt Society,* pp. 237–38. For an interpretation of the causes of Georgian corruption, see David Law, "Corruption in Georgia," *Critique* 3 (Autumn 1974): 99–107.

41. *Zaria vostoka,* February 28, 1973; *CDSP* 25, no. 13 (April 25, 1973): 6; Rakowska-Harmstone, "Dialectics of Nationalism," p. 15.

42. Two historians who wrote about the period 1917–1924, U. Sidamonidze and A. Menabde, were taken to task for their less than total condemnation of the Mensheviks and Georgian autonomists. In a speech to the Tbilisi party organization, Shevardnadze said: "There have recently been manifestations of a politically dangerous tendency, under the guise of restoring historical objectivity, to depart from a party appraisal of N. Zhordania, the Menshevik leader, double-dyed national chauvinist and inveterate enemy of Soviet Georgia, and others . . . We take a realistic view of the need for a scientific study of the historical past. However, this should help us to make better predictions of the future. One should look at the past through the eyes of the future, or the study of the past becomes an end in itself" (*Zaria vostoka,* February 8, 1974; *CDSP* 26, no. 8 [March 20, 1974]: 3). Even the official history of the Communist Party of Georgia, published in 1971, was attacked for being "unfree of subjectivism," especially in dealing with the period 1952–1970. The writing of history was a way to promote "nationalist prejudices," and the party leaders warned the academic establishment to beware of "a certain infatuation with antiquity" (*Zaria vostoka,* April 27, 1973; *CDSP* 25, no. 16 [May 16, 1973]: 5).

43. *Zaria vostoka,* April 27, 1973; *CDSP* 25, no. 16 (May 16, 1973): 5–6.

44. These rumors were reported to me in Tbilisi. In *Arkhiv samizdata* (hereafter, AS) document no. 2109, which can be found in the *Materialy samizdata* (hereafter, MS) 2/76, January 23, 1976, Georgian nationalists claim that those arrested for the fire were Jews and Armenians but that only Jewish names were released. This document claims that Vasken I, the catholicos of the Armenians, inspired this arson (p. 4).

45. *New York Times,* May 20, 1978. For reporting that Gamsakhurdia's televised expression of remorse might have been fabricated, two American journalists, Craig Whitney of the *New York Times* and Harold Piper of the *Baltimore Sun,* were ordered to retract their articles and were fined by a Moscow court. In July 1979 Gamsakhurdia asked for and was granted a pardon (*CDSP* 31, no. 27 [August 1, 1979]: 20).

Gamsakhurdia's writings have been published in the *Materialy samizdata, AS* 2581 in *MS* 28/76, August 25, 1976; *AS* 2444 in *MS* 16/76, May 14, 1976; *AS* 2580; *AS* 2757 in *MS* 42/76, December 31, 1976; *AS* 2809; and in other issues.

46. A Russian translation of Japaridze's speech was published in *AS* 2583 in *MS* 23/76, July 14, 1976.

47. *New York Times,* April 15, 1978; April 18, 1978; *Zaria vostoka,* April 16, 1978. On April 14, a similar clause was restored to the new constitution of the Armenian republic, and the same was done in Azerbaijan.

48. Interview with Professor Teimuraz Mamedovich Jafarli, deputy director of the Georgian Center for the Study, Formation, and Forecasting of Public Opinion, *Izvestiia,* August 21, 1983; *CDSP* 35, no. 34 (September 21, 1983): 11–12; RL 149/81, *Radio Liberty Research Bulletin,* XXV, 14 (3115), April 8, 1981.

49. The letter, which was first published in *Russkaia mysl'* in Paris, was published in English in RL 484/80, *Radio Liberty Research Bulletin,* XXIV, 52 (3100), December 26, 1980, pp. 4–5.

50. *XXVI s"ezd Kommunisticheskoi Partii Sovetskogo Soiuza, 23 fevral'ia-3 marta 1981 goda: Stenograficheskii otchet,* I (Moscow, 1981), p. 187. Shevardnadze's opposition to Georgian nationalism had political benefits for the non-Georgians in the republic who complained about discrimination. Even the Jews of Georgia, a group that historically had not suffered from anti-Semitic persecutions from the dominant community and that was well integrated into Georgian life, nevertheless began to emigrate to Israel and the United States in the early 1970s. After decades of hearing propaganda about the Soviet motherland (*rodina*) and the Georgian fatherland (*samshoblo*), the Georgian Jews sought their own homeland and national future outside the Soviet Union.

The Abkhaz people reacted against what they contended was Georgian interference in their national life and Tbilisi's failure to foster Abkhaz cultural and economic development. In December 1977, 130 Abkhaz intellectuals signed a letter of collective protest and circulated it widely. In May 1978, twelve thousand people gathered in the village of Lykhny to support the signers of the letter and to demand that Abkhazeti be allowed to secede from Georgia and join the Russian republic (RSFSR). After being deluged with letters and telegrams in favor of secession, Moscow dispatched I. V. Kapitonov, secretary of the Central Committee, to Sukhumi and installed a new party leader, Boris V. Adleiba, in Abkhazeti. Gently but firmly, Kapitonov told the local party *aktiv* that secession was impermissible. Shortly afterward, the government acknowledged the seriousness of Abkhaz complaints by decreeing a costly plan "for further development of the economy and culture of the Abkhaz ASSR" (*New York Times,* June 25, 1978; *Zaria vostoka,* May 26, 1978; June 7, 1978). For more on the conflict in Abkhazeti, see Roman Solchanyk and Ann Sheehy, "Kapitonov on Nationality Relations in Georgia," RL 125/78, *Radio Liberty Research Bulletin,* June 1, 1978; and Ann Sheehy, "Recent Events in Abkhazia Mirror the Complexities of National Relations in the USSR," RL 141/78, ibid., June 26, 1978.

51. For discussions of reformism versus preservation, see Stephen F. Cohen, "The Friends and Foes of Change: Reformism and Conservatism in the Soviet Union," in Stephen F. Cohen, Alexander Rabinowitch, and Robert Sharlet, eds., *The Soviet Union Since Stalin* (Bloomington: Indiana University Press, 1980), pp. 11–31; and George W. Breslauer, "Reformism, Conservatism, and Leadership Authority at the 26th Party Congress," in Seweryn Bialer and Thane Gustafson, eds., *Russia at the Crossroads: The 26th Congress of the CPSU* (London: Allen and Unwin, 1982), pp. 65–86.

52. *XXV s"ezd Kommunisticheskoi Partii Sovetskogo Soiuza, 24 fevral'ia-5 marta 1976 goda: Stenograficheskii otchet,* I (Moscow, 1976), p. 183.

53. Ibid.

54. *Ekonomicheskaia gazeta* 21 (May 1982), pp. 7–8; *CDSP* 34, no. 20 (June 16, 1982): 8–10, 35, no. 19 (June 8, 1983): 6–7; interview with E. A. Shevardnadze, *Pravda,* May 14, 1983.

55. *XXVI s"ezd KPSS,* vol. 1, p. 196.

56. *Pravda,* May 14, 1983; *CDSP* 35, no. 19 (June 8, 1983): 7.

57. *Pravda,* December 18, 1981; *CDSP* 33, no. 51 (January 20, 1982): 21.

58. *New York Times,* July 2, 1985; ibid., July 3, 1985. Shevardnadze was succeeded as party leader in Georgia by Jumbar Iliais dze Patiashvili, who had been serving as first secretary of the Gori district party committee, a secretary of the Georgian Central Committee, and a member of its bureau.

CHAPTER 14

1. *Kommunisticheskaia partiia Gruzii v tsifrakh (1921–1970 gg.) (Sbornik statisticheskikh materialov)* (Tbilisi, 1971), pp. 176, 265.

2. *Nauka i religiia,* (August 1981); *CDSP* 33, no. 45 (December 9, 1981): 15.

3. Mars and Altman, "Cultural Bases of Soviet Georgia's Second Economy," pp. 548–49.

Bibliographical Note

A full bibliography of sources and interpretations of Georgia's history is nearly as difficult to compose as a complete account of its three-thousand-year evolution. Most of the works used in preparation of this volume can be found in the notes. In this section some of the major writings about Georgia are listed for those who wish to do further reading.

Few scholars have attempted to cover the entire history of Georgia, and most have stopped short of the twentieth century. Among those who had dealt with the broad sweep of Georgia's past are:

Allen, W. E. D. *A History of the Georgian People from the Beginning Down to the Russian Conquest in the Nineteenth Century.* London: Paul, 1932; New York: Barnes and Noble, 1971.

Berdzenishvili, N. A., V. D. Dondua, M. K. Dumbadze, G. A. Melikishvili, and Sh. A. Meskhia. *Istoriia Gruzii: S drevneishikh vremen do 60-kh godov XIX veka,* vol. 1 Tbilisi, 1962.

Javakhishvili, Ivane. *kartveli eris istoria.* 4 vols. Tbilisi, 1928–1948.

Lang, David Marshall. *A Modern History of Soviet Georgia.* New York: Grove Press, 1962.

———. *The Georgians.* London: Thomas and Hudson, 1966.

On the prehistory of Georgia and its neighbors, the key works are:

Burney, Charles, and David Marshall Lang. *The Peoples of the Hills: Ancient Ararat and Caucasus.* New York: Praeger, 1972.

D'iakonov, I. M. *Predistoriia armianskogo naroda: Istoriia armianskogo nagor'ia 1500 po 500 g. do n.e. Khurrity, Luviitsky, Protoarmiane.* Erevan, 1968. For an English version, see Diakonoff, I. M. *The Pre-history of the Armenian People.* Translated by Loni Jennings. Delmar, N.Y.: Caravan Books, 1984.

Melikishvili, G. A. *Nairi-Urartu.* Tbilisi, 1954.

———. *sakartveloshi klasobrivi sazogadoebrisa da sakhelmtsipos tsarmokmnis sakitkhisatvis.* Tbilisi, 1955.

————. *K istorii drevnei Gruzii.* Tbilisi, 1959.
See also the relevant chapters in the *Cambridge Ancient History,* 3d ed. 12 vols.
Cambridge, England: Cambridge University Press, 1970– .

To begin a study of ancient and medieval Georgia the indispensable primary sources are the Georgian chronicles. Marie Brosset was the first modern scholar to publish and translate the chronicles, called in Georgian *kartlis tskhovreba* (The Life of Georgia). The original Georgian texts were published as *Histoire de la Georgie, depuis l'antiquité jusqu'au XIXᵉ siècle, publiée en géorgien, 1, Histoire ancienne, jusqu'en 1469 de J. C.,* 2 vols., St. Petersburg, 1849–1850; and *Histoire moderne, depuis 1469 jusqu'en 1800 de J. C., publiée en géorgien par D. Tchoubinof,* St. Petersburg, 1854. Brosset's translations were published in 5 volumes (St. Petersburg, 1849–1858).

Other modern editions of parts of the chronicles include:

Qaukhchishvili, S., ed. *kartlis tskhovreba: dedopliseuli nuskha.* Tiflis, 1942.
————. *kartlis tskhovreba: teksti dadgenili qvela jiritadi khelnatseris mikhedvit.* 4 vols. Tbilisi, 1955–1973.
Taqaishvili, E., ed. *kartlis tskhovreba: mariam dedoplis varianti.* Tiflis, 1906.

Pre-Christian and medieval Georgia and neighboring Armenia have been the subject of considerable monographic investigation. See, for example:

Abashmadze, V. V. *narkvevebi sakartvelos politikur modzghvrebata istoriidan.* Tbilisi, 1969.
Adontz, N. *Armeniia v epokhu Iustiniana: Politicheskoe sostoianie na osnove nakhararskogo stroia.* St. Petersburg, 1908; for an English version, see *Armenia in the Period of Justinian: The Political Conditions Based on the Naxarar System.* Translated by Nina Garsoian. Louvain-Lisbon, 1970.
Anchabadze, Z. V. *Iz istorii srednevekovoi Abkhazii VI–XVIII vv.* Sukhumi, 1959.
————. *Istoriia i kul'tura drevnei Abkhazii.* Moscow, 1964.
Charachidzé, Georges. *Introduction à l'étude de la féodalité géorgienne (Le Code de Georges le Brillant).* Paris, 1971.
————. *Le systeme religieux de la Géorgie paienne, analyse structurale d'une civilisation.* Paris, 1968.
Javakhishvili, Ivane. *dzveli kartuli saistorio mtserloba (V–XVIII ss).* Tiflis, 1921.
————. *kartuli samartlis istoria.* 3 vols. Tiflis, 1928–1929.
————. *Gosudarstvennyi stroi drevnei Gruzii i drevnei Armenii.* St. Petersburg, 1905.
Lordkipanidze, M. D. *Istoriia Gruzii XI–nachala XIII veka.* Tbilisi, 1974.
Manandian, Ia. A. *O torgovle i gorodakh Armenii v sviazi s mirovoi torgovlei drevnikh vremen.* Erevan, 1945. For an English version, see Manandian, H. A. *The Trade and Cities of Armenia in Relation to Ancient World Trade.* Translated by Nina Garsoian. Lisbon, 1965.
Meskhia, S. A. *Didgorskaia bitva.* Tbilisi, 1974.
Minorsky, Vladimir F. *Studies in Caucasian History.* London: Cambridge Oriental Series, 1953.
————. *The Turks, Iran and the Caucasus in the Middle Ages.* London: Variorum Reprints, 1978.
Mkrtumian, G. G. *Gruzinskoe feodal'noe kniazhestvo Kakheti v VIII–XI vv. i ego vzaimootnosheniia s Armeniei.* Erevan, 1983.
Sengalia, N. N. *seljukebi da sakartvelo XI saukuneshi.* Tbilisi, 1968.

Absolutely indispensable is the work of Cyril Toumanoff, whose numerous articles appeared in *Le Museon* and *Traditio*. Among his most important works are "Armenia and Georgia," *Cambridge Medieval History* (Cambridge, England: Cambridge University Press, 1966), vol. 4, pt. 1, pp. 593–637, 983–1009; *Manuel de généalogie et de chronologie pour l'histoire de la Caucasie Chrétienne (Arménie-Géorgie-Albanie)* (Rome: Edizioni Aquila, 1976); and his monumental *Studies in Christian Caucasian History* (Washington, D.C.: Georgetown University Press, 1963).

For the late Middle Ages and early modern period, see:

Allen, W. E. D., ed. *Russian Embassies to the Georgian Kings (1589–1605)*. 2 vols. Translated by Anthony Mango. Cambridge, England: Cambridge University Press, 1970.

Bagrationi, Vakhushti. *aghtsera sameposa sakartvelosa*. In vol. 4 of *kartlisa tskhovreba*, edited by S. Qaukhchishvili. Tbilisi, 1973. The Russian translation is *Istoriia tsarstva gruzinskogo*. Tbilisi, 1976.

Chardin, John. *Travels of Sir John Chardin into Persia and the East Indies, Through the Black Sea and the Country of Colchis*. London, 1691.

Lang, David Marshall. *The Last Years of the Georgian Monarchy, 1658–1832*. New York: Columbia University Press, 1957.

Megreladze, Darejan. *glekhobis klasobrivi brdzola peodalur sakartveloshi*. Tbilisi, 1979.

Meskhia, Sh. A. *Goroda i gorodskoi stroi feodal'noi Gruzii XVII–XVIII vv*. Tbilisi, 1956.

Tsagareli, A. A. *Gramoty i drugie istoricheskie dokumenty XVIII stoletiia, otnosiashchiesia k Gruzii*. 2 vols. St. Petersburg, 1891, 1902.

The century of tsarist rule has been treated in both documentary source books and monographs:

Antelava, I. G. *Gosudarstvennye krest'iane Gruzii v XIX veke*. 2 vols. 1962, 1969.

Antelava, I. G., E. A. Orjonikidze, and E. V. Khoshtaria. *K voprosu o genezise i razvitii kapitalizma v sel'skom khoziaistve i promyshlennosti Gruzii*. Tbilisi, 1967.

Arkomed, S. T. *Rabochee dvizhenie i sotsial-demokratiia na Kavkaze (s 80-kh godov po 1903 g.)*. Geneva, 1910; 2nd ed; Moscow-Petrograd, 1923.

Armani, Henry John. "The Russian Annexation of the Kingdom of Imeretia, 1800–1815: In the Light of Russo-Ottoman Relations." Ph.D. dissertation, Georgetown University, 1970.

Avaliani, S. L. *Krest'ianskii vopros v Zakavkaz'e* 2 vols. Odessa, 1912–1914.

Badriashvili, N. I. *Tiflis, Ot osnovaniia goroda do XIX v*. Tiflis, 1934.

Berzhe, A. P., ed. *Akty sobrannye kavkazskoiu arkheograficheskoiu komissieiu*. 12 vols. Tiflis, 1866–1912. This is certainly the most important document collection for the first half-century of Russian rule.

Chkhetiia, Sh., ed. *Dokumenty po istorii Gruzii. Seriia II. Tom 1, Gruziia v period burzhuaznykh reform (1862–1872), Chast' pervaia (1862–1866)*. Tbilisi, 1960.

———. *K istorii krest'ianskoi reformy v Gruzii (Dokumenty i materialy)*. Tbilisi, 1950.

———. *Tbilisi v XIX stoletii (1865–1869)*. Tbilisi, 1942.

Esadze, Semen. *Istoricheskaia zapiska ob upravlenii Kavkazom*. 2 vols. Tiflis, 1907.

Gugushvili, P. V. *Sel'skoe khoziaistvo i agrarnye otnoshenii II: Otmena krepostnogo prava*. Tbilisi, 1950.

Javakhishvili [Dzhavakhov], Ivane. *Politicheskoe i sotsial'noe dvizhenie v Gruzii v XIX veke*. St. Petersburg, 1906.

Khachapuridze, G. V. *Guriiskoe vosstanie v 1841 godu*. Tiflis, 1931.

———. *K istorii Gruzii pervoi polovine XIX veka*. Tbilisi, 1950.

Makharadze, F. *Gruziia v deviatnadtsatom stoletii: Kratkii istoricheskii ocherk*. Tiflis, 1933.

———. *Ocherki revoliutsionnogo dvizheniia v Zakavkaz'i*. Tiflis, 1927.

Markova, O. P. *Vosstanie v Kakhetii 1812 g*. Moscow, 1951.

Megrelishvili, G. *Gruzinskaia obshchestvenno-ekonomicheskaia mysl' vtoroi poloviny 19-ogo veka i nachala 20-ogo veka*. 2 vols. Tbilisi, 1959–1961.

Mochalov, V. D. *Krest'ianskoe khoziaistvo v Zakavkaz'e k kontsu XIX v*. Moscow, 1958.

Pantskhava, A. I. *K voprosu o razvitii agrarnykh otnoshenii v doreformennoi Vostochnoi Gruzii*. Moscow, 1957.

———. *Ocherki agrarnoi istorii Gruzii pervoi poloviny XIX veka*. Tbilisi, 1969.

Rhinelander, Laurens Hamilton, Jr. "The Incorporation of the Caucasus into the Russian Empire: The Case of Georgia." Ph.D. dissertation, Columbia University, 1972.

Semin, Orest. *Velikaia godovshchina. Agrarnyi vopros i krest'ianskaia reforma na Kavkaze*. Kiev, 1911.

Surguladze, A. N. *sazogadoebrivi azri XIX saukunis meore nakhevarshi*. Tbilisi, 1973.

Tsagareishvili, Sh. V., ed. *Revoliutsiia 1905–1907 gg. v Gruzii: Sbornik dokumentov*. Tbilisi, 1956.

Writing on the revolutionary and Soviet periods has been marred by partisanship and state censorship. Newspapers and published documents remain the most revealing primary sources, and in recent years a number of monographs have added to our knowledge.

Avalov, Zurab. *Nezavisimost' Gruzii v mezhdunarodnoi politiki, 1918–1921 gg.; Vospominaniia, ocherki*. Paris, 1924. For an English translation, see *The Independence of Georgia in International Politics, 1918–1921*. London: Headley Brothers, 1940.

Bor'ba za pobedu sovetskoi vlasti v Gruzii: Dokumenty i materialy (1971–1921 gg.). Tbilisi, 1958.

Bor'ba za uprochenie sovetskoi vlasti v Gruzii: Sbornik dokumentov i materialov (1921–1925 gg.). Tbilisi, 1959.

Gugushvili, P. V., ed. *Istoriia kollektivizatsii sel'skogo khoziaistva Gruzinskoi SSR (1927–1937 gg.)*. Tbilisi, 1970.

Hovannisian, Richard. *Armenia on the Road to Independence, 1918*. Berkeley and Los Angeles: University of California Press, 1967.

———. *The Republic of Armenia*. 3 vols. Berkeley and Los Angeles: University of California Press, 1971– .

Istoriia industrializatsii Gruzinskoi SSR (1926–1941 gg.). Tbilisi, 1968.

Kautsky, Karl. *Georgia, a Social-Democratic Peasant Republic, Impressions and Observations.* London, 1921.

Kazemzadeh, Firuz. *The Struggle for Transcaucasia (1917–1921).* New York: Philosophical Library, 1951.

Kharmandarian, S. V. *Lenin i stanovlenie Zakavkazskoi Federatsii, 1921–1923.* Erevan, 1969.

Kommunisticheskaia partiia Gruzii v tsifrakh (1921–1970 gg.): Sbornik statisticheskikh materialov. Tbilisi, 1971.

Lewin, Moshe. *Lenin's Last Struggle.* New York: Pantheon, 1968.

Lomashvili, P. N. *Velikii perevorot.* Tbilisi, 1972.

Natmeladze, M. V. *Istoriia rabochego klassa Gruzii (1921–1941 gg.).* Vol. 2. Tbilisi, 1981.

———. *sabchota sakartvelos mushata klasis istoria.* Vol. 1. Tbilisi, 1970.

Nove, Alec, and J. A. Newth. *The Soviet Middle East: A Communist Model for Development?* London: George Allen and Unwin, 1967.

Pipes, Richard. *The Formation of the Soviet Union: Communism and Nationalism, 1917–1923.* Cambridge, Mass.: Harvard University Press, 1957.

Suny, Ronald Grigor. *Armenia in the Twentieth Century.* Chico, Calif.: Scholars Press, 1983.

———. *The Baku Commune, 1917–1918: Class and Nationality in the Russian Revolution.* Princeton, N.J.: Princeton University Press, 1972.

———, ed., *Transcaucasia, Nationalism and Social Change: Essays in the History of Armenia, Azerbaijan, and Georgia.* Ann Arbor: Michigan Slavic Publications, 1983.

Uratadze, Grigorii. *Obrazovanie i konsolidatsiia Gruzinskoi Demokraticheskoi Respubliki.* Munich, 1956.

———. *Vospominaniia gruzinskogo sotsial-demokrata.* Stanford, Calif.: Hoover Institution Press, 1968.

Zhordania, Noe. *chemi tsarsuli (mogonebani).* Paris, 1958. The Russian translation is *Moia zhizn'.* Stanford, Calif.: Hoover Institution Press, 1968.

———. *Za dva goda.* Tiflis, 1919.

Index

DATE DUE

DATE DUE			
MAY 1 6 '90			
NOV 27 '90			
APR 1 1 1991			
SEP 2 0 '91 ILL			
DEC - 5 1991			
OCT 1 1 1993			
OCT 2 1 1993			
DEC - 9 1993			
NOV 2 4 1995			
JAN 1 1 1996			
261-2500			Printed in USA